Primordial American Terrorists

A True History of Events Leading
to the End of Slavery in the United States
#
by Robert Riggs

PROFILES IN TERRORISM ©
A SERIES

OTHER BOOKS IN THE SERIES (BY THE SAME AUTHOR):

SOFIA PEROVSKAYA, TERRORIST PRINCESS

Primordial American Terrorists

A TRUE HISTORY OF EVENTS LEADING TO THE END OF SLAVERY IN THE UNITED STATES

Part of a Series
Profiles in Terrorism ©

by Robert R. Riggs

© Global Harmony Press 2023, 2024
Berkeley, California

Global Harmony Press, Inc.
2625 Alcatraz Ave., Suite 124
Berkeley, California 94705
Deluxe Color Hardbound Edition, 2023

Copyright © Global Harmony Press, Inc., 2023, 2024

All rights reserved
under the laws of all nations including but not limited to United States, Canada, United Kingdom, Russian Federation, Republic of Italy. No part of this publication may be reproduced, stored in a retrieval system, or transmitted, in any form or by any person, without the prior written permission of Global Harmony Press

Primordial American Terrorists, A True History of Events Leading to the End of Slavery in the United States | Robert R. Riggs

Includes bibliographic references and index

ISBN 978-0-9991559-3-6 (Deluxe Color Hardbound)
ISBN 978-0-9991559-7-4 (Paperback)
ISBN 978-0-9991559-6-7 (Electronic)

Library of Congress Control Number: 2023921215

All materials used for this book are believed to be public domain, except as otherwise indicated. References to Internet Web Sites (URLs) were accurate at the time of writing. Neither the author nor Global Harmony Press is responsible for Web sites that may have changed since this book was prepared

Dedicated to the memory of Lawrence Ross

Acknowledgements

This work would not have been possible without the constant patience, support, guidance and encouragement of the author's wife, Dori Riggs.

The author extends thanks to:

Research resources
Doe Library, University of California at Berkeley
Wikimedia Foundation
Kansas State Historical Society
U.S. National Archives and Records Administration
Library of Congress

Museums
Ford's Theater, Washington, D.C.
Surratt House Museum, Clinton, Maryland
Dr. Samuel A. Mudd House Museum, Southern Maryland
Territorial Capital Museum, Lecompton, Kansas
John Brown Museum, Osawatomie, Kansas
Harriet Tubman Museum, Cambridge, Maryland

Research assistants
Jackson Kaiser
John Andre
Emily Jasper

Persons who generously volunteered their time for review, suggestions, logistics and moral support
Louisa Brandt
James Brown
Zoya Chakourski
Will Gorenfeld
Emily Riggs

Persons who provided critical financial support
Philip Connor Kidd III
Thomas McQuighan
Dana M. Wohlford

Introduction

WHAT IS TERRORISM? People argue it is an emotionally laden pejorative term, apt to be misused. Perhaps it is. But there is an enduring kernel of reality inside the concept. How then shall we define it? As we will use the term, terrorism is shocking, sudden violence. It is a ferocious attack perpetrated outside any attempt at legal justification against a relatively soft target, typically one or more unsuspecting, unarmed victims. So far, our definition also fits mall shootings and other acts of random gun violence that nowadays all-too-often shatter the safety of society. To be terrorism, it must be something more. Terrorism, by our definition, requires some form of social or political agenda, however inscrutable.

The impact of terrorism is ever more ubiquitous. One cannot attend a football game, enter a courthouse, or travel on an airplane without encountering a palpable preoccupation with its overhanging presence. The phenomenon continues to be poorly understood. Whenever a new act of terrorist violence bursts upon us, we strain to find the comfort of a logical explanation. That effort, though, is fraught with paradox. One of the most profound is the duality observed in the personality of the perpetrator. In lives apart from their defining act, terrorists frequently are lauded by friends and family as upstanding individuals, distinguished for kindness, good behavior, and charity. The pattern deserves close study. It has been noticed that terrorists, in their mental makeup, tend to resemble each other.[1] Our mission has been to address the questions: How and why?

---

[1] Walter Laqueur, *A History of Terrorism* (Transaction Publishers, London, 2007), pp. 4 – 5.

Primordial American Terrorists

The terrorist, in general, is not a natural-born child of the "cause." Rather, terrorists usually adopt their cause. They do so with fervent passion. Terrorism, indeed, ought to be classified as a crime of passion. Those who engage in it have a mystical and, to most people, distorted conception of reality. Their horrific attacks generally make no sense in terms of achieving any tangible goal. The terrorist, however, feels deeply that in killing or robbing victims whom he or she associates with the enemy, he or she is acting out of the most noble, self-sacrificing, devotional form of love. Very often, he or she brings to bear a strong religious sentiment. A divine power is felt to be standing behind, propelling, guiding, and sanctioning the egregious violation of mankind's laws. Because of the abhorrent nature of the behavior, the terrorist's only lasting accomplishment, most of the time, is to trigger a severe backlash of hatred and public overreaction against the very cause he or she seeks to promote.

The terrorist disorder, if one may call it that, appears to be a natural permutation of the human personality. Because an act of terrorism is inherently irrational, the search for explanation of cause and effect is usually fruitless. And yet, certain situations show themselves more likely to activate the terrorist. This work will explore a particular environment which gave rise to many terrorist acts. Our protagonists did not inherit a culture of political killings. They did not follow in anybody's footsteps. Rather, they felt their own way into action. And they exerted a surprisingly strong influence on each other, even when their "causes" were diametrically opposed.

A huge strength of the new United States, the "young Hercules"[2] on the international stage, was its dynamic political process. Freedom of speech, made the subject of explicit protection in its national constitution, was a bedrock pillar of

---

[2] See Matthew Karp, *This Vast Southern Empire* (Harvard University Press, Cambridge, 2016), p. 123.

that strength. Over its first fifty years, the pluralistic model of republican government hammered out by the founding fathers in Philadelphia yielded innovative ideas and effective measures for developing a land filled with wilderness and plentiful natural resources. However, the ethical objections and philosophical problems posed by the American institution of slavery were placed deep in political quarantine. Extraordinary efforts were made by slaveowners and their proxies to gag any debate over the issue, either in printed form or in the halls of Congress. Prominent abolitionists, too, distrusted and shunned the political process. Where effecting change through the political process seems hopeless, the desperation felt by passionate supporters of the cause can generate the suicidal emotional explosion associated with terrorism. That dynamic took effect in the young United States.

A related dynamic also proved to be a powerful catalyst. As a lineal branch descended from the original thirteen colonies, a distinctive culture evolved in the southern part of the United States. Expanding on the Enlightenment's rediscovery of the classics, elites here made a conscious decision to emulate the classical civilizations, particularly that of ancient Rome. The ruling aristocrats of those societies, it was theorized, had been freed to engage in valuable higher pursuits of military, scientific, political and intellectual activities by dint of the labor of slaves and their overseers. The southern United States was in the path of an unprecedented industrialization of the institution of slavery, the force of which generated the largest forced migration in human history. Ancient civilizations, including those in Mesoamerica, made extensive use of war captives to feed their need for slaves. The South, however, differed from all classical civilizations in that its institutionalized slavery was built upon a hereditary racial caste. Within a structure we recognize now as premodern and

Primordial American Terrorists

warped,[3] danger was perceived to lurk in free persons of African descent. Still more danger lurked in any expression of the dissenting opinion that the institution of slavery was entirely antithetical to the ideals of the American declaration of independence, and in any objection to the extremely troubling

---

[3] Debate rages over whether or not the American version of slavery was, in fact, a modern institution. See, e.g., Edward E. Baptist, *The Half Has Never Been Told: Slavery and the Making of American Capitalism* (New York: Basic Books, 2014), introduction p. xxiv; see also Karp, pp. 2-3, 150-51. We tend to endorse the more traditional view articulated as follows by Eugene Genovese, probably the leading 20th century student of American slavery:

> The premodern quality of the Southern world was imparted to it by its dominant slaveholding class. Slavery has existed in many places, side by side with other labor systems, without producing anything like the civilization of the South. Slavery gave the South a special way of life because it provided the basis for a regional social order in which the slave labor system could dominate all others. Southern slavery was not 'mere slavery' . . . but the foundation on which rose a powerful and remarkable social class: a class constituting only a tiny portion of the white population and yet so powerful and remarkable as to try, with more success than our neo-abolitionists care to see, to build a new, or rather to rebuild an old, civilization.

Eugene D. Genovese, *The Political Economy of Slavery* (2d ed., Wesleyan Univ. Press, Middlebury, Connecticut, 1989) pp. 3-4. We need not enter here into the "traditional" versus "revisionist" debate over the "modernity" *vel non* of slavery. Even if the antebellum Southern culture was, as we believe, an evolutionary dead end from the perspective of Western civilization, its participants were convinced their way of life was a permanent, noble and just one which should be upheld and enforced by law everywhere.

idea that any human being deserves to be born into a lifetime of enforced servitude.

The worldwide movement to condemn slavery, manifested in Great Britain's Abolition Act of 1833, posed an existential threat to the continuance of the "Southern" model of life. Southern intellectuals were well aware that history was poised to judge the viability of their vision of an aristocratic society resting on a paternalistic concept of master and slave. One tangible result was the post-1833 policy of strong support, by South-leaning Presidents and their appointed officials, of the three major New World states in which slavery remained a legal institution after 1833: Cuba, Brazil, and Texas (prior to its 1845 annexation by the United States).[4] The sense of existential threat produced an environment prone to terrorism. People who deeply feel a threat to prized cultural values are prime candidates to become terrorists. This observation applies to much of the terrorism that has recently emerged from the Islamic world, as well as the closely related form of violence initiated against civilian populations by contemporary paranoid regimes such as the Putin administration in Russia.

Now, let us examine our primordial American terrorists.

---

[4] See Karp, p. 87.

Chapter 1: The Coming of the Prophet

Sunday was the day of rest and relaxation granted to the servant class. That is why it was logical for Nat to select the Sabbath for his gigantic act. Nat was a prophet. The Lord had showed Nat things that happened before his birth, some thirty-one years earlier. His father and mother had often said in his presence that he was intended for a great purpose. Nat believed them. He had a phenomenally sharp mind, one that was restless and observant of everything. Nat learned to read without the benefit of any schooling. People found they had to give little Nat a book to shut him up from crying. His grandmother, observing his uncommon intelligence as a child, remarked along with others that Nat "had too much sense to be raised."[1]

Like his grandmother, Nat was very religious. Nat spent hour after hour with his Bible. When he grew big enough to work, all his time not spent in his master's service was devoted either to prayer or to practical science experiments. Nat never petty thieved, as did many other children growing up around his neighborhood. But those same mischievous teenagers, recognizing Nat's mental power, liked to carry him along whenever they were bent on roguery. Though he mostly held himself aloof, the others stood in awe of Nat's calling. Finding his judgments to be superior, the local people developed confidence in his divine inspiration. They found themselves deeply impressed by the ascetic manner in which Nat chose to live.

One day, as he prayed while ploughing a field, the same Spirit who spoke to prophets in the former days came and spoke to Nat in the words of the Scriptures. The Spirit spoke words on which Nat had much reflected: "Seek ye the kingdom of Heaven, and all things shall be added to you." The words of the Spirit reinforced Nat's knowledge that he was ordained for some high purpose in the hands of the Almighty. As Nat reached manhood, he found himself a little below average in height. But his intellectual faculties were well above average. While his highly inquisitive nature continued to absorb all kinds of learning about the world, Nat's attention kept returning to the holy object for which he knew he was intended.

Nat had been born into the status of a property. So had the majority of his neighbors. They shared with Nat a similar ancestry from a distant continent, as well as a similar heritage of being tied in racially stratified bondage by a confident and conceited society of colonizers. When his master placed him under the authority of an overseer, Nat ran away. Accustomed to an austere lifestyle, Nat dwelt in the woods for thirty days. All the neighbors thought Nat had surely found his way to another country, as Nat's father had done before him. But to their great astonishment, Nat returned to his plantation. The Spirit had appeared to Nat in the woods. It told him to reject the things of the world, to return, and to serve his heavenly purpose. When Nat went back to his earthly master, some neighbors snickered. For a time, Nat withdrew himself from having interactions with his fellow slaves. He sought more than ever to obtain true holiness before the great day of Judgment.

Nat practiced a ministry of baptism. Although due to his ancestry he was ostracized from performing sacraments in regular church, Nat baptized selected faithful in the waters of a local river. Both Nat's fellows, and Nat himself, were impressed with a belief that by the laying on of hands, Nat could cure diseases. There was a particular instance in which it was generally thought he had cured a neighbor in that way. Another of Nat's noted healings was accomplished through fasting and prayer. As much a cure of the spirit as it was of the flesh, this patient was a neighbor of European ancestry.

About the time Nat returned from his stay in the woods,

Chapter 1: The Coming of the Prophet

he had a stark vision. He saw black spirits and white spirits engaged in a battle. The sun was darkened, and thunder rolled. In place of the abundant gushing water of a Virginia storm, red blood flowed in streams. The Spirit said unto Nat: "Such is your luck, as you are called to see. Let it come rough or smooth, you must surely bear it." Other images followed. Lights glowed in the night sky. Nat alone recognized these lights for what they really were – the Savior's hands, extended broadly from east to west, just as they had been extended on the cross on Calvary.

The Spirit told him he would see more signs, to tell that it was time to take on the yoke of Christ and rise up to fight the Serpent. After watching an annular eclipse that covered 98% of the sun on February 12, 1831, Nat began organizing. Only a few of his most trusted neighbors were invited to share the secret. The uprising was intended for the symbolic national anniversary of freedom, July 4. Many and varied were the efforts made to screw up courage. July 4 came and went. Nat was sick with fear he would never be able to fulfill his purpose.

But on this Sunday, seven weeks later, Nat's preparations were ready. He had gathered in the woods the small group of disciples who believed in his mission. Nat had instructed them to prepare a hearty dinner. Hark, Nat's most trusted confidant, brought a pig to fortify them for the grueling night and day that lay ahead. Henry brought brandy for reinforcement. They were joined by Sam, Nelson, Will, and Jack. At around three o'clock in the afternoon, Nat left his customary Sabbath isolation to join them. The uprising was under way.

Will and Jack were new to the program. Nat asked Will why he was there. Will replied that his life was worth no more than those of the others. He was willing to lose that life if he did not gain liberty. Jack was Hark's brother-in-law, who lived on a different plantation. Nat accepted both newcomers and took them into his confidence.

Since the beginning of the previous year, Nat had been

living with a new master, a carriage maker named Joseph Travis. Technically, Joseph was not Nat's owner. Joseph had married Sallie, a widow from the Moore family, which claimed both Nat and Hark as its property. Nat and Hark grew close while working as fellow laborers in Joseph's establishment. Joseph was kind to Nat. If anything, Nat regarded him as overindulgent. Nat served directly under Joseph in the business, without any intermediate overseer. Neither Nat nor Joseph gave the other any particular cause to complain. To Joseph would be accorded the honor of receiving the first visitation from the Angel.

It is a pleasant sensation to be alive and out of doors on a warm summer evening in a mid-Atlantic state like Virginia. The evening of Sunday, August 21, 1831 was such a balmy night. Well after total darkness, Nat and his small cadre of followers arrived outside the familiar Travis home. There they met up with another waiting disciple, Austin. Together, the group made their way to the cider house. Each man drank to steel his nerve for what was to follow. All except Nat. He abstained, as always.

Hark went to the door of the house with an axe, to break it open. But Nat, reflecting, stopped him. He did not want to make any noise that could set off alarm in the neighborhood. Nat thought to enter through an upstairs window instead. He had Hark set a ladder against the chimney. Nat climbed up it, hoisted the sash and slithered through. As quietly as he could, he descended the stairs, unbarred the door, and removed the guns from their places.

It was decided that, symbolically, Nat must personally spill the first blood. Without a sound, Nat led the others into the room where Joseph lay asleep in bed. In the dark, Nat swung at Joseph with a hatchet. But Nat was far more skilled as a prophet than he was as a killer. The blow glanced off Joseph's head. It succeeded only in jarring him awake. Terrified, Joseph sprang from his bed and cried out for his wife.

Chapter 1: The Coming of the Prophet

It would be his final utterance. Will was an expert with an axe. One well-placed stroke split open Joseph's head, killing him instantly.

Sallie, Joseph's wife, soon shared a similar fate. It was no time to think of any past kindness, of any human feeling. A vigorous blow extinguished Sallie's life as she lay in her bed. Nat then led the way to the bedside of two boys, both sleeping peacefully. One was Putnam Moore, Sallie's 9-year-old son from a former marriage. Technically, Nat was the inherited property of young Putnam. The other boy was Joel Westbrook, an apprentice who had been working under Joseph. Both were slaughtered quickly, without words and without remorse. Just as silently, Nat and all his band exited the Travis house. But after they had already covered some distance, Nat remembered a problem. He had forgotten about the baby, asleep in a cradle. His instructions were clear. Neither age nor sex were to be spared. Henry and Will returned to snuff the life of the small creature. After a rapid decapitation, they dumped both the baby's body and its severed head into the fireplace.

Nat, Hark and the others looked over the booty from the Travis residence: Four guns that would shoot; several old muskets, with a pound or two of powder; and Moses, a boy of African ancestry, liberated to join the raiders. Nat formed Moses and all his other followers into a line. He had them practice the unfamiliar act of handling weapons, using military maneuvers he had long studied. Nat then marched his crew off to the next farm, some six hundred yards distant. This was the home of Salathiel Francis, who lived with just one companion, a butler of African ancestry. Nat had his band use a subterfuge. Sam, who worked for Salathiel's brother Nathaniel, went with Will to the door and called out that he had a letter for him. Salathiel opened the door. The two of them immediately seized Salathiel and dragged him out of the house. He was quickly hacked to death with a series of blows to the head. The butler was recruited to join the mission of rebellion.

Primordial American Terrorists

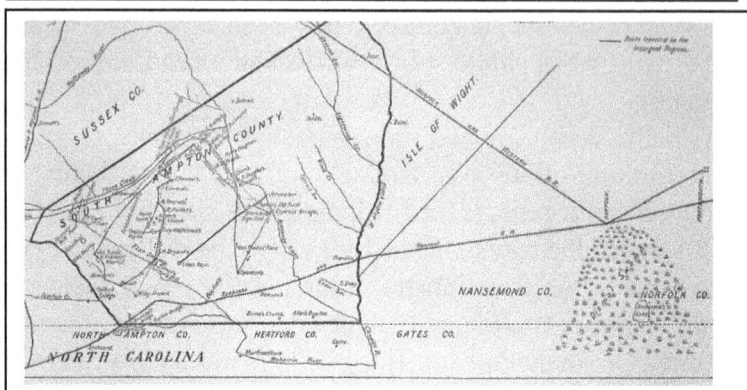

Map of routes followed by Nat Turner party, from Drewry, *The Southampton Insurrection*, 1900

Next the group went to the Reese home, again maintaining perfect silence on their march. There they found the door unlocked. Piety Reese was murdered in her bed, while sleeping. Her son William heard enough of the noise to rouse and ask, "Who is that?" Without a response, he was rapidly dispatched to the permanent sleep of death. Jack's eyes, surveying the contents of the house in the dimness, spotted a pair of shoes belonging to William. These shoes would fit his feet. He put them on before leaving.

Dawn was just breaking as the party of raiders arrived at their next destination, Elizabeth Turner's residence. Henry, Austin, and Sam went to the outbuilding used as a still. There they encountered the overseer, Hartwell Prebles. Hartwell was shot to death. The sound of gunfire awakened the women inside the residence. They barred the door. No matter. Relentlessly, Will smashed down the door with his axe. Elizabeth and her friend, Sarah Newsome, were inside the front room. Both were cowering, trembling, and begging for mercy. Nat's command was inexorable. They must die at once. While Will was tending to Elizabeth, Nat took Sarah by the hand. He smacked her over the head several times using a sword he had plundered. But Nat, being inexpert, and the sword, being

Chapter 1: The Coming of the Prophet

unsharpened, were not able to finish Sarah. Will turned away from the crumpled body of Elizabeth. Observing Nat's difficulties, he hacked Sarah apart with his axe. Heedless of the blood and gore of their victims, Nat and his band ransacked the home after the murders in search of ammunition, money and horses. They also made sure to recruit the enslaved people who lived on the premises. By the time Nat left the Turner residence, his force had increased to fifteen.

Nat's objective was to carry terror and devastation everywhere his gang went. He now divided his followers into two groups, so that the grisly work of inflicting death and destruction could proceed more efficiently and quickly. One group of six proceeded on foot to a home where they murdered Henry Bryant, his wife and child. Meanwhile Nat, with a mounted group of nine, went in another direction, to Caty Whitehead's plantation. They arrived about an hour after sunrise. Caty was a middle-aged, gracious woman, well known for her hospitality. Her grown son Richard was a Methodist minister. When Nat and his men rode up the driveway leading to the house, they saw Richard standing nearby, in a cotton field. They beckoned him to come over. Will, the executioner, quickly sent Richard to an immediate death.

As the raiders approached Caty's home, Nat saw somebody trying to scramble away. He pursued and caught the fugitive, only to find that it was a black girl. She would not be harmed. By the time Nat returned from this chase, the home had already been invaded by his men. Inside, three of Caty's daughters and a grandchild had been rapidly and ruthlessly put to death. Only one daughter, Harriet, was lucky enough to be concealed, with the help of one of Caty's house servants, underneath a bed. There, Harriet lay quivering, not daring to take a breath, while she heard her sister screaming desperately. She was being put to death only a few feet away from Harriet, in the same room. It was a horror Harriet could never forget.

As Nat approached the door to the Whitehead house he

saw Will emerge, dragging the struggling Caty with him. At the step, Will delivered an axe blow that nearly severed Caty's head and sent her blood-spattered body sprawling. Then Nat spied Caty's teenaged daughter Peggy, who was outside the house, trying to hide in a corner behind a cellar cap. Nat tried to grab Peggy, but she fled. The men in his group chased her. She was caught and held down by the men in his group. Nat seized a nearby wooden fence rail and used it to crush Peggy's head. Nat thus enriched the death toll with a victim whom he personally killed.

House servants were appalled by the massacre. But field help proved easier for Nat to absorb into his burgeoning army. Four more hands were added at the Whitehead property. Afterwards, they would say they were frightened and coerced into enlisting. As Monday morning wore on, Nat's growing band of marauders continued their rampage from house to house. They moved in a northeasterly direction, heading away from the Boykins district, where the Travis farm was located, in the direction of Jerusalem, the largest town in Southampton county. On one occasion, when they were passing the house of some poor whites, Nat said he would not kill them, because they did not think any more of themselves than they did of the blacks. But usually Nat and his followers spared no one not of African ancestry. Travelers encountered along the road, they killed. People they found at home or in fields, they executed.

One homeowner, Tom Barrow, went out on his porch and resisted a group of mounted raiders that Nat had sent on ahead. He was overpowered. After a struggle, Tom's throat was cut. As he was bleeding to death, Tom's wife Mary managed to escape. While she was running away, one of her house servants, a 20-year-old woman named Lucy, grabbed and held on to her for about a minute. Finally, another black house servant came along and managed to make Lucy let go. Lucy was the romantic partner of Moses, one of Nat's disciples.

Another stop was the residence of Levi Waller. This was

Chapter 1: The Coming of the Prophet

a central meeting place for the white community. A school was operated there. Before 10 o'clock in the morning, Levi heard that the blacks had risen and were murdering people. Levi sent his son to the school house about a quarter mile off, to warn his children to return home. William Crocker, the teacher, came to the house with Levi's children. Levi told William to go to the house to load the guns. But before he could accomplish this, William returned to Levi and informed him the blacks were already in sight.

To produce added terror, Nat sent ahead fifteen to twenty of his most reliable men on horseback to charge the houses being attacked. At the Waller residence these men galloped up very suddenly, before anybody there was prepared to meet them. Several pursued Levi as he sought to escape. Levi eluded them temporarily by jumping a fence and then crouching behind some high weeds. Fortunately for him, the attention of the raiding party was distracted by somebody else they saw running away. Levi afterwards thought this person was his blacksmith. Levi retreated into a swamp that was not far off. After remaining there for some time, Levi very cautiously approached his house, keeping himself hidden. From a remote vantage point he watched in silence as several of his family members were executed. Levi's wife and one small school girl tried to hide in a log building. Levi saw three of the raiders go into this building. Soon they emerged. Levi saw that one of them was holding his wife's necklace in his hand. Horrified, Levi decided to return to the deeper shelter of the swamp.

More time passed. Levi once again mustered the courage to creep toward his residence. The killing had subsided. Levi could see that the invaders were now drinking from his store of alcoholic beverages. Nat, whom Levi knew very well, was mounted on a horse and obviously in command. When Nat finally ordered his group to move on from the Waller residence, the mangled lifeless bodies of Mrs. Waller and nine children lay strewn about the premises. The only survivors, besides Levi, were the school-master William Crocker and a 12-year-old student, Clarinda Jones. Clarinda managed to get over the fence and into hiding, although she was hit in the legs by buckshot. The Wallers' baby girl, grievously wounded, would die two days later.

At another home, that of William Williams, while Nat and his band were occupied with slaughtering William and his two little boys, William's wife tried to run. She was pursued by the marauders, caught, dragged back to the house, and forced to lie down next to the corpse of her dead husband. Then she was executed by a gunshot.

By the time the sun ascended to high noon over Southampton County, fifty-five slaughtered men, women, and children lay decaying in the sweltering heat of a typical Virginia summer. Nat's forces had encountered no opposition other than Tom Barrow, whom they had dispatched fairly easily. The success of the attack had surpassed all his expectations. With the continuing impressment of numerous persons of African ancestry he and his men met along the way, he had now assembled what he estimated at fifty or sixty volunteers into his army. They were mounted on commandeered horses and mules, some of them two to an animal. Most of them were armed in some kind of way, with guns, axes, swords and clubs. But these hastily assembled farm workers and house servants did not form a disciplined fighting force. They were suffering the effects of an all-night orgy of violence, pillaging, and no sleep. To this was added the after-effects of a good deal of hard liquor that had been consumed. Many of the guns held the kind of ammunition one could use to shoot at birds or squirrels, not bullets to be relied on in a battle with armed opponents.

Nat's plan was to proceed to Jerusalem. Nat had a great desire to procure better arms and ammunition, and he hoped to obtain them there. But, as Nat and his crew were traveling along the road approaching Jerusalem, they passed a gate

CHAPTER 1: THE COMING OF THE PROPHET

leading to the home of James Parker. Nat knew James and his family were away from home, so there was no killing to be done there. Some of the men proposed to go into the Parker ranch, to gather his slaves to the cause. Nat opposed this. He did not want to delay getting to Jerusalem. But the men prevailed on Nat to wait, with a small party, at the gate while they made a side trip to round up people of color at the Parker residence, about a half mile in from the road. Against his better judgment, Nat stopped for them to do it.

Southampton County, although very peaceful, still recalled the fear of uprising that had swept through Virginia during the year 1814. As part of the broader conflict known in the United States as the "War of 1812," British commanders on nearby Chesapeake Bay had actively encouraged the enslaved populace to rebel. They had offered freedom to all who would desert. In response, some three to four thousand persons of color fled their colonial masters, the largest-scale emancipation of persons of African descent anywhere in the United States prior to the Civil War. A significant number of these refugees took up arms and fought with the British against the Americans. Collective memory of these events explained why, when word of the burgeoning insurrection was spread through the African American community like wildfire on Monday, August 21, 1831, they told that that the "British had returned" and were "going around killing white people."

Members of the ruling class also rapidly heard this alarming news. They reacted by mustering every available man into local militias. In a society that lacked any standing military or even a police force, volunteer citizen soldiers represented the established, and indeed the only, mechanism for quelling invasions, crimes and civil disorders.

As midday dragged on into afternoon, the wait at the Parker gate seemed like forever to Nat. He became impatient. He went into the property to gather and retrieve his men. As they were returning toward the road, they met with eighteen mounted men, part of a hastily assembled militia that was looking to find the track of the raiders. These eighteen men had already found and routed the small outpost Nat had left behind at the Parker gate. In the field between the Parker residence and the gate, Nat ordered the men with him to halt and prepare for a fight. A confused skirmish ensued. Horses being ridden by both sides spooked and defied their humans. In the mêlée, several of Nat's bravest followers were wounded. A few men in the militia were shot also. The rest retreated. Those shot by birdshot and other makeshift ammunition were merely stunned, but the raiders thought they were dead. Nat's followers rode on after the rest of the militiamen. But, after being pursued for about two hundred yards over a small hill, the militia reformed and united with another dismounted group of militia who had arrived on the scene. This new posse had already loaded their guns with real bullets, and they were ready to fire. The bristling guns panicked Nat's raw recruits. His force rapidly disintegrated and ran in all directions. Hark had his horse shot out from under him. Nat caught a loose horse so that Hark could remount.

Seeing his group in disarray, Nat sensed that retreat was his only option. So he gathered about twenty men and made for a private back road he knew would lead to Jerusalem another way. But after trying in vain to muster enough men to make an attack on the town, Nat decided to return to the Boykins district.[2] He was thinking his supporters, once dispersed, would return to their homes, from which they could join up with him later. As he traveled, some more African Americans flocked to Nat, causing his ranks to swell to around forty.

Nat decided to quarter for the night at a ranch called Buckhorn, owned by Thomas Ridley. Like other places he encountered after retreating from Parker's, Buckhorn was now occupied only by members of the servant class. Nat persuaded four of these to join his cause. Two agreed to move out in the morning to recruit more. At Buckhorn, Nat and his men were

CHAPTER 1: THE COMING OF THE PROPHET

able to eat and drink plentifully from the spoils of their plundering. Nat set out sentries and lay down to sleep for the night.

But soon, Nat was roused by a commotion. One of the sentinels had given an alarm of an impending attack. Nat sent some of his men to reconnoiter. But when they returned in the darkness, others mistook them for attackers, panicked, and ran off. Once again, Nat saw many of his new recruits flee in disarray. Nat was left with a force of about twenty. Nat decided to stay on the move. So he took his remaining men to the neighboring house of Dr. Simon Blunt, where they arrived shortly before daybreak. As they approached, Nat had Hark fire a shot into the air to alert the occupants to his presence. He expected that the white residents would all be gone. Nat and his lieutenants hoped to recruit Blunt's African Americans to join his force. But to their surprise, not only did it turn out Blunt was home, it turned out he and his people, including slaves, were waiting with guns, prepared to mount a stiff resistance. In the ensuing firefight, Nat beat a retreat, in the course of which he left behind several of his most reliable men, including Hark.

Nat's surviving party returned to the house of Newit Harris, which they had looted during their rampage the day before. When they came in sight of the house, they were spotted by a mounted militia stationed there. This militia immediately charged and attacked.[3] In the confrontation, Will stood his ground and was shot down, as were many of the other rebels. Nat managed to escape into a nearby swamp, accompanied by only two of his followers, one also called Nat, and Jacob. There, they hid. When twilight began to descend, Nat dispatched the two to seek out his four original disciples, Henry, Sam, Nelson and Hark. He instructed the other Nat and Jacob to gather them the next day, along with any new recruits, in the same wood where they had shared the preparatory Sunday dinner only two days earlier.

Nat made his way to the designated meeting place. No one

joined him. He remained there twenty-four hours, until Wednesday evening. During that time, the only people he saw were mounted white men, riding about intently as if they were looking for somebody. The prophet concluded his last followers must have been captured, and must have betrayed the meeting place. Nat vanished.

Investigation swiftly followed the defeat and dispersal of Nat's raiders. Plantation owners checked to see which of their human properties had been out all night on Sunday and Monday nights. Any man who could not account for his whereabouts those nights, if not summarily executed, was transported to jail at Jerusalem. The local citizens also arrested any African Americans they encountered who seemed to be out of their usual places or away from their home plantations. These detainees were taken to a plantation called Cross Keys, where they were interrogated. The interview notes were assembled to try to understand what was behind the overall insurrection. A muddled picture emerged. But prosecutors soon figured out that "General Nat" was in charge, and that Hark was one of the key commanders.

It took all of nine days from the time Nat's group was subdued at Dr. Blunt's until the attorneys and courts of Southampton County were ready to begin the trials of the accused. The first group went on trial Thursday, August 31. Over the next six weeks, a total of fifty-one trials unfolded at the Jerusalem courthouse. Five of the defendants were "free persons of color," who had the right to trial in regular Superior Court following a preliminary hearing. Four of these five were bound over for such a trial. Of the other forty-six defendants mentioned in the court minutes, seventeen were hanged.[4] Eleven were recommended to the Governor for clemency, which consisted of being "transported" to the deep South for hard labor, in lieu of hanging. Apparently these recommendations, when made, were always followed. Thirteen were found not guilty. Two were dismissed on legal

Chapter 1: The Coming of the Prophet

grounds, and three were discharged without trial. Those hanged included Lucy, who was the only woman defendant, and three of Nat's original disciples: Hark, Nelson, and Sam. Hark's brother-in-law Jack, also present at the last supper before bloody Sunday, was found guilty but "recommended for transportation."

The prosecutor was the same for all of the trials. Each of the defendants had one of three local attorneys appointed to represent them. The trials were all judged by panels consisting of five local white landowners. The citizens were rather nervous about keeping so many rebels on hand in the Jerusalem jail, so they formally requested that John Floyd, the Governor, provide a substantial force of soldiers to help guard the prisoners until they could be dispatched. These panels of juror-like justices decided in each case, first, if the defendant was guilty. If so, the defendant was sentenced to death by hanging at a particular day and time, to occur "in the usual place of execution." However, typically if the panel was persuaded that the defendant was a youth or went along with the rebellion under duress, then the justices recommended that the sentence be commuted to transportation.

One other matter the justice panels were called upon to pronounce was the value, in money, of every slave who was found guilty. This valuation was invariably announced at the same time as the prisoner's verdict and death sentence, because it was of great interest to the property owners. In an early example of a government bailout, the state of Virginia decided that the owners or their estates would receive compensation for the value of their human properties that were destroyed by judicially sanctioned execution, or exiled. The values they determined ranged from a low of $100 to the norm of $400 or $450 for an adult male, to a high of $600 for a blacksmith. Out of these government subsidies, the slave's owner (or the estate of the deceased owner, in the many instances where the owner had died at the hands of the insurgents) was required to pay the

Primordial American Terrorists

$10 per case in fees awarded to the defense attorneys who represented the defendants.

The trials had some unusual aspects. Persons of color who were accused in one trial were allowed to be called as witnesses for defendants in other trials. Some of these witnesses were even allowed to be called after they had already been sentenced to hang. For instance, Hark admitted he was one of the insurgents, and survivor Levi Waller identified him as one of the leaders, who was referred to by the other participants as "Captain Moore." He was sentenced to death on Saturday, September 3. However, Hark was then called to the stand as a witness in two other trials including one held September 7, so four days after his death sentence. He testified that five of the defendants had stated, prior to being captured, that they had separated from Nat. Several of these defendants were spared and "recommended for transportation." Valued at $450, Hark died by hanging on September 9.

By October 18, the trials were finished. The enslaved workers who were not dead or transported were back in the fields. But one mystery remained. What had become of Nat? The break in the case finally came when a pair of African Americans were out in the woods doing some hunting and their dog alerted. When they went to investigate, they were astounded to see a gaunt Nat emerge from a hole in the ground at which the dog was barking. Inside this hole, which Nat had dug with his unsharp sword, he had been concealing himself, with no apparent aid by anyone, for the better part of two months. Nat had led the life of an ascetic hermit. He had ventured out of his hole only under cover of complete darkness, returning to the empty Travis home to steal provisions. However, some of the provisions were meat, which the dog had smelled out and stolen while Nat was away on one of his nighttime forays. The dog remembered the location and returned to the hole, which is how he led his masters to it. Alarmed at Nat's appearance, the hunters fled. But Nat knew

CHAPTER 1: THE COMING OF THE PROPHET

others would be on his trail.

For two more weeks, Nat continued to evade the pursuit, moving about from place to place. He was spotted, shot at, and had several hair's breadth escapes, but he was not killed or caught. Finally, on Sunday morning, October 30, 1831,[5] he was discovered in another place of concealment underneath a tree by a poor white named Benjamin Phipps. Though he was armed, Nat surrendered to Benjamin without resistance.

"Nat, alias Nat Turner," was brought under guard to Jerusalem, where he was placed on trial the following Saturday, November 5. The result was a foregone conclusion. And Nat, too, was prepared for the day of Judgment. His hands were ready to be spread on the bar of the cross. Undaunted at the prospect of an impending public execution, he freely, even proudly, told the story of how he had heard the righteous word of the Lord and, in response, organized and carried out the attacks. The minutes of Nat's trial kept by the Virginians have a feel surprisingly similar to the records kept by the English concerning their 1431 trial of Jeanne d'Arc in Rouen, France. There is a manifest theater of the absurd when authorities bent on inflicting justice put on "trial" someone who looks them in the eye and tells them he or she was sent on a divinely inspired mission. Thus, the court record talks about Nat's testimony in the following terms. "He pretended to have had intimations by signs and omens from God that he should embark on his desperate attempt." And, "Nat went on to detail a medley of incoherent and confused opinions about his communication with God, his command over the clouds, etc., etc., which he had been entertaining as far back as 1826."

In his sentencing remarks presiding justice Jeremiah Cobb, after covering the atrocities committed and the innocence of the people, both white and black, who had perished, added a comment on Nat's holy mission. "If this be true, from my soul I pity you; and while you have my sympathies, I am nevertheless called upon to pass the sentence of the court. The time between this and your execution will necessarily be very short; and your only hope must be in another world."[6]

Here was a man who heard the voice of the Holy Spirit, a man who had so many noble characteristics, a prophet who may, in the fullness of time, come to be acknowledged as a holy martyr, if not a full-fledged saint. How could such a man perpetrate a cold-blooded carnage that brutally murdered dozens of unsuspecting men, women and children? We have arrived at the central paradox of the terrorist.

Chapter 2: Fighting the Serpent

Nat was not a deviant. Nor was he a sociopath. So far as we know, the worst conduct he ever engaged in before leading his night of rampage was a short-lived, peaceful escape attempt, which he himself ended voluntarily. Typical of terrorists, he made up his mind to die for the cause. It appears that, for terrorists, once this momentous decision is reached, the murder, or even mass murder, of innocent people associated with the enemy does not require an enormous stretch of conscience. Nat's killing spree was no ordinary crime. It was a nonverbal, but nonetheless extremely loud, exclamation of anger against a system he perceived as unjust. When combined with stealth tactics, and when combined with the unsuspecting and relatively defenseless situation of the victims, what qualifies Nat and his followers for the label of terrorists is the politically charged overtone of their actions.

Terrorism is a perverted form of political action by those who feel passion in support of a cause. It consists of dramatic violent, blood-letting, hostage-taking, property-destroying, or other abusive action that is entirely outside society's norms, as well as outside all established rules of engagement for conflict resolution. Terrorism does not attempt to produce reform within a political system. Instead, to the extent that it has a rational explanation, it is an attempt to shock and shake the political system itself. This helps explain one of the most persistent personality characteristics of terrorists. They are never, in political terms, highly articulate. Although usually they are capable of being exceptionally disciplined, that discipline does not shine through in terms of academic performance. Their resumés are replete with dropping out and otherwise failing in school settings. Though very convinced of the rightness of their beliefs, terrorists do not stand out for their advocacy. Stealth violence is their chosen mode of political expression.

Rudimentary power phenomena reminiscent of terrorism existed in ancient times. A fair number of these proto-terrorist groups made such a great impression that their names are now etched in the English lexicon. The "Zealots," for example, were a militant group that existed side by side with Pharisees, Sadducees, and Essenes in the Palestine of the New Testament epoch. They are known from Roman sources and the Jewish historian Josephus. A secret element within them, called the *sicarii*, formulated and used unorthodox tactics by surprise-attacking and stabbing their enemies to death during daylight, in the midst of crowds. Their typical victims were Jewish moderates and advocates of peace. Josephus reports that there was a frenzy of religious expectation among them, an inclination to regard martyrdom as something joyful. The Zealots held a belief that, after the fall of Jerusalem, when the sinful regime was no longer in power, God would reveal himself and deliver victory over the Romans.

The "Assassins" were made famous in the Western world by writings of Marco Polo. They arose as an Islamic splinter group in the late eleventh century, in the same arid region of the Middle East occupied more recently by the self-proclaimed Islamic State. Rather than confront an enemy in battle, the Assassins devised a strategy of stealth political killings directed personally against any rival leaders whom they deemed hostile or non-compliant, including prefects, governors, and caliphs. Their distinctive mode of attack was carried out with a knife or short sword. They often used disguises, subterfuge or other trickery in order to gain the needed proximity to their victims. Supposedly, a pair of Assassins stabbed to death Conrad of Montferrat, the Crusader

CHAPTER 2: FIGHTING THE SERPENT

rival of Richard the Lion-Hearted. The Assassins were in some ways more akin to extortionists than to terrorists, as they used their fearsome tactics to exact tribute and to maintain control of territory and cities.[1]

"Thugs" were discussed by Mark Twain in his 1897 work, *Following the Equator*. According to the colonizing British, the Thugs were adherents of a centuries-old secret tradition, which continued its depredations in the nineteenth-century India ruled by the English. The general mode of attack by a Thug was to strangle the victim using a turban, scarf, or noose. Thugs were known for deceiving and surprising their prey for purposes of robbery and murder. Their actual political aims were obscure. Reputedly, the Thugs acted from a quasi-religious motivation to engage in human sacrifice, by virtue of which they believed their taking of life would purify and protect society as a whole. Similar to modern terrorists, the Thugs often lived under multiple aliases to make themselves more difficult for authorities to identify.[2]

Scholar Walter Laqueur opened his seminal work on the history of terrorism with the following observation. "Terrorism, one of the most widely discussed issues of our time, is also one of the least understood."[3] Terrorism defies understanding in large part because of the dualism of the terrorist. The word conjures a vision of a wild-eyed fanatic, a killer of innocents. But that same terrorist, subjectively, acts out of the highest form of love. Selflessly he or she abandons his or her life for the sake of an oppressed people. As said by Laqueur, "[t]errorists have found admirers and publicity agents in all ages. No words of praise are fulsome enough for these latter day saints and martyrs."

After study, Laqueur arrived at the conclusion that the terrorist has a distinctive profile. "[T]errorism is not merely a technique. Those practicing it have certain basic beliefs in common. They may belong to the left or the right; they may be nationalists or internationalists, but in some essential respects their mental makeup is similar." Repeated observation in diverse cultural contexts has shown a constellation of personality traits which tend to be shared in common by terrorists:[4]

1. Suicidal ideation; embracing of death.
2. Above-average native intelligence and high IQ.
3. Highly empathic, particularly with children and animals.
4. Tremendous drive and determination.
5. Thirst for fame and glory.
6. Personal asceticism and capacity for an austere lifestyle.
7. Political views that are imbued with fantasy and lack of realism.
8. Lack of formal education – extensively self-taught as an "auto-didact."
9. Uncritical faith in their own ideas and plans of action (however hopeless or far-fetched they may seem to others).
10. Derive essential inspiration from works of literature.
11. Highly resistant to authority and organizations – even ones allied with or dedicated to their cause.
12. Domineering and intolerant; impose their views on others.
13. Extremely self-righteous micro-managers.
14. Slight disconnect from other people's view of reality.
15. Can be a failure in their ordinary walks of life (particularly with respect to a peer group of similarly

Chapter 2: Fighting the Serpent

intelligent, motivated, and self-disciplined individuals), with the failure often caused by their slightly distorted vision of reality.

16. Military training or military experience.

17. Extensive travel, often international.

18. Aristocratic or noble birth, or at least, a middle class to upper middle class upbringing that is not impoverished.

19. Strongly influenced in the direction of a parent's political views.

20. "In search of" ... adopting ... a cause to champion unto death, a cause as to which they are not personally aggrieved.

Their frequent behaviors:

A. Use of false names and/or disguises

B. Use of subterfuges

C. Use of religious style ideation and an appeal to the "authority of God" to justify violence and to whip up support for violent acts

D. Acting out in cold-blooded violence within a relatively short time after adopting the cause.

E. Substantially overestimating the willingness of the oppressed people whose cause he or she champions to rise up and engage in revolution to throw off the oppressor (relates to dissociation from reality, above).

F. Application of enormous pressure to radicalize persons who sympathize and agree with the "cause".

G. Maintaining a love–hate type relationship with sympathizing "legals" who do not share the willingness to engage in absolute dedication of their lives to the "cause," but who are willing to give money and other aid and comfort.

From what is gleaned from his *Confessions*, Nat fits the terrorist profile in many respects. He definitely had a high IQ. He was, so far as we know, entirely self-taught with no formal education of any kind. He was empathic, as attested by his repute as a healer. Personally, Nat was extremely ascetic, capable of living in the utmost austerity. He had no significant group allegiances. Obviously, Nat had enormously powerful religious ideation and an equally strong conviction of his righteousness. He invoked the authority of God to whip up support. Beyond that, he had an intangible deranged quality we see in many terrorists. It is not full-fledged psychosis, but rather a slight disconnection from mainstream humanity's perception of the nature of things. Terrorists typically construct and inhabit their own version of reality. Their frame of reference is just an eighth of a screw-turn out of alignment with that of everyday society.

Portrait of Nat Turner, from Drewry's *The Southhampton Insurrection*, 1900

Nat, to be sure, belonged to an oppressed class of people. But, on the level of his personal experiences, we do not have any reason to think that Nat was ever physically abused, taken far from loved ones, or denied the ability to have a family life. In his *Confessions*, Nat did not attribute his crusade to personal mistreatment, anger, or vendetta. Nat went out of his way to tell us that Joseph Travis, whom he murdered first, was a "kind master," and that he, Nat, "had no cause to complain of [Joseph's] treatment to me." The most direct way to understand

CHAPTER 2: FIGHTING THE SERPENT

Nat's persona and state of mind is to listen to his own words. Nat heard voices telling him he was righteous and destined for greatness, for he was a prophet. The time was fast approaching, when the first should be last and the last should be first. It was high time to fight against the Serpent. Hearing this, his auditor Thomas Gray reminded the captive his uprising had failed, and he was awaiting a certain and swift death. Thomas asked, "Do you not find yourself mistaken now?" Nat was ready with his reply: "Was not Christ crucified?"[5]

The actions Nat organized and led were not an organized attempt at a viable rebellion. They are far better understood as a violent lashing out, with political content. Nat knew from the start that his campaign would inevitably be suicidal. This is classic terrorist behavior. Martyrdom was a fate Nat embraced. Because he lacked role models, his terrorism was based on instinct. A necessary condition for that instinct to operate was Nat's personality. But there was also another very powerful factor at work. Slavery itself was inherently grounded on a bedrock of violence. It was a legalized underlying violence, one sanctioned by an entire social order and set of laws. And, beneath the peaceable, seemingly immutable surface appearance of such a social order, lurked the seeds of terrorism, an über-violent mode of lashing out in support of a cause that is recognized as politically hopeless.

Prior to Nat's eruption in August 1831, there was very little precedent in Anglo-American culture for terrorism in the modern sense. European colonists in the Americas were, however, familiar with terrorist-like phenomena perpetrated by desperate members of a rival culture, in the form of barbaric raids on settlements involving murder, mutilation, and kidnapping. These attacks came from bands of the aboriginal peoples they were rapidly displacing on the continent.[6] Such chilling massacres, generally carried out by warriors who were loving and neither harsh nor brutal within the context of their own civilizations, may be explained in a political context as a mute protest resorted to by societies whose way of life was rapidly becoming extinct under pressure from more developed forms of economic organization associated with the ever-expanding "Western" form of civilization. And it is of essential importance, with respect to understanding the factors associated with terrorism, to observe that a dynamic in many ways comparable resulted in the tension that drove persons who believed in the slave-holding civilization of the southern United States to commit acts of terrorism against representatives of a rival and more economically successful culture.

In a real sense, after the formation of United States in 1789, the American South, to the extent that it rested on a foundation of slavery, became a dying civilization. It was an archaic culture that ultimately could not survive the stress of competition with the more advanced form of economic organization that was emerging elsewhere in the United States and in Europe. Dispassionate observers, even many in the South, could sense that the "slaveocracy" was doomed and destined to die out because of its social and political weaknesses, not even taking into consideration its internal moral and religious contradictions.[7] The young United States was a testing laboratory for comparison of two contrasting republics on the same continent, with basically the same cultural antecedents. In the biting, if unpopular, words of a contemporary Southerner: "We find the one rising to a degree of almost unexampled power and eminence, and the other sinking into a state of comparative imbecility and obscurity."[8]

As of 1790, Virginia, which would be the home of four of the first five U.S. Presidents, was the dominant state in the Union. It had a population of 748,308, well over twice that of the state of New York, which was 340,120. Yet by 1850, the population of New York had swelled to 3,097,394, while Virginia's lagged far behind at less than half, 1,421,661. This exponential disparity in growth rate carried through to all other forms of economic indicators, including exports, manufactures, mining, and mechanic arts. In most of these categories, the state of New York outstripped Virginia by at least a factor of ten. Similar conclusions could be drawn from a comparison of the state of Massachusetts – which had about one fifth of the land area – with North Carolina. Not only did Massachusetts see enormously greater population growth, during the 1790 to 1850 period, it experienced about fifteen times more growth in terms of economic indicators. Its citizens also had a dramatically higher literacy rate, in comparison with North Carolina.[9]

South Carolina and its oligarchy regarded itself as the classical paradigm of a slaveholding republic. As we shall see, many of the institution's most ardent defenders in the U.S. Congress came from that state. But by every economic measure, South Carolina during the 1790–1850 period was seriously underdeveloped in comparison with any average "free" state, such as Pennsylvania. South Carolina's annual imports actually declined in real terms during the period, while Pennsylvania's boomed. The gross product of Pennsylvania was around twenty times that of South Carolina, by 1855. South Carolina flattered itself that its slaves had great value as "property," but even taking this dubious claim into consideration, Pennsylvania was still a place of far more total wealth, by a margin of $729,144,998 to $288,257,694.

The North had a clear superiority over the South in every category of manufacturing. By 1850, the South had to import most of the manufactured items that it consumed. Southern merchants regularly made pilgrimages to the North to purchase everyday items such as bibles, brooms, buckets, books, pens, ink, envelopes, shoes, hats, handkerchiefs, umbrellas, pocket knives, furniture, crockery, glassware, pianos, toys, primers, school books, fashionable apparel, machinery, medicines, and even tombstones. Although the South prided itself on agricultural resources, in point of fact the farm production of the "slave states" in terms of commodities was far inferior to the production of the North. Neutral observers saw an "inexcusable weakness, inertia and dilapidation everywhere ... manifest" in the Southern states.[10]

Terrorism is one reaction that emerges when a more primitive society – which a slave holding society is, in comparison to a free labor society – comes into an existential cultural conflict with a society that is more modern from a standpoint of economic organization. During the period we are about to examine in this work, passions surrounding existential cultural conflict became ever stronger, leading to the emergence, for the first time, of American terrorism.

But there was also another, and very important, factor at work.

Terrorism is the ultimate anti-democratic political tactic. Terrorists detest pluralism. They virtually never participate in a political process, except with the intent to wreak chaos. And, as the nineteenth century progressed, the defenders of the institution of slavery, both North and South, sought to keep issues of slavery's viability, morality, and future outside the arena of debate that is the lynchpin of the American-style political process. In so acting, they came into increasing tension and conflict with the ideal of an informed popular democracy that lay at the intellectual heart of the American revolution.

Beginning about 1820, the time of the first great political battle over the extension of legalized slavery into the new state of Missouri, the defenders of the institution of slavery in the United States slowly began to feel themselves besieged. In response, they bulwarked the institution against attack by forestalling the avenues of discussion, protest, and change normally available under a republican system of government. Those citizens who felt slavery to constitute an abomination to humanity, as well as an insult to America's explicit founding principle that "all men are created equal" and "endowed by

CHAPTER 2: FIGHTING THE SERPENT

their Creator with certain inalienable rights," were systematically hindered in expressing their views, either verbally, in print, or in political forums. The United States, from its inception, prided itself on resolution of issues through institutions of representative democratic government and the rule of law. Freedom of speech, and of the press, was the very first liberty guaranteed in its Bill of Rights. In such a context, the legally and judicially sanctioned gagging of advocacy of any abolition, alteration, or even restriction of slavery opened a path to terrorism on both sides of the issue as an avenue of quasi-political action. Slavery depended on a constant submerged pressure of violent control of human beings that was increasingly institutionalized. The thoroughgoing dampening of debate around the institution built up tension that made the threat of eventual violence ever more likely. Many sensitive observers who grew up in the South, in states where the relationships of master and slave were a way of life, and who were very aware and conscious of the bloody violent end of another nearby slaveholding regime in Haiti, felt a grim apprehension that one day ferocious rebellion would explode in the American South. And yet, in the young United States, wanton political violence by African Americans was not a common phenomenon.[11] The anti-democratic, speech-suppressing aspects of slavery's defense left a void in the political process that would attract the desperation of terrorism, on both sides. As we shall see, most of those who dedicated their lives to the diametrically opposing causes of protecting and opposing the institution of slavery did so through advocacy, and without violence. But a comparatively minuscule number possessed the distinctive personality characteristics that would lead them to become primordial American terrorists.

Chapter 3: A Precocious Frontier Puritan

In the year 1800 Nat, alias Nat Turner, was born. So, too, was John Brown.

The biggest single influence in shaping John Brown's beliefs, life, and destiny was unquestionably his father Owen Brown. Owen was part of a family of Puritan believers living and praying in the fervent hope of salvation. As a teenaged fatherless boy living in Canton, Connecticut, Owen was brought up by the Reverend Jonathan Hallock, a relative who was the minister of the town church. Owen later returned to apprentice in the home of Reverend Hallock as a young adult. Owen's older brother, also named John Brown, became a deacon in the church in nearby New Hartford, Connecticut. In 1793 Owen married Ruth Mills, granddaughter of the Reverend Gideon Mills. Ruth would become John's much beloved mother.

Owen plied a trade in leather, as a tanner, currier, and shoemaker, in addition to farming. Due to his consistently industrious, pious lifestyle, he and his family prospered and made themselves popular. But, for some reason, Owen felt restless. Twice he moved his entire business and farm from one town to another. Then, in the fall of 1804, he decided to completely uproot everything. He relocated the family during the following year to a frontier area in Hudson, Ohio. Ohio had then been a state for less than two years. The part of Ohio where Owen moved, adjacent to Lake Erie, had previously been mapped and reserved as a sort of projected western extension of Connecticut, called the "Western Reserve." According to Owen the indigenous people in the area, at the time of the family's arrival, "were more numerous than the white people, but were very friendly." They "brought us venison, turkeys, fish, and the like; sometimes they wanted bread or meal more than they could pay for at the time, but were always faithful to pay their debts."[1] Owen made helpful overtures to some members of the local tribe. His sentiments toward them were quickly absorbed by his young impressionable boy.

Owen and Ruth once again prospered in Hudson. Owen's businesses went well. He was soon recognized as one of the leading citizens in northeastern Ohio. He hosted "missionaries of the Gospel" and other eminent visitors. Through this social intercourse he rapidly became known to most of the "business people and ministers" (as he himself put it) not only in Ohio, but also in much of western Pennsylvania.

Owen Brown, father of John Brown
from Villard

But on December 9,

1808, a cataclysmic tragedy occurred. Hours after giving birth to her seventh child, Ruth Mills Brown died suddenly. Eight-year-old John was devastated. He would never fully recover from the emotional shock of losing his mother.[2]

John was a precocious and very bright boy. He learned extremely young that he could make himself useful through skill at driving cows and riding horses. He would have a lifelong heartfelt connection with animals. At age six he was "a rambler in a wild new country finding birds and squirrels, and sometimes a wild turkey's nest." When he was seven, he caught a live squirrel. The capture was evidently a violent struggle, John being bitten badly and tearing off the animal's tail in the process. But the "bobtail" squirrel became a much-beloved pet. John "got him perfectly tamed" and idolized him. When the squirrel disappeared, perhaps because it had been killed or had returned to the wild, John was, in his own words, "in mourning" for a year or two. For a long time afterwards he looked with longing at all squirrels to try to find his bobtailed pet. Soon afterwards John was given a lamb by his father as a present. The animal did fine until "it was about two-thirds grown," then it sickened and died. John tells us he experienced another storm of grief – which he hastens to tell us was an emotional, not a pecuniary grief – over this loss.[3]

John developed another lifelong characteristic at an early age. He could not bear to be "reproached." So in order to avoid having this happen, he became "addicted" (his word) to telling lies. John's candor and frankness in talking about this addiction, in the context of an autobiographical letter written in 1857 when he was not under any particular pressure to do so, is remarkably revealing. The better part of John's career would rest solidly on the faith and credit placed in him by others, generally people of wealth, who believed in John's outstanding character for integrity and trustworthiness. And yet, in matters of the utmost importance, John would revert to whopping deceits and falsehoods. He would also engage in elaborate

CHAPTER 3: A PRECOCIOUS FRONTIER PURITAN

deceptive subterfuges. Here we come into direct contact with the enigmatic dualism of the terrorist.

Energy was never lacking in John. He liked working and being busy. He performed feats we would today consider unbelievable for a child. By the time he was twelve years old, he was sent off by himself with a company of cattle for a journey of more than 100 miles. And, in his words, "he would have thought his character much injured had he been obliged to be helped in any such job." Transporting the cattle evidently was part of a profitable piece of business transacted by his father, selling and delivering beeves to American forces advancing northward through Ohio at the start of the War of 1812. Forty-five years later, John, speaking of himself in the third person, gave this account of what he identified as a strongly formative experience that happened during one of these journeys:[4]

> He was staying for a short time with a very gentlemanly landlord since a United States Marshall who held a slave boy near his own age very active, intelligent and good feeling; & to whom John was under considerable obligation for numerous little acts of kindness. *The master* made a great pet of John : brought him to table with his first company; & friends; called their attention to every little smart thing he *said or did* : & to the fact of his being more than a hundred miles from home with a company of cattle alone; while the *negro boy* (who was fully if not more than his equal) was badly clothed, poorly fed; *& lodged in cold weather;* & beaten before his eyes with Iron Shovels or any other thing that came first to hand. This brought John to reflect on the wretched, hopeless condition, *of Fatherless & Motherless* slave *children:* for such children have neither Fathers or Mothers to protect, & provide for them. He sometimes would raise the question *Is God their Father?*

John followed in his father's footsteps by taking up the trade of leather tanning and currying. From his indigenous friends Owen, after arriving in Ohio, learned the traditional way of curing buckskin. John, the observant boy, quickly learned that skill also. He prided himself in going about wearing self-cured buckskins. But John soon mastered, as well, all of the stages of Western-style chemical leather working. By the time he was fifteen, John was fully qualified and capable of acting as foreman of his father's tannery. He was then, by his own account, "very strong & large of his age & ambitious to perform the full labour of a man." During this period John developed his self-diagnosed obsession with perfection. James Foreman, who worked under him not long afterwards, recalled:[5]

> So strict was he that his leather should be perfectly dry before sold that a man might come ten miles for five pounds of sole leather and if the least particle of moisture could be detected in it he must go home without it … no compromise as to amount of dampness could be effected.

When he was sixteen, John was sent to Plainfield, Massachusetts to attend a religious preparatory academy, together with his brother Salmon, two years younger, and Orson Oviatt, son of the leading merchant in Hudson. The school was conducted in the home of the Reverend Moses Hallock, a relative of his father's old master Jonathan Hallock, and was known for producing ministers and missionaries.[6] However, the place was not a good fit for John. Within a span of several months, the trio left Plainfield and relocated to Litchfield, Connecticut, where they attended the even more religious Morris Academy. There John became an enthusiastic participant in "religious conferences and prayers." But after only a few more months, John dropped out of Morris Academy and returned to Hudson along with both of his companions.

CHAPTER 3: A PRECOCIOUS FRONTIER PURITAN

Given the substantial investment his father had made in sending both boys to New England for this education, the failure was a bitter defeat for John. It was not to be his last.

In relating to others what happened, John blamed his early exit from the school program on an "inflammation of the eyes." This explanation does not ring entirely complete. Throughout his extensive letters, which raise plenty of other physical complaints, we rarely hear of John having such a problem at any other time.[7] Also less than convincing is the excuse given by most of his sympathetic biographers, who attribute John's school troubles to a lack of background in the classical languages, Latin and Greek.[8] The reality is that at no time in his life would John ever be a willing participant or organizer in any group in which he was required to recognize and submit to the authority of others. John himself admitted:

> When for a short time he was sometimes sent to school the opportunity it afforded to wrestle & snow ball & run & jump & knock off old seedy wool hats; offered to him almost the only compensation for the confinement, & restraints of school ... he did not become much of a schollar."

Beyond schools, John's attitude of resistance to authority would include, in particular, skepticism about ecclesiastical figures. John would accept no interpretation of the Bible but his own. One who knew him remembered: "[H]e could not accept the creed .... [H]e was faithful to his own conscience."[9] He would assiduously avoid being enlisted in the military, fraternal organizations, and even antislavery societies.[10]

John certainly had no difficulty learning. Although he complained in his autobiographical letter that he did not learn much arithmetic in school, upon his return from Morris Academy John, from a textbook, mastered mathematics well enough on his own to become a capable land surveyor. From the age of ten he had "the free use of a good library," and, from it, he tells us he "acquired some taste for reading, which formed the principle [*sic*] part of his early education." (Spelling, obviously, was not John's strength.) He says he read the "lives of great, wise & good men." Plutarch's *Lives* was one of his favored works.[11] But the book to which he devoted the most time, and on which he became a recognized expert, was the Bible. He had an unusually complete memory of its contents. On many occasions later in life he would himself teach Bible classes, drawing favorable comparison to professional pastors and Bible scholars.

Whether it was in the context of studying the Bible, playing with children, raising a family, or running a business, John simply had to dominate. In his autobiographical letter, John displays insight on this trait when he repeats an expression his brother Salmon often used about him: "A King against whom there is no rising up." Again speaking of himself in the third person, John commented: "The habit so early formed of being obeyed rendered him in after life too much disposed to speak in an imperious or dictating way."[12] The 1882 reminiscence of Milton Lusk, who was three years younger than John and would become his brother-in-law, expressed the matter in the following terms.[13]

> I knew him from a boy, went to school with him, and remember well what a commanding disposition he always had. There was once a Democratic school and a Federal school in Hudson village, and the boys used to snow-ball each other. Brown and I were federalists, as our fathers, Squire Brown and Captain Lusk, were. Once day the Democratic boys found a wet hollow in the battlefield of snow balls, which were hard and hurt "masterly." John stood this for a while, – then he rushed alone upon the little Democrats, and drove them all before him into their schoolhouse. He did not seem to be angry, but there was such force and mastery in what he did, that everything gave way

CHAPTER 3: A PRECOCIOUS FRONTIER PURITAN

before him. He doted on being the head of the heap, and he was; he doted on his ability to hit the mark.

When he was eighteen, John followed further in his father's path by setting up, with his older foster brother Levi Blakeslee, an independent tannery outside Hudson. This was successful. He quickly acquired a whole stable of journeymen and apprentices working under him. At first John personally kept a "Bachelor's Hall," doing the baking and cooking for his crew. But soon John realized it would be more efficient to hire someone to do this type of work. Captain Amos Lusk, Milton's father, had died while serving during the War of 1812. John brought in his widow Mary to be the housekeeper. With Mary came Milton's 19-year-old sister Dianthe. John was particularly attracted to Dianthe because she was, as he put it, "remarkably plain." But she was also "neat, industrious & economical" as well as very religious. She was, according to Milton, "pleasant and cheerful, but not funny."[14] Her personality matched perfectly with John and his avowed "disdain of vain and frivolous conversation and persons." The two of them were married June 21, 1820.

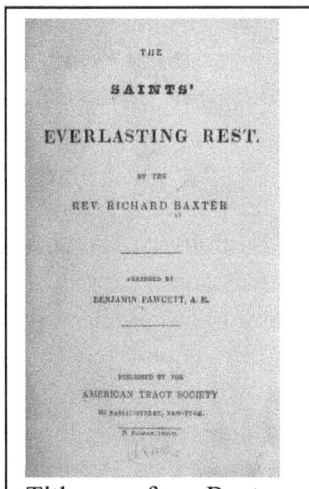

Title page from Baxter, *Saints Everlasting Rest*, 1840 edition

One of John's reading favorites was a classic Puritan treatise, written in 1650, Baxter's *Saints Everlasting Rest*. Besides glorifying death and the afterlife, this work strongly condemns any "profaning of the Sabbath," as that day is viewed as an earthly metaphor for the heavenly rest.[15] John severely irritated Milton with his attitude:

> When mother and Dianthe were keeping house for John Brown at the old log-cabin where he had his tannery, I was working as a boy at Squire Hudson's in the village, and had no time to go up and see my mother and sister except Sundays. Brown was an austere feller, and he didn't like that; one day he said to me, "Milton, I wish you would not make your visits here on the Sabbath." I said "John, I won't come Sunday, nor any other day," and I stayed away a long time. When Dianthe was married, I would not go to the wedding.

James Foreman came to work in 1820 as one of John's tanners. He lived with John and his family off and on for the next thirteen years. Foreman knew John well in the period before John had the first of his major failures, and long before he became a militant. Within a month after John's death, Foreman wrote a letter to a journalist who was putting together a rapid biography. His account expounds on several themes we have already seen: John's "iron will;" his passion for taming a new and wild country; his insistence on rigid observance of the Sabbath; his total command of the Bible, coupled with the ability to marshal scripture in support of his arguments; his unshakeable Calvinist belief in predestination. Tinted though they no doubt were by the charity John showed by giving Foreman a farm, as well as the afterglow of his feelings after John's terrorist exploits and death, Foreman's recollections are of considerable interest for understanding John's personality.

John, the future martyr, was obsessed with crime and punishment. This shines through several anecdotes that James Foreman chose to tell: [16]

> In the summer of 1824 a journeyman of his stole from him a very choice calf skin and the journeyman was suspected by Brown for the theft from the fact that he was rather opposed to good order and religious habits.

CHAPTER 3: A PRECOCIOUS FRONTIER PURITAN

> About a week after the theft a brother of the journeyman came to the tannery on business and shortly before he started home Brown sent two men ahead of the brother to secrete themselves and see if the brother was not carrying the calf skin home with him. Such proved to be the fact. They took the skin from him and brought it back and gave it to Brown who took the skin in his hand. He called the journeyman to one side and he owned up to the theft and cried like a child under the lecture Brown gave him. Brown told him he would not prosecute him unless he left, but if he did leave he would prosecute him to the end of the law. The journeyman stayed about two months through fear of prosecution and in the meantime all the hands about the tannery and the house were strictly forbidden speaking to him not even to ask him a question and I think a worse punishment could not have been set on a human being than that was to him, but it reformed him and he afterwards became a useful man.

On this same theme:

> In the fall of the same year his wife was taken sick under peculiar circumstances & Brown started for the doctor and some lady friends from his residence, a journey of one-and-one-half miles to the center of Hudson. On his way he spied two young men tying up two bags of apples and making ready to put them on their horses. Brown immediately tied his own horse, went to the men and made them empty their apples, own up to the theft, and settle up the matter before he attended to the case of his wife. Such was his strict integrity for honesty and justice.

And Foreman then tells yet a third story on this topic:

> In December 1829 a man living about sixteen miles

northeast from Meadville stole a cow in Meadville and started home with her. He was followed and about six miles down the road he was brought back on a warrant to Meadville. The owner of the cow learning the fact of the man being very poor took his cow and dismissed the man and started him home, but Brown being in Meadville next day & hearing the facts sent the constable and had the man rearrested and returned to jail where he was confined for some time. While he was in the jail Brown supplied his family with abundance of provisions regularly once a week until his release, and the principle he took was the man had committed a crime and must be punished but the family was innocent and must not suffer for the man's wrongs. It was always a standing principle with him that crime must not go unpunished nor honesty unrewarded.

Foreman's remarks are borne out by other people's descriptions about John. For example, Sanborn passed along the following account,[17] probably originating with the Reverend H.L. Vaill, one of the instructors at Morris Academy:

> A story of the two brothers is told, how John, finding that Salmon had committed some school offense, for which the teacher had pardoned him, said to the teacher: "Mr. Vaill, if Salmon had done this thing at home, father would have punished him. I know he would expect you to punish him now for doing this, – and if you don't, I shall." That night, finding that Salmon was likely to escape punishment, John made good his word, – more in sorrow than in anger, – giving his brother a severe flogging.

Foreman emphasized John's high reputation for personal honesty and integrity. "[I]t became almost a proverb that speaking of an enterprising man, 'He was as enterprising and

CHAPTER 3: A PRECOCIOUS FRONTIER PURITAN

honest as John Brown,' and as 'useful to the country'." Foreman found John highly empathic. He recalled:

> On one cold snowy Sabbath with the snow one and one-half feet deep Brown took it in his head that a family about four miles distant were destitute of anything to eat or wear and that the man being high-spirited might let his family suffer before he would make his wants known. So the next day he dispatched myself and wife as spies to find out their condition and, if needy, to propose to the man to come to Brown to get provisions and promise labor for it the next summer, and Brown says if I can only manage to get the provisions on to him without his knowing my object I will never take one cent from him and the ends of charity will be answered.
>
> The man & family we found destitute and proposed to him to come to Brown and get what was needed & pay in work next summer. He came, got the provisions and some clothing, but Brown utterly refused to receive any remuneration therefor.

John's obsession with crime and punishment, mixed with empathy for the offender, shines through in other accounts of him by family members. John once whipped his four-year-old son Jason with a switch after Jason told his mother a made-up story about a supposedly tame raccoon. He did this simply because the story Jason told was not true. John kept an "account" of lashes due his oldest son John Jr., who, as a young boy, was placed in charge of running a horse-powered mill to grind bark for the tannery. One day, after John Jr. lapsed for the umpteenth time by going out of the mill to play, the senior John remarked that it was time for a "settlement of the account." After taking John Jr. into the tannery and giving him lashes with a switch representing about one-third of the accrued "debt," to the son's "utter astonishment" John Sr.

stripped off his own shirt and ordered John Jr. to "lay it on" his bare back. John Jr. recalled:[18]

> I dared not refuse to obey, but at first I did not strike hard. "Harder!" he said; "harder, harder!" until *he received the balance of the account.* Small drops of blood showed on his back where the tip end of the tingling beech cut through. Thus ended the account and settlement, which was also my first practical illustration of the Doctrine of the Atonement. I was then too obtuse to perceive how Justice could be satisfied by inflicting penalty upon the back of the innocent instead of the guilty; but at that time I had not read the ponderous volumes of Jonathan Edwards's sermons which father owned.

John's daughter Ruth had this to say about him:[19]

> He used to whip me quite often for telling lies, but I can't remember his ever punishing me but once when I thought I didn't deserve it, and then he looked at me so stern that I didn't dare to tell the truth. He had such a way of saying, "tut, tut!" if he saw the first sign of a lie in us, that he often frightened us children. […]

> He showed a great deal of tenderness to me; and one thing I always noticed was my father's peculiar tenderness and devotion to his father. In cold weather he always tucked up the bedclothes around grandfather, when he went to bed, and would get up in the night to ask him if he slept warm, – always seeming so kind and loving to him that his example was beautiful to see.

In his autobiographical letter, John refers to himself as "a practical Shepherd." He says he "began early in life to discover a great liking to fine cattle, horses, sheep, & swine." Discussing a later period when John became a professional shepherd, Ruth

CHAPTER 3: A PRECOCIOUS FRONTIER PURITAN

says:[20]

> He would very often bring in a little dead-looking lamb, and put it in warm water and rub it until it showed signs of life, and then wrap it in a warm blanket, feed it warm milk with a teaspoon, and work it over with such tenderness that in a few hours it would be capering about the room. One Monday morning I had just got my white clothes in a nice warm suds in the wash-tub, when he came in bringing a little dead-looking lamb. There seemed to be no sign of life about it. Said he, "Take out your clothes quick, and let me put this lamb in the water." I felt a little vexed to be hindered with my washing, and told him I didn't believe he could make it live; but in an hour or two he had it running around the room, and calling loudly for its mother. The next year he came in from the barn and said to me, "Ruth, that lamb I hindered you with when you were washing, I have just sold for one hundred dollars." It was a pure-blooded Saxony lamb.

John emulated his father's restlessness by uprooting himself from the tannery in Hudson after five years and relocating to an entirely new country. His move, in May 1825, was actually eastward, a distance of around 100 miles across the Pennsylvania line to Randolph township, east of the town of Meadville in Crawford County. In his typically dominating fashion, John took with him not only his own growing family, but also his tannery employees, including James Foreman. Per Foreman, in Randolph John quickly "built a fine tannery, sunk vats, and had leather in vats tanning on the first of October besides clearing off twenty-five acres of new heavy timbered land."[21] He rapidly made himself very busy with multifaceted activities not only in his original occupation as a tanner, but also as a surveyor, a postmaster, and a community leader.

Foreman comments: "As a man he seemed always partial to a new country to improve and help subdue it and grow up with the improvements made & thus he was of great use in Pennsylvania in surveying out new roads, building school houses, procuring preaching and encouraging everything which would have a moral tendency to improve the country."[22] John also began branching out into acquiring and raising pedigreed animals, specifically blooded cattle.

John's major life events continued to follow in the path of his father Owen Brown. In 1832 John's wife Dianthe died of a heart ailment at age 31, three days after giving birth to their seventh child (who had also died shortly after birth). John and five surviving children moved out of the house and boarded for a time with James Foreman, who had just gotten married.[23] But early the following year, John and the children moved back to the family house. John was fairly easily able to replace Dianthe by repeating his tried-and-true formula of courting a relative of his tannery housekeeper. This time the object was the housekeeper's younger sister Mary Day, "a large silent girl of sixteen."[24] She accepted his proposal of marriage and, on May 11, 1834, the first of John and Mary's thirteen children was born.

By the beginning of 1835, John could well regard himself as blessed and successful in the life he had carved out in his ten years in Randolph township. He had taken a big role in taming a wild country. Twelve employees worked under him in his tannery establishment. He had overcome the loss of a good wife. He was continuing to follow God's command to be fruitful and multiply. He was a respected community leader. He was the resident postmaster. He was also the resident bible scholar, and was sometimes even called upon to preach a little. But suddenly, John uprooted himself and his entire family again. He left Randolph to move back to Ohio.

John never explained why he chose to make this curious move. But, by examining clues and context, we can venture a pretty fair guess that the reason, at bottom, was that John felt a deep-seated drive to do something big. Something glorious. He did not wish to remain king of an obscure backwater. He longed to be closer to the center of action, both financially and, as we shall see, politically. Winds of discontent were blowing and John, largely through his strong connection to his father Owen, felt them.

Chapter 4: The Rising Cause of Injustice

Benjamin Lundy was the first to discover that advocacy of the cause of abolishing slavery in the United States could be turned into a full-time livelihood.[1] The issue had festered for a generation since the new nation was born. Directly after the adoption of the Constitution, petitions were sent to Congress by Pennsylvania Quakers and others, asking that body to exert its full constitutional power for the abolition of slavery. But Congress quickly rejected these, unanimously agreeing that the national government had no power to interfere with slavery within the limits of any state. From that time the energy of anti-slavery action seemed to decline.[2] Although the importation of fresh Africans into American slavery was prohibited as of 1808, the ruling culture of the Southern states became ever more comfortable, and ever more stubbornly entrenched, in a paternalistic attitude toward its inherited African Americans. The majority, both North and South, held a sincere belief that enslaved people, under the benevolent tutelage of those of Western European descent, were better off than would be the case otherwise. They seemed oblivious that, in the words of James Fenimore Cooper, "Physical suffering … is not the prominent grievance of slavery. It is the deep moral degradation which no man has a right to entail on another."³ Cotton emerged as the latest major cash crop that could make effective use of the primitive slave labor system to generate giant profits.⁴

Benjamin Lundy
Library of Congress

Benjamin Lundy was born in 1789 in the very northern tip of New Jersey that is situated northwest of New York City. Both his parents were Quakers. At age 19, he traveled to Wheeling, then part of Virginia, on the Ohio River. There, he apprenticed in saddlery, and then he worked for eighteen months as a journeyman. Benjamin's wispy, mild-mannered appearance belied the force of spirit that lay within. Surrounded in Wheeling by young people he considered thoughtless and frivolous, Benjamin pointedly retained his plain style of dress. He kept going to Quaker meetings. He spent his spare time reading instructive books. He became quite distressed about the plight of the African Americans he occasionally saw being herded in chains through the streets of the city.⁵

Benjamin married and made a home in St. Clairsville, Ohio, 10 miles to the west. He went into business, in which he was fairly successful. In four years, he saved $3,000. He had two beautiful daughters. He was at peace with his neighbors, and he was not in debt. His life could be called prosperous. But none of this contentment was to last. Benjamin's deepening concern over the institution of slavery left him no peace of mind.

In 1815, Benjamin called together a few local friends and organized an association called the Union Humane Society. In a few short months, this society swelled from the initial five or six persons to nearly five hundred members. These included most of the influential preachers and lawyers, and many other respectable citizens, of several nearby counties. Benjamin, under a fictitious name, published an appeal on the subject of slavery addressed to "the philanthropists of the United States." Not long afterwards, Benjamin became involved in helping to edit a newspaper started by one of his friends, called *The Philanthropist*.

Benjamin left Ohio and traveled to Missouri for six months in order to sell items from his saddlery shop. When he returned, he found his business far too dull. At first he moved it 20 miles north, to Mount Pleasant, Ohio where *The Philanthropist* was printed. But shortly, he decided to take all three of his apprentices and his entire stock in trade and return with them to Missouri. Traveling by boat, the party arrived in St. Louis in late fall of 1819, right in the midst of hot national debate about the infamous "Missouri question," that is, the question of the toleration or prohibition of the institution of slavery in the proposed new state of Missouri. Benjamin plunged headlong into the controversy. He wrote several pieces for the local newspapers on the evils of slavery. But the other side of the question won the day. Missouri was formed with a constitution that contained no restriction on slavery.

A year and ten months after his departure, Benjamin returned home to Mount Pleasant, covering 700 miles on foot and in the winter. He had spent, and given up, thousands of dollars in his odyssey. But rather than return to saddlery, Benjamin decided to become a full-time abolitionist. He founded a newspaper, which he named *The Genius of Universal Emancipation*. The first publication of *The Genius* occurred in January 1821. It was something of a success. Within four months, he accumulated an ample subscription list. After eight monthly issues, at the urging of some friends Benjamin moved his operations to eastern Tennessee. After arriving he learned how to be a typesetter and printer as well as a writer. In addition to publishing *The Genius of Universal Emancipation*, he published a separate weekly newspaper and a monthly agricultural work. While in Tennessee, Benjamin

CHAPTER 4: THE RISING CAUSE OF INJUSTICE

received some threats based on the contents of *The Genius of Universal Emancipation*. But the threats did not result in violence, nor did they stop him from continuing.

The Genius of Universal Emancipation was, at the time, the only specifically anti-slavery paper in America. As such, it garnered a decent audience and circulation. Hoping to secure even better support, Benjamin decided to transfer its publication to an Atlantic city. Benjamin had made a few acquaintances in Baltimore, so he moved there. The first Baltimore number of *The Genius of Universal Emancipation* was published in October 1824. The paper, under Benjamin's stewardship, proposed a wide variety of schemes for ending slavery, most of which involved some form of gradual emancipation or purchase of freedom.[6] Presently he changed the format of the paper to a weekly. At the end of 1825, Benjamin went to Haiti. His mission there was to oversee the settlement of eleven African Americans, whom a North Carolina slave owner, after hearing Benjamin speak during a tour, had agreed to free. Benjamin sought the consent of the independent government of Haiti to receive more freed slaves. Over the next few years, he was responsible for resettling several hundred freed African Americans in Haiti. But Benjamin wound up being "detained" in Haiti, working on the resettlement project, much longer than he expected. Before he returned his wife died, and his children were placed in foster homes. By the time he arrived in Baltimore, Benjamin no longer had a home. From that point forward, Benjamin became essentially itinerant.

He continued to publish *The Genius of Universal Emancipation*. This evoked wrath. On January 7, 1827, Benjamin was attacked in broad daylight in the street by a prominent Baltimore slave trader named Austin Woolfolk, whom Benjamin had criticized in the pages of *The Genius*.[7] In response to the attack, Benjamin pressed a civil suit against Woolfolk. The judge found Woolfolk liable, but awarded

Benjamin only $1 in damages. He expressed the highly judicial opinion that by virtue of the assault, Benjamin "got nothing more than he deserved."

In June of 1828 Benjamin went on a tour of the Northeast for the purpose of raising money and securing more subscriptions to *The Genius*. While in Boston, he made the acquaintance of a 23-year-old journeyman printer named William Lloyd Garrison. Young Lloyd (as he was called) came from an extremely impoverished background. His father, a sailor, had deserted his mother and family when Lloyd was very young. Lloyd's older brother quickly developed into an alcoholic. His mother moved to Baltimore in search of a living, leaving Lloyd an orphan to be raised by his mother's fellow worshippers in the Baptist church of Newburyport, Massachusetts. Lloyd took advantage of free public schools and taught himself to read. Eventually he hooked on as a printer's apprentice. As he mastered the trade of typesetting, he branched out into occasionally writing pieces for the paper. When he finished his period of indenture in 1825, Lloyd borrowed money from his former master and started his own newspaper, of which he was editor. In print, he styled his name as "Wm. Lloyd Garrison." From the very beginning, Lloyd's trademark style was that of the harassing gadfly. He had the misfortune, or bad judgment, to harass his former master in print. This resulted in his loan being called, and his newspaper presses rapidly being sold to pay the debt.

At the time Lloyd Garrison met Benjamin Lundy, he had already gone through several more publishing gigs, all of which followed pretty much the same course as the first.[8] The papers he put out were technically excellent, but their sharp rhetoric soon got the editor into political hot water. Although Lloyd was prone to dunning citizens for their greedy and sinful behavior, he was not yet overly involved in the anti-slavery movement. But Benjamin's talks on that subject aroused his interest. In November 1828, Benjamin returned to Boston and

CHAPTER 4: THE RISING CAUSE OF INJUSTICE

tried to persuade the talented Lloyd to join him as assistant editor of *The Genius of Universal Emancipation.* However, Lloyd had previously committed to publishing another politically-oriented paper in Bennington, Vermont, and could not disengage from it.

In September of 1829 Lloyd, having run through his usual progression with the Bennington paper, and being once more unemployed, finally joined Benjamin in Baltimore as the co-editor of *The Genius.* Benjamin and Lloyd each published editorial matter under his own name. Lloyd the gadfly rapidly became an even more fervent abolitionist than Benjamin. In comparison to Benjamin, Lloyd was not as careful to avoid giving grounds for prosecution for libel in courts of a slaveholding state.

William Lloyd Garrison, at age 30
Library of Congress

In a prosecution that was largely political, Lloyd was charged and convicted of criminal libel for an article he had written about a New England slave trader. Unable to pay the $50 fine, he spent seven weeks as a martyr of sorts in the Baltimore jail (although in reality he lived relatively comfortably, in the home of the warden). During this experience, Lloyd began to acquire profound faith in the noble effectiveness of the political philosophy of turning the other cheek; in other words, of studied non-violence. Ultimately Arthur Tappan, a wealthy abolitionist from New York City, paid Lloyd's fine, bringing about his release, after Benjamin published a pamphlet that publicized the injustice of Lloyd's conviction.[9]

The libel prosecution campaign against Benjamin in Baltimore courts continued when he tried to restart *The Genius.* This legal pressure soon forced Benjamin to move the paper to

Washington City.[10] There, he continued his campaign to urge Congress to abolish slavery in the nation's capital. The presence of the slave system in Washington City contradicted American ideals, he wrote, and drew justifiable scorn from representatives of foreign powers. Even residents not participating in the system were becoming "contaminated by its deleterious and heart-corrupting influence."[11]

Meanwhile, the freed William Lloyd Garrison moved back to Boston and, on a financial shoestring, launched his own abolitionist weekly newspaper, *The Liberator*. The key issue on which Lloyd split with Benjamin was "colonization."[12] In the editorial of his opening edition of *The Liberator*, dated January 1, 1831, Lloyd published a small manifesto:[13]

> In defending the great cause of human rights, I wish to derive the assistance of all religions and all parties …. Assenting to the "self-evident truth" maintained in the American Declaration of Independence, "that all men are created equal, and endowed by their Creator with certain inalienable rights – among which are life, liberty, and the pursuit of happiness," I shall strenuously contend for the immediate enfranchisement of our slave population.

From the start, he denounced any more "gradual abolition." Lloyd's vitriolic indictment of the "colonization" movement was set forth in a separate book he published in May 1832. It included ten major averments:

1. The American Colonization Society is pledged not to oppose the system of slavery.

2. It apologizes for slavery and slave-holders.

3. It recognizes slaves as property.

4. It increases the value of slaves.

5. It is the enemy of immediate abolition.

CHAPTER 4: THE RISING CAUSE OF INJUSTICE

6. It is nourished by fear and selfishness.
7. It aims at the utter expulsion of the blacks.
8. It is the disparager of the free blacks.
9. It denies the possibility of elevating the blacks in this country.
10. It deceives and misleads the Nation.[14]

Nat's chilling rampage in Southampton County, Virginia occurred, as we have seen, in late August of 1831. This was only eight months after *The Liberator* began publication. Nat's terror attack produced an enormous backlash. The prevailing mood in the South turned ugly. No longer would published abolitionist advocacy of the Benjamin Lundy or William Lloyd Garrison stripe be tolerated in border areas such as Tennessee and Maryland. Many people, both North and South, blamed *The Liberator* for inciting the mass murders. Lloyd was indicted by a grand jury in the state of North Carolina. The legislature of Georgia offered a reward of $5,000 for his arrest and conviction for seditious libel.[15] Southern leaders quickly recognized the new prominence of the abolitionist movement as championed by Lloyd. They began passing laws barring the introduction of literature, particularly *The Liberator*, into the South via U.S. Mail. They began to correspond with Northern statesmen and officials with the aim of suppressing *The Liberator*.[16] In Boston, Lloyd on several occasions was attacked by mobs. He was extremely lucky to escape serious physical humiliation, injury, or death.

A hint of John Brown's thinking regarding his move from Pennsylvania back to the Hudson, Ohio area is in a letter he sent to his younger brother Frederick on November 21, 1834, only a few months before the move. This letter followed a visit to John's home in Randolph by Frederick, who was living in Hudson. John tells Frederick that, after fully consulting the feelings of his wife and his three boys, they agreed to get "at least one negro boy or youth," and "bring him up as we do our own." John explained that this upbringing would include "a good English education," the history of the world, business, general subjects, and "above all, try to teach him the fear of God." He says he and the family thought to obtain one, either by getting "some Christian slaveholder to release one to us," by getting "a free one," or if neither of the first two succeeded, by submitting to "considerable privation to buy one." The letter goes on to extol the virtues of this proposal. "If the young blacks of our country could once become enlightened, it would most assuredly operate on slavery like firing powder confined in rock." [17]

The letter is a clue that tells us that very likely, an important part of the context of John's thinking was a cause of injustice trumpeted on the pages of *The Liberator*.[18] Prudence Crandall, a 29-year-old woman, in 1831 opened a school in a large house in the center of the town of Canterbury, Connecticut. The leading citizens of Canterbury encouraged her to open the Canterbury Female Seminary, and many of them served on its advisory board. By the beginning of 1832 she had twenty students, who were placed with her to receive instruction in several branches of higher education. But over the course of the following year, Prudence acquired another interest. A young African American woman named Mariah Davis worked as a "family assistant" at the Seminary. She was engaged to a young man named Charles Harris, whose father, William Harris, was the local agent for *The Liberator*. Charles's sister Sarah, who was very close with Mariah, was a light-skinned girl, with a combination of European, African, and Native American ancestry, about seventeen years of age. Sarah had already attended a district school, but now she approached Prudence with the question of whether she might be admitted into the new Canterbury Female Seminary.

Prudence decided to take a stand by admitting Sarah, even

CHAPTER 4: THE RISING CAUSE OF INJUSTICE

Prudence Crandall portrait

though she knew doing so might offend some of the community members and parents. Sarah was a young lady of pleasing appearance and manners and, besides, was already well known to many of the pupils, having been their classmate in the district school. She had also been for some time a member of the church of Canterbury. No legitimate objection could be made to her admission into the school, excepting only her dark complexion.[19]

In a few days the parents of some of them called and remonstrated. Prudence pressed upon their consideration Sarah's eager desire for more knowledge and culture, the good use she intended to make of her education, her excellent character and lady-like deportment, and, above all, that she was an accepted member of the same Christian church to which many of them belonged. Her arguments were to no avail. Sarah belonged to a proscribed, despised class and, therefore, must not be admitted into a private school with their daughters. Appeals to their sense of right, to their compassion for injured fellow beings, did not change their minds. Prudence was threatened that, if she did not dismiss Sarah Harris, her white pupils would be withdrawn from her.

Prudence was obstinate to a fault. Rather than comply with such a demand, she decided on an even more dramatic and drastic action. On January 13, 1833, she wrote directly to Lloyd to ask his help in establishing an "all colored" school for women. This was a concept *The Liberator* had been pushing for several years. On February 24, 1833, Prudence announced to her students that, beginning with the next term, the school would receive *only* students of color.

Soon the whole town of Canterbury was in a flame of indignation. Prudence was immediately visited by the town leaders, who remonstrated with her severely over this program. She would not budge. On March 2, 1833, a prominent advertisement for the new "all colored" school appeared in *The Liberator*. The community was even more severely disturbed by the fact that this upstart young woman had decided to present herself as an outpost of organized anti-slavery. A town meeting was held March 9, with an agenda of devising and adopting such measures as "would effectually avert the nuisance, or speedily abate it, if it should be brought into the village."[20]

The mounting confrontation in Canterbury was trumpeted loudly in *The Liberator*. Sixteen local towns submitted petitions with numerous signatures asking Prudence to abandon the "all colored" school concept. Undismayed by the community's staunch opposition, Prudence received, early in April, black girls from Philadelphia, New York, Providence, and Boston. By the end of May, she had thirteen total students.[21] At first, local prosecutors threatened to apply an antiquated "vagrancy" law to the out-of-state students, which called for public "whipping on the naked body." Prudence and the students openly defied these threats. The community leaders then turned to other measures.

On May 24, 1833, the "Black Law" of the state of Connecticut was enacted. It read in part as follows:

> SECTION 1. Be it enacted by the Senate and House of Representatives, in General Assembly convened, that no person shall set up or establish in this State any school, academy, or literary institution for the instruction or education of colored persons who are not inhabitants of this State; nor instruct or teach in any school, or other literary institution whatsoever, in this State; nor harbor or board, for the purpose of attending or being taught or instructed in any such

school, academy, or literary institution, any colored person who is not an inhabitant of any town in this State, without the consent in writing, first obtained, of a majority of the civil authority, and also of the Selectmen of the town, in which such school, academy, or literary institution is situated ....

On receipt of the news that the legislature had passed this law, joy and exultation ran wild in Canterbury. The bells were rung and a cannon fired, until all the inhabitants for miles around were informed of the triumph. The abolitionist press was equally as outspoken in its condemnation of the disgrace of this law. The stage was set for a legal battle.

As soon as practicable, Prudence was arrested and arraigned before two local justices. The trial was brief, because the result was predetermined. Prudence was committed to stand trial at the next session of the Superior Court. She was remanded to jail. It was expected that Prudence's outspoken friends would rapidly post a bond to free her. By prearrangement, however, Prudence's abolitionist backers did not. As a sort of publicity stunt, Prudence was actually required to spend the night in jail. Prudence bore this with the spirit of a martyr. After she spent her symbolic night of detention in jail, Prudence's allies posted her bail bond the next day.

Arthur Tappan, the New York abolitionist philanthropist, was one of Prudence's original supporters in her idea of starting a school for African American women. He now came to Prudence's rescue financially. He and other benefactors hired an excellent team of attorneys to represent her. The first trial resulted in a hung jury. The retrial, before a judge more sympathetic to the Black Law, yielded a conviction. But Prudence's attorneys appealed this conviction to the state's highest court of errors on grounds that the Black Law was unconstitutional. The justices found a way to overturn the conviction on procedural grounds, without reaching the merits of the constitutional issue. Their decision was made on July 22,

1834. But on September 9, 1834, local bullies found another way to close Prudence's school. At midnight, the school house in Canterbury was assaulted by a number of persons with heavy clubs and iron bars. Five window sashes were demolished. Ninety panes of glass were dashed to pieces.

Prudence was finally ready to relent. Her pupils had become afraid to remain another night under her roof. The front rooms of the house were hardly habitable; and it seemed foolish to repair them only to be destroyed again. After due consideration with her friends, Prudence decided to abandon the school. *The Liberator* highly publicized all of this. The injustice done to Prudence, and the cause of raising and educating African Americans, reverberated in the letter written by John Brown to his brother only a few weeks later.

The most startling aspect of the Prudence Crandall persecution is that it was not carried out by slave owners, nor did it occur in a state where slaveholding was legal. These events occurred in New England. The burghers of Canterbury, even though they did not favor slavery, had absorbed the impact of the great wave of reaction that swept the nation following Nat's chilling terrorist attack carried out in Southampton, Virginia. In the wake of that attack there was a widely disseminated argument that the terrorism had its roots in educating, or "enlightening," African Americans. John Brown in fact made reference to this sentiment, in his letter of November 21, 1834 quoted above, when he spoke of an explosion that would result from enlightenment of young blacks acting like "firing powder confined in rock." The majority of people in New England and elsewhere who opposed slavery in the 1830s did not do so out of humanitarian motives. Their reasons were far more racist than altruistic: they simply did not want any persons of color in their midst. As unrealistic and cruel as it now appears, their solution was to ship all African Americans, no matter whether slave or free, to Africa to "colonize" that continent. This variant of anti-slavery was generally referred to as the "colonization" movement.

By 1834, northeastern Ohio stood at the eye of an erupting tempest pitting committed "abolitionists," who advocated immediate elimination of the institution of legalized ownership of human beings anywhere in the United States, versus "colonizationists." John's father Owen Brown, an ardent "abolitionist" and treasurer of the Western Reserve Anti-Slavery Society, was very near the center of this storm.[22] John found himself attracted to the political swirl around this issue. Shortly after the beginning of 1835, John accepted an offer to leave Randolph, move back to Hudson, and go into partnership to develop a new tannery with Zenas Kent, a wealthy acquaintance of his father whom John barely knew.

Prudence Crandall was one of the first militant abolitionists who found herself dealt with harshly and unfairly by a racist society. Lloyd would soon have many more such causes of injustice to trumpet on the pages of *The Liberator*.

Chapter 5: Sacrificing Life for Liberty

In December of 1834, just about the same time John Brown decided to move back to Hudson, a "revolt" occurred at Lane Seminary in Cincinnati, Ohio. A large group of students, known to history as the Lane Rebels, voluntarily accepted their expulsion from the seminary. Their reasons were expounded in a lengthy "Defense" published on the pages of *The Liberator*'s January 10, 1835 edition. The school fathers were not happy because the Lane Rebels, though otherwise model students, had determined to dedicate all their spare hours to active support of abolition, rejecting the more moderate anti-slavery approach of "colonization." The faculty told them they needed to stop their preoccupation with the issue. Their declaration of "Defense" summed up the grounds of their "secession" from the Seminary:[1]

> free discussion and correspondent action have been prohibited *by law*. We are commanded to discontinue anti-slavery society. We are prohibited from holding meetings among ourselves and from making statements and communications at table, or elsewhere, without permission. A committee of the board of

trustees is set over us to exercise censorship, and vested with discretionary power to dismiss any student whenever they may deem it necessary so to do, without consultation with the faculty and without assigning reasons either to them, to the individual dismissed, or to the community.

Among the fifty-one Lane Rebels who subscribed his name to the Defense was a 22-year-old Massachusetts native named Amos Dresser. Amos followed up his expulsion from Lane Seminary with an itinerant pilgrimage into the slaveholding republics. On July 1, 1835, he left Cincinnati to head southward to Nashville, Tennessee. In so doing he displayed a certain affluence, making the journey in his personal horse-drawn carriage.[2] Amos arrived in Nashville on July 11. His business was to sell two books: *The Cottage Bible*, which was a family-oriented study guide, and *Six Months in a Convent*, a best-seller written by a Protestant girl who had rebelled against a Catholic monastic order. The arrival of the cultured, educated Amos caused quite a stir in Nashville. Curious burghers rapidly discovered the contents of Amos's carriage to include abolitionist pamphlets and literature, such as pages from *The Liberator*, which Amos later said he had used as "wrapper" for the books. One item found in his box was a February, 1835 edition of *The Anti-Slavery Record*, which featured a provocative image of slaves being led in a coffle, the two in front depicted playing fiddles, with the American flag as well as the whip of a slave-driver flying in the background. When questioned, Amos made no secret of his anti-slavery sentiments. The effect was incendiary. Amos was promptly brought before a great "Committee of Vigilance" consisting of sixty of the most prominent citizens of Nashville on a charge of intent to distribute literature advocating the abolition of slavery.

Inflammatory woodcut found in Amos Dresser's trunk

On a Saturday afternoon and evening, before an overflowing courtroom audience, Amos played to the hilt the role of the unjustly accused. He denied any intent to post or sell anti-slavery literature. He did, however, admit that before reaching Nashville he had sold a copy of *Letters on American Slavery*, by John Rankin. This was an abolitionist work by any reasonable definition. Another copy of Rankin's book, as well as two other anti-slavery tracts, were produced from Amos's trunk, which was opened, with his permission, in court. Amos told the Committee these books were for his personal reference. Also extracted from the trunk was a letter to Amos from a person he calls "a very aged and venerable lady," which made reference to preaching "a stream of abolition two hundred and fifty miles long" from Cincinnati to Cleveland. Another letter, from one of Amos's friends who was a minister, remarked that during a recent visit to the East, "abolition had been the principal topic of conversation" by day, and that the friend had "preached on slavery" at night.

When called upon to make a statement on his own behalf, Amos proudly declared his sentiments on the subject of slavery. He told the assembled Committee and audience that he believed slaveholding to be inconsistent with the gospel, and a constant transgression of God's law. Emancipation contemplated that the slave should be put in possession of "rights which we have declared to be inalienable from him as a man" and the African American "should be treated as our neighbor and our brother." He denied, however, that he had ever incited violence, stating that in the "few instances" when he had casually conversed with slaves, he had recommended "quietness, patience, submission," relying on "the good conduct of the slaves ... and to the influence of argument and persuasion."

The courtroom was cleared for deliberation. Amos was escorted to a side room to await. The Committee reached their verdict by 11 p.m. They congratulated themselves on showing tremendous discretion, mature judgment and restraint by rejecting calls to impose a penalty of death, as well as other calls to inflict one hundred lashes. Amos was convicted of (1) being a member of an Anti-Slavery Society in Ohio, (2) having in his possession periodicals published by the Anti-Slavery Society; and (3) circulating these periodicals and advocating in the community the principles they inculcated. He was sentenced to receive twenty lashes on his bare back, which was felt to be a sufficient physical lesson and humiliation, and he was ordered to leave town within twenty-four hours. Amos was immediately taken to the main square of the city, he was stripped of his clothes, and just before midnight he knelt to be lashed with a cowhide whip by the city's chief constable (whom Amos, in his narrative, complimented for maintaining a professional demeanor throughout the proceedings). Next morning, the battered Amos sold his horse and carriage, at the loss of "at least two hundred dollars," and limped out of town in disguise. But his narrative sold many copies of the September, 1835 issue of *The Liberator*.

Two years later, in the humming Illinois town of Alton, the cause of abolition would witness the dark making of its first martyred hero. He was Elijah Parish Lovejoy, born in Albion,

Maine on November 8, 1802. Elijah was a Puritan through and through. His father was a prominent Congregational minister. From boyhood, Elijah displayed a phenomenal ability to memorize passages of literary works. Not only was he an outstanding student, he was also quite athletic, particularly in swimming. But his real passion was writing, including poetry. Elijah's poetry reflects an obvious fascination with death and the afterlife. Witness this concluding stanza from a poem called "The Little Star" that Elijah wrote while he was a student at Waterville:[3]

> But how or where—'tis doubt and darkness all
> Or oft times seems so, yet full well I know,
> There is beyond this sublunary ball,
> A land of souls, a heaven of peace and joy,
> Whose skies are always bright, whose pleasures never cloy
> And if to souls released from earth 'tis given,
> To choose their home thro' bright infinity,
> Then yonder star shall be my happy heaven,
> And I will live unknown, for I would be
> The lonely hermit of Eternity.

Elijah graduated in the fall of 1826 from what is now called Colby College in Waterville, Maine. He immediately headed west to St. Louis, Missouri. With his talent for writing, Elijah rapidly became editor of the *St. Louis Times*.[4] After a self-described period of four years as a skeptic, he embraced a thoroughgoing religious revival. In early 1832, he returned to the East to attend the Princeton Theological Seminary. Upon graduation, he was licensed to preach as a Congregational minister. But Elijah was not called to preach from the pulpit. His calling was to preach from the printed page of a newspaper. Elijah returned to St. Louis, where he took over as editor of a new paper called the *Observer*. Like William Lloyd Garrison, he was drawn to provoking controversy. Initially the

CHAPTER 5: SACRIFICING LIFE FOR LIBERTY

controversy centered on religious doctrine. He became unpopular with the Catholic church after he published lengthy diatribes against "Popery." Regarding the October, 1834 public dedication of the Basilica de Saint Louis (i.e., the new Catholic cathedral) in St. Louis, he denounced the very fact that the ceremony occurred on the Sabbath, as well as the display of soldiers and the American flag. The Catholic-oriented press, in response, bitterly criticized Elijah. Their foremost charge was that he was an abolitionist.[5]

In 1835 Elijah took up the cause of abolition in earnest. He published in *Observer* editorials explicitly urging Missouri to amend its constitution to forbid slavery. These, and other writings denouncing slavery as evil, drew attention from the same settled segment of society from which was formed the "Committee of Vigilance" that had previously passed judgment on Amos Dresser. Solid and sensible citizens felt the dissemination of abolitionist publications had too much risk of inciting bloody uprisings like Nat's.

A letter to the editor signed by nine persons on October 5, 1835 suggested "we have reason to believe that violence is even now meditated against the *Observer* office." Elijah as editor was urged to "pass over in silence every thing connected with the subject of Slavery." Public sentiment prevailed on the publisher of *Observer* to announce, while Elijah was absent on a religious retreat at the beginning of October 1835, that the paper would engage in "an entire suspension of all controversy upon the exciting subject of Slavery." But, upon his return, Elijah became all the more assertive. He was adamant that he would not change his published themes. Elijah attributed to "Popery" the criticism that had been leveled against him.[6]

A provocative event occurred on April 28, 1836. Francis J. McIntosh, of mixed African and European ancestry, was a cook on board the steamboat *Flora*, newly arrived in St. Louis from Pittsburgh. He was intent on visiting an African

American woman employed on another vessel docked in the harbor. McIntosh was arrested for reasons that remain somewhat unclear. Apparently, he interfered with two local deputies while they were trying to detain some other sailors. When McIntosh was being escorted to a jail cell, he drew a long knife, either due to a hostile remark by one of the deputies or possibly in an attempt to escape from custody. He lashed out with the blade at both of the deputies, first wounding one of them in the side, and then slashing the throat of the other, George Hammond. Hammond, spewing blood, managed to run down the street before he collapsed and died. McIntosh, meanwhile, fled the jail house, scaled a garden fence, and hid in an outhouse. A man nearby had seen the commotion. He followed McIntosh, smashed in the door to the outhouse, and seized both McIntosh and his knife. McIntosh was taken back to the jail, where a crowd rapidly gathered around. Its members were incensed at the murder of the well-known, well-liked George Hammond by an African American. Mrs. Hammond and her children drew more onlookers, and added to the crescendo of anger, as they came on the scene and wailed over George's body. The angry mob broke into the jail house, forced the sheriff to depart, and removed McIntosh from the holding cell. They then carried him to the outskirts of town, where they chained him tightly to a locust tree. They piled wood up to his knees and lit it. McIntosh pleaded with those in the crowd to shoot him, but they refused to do it. After 20 minutes of slow burning, McIntosh died.[7]

The next day Elijah visited the scene of the lynching. Appalled, he wrote: "We stood and gazed for a moment or two, upon the blackened and mutilated trunk, for that was all which remained – of McIntosh before us, and as we turned away, in bitterness of heart, we prayed that we might not live."[8] Elijah bitterly protested, on the pages of the *Observer*, the growing local practice of inflicting summary justice by an extrajudicial "mob."

CHAPTER 5: SACRIFICING LIFE FOR LIBERTY

A grand jury was asked to consider prosecution of the perpetrators of the McIntosh lynching. Its members decided against prosecuting anyone, after they were instructed by the presiding judge, with the hugely ironic name of Luke Lawless, that whether the grand jury should act to indict depends on "whether the destruction of McIntosh was the act of the 'few' or the act of 'the many'." What would go down in history as the "Lawless charge" was framed as follows:[9]

> If, on the other hand, the destruction of the murderer of Hammond was the act, as I have said, of the many – of the multitude, in the ordinary sense of these words – not the act of numerable and ascertainable malefactors; but of congregated thousands, seized upon and impelled by that mysterious, metaphysical, and almost electric frenzy, which, in all ages and nations, has hurried on the infuriated multitude to deeds of death and destruction – then, I say, act not at all in the matter; the case then transcends your jurisdiction – it is beyond the reach of human law.

Judge Lawless's legitimization of rule by "the multitude," as an exception to the rule of "human law," would reverberate.

Elijah published a scathing denunciation of the Lawless charge – saying, among other things, that the jurist was a "Papist" – and the "mob" rapidly responded. A group of vigilantes broke in and sacked the St. Louis office of *Observer*. Elijah was, at the time, already on the verge of moving his newspaper operation out of Missouri, across the Mississippi and a few short miles upstream, to the town of Alton, Illinois. While he told people in Alton that he did not particularly plan to focus on slavery, Elijah at the same time assured his readers that neither the theme nor the subscription list of the paper would change. The move did not fool the many who considered *Observer* to be highly subversive and dangerous due to its "agitation" of abolitionist views. No sooner did his surviving printing equipment arrive in Alton than a "multitude" seized it, while it lay on the riverside, and consigned it to the bottom of the Mississippi.

Elijah was now more determined than ever to persevere in the cause of abolition. In a letter to his mother dated August 31, 1836, he set forth his defining manifesto:[10]

> I have opened my mouth for the dumb, I have pled the cause of the poor and oppressed – I have maintained the rights of humanity, and of nature outraged in the person of my fellow-men around me, and I have done it, as is my nature, openly, boldly, and in the face of day, and for these things I am brought into these straits. For these things I have seen my family scattered, my office broken up, my furniture – as I was moving it to this place – destroyed – have been loaded with execrations, had all manner of evil spoken of me falsely, and finally had my life threatened, and laid down at night, weary and sick, with the expectation that I might be aroused by the stealthy step of the assassin. This was the case the last night I spent at St. Louis. Yet none of these things move me from my purpose; by the grace of God I will not, I will not forsake my principles; and I will maintain, and propagate them with all the means He puts into my hands. The cry of the oppressed has entered not only into my ears, but into my soul, so that while I live I cannot hold my peace.

Elijah had the terrorist's desperate passion for an adopted cause. He had the extreme stubbornness. He had the unwavering conviction that his mission was ordained by God. He was willing to give up material comforts for the sake of the cause. As we have seen, he had some suicidal ideation. He repeatedly expressed calm and contentment at the prospect that he may die a martyr's death. "I am sure I could have gone to the stake," he wrote in a letter to his brothers, "as cheerful as I ever was to go to a bed of rest."[11] But there were two extremely important and fundamental attributes that prevented Elijah from fitting the profile of the terrorist.

First, he demonstrated the ability to graduate from multiple higher education courses of study. That is something terrorists very seldom do.

Second – and this is absolutely critical – Elijah had enormous confidence in his ability to use the power of words to persuade the adversary to come over to his position. Terrorists virtually always disdain articulate engagement and argument with the adversary of their cause.

Another press was bought, shipped to Alton, and put to work. The *Observer* was duly published. On July 6, 1837, Elijah capped off an editorial appeal for the formation of a statewide Illinois Anti-Slavery Society with a castigation of the "bitter mockery" of Alton's July 4 celebration. On the anniversary of "the declaration that all men are born free and equal," he asked, how could the citizens "eat and drink with gladness of heart when our feet are on the necks of nearly THREE MILLIONS of our fellow men?"[12]

Five days later, a large public meeting was held in Alton to debate what should be done about *Observer*. As described in another local newspaper, the proceedings were

> not the intemperate ebullitions of excitement, or the temporary expression of a high wrought feeling; on the contrary, the proceedings throughout, manifest to us, the deep and settled purpose of men whose hospitalities have been slighted, and whose friendships have been abused, by one, who was bound by every moral and political obligation to have acted otherwise.

The meeting's participants, regardless of their views on slavery itself, agreed overwhelmingly that Elijah had breached a promise he had made the previous year when he came to Alton from St. Louis, that he would limit the *Observer* to being a religious journal. As a result, the public meeting determined to appoint five of its participants to meet with Elijah, in order to "ascertain whether he intends to disseminate through the columns of the *Observer* the doctrine of Abolitionism."

On July 20, *Observer* published a lengthy composition entitled "What Are the Doctrines of Anti-Slavery Men?"[13] Overall, it was a relatively temperate, measured presentation of the natural law basis of "immediate abolition." Unlike many of his other editorials, Elijah did not here include any harsh religious invective or anti-Catholicism. He started out from the premise that he, himself, had once opposed anti-slavery measures, and had since been won over to them. So in the spirit of revival, he urged his readers to follow along the same path. With great eloquence, his piece reviewed, one by one, the central moral problems associated with American slavery that underpinned his call for immediate abolition. We will condense them here:

1. One man cannot convert another into a piece of property.

2. Slavery is a sin, and whatever is morally wrong can never be politically right.

3. As all souls are born free of sin, there can be no merited status of slavery that passes from generation to generation and endures for all posterity.

4. Current slaveowners are responsible for perpetuating the institution; they cannot escape blame on the grounds that their forefathers introduced it.

5. The labor of a man is his fundamental property and cannot be given away without his consent.

6. Emancipation is not to be feared, because it means only that ex-slaves are to be treated like human beings.

7. Emancipation should be effected by the masters themselves, and not by revolt.

8. Slavery is just another of the many evils, such as gambling, bigamy, or drinking, that must be overcome by a civilized society.

9. Racial amalgamation is not something abolitionists advocate, nor is it inherent in emancipation. But, it is something that has obviously been practiced a great deal at the South by those who are the loudest in condemning it.

Elijah directed the five delegates from the public meeting to this piece, which he felt rebutted the hysteria of the charge that he was inciting terrorism. He also provided them with additional specific points of response to the citizens' demand that he cease his published advocacy of abolition. We will, again, condense them succinctly:[14]

1. Thank you for your courtesy.

2. I cannot accept you as an official organ of a public meeting.

3. I cannot accept that liberty of the press and freedom of speech are subject to supervision and control.

4. Liberty of speech is an inalienable natural law type right that came "from our Maker."

5. I do plan to engage in "important" agitation, but not "unwise" agitation.

However courteous, the "bottom line" of Elijah's response was flatly unacceptable to the vast majority of the citizens of Alton. It was only a matter of time before the players took to the stage for the final act.

Two unsuccessful attempts were made to "mob" Elijah's office. One failed because of a rain storm; the other, because the building was deemed too well guarded. But on Monday, August 21, 1837, at 10 o'clock at night, the *Observer* office in Alton was besieged by a determined band of fifteen or twenty citizen vigilantes. Several printing employees were in the office at that time. People in the crowd outside threw volleys of rocks at them through the windows. After one of the printers was hit on the head by a stone and seriously injured, all of them surrendered and left the building. The vigilantes then entered and proceeded with their work. The press, type, and everything else they could get their hands on was smashed into pieces, and dumped into the street outside the building. The necessity and success of this attack by ruffians was generally acclaimed. In the words of Elijah's brothers,

> had you on the next morning passed round from store to store, and from house to house, through the length and breadth of Alton, the expressions "good enough for him," "served him just right," and "glad of it," would oftener have been heard, than any words of reprobation or regret, ten to one.

Elijah, when this assault began, was out of the office performing a marriage ceremony. He returned while the crowd outside was conducting its siege. After he was recognized, he came very close to being tarred, feathered, and ridden out of town on a rail. But the crowd, after seizing him in the street, deliberated and decided to let Elijah go.[15]

Three days afterwards, Elijah issued an "appeal" to his friends and subscribers to contribute funds to re-establish *Observer*, despite its destruction. He urged them not to "let mob-ism triumph." The abolitionist press, including Garrison's *The Liberator*, publicized Elijah's plight.[16] From quarters far removed from Alton, Elijah received the outpouring of support he sought. The "friends and subscribers" promptly contributed the necessary money, and a new press was ordered from Cincinnati. Meanwhile, a tract opposing Elijah on religious grounds was circulated throughout the greater St. Louis area, written by a Presbyterian minister and theorist named James Smylie who lived in Mississippi. Smylie's pamphlet argued that slave holders did not need to go around with their heads "bowed like bulrushes" because the Holy Bible does, indeed, sanction the system of American slavery. Therefore, Smylie disagreed with Elijah that slave owners will feel God's "hot displeasure." Smylie argued that keeping wise patriarchal figures in charge of wives, children, and all other dependents, including slaves, was the best basis for a kind and just society.[17]

Part of Elijah's base expressed the sentiment that he should perhaps confine himself to publishing a religious paper. On September 11, he offered to resign as editor of the *Observer*, and turn over his list of 2,100 subscribers, on two conditions:

1. Whoever takes over must honor the *Observer's* obligations & debts to third parties; and

2. Elijah himself must be paid something to compensate him for the four years he put into building up the paper.

No one, including Elijah himself, seems to have taken this resignation offer seriously. It went nowhere. While Elijah was absent from town in September, visiting Edward Beecher and other Illinois Presbyterian church leaders, the new press arrived. It was taken by Elijah's friends to a local warehouse. The respectable citizens watched its arrival, which they did not intend to tolerate. Ten or twelve of them, with handkerchiefs tied over their faces, soon assembled outside the warehouse. The Mayor of Alton, John H. Krum, came on scene and politely requested that these gentlemen disperse and go home. They answered that they would certainly do so as soon as they had finished the little job they had on hand. They, in turn, advised the Mayor to go home so he would not get hurt. They promised to disperse just as soon as they destroyed Elijah's new press. Mayor Krum later commented, "he never witnessed a more quiet and more gentlemanly mob."[18]

Elijah returned to Alton to find his paper once more put out of business. On Sunday, October 1, he ventured across the state line to preach two sermons to the congregation of a Presbyterian church in St. Joseph, Missouri, the home of his wife's parents. There Elijah's young wife Celia, who was seriously ill, was resting in bed with their son, who was also sick. After the evening sermon, Elijah was alerted to be on his guard, because vigilantes were out looking to get him. At about 10 o'clock at night, two ruffians came to the in-laws' residence, which was on the second floor over a store. They knocked and asked for Elijah. Elijah, forthrightly and perhaps foolishly, poked out his head and asked what they wanted. "We want you downstairs, damn you!" They came in, grabbed Elijah, and started pulling him out of the house, punching at him when he resisted. Celia, feeble with illness as she was, came into the room, and she slapped the face of a man who tried to stop her. She put her arms around Elijah to protect him from further violence. It was a very frightening scene. The desperate efforts of Celia, her mother, and sister induced the intruders to leave the house. As soon as they did, Celia collapsed with exhaustion.[19]

The mob was by no means ready to desist. The vigilantes returned, forced themselves back into the upstairs room where Elijah was next to Celia's bedside, and once more set to dragging him out of the house. This time, however, one of the citizens was William Campbell. Even though he was a slave owner, he was also appalled by the crude behavior of the others. Campbell turned on the group and insisted that they leave. Eventually he persuaded some of them to join with him in turning the tide of intended violence to Elijah, and in inducing everyone to go back outside. As the mob was milling around in the yard, Elijah could overhear one of the most adamant among them, stirring up the crowd by telling them a story of how his wife, in Mississippi, had been raped by a black man, and that Elijah was at fault for instigating this act.

An emissary from the crowd came up the stairs to the residence a third time. This time he presented Elijah with a note. The note demanded that Elijah agree to leave town by 10 a.m. the next morning. Scornfully, Elijah refused. However, some of Elijah's defenders among the crowd came up and persuaded him to reconsider. After all, Elijah's home was in Alton, not St. Charles. So Elijah wrote out a pencil note saying he had ordered a stage to take him away by no later than the next morning at 9 a.m. Elijah's friends in the crowd were able to distract the remainder of the besiegers long enough so that he could slip out a back way. In the darkness, Elijah returned to the Alton area. He was ultimately joined there by Celia the next day.[20]

After this harrowing experience, Elijah and his brothers Joseph and Owen, who had come out to Alton from the East to join him in his struggle, carried muskets with them wherever they went. Elijah did not relent in his stubborn determination to continue *Observer*. Using his own personal credit, he ordered a fourth press to be shipped to Alton. To his brothers and others who questioned whether he should not move the publication to another place in Illinois, he replied, "we shall see."[21]

Elijah now fixed his attention and hopes on a "convention" to be held in Alton to form an Illinois Anti-Slavery Society, the organization he had advocated in his July 6 editorial. He had invited both locals and supporters of the cause from elsewhere in Illinois. Elijah was joined in this project by Edward Beecher. Edward and Elijah had a great deal in common. Both were Presbyterian ministers trained in outstanding theological seminaries. Both were also sons of noted Presbyterian ministers. Edward's father Lyman Beecher was president of Lane College, the seminary which, as we have seen, was operating in Cincinnati. Edward himself was now the president of Illinois College in Jacksonville, Illinois, 60 miles north of Alton. Like Elijah, he was convinced of his righteousness. In September, Elijah sojourned with Edward in Jacksonville. Edward persuaded Elijah that the "convention" should be held open to all persons interested in "free inquiry." He argued this would help rebut a charge that the outcome was pre-orchestrated. Edward placed an advertisement in a newspaper, inviting all persons interested in "free inquiry" to attend the convention, which was scheduled for Thursday, October 26.

Edward Beecher's plan for the open "free inquiry" convention backfired big time. The great majority of those who appeared at the Presbyterian Church in Alton to debate the question had no interest whatsoever in seeing the cause of abolition take another step forward. One of the leading speakers was Usher F. Linder, Attorney General of the State of Illinois. Those attending the "convention" agreed overwhelmingly in supporting a resolution Linder offered to adjourn the "convention" without forming any anti-slavery society.

Of course, the failure of the "free inquiry" convention did not cause Elijah to give up on his organizational project. The delegates bent on abolition met privately the next day, formed the Illinois Anti-Slavery Society, and elected Elijah as its corresponding secretary.[22]

More public meetings in Alton ensued, as the battle of wills between determined adversaries continued. Most citizens who participated in the meetings probably hoped, as their main goal, to prevent violence and bloodshed. A meeting attended by both sides occurred on Thursday, November 2, one week after the "free inquiry" convention. Edward Beecher tried to pass a series of "free speech" and "anti-mob" resolutions. Linder, the state Attorney General, led the opposition to these. The end product was something of a compromise, to appoint a committee composed of some partisans of both points of view. The meeting was then adjourned, to continue the following afternoon.

This resumed meeting, on Friday, November 3, was chaired by Linder. The very first thing he did was make a motion that no one from outside the county could be allowed to participate, other than to sit silently in the audience. This was an obvious move to muzzle Edward Beecher and other abolitionists who had come to Alton to support Elijah. The second thing was a resolution proposed by Linder, calling for reconciliation on both sides. But, as part of this resolution, it was deemed "indispensable" that "the late editor of the *Observer* no longer be associated with any newspaper establishment in this city." Various speakers debated whether or not Elijah had breached a promise not to publish on abolition when he relocated to Alton. Some argued that he had a right to change his mind on the subject. But at the conclusion of the debate, Linder's resolution proscribing Elijah's publishing activity was adopted.

Elijah then rose to address the meeting. His manner was calm and serious, but firm and decided. He gave a speech fit for inclusion in the annals of martyrdom:[23]

> Mr. Chairman – it is not true, as has been charged upon me, that I hold in contempt the feelings and sentiments of this community, in reference to the question which is now agitating it. I respect and appreciate the feelings and opinions of my fellow-

citizens, and it is one of the most painful and unpleasant duties of my life, that I am called upon to act in opposition to them. If you suppose, sir, that I have published sentiments contrary to those generally held in this community, because I delighted in differing from them, or in occasioning a disturbance, you have entirely misapprehended me. But, sir, while I value the good opinion of my fellow-citizens, as highly as any one, I may be permitted to say, that I am governed by higher considerations than either the favor or the fear of man. I am impelled to the course I have taken, because I fear God. As I shall answer it to my God in the great day, I dare not abandon my sentiments, or cease in all proper ways to promulgate them.

I, Mr. Chairman, have not desired, or asked any compromise. I have asked for nothing but to be protected in my rights as a citizen – rights which God has given me, and which are guaranteed to me by the constitution of my country. Have I, sir, been guilty of any infraction of the laws? Whose good name have I injured? When and where have I published any thing injurious to the reputation of Alton? Have I not, on the other hand, labored, in common, with the rest of my fellow-citizens, to promote the reputation and interests of this city? What, sir, I ask, has been my offense? Put your finger upon it – define it – and I stand ready to answer for it. If I have committed any crime, you can easily convict me. You have public sentiment in your favor. You have your juries, and you have your attorney (with a nod to Linder). I have no doubt you can convict me. But if have been guilty of no violation of law, why am I hunted up and down continually like a partridge upon the mountains? Why am I threatened with the tar barrel? Why am I waylaid every day, and from night to night, and my life in jeopardy every hour?

> You have, sir, made up, as the lawyers say, a false issue: there are not two parties between whom there can be a compromise. I plant myself, sir, down on my unquestionable rights, and the question to be decided is, whether I shall be protected in the exercise, and enjoyment of those rights – that is the question, sir – whether my property shall be protected, whether I shall be suffered to go home to my family at night without being assailed, and threatened with tar and feathers, and assassination; whether my afflicted wife, whose life has been in jeopardy, from continued alarm and excitement, shall night after night be driven from a sick bed into the garret to save her life from the brickbats and violence of the mobs; that, sir, is the question.

At this point, Elijah was overcome by feelings, and burst into tears. Many in the audience, including those who had just voted to shut down his paper, also wept aloud. Elijah continued:

> Forgive me, sir, that I have thus betrayed my weakness. It was the allusion to my family that overcame my feelings. Not, sir, I assure you, from any fears on my part. I have no personal fears. Not that I feel able to contest the matter with the whole community, I know perfectly well I am not. I know, sir, that you can tar and feather me, hang me up, or put me on the Mississippi, without the least difficulty. But what then? Where shall I go? I have been made to feel that if I am not safe at Alton, I shall not be safe anywhere. I recently visited St. Charles to bring home my family, and was torn from their frantic embrace by

> a mob. I have been beset night and day at Alton. And now if I leave here and go elsewhere, violence may overtake me in my retreat, and I have no more claim upon the protection of any other community than I have upon this; and I have concluded, after consultation with my friends, and earnestly seeking counsel of God, to remain at Alton, and here to insist on protection in the exercise of my rights.

Here, Elijah concluded by embracing his holy death: "If the civil authorities refuse to protect me, I must look to God; and if I die, I have determined to make my grave in Alton."

As soon as Elijah finished speaking, he left the building. Linder again took the floor. With all the confidence of a prosecutor who knows he already has his case won, Linder dismissed, as hypocritical cant, everything Elijah had just said. He held him up as a fanatic, as a dangerous man in the community. He condemned Elijah and all his friends as abolitionists.[24]

Elijah's latest press arrived in St. Louis on Sunday, November 5. The plan was to smuggle it into Alton at a small hour of the morning, when, hopefully, the town would be asleep. Monday night, November 6, Elijah assembled a militia of around forty to fifty of his sympathizers to guard the press. Mayor Krum knew all about the secret landing of the press, and he knew all about the militia. Later it would become a subject of legal controversy as to whether or not he had actually authorized the militia as an approved organ of the city government. When the press was landed in Alton Tuesday morning at 3 a.m., it was spotted by watching vigilantes. They blew horns to call the concerned citizens to their posts. However, even by this stratagem, at 3 a.m. they could not muster enough force to challenge Elijah's militia. So the press was successfully landed and transported to the second floor of a waterfront warehouse owned by a trading firm called Godfrey, Gilman & Co. Winthrop Gilman, one of the owners,

CHAPTER 5: SACRIFICING LIFE FOR LIBERTY

was sympathetic to Elijah.[25]

The next evening, the militia met again at Godfrey, Gilman & Co. Gilman asked them to stay overnight to protect the press. Nineteen, in all, agreed to stay. Within a short time a "mob" of twenty to thirty persons gathered outside. Edward Keating, a lawyer, and Henry West, a merchant, came to the door and asked to be admitted to see Gilman. They proceeded to advise him that unless the press was given up, the building would be burned down over their heads and every man killed. Keating later told his side of this story. He was actually not the one making the threat; he was trying to be a peacemaker and was trying to avoid violence. He was just making Gilman aware of how dangerous was the mob outside, and he was just urging everyone inside to give the mob what it wanted, to avoid bloodshed. A curt "reply" was given to Keating. Both the building and the press it contained would be defended.

The Godfrey, Gilman & Co. warehouse was only superficially well suited for defense. It actually consisted of two block buildings, one adjacent to the other, that were not interconnected. Although the second story of these buildings offered the advantage of firing down on the attackers, defenders on the second floor of one building could not directly see or communicate with those on the second floor of the other building. Much worse, all of the doors and windows were on the shorter ends of the buildings. The long sides had no windows. The attackers readily spotted this as a weak point. Persons inside were essentially blind with respect to the long side.

Some of the second floor defenders started rolling jugs and crocks out the doors onto the heads of the crowd beneath. The mob tried its usual method of throwing stones, but the force of these was much weaker than the force of the jugs and crocks raining down on them. In the melée, the sound of gunshots rang out. Some probably were fired over the heads of the attackers for effect. But soon there was an exclamation from outside that someone had been hit. A ruffian named Lyman Bishop had been struck while he was stooping to pick up a stone. Those inside, peeking out, saw four men pick up Bishop, one by each arm and each leg, and carry him to a nearby doctor's office. There, Bishop rapidly expired. The shock of the shooting and Bishop's death caused the mob to withdraw from the attack for a time.

Very soon, though, the crowd returned. Now it was angrier than ever. Voices yelled out that they were going to set fire to the building and shoot every damned abolitionist as they left the building. More shots were fired from inside, but again, over the crowd's heads. Mayor Krum, at that point, entered the building to talk with Gilman. He then emerged. Once again, he spoke in an effort to get the mob to disperse. But the vigilantes, many of whom had prior experience with scenes involving destruction of Elijah's presses, had no intention of standing down.

Now the attackers approached the blind long side of the building with an improvised double ladder. A boy climbed up the ladder with tinder and a match to set the roof on fire. Inside the warehouse, volunteers were called to go out and shoot whoever was on the ladder. Elijah was the first to say he would go. He was accompanied on the foray by two others. As they stepped out of the door to get at the blind side of the building, Elijah was met with a hail of bullets to his body. The other two were struck on their legs. Elijah turned back into the building and staggered up to the second floor, saying, as he went, "I am shot! I am shot! I am dead!" These were his last words. When he reached the top of the stairs, his life expired without any further struggle.[26]

Keating and West returned to the door to the warehouse, displaying a white handkerchief, and asked for Gilman. They said all the boys wanted was the press. If that was surrendered, they would put out the fire and leave the rest of the contents of the warehouse intact. Gilman reflected that his building contained a great deal of people's valuable goods that had been entrusted to him. So he, and everyone else present, resolved to give up the press. All the defenders except one of the wounded and one other man left the Godfrey & Gilman warehouse and went into a nearby hardware store. The vigilantes then entered. They went up to the second floor, took a good look at Elijah's dead body, and set about destroying the press. The next day, Elijah was taken out and quietly buried in Alton, just as he had foretold.[27]

Rendering of the attack on Gilman's store, Alton, Illinois, Nov. 7, 1837, resulting in the death of Elijah Lovejoy

Two criminal trials ensued in January of 1838. The first of them was directed to eleven of Elijah Lovejoy's supporters, plus Winthrop Gilman himself. They were charged with unlawfully and riotously and in a violent manner defending and resisting an attempt being made to break up and destroy a contraband printing press and, secondly, for unlawfully and riotously defending and resisting the attempt being made "by divers persons" to enter the storehouse of Godfrey and Gilman. In the second trial, eleven defendants were tried for acting in a riotous fashion to destroy the printing press, property of Godfrey and Gilman.[28]

The evidence in the first trial reflected a great deal of chaos that had happened on the night of November 7. The main contested issue was actually whether or not the actions of the defenders of the press, in shooting at their attackers, had been officially requested and sanctioned by Mayor Krum, so that they could not be deemed unlawful. Linder, the Illinois state Attorney General, took over the prosecution of the case, even though he was also obviously involved as a witness and protagonist of the events. The imagery evoked in Linder's closing argument was an appeal to fear of any public airing of abolitionist opinions. He obviously alluded to the lingering specter of Nat's Southampton insurrection.[29]

> But the press came at last; the press which was intended to preach insurrection, and to disseminate the doctrines which must tend to disorganization and disunion. With what delight they caught the first glimpse of their new-born child; with what joy they hugged it to their hearts!
>
> ...
>
> A press brought here to teach rebellion and insurrection to the slave; to excite servile war; to preach murder in the name of religion; to strike dismay to the hearts of the people, and spread desolation over the face of this land. Society esteems good order more than such a press; sets higher value upon the lives of its citizens than upon a thousand such presses. I might depict to you the African, his passions excited by the doctrines intended to have been propagated by that press. As well might you find yourself in the fangs of a wild beast. I might portray to you the scenes which would exist in our neighbor states from the influence of that press: the father aroused to see the last gasp of his dying child, as it lays in its cradle, weltering in its blood; and the husband awakened from his last sleep by the shrieks of his wife as she is brained to the earth.

The case was, however, well argued by defense counsel, that Gilman was entitled to resist the attack on his property. The Mayor had authorized the defense by militia of Gilman's warehouse. The jury required only 15 minutes to acquit.[30]

In the second trial, the evidence once again focused primarily on the amount of chaos involved. Most people who had entered the Godfrey and Gilman building testified they did so to witness the body of Elijah. It was never clear who was actually responsible for destroying the press. Defense counsel put the "press itself" on trial. The Lawless charge was well argued by the defense, that the deed had been done by a "multitude." In one hour, the jury acquitted.[31]

In both trials there was a remarkable absence of any testimony, evidence, or discussion about the exact circumstances of the shooting of Elijah Lovejoy.

News of Elijah's tragic death traveled East quickly. Lloyd devoted much of the November 24, 1837 issue of *The Liberator* to its coverage. He included a published account of the events by Mayor Krum. Many press clippings, primarily from New York or Southern papers, were included concerning Elijah's death. Most condemned Elijah for being very foolish, but they condemned even more strongly the mob that killed him. Even papers which totally detested abolitionism protested that Elijah's death would make him a martyr. Lloyd headlined his own commentary: "A Martyr for Liberty." He proclaimed the worthiness of Elijah's sacrifice, expressing a confident faith that his spirit would live on to terrify "a guilty, conscience-stricken people by its presence." However Lloyd was, at this time, busy defining a new and paramount political philosophy that he called "Nonresistance." In pioneering this concept, he would become the direct lineal forebear of Leo Tolstoy, of Mohandas Gandhi, and of Martin Luther King. He concluded his encomium to Elijah with a very important caveat:[32]

> We cannot, however, in conscience delay the expression of our regret, that our martyred coadjutor and his unfaltering friends in Alton should have

allowed any provocation, or personal danger, or hope of victory, or distrust of the protection of Heaven, to drive them to take up arms in self-defence. They were not required to do so either as philanthropists or christians, and they have certainly set a dangerous precedent in the maintenance of our cause, – though the fact does not in the least palliate the blood-thirsty conduct of their assailants. Far be it from us to reproach our suffering brethren, or weaken the impression of sympathy which has been made on their behalf in the minds of the people – God forbid! Yet, in the name of Jesus of Nazareth, who suffered himself to be unresistingly nailed to the cross, we solemnly protest against any of his professed followers resorting to carnal weapons under any pretext or in any extremity whatever.

News of events in Alton also flowed to northeast Ohio. Before the month of November was out, Laurens P. Hickok, a conservative professor of theology at Western Reserve College, became incensed when he read the story of the destruction of Elijah's presses, and his death. After reviewing the matter in an assembly of students at the college, he called a meeting to occur two days later at the Congregational Church in the town of Hudson. Smoldering with anger, the next day he rode all over town, calling at every house and inviting the people to attend. At this meeting Professor Hickok made an eloquent speech, culminating with, "Are we free, or are we slaves under Southern mob law?" Many others made stirring speeches expressing outrage, as well.

Over half a century later, two unrelated persons who attended would recall what happened near this meeting's conclusion. Owen Brown was there. Owen spit out a compelling image which compared Elijah to John the Baptist. He closed the meeting with a prayer. And his son, the 37-year-old John, was present. At the very end of the meeting, John stood, raised his right arm, and made a short declaration. "Here, before God, in the presence of these witnesses, I consecrate my life to the destruction of slavery."[33]

Chapter 6: A Star Bursts on the Scene

By the beginning of 1841, Lloyd was a full-time professional agitator. He had published *The Liberator* for ten full years. He constantly solicited and received ongoing financial support from sympathetic readers in order to keep the paper, as well as his meager family finances, afloat. To grow his subscription list, Lloyd traveled on frequent speaking tours. He maintained a network of abolitionist "agents" to promote the paper, mainly in New England, New York and Pennsylvania. He also made two successful trips to the British Isles, where slavery had already been abolished and where there was a willingness by many of the well-heeled to contribute financially to the sponsorship of abolitionist sentiments in the United States. Lloyd developed an effective speaking style. But his abolition theme could become repetitive and long-winded. So Lloyd regularly spiced up his anti-slavery revivals by calling on other interesting speakers who could draw more people into the audience.

One of these speakers was George Thompson, an eloquent and debonair native of Liverpool. Lloyd became friends with Thompson while the two of them traveled together on Lloyd's first British lecture circuit in the summer of 1833. The following year, English friends of abolition raised the money to subsidize sending Thompson to promote abolition in America. Within a short time Thompson was "[s]peaking eight to ten times per week in towns throughout New England." Thompson was a very effective fund raiser. His talents bailed *The Liberator* out of serious debt.[1] However, on the afternoon of August 21, 1835, Lloyd was nearly tarred and feathered, or worse, by a mob that invaded a Boston Female Anti-Slavery Society meeting at which Thompson was originally scheduled to speak. The women in this society became aware of public calls for a mob to lynch Thompson. They agreed among themselves that the handsome Englishman, for his own safety, should stay away from their meeting. Lloyd was selected to take to the podium in his place. The mob indeed hungered after Thompson. It entered the building before Lloyd could even get started with his speech. He escaped harm only because a couple of good Samaritans rescued him from the crowd's fury. Then the Mayor of Boston intervened and locked up Lloyd in jail overnight under a pretext, just to protect him.[2]

After Thompson returned to England, Lloyd found a new "draw" in the person of two former female slaveholders from South Carolina, Sarah and Angelina Grimké. They joined Lloyd's speaking tours. It was a provocative novelty unheard of at that time.[3] The controversy that ensued over Lloyd's tactic of relying on the Grimké sisters exacerbated a schism between Lloyd and other nationally prominent abolitionists. By this time Lloyd, the professional gadfly and agitator, was branching out into outspoken advocacy of righteous causes other than the immediate abolition of slavery per se. These included: the doctrine of nonresistance; the equal rights of women; and abstention from involvement in politics, on the ground that such involvement would inevitably taint ideological commitment with the sin of compromise. Lloyd also campaigned to eliminate the observance of Sunday as the Lord's Sabbath, on the ground that all days should be regarded as equally holy. Lloyd's stance on these issues provoked vitriolic conflict between Lloyd and many fellow abolitionists who did not subscribe to these other causes. Even though the others might tend to agree with the causes, they felt them to be a needless distraction from the focus of the problem of the institution of slavery. The moderates tended to be the wealthier, and the more connected to organized churches, among the anti-slavery advocates. Thus, they held much power within the abolitionist movement. Lloyd avoided being purged from his leadership position in the movement only because of the strong and unqualified support he consistently received from the African American community. To African Americans, Lloyd was a legendary hero due to his prolonged unrelenting fearless advocacy of the cause of immediate abolition.[4]

Another righteous issue Lloyd protested was the prevalence of overt race prejudice and segregation in the "free" North. On July 6, 1841 David Ruggles, an African American leader based in New York City, was ejected in a most unpleasant fashion from a train on which he held a valid ticket to travel from New Bedford, Massachusetts to Boston. The conductor ordered Ruggles off the segregated train without even allowing him to remove the suitcase he had stowed in the baggage car. When news of this outrage reached Lloyd, he and his friends swiftly organized a protest. They arranged to join a group of New Bedford African Americans on board a racially segregated steamer for the short trip from New Bedford to Nantucket Island, where a three-day abolitionist convention was scheduled. The large interracial group made a loud nonverbal statement by congregating all together on the ship's upper deck.[5]

One of the African Americans who made the pilgrimage with Lloyd on this nautical voyage to Nantucket was prodded

CHAPTER 6: A STAR BURSTS ON THE SCENE

into speaking at the ensuing convention by an abolitionist friend of Lloyd's, who had previously heard him speak to an all-black gathering in New Bedford. This unheralded young speaker, only 24 years old, had but recently made his escape from captivity. He took the podium briefly at the end of the Wednesday night session, then gave his real talk first thing on Thursday morning, August 12. Despite his youth, the talented speaker was already well-practiced and knowledgeable in techniques of rhetoric. Once he overcame his initial jitters, the young man's eloquent and thoughtful conveyance of his personal experiences completely captivated and enraptured his listeners. He had a brilliant mind. In public speech he combined philosophical musings worthy of an Aristotle with the vivid experiences of one born into the status of an involuntary servant for life. This speaker was so unheralded, the organizers were not even able to capture his name correctly in the minutes of the proceedings. That name, one newly invented upon the speaker's recent escape, was Frederick Douglass.[6]

It was the unexpected emergence of a brilliant star. Later, Lloyd would write:[7]

> I shall never forget his first speech at the convention – the extraordinary emotion it excited in my own mind – the powerful impression it created upon a crowded auditory, completely taken by surprise – the applause which followed from the beginning to the end of his felicitous remarks. I think I never hated slavery so intensely as at that moment.

On the spot, Lloyd and his organizers offered Frederick a full-time job as an abolitionist agent. And, after briefly deliberating, Frederick made the decision, on the spot, to leave his job as a New Bedford foundry worker to become a professional abolitionist.[8]

Frederick was given the name "Frederick Augustus Washington Bailey" when he was born in February, 1818 in a place called Tuckahoe, on the Eastern Shore of Maryland. His mother Harriet he met only rarely, just a handful of times in all before she died. Although Frederick tells us she was a hired-out field hand, important elements of her identity are clearly missing from his account. Her exact role in the Tuckahoe community remains a puzzle. According to Frederick, she could read, which was a rare skill indeed among African Americans in that Eastern Shore backwater. Her acquisition of this learning has never been explained. But one thing Harriet could not do was keep and raise her own children. All five of them were taken from her soon after their birth. Frederick remembered Harriet as a statuesque ebony beauty. Frederick's father was apparently of European ancestry. His identity was "shrouded in a deep mystery" that Frederick could never penetrate.

Frederick was nurtured by his mother's parents, Isaac and Betsy Bailey. His earliest memories were playing in and around their cabin. Betsy was respected in the community, white and black, for her cleverness. She was renowned for her ability to make quality fishing nets, and for knowing exactly how to position a sweet potato start to survive the frosty dead of a Maryland winter. Living happily in the small Bailey cabin with his grandparents and numerous cousins, Frederick, as he would later put it, "knew many other things" before he became aware that he had been born a slave.[9]

A passage Frederick wrote about his childhood provides an outstanding illustration of the depths of his insight as a psychologist, philosopher, and prose writer:[10]

> There is, after all, but little difference in the measure of contentment felt by the slave-child neglected and the slaveholder's child cared for and petted. The spirit of the All Just mercifully holds the balance for the young.

CHAPTER 6: A STAR BURSTS ON THE SCENE

The slaveholder, having nothing to fear from impotent childhood, easily affords to refrain from cruel inflictions; and if cold and hunger do not pierce the tender frame, the first seven or eight years of the slave-boy's life are about as full of sweet content as those of the most favored and petted *white* children of the slaveholder. The slave-boy escapes many troubles which befall and vex his white brother. He seldom has to listen to lectures on propriety of behavior, or on anything else. He is never chided for handling his little knife and fork improperly or awkwardly, for he uses none. He is never reprimanded for soiling the table-cloth, for he takes his meals on the clay floor. He never has the misfortune, in his games or sports, of soiling or tearing his clothes, for he has almost none to soil or tear. He is never expected to act like a nice little gentleman, for he is only a rude little slave. Thus, freed from all restraint, the slave-boy can be, in his life and conduct, a genuine boy, doing whatever his boyish nature suggests; enacting, by turns, all the strange antics and freaks of horses, dogs, pigs, and barn-door fowls, without in any manner compromising his dignity, or incurring reproach of any sort. He literally runs wild; has no pretty little verses to learn in the nursery; no nice little speeches to make for aunts, uncles, or cousins, to show how smart he is; and, if he can only manage to keep out of the way of the heavy feet and fists of the older slave boys, he may trot on, in his joyous and roguish tricks, as happy as any little heathen under the palm trees of Africa.

Frederick's happy time came to an abrupt end when he was six. He was taken away from his grandmother to reside with his master Aaron Anthony. Anthony himself was a subservient plantation manager for Colonel Edward Lloyd, a former Governor of Maryland and one of the wealthiest men in the state. Colonel Lloyd's Wye Plantation, where Frederick was sent to live, was renowned for its stately grounds, gardens and orchards. Colonel Lloyd and his family constantly hosted dignitaries and guests in a grand style. In the summer, the Wye Plantation was like a resort hotel for the wealthy and prominent. Young Frederick, however, had no shoes, no bedding, only the most rudimentary coarse clothes, and he often felt pangs of hunger.

The Wye Plantation, 1936

What was worse, he soon witnessed scenes of brutality. One such was described in his autobiography of 1855:[11]

> The reader will have noticed that, in enumerating the names of the slaves who lived with my old master, *Esther* is mentioned. This was a young woman who possessed that which is ever a curse to the slave-girl; namely, – personal beauty. She was tall, well formed, and made a fine appearance. The daughters of Col. Lloyd could scarcely surpass her in personal charms. Esther was courted by Ned Roberts, and he was as fine looking a young man, as she was a woman. He was the son of a favorite slave of Col. Lloyd. Some slaveholders would have been glad to promote the marriage of two such persons; but, for some reason or other, my old master took it upon him to break up the growing intimacy between Esther and Edward. He strictly ordered her to quit the company of said Roberts, telling her that he would punish her severely if he ever found her again in Edward's company. This unnatural and heartless order was, of course, broken. A woman's love is not to be annihilated by the

Chapter 6: A Star Bursts on the Scene

peremptory command of any one, whose breath is in his nostrils. It was impossible to keep Edward and Esther apart. Meet they would, and meet they did. Had old master been a man of honor and purity, his motives, in this matter, might have been viewed more favorably. As it was, his motives were as abhorrent, as his methods were foolish and contemptible. It was too evident that he was not concerned for the girl's welfare. It is one of the damning characteristics of the slave system, that it robs its victims of every earthly incentive to a holy life. The fear of God, and the hope of heaven, are found sufficient to sustain many slave-women, amidst the snares and dangers of their strange lot; but, this side of God and heaven, a slave-woman is at the mercy of the power, caprice and passion of her owner. Slavery produces no means for the honorable continuance of the race. Marriage – as imposing obligations on the parties to it – has no existence here, except in such hearts as are purer and higher than the standard morality around them. It is one of the consolations of my life, that I know of many honorable instances of persons who maintained their honor, where all around was corrupt.

Esther was evidently much attached to Edward, and abhorred – as she had reason to do – the tyrannical and base behavior of old master. Edward was young, and fine looking, and he loved and courted her. He might have been her husband, in the high sense just alluded to; but WHO and *what* was this old master? His attentions were plainly brutal and selfish, and it was as natural that Esther should loathe him, as that she should love Edward. Abhorred and circumvented as he was, old master, having the power, very easily took revenge. I happened to see this exhibition of his rage and cruelty toward Esther. The time selected was singular. It was early in the morning, when all besides was still, and before any of the family, in the house or kitchen, had left their beds. I saw but few of the shocking preliminaries, for the cruel work had begun before I awoke. I was probably awakened by the shrieks and piteous cries of poor Esther. My sleeping place was on the floor of a little, rough closet, which opened into the kitchen; and through the cracks of its unplaned boards, I could distinctly see and hear what was going on, without being seen by old master. Esther's wrists were firmly tied, and the twisted rope was fastened to a strong staple in a heavy wooden joist above, near the fireplace. Here she stood, on a bench, her arms tightly drawn over her head. Her back and shoulders were bare to the waist. Behind her stood old master, with cowskin in hand, preparing his barbarous work with all manner of harsh, coarse, and tantalizing epithets. The screams of his victim were most piercing. He was cruelly deliberate, and protracted the torture, as one who was delighted with the scene. Again and again, he drew the hateful whip through his hand, adjusting it with a view of dealing the most pain-giving blow. Poor Esther had never yet been severely whipped, and her shoulders were plump and tender. Each blow, vigorously laid on, brought screams as well as blood. *"Have mercy; Oh! have mercy"* she cried; *"I won't do so no more;"* but her piercing cries seemed only to increase his fury. His answers to them are too coarse and blasphemous to be produced here. The whole scene, with all its attendants, was revolting and shocking, to the last degree; and when the motives of this brutal castigation are considered, language has no power to convey a

Chapter 6: A Star Bursts on the Scene

just sense of its awful criminality. After laying on some thirty or forty stripes, old master untied his suffering victim, and let her get down. She could scarcely stand, when untied. From my heart I pitied her, and – child though I was – the outrage kindled in me a feeling far from peaceful; but I was hushed, terrified, stunned, and could do nothing, and the fate of Esther might be mine next.

As a boy living on the Wye Plantation, Frederick was never severely whipped. In fact, he found himself befriended by two important persons from the dominant social class. One was Daniel Lloyd, the youngest son of Colonel Lloyd, who took a liking to bright little Frederick. The two of them became, to some degree, playmates.[12] The other was Lucretia Auld, the newly married daughter of Frederick's master Aaron Anthony. Lucretia noticed Frederick, and made him into something of a pet. For his part, the boy enjoyed the attention. He developed a special means of communication with her. At times when he felt especially hungry Frederick, who was gifted with musical talent, would sing a gentle song underneath her window. It was his way of asking for a piece of bread and butter, a request which she seemed to enjoy and frequently obliged.[13]

Almost certainly due to Lucretia's intervention, at age eight Frederick was selected, out of all the slaves on the Wye Plantation, to go to Baltimore to serve as a personal companion to her husband's nephew Tommy Auld, a boy about Frederick's age. The gift was accepted with joy by Tommy's mother Sophie Auld. Sophie, a weaver by trade, never previously had any slave working for her. She had an excellent disposition, kind, gentle, and cheerful. Her natural and impulsive reaction was to treat little "Freddy" like a second child. Freddy, in turn, developed for Sophie the feelings of a child towards a mother. Before long, Sophie was busy teaching

Freddy to read. And Freddy proved to be an avid and fast learner. Sophie was proud of him, and she was proud of herself for being a good teacher. Freddy was pleased with his role taking care of Tommy. He vastly preferred his new life in Baltimore over the medieval darkness of the Wye Plantation.[14]

Aaron Anthony died suddenly, and without a will, when Freddy was about ten years old. Frederick was summoned back to the Eastern Shore to be inventoried and valued with the rest of Anthony's slaves and other property for purposes of the division of his estate. At the dock he had a tearful parting with Sophie, her husband (Lucretia's brother-in-law) Hugh, and Tommy. All of them, especially Freddy, were very anxious lest Freddy be inherited by Aaron Anthony's son Andrew, who was known for his profligacy. Luckily Lucretia, the guardian angel, wound up getting Freddy. She promptly sent him back to Baltimore to resume his life with the Hugh Auld family.[15]

But when Hugh found out about Freddy's progress in reading, he was shocked and dismayed. He peremptorily forbade Sophie to instruct Freddy any further. Freddy overheard him. "Learning would spoil the best nigger in the world," Hugh said. "Now, if you teach that nigger (speaking of Freddy) to read, there would be no keeping him. It would forever unfit him to be a slave. He would at once become unmanageable, and of no value to his master. As to himself, it could do him no good, but a great deal of harm. It would make him discontented and unhappy." Hearing these views expressed by Hugh in such crass terms stirred up an entirely new train of thought in Frederick. It was a special revelation. "From that moment," he would later write, "I understood the pathway from slavery to freedom."[16] He always credited Hugh Auld's remarks with yielding him a critical and valuable insight into the fundamental incompatibility of slavery and knowledge. And he admits, there was a kernel of truth to them. Freddy indeed soon found himself growing "gloomy and miserable" about his status as a slave, just as Hugh had

CHAPTER 6: A STAR BURSTS ON THE SCENE

predicted.[17]

Somewhat in spite of herself, Sophie heeded her husband's orders. She stopped her instruction of Freddy. At times, she even scolded Freddy when she found him poring over the pages of a newspaper. But Freddy rapidly found other even better teachers – immigrant children of ethnic European ancestry who hung out with him in the neighborhood. He became bosom friends with several local boys. They played games around learning new words. Frederick carried a dictionary with him everywhere. He constantly improved his comprehension and vocabulary. From his meager savings, he spent fifty cents to buy himself a used textbook on rhetoric, Caleb Bingham's 1817 compilation, *The Columbian Orator*.[18] Not only was this book filled with selected dialogues and passages from historical speeches and literature which Frederick found fascinating, its editorial selections conveyed, overall, a moral disapproval of the institution of slavery. Frederick read *The Columbian Orator* over and over again, absorbing its maxims and outlook.[19]

Frederick spent seven highly formative years growing up in the Fells Point area of Baltimore. During that period he experienced something of a religious awakening, one that filled him with spiritual love and compassion for fellow beings, even slave holders. He became attached to an elderly, very pious African American whom Frederick called "Uncle Lawson." Uncle Lawson filled Frederick with the thought that the Lord had a great work for him to do, and that it may involve preaching the gospel. Frederick imbibed a powerful sense of mission. Just as Frederick himself had learned from his neighborhood companions, he himself acted as a teacher for local young African American men, with several of whom he became close friends.[20]

When he was fifteen, a new abrupt development hit

Frederick. Hugh Auld got into a tiff with his brother Thomas. By this time, Frederick's Eastern Shore protector, Thomas Auld's wife Lucretia, had died. From her, Thomas had legally inherited Frederick. Thomas had married a new wife, Rowena. Thomas and Rowena sent Frederick's cousin Henny, who was crippled from serious burns she had suffered as a girl, to Baltimore to live with Hugh and Sophie. When Hugh informed Thomas and Rowena he had no use for Henny, and wished to return her, Thomas and Rowena became irritated. They curtly informed Hugh he would need to return Freddy, as well. So Frederick was once more loaded on a boat headed to the Eastern Shore. This time, the destination was Thomas and Rowena's home in St. Michaels, a peninsula on the eastern edge of the Chesapeake Bay.[21]

Immediately on arrival, Frederick felt like he had voyaged to a more primitive world. In Baltimore, he had forgotten all about feeling helpless about chronic pangs of hunger. Thomas and Rowena – and Frederick acknowledges that they were unusual among Southern slaveholders in this regard – did not give their slaves a sufficient allowance of food. This motivated the slaves to steal, when opportunity presented itself. Frederick reasoned, with some logic, that putting unauthorized food in his stomach was not really theft; it was a mere transfer of master's goods from one form of property to another. He looked on as Thomas Auld made a profession of religion at a Methodist spiritual revival. But, although Thomas became acclaimed as a high profile Methodist convert, the conversion did not lead him to emancipate any slaves.

There were, however, some people in Maryland whose social consciences were more troubled by the trappings of slavery than were those of the Methodist church fathers. A pious young man named Wilson asked Frederick to assist in teaching a new Sunday School for local African Americans. It was an assignment Frederick gladly accepted. He enjoyed the opportunity to make a "little Baltimore" in St. Michaels by teaching children how to read the Bible. But in only its third session, Wilson's Sunday school was violently dispersed by a mob, which was headed by two of the Methodist class leaders. The vigilantes drove off the students, wielding sticks and throwing stones. Some of the attackers hurled an accusation at Frederick as well. They said he "wanted to be another Nat Turner."[22]

Thomas Auld became fed up with Frederick's small acts of rebellion. He decided it was high time for the youth, now approaching sixteen, to learn his place as a slave. So effective January 1, 1834, Thomas contracted out Frederick to a local farmer named Edward Covey. Covey enjoyed a reputation, which he cultivated assiduously in the slaveholding community, for "training" young male slaves. Now for the first time, Frederick came under the oversight of a man determined to use the whip on a regular basis as an instrument of coercion and fear. Among the local African Americans, Covey was renowned for his "fierce and savage" disposition. Frederick understood ahead of time what he was in for with Covey. "I am given to understand, that, like a wild young working animal, I am to be broken to the yoke of a bitter and life-long bondage."[23]

Within three days of his arrival at Covey's, a pretext was found by Covey to administer to Frederick a whipping so severe that blood flowed freely. It left him with welts on his back as large as Frederick's little finger. The sores from this flogging remained open for weeks. The ground for punishment was a rollover accident that occurred when the greenhorn Frederick, inevitably, lost control of two semi-wild oxen who were pulling a cart loaded with firewood. Frederick caught on soon enough to the ways and rigors of farm life. Covey worked Frederick to the threshold of exhaustion. But bloody beatings continued, essentially on a weekly basis. Covey was regarded by Frederick and the other farm help as a snake, constantly slinking about to detect any indolence. Often he would pretend to leave the farm for the day, only to creep back by stealth, to see if any mischief was afoot. As a result, Frederick learned the hard way to see Covey behind every stump, tree, bush and fence on the plantation.[24]

Within a few months, Frederick felt himself crushed and broken in body, soul, and spirit. His intellect languished, and even his disposition to read departed. He was sometimes tempted to take the life of both himself and Covey, but something like – in his own words – a combination of hope and fear prevented him from doing it.[25]

On one of the hottest days of the month of August, Frederick was helping to thresh some wheat, using a "treading" process in which the grain was separated from the straw by virtue of horses' feet. The crew was in a hurry because they wanted to finish the work early in order to have a free hour before dark. Frederick then experienced heatstroke, something quite familiar to anybody who has tried to work for hours at an excessive pace in the extreme humidity of a sweltering Maryland day. His head spun out of control, he felt extreme dizziness, and in spite of himself, he collapsed. This brought the entire crew's treading work to a standstill. Covey soon came on the scene. After giving the helpless Frederick two bone-jarring kicks to the ribs, he smashed him over the head with a hickory stick. This inflicted a large gash from which blood ran freely. As Covey went to assist in getting the treading restarted, Frederick felt his head clear enough to get up. He resolved to walk the seven miles to Thomas Auld's residence in St. Michael's to complain of Covey's brutal conduct. Because he feared Covey would catch up with him on horseback, Frederick made his way not on the road, but through woods, bogs and briers. By the time he reached his destination, five hours later, he was scratched and bloody from head to toe.

CHAPTER 6: A STAR BURSTS ON THE SCENE

Thomas Auld, upon Frederick's arrival, did not sympathize. He backed Covey. But he let Frederick stay the night. The next morning, Frederick returned to Covey's farm, reaching it at about 9 a.m. When he entered the field adjacent to the house, Covey emerged from behind a fence corner, with a cowskin whip and rope in hand. Frederick instinctively retreated at full speed back into a cornfield, where he concealed himself as he made his way back into the woods. There he remained in hiding all day, praying for some kind of deliverance. Covey relied on hunger to drive him out. Indeed it would have worked, except that shortly before midnight, Frederick heard nearby footsteps which turned out to be those of Sandy, a slave. Frederick came out of hiding and asked Sandy to help him. Sandy was kindly. He also respected Frederick as the only African American for miles around who had book learning. Sandy took Frederick to the home he shared with his wife, who was a free woman. They gave Frederick a supper of ash cake which, to Frederick, was the best tasting meal he would ever receive in his life.

Sandy heard out Frederick's situation. Being something of a shaman, he gave Frederick a root to wear on his right side. With the help of this magical aid, Sandy predicted, Frederick would not be whipped. As an intellectual, Frederick was scornful of "pretenders to divination." But times were desperate, so he agreed with Sandy that there was nothing to lose with wearing the root. Next morning, as Sandy advised, Frederick openly returned to the Covey home. It was Sunday. Covey and his wife were leaving their home to go to church. To Frederick's surprise, Covey spoke to him benignly. He evidently did not care to take up the issue on a Sabbath, and in front of his wife. Sunday thus provided another day for Frederick to recuperate from his ordeal.

Monday morning was another matter. Shortly before

dawn, as Frederick climbed a ladder while going about his duties tending to horses, Covey took him by surprise and grabbed his legs. His plan was to get a lasso around them, so he could control Frederick for a whipping. But the rejuvenated Frederick astonished Covey by mounting a stiff resistance. He refused to be roped or tied. He grabbed Covey with a grip tight enough to draw blood with his fingernails. Covey growled at Frederick, "Are you going to resist, you scoundrel?" Frederick looked him in the eye and responded, "Yes, sir." The two of them wrestled each other to a standstill in the muck of a cow pen.

Covey's next move was to call upon bystanders for assistance. First he asked Bill Hughes, a white youth who worked for Covey as a farm hand. But as Hughes tried to grab Frederick's hand, Frederick, in a fighting rage, gave Hughes a sharp kick to the gut. The blow knocked the wind out of Hughes. With it, apparently, went all inclination to be involved in the fight. Next Covey tried to enlist help from Bill Smith, an African American whom Covey hired from an owner who had forbidden whipping Bill for anything short of a criminal offense. Smith pretended he didn't quite understand what Covey was asking. When Covey repeated his request and made it very clear, Smith then declined. He said to Covey: "My master hired me here, to help you work, and *not* to help you whip Frederick." Finally, Covey tried to summon the aid of the only other available person nearby, his cook Caroline, who was the one slave he owned. Oblivious to Covey's importuning, she too refused to participate in subduing Frederick.[26]

Two hours passed with Frederick and Covey still wrapped in a wrestling embrace. Finally, Covey gave in. Huffing and puffing with windedness, he told Frederick to go to work. Covey pretended to be victorious – saying, "I would not have whipped you half so much had you not resisted." But in reality, he was acknowledging a new reality of their relationship. For the remaining months of Frederick's time with Covey, he was

CHAPTER 6: A STAR BURSTS ON THE SCENE

never again subjected to the lash. Frederick did not discount the effect of the magic root. But his intellect told him Covey declined to push the issue because he did not want his embarrassment in the physical confrontation to become public knowledge. It was a turning point in Frederick's experience as a slave, and it kindled in him a renewed determination to be a free man someday.[27]

With the beginning of the year 1835, the contract for Frederick's labor was transferred by Thomas Auld to a new lease holder, William Freeland. In contrast to Covey, Freeland was a well-bred Southern gentleman. Frederick soon found him to be a good and just person with a sense of humanity, and free of mean and selfish characteristics. Frederick now not only had enough food, he had enough time to eat it. At age seventeen, besides working for Freeland, he also had the free time and energy to organize a Sunday School and, in winter, to teach three nights a week.

But Frederick remained discontented. The natural born philosopher grasped a bedrock existential truth.[28]

> When entombed at Covey's, shrouded in darkness and physical wretchedness, temporal well-being was the grand *desideratum*; but, temporal wants supplied, the spirit puts in its chains. Beat and cuff your slave, keep him hungry and spiritless, and he will follow the chain of his master like a dog; but feed and clothe him well, -- work him moderately – surround him with physical comfort, -- and dreams of freedom intrude. Give him a *bad* master, and he aspires to a *good* master; give him a good master, and he wishes to become his *own* master. Such is human nature.

With three of his companions, Frederick hatched a plan to flee during the Easter holiday of 1836. They were going to row to freedom up the Chesapeake Bay in a canoe. However, just as the four were preparing to depart, they were arrested. Their plan had been betrayed by someone. Frederick and the others were marched fifteen miles to jail in Easton. There Frederick remained while his fate was deliberated. He had every reason to expect that he would now be sent to permanent labor in the deep South. Thomas Auld told Frederick he intended to sell him to a friend from Alabama. But for some reason, he had a change of heart. Thomas Auld kindly decided to send Frederick back to his brother Hugh in Baltimore. Not only that, with good behavior he promised to free Frederick at age 25.[29]

Frederick arrived to find much had changed at the Hugh Auld residence. Tommy was little no more. He was now a man. He now had other friends and associates who were not African American. Tommy hired himself out on a brig called the *Tweed*, and it was a cold parting. Hugh hired Frederick out to work as a laborer in a Fells Point shipyard, where there was a shipbuilding project ongoing that had a tight deadline. Here Frederick had his first taste of racially based labor strife. Ethnically European immigrant laborers resented the competition of slave labor. The resentment eventually turned into open warfare. Frederick was attacked by a gang of four fellow apprentices, and by them, he was badly kicked and beaten. Frederick barely escaped. Frederick later said he nearly lost an eye. Hugh and Sophie were outraged at his injuries. They tried to press charges. But without white witnesses, a prosecution could go nowhere. And there was a Mafia-like conspiracy of silence among the many carpenters who had witnessed the attack on Frederick.[30]

Once again, the outcome of the violence worked to Frederick's benefit. Hugh got Frederick a place working in the same shipyard where Hugh worked as a foreman. Within a year, Frederick developed into an expert journeyman caulker, earning good wages. But he was still upset at the fact that his wages flowed into Hugh's pocket, not his.

CHAPTER 6: A STAR BURSTS ON THE SCENE

Eventually, in May of 1838, Frederick persuaded Hugh to enter into an agreement to hire his own time. Under this arrangement, Frederick could work anywhere he wanted, and earn as much as he wanted, but he must pay Hugh a flat rate of three dollars per week, and he must also bear the cost of his own room and board. It was a hard bargain for Frederick, because caulkers could only work in good weather, and they had to lay out money for tools and supplies. Still, Frederick was able to save up some funds. In addition, during this period he met Anna Murray, a young woman five years older than he. She had been born free, to a newly manumitted African American mother in the vicinity of Denton, Maryland, not far from Tuckahoe. Although Anna was not a slave, Frederick and Anna shared a common Eastern Shore heritage. Now Anna was relocated to Baltimore, where she was working as a domestic servant. Frederick shared his dream of freedom with Anna. The two of them planned to marry once that time came.[31]

The final chapter in Frederick's life of slavery was precipitated by his attendance at a religious camp meeting on the outskirts of Baltimore in August 1838. In order to travel with friends to this meeting, Frederick had to postpone delivering Hugh his weekly three dollars on Saturday night. Although Frederick promptly appeared with the money upon his return two days later, Hugh, in the meantime, had been very disturbed about his absence. He was concerned that Frederick had tried to escape. He immediately stopped the agreement to allow Frederick to hire his time. This, in turn, made up Frederick's mind to finally depart. In this he had the help of Anna and other "free" friends. He was fitted out with a convincing sailor's costume. He borrowed a "sailor's protection" document from an acquaintance who, superficially, had a similar physical description to Frederick. Disguised as a sailor and armed with a sailor's document, Frederick boarded a train bound from Baltimore to Philadelphia on September 3, 1838. Frederick easily fooled the conductor. But on the train itself, and also on the ferry ride across the Susquehanna River, he encountered some people who knew him and who were capable of denouncing his escape. But if these persons recognized him, they kept quiet. Frederick joyfully disembarked in Philadelphia. Soon he made his way onward to New York City.[32]

In New York, Frederick was helped by David Ruggles, who was providing the kind of assistance to fugitive slaves that would later come to be known as the "Underground Railroad." Ruggles provided a safe house for Frederick to stay. Frederick arranged for Anna to come to New York. The two of them were married at once. Ruggles suggested that the couple should settle in the town of New Bedford, which was, at that time, a burgeoning, bustling whaling town, later made famous by being portrayed on the pages of Herman Melville's *Moby Dick*. It was standard practice for escaped slaves to take on a new name, to help shield them from slave catchers. David Ruggles called him Frederick "Johnson," but when he arrived in New Bedford, Frederick found that there were already too many Johnsons. His New Bedford host, Nathan Johnson, rechristened him "Frederick Douglass." Nathan had just finished reading the epic 1810 poem by Sir Walter Scott, *Lady of the Lake*. The Scotsman James "Douglas" was a hero of that poem. Frederick added an extra "s", and "Frederick Douglass" was launched.[33]

Frederick's trade as a caulker was perfect for New Bedford. However, due to racial segregation and prejudice, he was frozen out of working that trade. Instead, Frederick found other jobs, first dealing with whale oil, and later stoking the fires at a brass foundry. He and Anna started a family. It was in New Bedford that Frederick first encountered *The Liberator*. He fell in love with its "immediate abolition" point of view. He

Chapter 6: A Star Bursts on the Scene

watched in rapt attention when William Lloyd Garrison came to town and announced "nearly all of his heresies." And Frederick continued his community evangelical and educational work, frequently preaching to all-black audiences in the New Bedford Zion Methodist Church.

It was in this church that William Coffin, an abolitionist who was active in Lloyd's movement, heard Frederick and was very impressed. Coffin recruited Frederick to attend the abolitionist convention in Nantucket, and it was Coffin who pushed him forward to speak to the gathering on August 11 and 12, 1841.[34] Thus, by the time he reached the podium, Frederick was ready made to become a star in the cause of abolition. Not only was he wise beyond his years due to his many and varied experiences, he was an experienced speaker, and he was a self-taught expert in rhetoric. Going on tour with Garrison and friends, Frederick would soon outshine all Lloyd's other speakers and sideshows as a rising star in advocating the cause of abolition.

Chapter 7: He Was an Honest Thief

When we last left him, John Brown was expressing anger and outrage over the mistreatment and demise of Elijah Lovejoy. In front of an audience, he pronounced that he was going to dedicate himself to opposing the evil of slavery. But he did little in the way of immediate acting on this decree. He never, at any time, joined an anti-slavery society or other organized abolitionist group.[1] John's main focus, from 1835 forward, was business. And, from the time he returned to the Ohio town of Franklin, near Hudson, after eleven years in rural Pennsylvania, the business went badly.

The first bad thing that happened is that John's partnership with Zenas Kent in the tannery project, his ostensible reason for relocating to Franklin, went nowhere. Tension soon arose between the two men. It was unendurable to John how Kent gave orders. With nineteen years of tanning experience, John resented Kent's meddling in the construction and outfitting of the tannery. He lacked the capacity to be an "organization man." Kent quickly gained an appreciation of this side of John's personality. Like most wealthy persons, Kent felt he had the wisdom and the right to give the orders. After all, the tannery was being constructed with his money. Marvin Kent, the son of Zenas and destined to be even richer than his father, came to know John at this time in Franklin. He did not think much of him. He found John to be so stubborn that "nothing short of a mental rebirth" could alter him. John was constitutionally incapable, Marvin said, of taking advice. He saw John as "a man of ordinary caliber with a propensity to failure in whatever he attempted."[2]

Between May and November of 1835, the struggle continued as Zenas Kent, de facto, vetoed John's ideas for the project by failing to advance funds for its construction. As a result, the tannery remained unfinished, and hides remained untanned. Many other people in the Hudson and Franklin area, at the time, were making money off speculative land transactions. John would later advance the dubious claim that he did not feel envious of their success. On top of a general prevailing atmosphere of prosperity and optimism about the future of the emerging Midwest, a new transportation project, the Pennsylvania–Ohio Canal, promised to make Franklin a center of commerce. As a result, property values skyrocketed.[3]

In November 1835, John suddenly decided to dissolve his partnership with Zenas Kent. He contracted himself out as a digger for the canal. Zenas did lend John enough funds to acquire a yoke of oxen and a plow. In the month that followed, John himself went into land speculation, buying the 95.5-acre Haymaker Farm, near Franklin, for $7,000. John planned to subdivide the Haymaker property into 150 industrial lots and sell them off for a profit. He made only a small down payment on the purchase, and borrowed the rest of the price from the seller. Within a month, he turned around and sold a one-half interest in this deal for $7,000 to his business associate, Seth Thompson. Thompson gave John $3,000 in cash and four promissory notes for $1,000, one each coming due annually over the next four years.[4] On paper, John had recouped his entire investment and doubled his money. Elated, he continued with more land purchases.

In February 1836, John bought another tract adjacent to Haymaker, paying $75 per acre. This acquisition was again heavily leveraged with debt. John then borrowed $6,000 from Western Reserve Bank of Warren. This loan was guaranteed by six personal sureties, including the notable Hudson merchant Heman Oviatt, whose son had accompanied John on the boarding school venture of his boyhood. With the proceeds of his Western Reserve Bank loan, John acquired a farm called Westlands, located on the outskirts of Hudson. John moved his family to Westlands from their rented accommodations in Franklin. He started a tannery there. He spent his days surveying and laying out the streets and lots of the "Brown and Thompson Addition" to Franklin, the subdivision John was creating out of Haymaker. He also supervised the construction of a large block building that was intended to serve as a hotel for the new town.[5]

But the boom that fueled the real estate development craze in the Franklin area would soon turn to bust. The change was already evident by July of 1836, when President Jackson issued his administration's "specie circular." This anti-inflationary executive order forbade federal government officials to accept anything other than specie, i.e., paper money backed by gold or silver, in exchange for government land sales. Much of the prosperity and inflation of the preceding years had been fueled by purchases made with notes issued on the credit of unregulated state banks. Now, this form of unofficial money would no longer be acceptable for buying large tracts from the federal government. It was part of a general tightening that greatly constricted the money supply. The predictable economic results were deflation and an unavailability of capital. Land prices in northeast Ohio went into decline.

On July 25, 1836, John wrote Seth Thompson to report that real estate sales in the Franklin area had virtually ceased. The situation did not improve. By year's end, John conceded

CHAPTER 7: HE WAS AN HONEST THIEF

to Thompson that if the Haymaker lands could be sold for "a fair price," he would agree to do so. In February 1837 John was focused on getting $8,000 for his 50% interest, but Thompson – no doubt more realistic – was ready to dump his half for only $1,000. John remonstrated with Thompson not to tell anyone he would be willing to take so little. These events highlighted a fundamental trait in John's personality. He had a very poor sense of reality when it came to market-driven changes in prices. Once he made up his mind about how much a thing was worth, he stubbornly adhered to that opinion, no matter what. In the world of business, this could be fatal.[6]

In March 1837, as Martin Van Buren was sworn in to replace Andrew Jackson as President of the United States, the growing recession reached catastrophic proportions. Banks began to fail nationwide. Major New York banks announced that they would no longer redeem commercial paper with hard money. The economic tailspin became even worse and grew into a "panic." By the fall, work on the Pennsylvania & Ohio Canal halted due to lack of funds. There was no hope for selling lots in John's "Brown and Thompson Addition" subdivision.

John, who had borrowed thousands of dollars on credit with no source of income other than land sales to make payments, faced ruin. Western Reserve Bank brought suit against him for the money it was owed. Soon it recovered a judgment for $5,260 against John's surety Heman Oviatt. John promised Oviatt that he would sign over Westlands to him. However, Westlands itself was subjected to other judgment liens. Creditors were closing in on John from all directions. Haymaker was after him. People to whom he had given Seth Thompson notes as payment were pressing claims as well. This was the crisis atmosphere that prevailed when John made his public declaration, in the Hudson meeting of November 1837, that he would now "consecrate his life" to fighting slavery.[7]

The year 1838 saw a small recovery in the Ohio economy.

Work on the Pennsylvania–Ohio Canal was set to resume and, as a result, real estate values in Franklin rebounded. But matters did not improve for John. In the fall, he led a drive to the East of several hundred head of cattle, organized by his father Owen and Heman Oviatt. This was at least a job that would earn some cash for John. But his other compelling motive for the trip east was to seek a loan of funds to bail him out of his financial mess. In search of such a loan he went to New York, where the cattle were delivered, and then to Hartford, and then to Boston. The potential financiers to whom John appealed dealt with him politely, even though some of them privately viewed him as a rather strange character. He came out of the meetings thinking his chances of getting a loan were far better than they really were. He kept assuring his creditors and associates that money was just about to arrive. This did not come to pass.

The delivery of such a large herd of cattle favorably impressed New York cattle merchants Tertius Wadsworth and Joseph Wells. They offered John a share of their partnership to go into the business of importing Ohio cattle to New York on a regular basis. John accepted.[8] As a result, after his return to Hudson at the end of February 1839, he soon organized a second cattle drive. Once again, his more pressing agenda was to renew his quest for a bailout loan.

Within a month, John was back on the road to the east with another herd of cattle. After delivering them in New York, in May he again made a trip to New England seeking loan money. He kept telling people he was "convinced beyond any doubt" that some unnamed person had made him a commitment to lend. But again, no loan materialized. On June 12, 1839, John reported to his wife in a letter: "The cattle business has succeeded about as I expected, but I am now somewhat in fear that I shall fail of getting the money I expected on the loan."[9] At some time during the next week, John misappropriated – that is, stole – $5,500 belonging to his partnership with

CHAPTER 7: HE WAS AN HONEST THIEF

Wadsworth & Wells, and used the money to make a payment demanded of him in order to redeem his contract to purchase Westlands. Most likely, the stolen money represented the sale proceeds to date of the cattle drive. And, John did not honor the pledge he had made to put title to Westlands in the name of Heman Oviatt. He recorded the deed in his own name.

Within a few days, the other partners of Wadsworth & Wells discovered the defalcation. They threatened John with arrest. To avoid this, John committed a third gross breach of fiduciary duty. George Kellogg, of the New England Woolen Company based in Rockville, Connecticut, on June 15 had advanced John $2,800 in cash to buy Ohio wool for the company.[10] To stave off immediate arrest for embezzlement, John took the money that had been entrusted to him by Kellogg and pledged it against his debt to Wadsworth & Wells. John later claimed he was hoping to get a loan within the next thirty days, the proceeds of which he could somehow pyramid into buying wool for Kellogg, plus paying all his other creditors. But this did not reflect reality. Kellogg's pledged money was taken to repay Wadsworth & Wells.

By August 2, 1839, Kellogg learned what John had done. He wrote John a letter asking for an accounting. After stalling for the better part of a month, John admitted defeat, insolvency, and bankruptcy. He confessed his guilt to Kellogg in a reply he sent twenty days later:[11]

> I have found it hard to take up my pen to record & to publish, my own shame, & abuse of the confidence of those whom I esteem, & who have trusted me as a friend, & as a brother. I flattered myself till now, with the hope that I might be able to render a more favorable account of myself, but the truth, & the whole truth, shall be told. When I saw you at Vernon (Connecticut), I was in dayly expectation of receiving a number of thousands from Boston, something over

five of which I owed for money I had used belonging to our cattle company (viz Wadsworth, Wells & myself). On the day I was to set out for home, as I was disappointed of the money I expected, I found no alternative but to go to jail, or to pledge the money you had confided to my trust, & in my extremity I did so with the most of it, pledging it for thirty days, believing that in less than that I could certainly redeem it, as I expected a large amount from a source I did believe I could depend upon.

John informed Kellogg that he had made a general assignment of his assets for the benefit of all his creditors. The best Kellogg now could do was await their final disposition and sale in hopes of receiving some share of the proceeds. Signing a second letter, "Your unworthy friend," he encouraged Kellogg to submit a full claim for damages plus interest to a former judge who had been appointed the trustee of John's creditors.[12]

Here we again encounter a bedrock dualism. By this time, John Brown was a fully formed 39-year-old adult. This person, who so prided himself on his high reputation for personal honesty and integrity, who was so obsessed with seeing that thieves are brought to justice, demonstrated through his conduct in a crisis that he himself was capable of seriously dishonest behavior and moral turpitude.

Eventually, John took advantage of a newly enacted federal law authorizing voluntary bankruptcy to obtain a discharge of all of his debts. Under the new bankruptcy statute, fiduciary defalcations and fraud were both express grounds for denying a debtor discharge. To avoid having his discharge contested, John pledged in court to repay the money lost by New England Woolen Company and Heman Oviatt, thus preserving their rights against him. By that time, John was actually employed by Oviatt, tending his sheep. Later on, John also had other wool business dealings with Kellogg. Remarkably, these men were persuaded that the circumstances surrounding the panic of 1837 had driven an upstanding man to desperation. Even though John was a thief, he was an honest thief.[13]

Westlands was another story. The farm was ordered sold in order to satisfy a judgment lien in favor of a creditor to whom John had given payment in the form of a worthless Seth Thompson note. The purchaser at auction, for a price of $1,681, was Amos Chamberlain, a Hudson resident John had known from his boyhood. John refused to turn Westlands over to Chamberlain. John contended that Chamberlain had acted unethically by bidding at the auction on what he should have known was rightfully John's. When Chamberlain came to claim his purchase, John had him arrested for trespass. Then John fortified an old log house on the property. He armed his three oldest sons with muskets and stationed them inside the makeshift fort, preparing them to shoot Chamberlain or anybody else who came to evict him. This resort to violence would foreshadow things to come.[14]

The county sheriff, however, outsmarted John. He did not take on the Westlands fort directly. Instead, he paid a visit to John's nearby tannery, where he easily took John into custody while he was busy sweating over hides. After the father was in custody, the sons readily surrendered their post. John and two of the boys were transported to jail in Akron. The sheriff apparently did not view them as real criminals, so he promptly released them. Chamberlain also declined to prosecute. In the meantime, though, he had swiftly entered Westlands and demolished the "fort."[15]

John considered a few possibilities for remaking himself in the wake of his financial ruin and bankruptcy. At the suggestion of his father, John thought about moving to western Virginia, in today's West Virginia, to help develop lands owned by Oberlin College, of which Owen Brown was a trustee. Oberlin's trustees were interested in having John survey these lands, which had been contributed to the notably progressive college by the wealthy abolitionist, Gerrit Smith. John spent time there in April 1840. He wrote a letter in which he was critical of the energy and intelligence of the inhabitants of the area, part of what we now call Appalachia. Probably because of his underlying aversion to submission to institutional authority, John delayed and vacillated to the point that Oberlin itself withdrew the offer for John to aid in the development.[16]

Returning to Hudson, John resumed tanning as a means of earning some cash to support his large family. He also fell back on his skills, and innate affinity, with animals. In the spring of 1841, he persuaded Heman Oviatt to let him tend to Oviatt's herd of wool-producing sheep. Over the next period of two-and-a-half years, John's activities in herding, breeding, and shearing Oviatt's sheep were successful.

Photo of John Brown, from Sanborn 1860

He rapidly developed a reputation for prowess in this field, to the point that, at the end of 1843, Simon Perkins, Jr. of Akron, Ohio, who owned a much larger herd of sheep, offered John a partnership. Perkins would supply the feed and the winter shelter needed for the herd, and John would supply the care of the animals. The proceeds would be divided evenly. The bargain also included a farmhouse near Akron owned by Perkins in which John could live with his family. John was extremely pleased with this deal, so much so that he could not resist writing a letter to his oldest son John Jr., in which he crowed, "It is certainly indorsing the poor bankrupt and his family, three of whom were but recently in Akron jail, in a

CHAPTER 7: HE WAS AN HONEST THIEF

Clipping from *Ohio Cultivator*, Sept. 1, 1845

manner quite unexpected."[17]

The wealthy Simon Perkins, unlike Zenas Kent, kept his hands off John's operations. John enjoyed acclaim as the active partner of "Perkins & Brown." He built up the Perkins & Brown flock through breeding with Saxony Merino stock, which were known for producing a superior fine wool. John actively promoted the breed's virtues. Using his pre-teen and teenage children as, essentially, unpaid slave labor, John once again achieved outstanding results. It helped that he personally accompanied his fleeces to market. That way, he came to the attention of people like Lowell, Massachusetts merchant Samuel Lawrence, who effused, "Mr. Brown's wool has ever been of the highest character, since he first brought it here, but this year it has amazed us."[18] The Perkins & Brown flock drew rave reviews in the agricultural press, both for the quality of its care and handling by John, and for the superior quality of the fleeces he was able to produce from that flock.[19] Part of this reputation was the result of a certain amount of overselling by John. For one example, he stated in a published article that he had been traveling all over the country "within the last ten years" to study sheep flocks. This was a substantial misrepresentation of his actual activities over that period, which we have just reviewed.[20]

By mid-1845, John's Perkins & Brown flock contained about 1,300 sheep.[21] The path was wide open to John to rely on the quality of his own wool product to continue the greatest prosperity he would ever enjoy. But John was not content to be a simple successful animal husband. Instead, John felt and followed an overpowering attraction and urge to adopt someone else's cause. In this instance, the adopted cause was that of the Midwestern wool grower.

In John's mind, these growers were being mistreated by New England textile manufacturers. They were not, he thought, getting fair enough prices for their high quality fleeces. In the words of Marvin Kent, "Brown saw everything large, and felt himself the equal of anything."[22] So, during the winter of 1845–1846, John developed a grandiose plan to introduce a new project for the benefit of wool growers throughout the United States. The idea was a sort of rudimentary cooperative. John would receive fleeces in a central Springfield, Massachusetts warehouse; there he would wash them and assign each of them to a "class" using a nine-tiered grading system of his own invention. He would then undertake to sell the fleeces at what he considered the "fair" price, given their quality, when the market was favorable. He would pay each grower based on the "average" price received during the season for the particular grade of wool, no matter at what price the grower's clip had actually sold.[23]

It was a highly visionary scheme, one worthy of an elaborate government program. Due to John's defining traits of uncritical faith in his own ideas, righteous stubbornness, and a slight lack of contact with the reality that markets composed of buyers and sellers have far more impact on commodity prices than does a "grading" system, John's wool cooperative project was destined to fail. It would be an even more spectacular failure and disastrous bankruptcy than the previous one John's financial backers and creditors had been forced to endure.

But all that was still in the future when John moved to Springfield in June of 1846 to devote himself full time to the wool cooperative. Initially his plan worked. In February 1847,

CHAPTER 7: HE WAS AN HONEST THIEF

John returned to Ohio to make a speech on the cooperative concept to a convention in Steubenville, Ohio, then the de facto capital of Ohio's wool country. His speech impressed the attendees. At the end, the convention recommended that wool growers should ship their product to Perkins & Brown's Springfield cooperative. John moved Mary and the younger children to Springfield in June 1847, leaving the three oldest boys to tend to the Perkins & Brown flock in Akron. During the first year of the cooperative, wool prices remained strong and the project went well.[24]

John's move to western Massachusetts marked the first time John lived in a town where a significant number of African Americans resided. Hudson, to be sure, was a hotbed of opposition to slavery but, while John resided there, any African Americans were generally just passing through en route to Canada or other parts north. Springfield, by contrast, had an active black community, one regularly proselytized by African American abolitionists. John was able to make the acquaintance of several of these, most notably Jeremy Loguen and Henry Highland Garnet. Loguen and Garnet, in turn, recommended John to Frederick Douglass. These two men met for the first time during a visit by Frederick to Springfield in late January or early February, 1848.[25]

Frederick's reason for visiting Springfield was to gather support for his newly founded newspaper, *North Star*. Frederick had just returned to the United States from approximately two very successful years spent in England and Scotland. There he was relieved to no longer feel the constant racial prejudice that traveled with him throughout the United States. He was highly acclaimed by the British public. His admirers in England raised the money necessary to "purchase" Frederick's legal freedom from Thomas Auld. While in England, Frederick decided to launch a newspaper upon his return to America. His friends took up a subscription of $2,500 to underwrite the newspaper venture. Frederick was convinced his skills as an orator could have an even greater impact if used on the printed page, *a la* Garrison. But, upon arriving in Boston on April 20, 1847, Frederick was surprised to find out Lloyd strongly opposed Frederick's newspaper project. Nevertheless, Frederick persevered. Frederick had been an eager and effective advocate and fundraiser for Lloyd and *The Liberator* ever since his "discovery" in Nantucket in 1841. In doing so, he had toed Garrison's party line. Now, Frederick began to differ with some of Lloyd's stubborn policy stands. One in particular that he questioned was Lloyd's steadfast determination never to become involved in politics, and never to support any particular political party or candidate. Another was "nonresistance." Frederick began leaning toward the view that African Americans would eventually need to rise up in order to gain their freedom.[26]

Henry Highland Garnet was another Maryland Eastern Shore native born into enslavement. As a boy, he had escaped with his family to freedom in the North. He grew into an educated, prominent abolitionist. As of 1843, Garnet began to preach the necessity of armed rebellion. John Brown emphatically agreed with Garnet that there would never be any progress eliminating slavery in the United States either through political action or moral suasion. Garnet was pleased with John's attitude, as well as his energy. For this reason he mentioned John's name to Frederick when Frederick came to Springfield. For his part John, who regularly read the *The Liberator*, was well aware of Frederick's identity as a "rock star" of the abolitionist world. John was very much looking forward to the opportunity to meet him. The meeting was soon arranged.

Frederick described, in memorable prose, his impressions from his encounter with John in Springfield.[27]

> Fortunately, I was invited to see him in his own house. At the time to which I now refer this man was a

CHAPTER 7: HE WAS AN HONEST THIEF

respectable merchant in a populous and thriving city, and our first place of meeting was at his store. This was a substantial brick building on a prominent, busy street. A glance at the interior, as well as at the massive walls without, gave me the impression that the owner must be a man of considerable wealth. My welcome was all that I could have asked. Every member of the family, young and old, seemed glad to see me, and I was made much at home in a very little while.

I was, however, a little disappointed with the appearance of the house and its location. After seeing the fine store I was prepared to see a fine residence in an eligible locality, but this conclusion was completely dispelled by actual observation. In fact, the house was neither commodious nor elegant, nor its situation desirable. It was a small wooden building on a back street, in a neighborhood chiefly occupied by laboring men and mechanics; respectable enough, to be sure, but not quite the place, I thought, where one would look for the residence of a flourishing and successful merchant.

Plain as was the outside of this man's house, the inside was plainer. Its furniture would have satisfied a Spartan. It would take longer to tell what was not in this house than what was in it. There was an air of plainness about it which almost suggested destitution. My first meal passed under the misnomer of tea, though there was nothing about it resembling the usual significance of that term. It consisted of beef-soup, cabbage, and potatoes – a meal such as a man might relish after following the plow all day or performing a forced march of a dozen miles over a rough road in frosty weather. Innocent of paint, veneering, varnish, or table-cloth, the table announced itself unmistakably of pine and of the plainest workmanship. There was no hired help visible. The mother, daughter, and sons did the serving, and did it well. They were evidently used to it, and had no thought of any impropriety or degradation in being their own servants. It is said that a house in some measure reflects the character of its occupants; this one certainly did. In it there were no disguises, no illusions, no make-believes. Everything implied stern truth, solid purpose, and rigid economy.

I was not long in company with the master of the house before I discovered that he was indeed the master of it, and was likely to become mine too if I stayed long enough with him. He fulfilled St. Paul's idea of the head of the family. His wife believed in him, and his children observed him with reverence. Whenever he spoke his words commanded earnest attention. His arguments, which I ventured at some points to oppose, seemed to convince all; his appeals touched all, and his will impressed all. Certainly I never felt myself in the presence of a stronger religious influence than while in this man's house.

One argument John laid out in this meeting, and one Frederick probably "ventured at some point" to question, was a plan to attack and weaken slavery by launching a guerrilla war on the slaveholding republics from mountain strongholds in the Appalachian chain. The idea is reflected in one of John's few scraps of writing that reflect substantive political advocacy, which he wrote right around the time of Frederick's visit to his home in Springfield. Apparently contemplated for submission to the *Ram's Horn*, a New York newspaper that had just been started by a free African American named Willis

CHAPTER 7: HE WAS AN HONEST THIEF

A. Hodges, the handwritten draft article was titled "Sambo's Mistakes."[28]

Viewed as a literary effort, John's essay was uninspiring, to put it charitably.[29] In form it purported to be narrated by an African American who was confessing, in a semi-satirical manner, to a litany of "mistakes" he had made in his lifetime. Some of these "mistakes" are plainly sops to John's peculiar and characteristic values, such as, a failure to practice self-denial (John's own lifestyle was extremely ascetic, as Frederick's narrative colorfully reveals); reading fiction and popular literature (John's own reading list consisted predominantly of the Bible, various Puritan treatises, and abolitionist tracts); using tobacco (although, John had published a study on using tobacco-infused tea as a remedy for head grubs in sheep); and joining organizations John viewed as a waste of time, such as Masonic lodges and temperance societies. Several other of the "mistakes" sound more like John's own vices: wasting time arguing over trifling theories, and stubbornly refusing to yield on minor disputes. John himself, as we have seen, was very stubborn, and he was also very prone to being doctrinaire; as a matter of fact, he had recently wasted an entire day of a wool grower's convention arguing the merits of "Saxony" sheep over other kinds of Merinos.[30]

But the core message embedded in "Sambo's Mistakes" was one John had shared with Frederick during his visit, as well as Garnet, Loguen, and other African Americans. It was an admonition to refuse any longer to peacefully submit to the indignity of being enslaved. John wrote, in his voice of "Sambo":

> Another trifling error of my life has been, that I have always expected to secure the favor of the whites by tamely submitting to every species of indignity, contempt, and wrong, instead of nobly resisting their

brutal aggressions from principle, and taking my place as a man, and assuming the responsibilities of a man, a citizen, a husband, a father, a brother, a neighbor, a friend – as God requires of every one (if his neighbor will allow him to do it).

This aspect of John's message appealed to Frederick. Frederick's "Editorial Comments" published in the February 11, 1848 edition of *North Star* included the following:

The most interesting part of my visit to Springfield, was a private interview with Mr. Brown, Mr. Van Renssalaer, and Mr. Washington. The first of these, though a white gentleman, is in sympathy a black man, and as deeply interested in our cause, as though his own soul had been pierced with the iron of slavery. After shaking my hand with a *grip* peculiar to Anti-Slavery men, Mr. Brown said that for many years he had been standing by the great sea of American bondmen, and anxiously watching for some true men to rise above its dark level, possessing the energy of head and heart to demand freedom for their whole people, and congratulated myself and the cause, that he now saw such men rising in all directions, the result of which, he knew, must be the downfall of slavery. Mr. Brown is one of the most earnest and interesting men that I have met in a long time.

However "earnest and interesting" he was as an abolitionist, the placement of commercial trust and confidence in "Yankee Brown" by many farmers turned out to be a serious mistake. John was more generous than shrewd, at least with the wool farmers, and more stubborn than cunning in his dealings with the manufacturers.[31] John overpriced the best wool, and underpriced the lower grades, with the result that manufacturers snapped up the lesser grades while refusing to buy the higher. This turned into a serious problem, given that the whole purpose of the wool cooperative was to force up the price of the finer wools to be used in the manufacture of broadcloths, doeskins, cashmeres, and satinettes.[32]

John felt hurt that farmers pressed him to sell their wool at less than he deemed its true worth, and that they blamed him for delay in getting it sold.[33] Because of his refusal to sell at prices he felt were not "fair," he needed to lease more space in which to store the unsold wool. He lacked the instincts of a trader. Said one business acquaintance:[34]

> He waited until his wools were graded, and then fixed a price; if this suited the manufacturers they took the fleeces; if not they bought elsewhere, and [John] had to submit finally to a much less price than he could have got. Yet he was a scrupulously honest and upright man, – hard and inflexible, but everybody had just what belonged to him. Brown was in a position to make a fortune, and a regular-bred merchant would have done so – benefitting the wool growers and the manufacturers mutually.

Aaron Erickson, a wool dealer of western New York, was initially suspicious of both John and his plan to classify wool. He felt that the prevailing method by which the manufacturers purchased ungraded wool from single farmers was eminently just. He found John to be a frank and simple man of "almost childlike ignorance," selling his lower grades for much less than they were worth, while pricing his finer grades substantially higher than manufacturers would pay. John had an inflexible confidence in himself and his classifications, willing enough to listen courteously to Erickson's many objections, but completely and utterly unimpressed. Erickson felt John was destined for ruin, a "victim of his own delusions."[35]

In 1848, Perkins & Brown suffered a loss of almost

$8,000. An account written out in John's hand records: Total paid: $57,884.48, total received: $49,902.67.[36] By early 1849 John was increasingly embroiled in a struggle with American woolen goods manufacturers, whom he believed were acting in concert to drive him out of business due to his idealism in "organizing" the wool producers.[37] In April of that year, John was in crisis. He fell seriously behind in grading wool and in answering correspondence. He was physically ill with malaria, a lifelong chronic ailment that became worse as he aged, and he was also exhibiting symptoms of depression. At home his youngest daughter was sick. She finally died on April 30 after a long illness. His wife Mary was also in poor health.[38] To defeat what he viewed as the malevolence of the American manufacturers, John engaged in an enormous gamble. He decided to ship his entire stock of high quality wool to London, England on the speculation that once there it would bring a price from English manufacturers closer to what it deserved. He would personally travel along with the wool. This London venture was a total "go for broke" risk. John agreed with Perkins not to buy any more wool in 1849; they decided to liquidate the firm unless John made a successful coup on his sales of wool in Europe.[39]

John shipped 200,000 pounds of wool to London in 690 bales during May, June, and July of 1849. He embarked for London by steamer *Cambria* on August 15, 1849. He arrived eleven days later, on August 26.[40] Meanwhile, with John's warehoused wool no longer overhanging the market, the price of fine wool in America immediately began to rise. Very soon it reached prices substantially higher than anything John could hope to receive in London. It became obvious to market observers that the fate of John's premium wool would be to ship it back to the United States.

Three days after his arrival, on August 29, 1849, John crossed to the continent. On August 30 he took a train to Paris. After meeting with a Paris wool concern, he took a five-day

CHAPTER 7: HE WAS AN HONEST THIEF

trip to Brussels and Hamburg.[41] Immediately after Hamburg, John's whereabouts are unknown for a period of ten days. He may have visited some of Napoleon's battlefields, according to tales he later told, but this is not contemporaneously documented. He was back in England on September 17. About 150 bales of his No. 2 wool were sold at auction for prices from 26–29 cents per pound, while the same grade was then selling in the United States for 35 cents per pound. He insisted that "not a pound" had been bought to be re-exported to the United States.[42]

In these September auctions, John was embarrassed and humiliated when the buyers' inspections revealed that some of John's bales had been contaminated on the inside with coarse unwashed wool, "filth," and waste matter. This was typical of what the English regarded with disdain as low-quality American product. Despite John's trumpeting of his grading system, some of the bales had not been thoroughly checked prior to their shipment to England.[43]

John finally ordered the British sales of his wool to stop, due to the low prices they were bringing compared to what the same wool was selling for in the United States. John's proud stubbornness precluded his shipping the remaining wool back to the United States, where prices were higher. Between September 28 and October 5, he tried, in vain, to broker the wool himself, during a tour of English mill towns. Finally on October 15 he sailed for home, with all his No. 1 and No. 2 wool sold in London for a loss, and the remainder, probably more than half of the 200,000 pounds shipped, still in London and not selling at the higher prices to which John had restricted it.[44]

On John's arrival, he immediately returned to Springfield, where he was buried in an avalanche of criticism from farmers. An English trader displayed to John one of John's own clips of wool, which he had bought for $0.52 per pound. This clip, John had sold for as low as $0.36 per pound in England, before ordering the sale to a halt. For the very same clip, three months earlier, the same English trader had offered John $0.60 per pound while it was still sitting in the loft, before any grading and baling. In the meantime, it had crossed the Atlantic twice.[45]

Once more, John returned with tail between his legs to a financial backer and patron. This time it was Simon Perkins. The net result of his London gamble had been total, catastrophic ruin for the partnership of Perkins & Brown. John plaintively protested that he was honest throughout; that he had sacrificed his own good in order to help other deserving farmers organize a collective that had worked to all of their benefit. Perkins' reaction to John's latest financial disaster was surprisingly benevolent. But for John's proud psyche, the wounds of failure continued to fester.[46]

Emulating the Phoenix, John was destined to rise yet again from the ashes of a crash and burn. It was a pattern he would repeat in his next, and final, incarnation.

Chapter 8: Henry Seward, a Boy Wonder

On March 11, 1850, William Henry Seward, a man known to his family and friends as "Henry," rose on the floor of the U.S. Senate to make what would be the most important speech of his career. Henry's life, to that point, was a counterpoint to that of John Brown. The two of them, born just about a year apart, each grew up in rural America. Both had socially prominent fathers. Henry was, like John, something of a child prodigy. Like John, he grew to abhor the relationship of human bondage. But Henry's personality was much different. He had a strong affinity for the classroom. A former family servant would tell a story about young Henry. "Unlike most little boys of the village, instead of running away from school to go home, Henry would frequently run away from home to go to school." At age 15, he was sent to attend Union College in Schenectady, New York, the only member of the family to have this honor and responsibility. He was placed as a sophomore on entry based on his existing degree of familiarity with classic books. Henry worked very hard in college, and he was successful. At the end of his junior year, he was one of a handful of students elected to Phi Beta Kappa.[1]

In the fall of 1818, Henry started his senior year of college. But during the Christmas holiday, he got into a dispute with his father over money. This led to his sudden departure from school, in January of 1819, to travel to Georgia. There, he met a man from New York who had just opened a new school in Eatonton, about 75 miles southeast of Atlanta, called Union Academy. After being interviewed, 17-year-old Henry was not only hired as a teacher in the Academy, he was made the rector. The school opened in April 1819. A sheepish Henry wrote back to his mentors at Union College in Schenectady, pleading with them to find a substitute to replace him so he could finish his degree. The substitute was indeed found, and eventually Henry returned to Schenectady to graduate. He then started to involve himself in politics. Whereas John Brown never voted in a presidential election, Henry Seward believed even intractable problems like the institution of slavery could be resolved using the American political process.[2]

After graduating, Henry studied law with attorneys for a year. Then he moved to New York City where he continued with work as a law clerk. He was admitted to the bar in 1822. He then moved to Auburn, in western New York between Syracuse and Rochester, where he joined the law practice of a retired judge. He ended up marrying the judge's daughter. At the wedding the red-haired Henry stood 5 feet, 6 inches, while his bride Fanny was an inch or two taller. Though somewhat diminutive, Henry was blessed with nonstop energy, never displaying tiredness or boredom. He was known to go virtually without sleep for several nights on end when he was working intensively to prepare a case or write a speech. His son Frederick later recalled his vigor:[3]

> He liked a large house, and plenty of people in it; a good fire, and a large family-circle round it; a full table, strong coffee, and the dishes "hot and sweet and nice." He preferred long rides, long and fatiguing

Chapter 8: Henry Seward, a Boy Wonder

walks; bathing in cold water or strong surf; working steadily for hours, and even taking recreation with determination and perseverance.

As a young lawyer in Auburn, Henry involved himself in politics. He opposed freemasonry, due to his disdain for its elitism and secretive oaths. Henry joined the newly emerging "Antimasonic" political party. As an Antimasonic candidate, he was elected to the New York state senate in 1830. Through their common political views, Henry met Thurlow Weed, the founder of an Antimasonic newspaper in Albany. Weed was a self-made printer-turned-pundit, in the mold of a Lloyd Garrison. Weed was as hard-working and effective as an influencer and politico as Henry was as a scholar and speechmaker. The two would become longtime allies.[4]

Thurlow Weed and Henry Seward become two of the charter members of the Whigs, a new political party organized to oppose President Andrew Jackson and his "Jacksonian" associates. As a result of Weed's vigorous lobbying (in which Henry did not personally participate), Henry was unexpectedly nominated as the Whig candidate for Governor of New York in 1834. He was only 33 years old. His main campaign issues were resurrecting the Bank of the United States and constructing internal transportation improvements such as canals. Due largely to a wave of prosperity that erupted in the midst of the electoral campaign, Henry lost the election to the Jacksonian Democratic party incumbent, William Marcy. Henry ran strong in western New York, but lost in New York and other cities.[5]

Henry then left his law practice to go into the real estate business, involving speculation in land in western New York. He did so in 1836, at almost the exact same time as John Brown went into land speculation in Franklin, Ohio. Henry, however, managed his land dealings more carefully. Although he too incurred high debts, he was able to generate enough income in rents to service them, even in the midst of the panic of 1837. The panic was blamed on the governing Democrats. As a result, the Whig party won a stunning landslide victory in the New York legislature elections in the fall of 1837.

Once more urged on by Weed, the Whigs again nominated Henry as their gubernatorial candidate in the fall of 1838. At age 37, the political boy wonder became the odds-on favorite to become Governor of America's most populous state. He was indeed elected, though by a fairly narrow margin. Wags joked that Weed was the "real" Governor. He certainly controlled Henry's patronage appointments. But Henry soon staked out his own policy agenda:

>1. The United States was destined to expand, both territorially and in terms of worldwide moral leadership.
>
>2. Education was vital, including, for blacks and immigrants. He sought to make education and schools universal. Bucking his own Whig party, he pushed for equal government funding of Catholic and Protestant schools.
>
>3. Immigrants should be treated fairly and without prejudice. He renounced the anti-Catholic prejudice prevalent among old-line New Yorkers.
>
>4. Internal improvements, such as canals, needed to be expanded. This was especially urgent in the wake of the fallout from the panic of 1837 and the associated monetary crisis. Several states were on the verge of debt default at the time.
>
>5. The state's judicial and administrative systems needed to be reformed.

Although some abolitionists, including Gerrit Smith, questioned Henry's commitment to anti-slavery during the 1838 campaign, in his capacity as Governor Henry showed fortitude on the issue. He presided over New York's enactment of personal liberty laws, which not only granted claimed fugitives a right to jury trial, but also required the state's district attorneys to intervene to represent them.[6] In a high-profile case, Henry defied a request from the state of Virginia for extradition of three black sailors who were accused of helping a slave to escape. But he also shrewdly maneuvered to avoid having his position on this request become an issue in his fall 1840 re-election campaign.

In the summer of 1840, the Whigs held their first national convention in Harrisburg, Pennsylvania. At this gathering, Weed was instrumental in denying the presidential nomination to Kentucky U.S. Senator Henry Clay. Instead, war hero William Henry Harrison was nominated. Even though Henry Seward did not even attend the Harrisburg convention, Clay associated his failure to become President with Weed and his pal Henry. He would hold something of a grudge. Harrison won the 1840 presidential election atop the Whig ticket. Henry was re-elected as New York's Governor, again by a narrow margin.[7]

Soon after his inauguration, in the spring of 1841, President Harrison died. The Virginian John Tyler, dubbed "His Accidency," took his place in the White House. He soon fired Harrison's entire cabinet, except for Secretary of State Daniel Webster. Webster and Henry then got into their first major confrontation, over the prosecution of a man named Alexander McLeod in connection with an attack on a vessel in New York waters that resulted in the fatal shooting of an African American sailor. The incident was allegedly related to McLeod's support of the British government in efforts to suppress an independence rebellion in Canada. Following his conscience on the issue, Henry favored requiring McLeod to stand trial for a perpetrating a crime. Webster favored dismissing the case to curry favor with Britain. He argued that the killing was not a crime, but an act of war. Moves and countermoves of the Tyler administration and New York officials with respect to McLeod's prosecution resulted in a bitter confrontation, in which Webster called Henry "a contemptible fellow." The crisis was defused when, in October 1841, McLeod was acquitted by a jury.[8]

Realizing that the cycle of public opinion had turned against the Whigs, Henry announced early on that he would not seek re-election in 1842. In general, during his four years as Governor, Henry was regarded by observers as an advocate for progressive causes who was not particularly successful in achieving legislation to support them. However, his stance on slavery, in particular, was effective. "As a mainstream political leader, Governor Seward highlighted and legitimized concerns about slavery and former slaves in a way that abolitionists, perceived as mere extremists, never could."[9]

After leaving office, Henry was several hundred thousand dollars in debt, part of which was a hangover from his real estate speculation, and part of which was a hangover from his rental of a stylish Albany house and large-scale hospitality as Governor. He only managed to escape the sea of debt because of his law practice. In particular, he made money off litigating patents. One of the cases went to the U.S. Supreme Court, where Henry was actually co-counsel with Webster.[10]

In 1844, Henry campaigned heavily in New York for Henry Clay as the Whig presidential candidate. Despite this, Clay lost the critical state by a very narrow 5,000-vote margin. As a result, Democrat James Knox Polk, who was very pro-slavery and favored annexing Texas as a new slave state, became President.[11] Four years later, going into the national Whig convention of June 1848, many thought a Henry Clay – William Henry Seward ticket would emerge. However, instead, Zachary Taylor, another war hero, and not Clay, was nominated for President. Taylor in turn selected Millard Fillmore of New York over Henry to be his vice-presidential candidate. This fateful choice posed an immediate political problem for Henry, because Henry and Fillmore were rivals for power within the New York Whig party. Regardless, Henry vigorously campaigned all across the state of New York, and also campaigned extensively outside the state, for the Taylor–Fillmore ticket. The visibility this gave him strengthened Henry's own chances of getting a U.S. Senate position, which at that time was filled by legislative appointment rather than a popular vote. In his campaign speeches, Henry consistently characterized the Whig party as standing for "freedom," and the Democratic party as standing for "slavery."

Zachary Taylor won the 1848 election for President. He prevailed handily in New York, while a Henry Seward protégé, Hamilton Fish, was elected Governor. Whigs dominated the New York legislature. Never-theless, because of Fillmore's new standing as Vice-President, getting a Senate appointment was still an uphill battle for Henry. Democrats in New York criticized Henry as "an abolitionist of the deepest dye." He pulled through, though, partly because he wrote a letter for publication suggesting he could live with slavery, although he would require it to be circumscribed within its present bounds pending its "constitutional, lawful, and peaceful" removal.[12]

Henry Seward, in 1848 portrait

His new seat in the Senate placed Henry in the eye of the biggest political storm to hit Washington in a generation, ever since the debates over Missouri Compromise of 1820. The agenda for debate was the admission to the Union of the state of California. Toward the end of the gold rush year of 1849

California's citizens, on their own initiative, had adopted a state constitution and applied for admission to the United States. President Taylor favored California's immediate and unconditional admission. Henry agreed with the President's position. But Senators from the Southern states were increasingly petulant over the rise of articulated anti-slavery sentiment. With some justification, they felt that acquiescence in Northern anti-slavery measures such as "personal liberty laws" posed a long term threat to their way of life. California's admission they viewed with alarm because its new constitution prohibited slavery. Adding another "free state" threatened to confer a majority of voting power in the Senate on states that outlawed human bondage.[13] Southern leaders were making a thinly veiled threat to withdraw from the Union over the issue. They set up a convention to be held in June in Nashville, Tennessee, in which secession would be the ultimate agenda for discussion.

When Congress met in January 1850, Henry Clay quickly proposed a compromise by introducing omnibus legislation. One major element added in his compromise measure was a new law that would involve the federal government in recapturing escaped slaves found anywhere in the United States. This was intended to mollify Southern concerns by effectively invalidating "personal liberty laws" such as the one Henry had helped enact in New York.

Daniel Webster, as a Senator from Massachusetts, gave a lengthy speech on March 7, 1850. His remarks were composed with his typical rhetorical brilliance.[14] They practically constituted a history treatise. His thoroughgoing review recapitulated the attitudes about slavery manifested by the ancient Greeks, the attitudes of the ancient Romans, and both sides of the difference of opinion about how biblical texts address the institution. Webster also gave lengthy attention to the history of how slavery had been treated by the founding fathers of the United States. He pointed out how James

CHAPTER 8: HENRY SEWARD, A BOY WONDER

Madison, the principal drafter, had assiduously avoided using the word "slavery" anywhere in the document, "for he said, he did not wish to see it recognized by the Constitution of the United States of America, that there could be property in men." He recounted that many delegates to the constitutional convention from Southern states had expressed a reprobation for slavery. Webster concluded that the founders: (1) expected that with the 1808 prohibition on the import of slaves, slavery would begin to die out; (2) gave Congress maximum powers to prevent the further spread of slavery; and (3) meant to leave slavery as they found it, within the control of the states rather than the national government.

Webster next discussed how times and sentiments had changed since the Constitution was adopted. The age of cotton, he said, had changed everything. It had caused Southern representatives to reconsider and abandon their former views on the inevitable dying out of slavery. Now, the issue was divisive. He identified the issue as the central focus of a recent eleven-year long debate over the admission of Texas as a new state in which slavery was permitted. He accused the "Northern Democracy" of provoking "extreme mortification" with its loudly expressed pangs of conscience over the extension of slavery into Texas. With respect to New Mexico and California, newly available for annexation due to the success of the United States in the Mexican–American war, he made a very lawyer-like argument. The physical geography of those places, Webster

Daniel Webster

asserted, by its very nature precludes slavery. Therefore, he argued, there was no need to "inflict a wound" on Southern sentiments by expressly prohibiting slavery in these new additions to the United States. In particular, he continued, New Mexico should not be subjected to any prohibition against slavery within its territory.

Webster's silver tongue then turned its attention to the fugitive slave issue:

> Mr. President, in the excited times in which we live, there is found to exist a state of crimination and recrimination between the North and the South. There are lists of grievances produced by each; and these grievances, real or supposed, alienate the minds of one portion of the country from the other, exasperate the feelings, subdue the sense of fraternal connection, and patriotic love, and mutual regard. I shall bestow a little attention, sir, upon these various grievances, produced on the one side and the other. I begin with complaints of the South; I will not answer, farther than I have, the general statements of the honorable Senator from South Carolina [John Calhoun], that the North has grown upon the South in consequence of the manner of administering the Government, in the collecting of its revenues, and so forth. These are disputed topics, and I have no inclination to enter into them.

> But I will state these complaints, especially one complaint of the South, which has in my opinion just foundation; and that is, that there has been found at the North, among individuals and among the Legislatures of the North, a disinclination to perform, fully, their constitutional duties, in regard to the return of persons bound to service, who have escaped into the free States. In that respect, it is my judgment, that the South is right, and the North is wrong. Every member

CHAPTER 8: HENRY SEWARD, A BOY WONDER

of every Northern Legislature is bound, by oath, like every other officer in the country, to support the Constitution of the United States; and this article of the Constitution, which says to these States, they shall deliver up fugitives from service, is as binding in honor and conscience as any other article. No man fulfills his duty in any Legislature who sets himself to find excuses, evasions, escapes from this constitutional obligation.

Webster next delivered a lashing to Lloyd Garrison and his ilk, who were gaining increasing strength and support within Webster's own home state of Massachusetts:

Then, sir, there are those abolitionist societies, of which I am unwilling to speak, but in regard to which I have very clear notions and opinions. I do not think them useful. I think their operations for the last twenty years have produced nothing good or valuable. At the same time, I know thousands of them are honest and good men; perfectly well-meaning men. They have excited feelings; they think they must do something for the cause of liberty; and in their sphere of action, they do not see what else they can do, than to contribute an abolition press, or an abolition society, or to pay an abolition lecturer. I do not mean to impute gross motives even to the leaders of these societies, but I am not blind to the consequences. I cannot but see what mischiefs their interference with the South has produced.

Webster concluded his speech by decrying vehemently the prospect of secession. He pointed out that its very idea was inadmissible, that "[t]here can be no such thing as a peaceable secession." Urging support for Clay's compromise, he attempted to uplift the chamber by appealing to the nobility of the American ideal, the ideal of constitutional government, and the freedom of the country from monarchical tyranny.

When Henry Seward took the Senate floor four days later, he had the daunting task of responding to Webster's great speech.[15] In substance, he was supporting the President's position that California should be admitted immediately and without being tied to the other, pro-slavery elements of Clay's "compromise" package. Henry, as usual, was determined to outwork his adversary. Ever the bookworm, Henry assembled facts and statistics to rebut Webster's clever argument that there was no need to injure Southern feelings because physical geography would prevent slavery from ever taking root in places like New Mexico or California. Henry pointed out that the world's largest "slave state" was currently Russia. He argued that "icebound Russia" has a climate totally unsuited for the typical slave-farmed monocrops, yet he brought out statistics showing that out of a total Russian population of 54,251,000, some 53,500,000 were serfs. "Sir, there is no climate uncongenial to slavery," he concluded.

Henry invoked Montesquieu, as well as several other political writers and philosophers, in support of his major thesis that any expansion of slavery must be halted as a matter of national policy:

> I cannot stop to debate long with those who maintain that slavery is itself practically economical and humane. I might be content with saying, that there are some axioms in political science that a statesman or founder of States may adopt, especially in the Congress of the United States, that among those axioms are these: that all men are created equal, and have inalienable rights of life, liberty, and the choice of pursuits of happiness; that knowledge promotes virtue, and righteousness exalteth a nation; that freedom is preferable to slavery; and that democratic governments, where they can be maintained by

acquiescence, without force, are preferable to institutions exercising arbitrary and irresponsible power.

It remains only to remark, that our own experience has proved the dangerous influence and tendency of slavery. All our apprehensions of dangers, present and future, begin and end with slavery. If slavery, limited as it is, now threatens to subvert the Constitution, how can we, as wise and prudent statesmen, enlarge its boundaries and increase its influence, and thus increase already impending dangers? Whether, then, I merely regard the welfare of the future inhabitants of the new territories, or the security and welfare of the whole people of the United States, or the welfare of the whole family of mankind, I cannot consent to introduce slavery into any part of this continent which is now exempt from what seems to me so great an evil. These are my reasons for declining to compromise the question relating to slavery as a condition of the admission of California.

Henry confronted, and challenged head-on, the threats of Southern representatives to secede. Such threats, he argued, cannot be allowed to block the path of "natural justice" and "Progress." Much of his speech was a ringing reaffirmation of Henry's faith in the genius of the American system of "democratic Federal government," with its "complex, yet effective, combination of distinct local elective agencies." He concurred with Webster and others "who say there can be no peaceful dissolution."

Henry did not actually use the words "higher law" in his three-hour speech. However, his national reputation would always be based on that catchphrase and, for that phrase, which he did not actually use, his speech was long remembered.[16] He laid out the thesis that natural law – a law ordained by God – trumps any compromises in the U.S. Constitution that sanction slavery:

> The law of nations disavows such compacts; the law of nature, written on the hearts and consciences of freemen, repudiates them. Armed power could not enforce them, because there is no public conscience to sustain them. I know that there are laws of various sorts that regulate the conduct of men. There are constitutions and statutes, codes mercantile and codes civil; but when we are legislating for States, especially when we are founding States, all these laws must be brought to the standard of the laws of God, and must be tried by that standard, and must stand or fall by it.

Henry metaphorically compared the fugitive slave clause of the U.S. Constitution, which the new law sought to explicitly require every state government as well as federal officers to enforce, to an "opaque spot" on the surface of a document that otherwise shines with the "splendor and power of the sun." "Your Constitution and laws convert hospitality to the refugee, from the most degrading oppression on earth, into a crime, but all mankind except you esteem that hospitality a virtue." He concluded by exhorting his colleagues to avoid a return to the "Dark Ages" of medieval times in which international compacts were made for the extradition of slaves.

Henry's speech cemented his national reputation for statesmanship. He had 100,000 copies printed and sent out, nearly half of which went under his signature using his franking privilege.[17] The position he advocated had the support of the President. At the June 1850 Nashville convention of Southern delegates, moderates prevailed and dismissed any notion of secession. But fate took a hand. At a July 4 fund-raising event in Washington City, President Taylor contracted cholera from eating tainted food. He died five days later. This

CHAPTER 8: HENRY SEWARD, A BOY WONDER

unexpected turn of events placed Millard Fillmore, Henry's political rival, in the White House. Fillmore lacked the conscience and statesmanlike qualities of a Henry Seward. He was rapidly seduced into supporting the Clay compromise. Fillmore appointed Webster as his Secretary of State. With presidential support, the compromise, including the Fugitive Slave Law, was enacted in the fall of 1850.[18]

The Fugitive Slave Law's enactment provoked a wave of fury among abolitionists. John Brown, too, was outraged, although, in his case, it was more a product of his fundamental raging nature than any specific reaction to a piece of legislation. He practically welcomed the law's advent, due to the potential it presented for fomenting anti-slavery violence.[19] In his "leisure" time in Springfield, while he was licking the wounds from his recent financial meltdown in the wool business, John put forth a concept for an organization intended for resistance by force by African Americans to any effort to return them to slavery.[20] To inspire the organization, John wrote a tract entitled "Words of Advice," dated January 15, 1851.[21] This was no Henry Seward speech. His "Words of Advice" provide by far the clearest indication of John's developing train of thought leading to his emergence as a terrorist. Due to his personality characteristics, John was instinctively feeling his way toward becoming a terrorist leader, even though the modern term "terrorist" would not exist for another 25 years, when it would be coined in Russia by the political philosophers of the *Narodnaya Volya*.

The "Words of Advice" urge the brand of tactics that we, today, recognize as terrorism. These include the defining terrorist modality of violence, the sneak attack on unsuspecting civilian victims:

> Let the first blow be the signal for all to engage; and when engaged do not do your work by halves; but make clean work with your enemies …. By going

about your business quietly, you will get the job disposed of before the number that an uproar would bring together can collect; and you will have the advantage of those who come out against you, for they will be wholly unprepared with equipment or matured plans; all with them will be confusion and terror.

"Words of Advice" also suggest another prototypical terrorist device, a primitive kind of bomb: "You may make a tumult in the court-room where a trial is going on, by burning gunpowder freely in paper packages."

John's "Words of Advice" strongly foreshadow propensities of modern terrorists. This starts with his purported "organization" itself. The "Words" are addressed to a "Branch of the United States League of Gileadites," and in fact, John's entire manuscript is framed as a sort of organic field manual and constitution for such a "Branch." However, the "United States League of Gileadites" is merely and solely an imposing name that John himself dreamed up. There was no such nationwide organization. Hence, the notion that John's organization was a "Branch" of such an impressive national body was purely a construct on his part. This is typical of the terrorist. Terrorists who have followed in John's wake, including those still erupting today, very commonly promote the image of a fictitious organization in order to substantially exaggerate their importance and numbers.

John's use of the word "Gileadites" in the name of the organization is also significant. It constitutes a conscious and explicit reference to an Old Testament story; in fact, in "Words of Advice" John expressly cites Judges, chapter 7, and Deuteronomy, chapter 20, verse 8. The proverbs of these texts advise never going into battle until all "cowards" are given free and full opportunity to absent themselves. "And the Lord reduced the thirty-two thousand who had first been under Gideon to only three hundred, knowing that the rest were cowards."[22] In "Words of Advice," John wrote: "Whosoever is fearful or afraid, let him return and part early from Mount Gilead." This reflects a core credo of the terrorist. Any sympathizers, or fellow believers in the cause, who urge moderation, restraint, political action, or other forms of non-violence must be purged from the terrorist group, even killed if necessary to preserve secrecy. It is paradigmatic behavior for the terrorist leadership to condemn such people as "cowards."

However, mainstream sympathizers do have an important role to play, according to "Words of Advice." Following the terrorist-style sneak attack, John recommends:

> if you are assailed, go into the houses of your most prominent and influential white friends with your wives; and that will effectually fasten upon them the suspicion of being connected with you, and will compel them to make a common cause with you, whether they would otherwise live up to their profession or not.

This gets into the subject matter of a recurring pattern discernible across terrorists of all stripes. A "love-hate" relationship typically exists between the terrorist, who has determined to give up his or her life in a passionate outburst of violence for the cause, and sympathizing "legals," who agree with the cause, and who give the terrorists financial aid and other forms of support, but who are not themselves interested in effectively committing suicide, becoming martyrs, or facing serious criminal charges. "Words of Advice" urges the "Gileadite" to mingle with these sympathizers in order to leave them with "no choice in the matter," lest they "flinch" at the violence.

The "Words of Advice" begin with an ode to those who had suffered death or disfigurement for the sake of the cause of abolition, including Elijah Lovejoy. Unrepentant martyrdom, after the fashion of the heroes of Foxe's *Book of Martyrs* (a

Puritan holy scripture chronicling and praising those who had been burned at the stake in Renaissance England for refusing to renounce Protestant practices), was glorified: "Stand by one another and your friends, while one drop of blood remains; and be hanged, if you must, but tell no tales out of school. Make no confession." The "Words of Advice" end with the sentiment that "a just and merciful God" will stand behind the righteous violence and carry the day.

To the "Resolutions" at the end of John's constitution are appended the names of forty-four citizens of Springfield, presumably all African Americans. However, these "signatures" were actually written out in John's handwriting. It is highly doubtful that the Springfield "Branch of the United States League of Gileadites" ever did much organizing, beyond being impressed and flattered at the energy John put into bulwarking their cause. Federal marshals did not come to disturb fugitive slaves in Springfield.[23] The field of battle for "Gileadites" would be found elsewhere.

Chapter 9: A Nightmarish Family Outing

Edward Gorsuch was a good man and a capable farmer. By the year 1849 he was 54 years of age. He was a church leader, sufficiently respected in the community that he was selected to arbitrate disputes among his neighbors. Edward's Maryland "Retreat Farm," which he had inherited four years earlier, was situated in a beautiful rolling area of Baltimore County, just 3 miles or so south of the picturesque town of Hereford. This was the northern rural periphery of Baltimore, a different and substantially more modern world than the primitive Eastern Shore. Edward was by no means a wealthy plantation owner like an Edward Lloyd, but his farm and family were reasonably well off, with forty cows, thirty sheep, and a dozen horses. Edward ruled his estate in the manner of a kind and benevolent father. Twelve slaves inherited by Edward along with the farm reinforced the agricultural prosperity. They were always well fed and well treated, never whipped or beaten. Every one of them had been promised his or her freedom in writing when they attained the age of 28.[1]

Alas, as Frederick tells us in his testimony, a person in bondage who has a kind and good master very often yearns to be a person with no master at all. And, in the fall of 1849, the urge to seek freedom came over four of Edward's capable bondsmen. Their departure was hastened by Edward's discovery of a major theft from the granary of Retreat Farm. Edward kept accurate accounts of the wheat stored in his corn house adjoining a main turnpike now called York Road. At his own mill, he processed this wheat for retail sale in Baltimore. The bin, he realized, was five bushels low. This was far too much to be attributed to factors such as normal shrinkage or rodents. A little investigation revealed that a quantity of wheat had been sold to a neighboring miller by one Abe Johnson, a free African American living 2 miles north of Retreat Farm. Gorsuch knew Johnson had neither land to raise wheat nor credit to buy it.[2]

Edward obtained a warrant for Johnson's arrest. But, before it could be executed, it was discovered he had fled north across the Mason–Dixon line into Pennsylvania. News of the search for Abe Johnson was rampant. People were suspicious that some of Edward's farm "boys" had helped Johnson raid the corn house and shared in his spoils. Perhaps the spoils provided a means for their travels. On the dark night of November 6, 1849, five young men, the racially mixed Noah Buley, the teamster Nelson Ford, two brothers, George and Joshua Hammond, and another African American, all made their escape from Retreat Farm and headed north up York Road into Pennsylvania.[3]

Life continued at the farm, but Edward Gorsuch, a diligent and conscientious man, felt he needed to do something about the absconding of his people. Edward was not particularly concerned about the escape for economic reasons. He probably realized his operations could be more profitable if they used hired help instead of slave labor. For the community leader and benevolent patriarch, their departure was more of a humiliating embarrassment. It was a matter of his personal pride and honor to get them to return home. It was not very hard for him to learn where they had gone. As a matter of fact, the refugees

CHAPTER 9: A NIGHTMARISH FAMILY OUTING

themselves sent messages back to the Gorsuch farm, asking to be sent various things that they needed. Their requests were accommodated.[4]

An appeal was made to authorities in Harrisburg, the Pennsylvania state capitol, to arrest and extradite Abe Johnson, and to assist in the recovery of the runaway bondsmen. No sympathy was shown for this by the Governor of Pennsylvania, William Johnston. Time passed, and the situation seemed to stabilize. Edward worked Retreat Farm for two crop years using other help. But still, Edward kept out feelers, looking for a way to retrieve his wayward charges. Finally he received a letter dated August 28, 1851 from a former Baltimore County resident named William Padgett. Padgett was now in Lancaster County, Pennsylvania. This letter told that Padgett knew where Edward's four men were located, and that they were all within 2 miles of each other. Padgett urged Edward to come right away, and recommended that he bring a force of "about twelve" so that "they can divide and take them."[5]

By this time, the Fugitive Slave Law had been enacted. Edward decided to handle the matter using its new procedure. After 1850 the pursuit of fugitive slaves became, almost like the Fugitive Slave Law itself, a matter of civic duty, more of a symbolic than a practical matter. The recovery of a slave under the new law often cost much more than the "market value" of the runaway. This was especially true of Edward's slaves, who had already been promised manumission and thus had very limited, if any, "cash value."[6] Edward's actions in this affair would show he was not in close contact with the reality that freedom was an intoxicant far stronger than the lure of a family hearth and home. Feeling much like a young man unexpectedly jilted by a partner in love, Edward cherished the notion that the objects of his affections would come to their senses and return to embrace him, if only he could just talk to them.

On Monday, September 8, 1851, Edward took an express

train from Baltimore to Philadelphia. Upon arrival, he went before Edward D. Ingraham, a federal commissioner appointed under the new law to issue fugitive warrants. Edward obtained, on that same day, four warrants to arrest escaped "persons held to service or labor," one each for Noah Buley, Nelson Ford, and the two Hammonds. The warrants were addressed to a deputy U.S. marshal who specialized, to a degree, in such captures. The marshal's name was Henry H. Kline. The next day, Edward met up with the friends and family he had enlisted to come along from rural Baltimore County on this adventure. The posse included: Thomas Pearce, a physician who was his sister's son and who also owned one of the escaped slaves; Joshua Gorsuch, a young man who was Edward's cousin; Edward's 24-year-old son Dickinson Gorsuch; and two neighbors, Nicholas Hutchings and Nathan Nelson. Edward also retained the services of two Philadelphia-area constables.[7]

Ordinary citizens in Lancaster County, and throughout eastern Pennsylvania in general, were resentful of the newly passed Fugitive Slave Law. The very idea of the law, making it "every man's duty" to cooperate with slave recaptures, was perceived as an affront to their sense of humanity and charity. In the spring of 1851 a political meeting was held at the Horticultural Hall in West Chester, about 30 miles east of the small borough of Christiana, in whose vicinity Edward's bondsmen were reported by Padgett to be located. At this annual meeting of the Pennsylvania Anti-Slavery Society, speeches were given denouncing the Fugitive Slave Law. Prominent residents of Lancaster County were in attendance. Resolutions were heartily passed, and thereafter published, encouraging vigilance, non-compliance and resistance to the law.[8]

What Padgett apparently did not know, and what he at any rate did not inform Edward, is that in going into the Christiana area of Lancaster County to effect his lawful right of recapture, Edward was up against a resistance organization very similar

CHAPTER 9: A NIGHTMARISH FAMILY OUTING

to the one whose outlines John Brown had drawn in his "Words of Advice to the Gileadites." The leader of this "Gileadite" style resistance was named William Parker. Parker, a 29-year-old African American, was self-liberated from his origins in slavery in Anne Arundel County, Maryland, on a plantation near today's Southern (of Harwood) High School, nearly due west across the Chesapeake Bay from St. Michaels. After escaping, Parker had made his way to the semi-rural Christiana area of Lancaster County where he was, by this time, well ensconced and respected in the local community. Parker had participated in an abolitionist revival where the headline speakers were Lloyd Garrison and Frederick Douglass. Before Edward's arrival, Parker and his local militia had been involved in a number of partisan scrapes and rescues with "slave catchers" who came into the area, several of whom reportedly wound up dead as a result of the festivities. Parker and his men also inflicted lethal violence on African Americans who were viewed as informers.[9] Just as it was a matter of honor to Edward to bring back his wayward minions, it was equally, if not more so, a matter of honor to Parker to see that none of them went back.

Edward's expedition encountered problems that might have caused a lesser man to reconsider the project. Marshal Kline left Philadelphia with the warrants the day after they were issued, on Tuesday between 1 and 2 p.m. The plan was for Kline to meet up with the Gorsuch party later that day in Penningtonville, the nearest town to Christiana about 2 miles to the southeast. For unknown reasons Kline did not, like Edward and his party, take a train to get there. Instead he hired a wagon, which broke down on the way. Kline then had to return to West Chester to get another vehicle. The time lost caused Kline to miss his meeting with Edward in Penningtonville. Not finding the Gorsuch party there, Kline went ahead to the town of Gap, 4 miles north of Christiana. He arrived extremely late and did not get to sleep until 3 a.m. on the morning of Wednesday, September 10. Finally, later that morning, he met up with Edward. By that time, the constables became disenchanted and announced they were returning to Philadelphia. Edward gave them more money and arranged for them to return on a train later that night. However, he would never see them again.[10]

The issuance of the fugitive warrants by Commissioner Ingraham was no secret. The posse's mission was rapidly discovered by the Philadelphia anti-slavery vigilance committee that was part of the "underground railroad." One of the dedicated agents of that committee was a rather portly man with a moderate amount of African American blood, named Samuel Williams. Williams copied out on a sheet of paper a summary of the warrants, including the names of the men whose arrests had been authorized. To give the targets warning of the expedition against them, he immediately boarded a train to Parkesburg, another town in Lancaster County not far from Christiana. Along the way he traveled in the same car with one of the constables, who recognized him. From Parkesburg, Williams continued west to Penningtonville. Williams was in a tavern in Penningtonville which Kline, upon his belated arrival on the night of Tuesday, September 9, entered looking for the Gorsuch party. Kline and Williams both knew who the other was. The two of them even spoke briefly. Williams then followed Kline when he took the train to Gap.[11] At that point, Kline had to realize Williams was conducting surveillance on the expedition.

While Kline and Edward spent most of Wednesday, September 10, resting and recuperating from the misadventures of the previous day, Williams was busy carrying news of the coming attempt at capture to the community in and around Christiana. Williams met with several local African Americans and abolitionists and filled them in on Kline's presence and its significance. He gave them the paper on which

CHAPTER 9: A NIGHTMARISH FAMILY OUTING

he had written down his summary of the warrants with the names of the targets. Word spread like wildfire. Parker mobilized his Gileadites. Very likely, Parker and his allies also alerted sympathetic non-African Americans to the impending confrontation. Parker was living in a two-story stone house a mile or so south of Christiana on a farm owned by Levi Pownell. The night of Wednesday, September 10, Parker had with him, in that house overnight, two of Edward's former servants: Nelson Ford, who was now called "Joshua Kite" by Parker, and who was also known locally as "John Beard," and Joshua Hammond, who was now called "Samuel Thompson" by Parker. Also in the stone house that night were Parker's wife Eliza, Eliza's sister Hannah, and Hannah's husband, Alexander Pinckney. Finally, there was a man named Abraham Johnson. It is likely this was the same "Abe Johnson" whose sale of grain had started the misadventures in the first place.[12]

Schematic map of Christiana vicinity, 1851

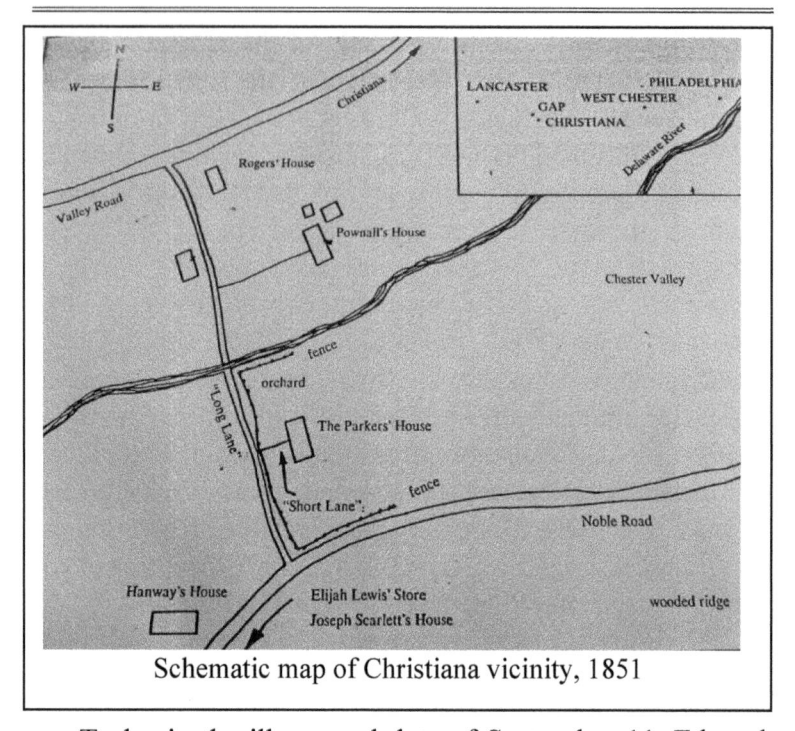

    To begin the ill-omened date of September 11, Edward and his entire company pulled an unscheduled all-nighter. At 11 o'clock Wednesday night, September 10, they went to the train station in Downingtown, 18 miles east of Christiana. There they waited in vain for the constables to return on the train from Philadelphia. The constables' failure to materialize did not daunt Edward. He and his party boarded the train from Downingtown westward to Gap, arriving at 1.30 a.m. In the middle of the night, they all walked the 3 miles south to Christiana. Along the way, they met up with Padgett. Somehow or other, Padgett knew Edward would be able to find several of the people he was seeking at Parker's. Before reaching Parker's, however, Padgett pointed out the way to another house, in the direction of Penningtonville from Christiana, where he said another of Edward's slaves could be found. Edward wanted to split off to claim this person, but Kline vetoed the idea. There was not enough time for such a

CHAPTER 9: A NIGHTMARISH FAMILY OUTING

diversion if the party was to arrive at Parker's at daybreak, which was the agreed plan. The group needed to avoid splitting up in Kline's opinion, which Edward accepted.[13]

It was a heavy, foggy morning. Padgett led the party southward to Parker's, taking a shortcut across some fields. They then continued along farm roads. Padgett pointed the group the rest of the way to Parker's place, then he left them. Padgett evidently did not want to be seen with "slave catchers" by Parker or anybody else. The group stopped to breakfast on some crackers and cheese. Pearce wanted to get some water to drink from a creek. Kline vetoed the idea. It was now near dawn, and there was no time to lose. They resumed their journey to Parker's. On the way, about 10 minutes before they arrived, they all heard the eerie sound of a horn being blown somewhere in the rolling hills to their right. With daylight barely peeking out from the horizon, they thought it was an oddly early time to be summoning people to work.[14] Edward and his party, in reality, were being watched. Their movements were being signaled. They were completely deluded in thinking they would enjoy any element of surprise.

To reach the Parker house, the Gorsuch party had to take a farm lane. The Parker house was to their left. As they approached the mouth of a shorter lane that led to the door of the house, they encountered a man whom Edward immediately recognized as his servant Nelson Ford. Nelson Ford was small and had a slender build unsuited for heavy physical tasks, so at Retreat Farm Edward

Rendering of William Parker home near Christiana, as of 1851

had assigned him to serve as his teamster. Ford evidently had been posted by Parker as something of a sentry. Seeing his former master, he immediately turned tail, sprinted into the house, and ran up the stairs to the second floor. Edward, Kline, and the entire party gave chase. In the twilight, Kline failed to see a low gate across the short lane leading to the house. He tripped and sprawled headlong over it, dropping both of the revolvers he was carrying.[15]

By the time Kline picked up the revolvers and himself, Edward had already reached the front door, which was left hanging wide open after Ford entered. Kline foll-owed Edward inside. Kline called up the stairs for the landlord. He got a reply that he was not coming down. Kline then announced up the stairs that he had two warrants, one for Nelson Ford and one for Joshua Hammond. Kline read out loud the warrants. Again came down a reply. There was no one here by those names. Kline then started up the stairs, with Edward behind him. Someone at the top of the stairs used a pitchfork-like implement to drive him back. Then an axe was thrown down at them. Stymied, Kline advised Edward to go outside to speak to the occupants through a window instead.[16]

Meanwhile, the other members of the Gorsuch party stationed themselves around the outside of the house. They immediately faced attack. Thomas Pearce was struck above the eye with an axe-like object thrown down from the second floor. Joshua Gorsuch was hit on the shoulder with another heavy missile. When Edward stepped out of the house at Kline's suggestion, a rifle shot very nearly hit him. The flash was visible to nearby Joshua Gorsuch between Edward's head and his shoulder. Kline stepped out of the house. He fired one of his revolvers up in the air, intended as a warning shot to the defenders.[17]

The firing and throwing of missiles then ceased. Various elements of conversation went back and forth between Parker, on the second floor, and Kline and Edward below, during a

Chapter 9: A Nightmarish Family Outing

standoff that lasted as much as an hour. Kline ceremoniously read out the warrants, in a loud voice, several times. Parker called out that Levi Parnell was the landlord, and suggested that Kline go get him. Kline replied that he would. Parker paraded himself, Pinckney, and Johnson at the second-floor window, each time asking, "Is this who you are looking for?" He was careful not to show the other two men. Kline made a show of writing a note on a piece of paper and handing it to Joshua Gorsuch, telling Parker it was a message to be taken to the sheriff to come with a hundred men. From the second floor, Parker responded to this ruse with a ploy of his own, asking for time to consider. At first, he asked for 10 minutes. Edward was encouraged that maybe his people would be surrendered peacefully to him, after all. They waited. When Kline announced that the 10 minutes was up, Parker called out to ask for 5 minutes more. While they waited, the Gorsuch party could hear sounds of spiritual singing coming from the occupants. They also heard the prominent sound of another horn blowing. This time, the horn sounds were coming from the second floor of the Parker house, from an instrument blown by Parker's wife Eliza. Parker's offer to parley was, in reality, merely a stall for time. The horn calls were a summons to battle.[18]

Joseph Scarlett, a local farmer and merchant, was Parker's employer, for whom Parker operated a threshing machine. Scarlett undoubtedly was in on the news of the slave-hunting party that Williams had brought the day before. When he heard, before dawn, the sound of the horns confirming that the "kidnappers" had indeed come, Scarlett mounted his horse and dashed around the area in Paul Revere-like fashion, summoning help here and there from African Americans for Parker and the fugitives he was protecting. Another important person who knew about the impending attack the day before was Isaiah Clarkson, a respected African American elder. Well before dawn, Clarkson arrived at the home of Elijah Lewis, a white storekeeper and postmaster, whom Clarkson knew would not approve of kidnappers coming to Christiana. He told Lewis that Parker's house had been broken into and that he was under assault. Lewis immediately decided to rush to the scene to see that "justice was done," as he would later put it. On the way, however, Lewis stopped at the flour mill of Castner Hanway. Hanway agreed to go to Parker's house as well. Hanway was not feeling up to the mile-long walk, so he took his horse. Thus, Hanway arrived at the Parker house before Lewis.[19]

When Hanway showed up on horseback in front of the low gate to the Parker house, Kline and all of the rest of the Gorsuch party, except Edward and his son Dickinson, went over to speak with him. Kline was hoping this white man – literally white, because he had flour from his mill sticking to his clothes – would perform his lawful duty to aid in the execution of his warrants. Kline identified himself as a deputy U.S. marshal who was there to execute arrest warrants for fugitives. Hanway was unsympathetic, if not outright hostile. He declined to give his name, curtly informing Kline it was none of his business. Kline gave Hanway the warrants to read. Hanway read them over several times. He remarked he thought the people in the house had a right to defend themselves. He expressed skepticism that Kline was going to be able to arrest anybody. Lewis, on foot, then arrived at the gate. Lewis, too, looked over the warrants, although he later claimed that because he forgot his glasses he could not make out much more than the name "Ingraham." Lewis also expressed to Kline the view that the "colored people" had a right to defend themselves. He advised Kline to clear out to avoid bloodshed.[20]

While Kline was talking with Hanway and Lewis for perhaps five to ten minutes, African Americans started arriving on the scene, coming from all directions. They were carrying all kinds of weapons. Some had "corn cutters," a kind of

CHAPTER 9: A NIGHTMARISH FAMILY OUTING

lightweight sickle. Some had clubs. And some had shotguns and rifles, weapons nobody in the Gorsuch party possessed. Ten to twenty militiamen assembled in the long lane, near the place where Hanway sat on his horse. Kline could hear the distinctive sound of rifles being loaded. At that point, Kline finally decided retreat was imperative. He declared to Hanway and Lewis, with a certain amount of bravado, that he would hold them responsible for the slaves. He asked the other members of the Gorsuch party who were standing around listening to go inside the gate and get Edward to withdraw. Pearce and Joshua Gorsuch went in. They told Edward it was time to give up and get out. They turned around and made their way back out, expecting Edward to follow.[21]

Edward's son Dickinson, who had remained with Edward outside the house, was also alarmed at the situation. He too urged Edward to withdraw. But Edward was prideful. He had not come all this way just to give up. Somehow, he still clung to the hope that his people would agree to come back, if he could only speak to them one on one. He replied to Dickinson that it would not do to give it up this way. And he hesitated about leaving.[22]

African Americans, meanwhile, continued to stream to the scene in large numbers. By now there was a crowd of seventy-five to a hundred milling about in the long lane outside the gate. Hanway rode over and said something to them in a low voice that Kline could not make out. Shortly after this, someone in the mob cried out, "He is only a deputy!" Somebody fired a shot at Kline. The shot missed, but it caused Kline to dive over the fence bordering the lane and take cover in the adjacent cornfield. The shot, and Kline's flight, seemed to break the tension. It rapidly led to much more action. The assembled crowd moved in the direction of the Parker house, passing Pearce, Joshua Gorsuch, and Dickinson, all of whom were leaving. Pearce recognized one of the men who went by him as

Noah Buley. As the militia entered, they were joined by Parker and the other defenders of the house, who now came out of the door and rushed forward to the attack.

The unarmed Edward probably did finally try to leave, but it was much too late. The mob swarmed him. Someone hit him over the head with a club, sending him to his knees. Edward gamely tried to rise. Someone else smashed him with another club, breaking his left arm. At about the same time, Edward was shot in the chest. Pearce saw his body go limp and collapse on the ground. Dickinson was the only member of the Gorsuch party who tried to come to the aid of his father. He waded into the crowd with a revolver and fired off a couple of shots. But he himself was struck with two crushing blasts from a shotgun. One hit him in the arm, which at the time he thought was a club; the other hit him in the side. Dickinson dropped his revolver, turned around and staggered out of the gate. Kline, who was just emerging from hiding, came to Dickinson, held him up, and helped him walk 40 yards or so down the lane in the direction opposite the creek, where he set down the fainting young man by the stump of a tree. Blood was coming out of Dickinson's mouth. Kline thought he was about to die.[23]

Guns were now firing off like crazy. The remaining people in the Gorsuch party turned and fled as fast as their legs could carry them. As he was jumping over to get out of the gate, Pearce was hit with a flurry of shots. He was struck by projectiles in the wrist, in the shoulder blade, and two of them lodged in his spine. His scalp was also grazed by a bullet. His clothes afterwards had twenty to thirty holes in them. Both Pearce and Joshua Gorsuch ran back up the long lane in the direction from which they had come. They were chased. Pearce probably avoided being shot to death only because he managed to shield himself by positioning himself on the other side of Hanway's horse opposite his attackers as Hanway began trotting away. Joshua Gorsuch tried to get Hanway to take him up beside him on the horse. Hanway declined. Someone in the

CHAPTER 9: A NIGHTMARISH FAMILY OUTING

mob caught up to Joshua Gorsuch and bashed him over the head with a club, knocking him out and inflicting a concussion. Fortunately, Joshua was wearing a fur hat, which slightly cushioned the blow and likely saved his life.[24]

Isaiah Clarkson took control of the situation at Parker's. After he spoke, the African Americans dispersed practically as rapidly as they had assembled. By the time a bystander to the action came into the yard a short time after the shooting ended, he found the body of Edward, not quite fully dead. He lay forty-nine steps from the front door of the Parker home, a little more than halfway from the door to the gate. Someone had removed the approximately $300 in cash he had in his pocket. All of the Gorsuch party, except Dickinson who was lying on the ground next to the stump, fled the scene. With some difficulty, Kline made his way to Penningtonville. On the road he met up with a disoriented Joshua Gorsuch. Ultimately, Edward's body was removed by some locals into the town center of Christiana for a coroner's examination. Dickinson Gorsuch was carried up to the Pownell house. Amazingly, after four weeks in bed, he managed to survive. Approximately eighty holes would be counted in his side, thigh, and right arm. Two African Americans also received relatively minor bullet wounds, which were treated by a local physician.[25]

Parker still had the sympathies of the local townspeople in Christiana. But he and his supporters realized this attitude would not be shared by authorities outside Lancaster County. That evening, all the former Gorsuch slaves, as well as Parker, Pinckney, Johnson, and the two African Americans who had been wounded, left town permanently for points north. Parker, Pinckney and Johnson traveled together, mostly by wagon but sometimes on foot, until they finally reached Rochester. There they stayed one night in the home of Frederick Douglass. The Christiana riot, as it came to be called, was in the headlines of national newspapers. Frederick and Julia Griffiths, his assistant editor of *North Star*, admired Parker greatly for his heroism in the resistance. Frederick gave Parker some money. Together with Griffiths, he helped Parker and his companions make their escape across the river to Canada. Before Parker left, he presented Frederick with Dickinson's revolver as a sort of war trophy.[26]

The cause of the slaveholding republics had now acquired a martyr of its own, in the person of the benevolent, law-abiding Edward Gorsuch. And nowhere was the sense of outrage over Edward's demise at the hands of a mob felt more acutely than in Baltimore. Four days after Edward's death, an "indignation meeting" with numerous speakers was attended by some 6,000 persons in Monument Square. To the north, near Edward's home in Baltimore County, public protest meetings took place in Cockeysville and elsewhere on September 13 and 15.[27]

The sense of outrage was only heightened because no one was ever convicted of a criminal offense with respect to the events at Christiana. Castner Hanway was placed on trial for treason, but the charge was difficult to make stick, given that Hanway was really only guilty of inaction. After a lengthy, high-profile federal court trial, the jury required only fifteen minutes to acquit. Numerous other locals, including Lewis, Scarlett, and Clarkson, were also arrested and charged with complicity in defying the Fugitive Slave Law. But after Hanway was acquitted, the cases against all the rest were dropped. Attempts at state court prosecution also proved abortive.

Within walking distance of Gorsuch's Retreat Farm, situated to the south along York Road, was the Milton School for Boys, an institution operated by a Quaker named John Emerson Lamb and his family. One of Lamb's pupils there was Thomas Gorsuch, the 15-year-old son of Edward, and younger brother of Dickinson Gorsuch. The sudden demise of Thomas's father was felt at the school like a tragic death in the

CHAPTER 9: A NIGHTMARISH FAMILY OUTING

family. It made a big impression on everyone associated with the school. And in attendance at Milton School at the time was a 13-year-old boy, not much as a student but highly sensitive and impressionable, by the name of John Wilkes Booth. The shocking, highly-publicized death of the father of one of his fellow students was a trauma he would long remember.[28]

Chapter 10: For Brutus Was an Honorable Man

John Wilkes Booth was born into a well-to-do Maryland family, as evidenced by his enrollment at a series of private boarding schools, including the Milton School. While Johnnie, as the family called him,[1] rubbed elbows in these schools with the children of slave owners, the money that sent him there did not derive from exploitation of slavery. Rather, the Booth family's money was earned by the career of Johnnie's father as a star of the stage on two continents. As in the case of John Brown, the father was a profound influence on the son, who would follow in his father's professional path.

Junius Brutus Booth was born in London in 1796, making him four years younger than the Romantic poet and writer Percy Shelley, whose *avant-garde* radical lifestyle and writings would be inspirational to Junius.[2] Junius's father Richard was a barrister, albeit one who had tried in 1777 to enlist in the cause of the rebellious American colonies against the British crown. That attempt was foiled by John Wilkes, a relative of Richard Booth's mother, then serving as the Lord Mayor of London, to whom Richard appealed for a letter of introduction. John Wilkes was the most outspoken and prominent radical politician of his day, but he did not approve

CHAPTER 10: FOR BRUTUS WAS AN HONORABLE MAN

of the young man's foray into revolution. So he tipped off Richard's parents, who had Richard arrested and returned home. Although he later kept a portrait of George Washington very prominently positioned in his office, Richard settled down to pursue a career in law. A law career was also envisioned for Richard's son Junius. But Junius very early stepped off the path of the straight and narrow. Two girls wound up pregnant by him, resulting in financial settlements paid by his father.[3] Junius joined an amateur theater company, where his acting was well received. It led to the thought of a professional debut, which Junius made on December 13, 1813, at the age of 17. At around that same time, an actor named Edmund Kean began taking London stage audiences by storm, pioneering a revolutionary, *avant-garde*, emotionally supercharged style of depicting tragic characters. Junius rapidly caught the fever of Romanticism inherent in this acting artistry. He would emulate Kean's method. Junius soon left home to join a theater company in traveling to Amsterdam.[4]

From Amsterdam, continuing acting gigs took Junius to Brussels. There he seduced Mimi (whose given name was Adelaide), a daughter of his landlord who was four years older than he. The two of them eloped. Junius continued to find various acting jobs in the French-speaking areas of the Continent. By the time they returned to England in May of 1815, Junius had just turned 19 and Mimi was four months into a pregnancy. A hasty wedding ensued. Resisting all enticements to go back into law, Junius stuck with acting. After spending a year or two playing insignificant bit parts, he finally got a break when Kean missed a performance due to illness. Thrust into the breach in the role of the central villain, Junius delighted the audience with his version of the same impassioned form of romantic acting artistry at which Kean excelled. Before long, he inveigled himself into starring roles on the London stage. On February 20, 1817, Junius played Iago to Kean's Othello before a packed house in London's Drury Lane theater, with Percy Shelley's father-in-law William Godwin among the enthused patrons in attendance.[5]

Over the next three years, Junius played steadily in leading roles, sometimes in London but more often in peripheral venues such as Gloucester, Bristol, and Glasgow. London audiences, in general, preferred Kean, and critics belittled Junius as an "imitator of Kean." In the fall of 1820, Kean left for a tour of America. Junius and his theater managers were disappointed that, during Kean's absence, customers stayed away in droves. After a major London engagement ended in financial disaster, Junius himself fled England for America at the end of January 1821. Leaving behind Mimi and their two children, Junius brought with him an 18-year-old flower girl he had met in London's Covent Garden theater. Her name was Mary Ann Holmes.[6]

Junius Brutus Booth, 1841
Photo by Matthew Brady, Library of Congress

Mary Ann and Junius arrived in Norfolk, Virginia on June 30, 1821. Junius quickly secured acting engagements in Richmond and Petersburg, earning badly needed cash and receiving favorable reviews from the theatrical press. On October 2, 1821, Junius debuted on the New York City stage. Acting what would become his most iconic role as Shakespeare's dastardly Richard III, Junius drew rave reviews for his closing death scene. Before the year 1821 was done, Junius headlined performances in Baltimore, Charleston, and New Orleans. Junius thus launched his 30-year American career as a touring stage star. It was a career that would have its ups and downs, to be sure, but more "ups." Junius earned a

Chapter 10: For Brutus Was an Honorable Man

reputation as one of America's foremost actors.

The lightning-like flashes of interpretation that London saw as Junius overacting, America received as the electrifying personification of a vivid and fanciful character. His grasp of characters reflected a marvelous clarity of insight.[7] When the critics in Baltimore said the acting talents of Junius were comparable to those of Kean, they meant it as a compliment. Junius came to consider Baltimore, where his performances were always well received, to be his home base. Soon he purchased 150 acres of land in semi-rural Harford County, 25 miles northeast of the city near the town of Bel Air. He moved there with Mary Ann and their newly born son, Junius Brutus Booth, Jr. Ingeniously, Junius bought an unused house from a neighbor, lifted it off its footings, and rolled it on logs to its new location on the parcel he called simply, "the Farm." His father Richard, that lover of all things American, soon emigrated himself, and he joined Junius on the Farm, helping to manage it during Junius's frequent traveling tours. In Maryland Junius, cured of his philandering habits, would have nine more children with Mary Ann. But three of them died in an epidemic of cholera within a one-month period of 1833, and another beloved son died of smallpox during a return by Junius to perform in England during 1836–1837. So the children who came later and survived were pampered by their parents. Johnnie, born May 10, 1838, was the ninth of the ten total children of Junius and Mary Ann. Boyish and full of fun, he was his mother's darling. Johnnie was regarded by many, including his older brothers, as a spoiled brat.[8]

Johnnie was "by no means a studious boy." As was the case with John Brown, young Johnnie's energy and intelligence far outstripped his ability to submit to the discipline of a classroom. One of Johnnie's elementary school mates recalled: "He was not deficient in intelligence and brains – very much in fact the other way – but he was not bookish, not devoted to his studies." At Milton School, he was very popular, a good swimmer, ballplayer, and tree-climber. But he was slow at books. Johnnie perplexed his schoolmasters, who liked him personally but were unable to make much headway teaching him subjects like arithmetic and grammar. Also similar to John Brown, Johnnie's writings consistently reflect an inability to spell words correctly. And yet again like John Brown, the young John Wilkes Booth enjoyed active, outdoorsy, roughhouse pastimes. From his earliest boyhood he was very skilled with a horse. He played pranks that caused some adults to frown, such as swooping down to snatch a smaller boy off the ground and hoist him up beside him on his galloping mount.[9] As a teenager Johnnie was nicknamed "Billy Bowlegs," after a Seminole chief but also an allusion to the curving shape of his legs, a characteristic Johnnie inherited from his father.[10] To fathom John Wilkes Booth, we must absolutely consider the other, less tangible, traits passed to him genetically from the strong, strange personality of his father.

Seemingly of a parcel with his power to movingly evoke *dramatis personae* on stage, Junius Brutus Booth suffered from a mysterious form of insanity. His "freaks" were legend. Sometimes they were blamed on drinking. However, even during his youth, well before he emigrated to America, Junius suffered a bout of what was called "apoplexy" on stage during the final scene of a performance at Newcastle-under-Lyme. After his American career got into full swing, such episodes became common. Junius was frequently written up in the press for his "mental derangement." The deranged behaviors took a wide variety of forms. On March 15, 1825, at the end of a performance at the Park Theater in New York City, Junius rolled over and made a strange remark to the audience. The next day, seemingly still in a trance-like state, he assaulted a fellow actor in a slashing knife attack and had to be disarmed by bystanders. The press, at the time, dismissed this as a temporary fit relieved by a night's sleep. Frequently Junius

CHAPTER 10: FOR BRUTUS WAS AN HONORABLE MAN

failed to appear for scheduled performances, later citing "indisposition." On December 7, 1829, he broke down on stage in Boston during a performance of *Evadne, the Maid's Tragedy*. Leaving the theater without a coat, he walked in the freezing cold all the way to Providence, Rhode Island. On November 9, 1835, Junius exited through the back door unannounced just before the curtain rose on his role of Iago in a performance of *Othello* at the Bowery Theater in New York City. He disappeared for two or three days.[11]

Some of Junius's deranged behavior was suicidal. On March 28, 1836, he attempted to hang himself. He was discovered by Mary Ann in time to save him. In March of 1838 (two months before Johnnie was born), during a sea voyage to Charleston, South Carolina, Junius lowered himself overboard into the ocean after he was notified by his traveling companion, theater manager Tom Flynn, that the ship had reached the point where William August Conway, a failed tragedian, had drowned himself. Flynn sounded the alarm, and Junius was fished out and rescued. Junius repaid Flynn for his kindness by attacking him with a fireplace tool in the hotel room the two were sharing in Charleston. In the resulting affray, Junius's nose was broken. Despite this unprovoked assault, Flynn forgave Junius. Within a week of his arrival in Charleston, Junius was performing to wild applause from a stage audience for one of his most consistently acclaimed roles, that of the evil Sir Giles Overreach in Philip Massinger's *A New Way to Pay Old Debts*.[12]

On November 5, 1832, after one of his unexcused failures to appear, Junius wrote a note to a Philadelphia theater manager which touched on some interesting subjects:

> Most reverend and illustrious Signor, How fare the showmen? I have absconded, alas left my name in the Bill and I understand the Devil's to pay in consequence thereof, but Jones – is it not [?] to act on

Friday, Jesus Christ and Mahomet died that Day, Adams and Jefferson also – many other great men have also made exalted Exits on that remarkable Day; it should be devoted to Prayer and Meditation. – Sunday, the Day of the Resurrection should be a time of rejoicing and pastime and good Deeds – I am willing to play gratuitously on that Day, provided the Surplus Proceeds of the House's Expense be given to the Relief of Orphans & Widows, the Deaf & Dumb Asylums & the emancipation of Negroes by Societies who may form for that laudable purpose. .... I am an Alien – not an Enemy & will become a citizen when my master Andrew Jackson commends me to do so; till then I am in politics neuter.

Or if you like crazy.

Junius's allusion to "great men" who had made their "exalted Exits" on a "Friday" would prove eerily prophetic. Fathers have a pronounced tendency to repeat sayings they think clever over and over in front of the family. No one will ever know for sure if this same reference was made by Junius in the presence of his young son Johnnie.

The mention of "Societies" formed for the "laudable purpose" of the "emancipation of Negroes" indicates Junius was at least aware of, and at least had some sympathy with, the efforts being made by Benjamin Lundy and Lloyd Garrison in Baltimore at around that time to promote the "genius of emancipation." Although African Americans worked for wages on the Farm in subservient roles as laborers and domestic help, Junius was never a slave owner.

Due to reading Shelley's *A Vindication of Natural Diet*, Junius became an avowed vegetarian. On September 28, 1835, a Philadelphia doctor who was summoned to minister to one of the children wrote the following entry in his diary:[13]

I had after leaving the room a long conversation on the

stair and afterward at the street door of the Hotel, with Booth himself on the subject of his habit of drinking – and said those numberless things of both warning and encouragement, which a sober man may and ought to say to one with naturally good feelings and high powers in art, but of habits that are rapidly reducing him to imbecility of mind and to crookedness of passions. This drinking has taken most of his appetite away, and he lessens even the little chance of his getting nourishment through a foolish freak, of eating no meat, – which he fell into from reading Shelley, one of your vain, wish-to-be-remarkable poets, and good-for nothing idle and mean complainers of the injustice of the world.

In support of a cause of "injustice of the world," Junius emphatically imparted his animal rights philosophy to his children. They were sternly forbidden to hunt or trap animals, or to eat any animal food. Mary Ann, however, was not particularly committed to the ideals of Pythagoras and Shelley. During the long periods when Junius was away from the Farm, the enforcement of his rules on this subject relaxed.[14]

For a remarkably long period spanning three decades, Junius successfully kept up the appearance with Mimi that he remained a husband who was merely in America temporarily. He regularly sent her money. Mimi continued to hold herself out as the wife of the famous tragedian. She did not become involved in a relationship with another man. One of their two children died, but the other, also named Richard Booth, became a classics scholar. During a nine-month return visit to England in 1825–1826, during which he performed extensively on the London stage, Junius hid his American family in an undisclosed location so that Mimi would not find out about them. He even commissioned a "family portrait" to be made with himself, Mimi and Richard.[15] When, ten years later,

Junius brought Mary Ann and five American-born children with him on his second lengthy return to play on the London stage, Mimi and Richard were in Brussels with her family. Junius managed to evade going there.[16] Finally, in 1843, using money provided by his father for that purpose, Richard emigrated to Baltimore. Richard toured with Junius for a time before he took up teaching Greek and Latin. Junius apparently said nothing to him, but it was not long before Junius's extensive American family was brought to Richard's attention by stage hands. Richard promptly informed his mother, who started making her own plans to travel to Baltimore. She arrived in December of 1846.

Mimi soon made a splash by presenting herself at the Farm and elsewhere as an outraged spouse. It created an embarrassing scandal, from which Junius and Mary Ann did their best to shield the kids. However, the Maryland children inevitably learned of their own illegitimacy. We have no direct evidence of the effect that this revelation had on the sensitive Johnnie. However, we do know from his older sister that one of Johnnie's few treasured pieces of reading material was Plutarch's *Morals*. His absorption of the contents of that book surely extended to the very first page, which Plutarch begins by stressing the importance of legitimate birth:[17]

> I would therefore warn those who desire to be fathers of notable sons, not to form connections with any kind of women, such as courtesans or mistresses: for those who either on the father's or mother's side are ill-born have the disgrace of their origin all their life irretrievably present with them, and offer a ready handle to abuse and vituperation... . Good birth indeed brings with it a store of assurance, which ought to be greatly valued by all who desire legitimate offspring. For the spirit of those who are a spurious and bastard breed is apt to be mean and abject: for as the poet truly says, 'It makes a man even of noble

spirit servile, when he is conscious of the ill fame of either his father or mother.'

Eventually Mimi sued for a divorce, which Junius did not contest, granting her a generous financial settlement. The divorce became final in March of 1851. Finally on May 10, 1851, which happened to be Johnnie's thirteenth birthday, Junius and Mary Ann were legally married and the Maryland children were retroactively legitimized.[18]

Junius, Jr., whom the family called "June," left medical studies at St. Mary's College in Baltimore in 1842 to seek his own career in theater. He married an established comedienne, who was eleven years older. They moved to New York, where June slowly began to secure bit parts on the New York stage. June eventually made a career in the theater, but his success was primarily as a manager, not an actor. June did try to emulate his father's dynamic style of acting, but observers felt that his performances were not enhanced with the same original interpretations and imaginative flourishes.[19]

In August 1848, Junius went on a traveling series of performances that took him first to Albany, New York. On this tour, he took with him his son Edwin, who was then 14. Edwin was allowed to go along to act as Junius's valet and, also, in an effort to curb his alcoholic episodes and "freaks." The strategy worked to a degree, as Junius was solicitous of the well-being of his son. However, the occasional failure to appear, usually accompanied by finding Junius somewhere in a stupor, did continue. In September, in New York City, the reviewers wrote that Junius was "the very best actor of the present day," although they said his voice and body were not so vigorous as they once were and that he was on "the downhill of life."[20] Touring together, Edwin got the benefit of watching his father, up close and personal, in many performances. Slowly, he too began to take on stage roles, often as a substitute for other actors. By September 10, 1849, Edwin appeared in a regular announced part in a performance of *Richard III* at the Boston Museum. Gradually, Junius's confidence in Edwin's abilities as an actor increased. By 1851, Junius was occasionally thrusting Edwin into unanticipated service as his understudy in starring roles.[21]

June, meanwhile, made his way to California on the heels of the Gold Rush. There he found that theater performances were in great demand and that quality actors were well paid. He returned to Maryland and convinced his father to head west. On June 21, 1852, Junius, June, June's mistress Harriet Mace, and Edwin left New York together on a steamer headed to Panama, where they made the short overland passage and continued on another ship to San Francisco. The party finally arrived on July 28. Audiences indeed paid well to see Junius, but the newspapers characterized him as a "splendid ruin" of his former self. He was "not in good voice" and "the effects of his tedious journey" were visible. The tour continued, in various theater productions managed by June, both in San Francisco and Sacramento. Saying he intended to retire, Junius left San Francisco on October 1, leaving behind Edwin and June to make their own professional reputations.[22]

The decision to travel by himself would be ominous. Junius made it through Panama and reached New Orleans, where he played a one-week engagement that included his classic roles as Richard III and Sir Giles Overreach. He again drew large audiences and favorable reviews, although it was noted that "time had eroded" his voice and physique. He intended to continue by water to Cincinnati. However, during the journey he became severely ill. Junius died on board the river boat, near Louisville, on November 26, 1852.

At the time of Junius's death, Johnnie was enrolled at St. Timothy's Hall, a military school in Catonsville, just west of Baltimore, that was founded by the progressive Episcopal Reverend Libertus Van Bokkelen. Van Bokkelen's school featured military style uniforms, drills, and training modeled

CHAPTER 10: FOR BRUTUS WAS AN HONORABLE MAN

after similar schools in Europe as well as the new U.S. Military Academy at West Point, New York.[23] While at St. Timothy's, Johnnie was involved in student unrest. He was part of a group of boys who had desired a change of diet, and were deprived of their two normal weekly holidays on account of their refusal to eat the food provided for them. The boys openly rebelled, ran away, and camped out in the woods. When a concerned group of teachers came on scene to "negotiate," Johnnie helped issue a protest letter to the teachers that was replete with Shakespearean phrases, such as, "Something is rotten in Denmark," "Foul meat, eaten with silver forks," and "All that glitters is not gold."[24]

Junius's death, and the loss of his income, put an end to Johnnie's unimpressive career in school. He returned to the Farm to help his mother and two older sisters manage. During this period of over three years, he became close to his sister Asia, who was two-and-one-half years older. Asia's later recollections, though tinged with sentimentality, shed light on Johnnie's personality. He had a pronounced tendency toward the ascetic. "His bed was the hardest mattress and a straw pillow," she wrote. "For at this time of his life he adored Agesilaus, the Spartan King, and disdained luxuries."[25] After Junius's death, the Farm fell on hard times, even famine. When visitors came, Johnnie was capable of going without himself, in order that the family could keep up the pretense of having an adequate supply of food.[26]

Johnnie had a violent episode, not on account of his own honor, but over the perception that his mother was disrespected. Asia told the story:[27]

> A man had the farm on shares, for our mother had tried various ways of making what she called "a living out of this useless land," and what Wilkes called "trying to starve respectably by torturing the barren earth." Great hopes were entertained that this fresh

attempt might be rewarded with success. The man was to work our horses, which he did mercifully enough at first, but he was ambitious of "turning out the best crops in Harford." He nearly ruined my mother by purchases of guano, and then he worked men, himself, and our beasts until her patience was exhausted. It was pitiable to see our dumb creatures droop in the fields, too tired to drag themselves homeward. Mother at last remonstrated, when he excitedly told her to "go mind her own business." She objected to let her horses go to the fields unless the men were allowed to return at sun-down, and the horses then be housed. The man became very insolent and called her and us vile names, which my mother related to Wilkes when he returned home in the evening. He was accompanied by a friend, who was a practicing lawyer. This gentleman told him "to come down to the lodge and demand an apology from the man, and then arrange about the hours of work for men and beasts."

"Apologize!" Wilkes said; "he's not the sort of man to do that. I'll get a stick ready."

He cut for himself a stout stick, and the two walked down to the lodge. The friend of Wilkes called out the farmer, and Wilkes demanded an apology being made to the ladies.

"First find your *ladies*," the farmer insolently retorted.

"Will you go up to my house this moment with me, and apologize to my mother and sisters for the abusive names you have called them?"

"Do you think I am going to lose my share of these crops just to save a lot of lazy dumb beasts and thick-skulled niggers from being *tired*? Apologize! That won't I!"

CHAPTER 10: FOR BRUTUS WAS AN HONORABLE MAN

"Then," said Wilkes, "I'll whip you like the scoundrel that you are."

And he let the stick fall heavily on the head and shoulders of the man who yelled out noisily that "he was killed and murdered."

Johnnie was prosecuted for this assault and battery. However, the provoking chain of events appears to have been regarded with some sympathy by the court. He got off with nothing more severe than, essentially, probation subject to a $50 bond posted by his mother.[28]

This was not Johnnie's only brush with the law. At an earlier period, before Junius's death while the family was staying at its city house in Baltimore, Johnnie got into trouble serious enough to bring him up before Baltimore police magistrates. He and a group of neighborhood kids, on a pleasant summer evening around dusk, were playing a game called "telegraph" that involved sending sparks through a wire stretched across the street. The "telegraph" wire toppled a man's hat when he walked unsuspectingly underneath. The man was not amused. He silently walked on to summon a nearby constable. The other boys and girls who had been playing the game rapidly vanished before the officer's appearance. The constable nabbed Johnnie. Johnnie's reported deportment on this occasion is of interest. He immediately and calmly asked the officer permission to unfasten and coil the wire, so it would not do any more damage. Once taken to the watch house, he declined the invitation to reveal the names of the other children who were involved in the game. "How is it only you were caught? For this gentleman declares there were a dozen of you boys," one of the magistrates asked. Johnnie responded: "Because that is my luck, sir, I guess."[29]

Johnnie was a thoughtful and sensitive boy. When returning to the Farm from Baltimore, he frequently brought back with him a bag of candy to pass out to the farm hands.[30] Asia wrote: "He was very tender of flowers, and of insects and butterflies. Lightning bugs he considered as 'bearers of sacred torches,' and would go out of his way to avoid injuring them." He once managed to catch a "katy-did" after nights of patient waiting and searching. Asia was eager to make it a specimen for her collection. "No you don't, you bloodthirsty female," Johnnie exclaimed. "Katy shall be free and sing tonight out in the sycamores."[31] Likely influenced by the attitude of his father, Johnnie could not bear to slaughter any of the livestock on the farm. Despite the hunger they faced, he refused to hunt or trap any of the wild animals and birds that frequented the Farm, looking upon them as "silent members of the family."[32]

The Booth Farm House, near Bel Air, Maryland
Library of Congress

Johnnie displayed a melancholy side. "He was a singular combination of gravity and joy," Asia recalled. He chose a bedroom that had a window facing east, rather than west, because he said he felt it would be too depressing to watch the setting sun every afternoon.[33] Although he had a lively sense of humor, he disliked stock jokes and pointedly avoided laughing at stories and anecdotes told at the expense of others. Even as an adult it would be observed that he merely smiled, and did not laugh at jokes.[34] Johnnie enjoyed songs that conveyed a feeling of suffering and sadness, especially African American spirituals.[35]

While Johnnie and Asia were trying to help their mother make ends meet on the Farm, they spent much of their spare time reading out loud their favorite books. Asia left us a valuable report about what specific pieces of literature were

CHAPTER 10: FOR BRUTUS WAS AN HONORABLE MAN

involved. In addition to Plutarch's *Morals*, mentioned above, another was *Plutarch's Lives*, his classic study of historical personalities, which, as we have seen, was also inspirational to John Brown. Another was Foxe's *Book of Martyrs*. And Shakespeare's *Julius Caesar* was recited and repeatedly acted out. Joe Hall, one of the African Americans employed on the Farm, remarked that in the olden days Richard Booth had often referred to his son Junius as "his noble Brutus." To which Johnnie responded with a classic quote from the play. "For Brutus was an honorable man."[36]

In November 1854, 16-year-old Johnnie worked as a volunteer in the successful Congressional campaign of Henry Winter Davis of the American party, better known to history as the "Know-Nothings." The American party was basically a "nativist," that is, anti-immigrant and anti-Catholic, faction of the disintegrating Whig party. The Know-Nothings strongly opposed Henry Seward, not necessarily because of his position on slavery, but because of his well-known sympathy for Catholics and immigrants.[37] On the issue of slavery, the American party position was officially neutral. Davis, interestingly, was personally against slavery. Later on in his career he would become a radical Republican. The "Know-Nothings" were as much a secret society as a political party. They got their name because, in response to any questions about what went on in their meetings, they were under instructions to answer that they "knew nothing." They were referred to by their detractors as "Kni-ists," a word linguistically similar to the Russian term "nihilists." Johnnie's involvement in the Davis campaign, according to Asia, consisted of acting as a sort of steward and color-bearer at a rally in Bel Air. To some, the American party was mostly about patriotic froth. "Three cheers for America," Johnnie wrote to a friend. He hung two crossed American flags above the door of the family home on the Farm.[38] This boyhood venture would prove to be the last involvement of John Wilkes Booth in any form of organized politics.

Chapter 11: A Battleground Called Kansas

During Henry Seward's so-called "higher law" discourse of March 11, 1850, a Senator from Mississippi interrupted him:[1] "Will the honorable Senator allow me to ask him, if the Senate is to understand him as saying, that he would vote for the admission of California if she came here seeking admission as a slave state?" To which question, Henry responded:

> I reply, as I said before, that even if California had come as a slave State – yet coming under the extraordinary circumstances I have described, and in view of the consequences of a dismemberment of the empire, consequent upon her rejection – I should have voted for her admission even though she had come as a slave State; but I should not have voted for her admission otherwise.

Although Henry later tried to walk back this off-the-cuff statement to a heckler, it helped plant the seeds for the great Kansas–Nebraska controversy.[2]

The United States of the early 1850s was riding a wave of

growth and prosperity. It looked westward to the plains of the Nebraska territory, comprised of the modern-day states of Nebraska, Kansas, eastern Colorado, parts of Montana and Wyoming, and the two Dakotas, not merely as fertile new lands to be domesticated into farms and ranches, but also as a vast expanse to be traversed by a national railroad that could connect to the new state of California. But carving up lands acquired in the 1803 Louisiana Purchase into states raised a persistent and troublesome question. Could the institution of slavery be allowed in these new states? Stephen Douglas, the Democratic Senator from Illinois, was politically invested in growth. He and his constituents wanted to push forward with opening up the Nebraska territory to settlement. Douglas seized upon the idea, suggested by Henry's concession during his "higher law" speech, of letting the settlers in the annexed territories determine the issue for themselves. "Popular sovereignty" became Douglas's new catchphrase. It sounded fair and democratic enough. But, in a broader context, "popular sovereignty" was a path to evade and, indeed, to *sub silentio* repeal, the major provision of the Missouri Compromise of 1820, "forever" prohibiting slavery or involuntary servitude, except as punishment for crime, in any part of the Louisiana Purchase north of the 36° 30' line of latitude.

In January 1854 Douglas, as chairman of the Committee on Territories, reported a bill to allow states formed from the territory of Nebraska to "be received into the Union, with or without slavery, as their constitution[s] may prescribe at the time of their admission." The bill was quickly amended to provide for the admission of two separate territories: one called "Nebraska," centered on the Platte River, and the other called "Kansas" (sometimes spelled "Kanzas"), a newly named rectangle due west of Missouri.[3] The intent to enact another "compromise" was obvious. "Kansas," despite its location north of the Missouri Compromise line of demarcation, would become an addition to the slaveholding republics, should the outcome of "popular sovereignty" produce such a result. Abolitionists were furious. Henry did his utmost to lead opposition to this latest appeasement of the slave power. But the allure of compromise again proved strong. The Senate passed the Kansas–Nebraska bill by a vote of 37 to 14.[4]

In the U.S. House of Representatives, vehement partisans on both sides literally came close to killing each other over the issue. President Franklin Pierce, a Northern Democrat who believed in tolerating slavery to preserve the Union, strongly backed the bill. He made its support a litmus test for federal patronage within the Democratic party. Even so, Northern Democrats were fairly evenly divided in their votes. But twelve Southern Whig congressmen crossed party lines to support the Douglas bill, which therefore passed by a vote of 113 to 100. This event would, in large measure, lead to the collapse of the Whig party before the year was over. But when the Senate formally enacted the Kansas–Nebraska Act at 1 a.m. on May 26, 1854, it was hailed in Washington City with celebratory cannon fire as yet another legal sleight-of-hand that would save the Union.[5]

The outcome was a battle fought on the frontier, predominantly over an ideological issue. Both sides sent foot soldiers to a distant land to fight for their positions. Henry expressed the spirit of confrontation. "Come on, then, gentlemen of the Slave States," he proclaimed. "Since there is no escaping your challenge, I accept it in behalf of the cause of freedom. We will engage in competition for the virgin soil of Kansas, and God give the victory to the side that is stronger in numbers as it is in right." [6] Wealthy New Englanders and Midwesterners rapidly organized "Emigrant Aid Societies" to financially sponsor the many courageous souls who were ready, willing, and able to seek a new life in Kansas. Among these wealthy philanthropists was Amos Lawrence, scion of a Massachusetts cotton mill family. Settlers he financed would name the "free state" headquarters of Lawrence, Kansas after him. By February 1855, an estimated 8,500 men, women and children had emigrated to Kansas. The majority of these emigrants, as well as their financial backers, were actually not abolitionists, even though Southern firebrands were quick to paint them as such. Many were even more racist than Southerners, as reflected in their overwhelming endorsement of a "free state" constitution banning all African Americans, free or slave, from the new state.[7]

Outraged and alarmed by the efforts being made in the North to send settlers *en masse* to Kansas, Southern leaders engaged in their own efforts to organize both settlers and militias, and to send them there in order to follow through with the hard-won opportunity to add to the lands available for expansion of the slaveholding republics. They held the strategic advantage, because President Pierce as well as many others in Washington viewed the Kansas–Nebraska Act as a de facto cession of Kansas to slaveholding interests. The President's initial appointees as territorial Governor and as territorial federal judges had a similar orientation.

David Atchison, a Democratic Senator from Missouri, was often referred to as Pierce's "Vice-President." The real elected Vice-President, William King of Alabama, had died before taking office, and there was at that time no provision for replacing a deceased Vice-President. So Atchison, selected by his majority party to be the presiding officer of the Senate, performed the Vice-President's constitutional duties. Atchison was a large man, given to blustery, bullying rhetoric. He wholeheartedly advocated the view that abolitionists were meddlers in other people's business who deserved to be tarred and feathered, or worse. "Vice-President" Atchison urged Missouri citizens to organize themselves to take political control of Kansas. In a speech in Platte County, Missouri, just across the border from Kansas, he threw down a challenge:[8]

The people of Kansas in their first elections will

CHAPTER 11: A BATTLEGROUND CALLED KANSAS

> decide the question of whether or not slaveholders can be excluded. Now, if a set of fanatics and demagogues a thousand miles off can afford to advance their money and exert every nerve to abolitionize Kansas and exclude the slaveholder, what is your duty, when you reside within one day's journey of the Territory, and when your peace, quiet, and property depend on your action? You can, without an exertion, send five hundred of your young men who will vote in favor of your institutions. Should each county in the State of Missouri only do its duty, the question will be decided quietly and peaceably at the ballot box.

In a pattern the world would later see recur in war-torn areas where conflicts having broader implications were fought by proxies, Kansas proved to be an ideal environment to foster the emergence of terrorism. And, in that environment, a primordial terrorist emerged.

In a letter written August 21, 1854, John Brown told his oldest son, John, Jr.:

> If you or any of my family are disposed to go to Kansas or Nebraska, with a view to help defeat *Satan* and his legions in that direction, I have not a word to say; *but I feel committed to operate in another part of the field.* If I were not so committed, I would be on my way this fall.

What John referred to in this letter as producing a feeling of being "committed" was his latest venture into partnership with a wealthy sponsor. [9] This new enterprise was not a tannery; it was not real estate; and it was not wool. It was a form of "professional abolitionism." At just about the same time John took the Perkins–Brown wool cooperative for its final suicide dive, he agreed with philanthropist Gerrit Smith to move his family to a harsh area in the Adirondacks that Smith had recently set up as a colony for resettling African Americans.

Gerrit Smith, although slightly eccentric, had ample intelligence and personal charm to accompany his enormous wealth. The source of that wealth was predominantly real estate speculation. Smith's father Peter, and Gerrit himself, were as adept at making fortunes accumulating and selling real estate, as John Brown was at going bankrupt. Gerrit Smith was a Renaissance man who used his wealth to sponsor a wide variety of progressive causes, including temperance, women's rights, and the abolition of slavery. He was a perennial candidate for elective office, including the Presidency. In August of 1846 he announced a new initiative to give away some of the less productive acreage in upstate New York accumulated by his father to deserving African Americans. The underlying conviction was that his African American homesteaders, if freed from the destructive influence of whites who looked down on them culturally, would achieve a laudable self-sufficiency, thus helping to bring about an end to the subjugation of African Americans in the United States. It was a visionary concept not closely tied to reality, and thus virtually doomed to failure from the start.[10]

John Brown's involvement in Smith's colonization project in the Adirondacks was a sequel of sorts to his earlier 1840 flirtation with the idea of moving to lands in the mountains of western Virginia that Smith had donated to Oberlin College with similar purposes in mind. John heard about Smith's new Adirondack land giveaway and, partly to escape his creeping malaise in the wool trade, he volunteered to go in on the project. John's asceticism, enforced on his large and well-trained family, and his highly developed pioneer skills, could prove useful, even inspirational, to the African American homesteaders. On April 8, 1848, John made the first of several pilgrimages to the Gerrit Smith mansion, which doubled as the headquarters of the Smith real estate empire, located in Peterboro, New York. This town, founded by

CHAPTER 11: A BATTLEGROUND CALLED KANSAS

Gerrit's father Peter, was roughly halfway between Syracuse and Utica. Smith agreed that John could be useful for the Adirondack colony project. In May 1849, just as he was planning his desperate gamble of shipping all his wool cooperative's goods to England, John moved his wife, four of his sons, and three of his daughters from their spartan home in Springfield, the one Frederick had visited only a year earlier, to a small log cabin in North Elba.[11]

To the eyes of outside observers, John rapidly established himself as a kind of frontier king in the mold of his former days in Pennsylvania.[12] But the texture of his life was now very much different. Essentially, he was itinerant. He soon left North Elba for his wool misadventure in England. After that turned into a financial wreck, he spent much of the next five years embroiled in litigation. To support his company's position in these various lawsuits and trials, John spent substantial time in such places as Boston, Massachusetts and Troy, New York, as well as Springfield, where he lingered long enough to write his "Advice to the Gileadites." John also spent a good deal of time in northeast Ohio, where his father Owen and his two oldest sons, John Jr. and Jason, were living. The day-to-day effort to wrest a living from the earth of the Adirondacks was left primarily to his wife Mary, his four younger sons, his adult daughter Ruth, and her husband Henry Thompson. So when, in August 1854, John wrote to John, Jr. that he felt "committed to operate in another part of the field," what he really meant was that he was aware he had not made very much progress on his pledge to Gerrit Smith to aid in the North Elba colonization project.[13]

But the fact of the matter was that Smith's Adirondack African American settlement project, however laudable in theory, was not the kind of activism that John was cut out to fulfill. It smacked of organizational work, something for which John lacked the patience or emotional outlook. He did nothing to advance the project during the nine months following his letter in which he told John Jr. he was "committed" to it. Indeed, John did not even go to North Elba. Rather, he and Mary occupied a rented farm near Akron, Ohio. There he dithered, suggesting he would take a vote of the African Americans in Essex County to see if they favored him helping them or instead going to fight for the cause in Kansas. He sought advice on the subject from Frederick Douglass, Gerrit Smith, and J. McCune Smith, a prominent physician and African American leader. Apparently, Frederick and McCune Smith did not express an opinion. Gerrit Smith, however, responded by telling John he thought he should keep his commitment to the project. John continued to prevaricate. His excuse for not going to North Elba was that he did not have sufficient funds to "move," a rather odd claim given that he was already supposed to be living on the lands he owned there.[14]

Finally, in June 1855, John returned to North Elba. But he stayed just a couple of days, only long enough to drop off Mary. On June 26, 1855, he went to Syracuse to attend the convention of the new "Radical Abolition" party. John, of course, had no intention of plunging into politics. His real reason for participating was to solicit consent for putting the North Elba project on an indefinite hold, and for going to Kansas instead, from Gerrit Smith who, along with McCune Smith and Frederick, was one of the convention's principal organizers. John went armed with two letters that John Jr. had recently sent to North Elba from Kansas. The letters depicted in graphic terms the erupting political hostilities, and they included a plea to send modern weapons – revolvers, rifles and Bowie knives – for purposes of self-defense. When Gerrit Smith dramatically read John Jr.'s letters to the convention assembly, he elicited an immediate outpouring of warm sympathy and financial support for John's mission. Gerrit Smith not only endorsed John's change of plan to go to Kansas,

CHAPTER 11: A BATTLEGROUND CALLED KANSAS

he immediately contributed $20 to that cause.[15]

After spending the rest of the summer getting organized, John traveled west, making much of the journey on foot. He arrived at the settlement created by his sons, dubbed "Brown's Station," on October 6, 1855. He regarded Brown's Station as being in a miserable condition. The sons and their families had no houses, and they were living in wagons and tents. They had as yet been unable to bring in any hay, so they lacked fodder for their animals. Worse, all of the party except for John Jr.'s wife Wealthy and his son Johnnie were sick to a greater or lesser degree with the fever and chills of malaria. So John's first efforts were to apply his ample pioneer skills. Under his direction, within a month the family erected a log shanty with a chimney capable of maintaining a fire. By the end of November, John was able to report in a letter to Mary that the illness epidemic was subsiding, that "both families" (i.e., those of John, Jr. and Jason) were "sheltered," and that part of the hay had been gotten in. He now turned his attention to the conflict regarding the institution of slavery.[16]

Up until John's arrival in Kansas, the competition between pro-slavery and anti-slavery forces in Kansas, although rowdy and boisterous, had not yet resulted in any overtly political violence.[17] There was kind of a "Wild West" feel to the territory. People were racing to stake out their homestead claims. The choicest lands, in the context of the Kansas prairie landscape, were the relatively scarce wooded areas bordering rivers and creeks. Disputes erupted over possession of the desirable land parcels containing timber, as settlers streamed into Kansas both from the North and from the South. A few conflicts over land resulted in murders. And, if the victim was considered "free state," or if he was considered "right on the goose" (the prevailing code phrase for pro-slavery), the homicide was apt to be interpreted in political terms. But as the end of 1855 approached, violent Kansas deaths were still few in number, and all of them had roots in conflict over property, rather than ideology or party loyalty.

Partisans of "the goose" used bullying as part of their arsenal of tactics. In particular, Missouri "mob rule" of the same general kind that Judge Lawless had sanctioned in the aftermath of the McIntosh lynching, and of the same kind that had been used to destroy Lovejoy's presses, was put into service by paramilitary "ruffians" dispatched to Kansas by Atchison and his allies. The biggest single instance of "mobism" was undoubtedly the election for a territorial legislature on March 30, 1855. The "slaveholding interest" and its sympathizers among Missourians made this election the focus of much advance organizing. Thousands from throughout the western part of Missouri felt it was their patriotic duty to volunteer for a grand expedition to overcome the "hordes of paupers, hirelings, and convicts" that had been sent to Kansas by "abolitionists, free-soilers and Emigrant Aid Societies." In the spirit of adventure, they entered Kansas in droves the night before the election and camped in the vicinity of the polling places.

Territorial Governor Andrew Reeder, a Pennsylvania Democrat appointed by President Pierce, had attempted to ensure a fair election by conducting a census of Kansas residents ahead of time and by requiring anyone who intended to vote to take an oath that he was a permanent resident of Kansas with the intention to remain in the territory. The Missourians argued that this proclamation was illegitimate and that all U.S. citizens who were present in Kansas on the day of the election had the right to vote. The invaders tied white tape or ribbons in their button holes to distinguish their party from "abolitionists." "Vice-President" Atchison personally led a group of eighty Missourians to one of the precincts. Through intimidating "mob" type tactics, the Missouri partisans overwhelmed election judges who tried to oppose them. They insisted on submitting their votes to the ballot boxes. In the end,

5,427 votes were tallied for the pro-slavery slate of candidates, as opposed to only 791 votes for the free state slate. Of the pro-slavery votes, 4,908 were subsequently found to be illegal by an investigating committee sent to Kansas by Congress the following year. At the time, however, the extent of fraud was not easy to prove. Governor Reeder invalidated the returns in only six of the thirty-nine districts, leaving the basic election results to stand. President Pierce, of course, accepted the outcome of the election.[18]

The slaveholding interest congratulated itself on winning the battle. The "bogus Legislature," as it would henceforth be dubbed, passed an aggressive set of laws. The "slave code" it enacted, reminiscent of laws in the South generally, made it an offense punishable by imprisonment to speak against the institution of slavery, or to possess abolitionist literature. The death penalty was prescribed for aiding an escaping slave. Loyalty oaths were required of all government officials, judges, jurors, and lawyers, pledging to uphold the Fugitive Slave Act. All native-born white American males over the age of 21 were authorized to vote, if they paid a poll tax of $1.[19] But the victory would prove rather hollow. The unsavory manner in which the "bogus Legislature" was elected, and the offensive nature of the "bogus laws" it passed, gave rise to a vehement adverse reaction when the news of these developments circulated in the East. It was part of this reaction that led Gerrit Smith to sanction John's abandonment of North Elba for Kansas. And, it was part of this reaction that led Amos Lawrence to purchase and ship one hundred breech-loading, highly accurate "Sharps" rifles – representing the latest in weapons technology – to Kansas, where they would arrive in the hands of James Abbott – whom the Kansas free staters called "Major Abbott" – in September 1855.[20]

By late June 1855, John Brown, Jr. had been in Kansas less than two months. Even though he and his family were still living in a wagon covered by a tent, he took several days to travel 40 miles north from Brown's Station to Lawrence to attend a "Free State Convention" that had been called by Kansas settlers who were opposed to the bogus Legislature. On June 25, this convention met and, within an hour, John Jr. had been selected to become one of five members of the "committee on resolutions." This committee worked throughout the day to produce the following "resolutions" that were adopted by the "convention" as a whole:[21]

> WHEREAS, certain persons from the neighboring state of Missouri, have, from time to time, made irruptions into this Territory, and have by fraud and force driven from and overpowered our people at the ballot box, and have forced upon us a Legislature which does not represent the opinions of the legal voters of this Territory; many of the members of said Legislature not being even residents of this Territory, but having their homes in the State of Missouri; and whereas, said persons have used violence towards the persons and property of the inhabitants of the Territory; Therefore,
>
> *Resolved*, That we are in favor of making Kansas a *free* Territory; and as a consequence, a free State.
>
> *Resolved*, That we urge upon the people of Kansas to throw away all minor differences and issues, and make the freedom of Kansas the *only* issue.
>
> *Resolved*, That we claim no right to meddle with the affairs of the people of Missouri, or any other State, but that we claim the right to regulate our own domestic affairs, and, with the help of GOD, we will do it.
>
> *Resolved*, That we look upon the conduct of a portion of the people of Missouri, in the late Kansas election

CHAPTER 11: A BATTLEGROUND CALLED KANSAS

as a gross outrage upon the elective franchise, and our rights as freemen, and a violation of the principles of popular sovereignty; and inasmuch as many of the members of the present Legislature are men who owe their election to a combined system of *force* and *fraud*, we do not feel bound to obey any law of their enacting.

Resolved, That the legally elected members of the present Legislature be requested, as good and patriot citizens of Kansas, to resign and repudiate the fraud.

Resolved, That in reply to the threats of war so frequently made in our neighboring State, our answer is, WE ARE READY.

Resolved, That the people of Kansas are opposed to the establishment of slavery here; and if established, it will be contrary to the wishes of three-fourths of our People.

Resolved, That Kansas has a right to, and does hereby invoke the aid of the general government against the lawless course of slavery propaganda with reference to this Territory.

John, Jr. was the only one of John Brown's many children who had any significant formal education. John himself had dropped out of school, as we have seen.[22] Over the months following the Free State Convention of June 25, 1855, John Jr. remained a participant in Kansas politics. Not only was he one of the drafters of the above free state resolutions, he was also appointed a vice-president of the committee on selecting free state officers. He attended a follow-up meeting of free state leaders at Big Springs, Kansas (halfway between Lawrence and Topeka), on September 5 and 6. At this meeting, an "executive committee" of free state advocates was organized.

John, Jr. was one of the twenty-three members appointed to this committee. Additional resolutions were adopted to urge peaceful opposition to the acts of the "spurious Legislature." The meeting's resolutions urged its supporters not to vote in the scheduled October 1 election, but instead to vote in an alternative election on October 9 for a free state representative to send to Congress. John, Jr. was appointed a member of the "Territorial Election Committee" to count the returns. Andrew Reeder was elected as the free state representative. A constitutional convention, with the agenda of creating a free state document (one also banning all African Americans), was set to occur in free state leaning Topeka. Meanwhile, the pro-slavery partisans on November 14 organized a party of their own, called "the Law and Order party," in the pro-slavery stronghold of Leavenworth.[23]

The kryptonite of all bullies everywhere is a determined, well-armed foe. Free state partisans in and around Lawrence had experience with bullying in the form of the "bogus" territorial legislature election of March 30, 1855. They also were very well aware of the Missouri mob rule that had been used to crush the likes of Elijah Lovejoy. Amos Lawrence's shipment of Sharps rifles was requested by the Kansas free state settlers with the explicit intent to counteract this type of intimidation. Major Abbott, who was the recipient of the rifle shipment, and other like-minded persons in the greater Lawrence area, organized and drilled a minuteman-like citizen militia, prepared to turn out and handle the rifles should the need arise. Soon, in late November 1855, the need arose.

On November 21 in a place called Hickory Point, about 10 miles south of Lawrence, Charles Dow, one of Abbott's militiamen who was, however, unarmed at the time, was shot down in the street by Frank Coleman. Coleman, a rival claimant for Dow's homestead, was from Virginia and leaned to the pro-slavery party. Dow and Coleman had a dispute over timber, but the killing of Dow was viewed immediately in the

Chapter 11: A Battleground Called Kansas

community as having political implications. Dow's murder was denounced by free state and pro-slavery settlers alike. The free state settlers were particularly upset at the lack of apparent concern about the crime among the "bogus" territorial authorities. As indignation and threats of reprisal over Dow's killing grew, Coleman was taken into the protective custody of Samuel J. Jones, a Virginia-born 35-year-old ally of Atchison, who had been appointed by the bogus Legislature to be the Douglas County Sheriff. Indignation about Dow's killing grew, and the atmosphere of violence reverberated. Even though an initial attempt to burn Coleman's cabin was snuffed out by moderates, his house was ultimately indeed burned, as was the house of one Buckley, who was one of Coleman's friends and allies.

At the time of his death, Dow had been boarding with a man named Jacob Branson, who was apparently a relative. Branson was suspected of fomenting the arson reprisal and of making threats against Coleman's life. A warrant for the arrest of Branson was issued by a local justice of the peace. Sheriff Jones went down to Hickory Point with a posse of fifteen men to take Branson into custody. The free state settlers viewed Branson's arrest with alarm, as being an attempt to silence a witness to the murder. They were very concerned about Branson's fate should he be transported to the pro-slavery stronghold of Leavenworth. Major Abbott immediately summoned the minutemen to rescue Branson. After unsuccessfully trying to track Sheriff Jones from Branson's house, the militia gathered with their rifles at Abbott's home, located about a half mile south of a bridge over the Wakarusa river called Blanton's Bridge, roughly halfway between Lawrence and Hickory Point. At around 11 p.m. Abbott's wife, from a vantage point on the doorstep, saw the Jones posse approaching from the south along the main road leading to Lawrence. The minutemen quickly grabbed their weapons and assembled in the road to confront Sheriff Jones with bristling guns. In the dim moonlight Abbott asked, "Is Branson there?" To which Branson called out, "Yes, I am here, a prisoner." One of the minutemen responded, "If you want to be among friends, come over here." Branson, who was 65 years old, was very stiff from three hours of sitting in the cold on a sharp-backed mule. Even though Sheriff Jones threatened to shoot him, Mrs. Abbott helped Branson dismount the mule and walk past the free state men. She led him into the house. Bitter words were exchanged. The Sharps rifles of the minutemen remained drawn and cocked. After a tense 15-minute standoff, Sheriff Jones and his party rode off, promising to exact dire vengeance.[24]

The next day, Sheriff Jones asked the new territorial Governor whom President Pierce had appointed, Wilson Shannon, to call up a militia to quell the "rebellion." Governor Shannon quickly agreed to his request. The Governor at first tried to call federal troops into service, but their commander, Colonel Edwin Sumner, refused to become involved without explicit orders from Washington. On November 29, pro-slavery backers organized the recruitment of a militia force of as many as 1,500 men. The intent of their leaders was to storm and sack Lawrence, take the "rebels" into custody, and destroy the "free state" printing press. But the free state defenders in Lawrence had themselves secured a howitzer to go along with their armory of Sharps rifles.[25] They showed their intent to mount a determined, well-armed resistance. The result was a mutually armed standoff.

News of the siege of Lawrence traveled the 40 miles south to Brown's Station. This was the type of action for which John had made his way to Kansas. On Thursday, December 6, he supervised the packing of a small lumber wagon with guns, ammunition, swords, blankets, and food. Leaving behind those who were still sick, John's sons John Jr., Owen, Frederick, and Salmon went along with him on the expedition. The party left

CHAPTER 11: A BATTLEGROUND CALLED KANSAS

just as the sun was setting. They camped overnight along the road. The next morning, on the way into Lawrence, they came to Blanton's Bridge, which a pro-slavery militia was guarding. A tense moment ensued. The militia eyed the five Browns warily as they passed, with each of them wearing a broad sword strapped to their waists, and with rifles, bayonets mounted on spears, and revolvers on full display. But nobody made any effort to block them. The Browns continued into town. Their conspicuous arrival made an impression, which buoyed the spirits of Lawrence's defenders. G.W. Brown ran a brief item in his December 15 issue of his free state newspaper, the *Herald of Freedom*:[26]

> About noon [Friday, December 7] Mr. John Brown, an aged gentleman from Exeter [actually, Essex] County, N.Y., who had been a resident of the Territory for several months, arrived with four of his sons – leaving several others at home sick – bringing a quantity of arms with him, which were placed in his hands by eastern friends for the defense of the cause of freedom. Having more than he could well use to advantage, a portion were placed in the hands of those who were more destitute. A company was organized and the command given to Mr. B for the zeal he had exhibited in the cause of freedom both before and since his arrival in the Territory.

This "company" consisted of Brown's own sons, plus fifteen other men, some of whom were also from the southern Kansas area where Brown's Station was located.[27]

The newly anointed Captain Brown promptly began causing trouble. He refused to take orders from any superior officers. He called for volunteers to go down to Blanton's Bridge and "make an attack on the pro-Slavery forces encamped there."[28] However, by the time John arrived, the tense situation was already well on the way to being defused by civic leaders who emerged on both sides.

Charles Robinson, a physician, had been sent to Kansas as a paid agent to take charge of its financial affairs by the founders of the Massachusetts Emigrant Aid Company. He would prove to be an articulate and respected political leader of the Lawrence free state party. Another, far wilder, free state leader was James Lane, formerly a Democratic congressman from Indiana and a military commander in the Mexican–American War.[29] Robinson and Lane arranged for Governor Shannon and several Missouri leaders to personally come into Lawrence. There they observed the body of a free state volunteer named Thomas Barber who had been shot to death outside Lawrence when, riding his horse, he refused to halt when ordered to do so by the pro-slavery militia that was patrolling the countryside.[30]

Charles Robinson, in 1857 portrait

This visible image of death in the form of Barber's corpse made an impression on Governor Shannon. To end the crisis, he negotiated a "Treaty of Peace" with Robinson and Lane that was signed on December 8, 1855, the day after John's arrival in Lawrence. Like most mediated settlements, the document contained points favorable to both sides. The pro-slavery advocates could feel they had achieved four major points:[31]

> 1. The "citizens" [i.e., free state settlers] denied that the "rescue" had occurred with their knowledge or consent.
>
> 2. They pledged to aid in the execution of any

Chapter 11: A Battleground Called Kansas

legal process against these rescuers.

3. They pledged to aid in the execution of the laws, especially criminal laws, in the town of Lawrence or its vicinity.

4. They pledged to aid the Governor in securing a posse if needed to enforce the laws.

The free staters, on the other hand, could feel that they had successfully resisted the onslaught of bullies backed by the federal government. Besides getting the invaders to leave the Lawrence area, they had achieved the following in the treaty:

1. Anyone arrested in Lawrence or the vicinity while any "foreign forces" remained in the Territory would have a right to examination before a federal district judge and to be admitted to bail.

2. The Governor pledged to use his influence to secure remuneration for any depredations committed by Sheriff Jones's posse.

3. The Governor represented that he had not called on residents of any other state to aid in executing the "laws" [referring to the enactments of the "bogus Legislature"], and that he would not attempt to do so, nor would he assert that he had the legal right to do so.

4. The signers "wished it understood" that they did not express any opinion as to the validity of the enactments of the territorial legislature [aka, the "bogus Legislature"].

Additionally, Governor Shannon, some said under the influence of liquor, signed a separate ambiguous document that would afterwards be much argued over. This one recognized the "citizen" volunteers as a militia of Kansas, and empowered its officers to call this Kansas militia out again when the safety of Lawrence or other portions of the territory might so require.[32]

Charles Robinson reported to the assembled free state minutemen, including John, that the committee had taken an "honorable position" in entering into the peace treaty. John demanded to know the treaty's terms in order to assure that no concessions had been made. John also tried to address the crowd of free state settlers that had gathered. But he was interrupted and was not allowed to speak. After Robinson and the negotiating committee assured the crowd that no concessions had been made to the bogus Legislature, the assembled militia retired to their homes. Peace having prevailed, John and his sons returned to Brown's Station. John hailed the outcome of this so-called "Wakarusa War" in a letter to his family as a great triumph. It was one he exaggerated by saying the Governor had "given up all pretension of further attempts to enforce the enactment of the bogus Legislature." But, in reality, John was likely a little disappointed that the conflict had been smoothed over though compromise instead of turning into a bloody clash.[33]

Chapter 12: A Primordial Terrorist Erupts

On January 15, 1856, a territory-wide election was held under the new "Topeka" free state constitution to elect a new Legislature to compete with the pro-slavery "bogus Legislature." Charles Robinson was elected Governor. John Brown, Jr. was elected to the Legislature from Franklin County. In the pro-slavery stronghold of Leavenworth (situated on the boundary with Missouri, 33 miles northeast of Lawrence), this election was viewed with much alarm. A new pro-slavery militia, drawn from settlers living in Kansas so as to conform to the non-intervention clause of Governor Shannon's "treaty," was named the "Kickapoo Rangers" after the town of Kickapoo that is near Leavenworth. The Kickapoo Rangers did their utmost to stop the election from going forward on January 15 in Leavenworth County. However, the free state partisans evaded the "mob" merely by adjourning the election in that county for two days, until January 17. One delegate elected to the free state Legislature from Leavenworth County at that time was a man named R.P. Brown (no relation to John).

The Kickapoo Rangers, frustrated over the holding of the "rebel" election despite their actions to enforce the laws that prohibited it, took into custody some of the politically active "free state" men, including R.P. Brown. A "mob" scene ensued. While leaders of the militia had cool enough heads to talk their followers out of notions of an organized lynching, several angry members of the mob surrounded Brown. One struck him over the head with a hatchet, splitting his skull. The wound was grievous, but not immediately fatal. Some of the militia members attackers took Brown to a local grocery store where they tried to dress his wound. Then they took him home to his wife. Brown died, however, the following day. Members of the Kickapoo Rangers made the rounds of the homes of known "free state" partisans in the area and, although hastening to say they had nothing against them personally, after the fashion of the prelude to Elijah Lovejoy's death, they "kindly" suggested that they should leave the area for the sake of their own safety.[1] By February 1, news of R.P. Brown's killing reached Brown's Station.[2]

The situation with two competing Legislatures each attempting to govern Kansas Territory was obviously unstable, although the severe winter weather put a damper on open hostilities. Reeder, the "free state" U.S. Representative, and J.W. Whitfield, the "bogus" U.S. Representative, were both in Washington claiming to be the legitimate congressman from Kansas. On January 24, 1856, President Pierce sent a special message to Congress denouncing the Topeka constitution, the election of a separate Representative to Congress, the election of a separate Governor, and the election of a separate territorial Legislature, all as being unlawful acts. He followed this up with a proclamation of February 11, ordering "all persons engaged in unlawful convention against the constitutional authority of the Territory" to disperse and retire. Jefferson Davis, the President's Secretary of War, issued an order directing Colonel Sumner to enforce this proclamation. Congress, however, moved in a much different direction than did the President. On March 24, it sent a special delegation of

CHAPTER 12: A PRIMORDIAL TERRORIST ERUPTS

three U.S. Representatives, two of whom were Northerners, to conduct a thorough investigation of affairs in Kansas, including the "bogus" March 1855 election that was the source of the "bogus" laws that the President's proclamation sought to bolster.[3]

John Brown, Jr.
Kansas State Historical Society

Meanwhile, John Jr. organized a militia of minutemen out of settlers in the area around Brown's Station, patterned after the group Major Abbott had organized in the Lawrence area. The minutemen called themselves the "Pottawatomie Rifles," named after Pottawatomie Creek that runs through the area extending west from Osawatomie. John, who was utterly incapable of taking orders from anyone, and especially from his own son, did not join the Pottawatomie Rifles.[4]

The first, and arguably most important, function of any government is to collect taxes. It was the collection of taxes that brought the tension between the two competing Kansas governments into the open in Franklin County, where Brown's Station was located, as well as neighboring Lykins County (now Miami County), site of the free state stronghold of Osawatomie and its pro-slavery counterpart, Paola. In the early spring of 1856, an assessor acting on behalf of the territorial government came through these areas and informed the residents that he would be making appointments to assess their holdings for the purposes of property taxes. On April 16, a settlers' meeting was held at Osawatomie to debate the matter of paying taxes, among other things.

The principal protagonists in this meeting were John, accompanied by several of his sons including John Jr., and a settler named Martin White, who was also a Baptist minister, and who resided on land just a few miles east of Brown's Station. White had come to Kansas as a "free white state" man. Originally a Kentucky native before coming to Kansas, he had resided in Illinois, where he had represented two counties as a delegate in the state legislature. White's territorial resumé portrays him as being a political moderate who attempted to get along with both sides in the stewing Kansas battle. He had been commissioned as Justice of the Peace under the territorial government on September 21, 1855. However, he still considered himself a free state man with respect to the institution of slavery. He was appointed and served as judge of the election of delegates to the Topeka constitutional convention, October 9, 1855, from the precinct of Stanton (near modern-day Rantoul). White also voted in the "free state" election of January 15, 1856.[5]

In the April 16 meeting, the Brown family presented a series of resolutions that had previously been adopted at another settler meeting in the "Pottawatomie" area. The text of these resolutions was incendiary:

> *Resolved,* That we utterly repudiate the authority of that ["bogus"] Legislature as a body emanating, not from the people of Kansas, but elected and forced upon us by a foreign vote; and that, therefore, the officers appointed by the same have no legal power to act.
>
> *Resolved,* That we pledge to one another mutual support and aid in a forcible resistance to any attempt to compel us into obedience to these enactments, let that attempt come from whatever source it may; and that if men appointed by that Legislature to the office

of assessor or sheriff, shall hereafter attempt to assess or collect taxes of us, they will do so at the peril of such consequences as shall be necessary to prevent the same;

Resolved, That a Committee of three be appointed to inform such officers of the action of this meeting by placing in their hands a copy of these resolutions.

Martin White spoke up in opposition. He urged, instead, a moderate policy of peaceful payment of taxes. He was answered in the meeting by John. There is no contemporary record of exactly what John said. According to White's later recollection, John avowed himself to be an abolitionist who would rather see the Union dissolved, and the country drenched in blood, than pay taxes under the territorial laws. This may be something of an exaggeration, but what we do know for sure is that White, along with a number of other "free state" moderates in attendance, left the meeting. The rump proceeded to adopt the Brown resolutions. The moderates conducted a follow-up meeting of their own at Stanton, in which resolutions urging obedience to the laws were adopted.[6]

On April 21, five days after the Osawatomie settler meeting, a territorial court convened at a place called "Dutch Henry's Crossing" on the south bank of the Pottawatomie, a place where the creek was crossed by the "California Road," at that time a major thoroughfare. Presiding was a Pierce appointee, U.S. District Judge Sterling G. Cato. Judge Cato was a native of Alabama. "Dutch Henry's" was the common name for the tavern and house of a man named Henry Sherman. Because Sherman was a native of Germany and spoke English with an accent, he was nicknamed "Dutch" (likely a corruption of "Deutsch") Henry. Dutch Henry had been in Kansas for a relatively long time, since at least 1847, and had established himself as a local merchant and cattle rancher.[7] He made no secret of his support of the "Law and Order" party. John and his family saw the coming court session at Dutch Henry's as a political opportunity and challenge with respect to their "Resolutions." John Jr. called up the Pottawatomie Rifles to "drill" nearby prior to the court session. Then he "released" the minutemen to attend court, to watch what would happen. A grand jury was sworn in consisting of local settlers who had been summoned to the makeshift courthouse for that purpose. After Judge Cato concluded his charge to the grand jury, John Jr. came forward and presented him with a short note, which read:[8]

> To the Court:
>
> Does this Court intend to enforce the enactments of the Territorial Legislature, so called?
>
> "MANY CITIZENS"

Judge Cato did not reply to this impertinent question. Instead, the court conducted some relatively minor business: (1) it approved payment of the jurors and court officers, (2) it imposed fines on people who had failed to appear when summoned for jury service, and (3) it returned three indictments, for such matters as killing two hogs belonging to someone else, selling liquor to Native Americans, and taking a shot, which missed, at a probate judge sitting in a neighboring county. None of this business had anything to do with the Browns.[9]

Meanwhile, pro-slavery partisans based in Leavenworth devised a clever strategy to divert the attention of the newly-arrived members of the investigating committee sent by Congress. Samuel Wood had been one of the more visible and vocal participants in Major Abbott's militia during the "Branson rescue" insurrection. On Saturday, April 19, 1856, Sheriff Jones came into Lawrence with a warrant for Wood's arrest. Wood, of course, refused to surrender. The December, 1855 "peace treaty" had explicitly promised that the free staters

CHAPTER 12: A PRIMORDIAL TERRORIST ERUPTS

would assist in making such an arrest. The following day, Jones returned. Without even attempting to look for Wood, Sheriff Jones called upon a number of men in the street to assist him in making the arrest. The promise of the free state advocates to raise a "posse" for this purpose was another explicit provision of the "peace treaty."[10]

Naturally, Sheriff Jones received no assistance from the citizens of Lawrence. Wood was nowhere to be seen. However, Jones was actually carrying out someone else's carefully designed plan. He left town armed with a new pretext to invoke the assistance and involvement of Colonel Sumner's U.S. troops, who until now had stayed out of the fray, against the "free state" rebels. On Wednesday, April 23, Jones returned to Lawrence accompanied by a detachment of federal soldiers from Fort Leavenworth. When the troops reached the central part of the city, a crowd gathered around them to ascertain their mission. The officer in command read a letter addressed to the Mayor of Lawrence from Colonel Edwin Sumner, the commander of the U.S. Army garrison at Fort Leavenworth. Sumner's wording betrays his awareness and sense of caution about having been dragged into a partisan dispute:

> Sir: – A small detachment proceeds to Lecompton this morning, on the requisition of the Governor, under the orders of the President to assist the Sheriff of Douglas County in executing several writs, in which he says he has been resisted. I know nothing of the merits of the case and have nothing to do with them. But I would respectfully impress upon you, and others in authority, the necessity of yielding obedience to the proclamation and orders of the General Government. Ours is emphatically a government of laws, and if they are set at naught, there is an end to all order. I feel assured that, on reflection, you will not compel me to resort to violence in carrying out the orders of the

Government.

Sheriff Jones then proceeded to arrest the citizens whom he had summoned on Sunday to assist him in the arrest of Wood. The Lawrence leaders were amazed at the boldness of this stratagem. But it was effective. Resistance to "bogus" laws and to "bogus" territorial officers was one thing, but resistance to the U.S. Army was quite another. The citizens named in Jones's latest warrant surrendered mildly and allowed themselves to be taken into custody.[11]

That night, Sheriff Jones camped in Lawrence with Lieutenant McIntosh, the commander of the federal troop detachment. At about 11 o'clock, the two of them went out of the tent to get some water from a barrel. While they were doing this, someone fired a shot at them. McIntosh, in the dark, tried to determine who had fired, but was unable to do so. The two returned to Lieutenant McIntosh's tent. About 10–20 minutes later, as they were seated inside it with some other men, another shot was fired from behind the rear of the tent at the silhouette of Sheriff Jones. It struck him between the right shoulder and spine. Sheriff Jones was rapidly carried out of the tent and into the Free State Hotel, the biggest permanent building in Lawrence and the only one that was built of brick and mortar, not the usual logs. There he received medical attention that was ultimately successful in saving his life.[12]

The attack on Sheriff Jones was an act of terrorism. Like all terrorism, its main effect was to produce an enormous uproar. Mainstream members of the community found the act repulsive. Free state "Governor" Charles Robinson, *Herald of Freedom* editor G.W. Brown, and other leading citizens of Lawrence in speeches and newspaper editorials roundly and loudly condemned the assassination.[13] However, they did not modify their political views. On May 10, the *Herald of Freedom* published the "resolutions" to defy the "bogus" laws, drafted by the Brown family, that had been adopted in the Pottawatomie and Osawatomie settler meetings. Apparently a

Chapter 12: A Primordial Terrorist Erupts

similar set of resistance resolutions adopted elsewhere in Kansas had previously been published. To the "Law and Order" pro-slavery party, this publication was defiance of the law. They were determined to deal with the imported Kansas "abolitionists" in the same way Dresser and Lovejoy had been treated. The free state press would be destroyed and thrown into the river, in just the same way as Lovejoy's offending presses had been destroyed.[14] In mid-May, a grand jury indictment was handed down in the court of U.S. District Judge Samuel Lecompte, formally condemning the *Herald of Freedom* and the *Kansas Free State* to be destroyed by the U.S. Marshal. And, for good measure, Lecompte also had his grand jury condemn the Free State Hotel to be demolished as a nuisance. These writs were placed for execution in the hands of U.S. Marshal Israel B. Donaldson. He issued a proclamation calling for a posse to assist in enforcing them. Probably a majority of them came from across the border, in Missouri. Donaldson's large and well-armed "posse" mobilized on a ridge west of Lawrence on May 21, 1856. "Vice-President" Atchison accompanied Donaldson and gave his men an inspirational speech.[15]

Rumors of the latest Lawrence-area developments spread to southeast Kansas. Here, there were no difficulties or dangers in the immediate vicinity, but minutemen were committed to go to the aid of Lawrence.[16] On May 21, a messenger riding south on the California Road carried news of the threat. "A proslavery army has concentrated, outside of Lawrence, and they have cannon! Send help at once."[17] By that afternoon the Pottawatomie Rifles, consisting of thirty-four militia volunteers including the leader, John Jr., and John's second oldest son Jason, mustered for action. Although John himself did not belong to the Rifles, not for anything would he miss out on this crusade. He mustered his own separate "company," being himself, his unmarried sons Owen, Salmon, Oliver, and

Frederick, and his son-in-law Henry Thompson. John's personal group accompanied the Pottawatomie Rifles as they moved northward in the direction of Lawrence.[18]

The militia camped overnight, then started north again the next morning. They were soon met by another messenger coming from Lawrence, who informed them that the free state leaders had decided not to fight and that the town was being destroyed. Despite some wavering, the group continued their march north. But as they bivouacked for breakfast about 5 miles south of Palmyra, yet another messenger arrived with a further update: The crisis was over; the Free State Hotel was already in rubble; the *Herald of Freedom* and *Free State* presses were destroyed, and much of the town was looted and burned, but no one had been hurt. U.S. troops had taken charge of the town. The posse that had done the damage was leaving. On behalf of Lawrence civic leaders, the messenger urged all the volunteers to return to their homes. Lawrence was drastically short of food and, in any event, there was nothing for them to do there now.[19]

The news of the sack of Lawrence was an outrage that caused John to snap.[20] The open alliance between the President of the United States and the "bogus" pro-slavery forces had been brought to bear and used with an overwhelming and crushing effect. The nation's political system, flowing from its highest officer, the President of the United States, through its appointed judges down to the U.S. Marshal and local Sheriff, had used legal process to destroy, under color of law, the headquarters and public voice of the free state leaders in Kansas. From this moment, May 22, 1856, and forward, John's persona and career would be that of a terrorist, using that term in its fully modern sense (which did not then exist). His preferred method would employ shocking deadly violence and property crimes against unsuspecting victims. He would never use this method to try to bring about a result within the political system. Instead, John would use the shudder of terror in a drive

CHAPTER 12: A PRIMORDIAL TERRORIST ERUPTS

to shake and topple the entire political system.

While John was traveling to Kansas, he had stopped along the way to raise funds and weapons for the cause. In Akron, Ohio, one of his sympathizers went into an armory and from it withdrew a stash of old artillery broadswords, which he gave to John. These short, heavy swords, thought to have nothing more than symbolic value for modern warfare, were in disuse. But John believed highly in the symbolic value of a sword. He had displayed these symbolic swords on his mission to the Wakarusa War. He had carried them when he and his family band traveled with John Jr. and the Pottawatomie Rifles. But now, the swords would become more than symbolic. On the morning of Friday, May 23, John had his sons get to work sharpening the blades of these swords. Much like Nat's axes, the swords would be useful for noiseless killings.[21]

John approached James Townsley, one of the men in John Jr.'s "Pottawatomie Rifles" force who had recently been indicted by a federal territorial court for assault with intent to kill.[22] Townsley agreed to use his two-horse wagon to transport John, four of his sons, and his son-in-law Henry Thompson on a secret mission to the Pottawatomie Creek area. John's two oldest sons, John Jr. and Jason, declined to go with their father. John Jr., in fact, remonstrated with his father not to leave the main group. But it was to no avail. Filled with passion and anger, John and his party left at 2 o'clock in the afternoon, heading south, away from Lawrence toward Brown's Station. They were joined by Theodore Weiner, a merchant who had just moved to the Pottawatomie Creek area. Weiner rode on his pony beside the wagon driven by Townsley that carried John and his sons.[23]

Exactly what John and his band did the rest of Friday, May 23, and during the day on Saturday, May 24, will never be known with certainty. Most likely, they camped overnight in a wooded area near the junction of the California Road and a small tributary 3 miles or so north of Pottawatomie Creek, roughly halfway between Brown's Station and Dutch Henry's Crossing.[24] There, John refined his plans. He briefed his followers on their roles. His sons were well practiced in carrying out John's orders. He could rely on them like a well-oiled machine. Townsley, on the other hand, felt sick at what he was being ordered to do. There was no way he was going home, however. He knew he would be killed as a traitor if he tried to leave the party now.[25]

James and Mahala Doyle lived with their five children in a log cabin on Mosquito Creek, a tributary of Pottawatomie Creek, about a mile north of Dutch Henry's Crossing. The family had been in Kansas only six months. At 11 o'clock Saturday night, all the Doyles were in bed when they heard strange people come into their yard. Somebody rapped at the door and called for James Doyle. James got up and went to the door. The men outside wanted to know where Mr. "Wilkson" lived. James said he would tell them. He opened the door and several, armed with pistols and swords, came into the house. John commanded the party. He said they were from the Northern army and announced that they were taking prisoners. James and his two oldest boys were unceremoniously ushered out of the house. John eyed the Doyles' third son, 16-year-old John. Sobbing, Mahala pleaded with John not to take him. After hesitating, he and the others left.

The next day, Mahala Doyle found the mangled bodies of her husband and her 22-year-old son William lying together, about 200 yards from the house. William's head was cut open. He also had stab wounds in his jaw and in his side. Her husband James had been shot in the forehead and stabbed in the chest. The "crimes" of which James and William Doyle were "guilty" were that they had served, respectively, as a juror and as bailiff in the federal court convened by Judge Cato on April 21. Also slaughtered was Mahala's 20-year-old son Drury. His brother found his body Sunday morning, lying in a ravine. His fingers

CHAPTER 12: A PRIMORDIAL TERRORIST ERUPTS

were cut off, both his arms were hacked off, and his head was smashed open.[26]

From the Doyle residence, John took his band to the home of Allen and Louisa Jane Wilkinson and their two small children. It was a log cabin situated on a land parcel due south of the Doyle property. The Wilkinsons were poor immigrants from Tennessee who had never owned a slave. Allen Wilkinson's "crime" was that he was a member of the territorial "bogus" Legislature. Additionally, he was the local postmaster, and he had served as acting district attorney during Judge Cato's April 21 court session at Dutch Henry's. Everyone in the house was asleep. When John's band arrived, it was after midnight. The Wilkinsons had a dog outside, which heard them approach and started barking.

Louisa was sick with the measles. She started up in bed and asked her husband what was the matter. He said it was just someone passing by on the road, and urged her to go back to sleep. Louisa was awakened again by furious barking. Outside, John's boys silenced the dog, dispatching it with their swords. Louisa heard footsteps. She saw a man's shadow pass by her window. Then came a knock at the door. "Who is that?" called out Allen Wilkinson. A voice replied, "I want you to tell me the way to Dutch Henry's." Louisa's husband started to tell them. The voice replied, "Come out and show us." Some discussion went back and forth. After a time, her husband told the intruders, in answer to some kind of question about whether or not he was a supporter of the territorial government, "I am." Then one of them announced, "You are our prisoner. Do you surrender?" "Gentlemen, I do," her husband replied.

The voice said, "Open the door." Allen asked them to wait until he could make a light. The voice refused. "If you don't, we'll open it for you." Against Louisa's wishes, Allen opened the door. Four men immediately forced themselves into the small log cabin. They ordered Allen to put on his clothes. They also expressed surprise that there were not more men in the house. They searched the house for weapons, taking a gun and a powder flask. Louisa begged the men to let Allen stay with her, because she was sick and helpless. Louisa did not know who John was, but she clearly understood the "old man" who had entered to be in command. He looked at her, he looked around at the children, and he remarked, "You have neighbors." Louisa said, "So I have, but they are not here, and I cannot go for them." "It matters not," was John's response. Allen wanted to put his boots on, but John and the others would not let him. They led Allen out of the house in his stocking feet. One of the other men came back in and took two saddles. Louisa asked John what he was going to do with Allen. He replied, "Take him a prisoner to the camp."

The next morning, Allen Wilkinson's body was found about 150 yards from the Wilkinson home. There was a gash in his head and in his side. His throat was slit.[27]

From Wilkinson's residence, John and a party of four other raiders went to the one room cabin occupied by James Harris. This was also positioned along the California road, near Dutch Henry's Crossing. There, Harris lived with his wife and child. They had been there for less than two months. At 2 o'clock in the morning, James, his wife and child were suddenly aroused by a company of men outside who said they belonged to the "Northern army." Each of the men was armed with a sword and two revolvers. James recognized John to be one of them, although at the time he knew him only as "Old Man Brown." He also recognized John's son Owen. John, Owen, and three other men came into the house. They announced that the occupants must surrender, that there was no point in any resistance. Three other men were sleeping in the house: John Whiteman, Jerome Glanville, and William Sherman, who was Dutch Henry's brother. Whiteman and Glanville had just bought a cow from Henry Sherman. They were stopping over at the Harris residence, which was owned

CHAPTER 12: A PRIMORDIAL TERRORIST ERUPTS

by Henry,[28] before returning home with their cow the next day.

John had his band search and ransack the entire cabin. They soon produced two rifles and a bowie knife belonging to the Harrises. The intruders took Glanville out of the house for a few minutes. Then they brought him back. Next, they took James Harris out. He was interviewed by John and one of his sons. They asked him if there were any more men about the cabin somewhere. He answered no. They then specifically asked where Henry Sherman was. James answered that he was out on the plains in search of some roving cattle. They asked if James had ever taken a hand in aiding pro-slavery men in coming to the Territory of Kansas, or if he had ever taken any hand in troubles at Lawrence. James said, "No." They asked whether he had ever done the free state party any harm, or intended to do that party any harm. James said, "No." They asked why he worked for Henry Sherman and lived in one of his cabins. He answered that he could get higher wages there than anywhere else.

John asked if there were any bridles or saddles about the premises. James replied that there was one saddle. The raiders made James put that saddle on a handsome gray horse belonging to Henry Sherman, which was at the cabin, so that they could take both the saddle and the horse. John then led James back into the house. The next man they took out was William Sherman. Two of the raiders stayed inside to guard the Harrises, Whiteman, and Glanville. James Harris heard nothing more for about 15 minutes. Then he heard a noise that sounded like a cap burst. The two invaders acting as guards then left. William Sherman did not return.

The next morning, James discovered William's body lying in Pottawatomie Creek, near the Harris house. His skull was split open in two places. Some of his brain had been washed out by the water. A large hole was cut in his chest. His left hand was cut off, except a little piece of skin on one side.

James buried the corpse.[29]

The uniform reaction by the local settlers, when the grisly carnage was discovered, was one of absolute shock. Everybody was appalled, no matter what their political views. John was rapidly identified as having been the leader of the massacre party, based on the accounts of the survivors. On Tuesday, May 27 the local settlers, without distinction of party, assembled and adopted resolutions. The chairman of the meeting was a pro-slavery man, C.H. Price, recently foreman of the Anderson County grand jury, while H.H. Williams, a notorious free state militant, acted the secretary. Their resolutions unequivocally denounced the terrorist spree, and pledged mutual cooperation in bringing the criminals to justice.

The day after the massacre, John and his band returned northward to the camp where his other sons, John Jr. and Jason had remained, near the Ottawa River. They arrived after midnight.[30] John evidently told John Jr. and Jason enough for them to fully comprehend the enormity of the horror he and the younger sons had carried out. Jason said to his father that the massacre had been an "uncalled for, wicked act." John responded, "God is my Judge."[31]

John Jr. had an even more dramatic reaction to his father's passage into terrorism. He was the oldest and most educated of the Brown children. Moreover, he was the only one among them who ever acquired any stature as a participant in public political life. He was a member of the "free state" Legislature, he was an officer in the "free state" convention, and he was a drafter of the "free state" constitution. John Jr. was respected enough by the community to be placed at the head of the settler militia, the Pottawatomie Rifles.

The horror arising from his father's actions caused John Jr. to lose his mind. He immediately resigned his captaincy of the Pottawatomie Rifles. Then he "plunged into the thickets" and remained there for several days. John Jr.'s brother Owen went to try to coax him out of the woods, but "he could do

CHAPTER 12: A PRIMORDIAL TERRORIST ERUPTS

nothing with him as his head was wild." A relative wrote that John Jr. was "beside himself" and had to be turned over to the authorities for his own safety. Sara Robinson, the wife of Governor Charles Robinson, was incarcerated with John Jr. shortly after the Pottawatomie massacre. She wrote in her diary that John Jr. "was still insane, and continued so during the whole of his stay in camp. Every day he walked up and down in front of the tents, with his hands behind him, looking up into the sky." In a letter written many years later John Jr.'s sister, Annie Brown Adams, stated: "[John Jr.]'s mind has always been more or less affected by the excitement, and trouble in Kansas."[32]

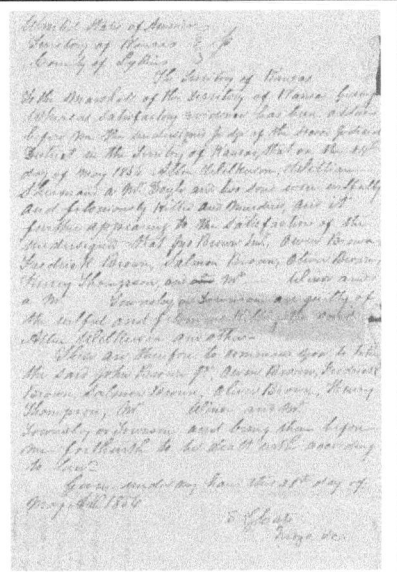

Federal arrest warrant for murder, issued for John Brown Sr. and sons, May 28, 1856
Kansas State Historical Society

How John avoided being brought to justice for his murderous rampage on the Pottawatomie was little short of a miracle, given the harsh condemnation his crimes elicited in local community members of all political stripes, given the multiple credible witnesses who promptly identified him as the leader of the nighttime terrorists, and given that his deadly outburst was essentially an attack on the justice system itself. John attributed his survival to endorsement of his executions by the divine being.[33] But he was critically aided by some fortuitous circumstances. The shock of his terrorist killings was overtaken in the public eye by outrageous provocations carried out virtually simultaneously by persons allied with the slave power. The shameless sacking of Lawrence was one of these. But an even bigger national furor was touched off by an egregious and unprecedented act of violence which occurred on the floor of the U.S. Senate.

Chapter 13: A Brutal Beating in the Senate

Judged strictly as a politician, Charles Sumner is one of the least likely people ever to serve in the U.S. Senate. He never held elective office at any level. He was, in modern terminology, a super nerd. His father Charles Pinckney Sumner had attended Harvard College, graduating in 1796. While there, he became friends with a student two years younger than he named Joseph Story. Story rose, in a meteoric career, to become one of America's most preeminent jurists. At age 32, he became the youngest person in history ever to be appointed to the U.S. Supreme Court. Story was also placed on the teaching faculty of the new Harvard Law School. Charles Sumner the younger was born in 1811, the same year Story was appointed to the Supreme Court. Although the elder Charles Sumner was not very successful in law practice, he at least won a reputation for being honest. He was eventually appointed as the Sheriff of Boston. From that office, he earned just enough to send his bright son to Harvard. The younger Charles was notoriously horrible in mathematics, but he made up for it with his ability to memorize and recite long literary passages, and with his proficiency in Latin as well as modern European languages. Young Charles went on to also attend law school at

Harvard. While doing so, he came to the attention of his father's old friend Justice Story. The bookish Charles became, in essence, Justice Story's law clerk and general assistant.[1]

Charles was utterly indifferent to feminine charms. His friends would occasionally wager successfully with sprightly and interesting girls that they could not keep his attention for a quarter of an hour. But Charles was highly sociable and generous with his time helping others. He rapidly made many friends among the young generation of intelligentsia living in the greater Boston area. After graduating from Harvard, he embarked on a law practice. His work as a lawyer never paid much, partly because he took frequent prolonged absences for various reasons. Charles greatly preferred the academic side of law to the nitty-gritty of representing clients. He became the editor of an admiralty treatise, and he also assisted Justice Story with his treatise on Equity. In that capacity he was so diligent and effective that soon Justice Story was deputizing Charles to teach his law classes at Harvard while the Justice was away hearing cases on the bench in Washington City.[2]

Charles closed down his law practice and traveled in Europe for two and a half years. During that time, he perfected his abilities in French and Italian. Carrying letters of introduction from his prominent New England friends, Charles was a hit in social circles, both on the Continent and especially in England, where his erudition and legal acumen were particularly well appreciated. The friends and contacts he made during this trip would be invaluable for his later career. When he finally returned to the United States in the year 1840, Charles made his residence with his mother, who was by now a widow. Not needing much income, Charles only dabbled at law practice, although the few cases he did handle were relatively high profile. He became close with Henry Wadsworth Longfellow, the poet, who also was Professor of Modern Languages and Literature at Harvard. In 1842 he also became good friends with a doctor named Samuel Howe, who was ten years older than Charles and who, like Charles, was a graduate of Boston Latin School. Howe, as well as Longfellow, were publicly outspoken abolitionists. Along with William Channing, who had graduated from Harvard in the same class with Justice Story, Howe and Longfellow influenced Charles to take a stance on the immorality of slavery.[3]

However, Charles's first entry into the public eye had really nothing to do with the institution of slavery or the abolition thereof. It came on April 24, 1845, when Charles was selected to give Boston's annual Fourth of July celebration keynote address. For that event he composed a speech which he entitled, "The True Grandeur of Nations." Its theme was universal peace. In contemporary political terms, the peace agenda translated into opposition to war with Mexico over Texas and possibly also California, and into opposition to war with England over Oregon territory. Charles's July 4 oration was a sensation. Over 10,000 copies of it were printed. Charles was so surprised and pleased with the reception given his July 4 speech that rather than continue pursuing his prior career goal of a faculty position at Harvard Law School, he decided to instead become a professional lecturer. Frequently his speaking gigs were associated with churches and reform movements, including abolition of slavery. His law practice nominally continued, but it failed to raise enough money to even meet its expenses.[4]

Charles's attitude toward effectuating change in relation to slavery contrasted sharply with that of Garrison. Charles read *The Liberator*, but he did not agree with its central political mantras. One was Garrison's insistence that the U.S. Constitution was a pro-slavery document and must therefore be radically amended. Another was Garrison's insistence on remaining entirely outside what he condemned as a morally compromised American political process. Charles, the ex-law clerk to a Supreme Court Justice, vehemently disagreed. He strongly believed in both the American political system and the United States Constitution.

In the wake of the nomination of slave-owning Zachary Taylor as the Whig candidate for President in 1848, "conscience Whigs" in Massachusetts rebelled and started a new major political movement, called the Free Soil party. Along with his friends Samuel Howe and Charles Francis Adams (son of ex-President John Quincy Adams), Charles, even though he had never previously taken part in politics, lent his name as one of the founders of this new organization.

The 1848 national Free Soil party convention nominated former President Martin Van Buren, an ex-Democrat, for President, and Charles Francis Adams, an ex-Whig, for Vice-President. The selection of Van Buren, formerly the staunch ally and Vice-President of the thoroughly proslavery Andrew Jackson, was highly curious. One way to interpret this unlikely nomination is that Van Buren was acting out a grudge he had with Lewis Cass, the 1848 Democratic party nominee for President. Van Buren's Free Soil candidacy took vital strength away from Cass. In fact, by splitting the Democrats it swung the overall election to Taylor by putting Taylor over the top in the popular vote of the crucial states of New York and Massachusetts.

Returning to Boston after the presidential campaign, Charles was quickly recognized as the ablest speaker of the Free Soil party. He won popular acclaim because of his reputation for honesty and idealism. Charles was nominated to run as a candidate for Congress from the Boston area on the Free Soil ticket. He lost this election to a former Boston Latin School classmate, Whig Robert Winthrop. However, Charles did come in second, ahead of the Democratic party candidate.[5]

Mainstream Whigs, including Winthrop, reacted with bitterness to the competition from the upstart Free Soil party. This drove the Free Soil leaders into the arms of the Democrats, who were desperate for a way to overcome prevailing Whig

CHAPTER 13: A BRUTAL BEATING IN THE SENATE

strength at the ballot box in New England. Despite their policy differences, Massachusetts Democrats made an expedient political alliance with the Free Soilers. The terms of the deal were that, if the allied parties were successful in defeating the Whigs, the Democrats would be rewarded with all appointed statewide offices, but the Free Soil party would get the U.S. Senate appointment to be made by the state legislature. In the Massachusetts legislative election of 1849, this strange and unlikely coalition indeed picked up a great deal of strength in both houses.

The enactment of the Fugitive Slave Law in 1850 evoked widespread popular outrage among Massachusetts citizens. One effect it produced was a strong protest vote for Free Soil candidates. As a result the alliance between the Free Soil and Democratic parties ended up controlling both houses of the Massachusetts state legislature in the 1850 election. Now the Democrats took their agreed statewide office spoils. On the other side of the bargain, Charles, who had never before held any public office, was selected as the Free Soil party's choice for the Senate appointment. This was confirmed quickly by the state Senate, but the battle over it in the Massachusetts House of Representatives was heated and protracted. Several Democratic representatives pointedly refused to vote for Charles, calling him a "one idea-d abolition agitator." They tried to make a deal with the Free Soilers to replace Sumner with a compromise candidate. But even though Charles, the non-politician, steadfastly refused to either campaign for the position, or to enter into any deals, the Free Soil party members refused to budge on his nomination. The opposition Whigs stalled for time, hoping nobody at all would be appointed and that they would get back control of the Massachusetts legislature the following year. But finally on April 24, 1851, after a four-month struggle, Charles was elected Massachusetts Senator on the twenty-sixth ballot.[6]

When Charles finally arrived to take his seat in Washington City, he found precious few Free Soil party allies. In the Senate, he had only two: John Hale, from New Hampshire, and Salmon Chase, from Ohio. The chances of advancing any "Free Soil" legislative agenda appeared dim indeed. For more than twenty years, the "slave power" (as Charles called it in his speeches) had been successful in bottling up any legislation aimed at restricting the institution of slavery. In fact, the slave power had prevented all such proposals from even reaching the stage of debate on the floor of either the House or the Senate. In 1836, the U.S. House of Representatives had enacted a "gag rule" requiring that all petitions and propositions relating to slavery be automatically tabled without being read, printed or acted on in any way whatsoever. The formal gag rule was repealed in 1844, but nevertheless, the leadership of both chambers steadfastly refused to allow any antislavery petitions to be received for debate.[7]

It was not the intention of either the Whigs or the Democrats to have any discussion of the institution of slavery during the 1851-52 session of Congress. Both parties were well aware of how divisive the issue had been in the previous session's battle over the Compromise of 1850 and the Fugitive Slave Act. Thus Charles, as a member of a fringe party, was bound to be frustrated by not getting a chance to take up the party's central issue on the floor of the Senate. Massachusetts Whigs played some dirty pool by disparagingly drawing his constituents' attention to Charles's impotent silence. To finally get the floor, Charles had to take the Senate by surprise. He devised a ploy to address the slave power when he rose to make remarks on an appropriations bill. This would be his only opportunity to address the Senate as a matter of right. He carefully concealed his intentions so the Senate leadership could not forestall his speech.[8]

When Senator Robert Hunter of Virginia introduced a

CHAPTER 13: A BRUTAL BEATING IN THE SENATE

small fiscal bill on August 26, 1852, authorizing reimbursement from the federal judiciary budget of ministerial officers of the federal government who incurred extraordinary expenses enforcing the laws of the United States, Charles seized the opportunity. He offered an amendment to the bill, providing in substance that no expenses relating to the Fugitive Slave Act could be reimbursed. And then, while he was at it, Charles threw into his amendment a sweeping closing phrase, "which said Act is hereby repealed." By means of this trickery, Charles finally got the chance to deliver on the Senate floor the speech denouncing the Fugitive Slave Act which he had been preparing for months.

The title of the speech was "Freedom, National, Slavery, Sectional." Charles brought to bear lengthy legislative history in support of an argument that the founding fathers had, in reality, opposed the institution of slavery, that they had sought to limit it, and that the Constitution itself was opposed to it. Charles argued that the extradition of fugitives clause in the Constitution had no application to slaves, but was only intended to cover the extradition of criminals and convicts. He mentioned various violent confrontations over enforcement, including the tragedy at Christiana, to show that the Fugitive Slave Act was a bad law leading to all kinds of misery and mischief.

When Charles's speech was finally over, his audacity drew ridicule and irate remarks from numerous Senators from many states, both North and South. But his Massachusetts constituents loved finally getting the chance to read a brazen confrontation of the slave power in the pages of the *Congressional Globe*. With them, his speech was enormously popular. Hundreds of thousands of copies were soon printed. It was even translated into German. The impact of Charles's speech defused behind-the-scenes attempts that were being made to, in effect, recall Charles from the Massachusetts

Senate post due to ineffectiveness.[9]

In several important ways, Andrew Butler was a South Carolina counterpart to Charles. He, too, could raise a strong claim to true blue-blooded American heritage. His father William Butler fought patriotically in the Revolutionary War, he was heavily involved in South Carolina's ratification of the United States Constitution, he played host to George Washington, he was a member of Congress, and then he was a war hero again in leading the defense of Charleston during the War of 1812.[10] The son Andrew, born in 1796, graduated from South Carolina College. Then he studied law, proving to have a great deal of natural ability in that arena. After serving in both houses of the South Carolina legislature, Andrew was appointed judge of a trial level court in 1833. He served in that capacity for eleven years. Consequently he was commonly called by the honorific, "Judge Butler."

Reminiscent of Charles, much of Judge Butler's female companionship came in the form of his formidable mother, war hero William Butler's widow Behethland Butler. Judge Butler married twice, but both wives died very soon afterwards. From 1834 on, Andrew remained unmarried and he moved in with his mother. Her farm was in rural Edgefield, in the part of South Carolina known as the Upcountry, not far from the Georgia border. As a Democrat, Judge Butler was appointed in 1846 to South Carolina's junior Senate seat, alongside the redoubtable John Calhoun.[11] He proved to be an effective legislator and by 1854 had risen to be the chair of the powerful Senate Judiciary Committee. He co-sponsored, along with Stephen Douglas, the Kansas-Nebraska Act.

In a strange twist of fortune, due to the "Democrat – Free Soil" alliance that led to his appointment, Charles occupied a "Democratic" seat in the Senate that was just behind that of Judge Butler. Charles and Andrew Butler engaged in memorable verbal jousting from their neighboring seats. The two of them did not merely exchange epithets. Andrew Butler

CHAPTER 13: A BRUTAL BEATING IN THE SENATE

was one of a select few Southern members of the Senate who felt himself capable of engaging with Charles on an intellectual level.

On June 26, 1854, Charles rose on the Senate floor to make remarks in support of a petition by citizens of Massachusetts to repeal the Fugitive Slave Act that had been presented by his fellow Massachusetts Senator, Julius Rockwell. The petition, called a memorial, followed in the wake of an emotional and controversial episode on May 25, 1854, in which an escaped slave named Anthony Burns had been captured in Boston and returned to his owner pursuant to the Fugitive Slave Act.[12] An attempt to incite forcible "mob" rescue, whipped up in part by a Faneuil Hall speech given by Charles's friend Samuel Howe, led to the death of one of fifty "special guards" enlisted by the U.S. Marshal to carry out the return of Burns to slavery. Charles pointed to this incident as yet another example of violence arising from an unwise enactment. He argued that many who originally supported the law in 1850 had since changed their views. Charles continued to condemn the Fugitive Slave Act as denying the fundamental right to trial by jury. In response to the charge that popular resistance to the law, such as the mob effort to stop the Burns rendition, was treasonous, Charles cited the example of America's revolutionaries, such as James Otis, John Hancock, and John Adams, who had forcibly opposed tyrannical edicts of the British crown.[13]

> It is true that the slave act was with difficulty executed, and that one of its servants perished in the effort. On these grounds the Senator from Tennessee charges Boston with fanaticism. I express no opinion of the conduct of individuals; but I do say, that the fanaticism which the Senator condemns is not new in Boston. It is the same which opposed the execution of the Stamp Act, and finally secured its repeal. It is the

same which opposed the Tea Tax. It is the fanaticism which finally triumphed on Bunker Hill. The Senator says that Boston is filled with traitors. That charge is not new. Boston, of old, was the home of Hancock and Adams. Her traitors now are those who are truly animated by the spirit of the American Revolution.

Charles urged the Senate not to summarily table the Massachusetts petition to repeal the Fugitive Slave Act. He turned to a citation from William Pitt. Speaking in the House of Commons in support of repeal of the Stamp Act, Pitt had decried the charge that speaking in opposition to the law was sedition. "Sorry I am to hear the liberty of speech in this House imputed as a crime."[14]

Andrew Butler entered the Senate chamber as Charles was speaking. When his remarks were concluded, Butler asked the chair what proposition had been under discussion. Informed, he responded with some pithy remarks of his own. Giving voice to a common Senate criticism of Charles, he decried his tendency to frame his remarks as an exercise in rhetorical oratory, rather than debate of specific measures. He condemned Charles's remarks as a "Fourth of July speech," not a proper Senate debate. But he also engaged with the substance of what Charles had said. He even injected Latin phrases, a rhetorical device often used by Charles. He accused Charles, in his "Fourth of July speech," of flagrantly misrepresenting history.[15]

> [T]here is one thing I wish to say in reply to the gentleman who sits near me [MR. SUMNER]. When Faneuil Hall was illustrated by eloquence, and immortalized by patriotism; when Otis spoke, and John Hancock acted, and John Adams made the declarations which have been so much applauded by the gentleman, they were the representatives of slaveholding States. They represented Massachusetts

Chapter 13: A Brutal Beating in the Senate

as she *was* – hardy, slaveholding Massachusetts. Sir, when blood was shed upon the plains of Lexington and Concord, in an issue made by Boston, to whom was an appeal made, and from whom was it answered? The answer is found in the acts of slaveholding states – *animis opibusque parati* ["open minds"]. Yes, sir, the independence of America, to maintain republican liberty, was won by the arms and treasure, by the patriotism and *good faith*, of slaveholding communities.

Judge Butler took the position that he was not particularly attached to the Fugitive Slave Act. He felt that even its absence, the Constitution itself required cooperation among states in the matter of extraditing fugitives from servitude. But, although Andrew Butler was generally an advocate of union over secession, he stressed the importance of unity on the issue of the return of fugitives for the future of the Union.

"Judge" Andrew Butler

> I have never made a threat on this floor; but I will tell him that if these agitations go on, the consequence will be that an issue will be made between North and South. Each section will become united – maintaining the position of units. I do not undertake to indicate those things; but will say, if sectional agitation is to be fed by such sentiments, such displays, and such things

> as come from the honorable gentleman near me [MR. SUMNER], I say we ought not to be in a common Confederacy, and we should be better off without it.

Butler, in a sense, expressed the obvious. A repeal of the Fugitive Slave Act would not solve the underlying issue.[16]

> If we repeal the fugitive slave law, will the honorable Senator from Massachusetts tell me that Massachusetts will execute the provision of the Constitution without any law of Congress? Suppose we should take away all laws, and devolve upon the different States the duties that properly belong to them? I would ask the Senator whether, under the prevalence of public opinion there, Massachusetts would execute that provision as one of the constitutional members of this Union? Would they send fugitives back to us after trial by jury, or any other mode? Will this honorable Senator [MR. SUMNER] tell me that he will do it?

To which question, albeit rhetorical, Charles responded:

> Does the honorable Senator ask me if I would personally join in sending a fellow man into bondage? "Is thy servant a dog, that he would do such a thing?"

The "dog" reference used by Charles was a quote from the biblical story of Hezael,[17] who reportedly made this remark after he was prophesied to become a brutal, bloody king. It was an academic, obscure allusion, even in an era in which biblical passages were far closer to the tip of educated tongues than they are today. His "dog" remark, which would eventually become one of his most famous, met with immediate derision and laughter on the floor of the Senate. Judge Butler suggested that it came from a book of rhetorical phrases Charles kept handy to throw around whenever he needed to sound superior. In further verbal sparring which followed, Charles clarified that

CHAPTER 13: A BRUTAL BEATING IN THE SENATE

he meant that he recognized no obligation to return escaped slaves under any circumstances.[18] Charles gave another "Fourth of July" type speech, in much of which he focused explicitly on Andrew Butler as well as Virginia Senator James Mason.[19]

The sequel to this pointed confrontation occurred two years later. It happened on May 19 and 20, 1856. The agenda for debate was no longer the Fugitive Slave Act. Now it was "Bleeding Kansas." James Lane, as a proponent of the "free state" Topeka Kansas constitution, came to Congress to present a statehood petition based on that constitution. Judge Butler and Stephen Douglas opposed any printing or debate about this petition. They rapidly got into confrontations over the issue on the floor of the Senate with both Henry Seward and John Hale, who were now, like Charles, pioneering members of the recently coalesced Republican Party.[20] Charles and Henry, while personal friends, had previously been members of opposing parties. Now, feeling the strength of a new alliance, the Republicans were gaining in confidence. More and more, they made "agitating" speeches railing against the institution of slavery in both houses of Congress. Charles intended to weigh in on Kansas with one of his typical scripted "Fourth of July" speeches. After being politely deferred for weeks on end in favor of other business, Charles finally was accorded the Senate floor on May 19, 1856. And he did not disappoint. Charles gave his longest Senate oration ever, lasting some five hours over two days.

Charles chose to, once again, focus his address extensively on Judge Andrew Butler. His opening drew an elaborate literary metaphor involving both Butler and Douglas,

> who, though unlike as Don Quixote and Sancho Panza, yet, like this couple, sally forth together in the same adventure. I regret much to miss the older Senator [MR. BUTLER] from his seat; but the cause,

against which he has run a tilt, with such activity of animosity, demands that the opportunity of exposing him should not be lost; and it is for the cause that I speak. The Senator from South Carolina has read many books of chivalry, and believes himself a chivalrous knight, with sentiments of honor and courage. Of course, he has chosen a mistress to whom he has made his vows, and who, though ugly to others, is always lovely to him; though polluted in the sight of the world, is chaste in his sight – I mean the harlot, Slavery. For her, his tongue is always profuse in words.

After engaging with Butler's historical arguments to the effect that New England had been a willing participant in the slave trade at the time of the U.S. Constitution, Charles moved on to address recent events in Kansas. Here, he repeatedly adverted to the concept of terrorism. In his speech, he accused the Border Ruffians of renewing "the incredible atrocities of the Assassins and the Thugs." Four separate times, he accused the proslavery partisans entering Kansas from Missouri of being "Assassins" and "Thugs."[21]

Charles was aware of the potential danger from the American version of "Assassins" and "Thugs." Mutterings had been heard in the wake of his speeches, and Charles had received threats of physical violence. Henry's wife Frances Seward had written a letter to Charles in which she expressed her "tears of gratitude" for his

Charles Sumner, 1856

CHAPTER 13: A BRUTAL BEATING IN THE SENATE

eloquence, but confessed to "some fears for your safety."[22] Other abolitionist senators, particularly Henry Seward and John Hale, remained far more restrained in their personal comments about Southern colleagues. But Charles was "constitutionally devoid" of fear. Several fellow members of Congress felt it wise to escort Charles home in the wake of his five hour speech. But Charles pointedly gave them the slip. He refused to take any special precautions.[23]

On Thursday, May 22, two days after Charles concluded his discourse on "The Crime Against Kansas," the Senate adjourned early for the day, at about 12:45 p.m. About a half hour later, only a sprinkling of people remained in the Senate chamber. One was Charles. Sitting at his desk number 9 in the back row, Charles was busy and intent on getting copies of his speech out in the mail to various constituents and friends. Engrossed in his work, he looked up when he was addressed by a large man he did not recognize, towering in front of him. "I have read your speech twice over carefully," the man announced. "It is a libel on South Carolina, and on Mr. Butler, who is a relative of mine … " Before he even finished the

PLAN OF THE SENATE CHAMBER IN 1856.

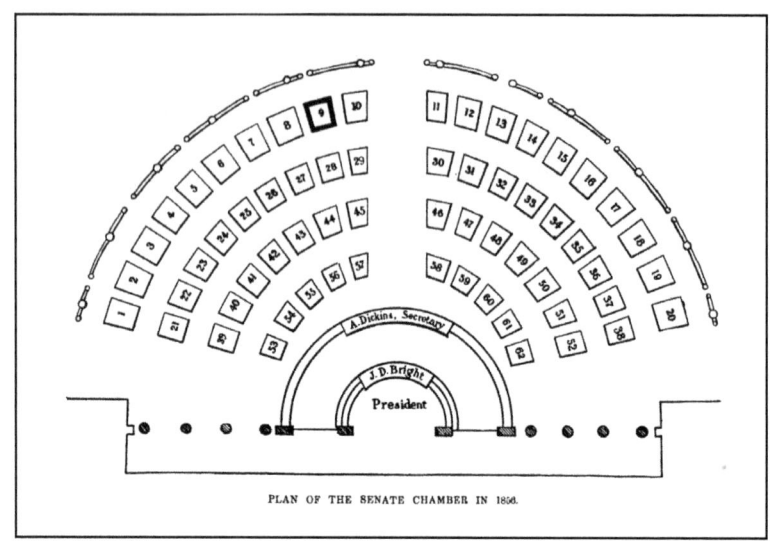

sentence, the man smashed Charles over the head with a walking cane. Made of a hard rubber called gutta-percha, the cane was similar in overall weight and stiffness to a hickory or whalebone cane. Hollow in the middle, it tapered from a diameter of about one inch at the handle to about five-eighths of an inch at the end.[24]

Charles started to rise from his seat. But the man before him was intent on using the element of surprise to administer a sudden and thorough beating. Without another word, he kept striking Charles over and over again, amazing onlookers with the rapidity and power of his strokes. As the blows rained down Charles managed to stand up, in the process toppling his desk, the legs of which sat perched on wood blocks inserted to raise the desk to accommodate his six foot, three inch frame. Screws which attached these blocks to the platform beneath were wrenched out. From being smashed over the head, Charles blacked out. He was out on his feet, to use a boxing term. In a confused state he flailed about, attempting in vain to clutch at the tormenting cane. His arms wildly waved in the air in an instinctive effort to ward off blows. The attacker kept after him,

CHAPTER 13: A BRUTAL BEATING IN THE SENATE

moving in a slow circle, striking again and again. More than a dozen times, he hit the target. Chunks of the hard rubber cane broke off from the force with which it kept hitting Charles. Still the attack continued relentlessly. Charles and his attacker engaged in a sort of crazed dance, in which the circling assailant mounted the level of Charles's overturned desk, while Charles staggered down to the next amphitheater level in front of the desk, six inches lower, so that the two essentially exchanged their initial positions. In the convulsive struggle, one of them knocked over desk number 29 that was located diagonally in front and to the left of that of Charles.[25]

The attention of everybody in the room was immediately captured by the sharp crack of the cane as it first struck Charles, followed by the crash of his desk to the floor. At that moment John Crittenden, an elderly Whig Senator from Kentucky, was speaking with James Pearce, a Senator from Maryland, at desk 23, about seven desks away from that of Charles. Recovering from his initial surprise, Crittenden was the first to reach the scene of the attack. As Crittenden expressed out loud his disapproval of the violence to no one in particular, Laurence Keitt, a Representative from South Carolina, also approached the area where the assault was occurring, coming up the center aisle that separated the two halves of the desks from the direction of the chair's desk in the front of the chamber. Brandishing a cane of his own, Keitt barked a sharp warning to Crittenden and the Senate doorkeeper not to intervene. Keitt growled, "Let them alone, god damn you," or something to that effect. Seeing Keitt's upraised cane, Senator Robert Toombs, a Whig from Georgia, urged him not to strike.[26]

When the attack began, Representative Ambrose Murray, a Republican from New York, was standing in the back left corner of the Senate chamber, farther away in the same direction as Crittenden and Pearce. He was chatting with Edwin Morgan, the chairman of the Republican National

Committee, and James Simonton, a reporter for the *New York Times*. In contrast to most of those present who simply stood or sat still in an apparent state of shock, Morgan and Murray rushed to help Charles. From their starting position, approximately fifty feet away, they took different routes. Murray went around the back of the chamber, came down the center aisle, and seized the attacker from behind, grabbing his arm so he could not strike another blow. Morgan, meanwhile, traveled by way of the pit in the front of the chamber, and came up the center aisle. Reaching the assault scene at just about the same time as Murray, Morgan caught Charles just as he was collapsing onto the floor.[27]

Charles was very seriously injured. Resting partially on overturned desk 29 and partially supported by Morgan, he was twitching spasmodically, unconscious, and bleeding profusely. Charles's clothes, and those of Murray, were drenched in his blood. After several minutes, Charles recovered his senses enough to be lifted to his feet by Murray and several others. They helped him stumble out of the Senate chamber and into a nearby anteroom, where a doctor and medic were summoned. Besides a myriad of bruises on Charles's shoulders, body and arms, the most serious wounds they observed were two deep, bloody gashes, both about two inches long, on Charles's scalp. The treating doctor later remarked that if he didn't know the weapon was a cane, he would have thought Charles was hit by bricks.

It was decided to stitch up these cuts on the spot to staunch the bleeding. In the pre-antibiotic age, these wounds were life-threatening.[28] Over the days that followed, one of them healed well, but the other became infected and festered, causing a high fever. In addition to the flesh wounds, Charles suffered brain trauma that lingered for years. Indeed, although it eventually improved somewhat, this trauma was never really fully resolved. Charles suffered from headaches for the rest of his life. Due to neurological symptoms such as weakness, pressure, dizziness and constant headaches, Charles, who had never previously been absent for even a single day, was unable to return to his Senate seat for three-and-a-half years.[29]

The attacker, though a complete stranger to Charles, was well known to the Southerners present in the Senate chamber. He was Preston Brooks, then a U.S. Representative from South Carolina. Preston was a 36-year-old first cousin once removed of Judge Butler. But Preston and Andrew Butler were actually much closer on a personal level than their degree of consanguinity, by itself, would indicate. Judge Butler was in essence an uncle to Preston. Preston's father Whitfield Brooks, an Edgefield, South Carolina attorney and planter, lost his mother at a young age. After that his aunt Behethland Butler, Andrew Butler's mother, became a surrogate mother to Whitfield. So Preston's father Whitfield Brooks and Andrew Butler grew up like brothers. As they matured, they continued to have much in common. Both had careers in the law, and both lived near each other in Edgefield. During the 1840's, when ex-judge Andrew Butler was appointed to the U.S. Senate, Whitfield was a frequent visitor to the home shared by Judge Butler and his mother Behethland, whom Whitfield called "Aunt Butler." Judge Butler also frequently visited Whitfield's home. When he was away, he wrote frequent letters to Whitfield.

Andrew Butler also enjoyed a constant relationship with Preston, Whitfield's eldest son, whom he saw very frequently. Preston felt Judge Butler to be a friend, in addition to a close family member.[30] Preston and Judge Butler were political allies who grew even closer after Whitfield's 1851 death, at the period when both of them were living and working in Washington City, representing South Carolina in Congress.[31]

Preston had recognizable aspects of the persona of the terrorist. Basically, he grew up spoiled in a well-to-do family. He was demonstrably prone to over-the-top adoption of the cause of others. At age twenty, he was expelled from South Carolina College for trying to break his younger brother out of jail at gunpoint. Shortly afterwards, when his father Whitfield was accused by a brash young attorney and politician named Louis Wigfall of cowardice for avoiding his challenge to a duel, Preston himself, unsolicited, took up with Wigfall the matter of the duel. On November 11, 1840, the confrontation took place on an island in the Savannah River. Both men's first shots missed. But they both persisted, and both hit their adversary with their second shots. Wigfall's shot entered Preston's body near his spine, passed through his left hip, and then a fragment entered his left arm, shattering the bone. Preston lingered near death for a long time before finally recovering. Part of the bullet remained permanently lodged in his hip.[32]

Preston later engaged in military training and service, leading a company of volunteers from Edgefield who enlisted to fight in the Mexican War.[33] But his war duty turned out to be less than fully satisfactory to him. He had to return to South Carolina due to illness. During his absence his younger brother, Whitfield Brooks, Jr., suffered a battle wound that eventually proved fatal. His cousin, Pierce Mason Butler, was killed in action at the battle of Churubusco. Preston ultimately returned to Mexico, but never saw combat duty.[34]

In plotting his terrorist-style attack on Charles, Preston was egged on by defenders of the "slave power" (to use Charles's term for it) who felt that Charles's unrestrained condemnation of the institution of slavery in the halls of Congress could no longer just be laughed off, because it was becoming a threat to their inherited way of life. A coterie of Southerners in Washington, whose membership will never be fully known, seized on Preston's close relationship with Andrew Butler as a pretext to assert a sense of outraged family "honor" over Charles's somewhat vulgar lampooning of Butler in his "Crime Against Kansas" speech.

Chapter 13: A Brutal Beating in the Senate

Convincing evidence, including Preston's own account, strongly indicates that Preston himself never even heard Charles's speech.[35] Judge Butler was absent from Washington at the time, as Charles noted in the speech, so he also did not hear what Charles said. Nor did he protest it to Preston. Preston might have glanced over the printed text of the first day of Charles's speech, but the strong inference from the actions and words of Representative Keitt, mentioned above, and of Representative Henry Edmundson of Virginia, as well as their subsequent defense of Preston's act on the floor of the House, is that they were in fact part of a conspiracy that devised and coordinated Preston's attack. These "slave power" devotees eagerly volunteered to act as Preston's "seconds" in a summary "punishment" of the super nerd Charles for his insolence.[36]

Reaction to the savage attack on Charles was highly polarized. Outside the South, the American public reacted with strong revulsion. The attack produced a prodigious sensation in Washington City. People were almost as angered at the Senate's rather blasé response as they were at the assault itself. The fact that anybody in a position of authority could justify such a cowardly surprise attack on an unarmed nonviolent statesman was a shocking revelation. The Senate appointed an "investigating" committee composed entirely of Charles's political opponents. This committee ruled that while the attack was a violation of the privileges of the Senate, the Senate had no jurisdiction to punish it. Any question of punishment was left to the House, of which Preston Brooks was a member.[37]

More politically balanced than the Senate, the House appointed a committee that lacked a majority of "slave power" members. This committee conducted a more thorough investigation. After hearing all the witnesses who agreed to come forward, the House committee recommended that Brooks be expelled, and that Keitt and Edmundson be censured. Members of the House rose to oppose this discipline, having the temerity to argue that Charles "deserved a good whipping." Notwithstanding, a majority of the full House voted to expel Preston Brooks and to censure Keitt. But they acquitted Edmundson, who was outside the Senate chamber during the attack. However, due to virtually unanimous opposition from Southern representatives, the vote fell short of the two-thirds majority required for the sanctions to take effect. Nevertheless, Brooks and Keitt were offended by the result. Both ostentatiously resigned, only to be rapidly returned to their posts by the near-unanimous vote of their South Carolina constituents.[38]

Representative Robert Hall of Massachusetts expressed a lucid evaluation of the attack and its aftermath in addressing the Speaker on the floor of the House, July 12, 1856:[39]

> Sir, the evidence ... shows that this attack was calmly premeditated ... It is not denied that the assault was violent; and notwithstanding the attempt of the gentleman from North Carolina to turn the whole into ridicule, and the adroit mystification of the physician's testimony by the gentleman from South Carolina, the whole proof goes to show that it was a case of unusual and aggravated violence. Sir, if the assault was not designed to destroy life, and I do not think it was, it was designed so to disgrace the Senator as effectually to destroy him in future influence, and to paralyze further exertion in the discharge of his high duties. It was designed to brutalize him under the influence of fear, and to strike from his brow his crown of manliness, and to crush down his spirit. The natural effect of this act of Mr. BROOKS was to deprive the Senate of the services and influence of one of its most distinguished members – to defraud a State of her fair representation – to insult the people who formed the constituency of Mr. SUMNER.

Chapter 13: A Brutal Beating in the Senate

Sir, this is not to be regarded as a mere personal quarrel – a simple congressional broil – a fracas between individual foes. The tone of levity which gentlemen have permitted themselves to use when endeavoring to make this representation, deserves sharp rebuke. No, sir, this striking down of a Senator in his place, within the very Senate-house itself, and for words spoken in that place under the sanction of the Constitution, is a graver offense than this. It is alike an indignity to an ancient Commonwealth, and an insult to her sovereignty, which must not pass unavenged. And then, sir, above and beyond all this, the transaction assumes a graver aspect, as a violence done to the great principles which underlie the fabric of this Government.

….

Sir, freedom of debate is the very breath of representative government.

Chapter 14: Fleeing to Escape the Peace

The headlines grabbed by the attack on Charles deflected the nation's attention away from John Brown's ruthless murders at Pottawatomie Creek.[1] John probably knew very well that, by choosing the path of a murderous terrorist, he would be an outlaw until the day of his death. Indeed, it is a prototypical terrorist act to cross this psychological Rubicon. From this moment forward, John had no more roots in ownership of Kansas farm land. From the night of the massacre until his ultimate final departure from Kansas, John Brown adopted the lifestyle of an underground guerrilla leader. Most of the time he holed up in secret "camps." He took advantage of the lawlessness of "Bleeding Kansas," a good part of which he himself had provoked, to avoid being brought to justice.

Posses scoured the area looking for the Pottawatomie massacre perpetrators. They did not catch John or any of his other followers who had taken part in the massacre, but his sons John Jr., Jason, and five others not involved who remained in the Brown's Station settlement were taken into custody by a force of Missouri militia. John Jr., who had lost his mental equilibrium over the massacre as we have seen, was chained to a post and beaten. Then the seven prisoners were shackled "two

CHAPTER 14: FLEEING TO ESCAPE THE PEACE

and two," in the manner of a slave coffle, and driven 75 miles on foot to Tecumseh. At issue was whether these men should be charged with treason for forcibly resisting the territorial laws. U.S. Commissioner Edward Hoogland, after a preliminary hearing, released Jason and four others, but bound over John Jr. and one other man to face the charge. When Jason returned to Brown's Station, he found everything in ruins. The Brown cabins and other buildings had been burned, and all the cattle and horses taken.[2]

From hiding, John received news of the reprisals being carried out due to the massacre. John continued his attacks on what he regarded as the enemy. On Friday, May 30, about seventy-five head of cattle belonging to "Dutch" Henry Sherman were stolen, probably by John and his band.[3] John then agreed with other free state militant chieftains to move northwards, in the direction of Lawrence, to carry out more retaliatory forays. Near a town called Palmyra, John and his sons set up a secret camp for guerrilla fighters, dubbed "Camp Brown." The fighters who filtered into Camp Brown lived with great austerity, surviving on stolen cattle, bread, and creek water.[4]

To James Redpath, a freelance journalist intent on covering the Kansas carnage who stumbled upon Camp Brown, John gave a hearty welcome. But he "forbade any conversation" on the Pottawatomie affair. John declared to Redpath that God was on his side; and that he would prevail because he had god-fearing men with strong principles standing with him. John's men reported to Redpath that John himself would frequently "retire to the densest solitudes, and after these retirings, he would say that the Lord had directed him in visions what to do."[5]

On June 1, John took his followers to nearby Prairie City to join forces with a band of fighters led by Samuel Shore, another militia leader. That night, they encountered and took prisoner four scouts from a group that was out looking for John. Combining his own men with Shore's, the next morning John led twenty-six volunteers in an assault at dawn on this force of roughly equal size, composed of pro-slavery irregulars deputized by the U.S. Marshal to hunt the Pottawatomie terrorists. The force was under the command of Henry Clay Pate. Little did Pate suspect the terrorists would get to him first. Pate was only 23 years old. His naivete and lack of experience would be telling in the encounter. After a three-hour skirmish dubbed the "Battle of Black Jack," in which several of John's fighters were badly wounded and many more of them ran off, Pate, fearing the arrival of free state reinforcements, sent out one of his men with a white flag to seek negotiations.[6]

John refused to speak with the white flag messenger. He demanded that Pate personally come out to negotiate. Pate blundered by doing it. Completely disregarding the sanctity of the white flag, John took Pate prisoner at gunpoint. By using Pate as a hostage, holding a gun to his head, and threatening to blow his brains out, John forced all of Pate's men to lay down their weapons. All twenty-five were then taken prisoner by John and his men.[7]

John next used a tactic often used by terrorists when they take hostages. He forced them to sign a statement he felt he could use for his purposes. John had Pate and his second-in-command Walter B. Brocket sign an "agreement" to the effect that Pate and the other prisoners would be exchanged on a one-for-one basis for a like number of free state prisoners then held in custody of the territorial government, including specifically, John's sons John Jr. and Jason. This remarkable document, signed under duress, totally disregarded that neither Pate nor Brocket had any authority to agree to release anyone held in lawful custody by the government.[8]

But before any further negotiations around a hostage exchange could occur, a force of fifty U.S. Army mounted troops commanded by Colonel Edwin Sumner and including

CHAPTER 14: FLEEING TO ESCAPE THE PEACE

Lieutenant Jeb Stuart[9] came upon Camp Brown. They took John into custody and freed his prisoners. One very fortuitous circumstance for John was that Sumner was Charles's cousin. In fact, Edwin and Charles were not merely cousins, but had been personally close from boyhood. Edwin's father Seth Sumner had acted as the guardian of Charles's father Charles for a long period of time. In that capacity, Seth Sumner supervised the elder Charles's education, including his studies at Harvard.[10] Charles continued to be friends with Edwin and he had, in fact, been out to visit Edwin during the summer of 1855, when he went on a tour of the West.[11] Edwin Sumner, like everyone else, was well aware of the brutal beating that had just been inflicted on Charles in the name of silencing his criticism of "the Crime against Kansas." Even though his boss was Secretary of War Jefferson Davis (the future President of the Confederacy), Edwin was inclined to avoid taking sides in favor of the Pierce administration in the Kansas struggle. Although he of course refused to honor John's coerced "prisoner exchange" agreement, and although he ordered John to disband his force at once, he then released John and his men. If Colonel Sumner indeed had any inkling that his prisoner John was under a federal court indictment for the terrorist Pottawatomie murders committed less than two weeks earlier, or that he had any responsibility to take John in to face charges on an indictment and accompanying arrest warrant that had already been handed down by the territorial federal court, he did not let on.[12]

John was extremely lucky (and, indeed, he explicitly attributed his good fortune to the hand of God) that he was not arrested and hanged when captured on this occasion, due to his guilt in orchestrating the Pottawatomie massacre. Despite the much publicized offering of hefty rewards for his capture, this would be the only time the terrorist killer of Pottawatomie would ever find himself in federal custody prior to his final attack of October 1859.

After the Pottawatomie massacre, Kansas became destabilized in a major way. Settlers did not sleep well, fearing more attacks by midnight marauders.[13] The naked outrage of John's cold-blooded execution of unarmed sleeping noncombatants touched off reverberating waves of crimes by both sides. Over time, the story of events on the night of May 24 was told in different ways to different people. Ambivalence about bringing John to justice spread fairly quickly within the free state community, since many were sympathetic with John's cause, and since they became ever more prone to overlook his guilt in the face of vicious reprisals committed by pro-slavery partisans.[14] In the retelling, John's Pottawatomie victims were demonized as bloodthirsty villains bent on sooner or later exterminating the Browns. So, their killing was justified in retrospect as an act of self-defense.[15] The feelings of horror induced by the massacre loosened normal civilized restraints on violent behavior. Crimes, particularly property crimes like arson and theft, became much more commonplace throughout the territory. These crimes were particularly cruel because of the abject rural poverty in which the average Kansas colonist family typically lived while trying to scratch out a living from previously untilled ground. Stealing their cattle, horses, and other livestock, generally speaking, placed these settlers in real jeopardy of starving to death. Destroying their homes placed them in real jeopardy of freezing to death. Whenever such a heinous crime was committed by partisans of one side, it encouraged the opposing partisans to retaliate in kind.[16]

In the wake of his narrow escape after being taken into custody by Colonel Sumner, John followed his primordial terrorist instincts. Adopting a classic terrorist behavior, he went underground. John spent the summer of 1856 hiding out in the Kansas bush, living off what his guerrilla band could steal from pro-slavery settlers and merchants and, in his words, "dwelling

CHAPTER 14: FLEEING TO ESCAPE THE PEACE

with the serpents of the rocks and the wild beasts of the wilderness."[17] During this lawless period, John's band was just one of perhaps a dozen "free state" militias that emerged in Kansas. Each one typically numbered twenty or thirty fighters, and each was led by its own chieftain. United in their hatred of the pro-slavery "ruffians," these bands had little organized coordination with each other. They lived off the land and they essentially operated independently, coming together only when a major confrontation with pro-slavery forces was contemplated. One such leader of a free state band was James Holmes. On the night of August 12–13, 1856, Holmes led a midnight raid against the home of Martin White and others of his neighbors who had not proven themselves sufficiently "free state." Ten "proslavery horses" were commandeered at gunpoint. On another occasion free state raiders, after driving off the inhabitants, and after stealing everything of any value, thoroughly burned a newly-founded settlement called "New Georgia," near Osawatomie.[18] This typified the rapine behavior of paramilitary forces on both sides. In the violence-racked vicinity of Lawrence, the chaos was so horrifying it caused the latest territorial Governor, Wilson Shannon, to be sacked. On his way out, he attempted to negotiate a "peace treaty" and a prisoner exchange, which brought about a very temporary and uneasy truce. John, who had been among the paramilitary leaders operating in this theater, headed south to the vicinity of Osawatomie.[19]

Just as Lawrence was the de facto headquarters of free state settlement in north Kansas, the town of Osawatomie was the de facto leading free state settlement in the central part of the state. As roving bands of marauders proved essentially impossible for authorities to catch, Osawatomie became a tempting target for reprisals by "pro-government" paramilitary forces. To protect against this, Osawatomie was informally garrisoned by the free state chieftains. However, their bands were not under any semblance of a unified command. They also needed to freeboot off settlers characterized as "the enemy" to sustain themselves. An opportunity to do so presented itself on August 25, when it was discovered that a large group of "Georgians" were camped in Linn County, approximately 10 miles due south of Osawatomie. The free state guerrilla chieftains quickly went to investigate. The next morning, they surrounded the camp and attacked it by surprise, quickly overwhelming the defenders. Besides taking thirteen prisoners, the free state chieftains obtained a nice booty: forty horses and mules, three wagons, a quantity of guns, ammunition, and camp equipment.[20]

John himself was not part of this capture, because he remained behind in Osawatomie at the time it happened. But that night, he traveled with his band to the "Georgian" camp, prepared to join in the attack. By then, the camp was already subjugated, occupied, and guarded by other free state chieftains. In the darkness and confusion, the infliction of serious casualties from friendly fire was narrowly avoided.[21] No doubt disappointed he did not get to share in the plunder of the camp, the next day John gathered a squad of approximately twenty-five free state militants and took them further south, toward Fort Scott, to do some more marauding. One of his victims this time was the wife of John's pro-slavery militia "namesake," John E. Brown, who was away at the time trying to search out and confront the free state militias. While robbing Mrs. Brown of all her cattle, as well as all of the men's clothes found in the house, John consoled her with the claim that he "never hurts women and children as her husband does." Indeed, John's admirers could later boast of his taking the high road by refraining from burning down the John E. Brown home, which was the frequent fate of reprisal victims in "Bleeding Kansas."[22]

On Thursday, August 28, John returned to Osawatomie with his newly-assembled herd of 150 cattle. The town's

CHAPTER 14: FLEEING TO ESCAPE THE PEACE

residents were extremely uneasy at the idea of him entering town with such a large trove of loot. They induced him to make camp north of the town, across the Marais des Cygnes river.[23] But this would not be enough to spare the town the wrath of the cycle of violence. The acting Kansas territorial Governor, Daniel Woodson, issued a proclamation of insurrection.[24] In response, a force of approximately 400 "pro-government" volunteer fighters was assembled. Under the command of John W. Reid, an attorney and Mexican War veteran who was christened "General" for the occasion, this force marched on Osawatomie on the morning of Saturday, August 30. Martin White, because he was a local who knew the terrain well, acted as the squadron's advance scout. As Reid's forces approached the town, they encountered three free state men near the home of Samuel Adair, John's brother-in-law. One of them was John's son, Frederick Brown. Frederick, who gave signs of being mentally disturbed and was known for acting out in a wild fashion, had in the past been a sentry for Camp Brown. Later, John would claim Frederick was not serving in any such capacity on the morning of August 30. Perhaps he was just up early feeding horses.[25] The advancing "pro-government" force, however, recognized Frederick as being a rebel. He was shot dead through the heart by Martin White.[26] Another deadly attack was on.

John, with his band of about fifteen stalwart followers he dubbed his "Kansas regulars," was camped north of the Marais des Cygnes having breakfast when word came that the town was under assault. Quickly he crossed the river and assumed the command of the rag-tag defenders of Osawatomie, consisting of a few local civilians and the band of another free state chieftain named James Cline, approximately the same size as John's Kansas regulars. When they saw General Reid's imposing army cresting a small hill to the west, John and everybody else immediately realized that their relative handful had no chance of holding the town against 400 men armed with cannon. He and the other defenders left the town and stationed themselves to the north, in the woods bordering the Marais des Cygnes. From there, they kept up a long-range rifle fire, which harassed Reid's men as they marched into town. John later exaggerated greatly when he claimed that seventy or eighty of the attackers were killed or wounded. General Reid's report stated that five of his men were wounded.[27] Cline's militia soon ran out of ammunition and retreated across the river. Reid sent part of his force around to flank his remaining opponents. After about 15–20 minutes of skirmishing, John decided to withdraw. By that time, the attackers were close enough to fire on John and his men as they fled. One was killed, and several more were wounded, while crossing the river.

John managed to get across the waterway and escape, although at some point in the flight he was struck by a gunshot. The ball did not penetrate the skin and merely caused a bruise. John attributed this survival to help from "the Lord." The Lord was not so helpful to the residents of Osawatomie, however. By nightfall, twenty-nine homes in the town were put to the torch and destroyed by fire.[28] According to his son Jason, who had fought alongside him, John watched the flames in tears. He pronounced, "I have only a short time to live – and only one death to die, and I will die fighting for this cause."[29]

The pro-government forces, including General Reid, half-believed and half-hoped that John, the feared terrorist, had been killed in the fight. But the Lord was, as he firmly believed, on John's side. Defying published reports of his death, John spent two days lying low with a few companions on a ranch near Osawatomie. Then he made his way out of the area and headed north to Lawrence, where the pro-government militiamen had relocated. When he arrived on Sunday, September 7, news of the "battle of Osawatomie" had preceded him. Upon his arrival John received cheers from the free state leaders assembled there. The free state chieftains, including James Lane, were at that time busy deliberating what to do. They were hanging in the balance, torn between their desire to raid and pillage nearby pro-slavery settlements and their need to defend Lawrence against imminent attack by Reid's "pro-slavery" army.[30]

An unexpected event rather quickly changed the dynamics of the whole situation. On September 7, the same day John arrived in Lawrence, John Geary was appointed the new Governor of Kansas territory. Geary was cut from an altogether sterner cloth than his predecessors. This new Governor would not view himself as a tool to implement the slave state destiny that had been envisioned for Kansas when Congress passed the Kansas–Nebraska Act. Rather, Geary saw his mission as being to restore civilized life to Kansas, without regard to the slavery controversy. He set out to accomplish this goal using a firmly clenched fist wrapped inside a glove of diplomacy. Upon his arrival in the territory on Tuesday, September 9, Geary immediately ordered the release of "Free State Governor" Charles Robinson as well as John Brown, Jr., two high-profile political prisoners who had been held in custody without charges all summer long. Then he personally went into Lawrence to meet with Robinson and other free state leaders. At first, they remained very suspicious of anybody "pro-government."[31] But Geary's actions soon convinced them he meant business.

Geary arrived in the town of Lawrence early in the morning, just after sunrise on Saturday, December 13. He met for two hours with Robinson. Later that day, Robinson wrote John a brief note:[32]

Captain John Brown,

Dear Sir, ... Governor Geary has been here and *talks very well.* He promises to protect us, etc. There will be no attempt to arrest anyone for a few days, and I think no attempt to arrest you is contemplated by him. He talks of letting the past be forgotten, so far as may be, and of commencing anew. If convenient, can you not come to town and see us? I will then tell you all that the Governor said, and talk of some other matters.

Very respectfully,

C. Robinson

The newly freed John Jr. was by now recovered from his bout of "insanity." He was always more willing to engage with political solutions than was his father. He wrote his own note to John on the back of Robinson's note. It read:

All seem to be pleased with Geary. They think that while he must *talk* of enforcing Territorial laws, he has intended to let them lie a dead letter; says no Territorial officer or court shall arrest or try. Although he says in his proclamation that all armed men must disband, yet he says our men better hold together a few days until he can clear the Territory of the *militia*; requests our men to enroll themselves, choose *their own officers*, and consider him as chief and themselves as his guard. I am inclined to the belief that unless something unusual shall turn up within a few days, you had better return home, as I have no doubt an attempt will be made to arrest *you*, as well as Lane, whom Geary says he is under obligation to arrest.

Robinson was favorably influenced toward John, at this time, by the demeanor and attitude of John Jr., who had been in prison with him near Lecompton. Robinson was so worried about the threat from what John Jr. referred to as "the militia" that he welcomed help from any quarter, no matter what baggage might be attached to it. John did indeed come into Lawrence town. He met with Robinson the following day. Robinson presented John with a glowing letter of praise and thanksgiving that the rumors of his death had proved false.[33]

Chapter 14: Fleeing to Escape the Peace

Captain John Brown,

My Dear Sir, ... I take this opportunity to express to you my sincere gratification that the late report that you were among the killed at the battle of Osawatomie is incorrect. Your course, so far as I have been informed, has been such as to merit the highest praise from every patriot, and I cheerfully accord to you my heartfelt thanks for your prompt, efficient, and timely action against the invaders of our rights and the murderers of our citizens. History will give your name a proud place on her pages, and posterity will pay homage to your heroism in the cause of God and humanity. Trusting that you will remain in Kansas, and serve "during the war" the cause you have done so much to sustain, and with earnest prayers for your health, and protection from the shafts of death that so thickly beset your path, I subscribe myself,

Very respectfully, your obedient servant,

C. Robinson

To the settlers of Kansas, ... If possible, please render Captain John Brown all the assistance he may require in defending Kansas from invaders and outlaws, and you will confer a service upon your co-laborer and fellow citizen.

C. Robinson

It was a letter Robinson would come to rue.

The force of 2,700 pro-slavery men under the command of Reid, huge by Kansas standards, advanced slowly from the east in the direction of Lawrence. "Vice-President" Atchison was among their leaders. A skirmish lasting about an hour occurred in the afternoon, when an advance contingent of Reid's army was greeted by about 100 free state defenders who came out to snipe at them from long range. Meanwhile, John roamed Lawrence's primitive fortifications, giving encouragement to the militiamen waiting there. But the decisive event occurred at around 9 p.m. when Governor Geary was able to maneuver a contingent of U.S. Army troops into a peacekeeping position on the hill in between Lawrence and its would-be attackers. This military intervention poured cold water on any idea of another sack of the town. General Reid's militia went back to their homes.[34]

Governor Geary then devised the innovative idea of swearing in both selected free state chieftains and selected pro-slavery militia leaders into the federal forces. He required them all to take oaths to cooperate and get along with each other.[35] The tactic proved effective in co-opting several of the main freebooters, and in getting the rest under a modicum of control. Geary gave an order for John's arrest, which caused him to heed his son's advice to leave the Territory. By September 30, Geary could report, with some pride, "Peace now reigns in Kansas."[36] John left the Territory on October 5. On October 7, the commander of the federal troops at Geary's disposal reported that he had just barely missed capturing "the notorious Osawatomie outlaw" as he crossed the border heading into Nebraska. John continued to the town of Tabor, Iowa, a favorable staging point for expeditions to and from Kansas by free state partisans. John's departure was no doubt one happening Geary had in mind when he announced on October 10: "Many notorious and troublesome agitators, claiming to belong to all parties, have left the Territory, and the beneficent influence of their absence is being already very sensibly felt."[37] Although sporadic assassinations and depredations continued from both sides, over the course of the months to follow Geary's persistent efforts at pacification of Kansas slowly bore fruit.[38]

John was not interested in being part of a peace process. Nor did he intend to become involved in any efforts to establish a properly representative civil government. John was separated by an invisible impenetrable barrier from political men like Robinson. Robinson and such did not trust John, because he was uncontrollable. John knew it.[39] Unlike them, John felt violence was the only solution. From now on, his obsession would be terrorist-style attacks on persons he identified with the institution of slavery.

Of course, John kept that focus almost entirely to himself. It was easy enough for him to don the public mantle of the abolitionist war veteran. During the months after his departure from Kansas, John spent his time on the road. Instead of returning to his wife and younger children, still living by themselves in the Adirondacks, he went on tour, raising money and weapons from supporters of the Kansas free state cause. When he learned that 200 Sharps rifles intended for

Signed portrait of John Brown, 1857

defensive use had been shipped to Tabor by a combined effort of the Massachusetts Kansas Committee and the National Kansas Committee, John set his sights on getting control of these weapons. In Chicago John was fitted, at the expense of supporters, with a suit of fine clothes. John did not do this because he had abandoned his plain and frugal lifestyle, but rather, because he wanted to make a good impression on well-heeled audiences. John then traveled back East. In Ohio he stopped long enough to obtain a letter of recommendation from a second prominent political leader, Republican Governor Salmon P. Chase. Chase conveniently wrote his endorsement on the back of Robinson's September 14 letter. John then stopped overnight in Rochester to have dinner with Frederick Douglass.[40]

John arrived in Boston on January 2, 1857. There Charles Sumner was laid up in bed, still recuperating from his beating at the hands of Preston Brooks. Friends of Charles would make a natural receptive audience for John's message that violence was the only viable answer to the slave power. Key among these friends of Charles were: Samuel Howe, Charles's longtime friend and mentor; his wife, Julia Ward Howe; and Theodore Parker, the firebrand scholar-minister. Samuel Howe and Parker had been involved in the forcible attempt at rescuing Anthony Burns from slavery, mentioned above.[41] These were all dedicated abolitionists deeply offended by the brazen assault on Charles. Aided in making connections to the wealthy abolitionists by a young admirer named Franklin Sanborn, John immediately commenced a whirlwind effort to raise money to support the armed struggle in Kansas. On January 5, at the home of Parker, John met Lloyd Garrison. The two of them debated, far into the night, over their deep disagreement about the method of promoting abolition. John quoted Old Testament passages on the deadly vindication of God's wrath, while Lloyd cited the New Testament in support of nonresistance. Their dialogue attracted a small group of listeners.[42] On January 7, John met Amos Lawrence, who would provide John with modest financial support. On January 9, John attended a dinner, set up by Sanborn, at the home of George Stearns, the chairman of the Massachusetts Kansas Committee (MKC). John charmed Stearns and his family with tales of the Battle of Black Jack. By the end of the evening, Stearns was ready to support putting John in charge of the MKC's 200 Sharps Rifles stored in Tabor, plus contributing $500 toward his Kansas expenses.[43]

CHAPTER 14: FLEEING TO ESCAPE THE PEACE

At a meeting of the National Kansas Committee (NKC) in New York City held January 23 and 24, John was the keynote speaker. He won confirmation from the NKC of his control of the free state arsenal of 200 Sharps rifles. The NKC also pledged to raise $5,000 for John's support, although very little of this money was ever actually paid. The support for John was voted in spite of a vehement warning by an NKC agent who had actually spent time in Kansas that John was much too ultra and that the Committee would not approve of what was done by him with the weapons.[44]

On February 18, John made another speech, this time in Boston before the Massachusetts Legislature. Very little was known in Boston at this time about the Pottawatomie murders, and still less about John's connection with them.[45] As part of his presentation, John movingly displayed chains he said had been used to bind John Brown, Jr. while he was a prisoner. He told the legislators what Kansas needed was men who "fear God too much to fear anything human." He would often recycle this turn of phrase throughout his fundraising tour.[46]

Yet, during the course of John's thus-far successful foray into professional abolitionism, several things happened that unmistakably betray John's true state of mind and intent. These things had very little to do with Kansas. In the same New York NKC meeting in which he received control over the 200 Sharps rifles, John gave a very curious answer to a question. When asked whether he would use these arms to invade Missouri and attack people in slave states – something the NKC pointedly did not authorize – he made this evasive reply:[47]

> I am no adventurer. You all know me. You are acquainted with my history. You know what I have done in Kansas. I do not expose my plans. No one knows them but myself, except perhaps one. I will not be interrogated; if you wish to give me anything I want you to give it freely. I have no other purpose but

to serve the cause of liberty.

In early March of 1857, during a visit to a small town near his Connecticut birthplace, John encountered a blacksmith named Charles Blair. He began negotiations that culminated in a written contract for Blair to fabricate, within three months, 1,000 six-foot long ash spears, each equipped with an iron spear head, for a discounted price of $1 each. John spent $550 of the Kansas aid money he had raised to make the deposit on these spears. They were odd weapons indeed, and they had no rational use in the Kansas conflict. All the Kansas protagonists were adept with firearms. John's secret plan, for which he was once again misappropriating precious funds entrusted to him for other purposes, was to place these spears in the hands of freshly recruited African Americans during a Nat Turner-style terror attack.[48] John himself described the spears as "a cheap but effectual weapon to place in the hands of entirely unskilled and unpractised men, which will not easily get out of order, and require no ammunition."[49]

In April 1857, John finally returned, after an absence totaling eighteen months, to the family homestead in North Elba. He brought with him a gravestone he had bought in Connecticut. He paid to have his dead son Frederick's name carved upon it, but he gave instructions to leave enough room for another inscription. He directed that his own name, and the date of his death, should be added in that space, when he should fall, as expected, in the conflict with the institution of slavery.[50]

Chapter 15: A Terrorist Replaces an Un-Terrorist

Terrorists can be visionaries. And, as we have seen, John Brown had a tendency toward a disconnect with reality, particularly in business dealings. His fundamental lack of sound judgment came to the fore once more with his decision to hire Hugh Forbes to function as the head drillmaster for the terrorist training camp he intended to launch at Tabor, Iowa.

Hugh was a credentialed revolutionary. However, had John researched the matter more carefully, he would have realized that Hugh's prior record in freedom fighting was largely associated with defeat. Born in England in 1808, Hugh attended Oxford University, graduating in 1826. He then received a commission in the Coldstream Regiment of Foot Guards, a storied unit in British military history. He was already retired from that army service, and was living a

Hugh Forbes

bourgeois life with an Italian wife and daughter in Siena, Italy, when the "republican" revolutionary fervor of 1848 broke out all across Europe.[1] In the northeastern region of Italy anchored by Venice, the Austrian-based government was deposed, and the "Republic of San Marco" proclaimed, on March 22, 1848.

At the end of April 1848, Hugh left Siena and volunteered to serve as an officer in the republican forces who were rallying to resist Austrian troops marching to put down the revolt. But the rebel Republic of San Marco, like so many companion upstart republics that popped up throughout Europe in the 1848–1849 period, proved short-lived. One by one, the Republic's territory and cities were reoccupied by Austria's military, until only the island city of Venice and two fortress outposts remained under republican rule. Hugh returned home at that time to Siena, but he had caught the republican fever. In October 1848, he embarked for Palermo to assist in defending the revolutionary republican government in Sicily. Once again, due to his military training and experience, Hugh was given command of untrained volunteers. But they were fighting in a losing cause. By the following April, the Palermo republican government surrendered to forces of the reconquering Spanish-based Bourbon kingdom. Hugh left Sicily and returned to the mainland, where the "Republic of Rome" had been proclaimed in the Papal States by Giuseppe Mazzini and others on February 9, 1849.[2] An international coalition of French, Spanish, and Austrian armies soon converged on Rome with the intent to restore order. By May, the only major Italian cities still under republican rule were Venice, Rome, and the Adriatic city of Ancona, and all of them were under siege. Ancona finally surrendered to Austrian forces on June 19, 1849. Hugh took command of the remnants of volunteer defenders, approximately 900-strong and mostly non-Italians, who made their way to the town of Terni, 63 miles north of Rome.

The valiant defense of Rome in 1849 by republican forces under the command of Giuseppe Garibaldi justly deserves its

CHAPTER 15: A TERRORIST REPLACES AN UN-TERRORIST

place in the pantheon of modern democratic revolutions. However, by July 1, the revolt's political leaders, including Mazzini, lost their nerve and decided to surrender. But Garibaldi, the fabled "hero of the Two Worlds," refused to accept defeat. With his pregnant South American wife Anita and an intrepid little force including some veterans of his prior freedom-fighting wars in Brazil and Argentina, Garibaldi abandoned the besieged capital on July 1, 1849. He began a brilliant, circuitous retreat through the surrounding hills. Eluding pursuit from all three foreign armies, by July 8 Garibaldi made it to Terni where he linked up with Hugh's legion. Hugh was not very popular with the citizens of Terni, who found him highly eccentric in his characteristic white English summer clothes and top hat. But Garibaldi's unexpected arrival revived their flagging republican spirits.[3]

Garibaldi had never previously met Hugh, but he came to appreciate his honesty and courage as the republican army continued its retreat northward from Terni. Garibaldi hoped to relieve the siege of Venice. He took his motley brigade, which included Hugh and his adult son Hugh Forbes, Jr., on another spectacular forced march over the high Apennine range that divides Italy like a spine. Several times, Hugh led detachments that successfully screened Garibaldi's army as it avoided major engagements with the Austrians. On July 31, Garibaldi's exhausted remaining army of about 1,500 arrived at the independent principality of San Marino. There, Garibaldi obtained a temporary respite from his pursuers. The leaders of San Marino negotiated a surrender for Garibaldi, which included the acceptance of an exile to the United States, but the local Austrian commander informed him the deal had to be ratified by his superiors in Bologna. This delay afforded Garibaldi a pretext to bolt once more, which he did that same night with a small cadre of 250 dedicated followers, including Hugh, who sneaked their way past the enemy lines.[4]

Garibaldi was even more experienced and accomplished as a naval tactician than he was as a commander of land forces. His latest plan involved the seizure of a port on the Adriatic from which to move his men by water to Venice. But his devoted wife Anita had taken sick during the long arduous retreat from Rome. Her condition, by now, was desperate. When Garibaldi's small force took over the lightly defended coastal town of Cesenatico on the night of August 1, Hugh was placed in charge of a rearguard detachment whose job was to cover the launch of a flotilla of vessels which Garibaldi commandeered from local fishermen. Garibaldi's plan, as usual, worked fairly well. But the launch was extremely difficult because of stormy conditions prevailing that night. It took a long time. Hugh had his men put up barricades at every possible exit from the town, with the objective of keeping the Austrians from learning what was happening. By doing so, he bought Garibaldi just enough time to get Anita and his remaining fighters loaded into boats, and to depart. This action, which probably saved Garibaldi's life, later made Hugh a minor Italian national patriot. Hugh was captured that night aboard a vessel that was heading north.

Garibaldi's nautical venture made it as far as Comacchio, just north of Ravenna, where Garibaldi went ashore. There, aided by some local partisans, he dramatically refused to flee. In hiding, he insisted on staying by Anita's bedside until she died, after a prolonged agony, on the night of August 4. Garibaldi miraculously escaped, but his top lieutenants were captured and summarily executed by firing squad. The Austrians, however, decided to spare Hugh. They merely consigned him to prison. Efforts by the British embassy and Hugh's wife eventually combined to persuade the Austrian government to release him two months later, in October 1849.[5]

Hugh was now *persona non grata* in Italy, being effectively exiled. In early 1850 he headed across the ocean to New York City.[6] There, over the next few years, he taught fencing and worked a variety of writing jobs, including translating, editing a newspaper, and reporting for the *New York Tribune*. He authored a two-volume work, entitled *Manual of the Patriotic Volunteer*, which was a sort of training guide for irregular forces engaged in revolution. It was this book, as well as the reputation earned through Hugh's New York and New England speaking engagements, that attracted John's attention to Hugh in the early part of 1857.[7]

On April 1, 1857, John instructed William Callender, a cashier of the State Bank of Connecticut, to pay to the order of Hugh Forbes the sum of $600. Hugh drew out his money in two installments at the end of April, directing it be paid to his bank in New York City.[8] This $600 was an advance on the sum of $100 per month that John promised to pay Hugh to act as drillmaster for his band of raiders.[9] Out of this advance, Hugh sent $120 to his wife who was living in Paris. Much of the rest he spent on publishing and promoting his book. Hugh lingered in New York, hoping to raise enough money from the book and from his venture training John's revolutionaries to bring his wife and family to the United States.[10]

In a note dated June 21, 1857, John expressed impatience, demanding that Hugh return the $600 if he was not prepared to come to Tabor immediately. Joseph Bryant, who was acting as an intermediary between John and Hugh at this time, did not deliver this letter to Hugh. He likely did not wish to trigger Hugh's volatile personality. Instead, after meeting with Hugh, he reported to John that Hugh planned to depart for Tabor in the next ten days, after finishing work on his book. John was very busy himself raising funds to support his own wife and family, an effort that caused serious discord with George Stearns, one of his important financial backers. John and Hugh both headed west to Iowa at roughly the same time, during July.[11]

When he arrived at Tabor on August 9,[12] Hugh found he

had nobody there to train except John and his son Owen. He and John thus had plenty of time on their hands to debate how best to attack the institution of slavery. Hugh's proposal (as he later summarized it) was:[13]

> With carefully selected colored and white persons to organize along the Northern slave frontier (Virginia and Maryland especially) a series of stampedes of slaves, each one of which would carry off in one night and from the same place twenty or fifty slaves; this to be effected once or twice a month, and eventually once or twice a week along non-contiguous parts of the line; if possible without conflict, only resorting to force if attacked. Slave women, as accustomed to field labor, would be nearly as useful as men. Everything being in readiness to pass on the fugitives, they could be sent with such speed to Canada that pursuit would be hopeless. In Canada preparations were to be made for their instruction and employment. Any disaster which might befall a stampede would at the utmost compromise those who might be involved in that single one; therefore, we were not bound in good faith to the abolitionists (as we did not compromise that interest) to consult more than those engaged in the very project. Against the chance of loss by occasional accidents should be weighed the advantages of a series of successful "runs." Slave property would thus become untenable near the frontier; that frontier would be pushed more and more southward, and it might reasonably be expected that the excitement and irritation would impel the pro-slaveryites to commit some stupid blunders.

But John had a much different plan:[14]

> He proposed, with some twenty-five to fifty (colored and white mixed), well armed and bringing a quantity

CHAPTER 15: A TERRORIST REPLACES AN UN-TERRORIST

of spare arms, to beat up a slave quarter in Virginia. To this [Hugh] objected that, no preparatory notice having been given to the slaves (no notice could, with prudence, be given them), the invitation to rise might, unless they were already in a state of agitation, meet with no response, or a feeble one. To this [John] replied that he was sure of a response. He calculated that he could get on the first night from 200 to 500. Half, or thereabouts, of this first lot he proposed to keep with him, mounting 100 or so of them, and make a dash at Harper's Ferry manufactury, destroying what he could not carry off. The other men not of this party were to be subdivided into three, four, or five distinct parties, each under two or three of the original band, and would beat up other slavequarters, whence more men would be sent to join him.

[John] argued that were he pressed by United States troops, which after a few days might concentrate, he could easily maintain himself in the Alleghenies, and that his New England partisans would in the meantime call a Northern Convention to restore tranquillity and overthrow the pro-slavery administration.

Initially, John was pleased with Forbes, calling him a "very capable teacher."[15] But friction soon developed, because neither Hugh nor John was about to acquiesce to the plan of the other. Their characters differed at a very fundamental level. Hugh, although a revolutionary, lacked the personality of the terrorist. For instance, no terrorist could have possibly written *Manual of the Patriotic Volunteer*. It is an erudite essay crafted in the liberal style of a Montesquieu, filled throughout with historical references and footnoted to a variety of sources, ancient and modern. Hugh both assumes and advocates rational and civilized behavior on the part of the revolutionary troops and their leaders. The *Creed of the Patriotic Volunteer and Militia-Man* contained in Volume Two of Hugh's *Manual* contrasts most starkly with the *Catechism of a Revolutionary*, which would be co-authored in 1869 by Sergei Nechaev and Mikhail Bakhunin, and that would, indeed, be a savage manual for terrorists and their deliberately uncivilized methods of operation.[16]

Above all, Hugh was not suicidal. John's Harpers Ferry terrorist plan, as Hugh and others exposed to it immediately recognized, meant suicide.

John and Hugh stayed together in Tabor for less than three months. During that time, Kansas was relatively free of violence. There was sentiment in supporters of the free state cause, both locally and in the East, that John's armed presence in Kansas would do more harm than good. But John decided to return to Kansas anyway, to gather soldiers for his attack, principally from among disaffected veterans of the violent summer of 1856. He left Tabor for Kansas on November 2. That same day, Hugh left Tabor to head back to the East.[17]

John's visit to Kansas was productive. During a relatively brief sojourn, he reassembled remnants of his 1856 terrorist band, his "Kansas regulars." To them he added several important new recruits to the cause. One of these had a personality far more suited to terrorism than did Hugh. John would soon use him in place of Hugh to direct the training of his followers. This man was Aaron Dwight Stevens.

Aaron Stevens was born March 16, 1831 in Lisbon, Connecticut. His father, also named Aaron, was a stone mason by trade, but his passion was music.[18] After young Aaron's mother died, the elder Aaron married her sister, and had more children. He spent much of his time directing a church choir as the growing family moved to nearby Norwich, near the Rhode Island border. Young Aaron Stevens did not finish school. He dropped out at age 14. Two years later, at age 16, he ran away from home and exaggerated his age to enlist in a regiment

CHAPTER 15: A TERRORIST REPLACES AN UN-TERRORIST

called the First Massachusetts Volunteers that was being assembled to take part in the Mexican war.

Young Aaron Stevens indeed traveled to Mexico, but the First Massachusetts Volunteers did not see any major combat. The unit became known for rowdy and undisciplined behavior as it remained in rear-area garrison duty through much of the war, arriving in Mexico City only after the fighting had ended. Returning home to Norwich, Aaron apparently apprenticed as a machinist. However, he was sufficiently disenchanted with civilian life that on April 1, 1851, less than a month after his 20th birthday, he enlisted to become a mounted soldier in the United States Army.

Stevens was soon assigned to duty as a private in Company "F" of the "First Dragoons," a storied cavalry unit operating in the thick of America's "Wild West."[19] Its role was partly that of a peacekeeping force, showing off its power to restrain Mexicans and Americans alike from engaging in depredations against the aboriginal denizens of the American Southwest. But, when the territorial government was bent on vengeance in response to deadly attacks in which settlers had been scalped, mutilated, or worse, the Dragoons were also called upon to tolerate, if not outright perpetrate, ugly massacres of men, women, and children belonging to aboriginal bands regarded as hostile.[20] Stevens himself regarded the primary function of the First Dragoons as being to "make tribes come to treaties" with the United States.[21] There is no direct evidence that he was personally involved in deadly battles with tribesmen.[22] But soldiers from his unit sometimes met a tragic fate. For example, on March 30, 1854, a group of men who had been detached from Company F to travel with another company were surrounded and trapped by Jicarillo Apaches on a New Mexico canyon trail and had to fight their way out. All 15 of the Company F participants in this ambush (now called the "Battle of Cieneguilla") were either killed or wounded. A total of 22 United States troops were killed, and 36 more were wounded.[23]

After this battle Stevens, with Company F, spent the remainder of 1854 "tramping around" New Mexico and Colorado for the purpose of finding the Apaches and inflicting vengeance on them for Cieneguilla. Stevens and Company F spent a whole month in the fall specifically chasing after hostile Apaches, without encountering any. He expressed a fatalistic attitude, remarking in a letter, "as luck would have it I have got off safe so far. But they might get me yet."[24] At some point in 1854, Stevens was appointed to serve as the Company bugler. Making bugle calls was a critical signalling function within the cavalry unit. It was a logical job for Stevens in view of his musical background and talents.[25]

On March 8, 1855, Company F, in preparation for another campaign against the Apaches, was ordered to march from Cantonment Bergwin, a military camp just a few miles south of Taos, New Mexico, to Fort Massachusetts, the first American outpost in what would eventually become the state of Colorado. At that time, Company F was under the command of Major Philip Thompson. Stevens was acting as Major Thompson's orderly. Major Thompson was a serious alcoholic, but he was personally charming and popular enough with the enlisted soldiers. On the other hand, Major George Blake, an experienced officer in overall command of Cantonment Bergwin and Fort Massachusetts, was not a drinker, but he was hated among the men of Company F because he was perceived as being constantly fault-finding, unnecessarily restrictive, and overly hard on them. The men also disliked Blake because he spent most of his time in Taos, away from the post he was supposed to be commanding. Blake, for his part, felt that the Company was highly undisciplined. One reason he consistently refused to grant leave was that he did not trust its men to be unsupervised in town.[26]

Major Thompson did two things that would turn out to

CHAPTER 15: A TERRORIST REPLACES AN UN-TERRORIST

cause serious trouble. First, he stopped his mounted company at a mill along the road to Taos, ostensibly to wait for pack mules and to get corn meal to carry as feed, but more importantly, to get a gallon or two of distilled liquor, which he ordered ladled out to provide an immediate drink for himself and all the troops. While the company was stopped, Major Blake passed them on his way to Taos. Thus, by the time the company reached the Taos town plaza, many of the troops were feeling the effects of the alcohol, and Major Blake was on hand to see, and disapprove, their drunken antics.[27]

When Company F arrived at the central town plaza of Taos at around 1 p.m., Major Thompson gave an order for half of the men to dismount and go into the stores surrounding the plaza, while the other half were instructed to hold their horses, awaiting a bugle call signaling the first group to return so the remainder could shop. Ostensibly, the men were to purchase sundries needed for their upcoming wilderness travels, such as tobacco, pipes, matches, and gloves. But many of them, as well as Major Thompson himself, viewed the liberty time as an opportunity to drink more liquor. By the time Stevens sounded his bugle to recall the first group, several of them were too intoxicated to mount their horses. The Company's men were behaving so riotously in the plaza that it caused town people to enter the bar and store of Peter Joseph, one of the leading merchants, to complain to Major Blake of the situation. Blake, who had many friends among the leading Taos citizens, was mortified.[28]

Blake approached Thompson, who was busy drinking in Joseph's store, and asked him to take the Company out of town. After some initial resistance on his part, the bedlam outside continued, and Thompson rather grudgingly agreed. Thompson had Stevens blow a call for the men of the unit to return to the plaza to assemble. As they did so a soldier, Private Jeremiah Sullivan, was too wobbly to get on his horse. Major

Thompson directed his lead sergeant, Thomas Fitzsimmons, to tie the man on his horse. The thoroughly inebriated Sullivan took serious offense at this affront to his dignity. He started punching at Fitzsimmons with his fists. He also tried to kick the sergeant in the face. Fitzsimmons smacked him right back. Blake, emerging into the plaza from a porch in front of Joseph's store, saw only the second half of this confrontation. He came over and demanded to know why Fitzsimmons had struck the man. Fitzsimmons responded that he would strike any man in the Company who hit him. Blake, observing Sullivan's woozy condition, believed it was impossible that Sullivan had struck Fitzsimmons. Accusing Fitzsimmons of being impertinent and lying, Blake summarily ordered Thompson to place the sergeant under arrest.

Thompson refused. He told Blake he could arrest the man himself. Blake then informed Fitzsimmons that he was under arrest. However, he made no move to have Fitzsimmons taken to jail. He simply went back into Joseph's store, and resumed writing dispatches.[29] Outside, the dragoons, most of whom were in a partial or total state of inebriation, were determined to get as much enjoyment as possible out of their precious moments in town. They continued to party and wreak frenzied havoc. After several minutes went by, the attention of everyone in Joseph's store was captured by the boisterous sound of five mounted cavalrymen who attempted to charge right up onto the store's wooden porch. They ran in and through a group of Americans and Mexicans lounging there. One of the horses, perhaps trying to avoid a collision, fell and threw its rider, a drunken private named John Cooper.[30]

The citizens of Taos did not dare breathe a word of reproach to the marauding soldiers. But Blake had had enough. He immediately exited Joseph's store and found Thompson in the plaza. He flatly ordered the major to take his Company out of town immediately. As Thompson was in the middle of stammering some reply, a mounted private named Joseph Fox

CHAPTER 15: A TERRORIST REPLACES AN UN-TERRORIST

rode up and issued a defiant statement. "You can't do it, Blake. You can take no man of this troop out of Taos." At this, Blake grabbed Fox and started pulling him off his horse.[31]

The resemblance of the daily lives of the soldiers of Company F, cooped up, confined, and regimented as they were in stark military camps, to the lives of slaves was not lost on the men of Company F. Under the effects of alcohol, the men's pent-up anger and hostility toward Blake reached its boiling point. They were incensed at being ordered out of town early. Blake was pointedly confronted by John Cooper. "We've been n**** driven long enough," Cooper said to Blake. "It's time you give us a little rest."

Blake, the 45-year old career officer, was not about to take such guff. His own frustration with the undisciplined men of the Company was also pent up. Seizing Cooper by the collar, he got in his face. "You are the damned son of a bitch I've been looking for and I'm glad I've got you at last." He slapped Cooper two or three times with the other hand. The muscular Cooper then grabbed Blake. The two of them tumbled to the ground and continued a grappling combat. With that, an all-out brawl was on.[32]

Men of the Company gathered around thickly to cheer on their comrade who was attacking the hated Blake. They yelled out encouragement, such as "Kill the son of a bitch!" and "Cut his throat!" To Kit Carson, the famed scout, frontiersman, Native American linguist and Taos resident who came out into the plaza soon after the violence erupted, it seemed the angry soldiers were very likely to kill Blake. Ramon Baca, a Mexican who worked for Carson, tried to intervene, but mounted dragoons immediately charged him, drew their weapons and chased him for some considerable distance before finally catching up to him and knocking him out with a saber blow.[33]

At some point, several officers and non-commissioned officers began to assist Blake in the fight. Blake managed to draw Major Thompson's sword from its scabbard. He used it to strike at Cooper. The tight quarters prevented Blake from wielding the weapon to full effect. However, his saber blows seem to have been sufficient to put a halt to the fight with Cooper. But just as Blake was freeing himself from Cooper, another soldier named John Steel came up and grabbed Blake by the neck. Sergeant Fitzsimmons went to pull Steel away from Blake. As he did, somebody yelled at Fitzsimmons, "Look out, you may get hurt!" He felt himself struck by a saber swung from his blind side by the mounted Fox. Fitzsimmons afterwards said he was sure this blow was actually intended for Blake.[34]

Lieutenant Robert Johnston was Thompson's second-in-command in Company F. At some point during the riot, Johnston asked Stevens, who was already holding his own horse and that of Major Thompson, to hold the reins to his horse. Johnston found it difficult to get through the crowd of soldiers surrounding Blake. He ordered the men to stand back, but they paid no attention to him. However, due to the combined restraining efforts of Thompson, Johnston, Fitzsimmons, and other non-commissioned officers, the fighting eventually ceased.[35]

Blake's face was a total mess, covered with dirt and blood. His scalp was swollen from a huge bruise, and he had a badly sprained ankle. But more than anything else, he was in a state of emotional shock over the indignity of the mutiny. He felt the powerful effects of adrenalin generated by his physical struggle with the younger soldiers. Pacing in front of the dragoons, he defiantly declared, "I can whip any man in this Company from right to left with either gun, pistol, or saber, and if there is any one of you who thinks yourself fit, step out here and I will show you if you can call old Blake a coward or not." Stevens, who had not been drinking, and who to this point had not taken any part in the riot, could not resist bursting out with a response. "By God, Major Blake, you can't do it. I accept your

Chapter 15: A Terrorist Replaces an Un-Terrorist

challenge!" Lieutenant Johnston immediately quashed the notion. He ordered Stevens to go away with the three horses he was holding to the far side of Joseph's store. Blake, escorted by a territorial judge named Perry Brocchus, turned away without answering and returned into the store to clean himself up. But before leaving the plaza, he asked Judge Brocchus to have the deputy marshal arrest Cooper, Fox, Steel, and Stevens, and take them all to jail.[36]

To Brocchus, it seemed Stevens might prove useful for defusing the lingering tense situation between Blake and the men of Company F. He afterwards said Stevens, holding the horses, looked "peaceful" and "orderly." Instead of immediately arresting Stevens, Brocchus sought to persuade Stevens to make an apology to Blake, both on behalf of himself and on behalf of the men of the Company. Brocchus spoke with Stevens at some length. Stevens apparently expressed a willingness to do so.

Brocchus escorted Stevens to near where Blake was now standing, at the edge of the porch outside Joseph's store. He said to Blake, "this man appears to be sorry for what he has done." Blake responded that if Stevens was willing to take back all that he had said, he would not proffer charges against him. Stevens answered him with an equivocal statement, something like, "If I have done anything wrong, I ask your pardon." Blake was unimpressed with this grumbling apology. He reiterated to the many watching bystanders that he was not afraid of Stevens or of the whole Company. He turned away, remarking to Brocchus, "Judge, I leave this matter with you."[37]

The perceived sneer by Blake caused the hot-tempered Stevens to flash instantly into rage. He exclaimed, "No, damned you, I'm as good a man as you are." At the same time, he took a step back with his right foot, loudly cocked his Sharps Rifle, raised it, and aimed it directly at Blake's chest. As he did so he growled, "I'll blow your heart out." Lt. Thompson, watching nearby, reacted immediately by reaching out to jerk Stevens's rifle upwards. Kit Carson also grabbed the rifle, and he forced it out of Stevens's hands. Stevens was then taken to jail by Judge Brocchus and deputy marshal E. N. Depew.[38]

For the mutiny, and Stevens's subsequent menacing of Blake, in May of 1855 Stevens, Cooper, Fox and Steel were all court-martialed and sentenced to be shot to death. However, the sentence had to be confirmed by the President. Secretary of War Davis, writing on behalf of President Pierce, declined to do so. In a letter dated August 8, 1855, he explained:

> It is proved that the commander of the company, and many of the company, then under arms, on a march, were drunk when the riot broke out. It would seem, too, that proper exertions were not made by the officers, non-commissioned officers, and soldiers to suppress the mutiny .... It appears that no proper discipline had previously been maintained in the company, and that the Major of the regiment, under whose command they had been serving, was greatly responsible for the utter lack of discipline which would have cost him his life in this mutiny, if he had not been rescued by the civil authority; and that part of the violence he suffered, in the riot, was invited by his challenging the company to fight him, man by man. Under these circumstances ... the President ... will not visit the whole consequence of the mutiny upon the four soldiers who have been convicted, nor execute in this case the sentence of death. Aaron D. Stevens, John Cooper, Joseph Fox, and John Steel, are hereby mitigated to hard labor for three years, under guard, without pay.

Little did Jefferson Davis imagine that he had just saved the life of a future American terrorist.[39]

Stevens was sent to serve his commuted sentence at

CHAPTER 15: A TERRORIST REPLACES AN UN-TERRORIST

Leavenworth. In January 1856 he managed to escape. He successfully concealed himself among some Native Americans for a few months. When he emerged, he assumed a false name, "Colonel Whipple."[40] Using that identity and his military training and experience, "Whipple" quickly became one of the marauding free state chieftains in the Kansas civil war. His band perpetrated a series of guerrilla-style raids on those perceived as allied with the slave power. Befitting the background of the former dragoon, "Whipple" specialized in stealing large numbers of horses from proslavery settlements.[41] But when the cycle of violence in Kansas was brought under control by civil authorities including Governor Geary during the course of 1857, "Whipple" once again found himself unemployed and bored. The prevailing peace left him without opportunities to plunder with impunity. "Whipple" was already an outlaw, so he had nothing really to lose by joining up with John in the fall of 1857. The handsome, six foot two inch Stevens would soon assume the place John had originally envisioned for Hugh Forbes as the head trainer of John's band of terrorists.[42]

Along with "Colonel Whipple," John also successfully recruited several more members of "Whipple's" guerrilla band. One of them was Ohio-born John Henry Kagi, a newspaper stringer on the fringes of "Bleeding Kansas." Kagi had self-taught skills in mathematics, English literature, Latin, and law. The most bookish of John's followers, Kagi was a passionate opponent of slavery. He also showed himself willing to unquestioningly obey John's directives, a most sought-after attribute in a terrorist organization.[43] Kagi would be trusted by John, and elevated by him to become the de facto second-in-command of his terrorist organization.

Another important addition to John's band was John Edwin Cook. Cook, a five foot seven inch tall, musically gifted young man with curly blond hair and intense blue eyes, was from a well-to-do family. He attended Yale, but dropped out. After spending some time as a law clerk, he decided to adopt the "Kansas free state" cause and headed west. He came upon "Camp Brown" shortly after the Battle of Black Jack, and he remained with John's small militia when it was dispersed by Colonel Sumner on June 5, 1856. In the fall of 1857, around November 1 he was summoned to meet with John at the home of a mutual acquaintance about 4 miles from Lawrence. Learning that John was forming a company to continue "armed resistance" to pro-slavery men, Cook quickly agreed to join. Soon he was informed of a rendezvous of John's followers set to happen in Topeka. Here he met up with "Colonel Whipple" and Kagi. This small group, the core of John's terrorist band, left Kansas to embark on a two-year journey that would end at Harpers Ferry. When they reached Tabor, they met up with John and other new additions to his budding terror organization, including Charles Tidd and Will Leeman.[44]

John took possession of the 200 Sharps Rifles stored in Tabor that belonged to the NKC and MKC, effectively misappropriating them from the Kansas use for which they had been purchased and earmarked. His weapons and followers meandered in a wagon train 300 miles easterly to Springfield, Iowa, close to the Illinois border, where John decided to have his men board with locals for the winter while drilling under the supervision of Stevens. While taking the weapons with him for safekeeping at his son's home in Ohio, John left his band of men behind on January 15 of the new year 1858. He was en route to the East, where he intended to do more fund raising before carrying out the sneak attack on civilians in Harpers Ferry, which he was already planning for the middle of May 1858.[45]

Hugh had other fund-raising ideas. History has heaped a great deal of scorn upon Hugh, but much of that rests on the viewpoint of writers who were hero-worshipping a terrorist they regarded as a martyr. In particular, John's first major

CHAPTER 15: A TERRORIST REPLACES AN UN-TERRORIST

biographer Franklin Sanborn was directly engaged in vitriolic dialogue with Hugh about money.

John, by his own later admission, originally contracted to pay Hugh $100 per month for at least the time Hugh "continued in his service," with the $600 payment in April 1858 serving only as an advance on the first six months of this agreement.[46] Exactly when the "first six months" commenced or ended was never clearly stated, not even by Hugh himself. But Hugh became alarmed about the destitute condition of his wife and children, then living in Paris, France. He considered it prudent to lobby the abolitionist community for more funds, even while he was with John in Tabor. Hugh's letters make reference to prior pleas he made for cash for his family to Gerrit Smith and Joseph Bryant in August and September 1857.

After November 2, 1857, when Hugh left Tabor, he went to the Ohio home of John Jr., where he checked to see if he had received any positive response to his requests for funds. He learned that the only response was a message that Gerrit Smith, having been very ill, had not even opened Hugh's letters. Shortly afterwards, Hugh went to see Frederick Douglass in Rochester. There he presented Frederick with a letter from John, urging Frederick to "receive and assist" Hugh.[47] Although not favorably impressed with the eccentric Hugh, Frederick did pay for him to stay in a local hotel, and he did give him a small sum of money. Frederick's German-born female admirer, Ottilie Assing, introduced Hugh to some of her German friends in New York City, but they did not contribute any funds to him.[48]

Hugh at this time received letters from his wife in Paris, which made him increasingly anxious about her well-being and that of their children. If Hugh's account can be believed, they were evicted from their home, lacked funds for food and clothing, and could not afford badly needed medical care. They were living, temporarily, on the charity of two Italian emigré benefactors. Hugh attributed their predicament to his own inability to send them the money he was due for heading up John's training program.[49]

Hugh took his complaints to Charles Sumner in two letters he wrote Charles shortly before the end of 1857. Probably Hugh chose to contact Charles at the suggestion of one of the numerous friends and connections that Charles had in England. It was a sound decision, because over the months of wrangling that followed, Charles would turn out to be the closest thing to an advocate for Hugh. Charles referred his letters to Samuel Howe, who in turn forwarded them to Sanborn, which was logical, because Sanborn was John's de facto fund-raising coordinator. Sanborn was the secretary of the MKC, and he had been instrumental in getting the NKC to commit the $5,000 to John in the first place. But now Sanborn was incensed that Hugh had written directly to Charles. No doubt, this was partly because Charles was still recuperating from the Preston Brooks attack, and so people were trying to shield him. But it was also partly because Howe, Sanborn, and John's other financial sponsors did not want the details of their dealings with a terrorist known to political men such as Charles. Sanborn wrote Hugh a curt, severe note dated January 1 in which he denied knowing anything about any financial commitment to Hugh by John or anybody else.[50]

This denial led Hugh to write Sanborn a lengthy response dated January 9. The high-strung Hugh felt he was being severely wronged because John was no longer paying the agreed $100 per month. Furthermore, he maintained that John's failure to fulfill his contract was not intentional on John's part but, rather, was a consequence of people Hugh called "New England humanitarians" reneging on their earlier financial pledges to John. Hugh called out two specifics: (1) the pledge of $5,000 given by the NKC in its meeting on January 23 and 24, of which only a small fraction had been paid;[51] and (2) a pledge of $1,000 given by citizens of New

CHAPTER 15: A TERRORIST REPLACES AN UN-TERRORIST

Haven, Connecticut, apparently on March 18, of which only $25 had been paid. Both these pledged donations were confirmed in John's correspondence.[52] Hugh harshly criticized the donors for failing to honor their pledges. John, he criticized only for being too lenient in declining to enforce the commitments. In shrill tones, Hugh accused the "humanitarians" of gross hypocrisy, unscrupulous deceit, and "cheating" by failing to deliver the funds they had promised.[53]

Sanborn wrote a response to Hugh, in which he enclosed $10. Sanborn admitted most of the relevant details about financing commitments that were alleged in Hugh's letter. Additionally, Sanborn conceded he knew about Hugh as early as the summer of 1857, but claimed this knowledge came from Gerrit Smith, rather than John himself. But Sanborn denied that the "gentlemen with whom I am associated" had breached any commitments. He suggested that John himself "may have mistaken *hopes* for *promises*." Of interest, Sanborn did not mention the far more obvious available response, which was that the NKC and other donors made their pledges of funds and rifles toward the cause of defending free state settlers in Kansas from border ruffian aggression, whereas John, as Sanborn well knew, now wanted to use the funds and rifles for an entirely different purpose, a terrorist attack on a community in Virginia.[54]

Hugh disdainfully returned the $10 to Sanborn. Pouring out more lamentations about his family's hardships, he continued to accuse the "humanitarians" of "cheating" by reneging on their financial commitments. Further pressing the point, Hugh accused them of "mismanagement and deception," and sought to compare the organization of the abolitionists unfavorably to that of their Southern counterparts:[55]

> [M]uch can be accomplished by a mere handful, if they are reliable and feel they can depend on each other. This is perceivable by counting how few in the

South rule the whole United States; for though that few has an abominable cause to sustain, yet the pro slaveryites do sustain it, simply because they stand by each other, and each man can rely on being supported.

Sanborn continued to be very distressed over Hugh's latest correspondence. For the first time, he felt doubts about John's competence. He wondered if John could be insensitive and mistaken in his judgment about character. Sanborn wrote to John, asking for more information about his relationship with Hugh and asking John to defend his "Boston friends." In response, John had his son John Jr. send a letter to Hugh, which John ghost-wrote. In its tone, the letter bore a resemblance to the type of communication John had previously sent to his partners during his failed business ventures of the 1830s and 1840s. It implies John still wanted Hugh as part of his enterprise. John asked his son to enclose with the letter a sum of money, $40. He told John Jr. he wanted to keep Hugh "a little encouraged" and to avoid any "open rupture" for the time being.[56]

When John ghost-wrote John Jr.'s letter to Hugh, he was staying with Frederick at his home in Rochester. This three-week stay kept John conveniently concealed from any potential law enforcement officers, but it also helped him with another objective. John was very interested in recruiting African Americans to carry out his Harpers Ferry attack plan. He felt that Frederick would be helpful for finding such volunteers. Additionally, he wanted Frederick's help and feedback on a new "constitution" for "proscribed, oppressed, and enslaved" persons whom John was concerned with enlisting. This organic foundation for revolution called for a President, Vice-President, Cabinet officers, Congress, and Supreme Court. All would be elected by a membership. All would be subject to the military rule of a separate Commander in Chief.

Almost certainly, Frederick helped write the preamble to John's "constitution," which is by far his most philosophical

CHAPTER 15: A TERRORIST REPLACES AN UN-TERRORIST

exposition and one highly uncharacteristic of John:[57]

> Whereas, slavery throughout its entire existence in the United States, is none other than a most barbarous, unprovoked, and unjustifiable war of one portion of its citizens upon another portion, the only conditions of which are perpetual imprisonment and hopeless servitude or absolute extermination; in utter disregard and violation of those eternal and self-evident truths set forth in our Declaration of Independence: Therefore:

> We, citizens of the United States, and the Oppressed People, who, by a recent decision of the Supreme Court are declared to have no rights which the White Man is bound to respect;[58] together with all other people degraded by the laws thereof,

> Do, for the time being ordain and establish ourselves, the following Provisional Constitution and Ordinances, the better to protect our Persons, Property, Lives and Liberties, and to govern our actions.

John's "constitution" strongly reflected John's lifelong obsession with crime and punishment. Of its forty-eight total articles, fully half deal with crime, punishment, or discipline.[59] During his stay with Frederick, John immersed himself in the "constitution." For him it was "the first thing in the morning and the last thing at night." John's constant dwelling on the document grew to the point that Frederick found it to be a bore. John also made a map, drawn on two planed boards, to illustrate the plan of fortifications he intended to construct in the mountains. Frederick's children found this exercise much more interesting than did Frederick.

Frederick heard John mention he thought he could take

Harpers Ferry with a few resolute men, and capture the arms stored there. But he paid scant attention to these remarks. He thought John's real plan was the same one that the two men had discussed previously over the past ten years – "railroad business on a more extended scale." Frederick believed John would divide his troopers into a series of small squads, each of which would cover a mountainous territory. Each squad would instigate local slaves to flee to the North, and then quickly to Canada. This large-scale escape of slaves would greatly reduce the value of slave property and thus place in jeopardy the entire slavery system. In sum, Frederick's understanding was far more similar to Hugh's plan than it was to John's real plan. Frederick thought instigating large-scale escapes to diminish the value of slave property was a rational strategy.[60]

John went directly from Frederick's home in Rochester to Gerrit Smith's home in Peterboro. Sanborn came on from Boston for the occasion. John laid before Sanborn and Smith the plan for the attack on Harpers Ferry. His hearers were astonished. Sanborn immediately saw and complained of the "manifest hopelessness" of the project. In a reaction typical whenever "legals" who support a cause are confronted with the nitty-gritty, criminal, and essentially suicidal activities of the terrorists they sponsor, Sanborn felt deeply ambivalent about the violence involved. He initially felt cornered, because his only alternatives were "betrayal, desertion, or support." But then he went for a long walk privately with Smith, who helped quell some of his anxiety. Sanborn remained somewhat reluctant to back a scheme to foment a mass slave uprising. John answered all doubts with an appeal to faith in righteousness: "If God be for us, who can be against us?"[61]

CHAPTER 15: A TERRORIST REPLACES AN UN-TERRORIST

Notwithstanding his reservations, Sanborn continued to follow an irresistible urge to help John gather support. Knowing he held a sway over the younger man by virtue of the depth of his dedication, John instinctively bolstered this urge. To reinforce the idea that he was at peace with a martyr's fate, John wrote a letter Sanborn would long cherish. In it John referred to the "cause" as being "enough to live for, if not to   for" (intentionally leaving blank space in place of the word "die"). He said, "I might not again have an equal opportunity." John added that he had felt a "strong, steady desire to die" for many years.[62] He followed it up with another letter in which he solicited noble book donations for the edification of his followers. John wrote that he wanted to equip his men with "Plutarch's Lives," "Life of Washington," and "the best-written Life of Napoleon."[63]

John Brown's primary financial backers, called the "Secret Six"

Sanborn organized a meeting of four of the principal financial supporters of John's plea, the year before, for funds for the "defense" of Kansas free state settlers. Now they would be asked to provide money for a course of action that was dramatically different. These supporters were Charles's friend Samuel Howe, George Stearns, Theodore Parker, and another firebrand minister, Thomas Higginson, who within the abolitionist community was one of the most outspoken advocates of armed resistance to the slave power.[64] Along with Sanborn himself and Gerrit Smith, they would come to be known to history as "the Secret Six." Their meeting occurred March 4, 1858 in John's room at the American Hotel in Boston. It started out with the others asking pointed questions to John about Hugh Forbes. While admitting he had indeed hired Hugh at $100 per month, and had paid him an initial $600 out of his "Kansas" money, John denied that the deal was good for a full year. He also assured them that Hugh did not know enough about the details of John's project to betray it.

    John then turned to a justification of his plan to sponsor a bloody insurrection. He appealed to the idea that efforts of the enslaved to fight to obtain their own freedom were of utmost symbolic importance. Only violence would prove to the stalwarts of the slave power and their Northern sympathizers that ethnic African Americans were not content to remain in bondage. John urged his hearers to keep believing in his virtuous character. They all, like Sanborn, had some initial reservations. But, much like his previous wealthy partners in land speculation and in the wool business, the Secret Six were ultimately swayed by John's spartan asceticism, by the passion of his embrace of Puritan values, and by his willingness to die for the cause. Parker, in particular, accepted and persuaded the others of the merit of John's argument that righteous violence by oppressed African Americans was purifying. By the time John ended his Boston visit four days later, the five agreed to go in with Gerrit Smith to raise a fresh $1,000 to back John's terror venture.[65]

Chapter 16: A Society Feeling Insecure

Under the distinctively American brand of federalist government, the Supreme Court is the most intellectually disciplined institution, even if that discipline is occasionally used for nefarious purposes to carry out a political agenda. The U.S. Supreme Court jumped into the fray over the institution of slavery in a big way on March 5, 1857, when it handed down its decision in the case of *Scott v. Sandford*.[1] The Justices were aware that they were making a significant decision, both for their contemporaries and for posterity. But they were not deciding the case in a vacuum.

By 1857, the Southern intelligentsia were constantly concerned about the long term future of their way of life.[2] They understood very well that their entire social order was moving on a divergent path in comparison with the North. Slavery gave the South a social system and a civilization with a distinct class structure, political community, economy, ideology, and set of psychological patterns. As a result, even as its exports flourished, the South's ruling aristocratic culture increasingly grew away from the rest of the nation and from other sections of the world, particularly in Europe.[3] Of course, its beneficiaries fervently believed that their system was better, stronger, more enlightened, and more modern. But the more educated and articulate among them were conscious that theirs was a culture facing existential threats. A decisive event for the Southern intellectuals was the phased, with compensation, emancipation declared by Britain in 1833. It placed fear in the hearts of the American slaveholding elite.[4] Southern leaders began to worry about moral isolation on the slaveholding issue. They increasingly began to view global politics through a lens of America's commitment to slavery and Great Britain's commitment to abolition. It was a sort of cold war between two competing ideologies. Proslavery observers were wildly paranoid about British intent to engage in "antislavery" action in Texas and the southwestern United States.[5]

The most influential and powerful Southern defenders of bondage had long evinced great concern for defense of the legitimacy and pedigree of chattel slavery. Major proslavery thinkers ventured all the way back to classical antiquity to establish a vital bond between Western civilization and property in human beings.[6] They fancied that the Africans had been improved and made happy by transport across the ocean, and subsequently by the birth of their offspring into a lifetime of servitude.[7]

Over the course of the 1850's, leading proponents of Southern ideology embraced a point of view that could be charitably termed "scientific racism." They portrayed subjugation of racial inferiors as being part of the modern experience. The enslaved peoples were argued to be naturally inferior to whites, thus justifying their enslavement by whites as being for their own good. The Caucasian race, according to a widely published essay by a Charleston editor, lacked the physical stamina to survive the tropical climate of the southern regions. Britain's and France's experiments with "free black labor" in the West Indies had failed miserably. Thus, the "reflecting parts of mankind" must accept the necessity of servitude. Slavery, the writer declared, was "the true progress of civilization."[8]

Disputing specifically the "Fourth of July" style speech given by Charles Sumner on the Senate floor in 1854, the *Southern Literary Messenger* took issue with Charles's assertion that slaveholding societies were in global retreat. It made much of the French and British policy, in the 1850s, of importing legally bound, woefully underpaid "coolie" laborers from China, India, and even Africa into the Caribbean. For Southern writers and editors, California's substitution of "Chinese slavery" for "African slavery" had exposed the impotence of Henry Seward's speech arguing that there is a "higher law" which forbids slavery. They confidently cited an "even higher" law – the demand for labor: cheap, inferior, and thus compulsory – labor. They argued the competitive advantage of such labor was "a law inherent in the nature of society," and thus a law "which denies all the villainy of abolition."[9] Southern "futurists," convinced theirs was the most successful and advanced society that history had yet developed, even fantasized about re-enslavement of African descendants in previously emancipated regions throughout the Caribbean, including Haiti.[10]

Despite this, all but the most optimistic of Southern intellectuals feared for the "security of their peculiar institutions," to employ their favorite euphemism.[11] The intellectuals were alarmed by the first postemancipation clashes, which came when American ships carrying slaves that ventured into British waters became stranded by storms or wrecked. In each case local British authorities freed the slaves on board.[12] The insecurity Southern elites felt about British disapproval of their "institutions" translated into a "foreign policy of slavery," the most pronounced characteristic of which was special solicitude for their fellow slaveholding societies in the Western Hemisphere, especially Cuba, Brazil, and the independent republic of Texas until its annexation into the

United States in 1845.[13]

But almost twenty years of scarcely interrupted Southern control of the machinery of the U.S. Government, inaugurated by the accidental presidency of John Tyler resulting from President Harrison's death in 1841, gave the slaveholding world view a strong upper hand not only in U.S. foreign policy but also on the bench of the U.S. Supreme Court.[14]

The Supreme Court cherry-picked the *Scott v. Sandford* case to address because its simplified facts[15] framed the paradigm of a problem that was being argued, at the time, by voices of the South. Dred Scott was an African American slave belonging to a Dr. Emerson, who was a surgeon employed in the U.S. Army. In 1834, Emerson took Dred to a military post at Rock Island, Illinois. Subsequently, in April or May 1836, Emerson was transferred from Rock Island to Fort Snelling, located on the west bank of the Mississippi River in what was then Wisconsin Territory and is now in the state of Minnesota. Meanwhile in 1835, a Major Taliaferro, also in the U.S. Army, took an African American slave named Harriet to Fort Snelling. There, in 1836, Dr. Emerson acquired Harriet from Major Taliaferro and gave his consent for Dred and Harriet to marry. Dr. Emerson, Dred and Harriet then returned to Missouri in 1838. Two daughters were born of the marriage, one on board a steamboat on the Mississippi River north of Missouri, the other on a military post in Missouri to which Dr. Emerson had been transferred.

Dred, Harriet, and their two daughters, according to the simplified facts, were all sold and conveyed to John Sandford. Dred then sued to obtain a decree of his family's freedom by virtue of the time they had spent on the "free soil" of Illinois and, subsequently, Wisconsin Territory. Although his suit for freedom was well supported by existing Missouri court precedent, and thus resulted in a trial court verdict and judgment in his favor, the Missouri Supreme Court overruled that precedent and reversed the judgment, instead holding that, under Missouri law, a slaveholder such as Dr. Emerson had the right to take his servants out of the state, into Northern territory, without ceding his rights of ownership. When Dred brought a separate complaint in federal court, the judge essentially instructed the jury that, in view of the Missouri Supreme Court's decision, Dred had no valid case. The inevitable decision against Dred was then appealed to the U.S. Supreme Court.

The case presented the Court with a model vehicle for a political statement, because it encapsulated in a simple, quasi-fictional, fact situation one central issue raised by Southern intellectuals, which was, namely, that they were being precluded by the laws of other states from taking their slaves with them into the North. In view of its political overtones, the Supreme Court took an inordinately long time to issue its decision. The Court elected to have the case held over into a second year and reargued. Then Justices in the majority leaked the most controversial aspect of the decision – holding the Missouri Compromise unconstitutional – to the incoming President-elect, Democrat James Buchanan, who heralded it in his inaugural address as a forthcoming solution to slavery-related issues. Every one of the nine sitting Justices issued an opinion of some kind. Their writings, collectively, occupy 233 pages in the Court's official reports of its decisions.

The Justices, predictably, divided along party lines. The seven Democrats, from North and South alike, joined in Chief Justice Roger Taney's majority opinion, with its pro-slavery holding. Eschewing several available narrower grounds of decision,[16] Chief Justice Taney framed the Court's holding in the broadest possible terms. The two non-Democrats dissented.

Although Roger Taney's 55-page opinion now is justifiably regarded as a result-oriented hatchet job, it was probably the most polished and coherent exposition ever written to support the institution of American slavery. Its central premise: As African Americans born into slavery, Dred Scott and his family were not "citizens" entitled to sue in federal courts. Chief Justice Taney's cold logic demonstrated why Abraham Lincoln would soon say, with respect to the legalized enslavement of African Americans, that none of the attempted compromises would hold, and the United States must therefore eventually be "all one thing or all the other."

U.S. Chief Justice Roger Taney, in 1856 photo

The Anglo-American legal system is all about following precedent. And Chief Justice Taney was able to invoke ample precedent to support his seminal observation that at the time of the Declaration of Independence, at the time of the Constitution, and beyond, the "unfortunate race" of Africans were regarded as members of an "inferior order" who had "no rights that the white man was bound to respect."[17] In fact, Taney went out of his way to cite precedents from Northern states, including specifically, the prosecution of Prudence Crandall by the state of Connecticut for attempting to educate African Americans, to show that, well into the nineteenth century, African Americans were not regarded by law as having any meaningful civil rights.[18]

Who *did* have historically recognized civil rights at the time of the Constitution, according to the seven-Justice Court majority? *The owners of slaves.* One concurring Justice, in his twenty-three-page opinion amplifying that of Taney, traced the sub-human status of slaves, and the right of their masters to own them, back to Roman times. He actually cited the Institutes of Justinian as precedent.[19] The right to own persons of African descent was deemed a fundamental one, which the Court's majority held to be clearly protected by the Fifth Amendment included in the Bill of Rights together with its guarantee that no person "shall be deprived of property" without due process of law.[20]

The corollary to this holding was also very logical. Neither Congress, in legislating for Territories such as the Wisconsin Territory, nor the states, such as the state of Illinois, had the power to deprive citizens of the fundamental right to own slaves as property. Thus the Missouri Compromise, in attempting to prohibit the institution of slavery in all territories north of the 36th parallel, violated the Constitution. Since the laws of Missouri were clear that Dred Scott was property, no court that was subject to the Fifth Amendment could alter that conclusion. It was a sweeping holding indeed, and one justifiably regarded with immediate alarm by the legal and intellectual community of the North. In one great motion, the Supreme Court had declared the entire platform of the new Republican party, to the effect that slavery should not be allowed in the territories, to be unconstitutional. And this *tour de force* by the "least dangerous branch" added a great deal of fuel to an already raging political firestorm.

Chapter 17: She Saw John's Head on a Serpent

Harriet Tubman is a legendary American hero. Her maiden name, as she called it, was Araminta Ross, or "Minty."[1] Harriet grew up in Dorchester County on the Eastern Shore of Maryland, in the same slaveholding community in which Fred Bailey, later rechristened Frederick Douglass, spent his boyhood. In fact Harriet, who was four years younger, and Fred shared a common network of acquaintances in the area, including Harriet's parents Ben Ross and Rit Green, as well as the slave-owning Thompson family for whom Ben worked for many years.[2] Harriet's experiences and grievances with being born into the oppression of human bondage were much like Fred's, but they did differ in one very important respect. Harriet, as a girl, did not have the good fortune to be taught to read. The written word would remain a lifelong mystery to her. She was, however, both highly intelligent and highly clever. She was also endowed with an uncanny sixth sense, both about danger and about future events, which another might attribute to psychic powers, but which Harriet herself would ascribe to direct communication with God.[3]

Starting with her earliest awakening as a small child, Harriet experienced the pain of being removed, along with her

Chapter 17: She Saw John's Head on a Serpent

mother, from her family home, and of being separated from her siblings due to the machinations of treating African Americans as property. She never got over the sense of frustration and injustice, and these feelings of bitterness were seriously exacerbated by dealings such as the "sales" of her sisters. She also felt the harsh lash of a whip that was administered as much to define and articulate a social order as it was to punish. In her later life Harriet dryly remarked, "there was good masters and missuses, as I've heard tell, but I didn't happen to come across them."[4] She felt an instinctive distrust of anyone who was a member of the European race. Every time she saw a white man, she was terrified about being carried away.[5]

Harriet was intelligent and resourceful enough to eventually discover a legal imbroglio involving her mother. In 1797, Rit's owner Atthow Pattison had died leaving a will that provided that Rit and her children would only be enslaved until they reached 45 years of age.[6] So under any reasonable application of the law, Rit should have been free as of 1834 at the latest. However, the heirs ultimately failed to recognize or honor this manumission provision. Through a series of events, Rit came to be owned by a woman, Mary Pattison, who then was widowed and in 1803 married Anthony Thompson. Thompson owned Ben Ross, an African American timber inspector and foreman. By this chain of circumstances Rit met Ben, and the two of them started a family together in 1808. Ben's skills were very valuable indeed in an era where lumber was an abundant and productive resource on the Eastern Shore. Ben and Rit lived together for fifteen years. Harriet was born to them in early 1822. But, shortly afterwards, due to discord between the European Americans who treated them as property, Ben and Rit were separated into different living quarters that were miles apart, although they continued to have more children together.[7]

Harriet's owners, and the other local families with whom

they placed her, found it impossible to train her into an effective house servant.[8] Thus, as an adolescent she was let outside to work as a field hand, and then later with her father in the timber trades. By the time she reached the age of 11, she was already doing heavy work in fields and handling timber.[9] Then, in an incident that occurred in a store, Harriet's skull was fractured by a two-pound weight that was thrown in anger at another recalcitrant African American. The traumatic head injury, much like that of Charles, disabled Harriet for a year or two. It caused lifelong after-effects, primarily epileptic-type seizures that caused her to suddenly doze off.[10]

She recovered enough, however, to return to being an effective field and forest hand. In fact, the diminutive young woman developed a reputation for feats of strength. She lifted "huge barrels" and towed boats "like an ox." She took pride in her ability to do a man's work. Similar to Frederick, she devised a way to hire out her time. Harriet was able to save enough money, besides what she was obliged to pay her master, to acquire a pair of $40 working steers. Using their labor, she was able to save even more.[11]

Sometime around 1844, Harriet married John Tubman, a free black man. Not much is known about their marriage. Harriet had no children. She continued working in the Dorchester County lumber industry with her father and others. This gave her father, and through him Harriet, access to a loose community of African American watermen who traveled extensively, and who were conversant with distant areas of Maryland, and perhaps even Delaware, New Jersey, and Pennsylvania, which Harriet herself had never seen. Some of these watermen were aware of a network of abolitionist sympathizers who might prove ready to assist refugees from slavery in making the journey north to freedom.[12]

Harriet was given even more reason to contemplate escape because of the financial misfortunes of her owner, Edward Brodess. Unsuccessful as a small farmer and mired in debt,

CHAPTER 17: SHE SAW JOHN'S HEAD ON A SERPENT

Brodess was subjected to creditors' remedies, which included the impoundment of his slaves as well as their forced sale. The treatment of human beings as items of property subject to levy was one of the more absurd, and heartless, aspects of the archaic slave-owning society.[13] Three of Harriet's older sisters were sold off to slave traders to satisfy Brodess's debts and settle some of his financial affairs.[14] Harriet was incensed over the trauma these separations caused her family. She was fearful that more of her brothers and sisters, and maybe even Harriet herself, would also be sold South. This fear began to approach reality when, on March 7, 1849, Harriet's master Edward Brodess died at age 47, leaving his widow Eliza to manage an essentially bankrupt estate. Although Harriet had not lived with the Brodesses for years, Edward's death had an immediate impact.[15]

In the aftermath of the death of Edward Brodess, controversy broke out over the legal status of Rit Green. In part, this dispute was tied to the move by the Brodess family and its creditors to sell Rit's descendants. If the Brodess title to Rit and her progeny expired at some future time, they could not legally be sold to a third party as property subject to a life term of slavery. However, Gourney Crow Pattison, Atthow Pattison's grandson and the plaintiff who sued Eliza Brodess, was not seeking anybody's freedom. Instead, he took the position that ownership of Rit, as well as all fruits of Rit's labor after she reached age 45, reverted to him under the residuary clause of Atthow Pattison's 1797 will. One collateral consequence of this rather tedious contention was that during the pendency of appellate proceedings the Brodess family's advertised sales of Rit's granddaughters (and Harriet's nieces) Kessiah, another also named Harriet, and niece Harriet's 2-year-old daughter Mary Jane, were temporarily stayed.[16]

Harriet was fed up over the helplessness that attached to the impending sale of her nieces. The whole family felt extremely close ties to them. Harriet later characterized these young women to biographers as her sisters. Harriet was also worried that her younger brothers would be sold as well. On September 17, 1849, Harriet and two brothers, Henry and Ben, departed the Bucktown area of Dorchester County. Their absence likely was not noticed for a few days. On October 3, a "$300 reward" advertisement was published by Eliza Brodess, asking for the return of "Minty, aged about 27 years, of a fine chestnut color, fine looking, and about 5 feet high."[17] Shortly afterwards, the three fugitives returned. Harriet's brothers, it turned out, did not yet have the nerve to leave behind their wives, a young child, and aging parents.

Undaunted, Harriet soon headed north a second time, all by herself. Most likely, she left from a property being forested in Poplar Neck, Caroline County, a day's walk north of Bucktown, where Ben and Rit were living at the time.[18] Not a whole lot of attention was paid to the departure of a partially disabled woman. Nobody pursued Harriet. Using information she had carefully assimilated, Harriet succeeded in reaching a series of good Samaritans along

Photo portrait of Harriet Tubman, 1868
Library of Congress

CHAPTER 17: SHE SAW JOHN'S HEAD ON A SERPENT

the way who were prepared to shelter and help her along. The first was a white woman in whom Harriet had confided. This woman gave Harriet the names of two other sympathizers and directed her on how to find the first one. This benefactor, in turn, helped her on to the second. Ultimately, Harriet reached the free air of Pennsylvania. When she crossed over the line, she felt like she was in heaven.[19]

It was a heaven Harriet was determined to share. What set Harriet apart from thousands of other escapees was her absolute rejection of the tyranny and injustice of forcing African Americans to abandon their family and friends as a price of choosing freedom. Harriet justly earned her fame for her persistent trips back home, putting herself inside the lion's jaws of the slaveholding republic. In total, she made thirteen trips, bringing away roughly 70 to 80 people. In addition, she gave guidance and instructions that were instrumental in liberating approximately 50 or 60 more.[20] Following her initial escape to the North, Harriet spent much of the next year in Philadelphia and Cape May, New Jersey, doing domestic labor for wages. She saved her earnings with a single-minded yearning to return, liberate, and reunite the family she had left behind on the Eastern Shore.

By December 1850, Harriet was in Fells Point, the same Baltimore community where Frederick had lived over a decade earlier. From there, she coordinated a successful plot to rescue her niece Kessiah and her two children, arranging for them to be literally snatched away from the auction block on which they had just been sold, and then helping them to be smuggled by Kessiah's husband across Chesapeake Bay in a sailboat fashioned from dugout logs lashed together.[21] On this occasion, Harriet did not personally return to the Eastern Shore. But her work of liberation was only beginning. A few months later, she returned again to Baltimore, this time to help smuggle her brother Moses and two other men to freedom.[22]

In the fall of 1851, Harriet did travel to the Eastern Shore on a mission to bring out her husband John Tubman. In this, she was severely hurt and disappointed. Harriet found that John had taken another wife, a free woman named Caroline. He refused to have anything to do with Harriet. But, putting aside her personal sorrow, she used her newly developed knowledge of sympathetic people along the route to bring out another group of African Americans who wanted to leave for freedom.[23] On either this or a later occasion, Harriet brought a group of eleven rescued refugees to Frederick's home in Rochester. From there, they made their way across the border into Canada.[24]

Harriet typically planned the escape she organized to begin on a Saturday evening, or, even better yet, over the Christmas holiday. Given that Sunday was the Sabbath, the absence of servants was not likely to be discovered until Monday, giving runaways the advantage of a two-day head start.[25] Harriet knew better than to venture onto the plantations herself. She arranged for a rendezvous point where she would meet the refugees and lead them from there. She almost always traveled with her party by night, and slept with the refugees she was escorting during the day. For this reason, she preferred to do her liberation work in winter, when the nights were longer. Absolute commitment was required from all members of her parties. She threatened to have someone in her party kill, with a revolver, anybody who gave up and went back. A dead fugitive could not inform.[26]

In December 1854, Harriet finally retrieved her brothers. She went to get them at Christmastime after learning – she afterwards attributed her knowledge to a "feeling that a great evil was hanging over their heads" – that the three of them were to be auctioned off on the following Monday. Harriet took them north from Ben & Rit's home on Poplar Neck. On the way they stopped at a much-used "Underground Railroad" station, reliable sympathizer Thomas Garrett's home in

CHAPTER 17: SHE SAW JOHN'S HEAD ON A SERPENT

Wilmington, Delaware. By December 29, Harriet and her brothers successfully reached Philadelphia.[27]

Because of increasing suspicions falling on him in view of the escapes of so many of his children, Ben Ross, although he had been technically "free" for fifteen years, decided he needed to take some precautions to promote his security. On June 11, 1855, he recorded a bill of sale memorializing his "purchase" of his wife Rit for $20.[28]

In May 1856, Harriet made another trip to the Eastern Shore in which she helped liberate four slaves. It was during this rescue that she became uneasy, feeling something was wrong and that her party was in jeopardy. She always seemed to sense when danger was near. In these moments her heart, as she said later, would go "flutter, flutter." Some 30 miles from Wilmington, intuition led her to suddenly change her planned route. Later she recalled that, "God told her to stop," which she did, "but then he told her to leave the road, and turn to the left." As they approached a "small stream of tide water," they looked for a boat or a bridge to cross over, but found none. Their only option was to wade across, but the water was cold and the depth of the stream was unknown, so the men refused to go in. Harriet was convinced they had no choice and that, if they did not cross, the risk of capture was too great. So she plunged in and waded across without them. The water nearly reached her shoulders, but no higher, and she safely reached the other side. Seeing Harriet had not drowned, her refugees reluctantly followed.[29] Like Jeanne d'Arc, Harriet was convinced she had divine support for her leadership. She assured colleagues in the "Underground Railroad" that she never went on a "mission of mercy" without God's consent.[30]

In October 1856, Harriet arranged the escape of "Tilly," a young woman of mixed African and European descent. Tilly's husband had previously been conveyed to the North on one of Harriet's prior expeditions. On this trip, to get away from the

Eastern Shore Harriet actually took Tilly southward, boarding a boat bound for Seaford, Delaware on the Nanticoke River. This was to avoid the attention the two African American women would have received had they been traveling northward. Once again, God seemed to smile on Harriet. Harriet herself carried a forged certificate of freedom, but she had nothing to cover Tilly's presence. Using the assistance of a friendly clerk, she managed to get Tilly a forged travel pass while she was on the boat. From Seaford, Harriet and Tilly took a train to Camden, Delaware, near Wilmington.[31]

Only a month later, Harriet was back in Caroline County. She was again unable to bring away her sister Rachel as she hoped, but she did arrange for the escape of another willing group. One of these men, Josiah "Joe" Bailey, was a skilled lumberman who had just been purchased for a price of $2,000. The new owner was extremely angry about his loss. He posted a reward of $1,500 for Joe's return. Harriet's journey along the route to Wilmington with this party of refugees was extraordinarily slow and difficult. Nevertheless, with the aid of her "Railroad operators," she evaded a very active pursuit and made it to Philadelphia, then moved on immediately to New York and Canada. The success of this miraculous odyssey cemented Harriet's reputation as "Moses." Harriet had tremendous charisma and fame among African Americans, who believed she had a "charm." It was said by many that "the Lord has given Moses the power."[32]

Harriet, who previously had worked for wages to support her rescue trips, now began to devote her time in between voyages to fund raising among abolitionists in the North. In the first week of April of 1857, she started south, from Philadelphia, with the objective of bringing her parents out of Maryland to join their other family members. By the end of May, she made it to Poplar Neck. She made a makeshift horse-drawn cart with which she transported Ben and Rit, both in their 70s, to Wilmington. They arrived June 4, 1857. Even

Chapter 17: She Saw John's Head on a Serpent

though Ben and Rit were both technically "free," they were still processed by the Underground Railroad operatives as if they were escaping slaves.[33] After getting them as far as Rochester, Harriet left her parents with others and set out to return to the Eastern Shore. She was still determined to bring out her sister Rachel and her two children. Again, she was unsuccessful in getting any of the three to leave. But Harriet did help a large group of bondsmen plan a mass escape, which they stunningly executed. This large-scale exodus of over forty African Americans in the fall of 1857, referred to in the press as a "stampede of slaves," threw the slaveholding community in Maryland into unprecedented turmoil. The attention attracted by the situation turned into a national media frenzy. The slaveholders who met at Cambridge on November 2 to consider what to do about the "stampede" had no idea that Harriet, who many of them knew personally from her earlier days in bondage, was a major adversary that they faced.[34]

Because of the uproar over the "stampede," Harriet had to stay away from the Eastern Shore for a while. She instead spent much of her time, during the winter of 1857–1858, in a refugee community she herself had done much to populate, in St. Catharine's, Ontario, just west of the U.S. border at Niagara Falls. But she also spent time in the home of Frederick Douglass, where she stayed during January 1858. John Brown arrived at Frederick's very shortly after Harriet's departure.[35] If John was not already familiar with Harriet and her exploits, he undoubtedly heard all about her from Frederick. John, as we have seen, was at this time very busy fleshing out his plans for a rebel state he hoped to project into the South. John and his key financial supporters were enticed by the notion that African Americans should "help their brethren" resist by force the shackles of hereditary slavery. In John's mind the rebellion would be, quite literally, spearheaded by African Americans. The problem was, he lacked the necessary corps of African

Americans. Harriet attracted his attention in this regard.

John and Harriet met for the first time in St. Catharine's on April 7, 1858. John immediately set to work on incorporating Harriet into his plan for the attack at Harpers Ferry. Harriet received John in her St. Catharine's residence, accompanied by a small group of her Dorchester County refugees whom she had assembled for the occasion.[36] Disregarding Harriet's gender, John wrote curiously of his enthusiasm in the wake of that meeting. "Harriet Tubman hooked on his [sic] whole team at once. He (Harriet) is the most of a man, naturally, that I ever met with. There is the most abundant material, and of the right quality, in this quarter, beyond all doubt."[37]

But this would prove to be yet another demonstrable instance in which John's glowing remarks reflect his disconnect with reality. John courted Harriet avidly over the course of the next several weeks. On April 12, John, who, as we know, was very short on cash himself, and who was busy at the time trying to raise funds, gave Harriet $15 to help pay her rent. Then, two days later, he gave her a draft from Gerrit Smith redeemable for $25 in gold. This may well be money that Smith gave John with the intent to convey it to Harriet, but John was accustomed to being on the receiving end of Smith's donative transfers. Despite the financial courtship, John's hopes for involving Harriet in his terrorist plot were sorely disappointed. On April 15, Harriet failed to appear for a meeting that John had scheduled. He sent a plaintive letter to William Day, an African American publisher, inquiring what had happened. "May I trouble you to see her at once?" he asked.

Unbeknownst to John, Harriet had already left St. Catharine's.[38] And this evasion would prove to be typical. Over the course of the next year, Harriet's expressed attitude toward John would always remain friendly and supportive. But with unspoken body language, she would assiduously avoid any

CHAPTER 17: SHE SAW JOHN'S HEAD ON A SERPENT

entanglement in his schemes.

Harriet, as we have seen, had qualities of a "sixth sense." Before meeting John, she repeatedly had a dream that she later emphasized to Sanborn. In the dream she was in a "wilderness sort of place, all full of rocks and bushes," when she saw a serpent raise its head among the rocks. As the serpent did so, its head became that of an old man with a long white beard. The man was gazing at her "wishful like, just as if he were going to speak to me." Then two other heads rose up beside him, younger than he. As she stood looking at them, and wondering what they could want with her, a great crowd of men rushed in and struck down the younger heads, and then also the head of the old man, still looking at her so "wishful." When she met John, shortly after, behold, he was the very image of the head she had seen on the serpent. Later, after Harpers Ferry, she realized that the other two heads were those of John's sons who perished there.[39]

Although both of them vehemently opposed the institution of slavery, Harriet and John, in terms of their personalities, were just about as different as two people can be. The absolute inconsistency of their character as human beings is a fundamental truth that has eluded their biographers. Harriet felt a powerful empathic love for her family and for everything associated with family. She was deeply and emotionally offended by the "sale" of her family members, probably just as much because of the shock and pain that the forced separation caused her parents as because of its effects on herself. Her escape from Maryland was fueled as much by revulsion at the advertised "sale" of her niece – whom she called a "sister" in speaking to her biographers – as by anything else. Harriet was bound and determined to find liberty, not just by herself, but with her family.[40] Harriet's passion for family was so strong that it far overflowed her actual biological family and attached itself to many others of a similar ethnic and cultural background. She fought to liberate them, as well. But Harriet did not have an appetite for initiating violence.

John, on the other hand, felt the ascetic's veiled disdain for family commitment, which George Orwell noticed typifies "saints" such as Gandhi.[41] He could separate himself from his wife and small children for years on end, and he could leave them to struggle on their own with a hardscrabble existence, in the name of fighting for a greater cause. He could lead his children to a near certain death. He could, and would, watch his children die with the same equanimity with which he viewed his own righteous martyr's death. John felt, and acted on, the emotion of hatred. He hated slave owners with a tremendous passion and he felt that not only slave owners, but anybody else who enabled the institution of slavery, deserved to die. His development and channeling of an attitude of deadly hatred toward a class of civilian "enemies" was the archetype of a terrorist's mentality.

Harriet, unlike John, did not hate slave owners. Harriet had the insight necessary to understand an entire social system that victimized the slave owners almost as much as it victimized their captives. She remarked as much to a writer who collected her stories:[42]

> I think there's many a slave-holder will get to Heaven. They don't know no better. They act up to the light they have. You take that sweet little child [pointing to a baby] – appears more like an angel than anything else – take her down there, let her never know nothing about niggers but they were made to be whipped, and she'll grow up to use the whip on them. No Missus, it's because they don't know no better.

On May 6, 1858, John brought nine of his "Kansas regulars" from Iowa to Chatham, Canada, where he had set up a "convention" for the purpose of ratifying his newly written "constitution." The purpose of the "convention" was also to

Chapter 17: She Saw John's Head on a Serpent

recruit African Americans from among the Canadian expats to carry the constitution into effect. John was still looking for Harriet, but she was nowhere to be found. The Chatham event went on anyway. Other African Americans were elected to hold the offices specified in John's constitution, but the convention was largely a disappointment. Harriet failed to appear, fewer men than John expected showed up to discuss his plan, and some of those who did come expressed the opinion that he would be disappointed, because the slaves would not know enough to rally to his support. By the end of the proceedings, John was too broke to even pay his hotel bill.[43] Besides, he now had another major problem. Hugh Forbes had re-emerged. Hugh's latest communications had touched off a shock wave in the minds of John's committee of financial supporters.

Charles Sumner was never a supporter of John's terror plan. Even though he personally had been a victim of savage political violence, he remained the same man who had first earned his way into the public eye with a speech in praise of universal peace. Charles heard out Hugh. He wrote several letters on Hugh's behalf to his friend Samuel Howe, who was among John's "Secret Six." Howe, on behalf of John's committee of fundraisers, sent a highly negative written response which Charles, acting in the role of an intermediary, then shared with Hugh.

On April 19, Hugh sent Howe a sharp reply to this letter, which challenged him, point by point. The first and most critical disagreement he raised was that "you have entire confidence in the integrity and capacity of Capt. John Brown." Hugh begged to differ. In support of his position he enclosed a copy of the letter he had previously written to John Jr., which laid out the fallacies of John's plan as well as the virtues of his own competing plan to attack slavery through operations that encouraged the type of "stampede of slaves" already experienced in Maryland. Hugh was offended at the idea that responsible "humanitarians," as he called John's financial supporters, would allow their strategy to be dictated by a lone, stubborn, man pursuing a highly dubious, and essentially suicidal, course of action. The question, Hugh wrote, should be resolved by the decision of "an appropriate committee." Hugh expressed confidence that any degree of rational deliberation would overrule John:[44]

> Were I addressing certain persons, I should say to them – See that Brown not be permitted to put into execution his own plan; let the "well matured plan," or mine, or some other better one be substituted; see that a proper committee of management be put at its head, and that leading men different from Brown be sought different from Brown in their humanity, integrity, truthfulness and capacity.

This letter, and another, similar letter that Hugh sent to Sanborn, panicked most of John's secret committee of supporters. They were especially concerned because Hugh's letters made it clear he knew most of the details of John's plan (contrary to what John had assured them in March) and, also, because they established in writing Hugh's awareness that Stearns, Howe, and Sanborn were all in on the project. Financially supporting somebody else's terror attack was one thing, but being traceable to a conspiracy to commit such crimes was quite another. On May 5, Sanborn, Stearns, Parker, and Howe all met to consider what to do. The "committee" did in fact override John, but not in the way Hugh had envisioned. They decided to order John to postpone his attack until a diversionary strategy vis-à-vis Hugh could be put into effect. John and his men would instead be supplied with money to return to Kansas to wait out the storm.[45] Their decision was reinforced by yet another letter from Hugh, dated May 6, in which Hugh explicitly informed Howe that he had discussed

CHAPTER 17: SHE SAW JOHN'S HEAD ON A SERPENT

the issue, in varying degrees of depth, with Senators Henry Seward and John Hale, as well as Charles Sumner.[46]

On May 10, Howe wrote a response to Hugh that was an intentional deception. He pretended to have no interest at all in the matter, other than a sincere desire to bring about free elections in Kansas. After reiterating his denial that he bore any responsibility for John's financial commitments, he informed Hugh that John was being sent back out to Kansas on a mission wholly inconsistent with the Harpers Ferry attack plan.[47]

> In order, however, to disabuse you of any lingering notion that I, or any of the members of the late Kansas committee (whom I know intimately) have any responsibility for Captain Brown's actions, I wish to say that the very last communication I sent to him was in order to signify the earnest wish of certain gentlemen, whom you name as his supporters, (in your letter and in the anonymous one,) that he should go at once to Kansas and give his aid in the coming elections.

The next day, Sanborn wrote another letter in an effort to bring along Higginson, who was adamantly opposed to postponement. Sanborn's principal argument was that the "three largest stockholders" in the venture, meaning Stearns, Smith, and Parker as the ones on John's "committee" who had the real money to contribute, all insisted on the delay associated with sending John to Kansas. But another argument he made in that letter betrays the awareness of the "Secret Six" about the true nature of John and his plan. Sanborn said he could not "quite yield" to Higginson's arguments, because Hugh had it in his power to remove "the terror" of John's attack.[48]

Chapter 18: A Massacre and a Midnight Murder

It was now inevitable that the political battle, if contested at all fairly, was going to be resolved in favor of the admission of Kansas as a "free state." The slave power was, in the final analysis, fighting a war largely with mercenaries. Most colonists from Southern states did not own slaves. They were not particularly interested in becoming slave owners themselves, nor were they interested in engaging in economic competition with plantations organized around slavery. The fate of an 1856 expedition of sponsored emigrants led to Kansas from Georgia and Alabama by Jefferson Buford, an Alabama attorney, illustrates how this played out. A good number of these Southern émigrés, after finding disillusionment, eventually changed their views to support free state principles.[1] By 1858, the meaningful political struggle in Kansas was not free staters versus partisans of the institution of slavery but, rather, between conservative and radical factions of the free staters. Instead of forcing the latest slave-state "Lecompton Constitution" down the throats of the settlers, as was originally proposed, Congress passed a bill

CHAPTER 18: A MASSACRE AND A MIDNIGHT MURDER

providing for this pro-slavery document to be addressed in a plebiscite, which was ultimately set for August 2, 1858.[2] It was well known that the pro-slavery party could win this electoral contest only by some kind of fraud, rather than by actual votes. Their only hope was to take advantage of any mistake the free state leaders might make.[3]

Northern Kansas, centered on the settlements of Lawrence and Topeka, Lecompton, and Leavenworth, had been largely pacified ever since the time Geary took over as Governor in the fall of 1856. The war-torn area now shifted to what was sometimes called "Southeast Kansas": Linn and Bourbon Counties, the area bordering Missouri immediately south and east of Osawatomie. As in Northern Kansas, the early conflict centered on ownership of farm land. And as in Northern Kansas, the initial Territorial machinery of government, installed from Washington, was proslavery. Courts and sheriffs looked with disfavor on free state settlers who staked claims to desirable property. They were ready, willing, and able to award legal title to Southern settlers instead. Linn and Bourbon Counties being so close to Missouri, a substantial number of pro-slavery settlers came across the border to displace free state settlers and have the authorities eject them from their new farms. This injustice, in turn, engendered tremendous resentment and bitterness.

James Montgomery emerged, in this environment, as a sort of frontier Robin Hood. Born in 1813, he was thirteen years younger than John Brown, with whom he had much in common. Like John, Montgomery grew up on the frontier. He was raised by his parents in Kentucky, mastering pioneer skills such as horsemanship and using guns. Like John, Montgomery gravitated strongly toward religion. He became an ordained minister in the fundamentalist Church of Christ, sometimes pejoratively called the "Campbellite" church. When the Kansas-Nebraska Act was enacted, he moved first to western

Missouri and, then, when Kansas was officially available for settlement, he moved across the border to an attractive claim in Linn County.[4]

James Montgomery, c. 1858

Like many other Kansas settlers, Montgomery rapidly acquired a distaste for the pro-slavery establishment and its bullying methods. In the late fall of 1855, he attended a meeting for the nomination of candidates for office being run by the government authorities at a Linn County town called Sugar Mound. Montgomery was appointed secretary of the meeting, in view of his literacy and education. But he rapidly expressed his disapproval of the pre-programmed pro-slavery agenda. He wanted the candidates to be required to define their positions. Montgomery's eloquence turned the meeting into something of a free state triumph, but it also made him some bitter enemies. One of them was George W. Clarke. Clarke was the pro-slavery chieftain responsible for killing Thomas Barber, whose corpse was placed on display, as we have reviewed, in the conflict outside Lawrence on December 5, 1855. In late 1856 Clarke brought a militia into Linn County and began systematically harassing free state settlers to induce them to leave their claims. Many were deliberately plundered of cattle, horses, goods, and crops; in many instances their cabins burned, and, on occasion, outrages of a sexual nature were committed. Montgomery believed the organs of "justice" were perverted in favor of the pro-slavery faction. So in response he participated in organizing a free state

Chapter 18: A Massacre and a Midnight Murder

militia called the "Self-Protective Company."[5]

Montgomery and his militia began using a bullying tactic of their own. They would "warn out," on pain of depredation or worse, those persons who had wrongfully taken over claims from free staters, as well as anybody else who was believed to be a militant adherent of the slave power. Those who did not leave within the specified time were visited again, when their houses were searched, and arms, ammunition, horses, and any other desirable property taken from them. Montgomery himself described "warning out" as follows:[6]

> The troops I have the honor to command are of the order called "guerrilla," and are bound by the rules of strict guerrilla warfare. We make not, as falsely charged, a war upon all who differ with us politically, but only on those who have been and are warring upon our people. The quiet, peaceable Pro-Slavery man has nothing to fear from us; he may remain among us, and enjoy his political opinions unmolested. We will protect, and have protected him in his rights.
>
> The violent pro-slavery man who will not give us the country we have fairly conquered, but still continues to molest, disturb, and kill the peaceable settlers; we go to and say to him, this country is ours; you and I have fought which shall have it, and we have fairly conquered you, and mean to have it. In so many days you must leave it.
>
> And as the idea of "guerrilla" is self-sustaining, we also say, if you have any money, we must have some of it, and if you have any horses, we must have them for service, etc. Yet I am very careful not to allow my men to take from any but persons of this description. If they do, I expel them immediately from my company, and restore the articles to their rightful

possessors.

Charles Hamilton and his two younger brothers, George and Al, came to Southeast Kansas with the Buford party from a town called Cassville, situated in Georgia about halfway between Atlanta and Chattanooga. Their father, Thomas Hamilton, was an outspoken advocate of the institution of slavery.[7] Charles had served in the Mexican War, where he had command of troops from Cassville. He was a burly five foot ten inches tall. Although occupying the polar opposite position on the issue of slavery, in the atmosphere of Kansas Charles, like John Brown, rapidly became far more interested in pillaging with a political agenda than in farming. He became a pro-slavery paramilitary chieftain, and he established himself in a fortified log cabin just over the border into Kansas from Missouri, near a pre-Territory settlement known as Trading Post. This log cabin was known to the locals as "Fort Hamilton." Sometime around May 1, 1858, James Montgomery and his militia gave Charles a "warning-out" ultimatum to pack up and leave Kansas Territory.[8] Charles heeded the warning, but he was angry. The settlers, fearing reprisal, kept a guard on watch for a time after Charles left. But by May 17, nothing had happened. The guards went back to their farms.[9]

On Tuesday, May 18, a meeting took place at the Missouri residence of Thomas Jackson, attended by numerous pro-slavery "delegates" from both Missouri and Kansas. They engaged in a heated debate about the best policy to adopt with respect to Kansas Territory. Some favored a continuation of essentially the original policy of harassment, still hoping that the free state settlers would become weary of strife and for the sake of peace leave the Territory. A minority favored indiscriminate slaughter of people who supported the free state political position. Charles was an advocate of the latter method. "[H]e urged the policy of striking terror into the enemy" by a means of a sneak attack.[10]

CHAPTER 18: A MASSACRE AND A MIDNIGHT MURDER

That same night, Charles returned to Kansas with a group of around twenty-five mounted men, including his two brothers and, as his "Lieutenant," Walter B. Brocket, the same Brocket whom John had captured along with Pate two years earlier at the Battle of Black Jack.[11] They took a slightly circling route in order to approach Trading Post from the west, crossing the Marais des Cygnes River at a point adjacent to the town, about 30 meandering miles downstream from the site of the battle of Osawatomie. A beautiful, quiet May day was just breaking when the raiders emerged from the timber bordering the Marais des Cygnes. The Hamilton men were greeted cheerfully by John Campbell, a young, unmarried clerk who worked in the Trading Post town grocery store. Perhaps, as Charles afterwards claimed, Campbell mistook them for Montgomery's militia. Charles surprised Campbell by taking him prisoner. Then his band pillaged the store. A customer in the store, and others in town who were accosted by the raiders, were let go. Charles made subjective judgments about whether or not particular locals were friends or enemies. At some point, the band encountered an Irish settler named Patrick Ross, who had previously been forced off his claim by paramilitary ruffians associated with Charles. They took Ross into their custody along with Campbell.

B.L. Read was a Baptist clergyman, 49 years of age, and a native of Connecticut. In July 1857, he and his wife had emigrated from Illinois to Kansas Territory. Read had acted as a judge of the "free state election," which is likely why Charles tabbed him as an "enemy" when he and his band encountered Read conversing with two other men at the entrance to the driveway of Sam Nichols, a settler who lived about a mile north of Trading Post. The other men were released, but Read was taken prisoner at gunpoint and his pony was confiscated.[12]

The Hamilton band blocked the road. At the roadblock it stopped and kidnapped a stranger in his 20s named William

Stillwell, who resided in Sugar Mound, when he came riding up in his two-horse wagon. In Stillwell, the ruffians smelled money. After commandeering his wagon and handing it over to a local whom they viewed as a sympathizer, and after unharnessing and taking his horses, they ordered Stillwell to fall into line with the other captives. The raiders then went into the Nichols home, looking to seize Sam Nichols. Sam Nichols was not present. Only his wife and children were at home, so they ransacked the place, stealing horses, guns, and ammunition.[13]

The Hamilton gang forced their growing collection of prisoners to trudge eastward, toward the nearby Missouri border. Charles sent detachments ahead to round up some other "enemies." One was 58-year-old William Hairgrove, a native of South Carolina and formerly a resident of Georgia and Mississippi. Hairgrove was conservative politically and had voted for President Buchanan, but Charles felt he did not adequately adhere to the pro-slavery cause. Al Hamilton found Hairgrove working in a field alongside the road. He took both William and his young son prisoner at gunpoint. They were brought to Hairgrove's residence, where several other local residents – Amos Hall, William Colpetzer, and Michael Robertson – had also been seized and assembled, along with Charles Snider, a man who was merely visiting the Robertsons from Illinois. The raiders, when taking the men away, assured their wives that they would not be harmed. At Hairgrove's place, the rampaging band commandeered a team of mules. Hairgrove's young son from the field was exchanged as a captive for his older 28-year-old son, Asa Hairgrove.[14]

The forced march continued. The raiders encountered Austin Hall, the brother of Amos Hall, driving an ox cart. He too was taken captive. Austin had been returning home from Charles's next intended destination, the shop and home of a blacksmith named Elias Snyder. The blacksmith was commonly called "Dutch" Snyder because of his German birth

CHAPTER 18: A MASSACRE AND A MIDNIGHT MURDER

and accent.[15] Charles and Dutch Snyder had history. The previous month, Snyder had been involved in a physical altercation with some of the men in Charles's militia at a saloon in Trading Post. Afterwards Charles himself had a heated discussion with Snyder, in which threats were uttered. Now, Charles left the main body of the raiding party with the collection of prisoners and took a small detachment to arrest Snyder at his shop and adjacent residence, located in a rolling, partly wooded area.

But Snyder, due to the feud, prudently kept a loaded shotgun handy. When the Hamilton band approached the open front of the shop where Snyder, accompanied by his brother and a customer, was working, Snyder called out to his son to get the shotgun. With it, Snyder fired a blast of buckshot which struck Charles's horse in the neck, disabling it and slightly wounding Charles himself. Snyder brandished the shotgun as if to shoot again, forcing the raiding party to temporarily withdraw. Snyder and the others then ran out the back of the shop. Although Dutch Snyder was hit by the raiders' fire, they all escaped into the adjacent thickly wooded area where the Hamilton mounted party could not easily follow.[16]

Charles's exact intentions, had he taken Dutch Snyder captive without resistance, are open to conjecture. In the wake of his wounding and Snyder's escape, he turned on his hostages with a terrorist's cold fury. All would be executed. After walking his injured horse back to where the captives were held, he ordered them to get on the march. In about a mile, they came to the ravine of a small stream. Charles instructed the prisoners to descend into the ravine, line up and face him. Then he commanded his own party, still mounted on horseback, to form their own line and "present arms." The unarmed prisoners stood looking up into gun muzzles about 10–12 feet away, their heads on roughly the same level with the horses' hooves. When not all of his men showed alacrity in obeying his order to prepare to shoot the captives, Charles cursed angrily and repeated his order. Brocket turned his horse away and declared he would not have anything to do with the gruesome act.[17] But when Charles drew his own revolver, his brothers and others in the band followed suit by also pointing their weapons. Charles shouted "Fire!" A volley of shots rang out. The victims collapsed to the ground.

Of the eleven unsuspecting men who had been led away from their homes and occupations that morning, five died in the ravine. Five others were seriously wounded by the terrorist gunshots. Only one prisoner, Austin Hall, was not hit. He, however, prudently dropped to the earth also, and lay very still, pretending to be dead. He was rapidly drenched with blood spewing from the men next to him.

The killers were merciless. Several dismounted and kicked the bodies to see if they were dead. Colpetzer rose and begged for his life. He was finished off with a shot in the head. Someone called out, "old Read ain't dead." This prompted a raider named Hubbard to remark that Read also ought to be shot in the head. A member of the militia fired a shot through the ear of the man he thought was Read, but who, in reality, was Patrick Ross. The real Read had received a rifle shot in the first volley, the bullet entering just below his arm and coming out his shoulder. Lying face down, he held his breath so he would look dead. William Hairgrove was hit both with buckshot and with a bullet that passed through his lungs. The killers rifled through Stillwell's pockets, looking for money. They stripped a watch off young Campbell, who was still alive although mortally wounded by a shot to the abdomen. They also removed the key to the store safe from Campbell's pocket. After what seemed an eternity, the survivors, who dared not open their eyes, heard the sound of horses leaving. Read warned the rest in a low voice to make no sounds. Read's wife Sarah was the first to arrive at the killing ground, passing the raiders as they were leaving the scene. She recognized the

CHAPTER 18: A MASSACRE AND A MIDNIGHT MURDER

terrorists as the kidnappers of her husband because they were leading her pony. They returned it to her when she pointed out that it was her animal. In response to her persistent questioning, they vaguely gestured in the direction where she could find her husband and the other captives.[18]

After Sarah Read reached the scene of the atrocity, the wounded Read sent her back to the Colpetzer residence to get help. Mrs. Colpetzer, too shocked and upset to go herself, sent her husband's wagon. Dutch Snyder, summoned by Austin Hall, also came on scene with his customer's wagon. The dead bodies were collected from beneath the waiting scavenger birds and transported to a house in Trading Post, where three of the corpses were displayed. The next day, an avenging posse composed of 200 men of all political persuasions marched 10 miles across the border to confront the people of West Point, Missouri, which was thought to be the staging point for Charles's band. None of the raiders could be found there, however.[19]

Charles rapidly made his way across Missouri to St. Louis, where he told a newspaper reporter that the entire affair had been an action to stop depredations of the local free state militia chieftain, James Montgomery. According to Charles, the prisoners he took at Trading Post were allied with Montgomery. One of them informed him that "a number of persons" in an armed party were at Snyder's shop. In a blatant falsehood, Charles claimed to the newspaper reporter that he had released all the prisoners, but that, instead of going home, they gathered at Snyder's. He further claimed falsely that the settlers killed near Snyder's died as part of a "skirmish."[20] An Arkansas newspaper further reported the incorrect information that Hamilton's party "was composed of both pro- and anti-slavery men, so that it was not a party fight, but a simple resistance to and punishment of outlaws."[21]

The horror of the atrocity, which became known as the

"Marais des Cygnes massacre," made it an instant sensation in the national press. If there was any lingering doubt in the minds of John Brown's supporters about funding his return to Kansas, it disappeared in the wake of this grim news. On May 24, the entire Secret Six, except for Higginson, met in person in Boston. They unanimously resolved that John must go to Kansas at once.[22] While grumbling about this order in his private comments to Higginson, John obeyed. John accepted $500 for expenses to take his "regulars" back out to Kansas. The only exception, the follower whom he did not bring with him, was the handsome, blue-eyed John Cook. Cook, at his own request, was posted to Harpers Ferry to embed himself in the local community as an advance spy for the terror expedition that John still planned to carry out there.[23]

John arrived in Kansas on June 25, 1858. The site of Charles's terrorist attack attracted John like a powerful magnet. Since his departure from the state John had grown a long, full beard, a disguise that hindered some people in recognizing him. Adopting the fake name "Shubel Morgan," John went instantly to Trading Post and attempted to purchase the entire Snyder claim with its blacksmith shop. Dutch Snyder at first agreed to sell, but later, due to legal complications and possibly having a better offer, he did not go forward with the contract. However, he did allow "Shubel Morgan" and his men to quarter on the property and to erect, near the shop, a structure that they dubbed "Fort Snyder." There, between July 12 and 15, 1858, Dutch Snyder, Snyder's brother and sons, James Montgomery, and William Hairgrove all joined in signing the "Articles of Agreement" for "Shubel Morgan's Company." These Articles were, in essence, a condensed reprise of John's Chatham constitution.[24]

Very soon, however, John was broke. Montgomery, in the wake of the universal horror provoked by the aftermath of the Marais des Cygnes massacre, had concluded a peace agreement with the latest Governor of Kansas Territory. This

CHAPTER 18: A MASSACRE AND A MIDNIGHT MURDER

peace agreement included a ban on any raiding or pillaging. Because of the "peace" accord, John was deprived of his usual source of income. By July 20, John was writing to Sanborn with a plea for funds. In August, he grew sick with a bout of malaria. John was forced to depart "Fort Snyder" for Osawatomie, where he rested in bed for the next two months in the cabin of his brother-in-law Samuel Adair.[25] When he recovered in mid-October, he went up to northern Kansas to seek money. In a stratagem borrowed from Hugh Forbes, John claimed that because the NKC had not delivered on its commitment to him for $5,000, he had the authority as its agent to collect on promissory notes Kansas settlers had given to the NKC. This was, of course, sharply disputed by the real Kansas agent of the NKC. However, using this method, John succeeded in collecting several hundred dollars.[26]

Upon John's return to Southeast Kansas, troubles started brewing once again. On November 13, Montgomery led a daytime raid on Paris, the pro-slavery county seat of Linn County, with his apparent objective being to suppress a "pro-slavery" grand jury indictment. John went along on this venture, but he was not interested in addressing legal papers. He remained apart, on the outskirts of town, while Montgomery conducted his business. The boldness of Montgomery's attack on the justice system drew the ire of Kansas Territory's newest acting Governor, Hugh Walsh. He recommended the establishment of a $3,000 reward for the capture of Montgomery and a $500 reward for that of John. Sheriff C.W. McDaniel and Captain Robert Mitchell, the same conservative free state leaders who had led the party that went into Missouri hunting the Marais des Cygnes killers, now took a posse to "Fort Snyder" to arrest John. John was not present at the time, being in Osawatomie. But, under the leadership of "Colonel Whipple," John's followers put up a stiff armed resistance that caused the posse to withdraw. "Whipple" then had his men sally forth to capture and humiliate McDaniel and Mitchell.[27]

Another "peace meeting" followed. But then on December 16, the fragile "peace" was broken by Montgomery, who made a raid on Fort Scott to free a prisoner named Ben Rice. In the fighting, the former U.S. Marshal J.H. Little was killed, and his store was plundered of $7,000 worth of goods. John himself stayed out of the fray, but many of his "Kansas regulars" participated under Montgomery in this attack. Two days later, one of John's men, George Gill, was approached by an African American named Jim Daniels who was selling brooms. Although he was at liberty to peddle cleaning tools, legally speaking Jim was held in the status of slave property, by an owner just across the Missouri line in Vernon County. Jim Daniels and Gill got into a conversation. Jim took Gill into his confidence and told him he was worried that he, his wife, and children were about to be included as part of an estate sale. Gill promptly reported this news to John at Fort Snyder. John found in it the perfect opportunity to get back into the business he cherished most: terrorism in support of the cause of toppling slavery.[28]

On December 20, 1858, at about midnight, Missouri farmer Harvey Hicklin was awakened by a voice outside. "Hello, damned you, get up and make a light!" Harvey jumped out of bed and, as he did, he could see in the blaze of a full moon that the yard outside his home was full of men. He immediately realized he was being robbed. The robbers were, in fact, already busily bashing down the door to his cabin. Harvey grabbed his wallet and stashed it underneath the featherbed on which his two small children were sleeping. Just after he did, the door gave way. Men pointing deadly rifles stepped into the cabin, which was only dimly lit from the glow of a fireplace. While he was held at gunpoint, the intruders began searching all four rooms of the cabin for money.

CHAPTER 18: A MASSACRE AND A MIDNIGHT MURDER

Then the bearded John stepped into the cabin. He remarked to Hicklin, "Well, you seem to be in a tight place, but you shan't be hurt if you behave yourself." John informed Hicklin that he knew Hicklin was not the owner, but that he was going to take all the African Americans who belonged to his father-in-law's estate and free them. This included Jim Daniels, his wife Narcissa, and their two children, as well as another African American. He was also going to take all the property and provisions that would be necessary to help them on their way to freedom. The items to be stolen included Hicklin's two horses, a yoke of oxen, harnesses, pork, lard, a saddle, a harness, an overcoat, a pair of boots, and several bed blankets. In a pleasant tone, John informed Harvey that he was doing the Lord's will and he was not at all ashamed of it. After about a half hour of chatting, one of the men came in and announced, "Captain, the wagons are loaded and all is ready." John departed at 2 a.m., leaving two of his riflemen to stand guard over Harvey, with orders to shoot him if he tried to escape. The guards stayed with Hicklin another hour.

When they finally left, Hicklin ran immediately to the home of his nearest neighbor, John Larue. There he found Larue's father Isaac, who informed him that a similar robbery had occurred. His son had been kidnapped to serve as a hostage, along with another man, Dr. A. Ervin.[29] Later he learned

The bearded John Brown in Kansas during 1858 adopted the fake name "Shubel Morgan"

that another local resident, David Cruise, had been shot to death in his home by a separate party of intruders led by "Colonel Whipple." "Whipple" gained entry by pretending to be a traveler needing shelter for the night. After "Whipple" and his band invaded the home, they announced that they were taking everything they could carry away, including Jane, a pregnant African American servant. When Cruise protested, "Whipple" shot him through the heart with his rifle. While David Cruise lay dying on the floor, his wife Lucinda was forced at gunpoint to help the raiders gather up all valuable property. Cruise was an inoffensive settler who had lived in his home for 20 years. He was not involved in the Hamilton raid or any other political violence.[30]

Aaron D. Stevens, John Brown's military second-in-command. He was an escaped convict who had been previously sentenced to death by a U.S. Army court martial. He used the fake name "Colonel Whipple."

John's raid into Missouri went far above and beyond the issues involved with the Southeast Kansas troubles. It drew immediate criticism from all parties, including James Montgomery, who had refused to participate in it and who publicly disavowed it in a letter written to a newspaper on January 15, 1859.[31] The local free state settlers were unhappy about the raid because it exposed them to retaliation, while John expected to leave the area. A settler named George Crawford wrote in a letter to Eli Thayer:

> I called Captain Brown's attention to the facts that we were at peace with Missouri; that our Legislature was

then in the hands of Free-State men to make the laws; that even in our disturbed counties of Bourbon and Linn we were in a majority, and had elected the officers both to make and execute the laws; that without peace we could have no immigration; that no Southern immigration was coming; that agitation such as his was only keeping our Northern friends away.

Crawford added the comment that in this conversation John seemed "very erratic … but very earnest."[32]

John, as an instinctive terrorist, was supremely comfortable with the righteousness of his actions, no matter how excessive or questionable they appeared to others. For this reason, shortly after his raid on Missouri he engaged in one of the most typical acts of the terrorist: He wrote a manifesto explaining and justifying his crime. It was a letter intended for publication in newspapers both in Kansas and in the East, an outright vindication of what could be considered a capital offense.[33]

JOHN BROWN'S PARALLELS

Trading Post, Kansas, January, 1859

GENTLEMEN, – You will greatly oblige a humble friend by allowing the use of your columns while I briefly state two parallels, in my poor way.

Not one year ago eleven quiet citizens of this neighborhood – William Robertson, William Colpetzer, Amos Hall, Austin Hall, John Campbell, Asa Snyder, Thomas Stilwell, William Hairgrove, Asa Hairgrove, Patrick Ross, and B. L. Reed, – were gathered up from their work and their homes by an armed force under one Hamilton, and without trial or opportunity to speak in their own defence were formed into line, and all but one shot, – five killed and five wounded. One fell unharmed, pretending to be dead. All were left for dead. The only crime charged against them was that of being Free-State men. Now, I inquire what action has ever, since the occurrence in May last, been taken by either the President of the United States, the Governor of Missouri, the Governor of Kansas, or any of their tools, or by any proslavery or Administration man, to ferret out and punish the perpetrators of this crime?

Now for the other parallel. On Sunday, December 19, a negro man called Jim came over to the Osage settlement, from Missouri, and stated that he, together with his wife, two children, and another negro man, was to be sold within a day or two, and begged for help to get away. On Monday (the following) night, two small companies were made up to go to Missouri and forcibly liberate the five slaves, together with other slaves. One of these companies I assumed to direct. We proceeded to the place, surrounded the buildings, liberated the slaves, and also took certain property supposed to belong to the estate. We however learned before leaving that a portion of the articles we had taken belonged to a man living on the plantation as a tenant, and who was supposed to have no interest in the estate. We promptly restored to him all we had taken. We then went to another plantation, where we found five more slaves, took some property and two white men. We moved all slowly away into the Territory for some distance, and then sent the white men back, telling them to follow us as soon as they chose to do so. The other company freed one female slave, took some property, and, as I am informed, killed one white man (the master), who fought against the liberation.

Chapter 18: A Massacre and a Midnight Murder

Now for a comparison. Eleven persons are forcibly restored to their natural and inalienable rights, with but one man killed, and all "hell is stirred from beneath." It is currently reported that the Governor of Missouri has made a requisition upon the Governor of Kansas for the delivery of all such as were concerned in the last-named "dreadful outrage." The Marshal of Kansas is said to be collecting a *posse* of Missouri (not Kansas) men at West Point, in Missouri, a little town about ten miles distant, to "enforce the laws." All proslavery, conservative, Free-State, and dough-face men and Administration tools are filled with holy horror.

Consider the two cases, and the action of the Administration party.

Respectfully yours,

John Brown

Chapter 19: Gathering for the Storm

Late at night on Thursday, January 27, 1859, John and Aaron Stevens, aka "Captain Whipple," reached the town of Holton, Kansas, 33 miles north of Topeka, in a driving snowstorm. Well aware that they were wanted by the authorities in connection with their recent Missouri murder and robberies, they were headed out of Kansas Territory. With them were twelve rescued African Americans bent on attaining freedom. Originally John and "Whipple" had liberated eleven, but then Jane, the woman taken from the slain David Cruise, had given birth since leaving Missouri. John, "Whipple" and a coachman spent the night in the Holton Hotel, operated by Thomas Watters, while the African Americans remained out of sight, bunked together in the covered wagon. Before daylight they got under way again, heading north. But when they reached Straight Creek, 5 miles north of Holton, they found its waters so swollen from recent storms that it was impossible to cross.[1]

John used an empty cabin on the bank of the creek to shelter his African American charges. He himself, along with "Whipple," quartered in the nearby home of a free state sympathizer, Dr. Fuller. At about 10 o'clock the next morning, a small group of mounted pursuers reached the creek crossing.

CHAPTER 19: GATHERING FOR THE STORM

But John and "Whipple" held a critical advantage over them. They were bent on fighting to the death, while those out looking for them were on something of a lark. As they were investigating the occupants of the previously empty cabin, "Whipple" surprised them by pointing his Sharps rifle at their leader and ordering them to surrender. One did, but the other five put spurs to their horses and made a fast escape.

Word that John was in the vicinity spread like lightning. A request was made to the federal troops, quartered in Leavenworth, to send a force to capture him. However, these troops were again commanded by Colonel Sumner. As before, Charles's cousin reacted very slowly when asked to commit U.S. Army forces in a conflict involving John. A doctor and Deputy U.S. Marshal named J.P. Wood, who had been a thorn in the side of the Kansas free state party ever since the early days of 1855, decided to raise his own posse to catch John. He enlisted approximately twenty-five volunteers, who had no military experience or training. Their greenness would be on display very quickly when put to the test of fire.

Wood and his posse reached the residence of Dr. Fuller at around 3 p.m. John and "Whipple" had been joined, in the meantime, by a free state partisan from Holton named William Creitz, who had previously served as a member of "Whipple's" militia. Wood demanded the unconditional surrender of all the house's occupants. John peremptorily refused. Wood threatened to burn down the house. At this point, John and Wood agreed to allow the neutral non-combatants, Dr. Fuller, his family, and two neighbors, to leave. This left inside only John, "Whipple," Creitz and the prisoner taken earlier, who John kept in handcuffs as a hostage. John, "Whipple," and Creitz barricaded all of the doors and windows with furniture and sacks of flour. In the walls they dug out loopholes that could be used to fire at attackers from any direction. John and "Whipple" had every intention of fighting to the death, and they were determined to kill as many of the attackers as possible.

Wood and his posse had a fantasy that by sheer force of numbers they would be able to arrest John without violence. They were not terribly interested in risking their own lives in this adventure. Painfully aware of the accuracy of "Whipple's" Sharps rifle, they took care to stay outside of its range. They could see guns sticking out through holes in the chinking of the Fuller cabin. From inside the residence, Creitz could hear some in the posse suggest to Wood that they ought to retreat. Eventually Wood gave in and granted permission for his motley group to withdraw until more help arrived.[2] The posse thus enlarged, Wood now assembled them to guard the road at a place called Eureka, on the other side of another creek crossing about a mile north of the place where John was boarding with Dr. Fuller.

Freed from immediate pressure, John sent a messenger of his own to Topeka for help. Several of his "Kansas regulars" had been left behind there to gather provisions. They quickly gathered a group of fifteen free state volunteers with Sharps rifles to go to John's defense. Upon their arrival at 10 o'clock in the morning on Monday, January 31, John immediately got them on the march to confront Wood. Straight Creek now was crossed. John's newly assembled militia proceeded toward Eureka. Even though it appeared at first that Wood and his men would meet them in a battle line, as soon as the free state militia came into rifle range Wood's posse panicked once again and retreated to safety. Not content with simply crossing the creek at Eureka, John sent his men in hot pursuit. They soon captured three members of the posse and four horses, which were appropriated on the principle that "to the victor belong the spoils." Taking them along as hostages, John and his Topeka escort soon made their way to the Iowa border. On February 1, 1859, John, "Whipple," and their party of refugees departed Kansas for the last time.[3]

John rapidly crossed through Nebraska and went to Tabor, Iowa. Even though he had previously been received there with great hospitality and treated in the friendliest manner, now the very same citizens condemned his terrorist behavior. They curtly informed him that they did not consider his killing and thievery to be consistent with Christian principles. A public meeting repudiated John's conduct and threatened to take him into custody. As a result, John had to hastily leave town and flee eastward to his former haven in the Quaker community of Springdale, Iowa. There he spent two weeks in late February and early March. Even in Springdale, he had to be on the lookout for attempts to take all the fugitives, John included, into custody.[4]

Perhaps in response to the general hostility to his Missouri raid he faced from residents in Iowa, Brown penned another manifesto, entitled "Vindication of the Invasion." John's proffered justifications are a telling indicator of his thought process. First, "It was in accord with my settled policy." Second, "It was intended as a discriminating blow at slavery." Third (and "over and above all others"), "It was *right*."[5] The terrorist convinces himself or herself so thoroughly of the abiding "rightness" of his adopted cause that he, or she, becomes blinded to the horror and brutality of the act of terrorism. What John fundamentally underestimated, as many terrorists to follow would underestimate as well, is the utter revulsion that ordinary, upstanding citizens invariably feel about a terrorist act. Thus, even people who took no part in slaveholding, and who had no fondness for the institution of slavery, would firmly resist John's path of violence against unarmed civilians.

In general, the farther east John traveled, the warmer the reception he received from the abolitionist public. The farther east he traveled, the easier it became for him to minimize his acts of nighttime violence against civilians and place a favorable spin upon his raid into Missouri.[6] He showed off the African Americans he had rescued, raising money in Chicago to pay for their travel to Detroit and passage into Canada. John profited financially from bragging to audiences about his raid to liberate slaves and about his exploits in shepherding them to freedom. In a speech to abolitionist supporters in Cleveland, Brown proudly discussed the fact that the Governor of Missouri had offered a reward of $3,000, and U.S. President James Buchanan $250 more, for his capture. He sarcastically remarked that John Brown would give $2.50 for the safe delivery of the body of James Buchanan in any jail of the free states. He added that he would never submit to an arrest, as he had nothing to gain from submission. A resolution approving of John's course of action was introduced and adopted by the audience. He thanked the Cleveland audience very sincerely for its endorsement, although he was perfectly sure his course was right before.[7]

On April 11, 1859, John arrived at the Peterboro home of Gerrit Smith. With him was one of his newer "Kansas regulars," Jeremiah Anderson. Jerry, as the others called him, was a swarthy young man, described by one of his teachers as "morose" and "eccentric." Although he was perceived as "studious," Jerry like John had dropped out of school prior to graduation. Jerry was selected by John, out of all of his "regulars," to accompany him everywhere as a sort of adjutant. Gerrit Smith was pleased with the visit, and also with John's report on the Missouri raid. He immediately gave John $400. Two nights later, in a more public gathering at Smith's home, John made a speech in which he put his intended martyrdom for the cause on full display. Sanborn's former classmate Edwin Morton, who was then residing with Smith, wrote a letter to Sanborn describing this meeting:[8]

> You must hear of Brown's meeting this afternoon – few in numbers, but the most interesting I perhaps ever saw. Mr. Smith spoke well; G.W. Putnam read a

spirited poem; and Brown was exceedingly interesting, and once or twice so eloquent that Mr. Smith and some others wept. Some one asked him if he had not better apply himself in another direction, and reminded him of his imminent peril, and that his life could not be spared. His replies were swift and most impressively tremendous.

On his return to Massachusetts, John soon discovered that public donations for the anti-slavery cause had dried up, largely due to the peace that now prevailed in Kansas. John's studied vagueness about exactly what he planned to do with the money was also a probable factor in his meager receipts. John was warmly received as "manly" and righteous in the meetings but, apart from the Secret Six, he did not generate significant cash.[9]

Probably a typical reaction was that of John M. Forbes, a public-spirited and broad-minded businessman of Boston. Forbes became acquainted with John during May 1859. He observed, in a contemporary letter, that there was a "little touch of insanity" about John's "glittering gray-blue eyes." Forbes wrote that John "repelled, almost with scorn, my suggestion that firmness at the ballot-box by the North and West might avert the storm; and said that it had passed the stage of ballots, and nothing but bayonets and bullets could settle it now."[10]

The thinly veiled suicidal ideation expressed by John in his fund-raising speeches was disturbing to some of his backers. At a meeting in Boston, John presented George Stearns with a pearl-handled bowie knife, which he identified as the weapon he had taken from Henry Clay Pate at the Battle of Black Jack. He told Stearns he was giving it to him with the thought that the two of them would probably "never meet again in this world." Stearns found the sentiment upsetting. For months he had been led to believe that John expected to come away from his venture alive and ready to command a mountain fortress full of slaves.[11]

Stearns was also concerned by the angry exchange that took place between John and Henry Wilson after the presentation. Wilson, the more junior Massachusetts colleague of Charles Sumner in the U.S. Senate, was a charter member of the Free Soil party, a key supporter of Charles in his initial appointment to the Senate, and a vociferous opponent of the slave power.[12] But the year before, he had been exposed to Hugh's critique of John's strategy. Now he was seriously distressed by John's Missouri raid. In the meeting attended by Stearns, Wilson made it clear that he did not in any way approve of the use of violence. His censure, of course, drew a sharp rebuff from John.

Stearns was shocked by the vehemence of Wilson's comments. He realized, perhaps for the first time, what his relationship with John might mean for his future standing in the political abolitionist community of Massachusetts. Still, Stearns contributed $1,200 to support John's terror venture, well over half of the total funds Brown would raise during his final tour of New England.[13] John raised total funds of "almost $2,000" before departing Boston on June 3, 1859. This enabled him to stop at Collinsville, Connecticut, and make his final payment of $300 on the thousand custom-made iron-tipped pikes he had ordered two years earlier.[14] John had the spears boxed and shipped to "Isaac Smith & Sons, Chambersburg, Pennsylvania."[15]

John intended these weapons to be used by large numbers of rebellious slaves. He badly needed African American followers to carry out this plan. He felt such disciples would be much more able than whites to generate an instant uprising in the slave community. His inability to recruit significant numbers of African Americans into his terrorist plot was a continuing source of disappointment and anxiety.[16]

One person whose help John remained very eager to secure in this regard was Harriet Tubman. Since her last contact with John, Harriet had finally acquired a residence for

CHAPTER 19: GATHERING FOR THE STORM

the extended family she cherished. A home in Auburn, New York was sold to her, in a sweetheart deal, by Henry Seward. Now, during the spring of 1859, Harriet herself was busy with fund raising. She was intent on paying off her debt to Henry for the home purchase. Encountering a warm and enthusiastic reception in the abolitionist community for the marvelous stories of her rescue expeditions, she began to see financial rewards. Her talk at Higginson's church was very well received. On July 4, Harriet addressed a Massachusetts Anti-Slavery Society meeting at Framingham in which Higginson welcomed her to the platform. Harriet spoke as "Moses, the deliverer," rather than in her personal name. Once again, her appearance was a sensation. From it she raised $37, which she paid to Henry.[17]

Harriet shared the stage with John in at least one abolitionist revival meeting. She expressed support for John's fundraising, which, as we have seen, was largely unproductive outside of the Secret Six. John, however, wanted another kind of help from her. He was anxious for Harriet to return to Canada and gather black recruits for him. But in early June 1859, Harriet informed Sanborn that she could not or would not go. Harriet diplomatically, but assiduously, evaded any entanglement in John's actual plot. At the critical moment, she mysteriously disappeared. John Brown, Jr. expected to see Harriet in Boston in the middle of August, but their meeting did not materialize. On August 27, Sanborn wrote a letter to John, who had apparently inquired about her whereabouts, telling him that she was "probably in New Bedford, sick." In September John, "impatient and anxious," sent inquiries to Sanborn and others in search of her. Lewis Hayden wrote to John on September 16 to tell him that he had just written Harriet, asking her to hurry back to Boston. But by the end of September, Harriet had still not been heard from. With her extraordinary insight and survival instincts, she was aware that

John's attack plan was suicidal. She had suffered personally from the evils of bondage, she was very courageous, and she was just as opposed to the institution of slavery as anyone, but Harriet simply never believed in terrorist-style violence. Not only did she stay away from John's plot herself, she made sure none of her many friends or family members became involved in it either.[18]

John Unseld lived on a farm in western Maryland, just a short distance up the Potomac River from Harpers Ferry, Virginia. A small-time slave owner, he lived off the income from another farm he rented out, and some other investments. On the morning of July 4, 1859, Unseld was walking toward Harpers Ferry along the road near his home when he encountered a bearded old man with three men who appeared to be in their 20s. The older man introduced himself as Isaac Smith. "Smith" then introduced two of the younger men as his sons, Oliver and Watson. The other was Jerry. "Smith" explained that the four of them were farmers from northern New York, where their crops had been ruined by cold weather, and that they were seeking farmland further south.

Upon his return from town that afternoon, Unseld once again encountered this same group. This time he chatted with them at more length. Smith remarked favorably to Unseld on the looks of the local land. He asked whether Unseld knew of any nearby farm that might be available for rent. Unseld, in response, pointed out to Smith a small nearby farm with a house and a cabin that had been owned by a Dr. Kennedy, who had recently died, and that was for sale. Smith soon leased this farm from Kennedy's widow through March 1860 for a total prepaid rent of $35.[19] Over the next three months Unseld, while riding on horseback, stopped by the Smith residence every week or so just to say hello, but he declined Smith's invitations to get off the horse and come inside. Unseld questioned aloud how Smith could make a living off such a small farm. "Well," replied Smith, "my business has been buying fat cattle, and

CHAPTER 19: GATHERING FOR THE STORM

driving them to the State of New York, and selling them, and we expect to engage in that again."[20]

In reality, of course, "Isaac's" real name was not "Smith." It was John. John picked the Kennedy farm, about 4 miles north of the town of Harpers Ferry along the main road on the Maryland side of the Potomac, to use as the safe house and staging area for his raid on the town that lay across the river, on the Virginia side. The 1,000 steel-tipped pikes, as well as the fifteen boxes of Sharps rifles whose control John had managed to wrest from the MKC, were all delivered to the Kennedy farm from John's other safe house in Chambersburg, Pennsylvania, 50 miles to the north.[21] In small groups, John's "Kansas regulars," augmented by a handful of Quaker abolitionists whom Brown had recruited during his stays in Springdale, Iowa, were slowly filtered into the farm. The militia men were at all times carefully concealed inside the house, so that they could never be seen by neighbors. The only residents of the Kennedy house whom Unseld ever saw, besides "Isaac Smith" and sons, were Smith's daughter Anne, and Martha, Oliver's wife. Anne and Martha stayed at the Kennedy farm house from shortly after it was rented in July until the end of September. Oliver and Martha had recently married on April 7, 1858. He was 20 years old, and she was 17. Martha's role with the Brown gang at the Kennedy farm was to act as housekeeper and cook. Anne's

Sketch of the house at the Kennedy Farm, where John Brown staged his men and organized his attack on Harpers Ferry

main job was to stand watch. She had to be ready to stall any visitors until John's band could rush up to the attic loft to hide.[22] The attic loft served as a gymnasium, prison, and hiding place, during the day, and as the sleeping quarters for John's men at night.[23]

John, aka "Smith," adjusted his disguise by again changing his facial hair. He now shortened his long gray Kansas beard into one only an inch and a half long.[24] John's communications, and those of the people involved in his terrorist organization, were couched in code. He had his associates refer to their project, in letters, as "coal mining."[25] By mid-August, the men concealed at the Kennedy farm included three of John's sons, two brothers of his son-in-law Henry Thompson, and eight of the "Kansas regulars." They spent their confinement in the house playing games such as checkers, singing songs, and reading and rereading Hugh Forbes's warfare guide, *Manual of the Patriotic Volunteer*.[26] They also wrote their "goodbye" letters to loved ones. Several of these doubled as terrorist manifestoes. The letter written by John's youngest "Kansas regular," 20-year-old Will Leeman, to his mother on October 2, 1859 is a classic of the genre:[27]

> Dear Mother – I have not written you for a long time, and have not heard from you for a longer one. I am well, and anxious to hear from you. I am now in a Southern *slave State*, and before I leave it, it will be a free State, and so will *every other one in the South*. Yes, mother, I am warring with slavery, the greatest curse that ever infested America. In explanation of my absence from you for so long, I would tell you that for three years I have been engaged in a secret association of as gallant fellows as ever pulled a trigger, with the sole purpose of the extermination of slavery. We are now all privately gathered in a slave State, where we are determined to strike for freedom, incite the slaves to rebellion, and establish a free government. With the

CHAPTER 19: GATHERING FOR THE STORM

help of God we will carry it through. Now you will see, mother, the reason why I have stayed away from you for so long – why I have never helped you when I knew you was in want, and why I have not explained to you before. I dared not divulge it. Now we are about to commence, and it does not make any difference; but, mother dear, I charge you not to divulge a word in this letter outside the family, until you hear from me in actual service. I don't want you to worry yourself about me at all. I shall be in danger, of course, but that is natural to me. I shall not get killed. I am in a good cause and I am not afraid. I know my mother will not object. You have a generous heart. I know you will sacrifice something for your fellow beings in bondage. I knew one lady in New York that bid her husband and four sons to take up arms in our cause, and they are here with us now.

Aaron Stevens, using his fake name "C. Whipple," expressed his terrorist ideation in a manifesto letter he wrote to a potential love interest.[28]

I hope your heart will be with me in this cause. Oh! There is so much happiness in trying to make others happy. I feel at times that I am in heaven. There is hard and trying times, now and then, but it is thrice washed // away by the happy feelings that spring from the thoughts that we have not lived for naught, that is we have accomplished some good in the world, and instead of keeping our fellow beings back, that we have healped them forward.

John passed a harsh judgment on those of his former followers who declined to join the terrorist mission. George Gill, for instance, had been one of the men who joined John's Vernon County, Missouri expedition, and who afterwards helped him escape pursuit in Kansas, but he declined to join John in Maryland, blaming an attack of rheumatoid arthritis. John criticized him in a letter written on August 6, 1859: "George G. will so far redeem himself as to try: & do his duty after all. I shall rejoice over 'one that repenteth.'" John Jr. provided some logistical support, but his efforts at recruitment were unsatisfactory to his father. Kansas veterans Jason Brown, Henry Thompson, and Salmon Brown all explicitly refused to join the Harpers Ferry venture.[29]

John was still desperately trying to assemble the main missing element of his planned strike, African American followers.[30] So far, he had just one such recruit: Dangerfield Newby, a mixed-race blacksmith who was freed when his Virginia owner allowed him to move to Ohio. John met Newby while he was staying in Ashtabula County, Ohio in late March and early April of 1859. It seems Newby was motivated to join John partly because he hoped to somehow free his wife, who, along with his seven children, was held in bondage about 30 miles south of Harpers Ferry.[31]

John turned his attention to his good friend Frederick Douglass. He arranged to meet Frederick in Chambersburg, Pennsylvania on August 19, 1859. John was accompanied by John Henry Kagi, while Frederick was accompanied by Shields Green, an escaped slave from South Carolina, whom John had met previously when he was visiting Frederick in Rochester. Over a three-day

John Henry Kagi

CHAPTER 19: GATHERING FOR THE STORM

weekend, they engaged in long discussions at the site of an abandoned quarry outside the main part of town. Frederick, quite simply, was not a terrorist. Nor was he in sympathy with a terrorist suicide mission. In his 1881 autobiography, Frederick gave the following account of this meeting:[32]

> We – Mr. Kagi, Captain Brown, Shields Green, and myself – sat down among the rocks and talked over the enterprise which was about to be undertaken. The taking of Harpers Ferry, of which Captain Brown had merely hinted before, was now declared as his settled purpose, and he wanted to know what I thought of it. I at once opposed the measure with all the arguments at my command. To me such a measure would be fatal to running off slaves (as was the original plan), and fatal to all engaged in doing so. It would be an attack upon the Federal government, and would array the whole country against us.
>
> Captain Brown did most of the talking on the other side of the question. He did not at all object to rousing the nation; it seemed to him that something startling was just what the nation needed. He had completely renounced his old plan, and thought that the capture of Harper's Ferry would serve as notice to the slaves that their friends had come, and as a trumpet to rally them to his standard. He described the place as to its means of defense, and how impossible it would be to dislodge him if once in possession.
>
> Of course I was no match for him in such matters, but I told him, and these were my words, that all his arguments, and all his descriptions of the place, convinced me that he was going into a perfect steel-trap, and that once in he would never get out alive; that he would be surrounded at once and escape would be

impossible. He was not to be shaken by anything I could say, but treated my views respectfully, replying that even if surrounded he would find means for cutting his way out; but that would not be forced upon him; he should, at the start, have a number of the best citizens of the neighborhood as his prisoners and that holding them as hostages he should be able, if worse came to worse, to dictate terms of egress from the town.

I looked at him with some astonishment, that he could rest upon a weed so weak and broken, and told him that Virginia would blow him and his hostages sky-high, rather than that he should hold Harper's Ferry an hour. Our talk was long and earnest; we spent the most of Saturday and a part of Sunday in this debate – Brown for Harper's Ferry, and I against it; he for striking a blow which should instantly rouse the country, and I for the policy of gradually and unaccountably drawing off the slaves to the mountains, as at first suggested and proposed by him.

When I found that he had fully made up his mind and could not be dissuaded, I turned to Shields Green and told him he heard what Captain Brown had said; his old plan was changed, and that I should return home, and if he wished to go with me he could do so. Captain Brown urged us both to go with him, but I could not do so, and could but feel that he was about to rivet the fetters more firmly than ever on the limbs of the enslaved.

In parting he put his arms around me in a manner more than friendly, and said: "Come with me, Douglass; I will defend you with my life. I want you for a special purpose. When I strike, the bees will begin to swarm, and I shall want you to help hive them." But my discretion or my cowardice made me proof against the dear old man's eloquence – perhaps it was something of both which determined my course. When about to leave I asked Green what he had decided to do, and was surprised by his cooly saying, in his broken way, "I b'leve I'll go wid de ole man."

Here, we separated; they go to Harper's Ferry, I to Rochester. There has been some difference of opinion as to the propriety of my course in thus leaving my friend. Some have thought that I ought to have gone with him; but I have no reproaches for myself at this point, and since I have been assailed only by colored men who kept even farther from this brave and heroic man than I did, I shall not trouble myself with much about their criticisms. They compliment me in assuming that I should perform greater deeds than themselves.

At the end of August 1859, U.S. Secretary of War John B. Floyd, in his office in Washington City, received an anonymous letter, which essentially told him everything he would have needed to know to prevent John's terrorist raid. The letter read:

Cincinnati, August 20.

Sir: I have lately received information of a movement of so great importance that I feel it my duty to impart it to you without delay.

I have discovered the existence of a secret association, having for its object the liberation of the slaves at the South by a general insurrection. The leader of the movement is *"Old John Brown,"* late of Kansas. He has been in Canada during the winter, drilling the negroes there, and they are only waiting his word to start for the South to assist the slaves. They have one of their leading men (a white man) in an armory in Maryland – where it is situated I have not been able to learn. As soon as everything is ready, those of their number who are in the Northern States and Canada are to come in small companies to their rendezvous, which is in the mountains in Virginia. They will pass down through Pennsylvania and Maryland, and enter Virginia at Harper's Ferry. Brown left the North about three or four weeks ago, and will arm the negroes and strike the blow in a few weeks; so that whatever is done must be done at once. They have a large quantity of arms at their rendezvous, and are probably distributing them shortly.

As I am not fully in their confidence, this is all the information I can give you. I dare not sign my name to this, but trust you will not disregard the warnings on that account.

The authorship of this impressively accurate warning letter remains uncertain. Eventually, four decades later, "credit" was taken by two brothers, David and Benjamin Gue. Benjamin Gue, who himself had become a historian, claimed that he and David, as young men, had been members of the Quaker community near Iowa City, Iowa and, in that capacity, came to learn many of the details of Brown's plot from another Quaker in the area who was in Brown's confidence. According to Benjamin Gue, the letter to Secretary Floyd was actually written in an effort to save the lives of John and Cook, by foiling a plot that was bound to be suicidal.

However, Floyd, a notably incompetent administrator, after reading the letter put it aside and paid no more attention to it. Inexplicably, he failed to make the connection between the "Old John Brown" discussed in the letter and the John Brown for whom the President had offered a large cash reward

CHAPTER 19: GATHERING FOR THE STORM

based on his murderous crimes in Kansas and Missouri. Floyd would later testify he also disregarded the letter because he did not believe any U.S. citizen would be capable of such "wickedness and outrage." Also, he said he dismissed the letter because it described the Armory as being in "Maryland," and there was no Armory in Maryland.[33] So, despite the warning letter, John's plot was not uncovered.

John was cheered by the addition of Shields Green. Being a fugitive, Green already went by a code name, which was "Emperor."[34] But John continued to be dismayed at the paucity of his African American recruits. Out of the dozens of persons of African ancestry whom John had gathered in May of 1858 for his Chatham convention, he was only able to persuade one, a free-born newspaper helper named Osborne Anderson, to join his mission. He did, however, get some help from friends and family in Oberlin. This came in the form of recruitment of two African Americans who had been involved in a high-profile rescue of a fugitive slave named John Price. Price, after living quietly in Oberlin for two-and-a-half years, was captured in an ambush that took place on a farm, by slave catchers acting under federal authority, on September 13, 1858. Their dirty deed was quickly denounced, however, and in response, over 200 enraged local citizens rapidly mustered themselves into an angry mob, which surrounded the hotel where Price was being held. They stormed the top floor, where Price was located, and forcibly removed him from the grasp of his captors. Price was whisked away to safety, but about forty of the rescuers were later indicted by the Ohio federal court. As was typical of "mob justice" cases, only two of the rescuers were actually tried, in a sort of test case. This trial, held in Cleveland, commenced April 7, 1859. John happened to be in the area on his fund-raising tour of northeast Ohio when it began. He and his band took a great interest in the much publicized affair. Kagi, second-in-command of his Kansas regulars, visited the defendants at the

Cleveland jail where it was being held.[35]

Two African American Oberlin residents who had been involved in the Price rescue were ultimately, at virtually the last minute, recruited to join John's raiders in Harpers Ferry. They were John Copeland and Lewis Leary.

John Copeland was born into a free mixed-race family in Raleigh, North Carolina in 1834. While he was still just a boy, his family decided to emigrate to the North. After entering Ohio, they encountered Amos Dresser, who now, eight years after his youthful misadventures in Nashville, was settled in as a practicing minister of a congregation in southern Ohio. Amos strongly recommended that the Copelands should relocate to Oberlin, and they heeded his advice. His family put down roots there and, ultimately, John Copeland attended Oberlin College. He was one of the leading participants in the Price rescue and, although indicted, was never arrested. By the time he was recruited to join John, in September of 1859, the trial of the Price rescuers had basically blown over. The lead defendants received fines, and the charges against the balance of the defendants were dismissed in exchange for the dismissal of state criminal charges against the slave catchers.[36]

Lewis Leary, like Copeland, was born into a free mixed-race family in North Carolina. While identifying as ethnically African American, Leary's family was in the upper middle class in terms of its socioeconomic status. His father, in fact, owned slaves of his own. Young Lewis, in terms of his personality, was hotheaded and rash. He got into some local troubles, as a result of which, he was advised to leave the state. In 1857, he arrived in Oberlin. There he took up his father's trade as a harness and saddle maker, married, and had a child. He apparently was involved in the mob that rescued Price, but his presence did not come to the attention of the authorities, and he was not included in the indictment. This seems to have rankled his pride. Lewis closely followed the trial and, when John came to Cleveland to speak in late March of 1859, Lewis

CHAPTER 19: GATHERING FOR THE STORM

was in attendance. He was impressed with John and his speech. John Jr. successfully recruited him to join John's raiders in August of that year.[37]

Copeland and Leary knew each other, both being from North Carolina and being related by marriage. Apparently they decided jointly to answer John Jr.'s recruiting call for African Americans to join John's band. Neither Copeland nor Leary likely knew the exact nature of John's project they were volunteering to join. But it is clear from the remarks they made before departing that they knew it involved freeing slaves and that their lives would be seriously at risk in the enterprise. On September 8, Leary wrote a letter to Kagi, who went by the fake name "J. Henrie," saying in coded language that he and another "handy man" were "competent to dig coal," but that they needed "tools." Leary was directed to Ralph Plumb, an Oberlin lawyer who had also been involved in the Price rescue. Plumb provided $17.50 for Leary and Copeland to travel to the terrorist safe house in Chambersburg.[38] From there, they traveled south to the Kennedy Farm, where they arrived October 12, 1859.[39]

In addition to his followers concealed inside the Kennedy farm house, John had another important member of his band planted in the Harpers Ferry community. He was John Cook, one of his "Kansas regulars," whom John had dispatched to Harpers Ferry to act as an advance scout to case the town when he was forced to postpone the attack in May 1858. In the meantime, Cook had kept himself busy. He got into a love affair with his landlady's daughter, whom he then was forced to marry because she was pregnant with his child.[40]

John undoubtedly hoped to recruit more people. But John had to move, because he was running out of money. He was reduced to shaking down his own minions for their last penny, a late-stage pre-attack action typical of terrorist leaders. From a 20-year-old follower, the girlish Barclay Coppoc, John extracted $40 in gold. Then, on October 10, he received an unexpected infusion of $600 in gold delivered by a new volunteer named Francis Jackson Merriam. Francis Merriam was the 22-year-old grandson of Francis Jackson, a prominent abolitionist and wealthy patron and friend of Lloyd Garrison. Young Merriam, erratic and unbalanced, was blind in one eye and felt himself to be dying. He was motivated to go on a suicidal crusade before he passed. On his way to join John, Merriam stopped in Baltimore to pick up some ammunition. Merriam stayed overnight at the Wager House, a hotel in Harpers Ferry, and then came up to the Kennedy Farm on the morning of Sunday, October 16. With his arrival, the stage was set for John's last and most high profile terrorist attack.[41]

Chapter 20: The Other Washington

"Washington." Lewis awoke with a start to the sound of his name being called from outside his bedroom door.[1] It was 1:30 in the morning. A hopeful thought flickered across Lewis's mind that perhaps it was just some friend who had arrived late and who was let into the house by the servants. Nighttime home invasion was not a normal worry in sleepy Halltown, Virginia.

Hastily, Lewis rose. He stuck his feet in his slippers and opened the door.[2] His hope for a friend was dashed in an instant by the sight of bristling gun barrels pointed directly at his face. There stood four armed intruders. One held a wooden torch in his left hand, by the light of which Lewis could see a large revolver in his right hand and three cocked rifles trained on him by each of the other men. The gestures and manner of the tallest of the intruders, a bearded young man, gave Lewis to understand that he was the leader. The leader asked Lewis if he was Colonel Washington.[3]

Lewis Washington, 1861 portrait

Lewis stood for a moment in shocked silence.[4] The leader repeated the question to one of the other intruders, whom Lewis, to his surprise, recognized as John Cook.[5] The talkative, musically gifted young man with curly blond locks had arrived in the neighboring town of Harpers Ferry the previous summer. Cook and the pregnant Mary Kennedy had been married in town six months ago. Everybody knew him. Just three weeks ago, in fact, Cook had stopped by the farmhouse to chat with Lewis. Lewis enjoyed Cook's visit, and gave him a friendly tour of the farm. Believing Cook to be employed at the federal armory in nearby Harpers Ferry, Lewis showed Cook his gun collection. Cook had produced two of his own revolvers, which he told Lewis he wore to get his hips adjusted to carrying them. Cook had invited Lewis to do some shooting with the pistols and, while doing so, Lewis had remarked that the pistol he used was engraved with the name "John E. Cook" on the handle. This engraving was how Lewis remembered Cook's name. Cook had volunteered that he had done the engraving himself.[6] Lewis never dreamed he was being scouted by terrorists.

"Is this Colonel Washington?" repeated the leader. "Yes, Captain," Cook answered quickly.[7] Lewis quickly raised his hands to emphasize to the intruders that he was going along with them and putting up no resistance. But verbally he asked, "Would you mind telling me what is the meaning of this, Cook?"[8]

"You are our prisoner," the bearded leader replied brusquely. "We have come to abolish slavery. You must come with us to the Ferry at once. So get ready."[9]

"Abolitionists!" Lewis muttered to himself. Lewis did not share their beliefs. He viewed as benign his relationship with the modest collection of slaves who worked his farm and kept his house and grounds. Some he actually hired from other owners. Most of the field hands went home on weekends. Lewis at times felt himself burdened with a weight of responsibility for the servants' well-being. To Lewis they seemed like family, retainers who were perhaps less than fully capable of taking care of themselves on their own. Halltown was not the deep South. Lewis's farm called Beall Air, although prosperous, was not a cotton plantation.

When an ember from the raiders' blazing torch fell to the floor, Lewis was seized with fear that his house would catch fire and burn. He asked the leader if he would have his men come into the bedroom and light the candles so that he could see to get dressed.[10] The Captain nodded a silent assent. As Lewis began to fumble around, looking for warm clothes to wear in the chilly October night air, the Captain left Cook and others in the band of raiders to guard Lewis.

After Lewis was dressed, with his boots on, he was escorted from his bedroom into the dining room. A young African American woman who was one of Lewis's house servants was busy reviving the fire in the fireplace.[11] As the intruders warmed themselves, they looked around the room. It seemed to Lewis as if they were waiting for the Captain's return. Lewis began pacing to and fro, wondering to himself whether he might yet be able to talk them out of the kidnapping.[12]

After a few tense minutes that seemed an eternity, Lewis heard the voice of his coachman Jim coming from outside the house, together with voices of others in the band of kidnappers whom Lewis had not previously seen. He also heard other noises, which told him that his horses were being removed from their stalls and harnessed, and that his vehicles were being moved about.

The Captain entered. Lewis played for time. He went to the sideboard and took out a bottle of whiskey. "May I offer you something?" he asked.

"No," returned the Captain, politely but firmly.

"I presume you have heard of Osawatomie Brown?" the Captain continued. "No, I have not," Lewis responded. "Then you have paid very little attention to Kansas matters," said the Captain.

Lewis, in reality, was well aware of the issues and events in Kansas. But at the moment, Lewis did not wish to be associated with the Kansas controversy in the minds of his midnight callers. He was, however, stung by the injustice of the Captain's implicit accusation that he was somehow associated with the attacks and atrocities by the Missouri-based ruffians. Lewis parried. "I have become so much disgusted with Kansas, and everything connected with it, that whenever I see a paper with 'Kansas' at the head of it I turn it over and do not read it."

"Well," replied the Captain, returning to the subject of John, whom the Captain himself had referred to as "Osawatomie." "You shall see him this morning."

"You have some firearms, do you not?" the leader asked Lewis. When Lewis did not immediately answer, Cook interjected. "They are kept over here, Captain." Cook pointed to Lewis's rifle closet. The Captain returned his attention to Lewis. "Give us all of your weapons, including your rifles, your pistol and the Frederick sword."

A wail of protest involuntarily escaped Lewis the moment he realized that the raiders were out to rob him of the family's most prized and precious possession. It was an heirloom from Lewis's most distinguished relative, General George Washington, who had been the military leader of the American Revolution and first President of the United States. Lewis now bitterly recalled how proudly he had displayed this ceremonial sword to Cook during his recent visit. The Captain, Cook, and the others, alarmed by Lewis's emotional outburst, indicated with renewed gestures of their rifles that their threat was extremely serious and that they would brook no further mischief or delay. The Captain, whose real name was Aaron Stevens, aka "Colonel Whipple," had a record of threatening to blow out people's hearts with rifles, as well as a record of being trigger happy. The last victim of one of his midnight home

Chapter 20: The Other Washington

invasions was fatally shot through the heart. Again holding his hands raised, Lewis slowly crossed the room to the closet where he kept his firearms. He slowly opened the door for Cook to handle and remove the contents. Cook removed a double-barreled shotgun, a hunting rifle, a horse pistol, and an antique pistol that was forged in Harpers Ferry in 1806. The captors looked pleased with themselves. One of them, a fellow whose name Lewis later learned was Tidd, slowly looked over each weapon, then carried them all outside.

"Now, the Sword," the Captain prodded. According to family tradition, it had been a gift sent to George Washington by King Frederick the Great of Prussia. Lewis let out another protest. "I am going to speak very plainly," Lewis blubbered. "You told me your purpose was philanthropic, but you did not mention at the same time that it was robbery and rascality."

Stevens, the Captain, appeared unmoved. Once more he cocked his rifle and trained it on Lewis. With a deep sigh, Lewis slowly crossed to where the sword occupied its position of importance, on the wall over the fireplace. Lewis removed it from its mounting, holding it by the blade. As he turned, Stevens gestured to one of the other men in his band with a wave of the hand. "Step forward and take it." In his anxiety, Lewis failed to notice that this robber was Osborne Anderson, a man of partial African American ancestry. Having a man of color personally take the sword from Lewis's hands held a symbolic importance to the abolitionist invaders.

"Secure him and take him out," Stevens ordered. One of the men stepped forward and produced a length of rope that had evidently been prepared in advance for the occasion. Lewis now impassively extended his arms behind his back and allowed himself to be tied. Lewis's two female house servants, who had been watching, finally lost the composure they had each been struggling to maintain. One just sobbed out loudly. The other leaped to her feet and approached the Captain, fastening on him a piteous gaze. "Oh, sir, please don't take him, please *please* sir, don't," she cried. "I'm sorry," replied Stevens, unmoved. "It's orders."

When Lewis went out, he saw a dark-skinned African American, one of the raiders whom he had not seen before, driving his carriage. The others called him "Emperor." Lewis was loaded into the backseat, alongside one of his captors. He noted at a glance that the horses were incorrectly paired. The shorter of the two horses was hooked to a longer harness, which was fitted to the taller of the two animals. Predictably, the horses stopped short very soon after they were started. "These horses will not drive in that way," Lewis called out. "They are on the wrong sides."

The Emperor jumped down and set about rearranging the horses and the harnesses. Another raider conferred with him. Lewis's coachman Jim, being far more familiar with the animals and the equipment, was asked to step up and drive the carriage in Emperor's place.

Lewis's heavy farm wagon, hitched to four of his other horses, bumped along behind the carriage. Since he was tied facing forward, Lewis was unable to see who was riding on the wagon. "We ordered your wagon to take your slaves," his guard informed him. From the sound of voices Lewis believed that one or two of his male African American servants were riding in the wagon along with some of the other invaders.

By the light of a newly risen moon, the procession started for nearby Harpers Ferry. After a few minutes, Stevens, from the wagon, called out to Jim to halt the carriage in front of the home of Richard Henderson, one of Lewis's neighbors. Lewis decided to speak. "There is nothing for you here. Mr. Henderson recently passed away and there is only Mrs. Henderson and four or five daughters in the house." Tidd jumped down and went back to the wagon to confer with the Captain. After a brief moment, he returned and directed Jim to resume the procession.

CHAPTER 20: THE OTHER WASHINGTON

As the carriage approached the top of a small hill, one horse's harness suddenly came loose. The carriage quickly came to a stop as the driver jumped down and reattached it.

Just over the crest, the carriage again halted. The little caravan was now in front of the farm of John Allstadt. With the help of Washington's freed slaves, the raiders quickly removed a rail from a criss-crossed series of boards, called a Virginia worm fence, that lay along the road opposite Allstadt's place. Lewis guessed the raiders intended to use the rail as a ram in order to bash down Allstadt's door. The surmise was quickly confirmed by the sickening sound of the door at Allstadt's giving way to the force of the raiders' sudden assault with the rail. Lewis heard the women in Allstadt's house screaming with terror and alarm.

Lewis sat considering the strange turn of events for another interminable period. More piteous cries and pleas came from the women in the Allstadt house. Lewis knew what it meant – Allstadt, too, was being kidnapped. Finally, a group returned to the parked wagons. Lewis could tell from the noises that Allstadt was being forced to mount the platform of his trailing farm wagon. Then Tidd returned to the front seat of the carriage, alongside Jim, and asked him to drive down the road. Jim willingly complied.

The caravan's journey to the Ferry was slow and halting. Lewis could not make out why. In actuality, even though it was the deepest part of the night, the little band of abolitionist invaders was busy recruiting supporters for the cause of rebellion from among the local African American population.

Eventually, the carriage bearing Lewis arrived at the gates of the Ferry's United States Armory, situated not far from the confluence of the Potomac and Shenandoah Rivers. It was still dark. "All's well," Stevens cried out. "All's well," came a response from behind the gate. After some preliminary clinking, the gate swung open. The carriage, followed by

Lewis's four-horse wagon, rumbled out of the street and into the Armory grounds.

Lewis looked around in surprise. Up until that moment, he still thought it possible that he had simply been kidnapped for

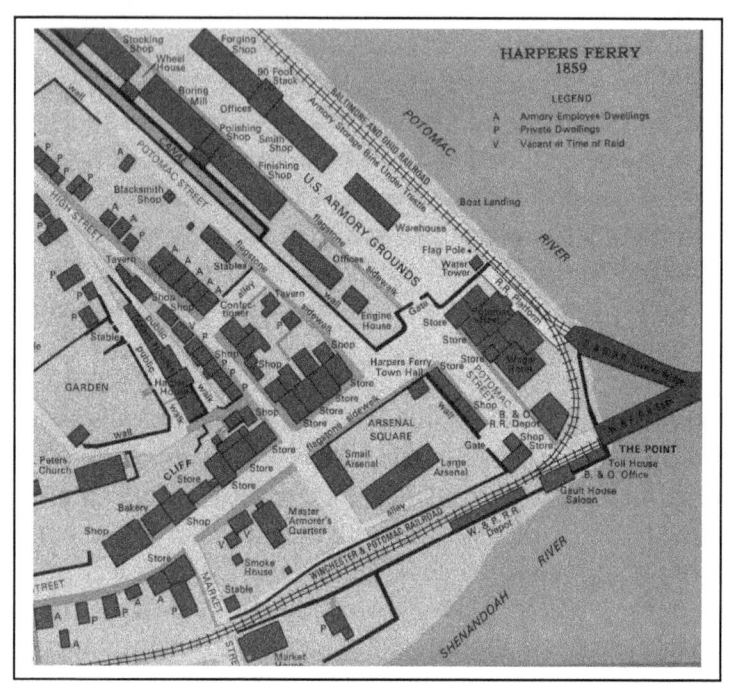

ransom by bandits. Now, he realized that the band of invaders were indeed part of a much larger force. As the carriage entered the yard, a man much older, but dressed in just as unkempt a fashion as any of the other raiders, came forward to receive him. The old man quickly gave an order for the raiders to remove Lewis's bindings. Lewis realized he was facing "Osawatomie," leader of the Abolitionist band.

"You will see a fire in here, sir," John said to Lewis, motioning for one of the raiders to escort Lewis into the Armory's watch room, adjacent to its engine house. "It is rather cool this morning." "Osawatomie" appeared to know who Lewis was. Lewis studied him for a moment as he entered the

CHAPTER 20: THE OTHER WASHINGTON

watch room. John's face was cragged, weathered, and dominated by a gray beard. Although John was clearly past middle age, his body remained slender and muscular. He was not overly tall.

Thus far, John's plan had gone off like clockwork. He and his group of followers now held undisputed possession of the United States Armory at Harpers Ferry. The previous night, John and his band had surprised and quickly overpowered the unsuspecting night watchman. John faced no other security. His raiders also took over the nearby United States Arsenal, and the nearby rifle factory. The train station's porter, ironically enough a free African American, had refused to obey the raiders and was shot, mortally wounded. The others, who more prudently surrendered, were taken prisoner, and were herded into the Armory's watch room before Lewis was brought in.

Inside the watch room, in the fire's dim glow, Lewis recognized four or five of the other local citizens who were already being held as captives. One of them was John Daingerfield, the Armory's paymaster clerk. Several of the raiders, including Cook, also sat beside the fire, trying to dispel the chill they had acquired from the nighttime outing. As Lewis looked about, Allstadt was also ushered into the room. Completely cowed at the unexpected conquest of the Armory and the seemingly substantial numbers that the terrorists possessed, the captives in the watch room made no attempt at resistance and waited passively for the captors' next move.

In a few minutes, John entered. Sensing that Lewis, as well as the other prisoners, were acting quiet and uncommunicative, John seemed intent on improving their mood. He volunteered, "I think, after a while, possibly, I shall be enabled to release you, but only on the condition of getting your friends to send in a negro man as a ransom." Lewis and one or two other captives nodded with approval at the suggestion. "It is too dark to see to write at this time," John continued. "But when it shall have cleared off a little and become lighter, if you have not pen and ink, I will furnish them to you, and I shall require you to write to some of your friends to send a stout, able-bodied negro."

But as dawn's light broadened, John and his raiders made no move to release Lewis or any of the others. With frenetic energy, the raiders kept coming in and out of the watch room. They kept bringing in more prisoners. Many of these were the Armory's regular staff, who were being arrested as they reported to work. John's men, including the slaves whom he had recruited overnight, also kept coming into the watch room to warm themselves from the cold, rainy conditions outside. All of the slaves were carrying long wooden spears that the raiders had given them to use as weapons. Lewis thought to himself that they did not look very comfortable doing it. The African Americans avoided any eye contact or conversation with the prisoners, including Lewis and the other slave owners present.

Without any prompting, John announced the reasoning for his raid:

> This slavery thing must be put a stop to. I have spent years fighting against this accursed system of slavery. I now have the power to do it, and I will carry it out.[13] By noon today we will have fifteen hundred men here ready to move forward with us.[14]

To Lewis, he continued:

> I shall be very attentive to you, sir, for I may get the worst of it in my first encounter, and if so, your life will be worth as much as mine. I shall be very particular to pay attention to you. My reason for taking you was that, as the aide to the governor of Virginia, I know you would endeavor to perform your duty, and perhaps you would have been a troublesome customer

for me. And apart from that, I wanted you particularly for the moral effect it would give our cause, having one of your name as prisoner.[15]

Stevens entered the watch room and approached the fire to get warm. After a few moments he turned to one of the prisoners, a young man whose name Lewis did not know, and asked him about his view in reference to the institution of slavery. "Of course, being born South, my views are with the South on that subject," the man replied. Stevens asked if the man owned any slaves. He said he did not. "Well," Stevens remarked disdainfully. "You would be the first man I would hang, for you defend a cause not to protect your interest in doing so."[16]

For the first time, Lewis saw a local African American named Catesby enter the watch room. He, also, was carrying a spear. Catesby actually was the property of a neighbor named Dr. Fuller, but he had been hired by Lewis to work at Beall Air. Catesby apparently had heard about John's raid during the night and had made haste to meet up with his men, joining the group at Allstadt's residence and riding from there in the wagon.

At around 9.30 in the morning, Terence Byrne was brought into the watch house with Lewis and the other prisoners. Byrne was another slave-owning farmer from the Maryland side of the Potomac, some 5 miles from the Ferry. "Good morning, gentlemen" Byrne remarked as he entered the room. "I hope I am in good company." Lewis guessed the rebels were still adding to their forces, rounding up more slaves to join their cause, as well as slave owners to hold as hostages.[17] By now, thirty or so prisoners sat on the floor in the watch room. They were guarded by only two or three raiders. But feeling that the captors were still in control of the situation, they made no move to try to escape.

Meanwhile, John Henry Kagi, stationed at the rifle factory

and federal Arsenal across the street from the federal Armory, was frantically sending John message after message urging haste in gathering up the raid's loot and departing before nearby militias could mobilize.[18] John ignored these messages from his second-in-command. He refused to budge from his position in the Armory. Osborne Anderson, one of John's few surviving followers, would later write that John appeared "puzzled" by the situation. John's admiring biographers, likewise, have been puzzled by John's strange lack of action on the morning of Monday, October 17, 1859.[19] The raiders' plan called for them to quickly gather up the spoils of victory, to leave town before any major opposing force could arrive, and to head into the Blue Ridge mountains across the Shenendoah. From there, the raiders and the recruits would use the same route, dubbed the Great Black Way, that was already in use for purposes of the Underground Railroad.[20] John's sponsors and followers expected him to lead a guerrilla war, using the dense wilderness and caves of the rugged country as a refuge in which to evade the forces of law and order that would be brought against them.[21]

John, as we have seen, believed that only aggression could quell the manifest evil of the American slave power. He sold himself to his abolitionist financial backers as a man of action. Why, then, did he remain so passive after his initial victory at Harpers Ferry, awaiting the inevitable destruction of himself and his mission? John must have realized that help for the conquered town would soon be on the way. Every moment was precious.[22] And, why did John personally persuade the reluctant conductor of the overnight train, which his men had stopped, to depart in the direction of the eastern cities? He even escorted the engine personally across the Potomac bridge. Why? The conductor and passengers would, of course, rapidly spread the shocking news of the raid to the four corners of the wind, using a marvelous new innovation, the telegraph. John's decision about the train presents another puzzle. John

CHAPTER 20: THE OTHER WASHINGTON

obviously knew all about the importance of cutting communication. Under his carefully scripted plan, at the very start of the raid John's men had disconnected the telegraph lines connected to Harpers Ferry, to keep them from being used to broadcast an immediate call for help.

There is only one convincing explanation for John's seemingly irrational behavior. His vision of "victory," like that of a modern suicide terrorist, was entirely abnormal.

Armistead Ball, one of the Armory staff members who had been captured as he came to work, asked the raiders if he could go to his home nearby, to tell his family that he was safe. The question was presented to John, on his next visit to the watch room. John came back with two of the raiders, who were assigned to escort Ball to his residence and back. When they returned, Ball told John he had arrived at home to find that people were still in bed and his breakfast was not yet ready. John allowed Ball to go home under escort a second time an hour later, when his food would be waiting.

Magnanimously, John announced that breakfast from the Wager House, the hotel across the street from the Armory, was being served in the Armory yard. Lewis did not like the idea of eating food brought under forced circumstances. Besides, he worried that it might be drugged, to save the captors the trouble of having to stand guard in the watch room. Lewis advised several of his fellow captives not to take John up on the breakfast offer.

Not long after breakfast was finished, the relaxed attitude of the captors came to an abrupt end. Lewis heard the telltale sounds of a gun battle going on outside the Armory compound. To him, it sounded like the firefight went on for about 10 minutes before subsiding.

John made another appearance in the watch house. He no longer wore an air of benevolence. He was more imperative and hurried. He looked around and tapped Lewis on the shoulder. "I will have you, sir," he said, gesturing him to go with a waiting raider escort. He tapped four others, saying the same to each.

Lewis and the other prisoners John had picked out of the assemblage were escorted out of the watch room and into the adjacent engine house, a space perhaps 25 feet square, where the Armory's fire engines were stored. It was under the same roof, part of the same brick building, but no door connected the larger room, where the vehicles were housed, and the watch room. In the front of the engine house were two large double doors, between which was a stone abutment. Within were two old-fashioned, heavy fire-engines, with a hose-cart and reel standing between them, and just back of the abutment between the doors. They were double-battened doors, very strongly made, with heavy wrought-iron nails.[23]

John gestured with the Frederick the Great sword for Lewis and the others to sit on the floor in the left rear corner of the structure.[24] A short time later, Allstadt, Daingerfield, Byrne and two others were also escorted into the engine house, where they joined the huddled prisoners.

The arched front double doors of the engine house had been barricaded with the hand brakes of the fire engines, and tied shut with a rope. Although the door was thus barricaded and secured, the raiders could push the door open just far enough to see what was happening outside, to enter and exit, and to shoot at attackers. The door opening was their only way to see out of the sturdy brick structure, which John had selected as a stronghold due to its fortress-like construction.

Lewis could tell that one of the raiders had evidently been wounded in the fight outside. He struggled into the engine house, moving gingerly, but carried his gun and took up a firing position next to the front door.

Still grasping the Frederick sword, John returned to the back of the engine house and again addressed the captives. "Gentlemen, perhaps you wonder why I have selected you from the others. It is because I believe you to be the most influential, and I have only to say now that you will have to share precisely the same fate that your friends extend to my men."[25] John added, "I am too old a soldier to yield the advantage I possess, holding hostages." Eyeing Lewis, whom he seemed to regard as the de facto leader of the prisoners, he asked, "What do you think about this idea?" John proposed to the prisoners that he would take the hostages across the bridge to the Maryland side of the Potomac, and then release them once he received safe passage. The captive Lewis, being in no position to argue, said it sounded fine to him.[26]

John handed Daingerfield a pen and a piece of paper, and asked if he would be good enough to write out the peace proposal. Daingerfield agreed to do it. John then dictated his proposal for Daingerfield to write out. When he had finished, John read the note and again asked the prisoners if they agreed to it. Lewis saw no point in making any objections.

John looked over the hostages. "Which one of you would be willing to volunteer to carry a flag of truce?" No one seemed particularly eager. Archibald Kitzmiller, a clerk at the Armory, finally stepped forward after a few moments of hesitation. "I will do it." John turned to Stevens, who had fashioned a makeshift white flag out of a torn piece of cloth. "The two of you will go together to carry the proposal." John seemed to be referring to the proposal he had just asked Daingerfield to write out.

Two of the raiders cracked open the barricaded door to the engine house so that Stevens and Kitzmiller could emerge. The occupants of the engine house, including Lewis, waited anxiously. It was not thirty seconds before Lewis heard the report of gunfire, followed by a scream of pain. Stevens had been hit by several bullets fired by one of the militiamen posted outside. The raiders scrambled toward the door to try to get a look at what was happening. Lewis, however, could not see anything except the raiders from his position in the rear, behind the fire engines. John, for the first time, showed a flash of anger. He spat, "Those dirty devils showed no regard whatever for a flag of truce," bitterly and loud enough so that all the captives could hear him.

Just then, it began raining hard outside the engine house. One of the prisoners, Joseph Brewer, went forward to peek out the front doors. He saw Stevens bleeding and lying unprotected from the chill rain that was falling outside the engine house. He turned to John. "I would like to go to help that man. On my word of honor, I will just help him get to cover, and then I will return to take my place." John studied Brewer and considered his proposal for a brief moment. Then he nodded his approval and indicated for Brewer to go out. Lewis could not see what was happening. However, 15 minutes later, Brewer duly returned to the door and knocked to be let back in. The raiders admitted him.

John went over to tend to the wounded raider who had struggled in earlier. He was now lying crumpled against the wall opposite the captives. "He exerted himself too much," John remarked to no one in particular. The prisoners were not yet aware that the wounded raider was in fact one of John's sons.[27]

The hostages sat next to one another on the floor in the back of the engine house, behind the fire engines. Near Lewis and the other prisoners stood the newly freed slaves, including Lewis's own house servant. Lewis noticed the house servant had now discarded the spear he had been carrying earlier. It seemed the slaves were no longer feeling quite so much confidence about their rescuers, now that they were under fire and essentially confined, along with the hostages, in the engine house. From their position in the rear, slave owners and slaves alike watched the raiders as they took fighting positions in the front part of the little building. Each one held a rifle, with another loaded revolver beside him.

CHAPTER 20: THE OTHER WASHINGTON

Allstadt left the group of prisoners and went toward the front of the engine house. The raiders were nervously looking out the front door, prepared to repel any assault that might be attempted by the citizens outside.

A citizen, who happened to be the Mayor of Harpers Ferry, came around a corner and took a look at the engine house. "If he keeps on peeking like that, I'm going to shoot," declared one of the raiders. The man peeked around the corner again. The raider fired a shot, that missed. "For God's sake, man, don't shoot," cried one of the prisoners. "They'll shoot in here and kill us all." The man came out again to look at the engine house. The raider shot again and, this time, the Mayor promptly collapsed in a heap. "Dropped him," said the raider. One of the other citizens came out to take a look at him, quickly concluded he was beyond any possible help, and retired. Although he was in easy range, the raiders did not fire at this person.

One of John's followers sat in the engine house doorway, watching for signs of attackers. As he did, he spotted someone sighting a gun at him over a railway trestle about 30 yards away. He raised his rifle to shoot but, as he did, the other sniper shot first, hitting the raider in the abdomen. The raider crumpled to the floor, but did not die right away. "It's all up with me," he cried. In a few moments he seemed to die. John went over to take a close look at him. He shrugged and went back to keeping watch on the attackers.

U.S. Arsenal at Harpers Ferry, including the Engine House, in 1862 photo
U.S. Parks Service

Later, Lewis would learn from John that this young raider was another of his sons.

A short while later, another raider was also shot as he attempted to fire out of the doorway. He died rather quickly. His body was dragged into the rear corner of the engine house, and left near where the hostages were huddled.

John and his men were growing agitated at their difficulty in safely returning the increasing gunfire that was now being directed toward the engine house. John turned to a muscular-looking African American, one of Allstadt's slaves. John called him by his name. "You are a hearty fellow, Phil. Can you knock some loop holes in the walls for us to shoot through?" "Yes, sir," Phil replied. One of the raiders handed Phil a hammer and a steel chisel. Phil commenced chipping a hole though the mortar holding the brick walls of the structure. As Phil worked, Lewis could hear the whine of projectiles being fired at the engine house by the fully aroused citizenry without. A steady rain of lead was hitting the walls, windows, and doors of the engine house. All of the windows were shot out. Some of the rifle balls penetrated and made holes in the stout wooden doors, which John and his raiders had barricaded with heavy bars. For the time being, however, none of the raiders or prisoners was hit.

Phil hesitated for several moments as heavy firing coming from outside kept hitting near the spot where he was working on drilling out holes. "It's getting too hot for Phil," John remarked laconically. He went forward, took the hammer and chisel from Phil's hands, and began hammering energetically until the holes started by Phil were large enough to stick a rifle barrel through.[28] Lewis was impressed at how well John concentrated on the task at hand, oblivious to the splatter of bullets striking on the same wall he was attacking.

The prospect of return fire, plus the advent of a more prolonged rainstorm, caused the besiegers to halt their efforts to dislodge John and his band from the engine house on

Monday. The militias did not want to provoke any unnecessary harm to the hostages. They knew that U.S. Marines were on the way to take charge of the situation. The militia leaders also could see that John and his men were guarded by the surrounding armed forces practically as securely in the engine house as they would be in any jail. A series of negotiators were sent in to try to convince John to give up. They had no success. John kept on insisting that he and his men be granted safe passage across the Potomac bridge. The rescuers, who now had John and his followers thoroughly bottled up, found these terms wholly unacceptable.[29]

John's seven surviving followers, his dying son Watson, and his ten hostages, spent an extremely miserable night, shivering, cold, and hungry on the floor of the unheated Armory.[30] The dead bodies of Oliver Brown and another of John's men lay in the corner, next to the hostages. John kept the Frederick the Great sword in his hand. He urged his men to be ready. To his hostages, and to the negotiators, John repeatedly argued the point that he could have easily burned the entire town of Harpers Ferry while he had possession of it, but that he had not.[31] The thought of committing a full scale "Bleeding Kansas" style atrocity had clearly crossed John's mind. He argued he should be given "credit" for not doing it. John expressed out loud his resolve to die in the morning. To Lewis Washington, he seemed an extremely brave man.

Daingerfield was one of the captive Armory employees with whom John had extended conversations inside the pitch-black engine house during the marathon night-long vigil. He found that John was "as brave as a man could be, and sensible upon all subjects except slavery. Upon that question he was a religious fanatic, and felt that it was his duty to free the slaves, even if in doing so he lost his own life."[32]

At 11 o'clock Monday night, Colonel Robert E. Lee arrived at the Armory with a force of ninety Marines. Lee's troops promptly relieved the militias who had been guarding the engine house.[33] He sent his Lieutenant, Jeb Stuart, to ask if John was willing to surrender peacefully. When Stuart entered, after a lantern was lit he recognized John. He remembered John from their Kansas encounter after the Battle of Black Jack. John declined Stuart's suggestion, conveyed from Colonel Lee, that he surrender and seek clemency. He told Stuart, "I prefer to die here."[34]

When dawn broke, Lee had his forces, clad in bright blue U.S. Army uniforms, positioned for storming the engine house. Lee himself stood on a small rise only about 40 feet away.[35] The troops were instructed to avoid firing and to instead use bayonets, in hopes of avoiding casualties to the hostages.[36] Stuart approached the front doors of the engine house with one last request for John to surrender. John replied that he would agree to come out of the engine house if it was agreed to let him cross the bridge with his men so that they could try to escape. At this, Stuart immediately jumped to the side of the doors, and waved his plumed hat, which later was to become a famous personal trademark of Stuart. This wave of the hat was the Marines' prearranged signal to begin the final assault.

Lieutenant Israel Green led the charge of the Marines. At first, his men tried to bash down the double doors of the engine house using sledge hammers. John had the doors barred and tied securely, but with enough give so that the energy of the sledge hammers did not break the doors.[37] With the increasing daylight, Green noticed a wooden ladder that was lying in the Armory yard. He had his twelve-man reserve pick it up to use as a battering ram against the doors. On the second try, the lower part of one of the doors finally gave way. Green was the first soldier to rush in through the hole. One of John's followers yelled out, "I surrender." Others kept shooting at the attackers. None of this slowed the Marines. In the dimly-lit engine house it was not easy for them to see what was happening. After circling around one of the engines, Green saw Lewis

Washington. Washington quickly pointed out John, crouching near the door with his Sharps rifle. Green jumped toward John and reached him just after he fired a shot that proved fatal for a Marine who had followed Green through the hole in the door. As other storming Marines rushed in and quickly bayoneted two of John's followers, Lieutenant Green tried to run John through with his saber. But the saber was only a light dress-uniform model. Instead of penetrating John's body, its blade bent backwards when it encountered John's clothing. Green then attempted to hit John over the head with his twisted saber, but John moved aside to try to escape the blow, so that the saber instead struck the back of John's neck, knocking him unconscious. In this struggle, John did not suffer any deep wounds. He came to immediately after being carried out of the engine house.[38]

John would no doubt view this miraculous survival as yet another meaningful act at the hand of an intervening God. It fulfilled his lifelong quest to occupy a pulpit.

John's followers who did not escape met with the same fate as did the followers of Nat. Of twenty-one who participated in the attack on Harpers Ferry and its environs, nine were killed in the fighting or died soon afterwards of mortal wounds. The dead included John's sons Oliver and Watson, as well as his second-in-command John Henry Kagi. One other disciple, John's relative by marriage William Thompson, was shot by angry citizens immediately after being captured. The remainder of those caught all died dangling at the end of a noose. Aaron Stevens, aka "Colonel Whipple," was riddled with bullets, but he slowly recovered and eventually was put on trial. He met his end on the gallows, March 16, 1860. Besides Stevens, five others were hanged. But five in the attack squad, including John's son Owen, managed to escape.[39]

Chapter 21: Ecstasy of the Martyr

At 2 o'clock on the afternoon of Wednesday, October 19, 1859, the day after he was captured, in the paymaster's office of the U.S. Armory, John gave a sort of three-hour "press conference" in which the questions were asked of him by a combination of reporters, U.S. Senators, Congressmen, military officers, and the Governor of Virginia. To modern ears accustomed to the aftermath of terrorist attacks, their questions have a familiar ring. Why did you do it? What else did you plan to do? Who else is involved in supporting the plot? Who provided your financial support? The press conference abundantly fulfilled John's desire to publicize his cause. The transcript of questions and John's answers made front page news in the *New York Herald* and other major newspapers, whose readers were thirsty for every drop of news about the sensational attack and the man behind it.

John's absolute contempt for the world view of his captors, and his similar contempt for the death by hangman's noose that inevitably awaited him, gave the dialogue an almost surreal aspect. John articulated several themes which would become typical in future manifestations of terrorism:

CHAPTER 21: THE ECSTASY OF THE MARTYR

1. John's raid was a holy mission ordained by God.

Clement Vallandigham (U.S. Representative from Ohio). Mr. Brown, who sent you here?

John: No man sent me here; it was my own prompting and that of my Maker, or that of the Devil – whichever you please to ascribe it to. I acknowledge no master in human form.

* * * *

James Mason (U.S. Senator from Virginia). How do you justify your acts?

John: I think, my friend, you are guilty of a great wrong against God and humanity – I say it without wishing to be offensive – and it would be perfectly right for anyone to interfere with you so far as to free those you willfully and wickedly hold in bondage. I do not say this insultingly.

Senator Mason. I understand that.

John: I think I did right, and that others will do right who interfere with you at any time and at all times. I hold that the Golden Rule, "Do unto others as ye would that others should do unto you," applies to all who would help others to gain their liberty.

Lieutenant Stuart. But don't you believe in the Bible?

John: Certainly I do.

* * * *

A Bystander: Do you consider this a religious movement?

John: It is, in my opinion, the greatest service man can render to God.

Bystander: Do you consider yourself an instrument in the hands of Providence?

John: I do.

Bystander: Upon what principle do you justify your acts?

John: Upon the Golden Rule. I pity the poor in bondage that have none to help them. That is why I am here, not to gratify any personal animosity, revenge, or vindictive spirit. It is my sympathy with the oppressed and the wronged that are as good as you and as precious in the sight of God.

2. John's violent actions and motives were righteous, while those preparing to hang him faced a stern and wrathful judgment by God and history.

Bystander. I know it. I think you are fanatical.

John: And I think you are fanatical. "Whom the gods would destroy they first make mad," and you are mad.

* * * *

Henry Wise, Governor of Virginia. Mr. Brown, the silver of your hair is reddened by the blood of crime, and it is meet that you should eschew these hard allusions and think upon eternity.

John: Governor, I have, from all appearances, not more than fifteen or twenty years the start of you in the journey to that eternity of which you kindly warn me; and whether my tenure here shall be fifteen months, or fifteen days, or fifteen hours, I am equally prepared to go. There is an eternity behind and an eternity before, and the little speck in the centre, however long, is but comparatively a minute. The difference between your tenure and mine is trifling and I want to therefore tell you to be prepared; I am prepared. You all have a heavy responsibility, and it behooves you to prepare more than it does me.

3. John's one and only objective in undertaking the raid had been to free slaves, not to kill slave owners.

Senator Mason. What was your object in coming?

John: We came to free the slaves, and only that.

* * * *

Bystander: Have you read Gerrit Smith's last letter?

John: What letter do you mean?

Bystander: The *New York Herald* of yesterday, in speaking of this affair, mentions a letter in this way: "Apropos of this exciting news, we recollect a very significant passage in one of Gerrit Smith's letters, published a month or two ago, in which he speaks of the folly of attempting to strike the shackles off the slaves by the force of moral suasion or legal agitation, and predicts that the next movement made in the direction of negro emancipation would be an insurrection in the South."

John: I have not seen the *New York Herald* for some days past; but I presume, from your remark about the gist of the letter, that I should concur with it. I agree with Mr. Smith that moral suasion is hopeless. I don't think the people of the slave States will ever consider the subject of slavery in its true light till some other argument is resorted to than moral suasion.

Congressman Vallandigham: Did you expect a

general rising of the slaves in case of your success?

John: No, sir; nor did I wish it. I expected to gather them up from time to time, and set them free.

* * * *

Q. Brown, suppose you had every nigger in the United States, what would you do with them?

John. Set them free.

Q. Your intention was to carry them off and free them?

John. Not at all.

A Bystander: To set them free would sacrifice the life of every man in this community.

John: I do not think so.

* * * *

Q. Was it your only object to free the Negroes?

A. Absolutely our only object.

Q. But you demanded and took Colonel Washington's silver and watch?

A. Yes; we intended freely to appropriate the property of the slaveholders to carry out our object. It was for that, and only that, and with no design to enrich ourselves with any plunder whatever.

4. John and his men were to be commended because they had refrained from unnecessarily taking lives during the raid.

Senator Mason. But you killed some people passing along the streets quietly.

John: Well, sir, if there was anything of that kind

Chapter 21: The Ecstasy of the Martyr

done, it was without my knowledge. Your own citizens who were my prisoners will tell you that every possible means was taken to prevent it. I did not allow my men to fire when there was danger of killing those we regarded as innocent persons, if I could help it. They will tell you that we allowed ourselves to be fired at repeatedly, and did not return it.

A Bystander: That is not so. You killed an unarmed man at the corner of the house over there at the water-tank, and another besides.

John: See here, my friend; it is useless to dispute or contradict the report of your own neighbors who were my prisoners.

5. John was eager to be interviewed in the press conference.

Senator Mason. Does this talking annoy you?

John: Not in the least.

* * * *

John: ... I want you to understand, gentlemen, and [to the reporter of the *Herald*] you may report that – I want you to understand that I respect the rights of the poorest and weakest of colored people, oppressed by the slave system, just as much as I do those of the most wealthy and powerful. This is the idea that has moved me, and that alone. We expected no reward except the satisfaction of endeavoring to do for those in distress and greatly oppressed as we would be done by. The cry of distress of the oppressed is my reason, and the only thing that prompted me to come here.

* * * *

Reporter: I do not wish to annoy you; but if you have anything further you would like to say, I will report it.

John: I have nothing to say, only that I claim to be here in carrying out a measure I believe perfectly justifiable, and not to act the part of an incendiary or ruffian, but to aid those suffering great wrong. I wish to say, furthermore, that you had better – all you people at the South – prepare yourselves for a settlement of this question, that must come up for settlement sooner than you are prepared for it. The sooner you are prepared the better. You may dispose of me very easily, I am nearly disposed of now. But this question is still [to] be settled, this negro question I mean; the end of that is not yet. These wounds were inflicted upon me – both saber cuts on my head and bayonet stabs in different parts of my body – some minutes after I had ceased fighting and had consented to surrender, for the benefit of others, not for my own. I believe the Major would not have been alive; I could have killed him just as easy as a mosquito when he came in, but I supposed he only came in to receive our surrender. There had been loud and long calls of "surrender" from us, as loud as men could yell: but in the confusion and excitement I suppose we were not heard. I do not think the Major, or anyone, meant to butcher us after we had surrendered.

6. *John's attack was supported by innumerable unnamed persons.*

Congressman Vallandigham: Have you had correspondence with parties at the North on the subject of this movement?

John: I have had correspondence.

* * * *

CHAPTER 21: THE ECSTASY OF THE MARTYR

Vallandigham: Who are your advisors in this movement?

John: I cannot answer that. I have numerous sympathizers throughout the entire North.

Vallandigham: In northern Ohio?

John: No more than anywhere else; in all the Free states.

Vallandigham: But you are not personally acquainted in southern Ohio?

John: Not very much.

Colonel Robert E. Lee, the same day, wrote his own succinct assessment on John and his terrorist exploit.[1]

He avows that his object was the liberation of the slaves of Virginia, and of the whole South; and acknowledges that he has been disappointed in his expectations of aid from the black as well as white population, both in the Southern and Northern States. The blacks, whom he forced from their homes in this neighborhood, as far as I could learn, gave him no voluntary assistance. The servants of Messrs. Washington and Allstadt, retained at the armory, took no part in the conflict, and those carried to Maryland returned to their homes as soon as released. The result proves that the plan was the attempt of a fanatic or madman, who could only end in failure; and its temporary success, was owing to the panic and confusion he succeeded in creating by magnifying his numbers.

John's audacious strike produced the two most common modern terrorist accomplishments: an immediate political overreaction and a security crackdown. Throughout the slaveholding republics of the American South, rumors and fears abounded of a wave of incipient slave revolts. To protect against a further "Harpers Ferry" style uprising, many communities within the slaveholding republics now assembled militia units and organized civil defense companies. Southern residents who expressed any sympathy for John's aims were severely punished as criminals.[2] The raid bolstered the position of those in the Southern states who were already advocating "disunion" due to the cultural clash over the institution of American slavery.

The Virginia authorities wasted no time in bringing the "mad man" to trial. They had no intention of granting him mercy. The case was presented to a grand jury on Tuesday, October 25, six days after John's press conference. The grand jury rapidly, as in the next day, found to be a true bill an indictment which charged John with three capital counts: (1) "conspiring with Negroes" to produce insurrection; (2) treason against the commonwealth of Virginia; and (3) murder. John's trial started immediately. He made a series of requests for postponements, which were denied. The trial proceeded with the still wounded, but rapidly recovering, John lying on a cot in the courtroom, mostly listening passively. He was represented by a series of attorneys: two local attorneys, then a young lawyer sent from Massachusetts, and then two more experienced lawyers sent from Ohio. These last argued the case, on Monday, October 31.

Interestingly, John's attorneys did not venture any argument that there existed either a moral or a legal justification for his raid. Instead, they argued technicalities: John could not be guilty of treason against a commonwealth of which he was not a citizen. John personally did not wish to see anybody killed in the raid. These quibbles gave the jury no pause, as it returned a guilty verdict in just 45 minutes. On Wednesday, November 2, the judge sentenced John to a death by public hanging, to occur on December 2.

Chapter 21: The Ecstasy of the Martyr

John, upon his sentencing, went into a state of ecstasy. He had succeeded in achieving his longtime goal, public martyrdom in the name of a holy cause, a modern-day death very much like the heroes of Foxe's *Book of Martyrs*. On November 3, John added a postscript to a letter which he had already written out to his wife. "Yesterday, Nov. 2, I was sentenced to be hanged on Dec. 2d next. Do not grieve on my account. I am still quite cheerful."[3] John expounded on this ideation in a follow up letter he wrote to Mary and the North Elba children on November 8.[4]

> I am, besides, quite cheerful, having (as I trust) the peace of God, which "passeth all understanding," to "rule my heart," and the testimony (in some degree) of a good conscience that I have not lived altogether in vain. I can trust God with both the time and the manner of my death, believing, as I now do, that for me at this time to seal my testimony (for God and humanity) with my blood, will do vastly more towards advancing the cause I have earnestly endeavored to promote, than all I have done in my life before....
>
> Remember, dear wife and children all, that Jesus of Nazareth suffered a most excruciating death on the cross as a felon, under the most aggravating circumstances. Think, also, of the prophets, and apostles, and Christians of former days, who went through greater tribulations than you or I; and (try to) be reconciled.

In a letter in April 1857 to John Jr., John had discussed a family gravestone that he had obtained and was then shipping to North Elba. He stated that it had room for further inscriptions and that in 100 years the stone would be a "great curiosity."[5] John's correspondence during his final month reflects a serenity, indeed almost a joy, at the glorious death awaiting him. "Be of good cheer," John wrote to his wife. We shall "soon come out of all our great tribulations" and "God shall wipe away all tears from our eyes."[6]

John articulated his ecstasy around martyrdom even more explicitly in a letter he wrote on November 15 to his former Connecticut school master, Reverend H.L. Vaill:[7]

> Allow me here to say, that notwithstanding "my soul is amongst lions," still I believe that "God in very deed is with me." You will not, therefore, feel surprised when I tell you that I am "joyful in all my tribulations;" that I do not feel condemned of Him whose judgment is just, nor of my own conscience. Nor do I feel degraded by my imprisonment, my chain, or prospect of the gallows.

The jailer in Charles Town, John Avis, was kind to John during his month awaiting death. He was freely permitted to receive visitors. He also received a veritable flood of letters from sympathizers and admirers. He responded to most of them with the unlimited writing materials that were apparently put at his disposal. Many of John's correspondents expressly refrained from approving his choice of methods, although they praised to the heavens his willingness to die for the cause. John, in his replies, generally sidestepped the implicit criticism. His response to "a Quaker lady" was typical:[8]

> I am a prisoner in bonds. It is solely my own fault, in a military point of view, that we met with our disaster – I mean that I mingled with our prisoners, and so far sympathized with them and their families, that I neglected my duty in other respects. But God's will, not mine, be done.
>
> You know that Christ once armed Peter. So also in my case; I think he put a sword into my hand, and there continued it, so long as he saw best, and then kindly took it from me. I mean when I first went to Kansas. I

CHAPTER 21: THE ECSTASY OF THE MARTYR

wish you could know with what cheerfulness I am now wielding the "sword of the Spirit" on the right hand and on the left. I bless God that it proves "mighty to the pulling down of strongholds."

Though many prominent New England intellectuals and abolitionist leaders initially criticized John's raid due to its terrorist methods, their sentiments fairly quickly evolved into a consensus that good would come of John's righteousness, when he was put to death for his deeds.[9] Thus they too welcomed his impending martyrdom. The reaction of Henry Ward Beecher, brother of Edward Beecher as well as *Uncle Tom's Cabin* author Harriet Beecher Stowe, was typical: "Let no man pray that Brown be spared!" He continued, "Now, he has only blundered. His soul was noble, his work miserable. But a cord and a gibbet would redeem all that, and round up Brown's failure with a heroic success." John left behind a newspaper account of this sermon, with the word "Good" scratched above it.[10]

By no means was all of John's mail in the wake of his death sentence sympathetic. He received a letter dated November 20 from Mahala Doyle in Chattanooga, Tennessee. She wrote:

John Brown, Sir

Altho vengence is not mine, I confess, that I do feel gratified to hear that you ware stopt in your fiendish career at Harper's Ferry, with the loss of your two sons, you can now appreciate my distress, in Kansas, when you then and there entered my house at midnight and arrested my husband and two boys and took them out of the yard and in cold blood shot them dead in my hearing, you cant say you done it to free our slaves, we had none and never expected to own one, but has only made me a poor disconsolate widow with helpless children while I feel for your folly. I do hope & trust that you will meet your just reward. O how it pained my Heart to hear the dying groans of my Husband and children if this scrawl give you any consolation you are welcome to it.

Mahala Doyle

Probably the people who panicked the most in the wake of the Harpers Ferry fiasco were John's secret committee of six supporters. On Tuesday afternoon, October 18, after everyone in John's band at the engine house was killed or captured, Jeb Stuart and some of his men inspected the terrorist headquarters at the Kennedy Farm. They found a carpetbag John had left inside a locked trunk, filled with insurrection documents and incriminating letters from Sanborn, Howe, Stearns, and Smith. When this hit the national news, Samuel Howe went into a state of emotional turmoil. He became paralyzed by fear of being implicated in the venture. Although he joined the hastily organized "defense committee," he vehemently opposed any attempt to use extralegal means to bring about John's rescue.

Sanborn and Stearns decided to run to Canada for safety. They arrived in Quebec on Friday, October 21. Somewhat sheepishly, they realized that their flight made them look guilty, so they returned to Boston six days later. But Sanborn, once John's most devoted supporter, now involved himself in trying to silence other committee members who might reveal the true dimensions of the terrorist conspiracy.[11]

Gerrit Smith had a nervous breakdown, as a result of which, family members checked him into the Utica Asylum for the insane. He did have enough presence of mind to send his son-in-law to Boston to collect all other letters that might link him to Harpers Ferry. Like his co-conspirators in Boston, Smith had contemplated John's possible failure, but he had not prepared himself to face it, nor was he prepared to face the possibility of his own public implication in the affair. Nobody

CHAPTER 21: THE ECSTASY OF THE MARTYR

dreamed that John would leave all his letters behind at Harpers Ferry, rather than burning them. Smith was also baffled over John's seeming ineptitude after his initial seizure of the U.S. Armory. The distraught Smith rambled about going to Virginia himself to assist John, but the specifics remain a mystery. In response to his rantings, Smith's family had him committed to Utica Asylum. He wound up staying there until shortly after John went to the gallows. He finally returned to his home in Peterboro on December 29, seemingly recovered.[12]

Frederick was in Philadelphia, on the lecture circuit, at the time John pulled off his Harpers Ferry raid. He too was identified as one of the potential conspirators from the letters found in John's possession. Although he was, of course, no more implicated than the Secret Six, he had far more than they to worry about, due to his racial origins. Warned by anti-slavery sympathizers, Frederick quickly left town late at night on Wednesday, October 19, the day after John's raid was finally crushed. He first took a train to Hoboken, New Jersey, where he hid out in a residence where one of his female admirers, Ottilie Assing, was a boarder. In the meantime, Governor Wise made a formal request to President Buchanan for nationwide assistance in finding and arresting Frederick, whom he characterized as "a negro man ... charged with murder, robbery, and inciting servile insurrection." Frederick took an obscure route by train to Rochester, where he paused only briefly before crossing the river into Canada. From there he would depart for an indefinite exile in England, leaving Quebec on November 12.[13]

In contrast to the Secret Six, some of John's associates from Kansas battles, as well as some abolition supporters in Boston, thought about mounting an attack to rescue him from the execution. John himself did nothing to encourage such an attempt. John explicitly denied consent for any such effort to a scout sent by the defense committee from Boston to Charles

Town, posing as an attorney sent to assist in John's defense. The scout wrote back to his financial supporters, indicating:[14]

> There is *no chance* of his ultimate escape. There is nothing but the most unmitigated failure and the saddest consequence which it is possible to conjure up to ensue upon an attempt at *rescue*. The country, all aroused, is guarded by armed patrols and a large body of troops are constantly under arms. If you hear anything about such an attempt, for Heaven's sake do not *fail to restrain the enterprise.*

John was equally resolute in shunning the notion, proposed by several attorneys, of presenting a plea of insanity to Governor Wise.[15]

To guard against any rescue attempt, and as part of the general outrage and security reaction to John's startling Harpers Ferry attack, Governor Wise called up into active duty, and summoned to Charles Town, citizen militia companies from throughout the State of Virginia. One of these patriotic groups, based in Richmond, was formally known as "Company A, 1st Regiment of Virginia Volunteers." More commonly, they called themselves the "Richmond Grays" due to the color of their uniforms.[16]

John Wilkes Booth was not a member of the Richmond Grays. Johnnie was, at that time, perfecting his trade, working as a stock actor in Richmond's Marshall Theater. Seeking to escape the shadow of his legendary father, Johnnie at this time went by the stage name, "John Wilkes." Johnnie seemed drawn by an irresistible force to follow in his father's career footsteps. But he had gotten off to a rough start. In his first public stage performance, in Philadelphia, 19-year-old Johnnie flubbed his line in Hugo's *Lucretia Borgia*, when he was supposed to come on stage and say "Madam, I am Petruchio Pandolfe." What Johnnie instead blurted was, "Madam, I am Pondolfio Pet-Ped-Pat-Pantuchio Ped – damn it! What am I?" The audience

CHAPTER 21: THE ECSTASY OF THE MARTYR

laughed, but as his problems continued, he found himself booed and hissed off stage. The next night, when he came on stage and heard the audience hissing, he experienced fright and was unable to say a word.[17] Nevertheless, Johnnie persisted. With a newly discovered capacity for self-discipline, Johnnie developed pneumonic tricks to surmount his learning difficulties.[18]

Starting in September of 1858, Johnnie was engaged as a stock actor at the Marshall in Richmond. With regular performances, he began to put his natural personal magnetism and talent on display. One Virginian remembered Johnnie during this period as "a man of high character and social disposition, and liked by everyone with whom he associated." Good qualities consistently shine through in recollections of people who knew him while in Richmond. He was called thoughtful, tactful, and forgiving.[19] A woman described him as "brave, ardent and affectionate." She said he was "ready for a fire or ready for a fray." The reference to a "fire" likely refers to an incident that happened on December 20, 1858, when he rescued an actress whose dress had caught on fire from the stage gas footlights.[20] John Barron, a fellow actor who came to know Johnnie well during his days as a Richmond stock actor, was highly impressed:

> He, like his brothers, was as generous as the balmy air on a glorious summer eve. Modest as a maiden, gentle, kind and considerate. While he was not much as a conversationalist, he was exceedingly companionable. John was quick in action and had eyes that were piercing and most expressive, with a perfect physical beauty and stately bearing.... The man was like Edwin [his brother] – born with the divine spark. He was the mold of form, delicately organized physically, with beautiful hands and small feet, graceful by nature, and in all a most effective actor. His eyes, like all

the Booths, were exceedingly brilliant and expressive of all the phases of his characters.

John Mathews, an actor who met Johnnie later, at the beginning of 1865, summed up his impression of Johnnie very succinctly, just after Johnnie had died an arch-villain. "A most winning, captivating man. That was the opinion of everyone who came into contact with him."[21]

As for being "ready for a fray," Johnnie put that quality on display very promptly in the aftermath of Governor Wise's summons. Without any prior warning to theater management, on November 19, 1859 he suddenly threw off his acting job at the Marshall and prevailed upon the Richmond Grays to let him accompany them on their mission to Charles Town. One member of the Grays later recalled the scene:[22]

> Louis F. Bossieux and I were placed as a detail from the Grays in the baggage car of the train in charge of the company's luggage. Booth appeared at the door of the car and asked if he could go with us to Harper's Ferry. We informed him that no one was allowed on the train but men in uniform. He expressed a desire to buy a uniform, since he was very anxious to go. So, after some consultation with him, Bossieux and I each gave him a portion of our uniforms, took him in the car, and carried him with us.

The Grays took the train as far as Aquia Creek, on the Potomac opposite southern Maryland. From there, they took a boat the remaining 40 miles to Washington, arriving around daybreak. Led by the Governor, the troops marched down Pennsylvania Avenue past the White House en route to catching another train for Harpers Ferry. In this procession, Johnnie walked directly behind Governor Wise.[23]

The Grays, along with Governor Wise, arrived in Charles Town in the late afternoon of Sunday, November 20. Johnnie and the Grays were temporarily quartered in an old tin factory.

CHAPTER 21: THE ECSTASY OF THE MARTYR

Johnnie was assigned the temporary rank of Quartermaster Sergeant, and with diligent service, soon wormed his way into good graces of the officers. It did not hurt that Johnnie regularly amused the soldiers every night with dramatic recitations of Shakespeare. With approximately 1,200 men from all over Virginia patrolling day and night, Charles Town turned into a virtual military camp. Cannon commanded the streets, schools were closed, ordinary business was suspended, and military law prevailed.[24]

Johnnie was quite familiar with Foxe's *Book of Martyrs*, as it was one of his most-read books as a teenager.[25] John Brown's impending addition to the rolls of martyrdom was not at all lost on the young Shakespearean actor. Johnnie was proud to be personally handed one of John's pikes by Lewis Washington. The pike, which became a family memento, was inscribed in large letters, "Major Washington to J. Wilkes Booth."[26] Johnnie was determined to make the acquaintance of the man who was now the center of attention. John, for his part, welcomed his celebrity status, generally making it a point to shake the hands of each of his many visitors. Johnnie volunteered for sentry duty outside the jail. The day before the execution, Johnnie prevailed on the Sheriff to grant him a visit with the condemned man. While the details of the visit are not preserved, Johnnie's sparse subsequent political writings and manifestos leave no doubt that John's actions and demeanor made a lasting impression on the young actor.[27]

The appointed day for Brown's hanging was December 2, 1859. At around 11 o'clock in the morning, he was escorted out of the Charlestown jail, wearing the same clothes he had worn in the battle at the engine house. The noose was already in place around his neck, but concealed from view underneath a black frock coat.[28] Among the guards accompanying him on his last ride were the head jailer, John Avis, and the local sheriff, James Campbell.[29] Brown had forged a respectful, almost friendly, relationship with each of them during his last month in jail.[30] Avis had hosted Brown and his wife in his quarters, attached to the jail, for a last supper the night prior. After saying goodbye to Stevens, Copeland, and "Emperor" Green, each of whom would soon meet with a similar fate, Brown rode to the gallows seated on a box containing his own coffin, in the back of a wagon drawn by two large white horses. Just before his arms were tied at the elbows, he handed a note to one of the guards with his last written words:[31]

> Charlestown, VA, 2nd December, 1859.
>
> I, John Brown, am now quite certain that the crimes of this guilty land will never be purged away, but with Blood. I had, as I now think, vainly flattered myself that without very much bloodshed, it might be done.

Artist's rendering of the hanging of John Brown, published 1859

The execution ground, where Johnnie and the other military personnel were assembled to prevent any trouble and witness the hanging, was on the outskirts of town, approximately three quarters of a mile from the jail. One of the

CHAPTER 21: THE ECSTASY OF THE MARTYR

onlookers was Thomas J. Jackson, then an obscure professor at the Virginia Military Institute, but soon to earn lasting glory during the American Civil War as a general nicknamed "Stonewall." Jackson wrote in a letter to his wife the same day that John "ascended the scaffold with apparent cheerfulness."[32] The noose was adjusted, the rope tied to the bar, a white hood placed over John's head, and he was guided into his final position. His last words to the sheriff were, "Don't keep me waiting." But more than 10 minutes passed with John standing still and upright over the trap door, poised for death, as the troops slowly finished filing into their assigned positions for the event. No one present detected any signs of flinching. Finally, the call was shouted, "We are ready." Below the platform, the sheriff raised a hatchet. He severed the rope with a single blow.[33]

Chapter 22: A Primordial Political Genius

On February 27, 1860, 1,500 persons braved a snowstorm and shelled out 25 cents apiece to hear a politician from Illinois give an address in the brand new Cooper Union for the Advancement of Art and Science in lower Manhattan.[1] To his listeners, Abraham Lincoln was a novelty. Lincoln was tall, thin, and rather unsteady in his gait. A reporter in attendance described an involuntary comical awkwardness that marked his movements while speaking. Though powerful at times, Lincoln's voice had a tendency to dwindle into a shrill and unpleasant sound. And yet it was impossible for the audience to avoid noticing how marvelously quick he was in his thoughts and perceptions. His enunciation, however, was slow and emphatic. A peculiar characteristic of his delivery was the remarkable mobility of his features, the frequent contortions of which evoked a merriment that his words alone could not have produced.[2]

Although he was an experienced speaker, both in campaign settings and in courtrooms, Lincoln was painfully aware of his tendency to bore audiences whenever he digressed from the realm in which he was a natural master, that of politics. On this snowy night in New York City, Lincoln would stick to just a few strong themes. His purpose was to speak on behalf of the new Republican party, now a vibrant entity, one rapidly gaining strength not only from former Whigs, but also from many who were disillusioned with the dough-faced Democrats led by President Buchanan, and with the jingoistic "Know Nothing" party. The central premise of Lincoln's talk was to oppose, on an intellectual level, the historical premise underlying Chief Justice Taney's decision in *Scott v. Sandford*. It was a topic he had been researching for several months: that the opposition of Republicans to expansion of the institution of American slavery in the national territories was more in keeping with the actual thinking of the founding fathers than was the version of history articulated by Democrats, most prominently in Taney's lengthy opinion. Continuing a technique he had developed in his Illinois speeches, Lincoln structured his speech as a parody of the view that the "framers of the U.S. Constitution" knew better than anyone how to address slavery.

To his enthused listeners, Lincoln presented his evidence that a clear majority, twenty-one of the thirty-nine men who signed the U.S. Constitution, had at one time or another voted in favor of, and that George Washington as President had signed into law, legislation incompatible with the view adopted by the Supreme Court in *Scott v. Sandford* – that the Constitution granted the federal government no authority to prohibit or regulate slavery in the territories. To loud applause, Lincoln argued that the framers, including such men as Washington, Thomas Jefferson, and James Madison, who themselves held slaves, viewed the institution "as an evil not to be extended, but to be tolerated, and protected only because of and so far as its actual presence among us makes that toleration and protection a necessity." [3]

Lincoln then addressed "a few words to the Southern people." Rhetorically, it was to them that he broached his views on John's attack at Harpers Ferry. The aftermath of John's terrorist raid, to this point, was a general revulsion felt by most civilized Americans, other than radical abolitionists and some African Americans.[4] Lincoln was very concerned with rebutting the charge that "Black Republicans," as they were pejoratively labeled, stood solidly behind John's actions: "You charge that we stir up insurrections among your slaves. We deny it; and what is your proof? Harpers Ferry! John Brown!! John Brown was no Republican; and you have failed to implicate a single Republican in his Harpers Ferry enterprise." Lincoln was also very concerned with rebutting the charge that Republicans were in sympathy with fomenting violent insurrections. Overreaction to the terror of Nat's attack, as well as John's, still dwelt near the forefront of everyone's minds:

> Slave insurrections are no more common now than they were before the Republican party was organized. What induced the Southampton insurrection, twenty-eight years ago, in which, at least three times as many lives were lost as at Harper's Ferry? You can scarcely stretch your very elastic fancy to the conclusion that Southampton was "got up by Black Republicanism." In the present state of things in the United States, I do not think a general, or even a very extensive slave insurrection is possible. The indispensable concert of action cannot be attained. The slaves have no means of rapid communication; nor can incendiary freemen, black or white, supply it. The explosive materials are everywhere in parcels; but there neither are, nor can be supplied, the indispensable connecting trains.

Lincoln expressed an insightful grasp of the fundamental nature of a terrorist act.

> John Brown's effort was peculiar. It was not a slave insurrection. It was an attempt by white men to get up a revolt among slaves, in which the slaves refused to

CHAPTER 22: A PRIMORDIAL POLITICAL GENIUS

participate. In fact, it was so absurd that the slaves, with all their ignorance, saw plainly enough it could not succeed. That affair, in its philosophy, corresponds with the many attempts, related in history, at the assassination of kings and emperors. An enthusiast broods over the oppression of a people till he fancies himself commissioned by Heaven to liberate them. He ventures the attempt, which ends in little else than his own execution. Orsini's attempt on Louis Napoleon, and John Brown's attempt at Harper's Ferry were, in their philosophy, precisely the same. The eagerness to cast blame on old England in the one case, and on New England in the other, does not disprove the sameness of the two things.

Felice Orsini, to whom Lincoln explicitly compared John Brown, was another primordial terrorist. He was born into a well-to-do family. His father Andrea was a military officer, a captain who had served in Napoleon Bonaparte's Italian legion during several of his campaigns, including his ill-fated invasion of Russia in 1812.[5] Andrea Orsini became an early patriot for Italian nationalism, taking part in an ill-fated attempt in 1831 to unite the fractured Italian states into a national entity. In an extreme piece of historical irony, one of the leaders of this nationalist uprising who fought alongside Andrea Orsini was a young Louis Bonaparte, nephew of the famous French Emperor, and the future ruler of France under the title of Napoleon III.[6]

The younger Orsini followed in his father's militant footsteps, taking up underground rebellion against the Papal State that controlled much of the southern part of the Italian peninsula. After being arrested, convicted, and sentenced to life in prison for his participation in a nationalist plot, Felice was on the point of attempting escape when Pope Gregory XVI died. His successor, Pius IX, issued a general amnesty, as was customary for new pontiffs. As a result, Felice was released.[7] He then obtained some military experience fighting with rebel forces against the Papal State and its allied continental powers during the Revolution of 1848, first in the Venice area, and then further south at Ancona.[8] After France and Austria came to the military rescue of the Papal State, the 1848 revolution in Italy collapsed with Garibaldi, accompanied by Hugh Forbes, making a dramatic retreat, as we have already reviewed.

Once the revolution failed, Felice Orsini relocated to Nice, in the French Riviera. There he spent his only period engaged in normal commerce, assisting for a time in his uncle's hemp business. He temporarily indulged in a wife, and had two children. It was a brief interlude. By the fall of 1853 he returned to Italy, the Lunigiana area situated in the mountains east of Massa, where he tried to incite a general revolution in the name of Italian nationalism. But when his followers were confronted by armed forces of the local Savoy government, they immediately dispersed to their homes. Felice was arrested and deported. He made his way to London, where he joined a community of Italian nationalist expats led by Giuseppe Mazzini. On February 21, 1854, Felice, together with a pantheon of revolutionary guests including the Hungarian nationalist Lajos Kossuth, Mazzini, Garibaldi, and the Russian radical Alexander Herzen, was invited to attend a dinner party hosted by George Sanders, the 42-year-old United States consul to England, and also attended by the U.S. Ambassador to England, the future President James Buchanan. Sanders was exceptionally sympathetic to these dissidents, a tendency deemed so dangerous it ended up getting him recalled from his position as consul shortly after the dinner. Sanders's dinner toast would foreshadow his future as a sponsor of terrorism: his expressed wish was "to do away with the Crowned Heads of Europe."[9]

Felice's tolerance for any mainstream political agitation was very small. The following month, in March 1854, he

CHAPTER 22: A PRIMORDIAL POLITICAL GENIUS

returned to Italy to resume fomenting uprising in the Lunigiana. Again the plot failed, this time because his band of rebels were poor mariners. They shipwrecked in the Gulf of La Spezia.[10] Felice then traveled to Switzerland under the fake name of Tito Celsi. Another alias he used to obtain a false passport was George Hernagh. Despite these subterfuges, he was arrested and handed over to the Austrians, who promptly detected his real identity.[11]

After spending months locked up in a castle in Mantova, south of Verona in the Austrian-ruled sector of Italy, on March 29, 1856, Felice managed to pull off a daring solo escape from his maximum security cell. Over a period of weeks, he used smuggled saw blades to sever two sets of bars on his exterior window, painstakingly disguising his cutting with wax. When the opening was finally ready, he used a makeshift rope fashioned from purloined sheets to make the descent of around 60 yards to the ground below. Felice severely injured his ankle when he plummeted the last few feet to the ground. He was lucky to be helped by a friendly peasant to get over the moat that surrounded the castle.[12] After spending fifteen days hiding in Genoa while recuperating from his injury, Felice made his way back to London. But he quickly got into renewed conflict with the "political" exiles there, including Mazzini. Felice was all about action, no matter how hopeless or irrational it seemed to others.[13]

Now, Felice convinced himself that the key to a unified Italy would be the death of the French Emperor, his father's old ally Napoleon III. He began giving his attention to making bombs that would detonate on impact. Felice also adopted another false name, "Thomas Alsopp." At the end of 1857 "Alsopp" departed England to go to Paris, via Belgium. With the help of several conspirators, he smuggled parts for the explosive devices from England. On January 9, 1858, three fellows whom "Alsopp" had recruited for his bomb squad joined him in Paris. They were: Carlo Rudio, age 23, a language teacher from Belluno (in the Italian Alps); Andrea Pieri, age 50, a language teacher from Lucca, and Antonio Gomez, age 29, a domestic worker from Naples.[14] The plan was to attack during the Emperor's planned visit to the theater to see a performance of Rossini's *William Tell* on the evening of January 14, 1858.

A few minutes before the Emperor's arrival, an officer recognized Pieri's face from a security bulletin. He was arrested. Besides the bomb Pieri carried, they found him in possession of a knife and a revolver with six loaded bullets. But the Emperor's theater visit went forward. As his carriage approached the colonnade outside the theater, it stopped so the Emperor could exit into the hallway leading to the royal box. At that moment the terrorists, in quick succession, hurled three bombs intended to kill him. The first blew up in front of the carriage, the second closer to it and to the left, and the last one underneath. The shock of the explosions extinguished all the gas lights and shattered the windows of the entry vestibule of the theater. Fifteen unsuspecting people, among them escorts, police officers, and bystanders, were killed. Hundreds were severely wounded. Besides the two horses pulling the Emperor's carriage, twenty-four horses in his procession of lancers were hit. Two died on the spot, and three others the next day. The horses not killed were extremely frightened, and they trampled over the fallen horses and injured bystanders. Sixteen projectiles from the bombs hit the imperial carriage. However, the carriage had been reinforced with armor, and the Emperor and his wife were unhurt. Felice himself was hit in the head with a projectile, which caused him to bleed very profusely. He had to abandon his second bomb instead of throwing it.[15]

Felice went back to his apartment, where he was arrested a few hours later. The police had captured Gomez, in addition to Pieri. From them they soon learned Felice's role as the leader of the terrorist attack, as well as his location. He at first gave his name as "Thomas Alsopp," but it was quickly discovered that he was really Felice Orsini. He remained single-minded in his fanaticism for Italian unity, writing an appeal on the subject to his intended victim, Napoleon III. After trial, conviction, and sentence, he was put to death by public guillotine on March 13, 1858.[16]

Lincoln's identification, in his historic Cooper Union speech, of the "philosophy" of Felice Orsini with that of John Brown displays his power of analysis. If Orsini and Brown can be called primordial terrorists, Lincoln can be called a primordial political genius. He was born with a natural disposition and talent wonderfully suited for the American political process.

Of all the characters chronicled in this work, Lincoln started from the humblest origins. Born February 12, 1809, he was painfully impressed with the extreme poverty of his early surroundings. To a campaign biographer in 1860, he summed up his entire youthful life in one phrase taken from Gray's *Elegy*: "The short and simple annals of the poor." Lincoln believed his mother, Lucy Hanks, was the illegitimate daughter of a well-bred Virginia planter. To that genetic source he attributed his masterful innate power of analysis, his logic, his mental activity, and his ambition. His father, Thomas Lincoln, although not stupid, was inordinately lazy. After the younger Lincoln achieved worldly prominence, many people who knew both he and Thomas constantly pointed to the lack of resemblance between the shiftless father and his industrious son. Other evidence indicates that young Lincoln also had a tendency to be lazy, to a degree, but that he thoroughly trained himself to overcome it. A neighbor remarked, "He worked for me ... but was always reading and thinking. I used to get mad at him for it. I say he was awful lazy ... He said to me one day that his father taught him to work, but he didn't teach him to love it." Thomas Lincoln did have a liking and reputation for telling jokes and stories, a quality that would become one of his son's lifelong trademarks.[17]

After relocating his family to Indiana from Kentucky, Thomas Lincoln built a "half-faced camp" for his family to live in, a most primitive structure 14 feet long by 14 feet wide with one side open to the elements. Later he built a somewhat larger enclosed cabin, but its contents were equally rustic. Inside was nothing but a dirt floor and the crudest possible stools, even though Thomas was a carpenter by trade. The only bed was supported by a stick. The densely forested area was wild, with many animals including bears. Young Abe became very proficient in handling an axe. In October 1818, when the boy was 9, Nancy Hanks Lincoln died of an unsuspected form of poisoning from a weed that was transmitted through cow's milk.

Thomas Lincoln returned to Kentucky, where he successfully courted Sally Bush, a widow, to replace Nancy Hanks as the family matron. The new Mrs. Lincoln had three children of her own, and she owned a goodly stock of household goods. She proved to be a good influence on her new husband. Sally made him put a floor in the cabin, as well as install doors and windows. The cracks between the logs were finally plastered up. The children's crude mat of corn husks gave way to a much more comfortable featherbed. With her stepson Abe, Sally was gentle and affectionate. It was finally arranged to send him to school, where he proved to be a good student. He soon became studious. He frequently read and studied at home as well as at school.[18]

Young Lincoln's real progress in terms of learning came almost entirely on his own. Typically he would lie down to read and study. He kept the Bible and *Aesop's Fables* always within reach, and he read these works over and over again. Eventually, after leaving home and moving to Illinois, he caught on to the fact that it was possible to teach yourself to be an attorney. He did just that, learning enough to become a professional lawyer

CHAPTER 22: A PRIMORDIAL POLITICAL GENIUS

just from reading books and treatises lent to him by a local attorney. From a mental standpoint Lincoln was one of the most energetic young men of his day. He dwelt altogether in the land of thought. No one had a more retentive memory. If he read or heard a thing that interested him, it never escaped him. His powers of concentration were exceptional and intense.

From the earliest days Lincoln was a popular speechmaker and storyteller. He devoured the newspapers and frequently spoke on political themes. He also attained local notoriety for his remarkable physical strength. In the rough and tumble world of pioneer life, these were talents he was able to parlay into a popularity that helped win electoral contests. In 1834, after a campaign based largely on hand shaking, Lincoln was elected to the Illinois state legislature at the age of 25.[19]

In his politics, Lincoln was a Whig. As it happened, he developed a long-term rivalry relationship with another political prodigy who was a Democrat, Stephen A. Douglas. Douglas was actually four years younger than Lincoln. The gawky Lincoln, who was 6 feet, 4 inches, and the stout Douglas, standing just over 5 feet tall with a huge head and broad shoulders, were physical polar opposites. Of the two, Douglas was a much smoother orator. He and Lincoln originally met during Lincoln's first term in the Illinois state legislature. Douglas had just moved to Illinois from his native Vermont, and he was busy trying to get himself appointed as State's Attorney for the First Judicial District.[20] Soon Douglas used the newly invented system of political party conventions to catapult himself into the state legislature, as well.

As a Whig, Lincoln of course favored spending for "internal improvements" such as railroads and canals, which became the subject of extensive borrowing by the state government. However, Douglas also championed these public works projects, and he did so perhaps even more strongly.

Lincoln became involved in using public works spending bills as a vehicle for "log rolling" to garner support for his own pet project, moving the state capital of Illinois from Vandalia to its present-day location of Springfield. Lincoln clashed sharply with Democrat Usher F. Linder over the relocation of the capital, at just about the same time when Linder was taking a leading role in opposing Elijah Lovejoy's anti-slavery newspaper activism.[21]

With his political skills, Lincoln and his Whig allies succeeded in getting the capital changed to Springfield. Lincoln then personally moved to the new capital, where he lived as a boarder with Joshua Speed, who kept a store in town. Speed's store, in the evenings, became a kind of frontier salon for political discussions. Lincoln and Douglas, along with others, were regular participants in these conversations. Douglas was a vigorous advocate of the Democratic point of view on the central issues of the day, such as monetary and banking policy. One night he laid down a challenge to his Whig adversaries to take their dialogue to a more public forum. It was agreed and arranged to conduct a series of public debates, tag team style, on four consecutive evenings, with four Democrats debating four Whigs, one on each night. Douglas led off for the Democrats, while Lincoln spoke the last night in the anchor leg for the Whigs. It was the opening chapter of the most famous political dialectic in U.S. history.[22]

In 1840, Lincoln was selected to be an elector for the Whig presidential candidate, William Henry Harrison. In that capacity, he went on the stump, making speeches for Harrison and the Whigs. He frequently met Douglas, who was doing the same thing for the Democrats and their presidential candidate. It was at around this time that the two of them engaged in an entirely different form of rivalry, this time for the hand of a woman.

Mary Todd came from a well-to-do, influential family. Her sister Elizabeth was married to one of Lincoln's close

Chapter 22: A Primordial Political Genius

Whig political allies, Ninian Edwards. When she moved to Elizabeth's home in Springfield in 1839, Mary was 21 years old. She was of average height, compactly built with a round face, rich dark brown hair, and bluish-gray eyes. Mary was a passionate and well-educated woman with a quick intellect and an equally quick temper. She was capable of biting sarcasm. Courting her was a good career move for Lincoln, who came from very humble origins as we have seen. Through the influence of his landlord and friend Speed, Lincoln began to call on Mary. In these visits he appeared somewhat shy. In fact, he hardly said a word, allowing her to always lead the conversations. Mary seems to have been impressed with her suitor partly, if not entirely, because she appreciated that he was already on his way to a promising career in politics. She told people she intended to marry a future President, a remark that seemed to them, at the time, just as crazy as it sounded.[23]

While Lincoln was courting Mary Todd, Stephen Douglas appeared on the scene as a competing candidate for her affections. Douglas was closer in age to Mary, and he had far more social graces than did the awkward Lincoln. Mary sometimes walked the streets of Springfield arm-in-arm with Douglas. Apparently feeling some distress at her need to decide between the two men, Mary fell ill. Ultimately, she asked Douglas to quit his pursuit. Lincoln, however, felt the sting of the rivalry. He asked Mary to marry him. Exactly what transpired between the two remains shrouded in mystery and controversy. What is clear and incontrovertible is that Lincoln had a nervous breakdown founded in depression and doubt about his own ability to commit to the relationship. For the first time, Lincoln absented himself from his law practice and his seat in the Illinois legislature. He left the state to go into a lengthy retreat at the home of Speed's parents, in Kentucky near Louisville. After about eight months, he finally pulled himself together, returned to Springfield, resumed his career and, with the help and encouragement of a friendly society lady, resumed his courtship of Mary. In November of 1842 they were married. However, some close to Lincoln felt that the relationship never fully recovered.[24]

In 1841, the Democrats gained ascendency in the Illinois legislature. They pushed through a court-packing plan that increased the number of justices on the Illinois Supreme Court from four to nine. Douglas, still in his 20s, was one of the new justices appointed. From that point forward many, including Lincoln, referred to him as "Judge Douglas." But in the fall of 1846, Douglas was appointed by the Democratic-controlled legislature to become a U.S. Senator. In the same election cycle Lincoln, after a brokered political deal within the Whig party got him the nomination, won a seat as U.S. Representative in the lone Whig Congressional district in the state. So, both Lincoln and Douglas moved to Washington at the same time. Lincoln and Mary boarded there in the same house with Joshua Giddings, the stalwart abolitionist congressman from Ohio, and they became fast friends.[25]

While in Congress, Lincoln did little of note aside from a speech criticizing the pretext on which the United States had started the Mexican War. The speech was highly unpopular in his home state. The deal Lincoln had made to get the Whig nomination called for him to step down after just a single two-year term. He kept his promise. Starting in 1849, Lincoln's political career lay dormant as he went back to law practice. Five years later, it was the brainchild of Douglas, the Kansas–Nebraska Act of 1854, which aroused a tide of indignation that revived and piqued Lincoln's political instincts.[26]

Lincoln, the ultimate self-made man, had an instinctive aversion to the institution of slavery. As early as the fall of 1836, when the Illinois legislature overwhelmingly passed a resolution banning anti-slavery memorials (a measure specifically targeting those proffered by Elijah Lovejoy's Anti-Slavery Society at Alton), Lincoln was one of the very small handful who voted against it. He was, however, cautious to avoid moving far in advance of public opinion on the issue. For instance, while his speeches condemned the "mob rule" involved in the lynching of Macintosh, he avoided any comment on the controversial events leading to Lovejoy's death in Alton.[27] Afterwards he became good friends with Elijah's brother Owen Lovejoy. But, publicly, he distanced himself from Owen's radical abolitionist point of view, and when he participated as one of the founders of the Republican party in Illinois in 1856, he took pains to avoid being perceived as associating with the abolitionists. Lincoln consistently espoused recolonization as the solution to the question of what to do with emancipated slaves.[28] As we have seen, this was regarded as serious heresy by Lloyd Garrison, Frederick Douglass, and their allies.

Lincoln's seminal analysis of the American slavery issue was summed up in his often-repeated biblical proverb:[29] "A house divided against itself cannot stand." In the light of the Kansas struggle and the Supreme Court's reasoning in *Scott v. Sandford*, Lincoln saw clearly that the United States would eventually become either a nation in which owning slaves is entirely legal and protected by law, or one in which it is entirely forbidden and illegal. Lincoln introduced the expression in a speech he made on the occasion of the Republican nominating convention for U.S. Senator on June 16, 1858. This occurred at a critical juncture in Lincoln's career, because he was now being threatened by Douglas in a wholly new and unexpected way.

Even though the doctrine of "popular sovereignty" championed by Stephen Douglas was regarded by many as a mere pretext for expansion of the slaveholding republics, Douglas himself took it very seriously. By 1858 he became embittered with a Buchanan presidential administration bent on disregarding the clear will of the settlers in Kansas to exclude both slavery and African Americans. Douglas complained publicly, and due to his bold criticism of the incumbent Democratic president, some Republicans felt Douglas would be an ideal recruit for their newly burgeoning party. Horace Greeley, the powerful editor of the *New York Tribune*, was one of the most outspoken Douglas advocates. Greeley signaled early and often that he would throw his support to Douglas over Lincoln in Illinois politics, should Douglas switch to the Republican party. Lincoln's speech at the 1858 Republican nominating convention in Illinois was primarily a defense against this flank attack. With his usual aplomb, Lincoln succeeded in reminding his fellow Republicans that he was one of the founders of the party, and that the main reason the party had been formed was to oppose Douglas. The Illinois Republicans ignored out-of-state pundits such as Greeley and overwhelmingly endorsed Lincoln, going out of their way to select him in advance as their choice to challenge Douglas, the incumbent Democratic Senator.[30]

The Lincoln–Douglas contest for the Illinois U.S. Senate seat in 1858 served as the stage for a classic series of debates. As in previous campaigns, Lincoln started the dialogue by "following" Douglas appearances with speeches of his own. On July 16 and 17, 1858, Douglas spoke at Bloomington and Springfield. On July 17, in the evening, Lincoln spoke in reply. Then, on July 24, Lincoln sent his longtime nemesis a formal challenge to engage in a series of debates. On July 30, Douglas accepted. It was soon decided to have seven debates, one in each Illinois Congressional district, starting August 21 and ending October 15, in Alton. The format was three hours: opening, one hour; response, an hour and a half; reply, a half hour. Douglas got to open and close four times, Lincoln three.[31] In terms of subject matter, the most remarkable aspect of the

CHAPTER 22: A PRIMORDIAL POLITICAL GENIUS

Pre-Presidency photo portrait of Abraham Lincoln
Library of Congress

debates was the extent to which economic and fiscal issues were almost completely pushed aside in favor of a preoccupation by both candidates with the issue of the institution of slavery in America.[32]

One newspaper writer would later comment, "Without Douglas, Lincoln would be nothing."[33] During the course of the debates, Lincoln maneuvered his adversary into a position of having to defend, if not the relationship of slavery itself, then the position that a society in which owning slaves is a legal way of life can be a legitimate choice. Lincoln parodied the position of Douglas as boiling down to: "If one man chooses to enslave another, no third man has the right to object." In the final debate in Alton, Lincoln closed his speech with a stirring summary:[34]

> [The institution of slavery] is the real issue. That is the issue that will continue in this country when these poor tongues of Judge Douglas and myself shall be silent. It is the eternal struggle between these two principles – right and wrong – throughout the world. They are the two principles that have stood face to face from the beginning of time, and will ever continue to struggle.

In the state election on November 2, 1858, Lincoln received around 4,000 more votes, but Douglas succeeded in retaining his Senate seat. The Democrats continued to control the legislature due to the way the districts were apportioned. However, from the debates, Lincoln attained his first national attention and acclaim.[35] They proved to be a dynamic battle, in the course of which both candidates shifted their positions somewhat toward middle ground. Lincoln took a moderate position, for example, by denying that he had ever advocated racial equality. Abolitionists regarded him with distrust, calling him a "Henry Clay Whig." Lloyd Garrison, for instance, deprecated him as a candidate who would "do nothing to offend the South." Douglas, on the other hand, moved slightly in the direction of repudiating the constitutional rationale of *Scott v. Sandford* by affirming his view that residents of a territory had the power to vote to exclude slavery before the formation of a state.[36] This "Freeport doctrine," so-called because it was first clearly stated by Douglas during the debate in Freeport, had a very important consequence: Douglas was now ostracized and regarded as unacceptable by a major segment of Southern political thought. Lincoln, on the other hand, benefitted in the North because he was perceived as more of a moderate on the "abolition" issue than Henry Seward, even though the actual views of the two men were in fact very similar. Lincoln held the advantage over Henry of being a newcomer without much of a record. The Southern press was vitriolic in its attitude toward Henry, causing important people to oppose his presidential nomination even though he was generally regarded as the Republican front-runner. Whispers circulated that a Seward administration would be corrupt because of the inevitable power of a Thurlow Weed over patronage. Fears were expressed that Henry had overly alienated the nativist Know Nothings. The invitation sent by New York Republicans to Lincoln to make his Cooper Union address was basically a stalking horse for wresting the presidential nomination away from Henry Seward.[37] Henry, in response, sought to stake out a moderate position. In a February

CHAPTER 22: A PRIMORDIAL POLITICAL GENIUS

1860 Senate speech, Henry denounced John's Virginia attack as treason, and applauded his swift execution.[38]

The 1860 Republican National Convention was held in Chicago, within Lincoln's home state, which proved to be a critical advantage. The gallery was packed with vociferous Lincoln supporters. On the first ballot conducted May 18, 1860, Henry received 172 votes, 60 short of the number needed to nominate, while Lincoln was second with 102. However, the large Pennsylvania delegation, after giving its initial ballot to its Governor, moved to Lincoln on the second ballot. The switch produced the decisive momentum. The darling dark horse candidate from Illinois was nominated by acclamation on the third ballot.[39] It is recorded that Henry in Auburn, upon receiving a telegram with the news, "Abraham Lincoln nominated," exclaimed, "Well, Mr. Lincoln will be elected and has some of the qualities to be a good president." [40]

Henry was absolutely correct in predicting that Lincoln would be elected. The incumbent Democrats splintered and self-destructed. During his 1856 campaign, Buchanan had promised not to seek a second term and, as a practical matter, he lacked support for doing so anyway, because his administration was widely regarded as corrupt. With the incumbent on the sidelines, Stephen Douglas was the Democratic front-runner and natural candidate. But Buchanan, who was still angry over Douglas's position showing independence on the Kansas issue, refused to endorse him. The Democratic National Convention took place during the last week of April in Charleston, South Carolina. It was the worst possible venue for trying to unite the party around Douglas.[41] The delegates split over the party platform. Southern leaders, including Jefferson Davis, advocated enacting a territorial "slave code" that would guarantee the right to own slaves throughout the national territories. On this plank they were outvoted by the Northern Democrats, who adopted Douglas's "popular sovereignty" concept. The Southern delegates then bolted from the convention. Party rules were interpreted to require that, with less than two thirds of the delegates present, no candidate could be nominated. The rump of delegates agreed to reassemble in Baltimore in June. But in that new convention the Southern delegates once again departed rather than participate in nominating Douglas. This time, the convention did choose Douglas to be the party candidate, but the breakaway "Southern Democrats" met in Richmond and nominated John Breckinridge of Kentucky, the incumbent Vice-President who was endorsed by President Buchanan.[42]

As an over-the-top excess reaction to the terror of John Brown's attack, Southern voices in politics and the press linked John with a conspiracy of "Black Republicans" – the association Lincoln attempted to rebut in his Cooper Union address. Many in the South began to talk publicly about the prospect that their states would secede and withdraw from the Union if Lincoln were elected President. In May, a new party called the "Constitutional Union" party, formed from remnants of the Southern Whig party and the Know Nothing party, met in Baltimore to choose a presidential candidate whose only meaningful platform would be support for compromise and the preservation of the Union. John Bell, a Whig Senator from Tennessee, was selected to be the Constitutional Union candidate, with Edward Everett of Massachusetts nominated as Vice-President.[43] The formation of this new party, in addition to the schism of the Southern Democrats, severely sapped support for Stephen Douglas throughout the nation, and made it virtually impossible for him to prevail in the presidential election.

In view of his disorganized and divided opposition, Lincoln had to do almost nothing to win the presidential election. In fact, the only candidate who campaigned extensively was Douglas. Douglas exhausted himself on a prolonged tour of the country, with many stops and speeches.[44]

But on October 9, 1860, an election for Congressional representatives and state officials in the large Northern states of Pennsylvania, Indiana, and Ohio yielded large majorities for the Republicans. The handwriting was on the wall, easily visible to all experienced political observers, including Douglas. He confined his further campaign efforts to a tour of the Deep South, including Montgomery, Alabama, where he and his wife were pelted with rotten eggs. Douglas made a speech in Montgomery on November 2, 1860, which urged his listeners to cherish the Union and desist from the notion of secession in the aftermath of a Lincoln victory. He said in this speech that the nation that the founders created was the "greatest blessing ever conferred on a free people." He also warned that there is a "conspiracy on foot to break up this Union."[45]

In the end, essentially two elections took place. In the South, where Lincoln received essentially zero ballots, Bell received about 40% of the votes and carried three states: Virginia, Kentucky, and Tennessee. Breckinridge carried the remainder, including Maryland and Delaware. Douglas, although second with 29% of the overall popular vote, carried only Missouri, a split ballot in New Jersey, and nothing else. Lincoln, with 40% of the overall popular vote, carried every Northern state, flipping the important states of Pennsylvania, Indiana, Illinois, and California to the Republican side of the ledger. With 180 electoral votes, representing 59% of the total, he was easily elected.[46]

The nation held its collective breath, awaiting a dramatic swing of the political pendulum.

Chapter 23: "Alow Me a Few Words"

When Stephen Douglas spoke in Montgomery four days before the presidential election, one on hand who paid very close attention to his rhetoric was John Wilkes Booth. By sheer coincidence, Johnnie was also in Montgomery, playing in a starring role that very evening in Shakespeare's *Romeo and Juliet.* Matthew Canning, a Philadelphia lawyer turned theater impresario, had engaged Johnnie, still billed as "Mr. Wilkes," to tour as the leading man with his Southern theater company.[1] The new starring role was a major step forward in his career. His first night on stage with Canning's troupe was on October 1, 1860 in Columbus on the Georgia–Alabama line. His performance as Romeo was an instant hit. The following year, a reviewer for the *Chicago Times* would write of Johnnie's Romeo:[2]

> He has a capacity for sentimental parts which should lead him in his search for fame…. As *Romeo* he is impressive and often fervent. There is an emotion, an earnestness, a pathos in the very tones of his voice, which attracts independent of the pervading warmth imparted by the poetic flow of the text.

Chapter 23: "Alow Me a Few Words"

Johnnie's exceptionally creative, emotive, and naturalistic interpretations attracted immediate notice from the public as well as reviewers. His performances first in Columbus, then in Montgomery, packed the theaters to the point that it was difficult for critics to even enter the houses. And while Johnnie was well received for his tragic heroes like Romeo, the real raves came for his personification of dastardly villains, particularly, Pescara in Sheil's *The Apostate* and Richard in Shakespeare's *Richard III*.[3] Instantly the reviewers recognized that Johnnie reincarnated, and perhaps even exceeded, his father's famed stage brilliance in these roles. The father–son resemblance was all the more uncanny because Johnnie had never even seen his father act professionally.[4] But he won praise, and attracted large audiences, as a "chip off the old block." By the end of the tour, Johnnie finally relented and allowed himself to be billed, for the first time, under the name of "Booth."[5]

Johnnie also emulated his father's penchant for bizarre behavior. Such an episode occurred on Friday, October 12, 1860. In a tussle with his manager, Johnnie was shot in the leg with Canning's revolver. The flesh wound he sustained, which reportedly almost rendered him a eunuch, was staunched in time to save him. But the injury kept him from performing on stage for seventeen days, during which time the revenue of the Canning troupe's performances dropped precipitously. Johnnie mustered enough strength to simply recite the lines of Mark Antony over the dead body of Julius Caesar for the closing performance in Columbus eight days after being shot. After that, the troupe went on to Montgomery. Johnnie had to sit out the initial week. But just as he received kudos from the critics for being a hard worker, he overcame the leg injury from the bullet in far less time than they expected. On October 29, he returned to the stage in the role of Pescara. The reviews, while noting his hobble, were excellent. Soon crowds were again swarming to see his performances.[6]

As a result of the financial success of Canning's tour, Johnnie enjoyed, for the first time, substantial theater earnings. Part of these he invested in the services of a Montgomery brothel operated by Madame Jennie Garborough. The Madame assigned Johnnie to a pretty 18-year-old inmate of the residence, Louise Wooster. Louise had been born into a respectable Mobile family, but she had moved to Montgomery to take up a life of prostitution after both of her parents died, and after she was then subjected to sexual molestation by a man who took her in at age 11. In keeping with his avid interest in all classes of people, Johnnie let his natural feelings of compassionate attraction take over regarding Louise. Louise, for her part, idolized Johnnie. She found him "an ideal man, handsome, generous, affectionate and brave." During a little over a month he spent in Montgomery, they developed a warm romance on top of the physical relationship. Johnnie, immersed in mastering the many roles needed for his theatrical repertoire, enjoyed doing "little rehearsals" with Louise. Together they dreamed of freeing Louise from her life in the brothel and of turning her into a stage actress.[7] It was the beginning of what, for Johnnie, would turn into a series of love affairs with professional sex workers.

To Louise, Johnnie poured out his heart. And, more than anything else, his heart was filled with emotions directly

John Wilkes Booth in photo, published 1925

inspired by Douglas's message of November 2. Johnnie was passionately in love with the idea of the Union. Furthermore, an underlying strand in his mental makeup was strong opposition to prevailing political sentiments. Because people in Montgomery were all aflame with eagerness for secession, Johnnie disagreed with them vehemently. He expressed his mind on that subject, not only to Louise but to others.[8] He did so incautiously, because in the overreaction that followed Lincoln's election as President, Montgomery quickly melted into a seething hotbed of secessionist sentiment. When his gig in Montgomery ended on December 1, 1860, Johnnie came under pressure to pledge his allegiance to the Southern cause. Johnnie panicked, because he did not wish to be trapped behind the lines in the event Southern independence was declared. He ended his engagement and departed in haste, promising Louise he would return for her in a matter of weeks, or months at the most. "Such a glorious country as ours cannot be broken up by a few fanatics," he assured her. Left behind, Louise would never see Johnnie again. But Johnnie had been kind to Louise, despite her despised status as a fallen woman. For that she would always remember him fondly and would cherish his memory, even into the next century.[9]

Lincoln's election added to the malaise felt throughout the South as a result of John's terrorist raid at Harpers Ferry. His ascent to the Presidency was trumpeted by firebrand Southern leaders as, in itself, an intolerable overt act of hostility to the South and its social system.[10] In the gathering torrent of passion for secession, all of the federal judges and prosecutors in North Carolina and South Carolina immediately resigned.

By December 3, 1860, when outgoing President Buchanan addressed the growing crisis in his final State of the Union message,[11] he opened with a question. Why, when the country was in the midst of the greatest plenty and prosperity in its history, and was rapidly growing into one of the world's strongest powers, was such a state of discontent extensively prevailing throughout the nation? He immediately provided a one-sentence answer to his own question: "The long and continued and intemperate interference of the Northern people with the question of slavery in the Southern states." What he called the worst aspect of the problem was not the efforts of territorial legislatures to exclude slavery, nor was it defiance to enforcing the Fugitive Slave Act. It was a direct overreaction to the terrorist acts by Nat Turner and John Brown. Buchanan said:

> The immediate peril arises not so much from these causes as from the fact that the incessant and violent agitation of the slavery question throughout the North for the last quarter of a century, has at last produced its malign influence upon the slaves and inspired them with vague notions of freedom. Hence a sense of security no longer exists around the family altar. This feeling of peace at home has given place to apprehensions of servile insurrection. Many a matron throughout the South retires at night in dread of what may befall herself and her children before the morning.

Buchanan attributed the unwarranted agitation against slavery to "the public press," to "State and County conventions," and to "abolition sermons and lectures." He deprecated sentiment in favor of granting any fundamental rights to African Americans, urging that each state must be allowed to "manage their domestic institutions in their own way." In support of his view that there is nothing about slavery that shocks the conscience, he pointed to the existence of "similar institutions" in Russia and Brazil. Although he was a former U.S. Ambassador to England, President Buchanan chose not to mention the abolition of slavery throughout the British empire, which at that point had occurred over 25 years

CHAPTER 23: "ALOW ME A FEW WORDS"

earlier.

Buchanan's next major theme was that Lincoln's election was no just cause for dissolving the Union. He denied that any state had the right to secede. The forefathers had devoted many years of toil, privation, and blood to establish the Union, which was no "rope of sand" to be dissolved by a wave of public opinion. Secession, not being permitted under the Constitution, was nothing short of revolution. Such a resort to revolutionary resistance would be justified only by a "deliberate, palpable, and dangerous exercise" of "powers not granted by the Constitution." The mere election of Lincoln was not such an overt act. From "the very nature of his office," the next President "must necessarily be conservative," Buchanan argued. Congress was not in a mood to take away the South's right to property in slaves. The Supreme Court, "only three days after my inauguration" as Buchanan put it, had solemnly decided that slaves are property, and that like all property, their owners have the right to take them into the common Territories, under the protection of the privileges and immunities and due process clauses of the Bill of Rights. The next President would be bound to uphold these constitutional provisions.

Buchanan then addressed head-on the looming specter of secession by Southern states. Any President, he said, would lack the authority to recognize the de facto government of such states. But, on the other hand, after "much serious reflection" he had concluded that any attempt to oppose their secession by force would be unconstitutional. He pointed out that James Madison, the principal architect of the Constitution, had successfully opposed, on May 31, 1787, a provision that would have expressly granted Congress the power to coerce a recalcitrant state into submission. An attempt to put down secession by force would also be unwise, Buchanan argued. It would produce nothing but ill-will on both sides and would "destroy the greatest temple which has ever been dedicated to human freedom since the world began." As his departing prescription for the impending crisis, Buchanan concluded by urging the nation to adopt an "explanatory amendment" to the Constitution, one that would essentially "lock in" the view of the Constitution and Bill of Rights expressed by the majority decision in *Scott v. Sandford*.

Ten days later, on December 13, 1860, an estimated 50,000 people crowded into Independence Square in Philadelphia in front of a huge banner that read, "Concession Before Secession" to attend a mass rally dubbed the "Great Union." Philadelphia's Mayor Alexander Henry presided. Prominent figures made speeches in support of compromise and gestures of support for the South. Resolutions were passed to "search the statute books" to repeal any law which "in the slightest degree" invaded the constitutional rights of the citizens of a sister state. A pledge was made to "cheerfully submit" to the Supreme Court decision in *Scott v. Sandford*. There was a general frowning on all "denunciations of slavery."[12]

Johnnie was, again, a very interested observer in personal attendance at the Great Union rally. He was at that time freshly arrived in Philadelphia from Montgomery.[13] When he listened to the Great Union speakers, he was once more strongly moved on an emotional level. He promptly wrote a lengthy speech that he never, so far as anyone knows, delivered. However, it is by far and away the most extensive and longest of Johnnie's extant writings and, as such, it gives the deepest and most direct available insight into his thought processes around political matters.

Johnnie's speech began with one brief sentence, perhaps intended as a title: "Alow Me a Few Words."[14] In the way it betrays a strong desire to shape issues of political importance, and also, in its degree of spelling and punctuation errors, "Alow Me a Few Words!" is very similar to the "Historic

CHAPTER 23: "ALOW ME A FEW WORDS"

Diary" that would be penned approximately 100 years later by a young man named Lee Harvey Oswald.[15] In this work, Johnnie personalized and expanded upon concepts he had absorbed from the speeches of Douglas in Montgomery, President Buchanan's State of the Union message,[16] and the Philadelphia "Great Union" speakers.

Johnnie wholeheartedly endorsed Buchanan's thesis that advocacy of abolition was the root cause of America's discontent. In his own words, he repeatedly urged suppression of the speech rights of "trators" (his spelling) around the slavery issue:

> Now, Mr. Theodore Cuyler in his speech of Dec. 13th: says that liberty of speech and license of speech are very different things. I agree with him and can safely say, It is that very liberty of speech *abused*, which has brought us to the brink of where we stand, You will all admit my liberty of speech does not extend to my speaking my mind freely in society, or I should be kicked out. No more does it warrant my using profane language in a church. Then why should free use of speech have license to destroy a country.

The press was not spared Johnnie's invective:

> Can a paper be just that exaggerates the evils of man, and turns his good into crime. Can a paper be just which shows only one side of a question, leading its readers into darkness and despare. Show me a paper and for one word of truth you can find a hundred lies. Calculated to lead mankind into folly and into vice Ay false master which has brought on all these troubles by which we are surrounded instead of binding us closer in a loving brotherhood. It belies its calling: that is my view of it as a northern man. I am not a southerner, but viewing it as a southern man I will

speak of it thus, It belies its calling. It makes me hate my brothers in the north.

Johnnie admitted that he was "no politician," and that he was not a practiced speaker. He regretted lacking the eloquence of a "Dimothanies" or a "Ciciro" (an odd statement, because his budding Thespian career was a form of public speaking). He further admitted that his speech may exceed the "bounds of prudence." His general attitude throughout was entirely consistent with that of a John Brown, disdaining reasoned dialogue and political action. While convinced he was entirely right, he was also unwilling to engage in any form of debate to defend his position. Thus, he wrote:

> [I]n sooth my friends, I have been in constant dread scince my speech began, lest some mouthing politician should call upon me to answer questions, or argue this, or that subject. I cannot argue. I am gifted with no such powers. I can tell you the truth which is better than argument the world over. I can tell you the truth, shuch as you know it to be yourselves! I can use my weak voice and perhaps *vain endeavors* to call you back to reason.

Johnnie advocated the ultimate "truth" of a violent solution: Death to "trators":

> Then what should be done with such men who are cold to all the blessings of the freedom they possess? who laugh at our country as it is, Scoff at her institutions as they are, And who would not only cry for a King, but endeavor to lead others in their views and spread their d—-d opinions throughout the land. Now I call it treason to our common country, and it should not be allowed, don't you, my friends. Aye, then where is their liberty of speech. I tell you that liberty of speech can be abused and should not be tollerated to the abuse thereof. Men have no right to

Chapter 23: "Alow Me a Few Words"

> entertain opinions which endanger the safety of the country. Such men I call trators and treason should be stamped to death and not alowed to stalk abroad in any land. So deep is my hatred for such men that I could wish I had them in my grasp And I the power to crush. I'd grind them into dust!

In a revealing paradox, the one abolitionist for whom Johnnie expressed grudging admiration was John Brown himself, due to his bold and unabashed use of violence:

> The Abolition party must throw away their principals. They must be hushed forever. Or else it must be done by the punishment of her aggressors. By justice that demands the blood of her oppressors. By the blood of *those*, who in wounding her have slain us all, with naught save blood and justice. Ay blood, in this case, should season justice. You may not agree with me. thousands do. The whole South does. For John Brown was executed (yes, and justly) by his country's laws for attempting in another way, mearly what these abolitionists are doing now.

Johnnie's writing in his speech betrayed a more than subtle hint of influence from John's violent actions at Harpers Ferry. Adverting to an ancient metaphor of statecraft lexicon, he evoked in John a "noble" figure of rule by force, strength, and respect in the image of the Lion, as contrasted with one exercising power through political and diplomatic intrigues, as symbolized by the Fox:[17]

> I saw John Brown hung. And I blessed the justice of my contry's laws. I may say I helped to hang John Brown and while I live, I shall think with joy upon the day when I saw the sun go down upon one trator *less* within our land. His treason was no more than theirs,

for open <u>force</u> is <u>holier</u> than hidden <u>craft</u>. The Lion is more noble than the fox.

Johnnie was filled with passion around politics. And "Alow Me a Few Words" was, in its essence, a tremendous outpouring of patriotic emotion. He intentionally and explicitly informed his listeners that his goal in making the speech was to evoke in his listeners the same level of emotion about the growing crisis that he himself felt. He declared that his mission was:

> To fan the dieing embers of patriotism now slumbering in your hearts. To wake that love of country which I know you to possess. Indeed *I* love her so that I oft mentally exclaim, *with Richelieu.* O my native land let me but ward this dagger from thy heart! and die upon thy bossom. Such is my love that I could be content to crawl on to old age. With all the curses, that could be heaped upon me, *to see her safe from this coming tempest!* If there is any man here who can lay his hand upon his heart and say he would not do the same, *that man* I deem unworthy to hear me. But I am sure there is no such man.

Displaying a fundamental disconnect terrorists tend to share in common, this son of an immigrant invoked a powerful image of his father dying for his son's liberty. It was an image that was entirely fanciful and inapplicable to his own personal history:

> Think of the lives nobly spent and lost in rearing aloft this great temple of liberty. Think of all the blood spilled to cement the work. Think upon the actions of our fathers, who endured evry privation, who even died to secure us (their sons) this glorious heritage of freedom. A heritage unstained by injustice, unstained by treason, unstained by any wrong, a heritage upon which God smiled and poured his blessings. A

Chapter 23: "Alow Me a Few Words"

heritage which the memory of our fathers, *Commands us to maintain.* Do you think my brothers that the spirit of those peaceful dead will smile upon us when this union is destroyed. No No this union must and shall be preserved. We'l all stand by her, And keep her in her original purity, or die. Grant but impartial justice and our country will stand the shock of ages. Ay, grant love to all, justice to all. With death to trators and she can never die.

In his draft speech, Johnnie took one small element of Buchanan's State of the Union address and stretched it toward what would eventually become, for Johnnie, an obsession: Kings and other absolute rulers.

Buchanan, speaking of secession:

> By such a dread catastrophe the hopes of the friends of freedom throughout the world would be destroyed, and a long night of despotism would enshroud the nations.

Johnnie, in his draft speech:

> O what a triumph for the crowned world will it be to see this once proud union bend its head unto the dust! To see the bird that is the emblem of our freedom and our strength break its majestic pinions and fall fluttering to the earth....

> The South is leaving us. O would to God that Clay & Webster could hear those words. Weep fellow countrymen, for the brightest half of our stars upon the nations banner have grown dim. Once quite out my friends, all will be dark and dreary. Where once reigned shuch a dazzling & celestial light to strike with awe the enthronéd Monarchs of the world.

Johnnie declared himself in search of a cause of injustice for which to fight to the death:

> Thank God I have a heart big enough for all the states. If Main was wronged by her sister states, and struck for justice, I'd fight for Main. If Florida was wronged by her sister states, Id fight for Florida. If Delaware was wronged by her sister States, I'd fight for Delaware. And so for all the rest, though I struck the first blow at my own dear Maryland. If this sectional feeling is so strong we may as well say we will only fight for the house in which we first drew breath. Or only for the mother that bore us, or in fact we wont fight at all. No gentlemen the whole union is our country, And the Cry for justice should be heard & heeded from whatever extremity it may come.
>
> . . . .
>
> We should act with coolness and judgment, all should be done in peace. For God be my witness that I love peace, that I would give my all to maintain it, but Gentlemen there is a time when men should act for themselves and not under the guidance of a few political leaders who use them only for their own ends, I tell you Sirs when treason weighs heavy in the scale, it is a time for us to throw off all gentler feelings of our natures and summon resolution, pride, justice, Ay, and revenge, to take the place of those nobler passions in the human heart, respect, forgiveness and Brotherly-love.
>
> . . . .
>
> Would you not all die to save your country. Yes. I know you would. Why then will you allow her to be destroyed. The cesessionists of the south say that all argument has been exhausted, that they can and will

Chapter 23: "Alow Me a Few Words"

use it no more. we have been deaf to the voice of justice. We cannot blame them. What is to be done? If argument has no more resources, it is time for all good citizens who are, or would be conservative to their country, in, this, her hour of need to come to action. And not stand Idly by hoping to save a country by *fast* and *Prayer*.

. . . .

Ay, grant love to all, justice to all. With death to trators and she can never die. I would go on but know not what to say to you, you are all better judges of this subject than I, I am unused to speak upon the spur of the moment. I am gifted with no powers of oration but am a mear child of a boy, to some I see around me. A child indeed and this union is my Mother. A Mother that I love with an unutterable affection … O would that I could place my worship for her in anothers heart, in the heart of some great orator, who might move you all to love her, *to help her now when she is dieing.* No, No. I wrong you. You all do love her. You all would die for her. Yet hesitate upon the way to save her. God grant, it may be done in a peaceful way. If not, it must be done with blood. Ay with blood and justice.

The problem that becomes apparent from Johnnie's draft speech, and the most likely reason he never finished it, is that the exact "cause" for which to fight was difficult to fathom. The South, for whose justice he cried, was all aflame for secession, while Johnnie at that time passionately opposed the idea. Thus, while he did not "intend to argue," and while he wished to "speak clearly" of the "truth" he "knows," and of what he "intends to do," he would not bring himself to condone the South's flight:

I will not fight for cesession. No I will not fight for disunion. But I will fight with all my heart and soul, even if theres not a man to back me, for eaqual rights and justice for the South. As I would do for the North in like position.

The problem was, the South's momentum toward secession was overwhelming. Spurning the Great Union, South Carolina, on December 20, 1860, became the first state to formally secede from the United States. Six other Deep South states rapidly followed suit. President-elect Lincoln, getting organized to confront the crisis, showed that his instincts were far more political than they were ideological by appointing his four main rivals for the Presidency to top cabinet posts. He appointed the number one rival, Henry Seward, to be his Secretary of State on December 28. Henry promptly drew the ire of abolitionists, and even his wife, when he made a major speech in the Senate in which he put forth five points of compromise, including endorsing the idea proposed by President Buchanan of a constitutional amendment to protect slavery from any Congressional interference. All overtures were in vain. On January 10, 1861, South Carolina artillery fired on *Star of the West* as she attempted to resupply the federal government's garrison at Fort Sumter in Charleston Harbor.[18]

Matthew Canning persuaded Johnnie to follow up his well-received and financially successful Southern tour with a tour of Northern venues. On January 21, 1861, Johnnie opened a two-week engagement at the Metropolitan Theater in Rochester, New York. He received extremely positive reviews, especially regarding his villainous "Richard," a role in which he invariably drew comparisons to his father Junius Brutus Booth.[19] A reporter wrote that his "full and crowded houses" were all the more remarkable because they came at a time when theater in general was "languishing".[20]

CHAPTER 23: "ALOW ME A FEW WORDS"

This fact speaks more than anything else that can be said as a tribute to this genius. He has played a round of characters calculated to show the scope and versatility of his power, as well as to put his ability to the test of criticism. And all he has done well, making new friends and admirers in each new phase of character that he assumed. His Othello, Richard, and Romeo were as faultless as the same characters in the hands of his illustrious sire at the same age, and there is no reason to doubt that he is destined to fill his place upon the stage, and add new luster to the name he bears.

Johnnie moved on to Albany, the New York state capital. The second night, while falling as part of the performance, he accidentally landed on his dagger, stabbing himself in the right armpit. It was another potentially very serious injury. However, once again luck was on his side. The knife did not rupture any of his vital organs. Six days later he was back on stage, fencing left-handed with his right arm strapped to his side, acting the part of the villain Pescara. The audience was spellbound by, in the words of a reviewer, Johnnie's "artistic conceptions of the characters he performs." That same evening Lincoln, on his way to Washington to be inaugurated, was also in Albany giving a much less riveting performance, a speech only a few blocks away.[21]

After closing Albany, Johnnie went on to Portland, Maine, where he opened a series of performances on March 18 by again playing Richard. He was so well received that the troupe's booking was extended to include a second week.[22] When the two weeks in Portland concluded, Johnnie returned to Albany to prepare for a return engagement set to begin on April 22.

Meanwhile, the national secession crisis deepened. Delegates from the seven Deep South states that had seceded met in Montgomery during February 1861 and hammered out a constitution for the new Confederate States of America, or CSA. The militants recognized the value of appointing mainstream politicians to hold the leading offices. On February 9 they tabbed Jefferson Davis, the former Secretary of War and Senate colleague of Henry and Charles, to be the CSA's President. Alexander Stephens, a Georgia moderate who had supported Douglas during the 1860 campaign, was selected to be Vice-President. On February 16, new President Davis made a speech that catered to the militants, promising to meet any attempt to interfere with the new Confederacy with "Southern powder" and "Southern steel." The Upper South states teetered as both camps vied for their loyalty. Out of prudence, Lincoln agreed to use a ruse to frustrate any possible attempt by pro-slavery radicals to interfere with his passage through Baltimore en route to the seat of the federal government in Washington. On March 4, the very day of the inauguration, the Senate passed a proposed constitutional amendment guaranteeing the right to own slaves in the South. It was a measure Henry had advocated in his January speech. Republican legislators were so upset over this peace offering that more than twenty of them opposed Henry's confirmation as Secretary of State. Henry also helped water down Lincoln's inaugural address, which was very conciliatory toward the South.

The militants who had gained ascendency in the Deep South were determined to show they meant business. The most immediate flash point revolved around a struggle for control of federal military outposts located in Deep South states. Fort Sumter, built on an island that dominated Charleston harbor, was placed under de facto siege due to the refusal of South Carolina officials to allow any U.S. government ships to land on the island. In his first major showing of presidential resolve, Lincoln refused the advice of a majority of his Cabinet to abandon the fort. On April 6 he informed Governor Francis Pickens of South Carolina – a state official with whom he could

Chapter 23: "Alow Me a Few Words"

correspond without recognizing the new Confederate government – that a supply mission would be sent without adding to the troops there. CSA President Davis in Montgomery promptly instructed forces in Charleston to preempt any such relief mission by demanding Fort Sumter's immediate surrender, and to take the island by force if it refused. The demand to surrender was refused, so, at 4.30 a.m. on April 12, Confederate cannons opened fire from shore. The steady bombardment, coupled with the garrison's lack of ammunition and supplies, forced its capitulation within a matter of less than two days. While symbolic, the Confederate capture of Fort Sumter was also a decisive event. It brought home to everyone in America the fact that the declaration of rebellion by the new CSA was more than just theoretical. The event was felt in the North as a huge emotional shock. President Lincoln immediately received enthusiastic support for a proclamation to raise 75,000 federal troops to put down the rebellion.[23]

Just as Johnnie had chafed and taken umbrage in the face of a wave of secessionist sentiments in Montgomery five months earlier, now he chafed and took umbrage at the surge of anger that was felt in New York and elsewhere against the South. On April 19 a local Albany paper, in a piece addressing his upcoming theater engagement, complained about how Johnnie had "unfurled his colors" publicly. His intemperate remarks praising the "heroism of the South" caused people to become incensed. This was not good for business. Manager Canning insisted Johnnie cut out the political rhetoric. Cowed, he complied.[24]

However, Johnnie's personal life soon took another bizarre turn. On the Rochester and Albany stages, the co-star who played Juliet to Johnnie's Romeo, five years older than he, was an experienced actress named Henrietta Irving.[25] Evidently, some of Johnnie's nighttime "rehearsals" with

Henrietta went far above and beyond. However, Johnnie had no intention of getting into a long-term commitment to her. Henrietta, whose personality was reportedly something less than pleasant, became enraged and depressed. Neither of them ever discussed exactly what precipitated their extracurricular drama. Rumors swirled about an element of jealousy over attraction between Johnnie and Henrietta's sister Maria, who was also an actress in the same troupe. What is incontrovertible is that on the night of April 26, 1861, Henrietta, in Johnnie's room in Albany's Stanwix Hotel, slashed him viciously across the face with a knife. She then retreated to her room and turned the knife on herself, although she was not seriously wounded.[26]

Luck, yet again, was on Johnnie's side. The knife attack produced a large bloody gash that had to be repaired with many stitches, but it barely missed Johnnie's face. Instead, the wound was on his upper forehead, where its effects could be concealed by a lock of his hair. Still, this latest injury forced Johnnie to cancel all his remaining performances in the spring of 1861. He returned to Philadelphia, where his mother, Mary Ann, for his 23rd birthday, gave him a two-volume set of John S.C. Abbott's *The History of Napoleon Bonaparte*. It was inscribed with his new stage name, "J. Wilkes Booth." Johnnie conspicuously idolized Napoleon, often approaching and kissing his sculptures and busts. But he also admired Felice Orsini, the would-be assassin of Napoleon's nephew Napoleon III. Concerning Felice, Johnnie commented sardonically that if he had undertaken such a job, he would not have bungled it.[27]

While Johnnie was recuperating from his knife wound, the teetering dominoes of the Upper South largely fell into place. In a sort of ironic re-enactment, a Virginia militia, acting pursuant to a plan conceived by the same former Governor Henry Wise who had presided at John's post-arrest "press conference," overwhelmed the defenders, took over, and pillaged the federal armory at Harpers Ferry. At a secession convention in Virginia, militants were swept into power by passions generated in the wake of Fort Sumter. On April 27 they issued an invitation to the new CSA government to make Richmond its permanent capital, even though Virginia had not yet formally ratified secession. The ratification, in a plebiscite that occurred May 23, was an important development, for Virginia was by far the most populous and industrialized of the slave states other than Maryland, Kentucky, and Missouri, none of which seceded. But the notion of secession had its dissenters, particularly in the mountainous part of the state, essentially everything west and south of Harpers Ferry. Leaders there promptly held their own convention and elected an alternate set of loyalist "Virginia" Senators, who were quickly recognized and seated by Congress in Washington.[28] This "secession from the secession" ultimately resulted in the new state of West Virginia.

Maryland, Kentucky, and Missouri all remained in the United States. After some initial chaos, rioting and bridge burning following Fort Sumter, under the strong hand of Henry Seward Maryland was swiftly occupied and garrisoned by forces arriving from the North. On April 27, Lincoln and Seward exercised the federal power under Article 1, Section 9 of the U.S. Constitution to suspend the writ of habeas corpus on an emergency basis in portions of Maryland, thus authorizing the arrest and detention, without formal charges, of suspected Confederate sympathizers. This resulted in a political stabilization. On June 13, Unionist candidates won all six Maryland Congressional seats in a special election. The state declared "neutrality" in the North–South conflict, and declined to allow a secessionist convention. Similarly, in Kentucky, five of the six prevailing candidates in a special election for Congress were Unionist. Kentucky also "declared neutrality."

Meanwhile in Missouri, Nathaniel Lyon, the highly enterprising commander of the United States Arsenal, launched a preemptive attack on a pro-secession militia that was threatening the arsenal with cannon. The militia surrendered without even firing a shot. Lyon proceeded to use his troops to occupy practically the entire state of Missouri, acting in defiance of the state's Governor and legislature who were openly pro-secession.[29]

One Maryland official who was arrested and detained without charges was George P. Kane, Baltimore's Police Marshal. Kane was a theater supporter and a personal friend of Johnnie's. When he refused to allow federal troops to seize arms from a Baltimore city arsenal, he was tabbed as an enemy of the United States. On June 27 at 3 o'clock in the morning, he was arrested at his home without a warrant and placed in indefinite custody on a vague suspicion of being involved in blowing up bridges and severing telegraph lines to the North. Kane's arrest and detention seriously angered Johnnie. He saw it as a cause of injustice. George Kane ultimately spent a year and a half languishing in prison without any charges, or even any explanation for his detention. Kane blamed Henry Seward rather than Lincoln for his treatment, because Henry was personally in charge of the program of Maryland arrests and detentions.[30] Johnnie was undoubtedly aware of this. Johnnie eschewed the example of numerous of his boyhood friends who headed South to join CSA forces and went on to resume his acting career in the fall of 1861. But he continued to seethe over Kane's unjust detention. During a rehearsal in New York City in March 1862, a cast member casually remarked that the person who ordered Kane's arrest

George Kane, in photo published 1861

CHAPTER 23: "ALOW ME A FEW WORDS"

should be shot. Johnnie, silent in the conversation to that point, surprised the company with an emotional outburst:[31] "Yes, sir, you are right! I know George P. Kane, he is my friend, and the man who could drag him from the bosom of his family for no crime whatever, but a mere suspicion that he may commit one some time, deserves a dog's death!"

Chapter 24: An Extraordinarily Lifelike Villain

In the performing arts of the 1860s, an invitation to play in New York was the requisite of any "A-list" actor. In March 1862 Johnnie got his first such engagement on the New York stage. It came about due to a combination of circumstances. Mary Provost, a veteran actress, was disappointed at her treatment by New York venues. She decided to open her own production at the Wallack Theater on Broadway. Because she was not yet established and could not get established stars, she had to turn to new and rising talent who "had not yet been given a metropolitan hearing." Johnnie was in this category. Additionally, Johnnie's older brother Edwin, by now an established fixture on the New York thespian scene, was away in England. With Edwin absent, Johnnie did not need to intrude on his brother's turf to play in New York. Mary Provost invited Johnnie to play in her newly opened theater because of his novelty and because of his reputation for drawing big houses in "the provinces," as the critics termed other cities.

Decades later, those present remembered Johnnie's first Monday morning rehearsal with the Mary Provost troupe in

CHAPTER 24: AN EXTRAORDINARILY LIFELIKE VILLAIN

Manhattan. A stage veteran, who had previously performed with Johnnie in Georgia, had advised them to expect something extraordinary. He said, "This boy is the first actor that ever (to use a professional term) knocked me completely off my pins, upset and left me without a word to say!" The others assembled, including Mary, were incredulous. One recalled:[1]

> At that moment, a commotion was heard at the back of the stage ... And striding down the center of the stage came the young man himself who was destined to play such an unfortunate part in the history of our country afterwards. The stage being dark at his entrance, the foot and border lights were suddenly turned up and revealed a face and form not easily described or forgotten. You have seen a high-mettled racer with his sleek skin and eye of unusual brilliancy chafing under a restless impatience to be doing something. It is the only living thing I could liken him to. After the usual introductions were over, with a sharp, jerky manner he commenced the rehearsal. I watched him closely and perceived the encomiums passed upon him by the old actor were not in the least exaggerated. Reading entirely new to us, he gave; business never thought of by the oldest stager, he introduced; and, when the rehearsal was over, one and all admitted a great actor was amongst us.

Johnnie considered his interpretation of the villainous Richard in *Richard III* to be his masterpiece. He almost always opened his engagements in that role and, if not, he played it on the second night. Often, he concluded with it as well. His Richard was a great hit on the New York stage. Johnnie sent Edwin a clipping about his opening, which appeared in the *New York Herald* on March 18, 1862:[2]

Mr. Booth undertook no small task when he attempted

to act a character in which his father was famous, and which his brother Edwin plays so well; but the result justifies the undertaking. As Edwin in face, form, voice and style resembles the elder Booth, so the debutant last evening is almost a facsimile of Edwin, and in the first three acts of the play these brothers could no more be distinguished than the two Dromios. But in the fourth and fifth acts, J. Wilkes Booth is more like his father than his brother. He reads the play capitally, and makes all the well known points with ample effect. But in the last act he created a sensation. His face blackened and smeared with blood, he seemed Richard himself; and his combat with Richmond (Mr. Tilton) was a masterpiece. An audience packed and crammed beyond the usual limits of the theatre applauded him to the echo. Mr. Booth has had much experience in the provinces, and his conception and rendition are most mature, his self-possession extraordinary.

Johnnie's riveting performance as Richard drew such packed houses that it was returned to the stage eight times during Johnnie's three-week Manhattan engagement.

Johnnie's New York success cemented his status as a national star, but it did not alter the charming nature of his personality. He was willful and impetuous, but tempered with a "sweet disposition" and a "general kindness of heart." In their recollections, people consistently described Johnnie in terms of being a pleasant and thoroughgoing "gentleman." Joseph Southall, a medical student, said he presented himself well and impressed acquaintances as a respectable person, neat and careful in his dress, "but never at all gaudy or flashy." James Ferguson, who kept a tavern adjoining Ford's Theater in Washington, reported, "I have heard him talk by the hour, but never heard a vulgar, obscene, or ungentlemanly expression fall from his lips." George Crutchfeld, a bank clerk,

CHAPTER 24: AN EXTRAORDINARILY LIFELIKE VILLAIN

commented, "he was a man of high character and social disposition and liked by everyone with whom he associated."[3] Kathryn Evans, an actress, said in a 1926 reminiscence: "I have nothing to say in favor of Booth, because he committed one of the worst crimes in history ... but I cannot refrain from telling those who never saw him that he was the finest gentleman I ever met."[4]

Johnnie was highly charismatic. William Howell, an actor who played with Johnnie in his early days at the Arch Theater in Philadelphia, and who let Johnnie share his room in Baltimore for a time during the summer of 1861, in an 1899 reminiscence described him as "quick, impulsive, fiery, big-hearted, generous, captivating and magnetic." He had not liked Johnnie at first, but after you came to know him,[5]

> you would scale the mountain's peak, breast the ocean's billows or pour out your heart's blood to serve him ... You could not resist his captivating manners, his genial smile and his personal magnetism ... His heart and soul beamed out of his eyes ... He was that sort of man that if you ever came within the range of his personal magnetism and fascination you would be involuntarily bound to him as with hooks of steel.

George Alfred Townsend, a newspaper reporter, met Johnnie for the first time in Washington in 1865. In an otherwise unsympathetic account, Townsend grudgingly expressed his appreciation of Johnnie's attractive power:

> His address was winning as a girl's, rising in effect not from what he said, but from how he said it. It was magnetic, and I can describe it therefore by its effects alone. I seemed, when he had spoken, to lean toward this man. His attitude spoke to me; with as easy familiarity as I ever observed he drew near and conversed. The talk was on so trite things that it did

not lie a second in the head, but when I left him it was with the feeling that a most agreeable fellow had passed by.

Johnnie made a lasting impression, as well, with his attitude of kindness toward "little people." He joked with everyone he came into contact with, even girls in the laundry where he left his collars and cuffs. By relatively unlettered persons who came in contact with him, he was almost idolized. His graciousness to that class was proverbial, his liberality unstinted.[6] His kindness extended to aspiring actors as well. Martin Wright met Johnnie when he was starting his acting career in Cleveland's Academy of Music in 1863. He had this to say:[7]

> [A]ny supernumerary could go to him for advice. Whoever went to him was received with gentle courtesy and generally came away an admirer. Of all the stars that came to play with us the one we loved and admired most was John Wilkes Booth. He was not high and mighty like most of the stars. There was never a better fellow.

Johnnie went out of his way to pay kind attention to children. An actress named Clara Morris wrote this about Johnnie in her 1901 autobiography:[8]

> Dashing out of the stage door to the telegraph office one day, he precipitately capsized a child, 'a roamer of the streets.' Lifting the youngster swiftly to his feet Booth drew his handkerchief from his pocket, wiped the child's dirty face, kissed him, filled his hands with coins, and then rushed on his way to dispatch his message ... He knew of no witness to the act. To kiss a pretty, clean child under the approving eyes of mama might mean nothing but politeness, but surely it required the prompting of a warm and tender heart to make such a young and thoughtless man feel for

and caress such a dirty, forlorn bit of babyhood as that.

Another actress, who played with Johnnie in his Richmond days, remembered his attitude toward a small girl who had a bit part in a production of *The Sea of Ice*. Johnnie was so tender to her "that she would nestle in his arms until her time came to go on stage."[9] Roland Reed, later a famous comedian, was working as a 10-year-old stage boy in Philadelphia when Johnnie suddenly took notice of him for no particular reason. He stopped, turned around, and shook hands with the boy. When Roland looked at his hand, he found a dollar in it.[10] In January 1864, when Johnnie was stranded for a while in Missouri due to a snowstorm, he ventured outside to engage in playful snowball fights with local children.[11]

John Wilkes Booth, in photo by Charles D. Fredricks & Co. Library of Congress

Within the United States, Johnnie was a national sex symbol. Both men and women everywhere considered him the handsomest man in America, and not just because of his good looks, but because of his overall demeanor and bearing. Many later remarked how photographs did not fully convey his attractiveness. William Ferguson, for instance, commented: "Pictures in the main disclose him as saturnine. They show nothing of his quick excitability, nothing of his love of fun, no trace of his joyousness."[12] Townsend wrote:

None of the printed pictures that I have seen do justice

to Booth. Some of the *cartes de visite* get him very nearly. He had one of the finest vital heads I have ever met. By this I refer to physical beauty in the Medician sense – health, shapeliness, power in beautiful poise, and seemingly more powerful in repose than in energy.[13]

In the words of Clara Morris:[14]

> [Johnnie's] striking beauty was something which thousands of silly women could not withstand ... His mail each day brought him letters from women, weak and frivolous, who periled their happiness and their reputations by committing to paper words of love and admiration which they could not refrain from writing.
>
> It is scarcely an exaggeration to say the sex was in love with Booth ... At depot restaurants those fiercely unwilling maiden-slammers of plates and shooters of coffee cups made to him swift and gentle offerings of hot steaks, hot biscuits, hot coffee, crowding around him like doves around a grain basket.

Charles Wyndham, a British actor and abolitionist sympathizer who played with Johnnie for two months, recalled in 1909:[15]

> Seldom has the stage seen a more impressive, or a more handsome, or a more impassioned actor. Picture to yourself Adonis, with a high forehead, ascetic face corrected by rather full lips, sweeping black hair, a figure of perfect youthful proportions and the most wonderful black eyes in the world. Such was John Wilkes Booth.
>
> At all times his eyes were his striking features but when his emotions were aroused they were like living jewels. Flames shot from them. His one physical defect was his height (for certain heroic characters), ... but he made up for the lack by his extraordinary

CHAPTER 24: AN EXTRAORDINARILY LIFELIKE VILLAIN

presence and magnetism ...

The theatrical press, at the time, lauded Johnnie for having a great deal of acting talent, for youthful good looks and energy, and for adding a huge amount of creative innovation to his performances. And yet, to the discerning reader, some storm clouds were on the horizon. Experienced reviewers tempered their praise by observing that Johnnie was raw, unstudied, and undisciplined. Even his positive writeups tended to include caveats such as "promising young actor," "still developing great future promise," and "there is the stuff in him to make him a first class tragedian, if he chooses to correct by study the extravagances that disfigure his impersonations."[16] Remarks were made that Johnnie would not exert himself to a word-for-word rendering of his parts but, rather, would skim over the roles and improvise, thus causing confusion on stage because other actors would miss their cues. His new interpretation of classic roles brought him praise by some and censure by others.[17]

In an ominous sign, the most enthusiastic raves Johnnie always received were for his extraordinarily lifelike portrayal of psychotic villains. A New York stage critic commented:[18] "He seems to revel in rascality, to enjoy the devilish tricks he puts upon his victims, to glory like another Lucifer in the misery he has caused. His Mephistophelean sneer, his demonic glare, and pity-murdering laugh, fairly curdle the blood, and haunt one like the spectres of a dream." In the role of the doomed political murderer Macbeth, the same reviewer commented that Johnnie, though lacking "delicacy of execution," finely portrayed the "irresolution" of the character. Charles Wyndham recalled:[19]

> I was strongly attracted to him in the first place by his effective, thrilling presentation of Hamlet. Edwin's was a reflective Hamlet. As John Wilkes Booth

played it, the Danish Prince was unmistakably mad throughout. Edwin's conception of the part was that of uneven and unbalanced genius, and wonderfully he portrayed it. But John Wilkes leaned toward the other view of the character, as was in keeping with his own bent of mind. His Hamlet was insane, and his interpretation was fiery, convincing, and artistic.

Immediately after concluding the New York engagement, Johnnie went to open in Boston, where he met with discerning critics. In a comment that would prove prescient, one of them criticized Johnnie for failing to master basic principles of elocution and for not using his voice properly:[20]

> [W]e have taken pains to see him in each of the characters which he assumed during the last week: Richard III, Romeo, Charles de Moor, and Hamlet. We have been greatly pleased and greatly disappointed. In what does he fail? Principally, in knowledge of himself – of his resources, how to husband and how to use them. He is, apparently, entirely ignorant of the main principles of elocution. We do not mean by this word merely enunciation, but the nature and proper treatment of the voice, as well. He ignores the fundamental principle of all vocal study and exercise – that the chest, and not the throat or mouth, should supply the sound necessary for singing or speaking.

In Philadelphia, another sophisticated venue where Johnnie played for two weeks in March 1863, "established" people in the thespian world, such as Arch Street theater owner Louisa Lane Drew and veteran Shakespearian actor Edwin Forrest, did not find his raw, improvisational style at all engaging. Perhaps they were, in some measure, jealous of young Johnnie's indisputable box office power. Partly to avoid his critics, partly to take advantage of, in the words of a New York pundit, the

CHAPTER 24: AN EXTRAORDINARILY LIFELIKE VILLAIN

"undiscriminating applause of country audiences," and partly to avoid infringing on the capitals of the American stage world in which his brother Edwin was a growing and recognized star, following his successful engagement at Mary Provost's theater during March 1862 Johnnie never returned for another. He stayed extremely busy and accumulated a fair amount of wealth during the remainder of 1862, 1863, and the beginning of 1864. With the exception of two performances in Brooklyn and a single two-week engagement in Philadelphia, he made his money playing "the provinces" – "border" venues such as Louisville, Nashville, Cincinnati, and St. Louis, and "western" venues such as Chicago, Indianapolis, and Cleveland, mixing in occasional engagements in New England and Washington City. And money he indeed made. During the peak of his career, Johnnie's income averaged $20,000 per year, a princely sum in the 1860s.[21]

While Johnnie's reputation, audiences, and earnings soared during 1861, 1862, and on into 1863, there was not a whole lot to disturb him in terms of the progress of efforts by President Lincoln and his Secretary of State Henry Seward to quell the rebellious South. Politics and war proved uncomfortable bedfellows. Lincoln ordered an advance into Virginia by the first wave of enthusiastic volunteers, in the face of disagreement from his army commander, General Winfield Scott. The raw Union soldiers were quickly routed on July 21, 1861, at nearby Manassas Junction in a battle dubbed "Bull Run." Only a similar degree of inexperience by the Confederate commanders prevented them from seizing the nearby U.S. capital in Washington City. Pro-slavery advocates in Maryland were emboldened by the victory, and they attempted to reorganize a secession convention. The defeat at Bull Run prompted Lincoln to promote a young and promising West Point graduate, George McClellan, to command the army charged with defending Washington. Yet McClellan's appointment was also partly political. As a Democrat, McClellan's elevation was a sop to the national unity platform Lincoln continued to advocate.[22]

Lincoln's authority as President and Commander-in-Chief, with Henry as his key policy advisor, was challenged by John C. Frémont, the 1856 Republican party presidential candidate and one of his continuing rivals for control and influence within that party. Typical of Lincoln's politician's approach, he had placed Frémont in military command of the western theater of operations, centered in Missouri. Frémont soon proved more concerned with giving out political perks and patronage than he was with formulating and carrying out an effective war effort. Nathaniel Lyon, the intrepid Union field commander, was poorly supported by Frémont and was killed in a battle in southern Missouri on August 10, 1861. Frémont pandered to radical elements in the Republican party by issuing an edict freeing the slaves of everyone who took up arms against the federal government. Lincoln grasped the importance of the issue. He strongly insisted that any decision on liberating slaves was a political decision to be made exclusively by the central government in Washington, not by military personnel. Lincoln decided he had to remove Frémont, but was forced to do so stealthily, sending the replacement order by a secret messenger so that Frémont would not be able to marshal political opposition. As it was, Frémont's removal generated a storm of protest among abolitionist Republicans.[23]

The radical wing of the Republican party was also unhappy over McClellan, their political adversary, who was placed in overall command of the combined Union forces by Lincoln on November 1, 1861. He was perceived by them as dawdling and inactive for not launching a winter campaign. In late December, McClellan fell ill, further adding to the sense of frustration and seething anger. In January 1862 critics of McClellan and the Lincoln administration's war policy, including Charles Sumner, formed a "Committee on the

CHAPTER 24: AN EXTRAORDINARILY LIFELIKE VILLAIN

Conduct of the War" to investigate McClellan's inaction. Lincoln termed the Republicans who were attacking him "Jacobins," after the radicals who perpetrated the reign of terror in revolutionary France.[24]

Henry and Lincoln adopted a cautious policy in international affairs. They were above all petrified that England would enter the war on the side of the CSA. In August 1861, a Union naval vessel boarded the British mail steamer *Trent* in the Bahama Channel and discovered she had on board two Confederate government representatives, James Mason and John Slidell. Mason, only a year and a half earlier in his capacity as a U.S. Senator from Virginia, had chaired the Senate committee that investigated allegations of conspiracy regarding John's raid on Harpers Ferry. Mason and Slidell were essentially being sent as the CSA ambassadors to England and France, respectively. Mason and Slidell were taken off *Trent* into custody and jailed in Boston, provoking howls of outrage from the British government. Hawkish forces in England pushed for an ultimatum demanding their release, or else war. After an all-day Cabinet meeting on Christmas Day 1861, Henry and Lincoln decided to back down. They ordered Mason and Slidell unconditionally released and allowed to continue with their respective diplomatic missions.[25]

Lincoln took very seriously his constitutional responsibility as Commander-in-Chief of the Union forces. He applied his usual analytic powers to the job. His grasp of the fundamental dynamics of the war was shown in a letter to his Midwest commander, Don Carlos Buell, in early 1862:[26]

> I state my general idea of the war to be that we have *greater* numbers, and the enemy has the *greater* facility of concentrating forces upon pockets of collision; that we must fail, unless we can find some way of making *our* advantage an over-match of his; and that this can be done by menacing him with

superior forces at *different* points, at the *same* time, so that we can safely attack, one or both, if he makes no change; and if he *weakens* one to *strengthen* the other, forbear to attack the strengthened one, but seize, and hold, the weakened one, gaining so much.

There was much truth to the concept, grasped early on by Henry Seward, that the South, with its antiquated institution of slavery, was a far more primitive economic organization than was the thriving balance of the United States. Even before the war, Henry saw the slaveholding republics of the South as relics of a bygone era; aristocratic and retrograde, out of step with the progressive currents sweeping the nineteenth-century world.[27] The North, with its far more advanced and industrialized social organization, would hold a critical upper hand throughout the conflict in terms of numbers of soldiers, transport, weapons, and wartime industrial production.

Despite this, in its drive for independence the South possessed some very important advantages.

First, the war was fought almost exclusively on the South's territory. This yielded the signal advantages of familiarity with the wilderness and the terrain, and of having more sympathetic locals available to give aid and comfort to its troops.

Second, the culture of the South, while more backwards than the North in terms of its economic organization, was also more "medieval" in the sense of having a more militaristic orientation. Prior to the war, aspirations to a military career were far more common in Southern communities than in their Northern counterparts. Virginia had an extensive network of volunteer militias typified by the Richmond Grays, young men who were already drilled and prepared as soldiers before the war began. Many leading officers in the U.S. Army were Southerners at the time the war started. For example, Robert E. Lee at the outset of hostilities was offered, and declined, overall command of the U.S. war forces.[28] A large number of

Southerners had experience fighting in previous conflicts, particularly the Mexican–American War.

Third, the forces mustered by the South were usually fighting in a defensive posture. Given the military technology of the day, in a battle fought with relatively even numbers of troops, well-supplied defenders supported by artillery generally prevailed in repulsing frontal assaults.

Fourth, and perhaps most important, the CSA soldiers and their leaders felt that they were fighting to preserve their way of life. For their opponents, the central issue of preserving the Union was far more abstract. Many Union troops, and their political leaders, favored a "free white society" that basically excluded all African Americans. The ambivalence stemming from a combination of racial attitudes and a desire by many to placate the South would plague the war effort for several years.[29]

Lincoln had long disclaimed "all intention to bring about social and political equality between the white and black races." In his political campaigns of 1859 and 1860, it was his advocacy of the "rights of northern free labor" that resonated most strongly with his audiences. To the extent that he focused on the issue at all, Lincoln was a longtime exponent of "the separation of the white and black races" – meaning in sum, the deportation of African Americans for "colonization." The Blair family, his political allies from Missouri who were among the most prominent anti-slavery activists from any slave state, with Lincoln's approval looked to Central America, not Africa, as the primary target for colonization.[30] Lincoln's official attitude continued to be that the Southern states were still legally part of the Union. He recognized a "Virginia governor" for West Virginia, the Washington City suburbs, and Norfolk, areas that were under Union control. For other seceded states partially under Union control, he appointed military governors. Andrew Johnson of Tennessee was one of these. Many of the military governors were still pro-slavery, and most of them, like Johnson, were hostile to African American civil rights.[31]

Under bitter attack by Republicans for the failure of McClellan to undertake a winter campaign with his "Army of the Potomac," Lincoln flirted with the idea of taking to the field himself to personally command the Union armed forces. But after a tense Cabinet meeting on January 10, 1862, McClellan finally revealed his strategy, which Lincoln's other generals backed. He would largely abandon the fortified position protecting Washington and, taking advantage of Union naval superiority that gave it clear control of the Chesapeake Bay, move his army down to the peninsula in eastern Virginia situated between the tidewater York and James rivers. The Union had an existing bridgehead established by the U.S. Navy already in place on this peninsula, called Fortress Monroe. From this starting point, he would advance north and west on the CSA capital in Richmond, which lies astride the James. Still, McClellan was extremely slow and cautious. On January 27, Lincoln issued a war order commanding a general advance of all Union armies on or before February 22.[32]

McClellan moved almost all his army to the Yorktown peninsula, but his advance toward Richmond was slow. Preferring to fight from a defensive position, he felt the need to conduct repeated siege operations, rather than frontal assaults. In terms of avoiding heavy casualties, he was correct in this judgment, but to the politicians in Washington, including Lincoln, the glacial pace of McClellan's progress, coupled with a perception that the rebels kept on conceding to the Union's superior numbers by abandoning their positions and retreating to evade engagement, was maddening. On May 6, Lincoln went personally to Fortress Monroe with two of his most hawkish Cabinet members, Edwin Stanton and Salmon Chase. Together they organized an assault on the port of Norfolk, at the base of the James opposite the Yorktown peninsula, which McClellan had feared to challenge. To the General's surprise,

CHAPTER 24: AN EXTRAORDINARILY LIFELIKE VILLAIN

the force Lincoln personally dispatched was not only successful in capturing the city of Norfolk and its garrison of 6,000 defenders, it also secured the scuttling of the *Merrimac*, the Confederacy's new "ironclad" warship, which represented its one and only serious attempt to contest Union naval dominance.[33]

Lincoln was then distracted by the activity of a Confederate force in the Shenandoah Valley, commanded by Thomas J. Jackson, the same who, as a Union Army officer, had written an account of John Brown's hanging. Jackson was dubbed with the nickname "Stonewall," but in Virginia combat he specialized in moving his troops with great swiftness. As a result, he was usually able to surprise and overwhelm Union detachments that were inferior in numbers and ill prepared for combat. Jackson posed a threat to attack Washington. Lincoln therefore dispatched two detachments to encircle and capture Jackson. These troops were commanded by generals who were Lincoln's former political and personal rivals: James Shields (with whom Lincoln had come close to fighting a duel in an affair over a newspaper article in 1842) and John Frémont (Lincoln's rival within the Republican party whom he had recently removed from command in Missouri). But the Union forces were neither sufficiently coordinated nor sufficiently agile to hem in Jackson as Lincoln intended. On June 8 and 9, Jackson defeated Frémont and Shields successively in separate engagements. Then he made one of his trademark rapid marches to join up with the Confederate defenders of Richmond.[34]

Meanwhile, these defenders had launched a counterattack on McClellan's advance guard, which had moved to within 5 miles of the CSA capital. The Confederate general in charge, Joseph Johnston, who had been McClellan's close personal friend prior to the war, was wounded in the fighting. Johnston was replaced as Commander by his West Point classmate,

Robert E. Lee. McClellan wrote Lincoln: "I prefer Lee to Johnston." The comment would soon prove one of the more foolish remarks ever made. Lee, reinforced by Jackson, continued the assault on McClellan's forces, which were divided by the Chickahominy River so that Lee was able to gain numerical superiority at the point of attack. After a series of bloody fights later dubbed "the Battle of Seven Days," the Confederates forced McClellan to abandon his positions and retreat to a base on the James called Harrison's Landing, where his forces could be protected by the navy. At the beginning of August, Lincoln, advised by experienced generals, ordered the entire McClellan expedition to be pulled and repositioned back in northern Virginia, in front of Washington. Essentially, the Peninsular campaign had wasted the better part of a year and had accomplished little or nothing.[35]

Lincoln relieved McClellan of overall command of the Army of the Potomac and gave it to John Pope, a dashing young officer whose father, an Illinois federal judge, had presided in cases tried by Lincoln during his days as a lawyer. Pope declared that the order of the day would now be attack, not defense. But at the end of August 1862, as Pope prepared to advance south across the Rappahannock, Lee and Jackson took him by surprise. Jackson drove his force on a fast encircling movement and, striking swiftly, captured Pope's entire supply depot at Manassas Junction, very near where the first battle of the war had been fought. Lee and his commanders

CHAPTER 24: AN EXTRAORDINARILY LIFELIKE VILLAIN

then outmaneuvered Pope's army, sending the Union forces into full-scale flight. This "Second Battle of Bull Run" was a disaster for Pope and his troops, as they were forced to straggle back to Washington. Once again, McClellan was blamed for the defeat. He had refused to use his defense force to reinforce Pope, declaring that protecting the capital was paramount. Notwithstanding, and defying vocal critics in his own Cabinet, Lincoln continued to keep McClellan in charge of the garrison defending Washington.[36]

Lee was emboldened by his army's success at "Second Bull Run." Moving his main force west and north, on September 4 he advanced into western Maryland. This unexpected development drew applause from Confederate sympathizers in Maryland, including Johnnie. At the time, Johnnie was spending the annual summer stage hiatus for heat and humidity hanging out at the old family home in Bel Air. Using his gymnastic skills to scale a tower composed of barrels, he cut letters out of a circus poster and rearranged them to make his own huge banner that announced, "JEFF IS COMING!"[37]

McClellan and his forces ultimately succeeded in beating back Lee and his Confederate army at the battle of Antietam on September 17, although both sides took dreadful casualties. Due to his typical caution, McClellan failed to destroy or capture Lee's defeated army, which was able to retreat to a defensive position south of the Rappahannock. Shortly afterwards, on October 4, 1862, with the aid of two invading forces that had entered the state at about the same time Lee entered Maryland, a Confederate was installed as the new state Governor in the Kentucky capital of Lexington. The Confederates hoped to provoke a general rising of popular sentiment in favor of secession. Their armies were able to enter and take over Lexington because Kentucky had been kept largely free of Union forces out of Lincoln's deference to

Kentucky's declared "state of neutrality" in the conflict between the CSA and the rest of the United States. Buell's Union Army of the Ohio responded promptly, however, to the Confederate takeover of the reins of Kentucky state government. On October 7 and 8, Buell engaged with the Confederate army 45 miles southwest of Lexington in another extremely bloody fight that would be dubbed the "Battle of Perryville." There the Confederates, under General Braxton Bragg, extracted a hard fought tactical victory, but in the aftermath, their overextended forces had no real choice except to retreat into Tennessee. Without their support, the new "Confederate" Kentucky state government had to vacate quickly.[38]

A mere two weeks later, on October 23, Johnnie opened his 1862–1863 season with a two-night engagement at the small venue Lexington Opera House, playing in his signature role as the villainous Richard III.[39] It was as close as Johnnie would ever come to entering Confederate-controlled territory.

Chapter 25: The Crushing of the Rebellion

As the war dragged into its third year, Union land and naval forces had made inroads into territory of the seceded CSA, particularly in the Midwest and West. However, to contemporary eyes it was still very plausible to see eventual Southern independence as its end product. The last two major conflicts fought on American soil during the previous century had both ended with Great Britain, the more dominant power in terms of overall wealth, military might, and naval strength, capitulating to the United States on the issue of independence. This result had obtained even though England occupied Philadelphia, seat of the rebel government, as well as New York City, during the Revolutionary War, and even though it captured Washington City, the U.S. capital, during the War of 1812.

War, however, is ugly. It becomes even uglier as the flower of a young generation dies and is maimed over and over on tragic battlefields. And, it grows uglier still when so many thousands more fall sick and die of the infectious diseases that characterized military encampments of the 1860s. After the initial righteous enthusiasm wore off, the ugliness of war brought about a sea-change in the attitude about the rebellious states, as well as the attitude about tactics to be brought to bear in the conflict. The original conciliatory attitude toward the rebellious states, exemplified by Lincoln's own attitude, ebbed. Early Union commanders like McClellan, who felt the war should be conducted in a "civilized" fashion and with methods that would minimize casualties, were replaced by new more aggressive commanders, typified by Ulysses S. Grant, who were willing to stay engaged with the enemy and grind out battles, even though it meant unheard-of numbers of deaths among his own troops, in order to inflict an equivalent carnage on a foe that could not withstand the attrition.[1] Over time the viciousness of the fighting, and its appalling toll in terms of human life, gave rise to an increasing public sentiment that the will to resist should be taken out of the rebellious South using something approaching the modern concept of "total war."

One of the most obvious weapons in the strategic arsenal available to the United States was to proclaim the freedom of the "slave property" of all who defied federal authority. This would serve the dual purpose of punishing the rebels, while at the same time opening up the potential for them to face their own rebellion on the home front. It was not a new idea. As we have seen, the British already employed the same tactic extensively in Virginia during the War of 1812. However, the resemblance between such a strategy and that of a John Brown was obvious to both Lincoln and Henry. In declining one emancipation entreaty, made by Quakers during early 1862, Lincoln alluded to John. He did not want to be seen as trying to foment a violent slave uprising. He told them: "If a decree of emancipation could free the slaves, John Brown could have done the work effectively."[2]

As soon as he heard of the first shots fired at Fort Sumter, Charles Sumner rushed to the White House and advised Lincoln "that under the war power the right had come to him to emancipate the slaves." Lincoln, however, maintained that because secession was unlawful and unrecognized, legally speaking the Southern states remained in the Union with all their constitutional rights (including the right to have legalized slavery) intact. But the outbreak of the war triggered an immediate flux of African Americans into Union lines, seeking to escape bondage. Thus, an immediate policy decision was required as to what to do with them. His military commanders mostly wanted to encourage the exodus, and take advantage of the manpower yielded. But Lincoln preferred to conduct the war in a constitutional manner. He continued to advocate gradual, compensated emancipation, coupled with colonization. Congress, in a special session immediately after the First Battle of Bull Run, overwhelmingly passed a resolution affirming that the war was being waged solely to maintain the supremacy of the Constitution and not "for the purpose of overthrowing or interfering with the rights or established institutions of these states." Even abolitionists abstained rather than voting no.[3] But the ugliness of war would soon impinge upon these lofty sentiments.

Escaped slaves were viewed as allies and friends by those engaged in the life and death struggle on the war front. This created powerful pressure favoring granting them freedom. In May 1861 at Fortress Monroe, General Benjamin Butler initiated the concept of treating prisoners escaped from rebels as "contraband of war" and seizing them on that basis, rather than returning them to owners behind enemy lines. Butler was hardly an ideologue. He was actually a staunch pro-slavery Democrat who had supported Breckinridge during the 1860 campaign. Lincoln at first laughingly approved of what Butler had done. But later he realized it had much broader political overtones. On August 6, 1861, Congress formalized Butler's action by passing the Confiscation Act, confiscating property, including slaves, intended for Confederate military purposes. Lincoln was nervous about this measure and signed it "with great reluctance."[4]

Lincoln and Henry continued to display politically

CHAPTER 25: THE CRUSHING OF THE REBELLION

motivated ambivalence around the issue. We have already seen that in the fall of 1861, when John C. Frémont issued an emancipation order in Missouri differing only in some technicalities from the Confiscation Act, Lincoln voided it and removed Frémont from command. On May 9, 1862, General David Hunter, who was commanding the Department of the South (comprising the entire states of South Carolina, Georgia, and Florida, although as a practical matter within that area the Union at that time only controlled a few islands off the coast of South Carolina) issued a proclamation that declared "forever free" all of the 900,000 persons of African descent within his Department, and encouraged them to volunteer to fight. This sweeping edict was countermanded by Lincoln a week later. But, even so, Lincoln left open the possibility of using his authority as President to order something similar in the future.[5]

Lincoln's preferred approach to the issue of ending slavery continued to be a measure calling for emancipation that was "gradual," in the sense that it would provide that absent payment of compensation, all persons born into slavery must be freed by the time they reached a certain age. In November 1861, Lincoln personally drafted such a gradual and compensated emancipation bill for the State of Delaware. As far as what to do with the persons made independent in these ways, Lincoln continued to envision colonization as the best solution. In his annual message to Congress in December 1861, Lincoln urged the appropriation of funds to pay for a mass migration. The press referred to a potential new colony for African Americans as "Lincolnia." Radicals were enraged by Lincoln's message, while Democrats and moderate Republicans applauded it.[6]

But, "War is Hell." It was almost solely due to the enormous overreaction of the South to John's raid, followed on by its related overreaction to Lincoln's election by declaring secession, and then violently taking up arms and starting a civil war, that public majority sentiment in the North swung in favor of outlawing slavery. But for the overreaction, majority support in every state, as well as the support of Lincoln and other moderate Republicans, would have remained in place for "letting slavery alone" in the Southern states. At all times, the policy of Lincoln, the born politician, on the subject of emancipation was very carefully modeled on his gauging of public opinion.[7]

Propelled by impatience to get the war moving, in its second year, 1862, abolitionists began to get a much broader hearing. The idea of confiscating or broadly emancipating all slaves without compensation gathered more popular support. Lincoln was sensitive to this shift in opinion. On April 16, 1862, he signed into law an Act providing for partially compensated emancipation of African Americans in the District of Columbia. In an ironic twist, a professional slave trader actually had to be brought in from Maryland to appraise the value of the freed slaves for purposes of determining the compensation. On June 19, 1862, Lincoln signed another bill abolishing all slavery in the federal territories. This directly contradicted the *Scott v. Sandford* holding and, of course, it also defied its authority.[8]

Even though Lincoln continued to push his gradual and compensated border state emancipation plan, he came under increasing pressure to attack the rebellion in every way, including freeing the slaves. On July 4, 1862, Lincoln rebuffed Charles's plea that he issue a general decree of emancipation. However, during the summer of 1862, Congress became active, pushing for harsher policies toward the rebels. The measures under consideration included even more sweeping emancipation, and/or confiscation, of their slaves. They also included such newer, harsher measures as the possible death penalty for rebels. The removal of McClellan as the top Union field commander in the wake of his failed Peninsular campaign also made way for a change of policy regarding emancipation.

McClellan had continued to strongly oppose violation of civilian property rights and "forcible abolition of slavery."[9]

On July 14, 1862, Lincoln sent Congress a bill that pledged to set up federal bonds to finance any state that would enact compensated emancipation. The bill also had a provision for allowing a future decision by such a state to reinstitute slavery. Radical Republicans ridiculed this proposal, and it went nowhere. As this was happening, Lincoln privately acknowledged to Henry, as well as Secretary of the Navy Gideon Welles, that military necessity was pushing him strongly in the direction of a decree of emancipation. On July 21, Lincoln presented a draft Emancipation Proclamation to his Cabinet. Henry was the key advocate who persuaded Lincoln against issuing this document immediately. He felt it may make England more likely to enter the conflict, and that it would appear to be an act of desperation, similar to the freeing of slaves in the Nat Turner and John Brown terror attacks. Lincoln was persuaded by Henry's argument that, given the Union's high-profile setbacks in the Peninsular campaign and then at Second Bull Run, the moment was not opportune to issue the Proclamation.[10]

Lincoln kept pushing to establish a colony at Chiriquí (in modern-day Panama). On August 14, 1862, he met with a group of African American representatives in a Washington black church. The phrases Lincoln used in this meeting, such as, "You and we are different races," and "even when you cease to be slaves, you are yet far removed from being placed on an equality with the white race," were a frank acknowledgement of the permanence of racism in America. Those in attendance listened politely as he tried to convince them of the benefits of accepting "colonization." Nothing at all came of this initiative, as colonization basically met with a near-total lack of acceptance in the African American community.[11]

On September 22, 1862, after Union forces finally won a victory at Antietam, Lincoln issued his "preliminary" Emancipation Proclamation, threatening to liberate all slaves in Confederate states if resistance was not ended by January 1, 1863. The decree was highly unpopular in the border states and among Unionists in the South. Moreover, it still left unresolved the future status of the liberated slaves. Lincoln appeared to hope many would accept colonization. During this period, Lincoln and Henry became very close. However, Henry never agreed with Lincoln that colonization was either desirable or feasible. It was the one political subject on which they disagreed.[12]

In the Congressional elections of the fall of 1862, Democrats made major gains, and retook legislative control of several Midwest states, including Illinois. Lincoln allies lost their seats. The lack of apparent military success was one factor. Even though, in hindsight, the Union had just won two of its most important victories, at Antietam and at Perryville, there was not yet sufficient perspective for the general public to recognize their significance. Another factor in the election was the success of the Democrats in portraying the Republicans as "n*** worshippers."

On November 5, 1862, the day after the disastrous midterm elections, Lincoln signed an order removing McClellan as Commander of Army of the Potomac. Lincoln was upset because McClellan had allowed Lee to slip back into a defensive position vis-à-vis Richmond. But this was also in part a replacement of a Democrat who allowed his political views to temper his military aggressiveness, trying to run a "civilized" war. McClellan was replaced with 38-year-old General Ambrose Burnside. Burnside decided to strike immediately at Richmond, through Fredericksburg. But Lee was able to assume defensive positions behind the Rappahannock while Burnside was fording it with his army. The battle, which took place between December 11 and

December 15, turned into a slaughter, as Burnside vainly threw his bridgehead force into Lee's defensive positions. The bloody defeat at Fredericksburg was yet another major shock for the Union forces. It prompted immediate criticism of Lincoln and calls for the firing of Henry as his Secretary of State. Chase, among others, led the cabal against Henry, who was viewed as being too dovish toward the South. After two days of meetings with the rest of the Cabinet and various Senators, Lincoln convinced them to relent. He rejected Henry's tender of resignation.[13]

Lincoln duly issued the Emancipation Proclamation, as promised, on January 1, 1863. It was a blatant war measure. Besides the "border states" of Maryland, Kentucky, and Missouri, it exempted the entire state of Tennessee (a concession to Andrew Johnson), the tidewater counties controlled by the Union in Virginia, and the parishes controlled by the Union in Louisiana. It was not framed as a declaration of the rights of man. Lincoln was nervous that it would be declared beyond his constitutional authority. For example, Justice Curtis, who had dissented in *Scott v. Sandford*, had written a pamphlet expressing the view that it was unconstitutional. The Proclamation also broke new ground by welcoming African American soldiers into the Union Army. This was a reaction to the increasing difficulty the Union was having in securing enough enlistment for the bloody and protracted conflict. Overall, to people with a favorable orientation toward Southern independence, the Emancipation Proclamation looked like a desperate war tactic. It really had almost no immediate effect, since it expressly exempted most of the areas already under Union control, except eastern North Carolina and the South Carolina Sea Islands. Nor did it foment a black uprising in the South.[14]

After the defeat at Fredericksburg, Lincoln surprisingly replaced Burnside with Joseph Hooker, Burnside's harshest critic within the circle of generals whom Burnside had been trying to blame and relieve of command. Hooker decided to undertake the flanking action with respect to Lee's "Army of Northern Virginia" that Burnside had eschewed. The end result was, however, very similar – another bloody defeat in the battle of Chancellorsville, April 30–May 3, 1863. In the fighting, though, the Confederates also sustained serious losses, including the death from friendly fire of General "Stonewall" Jackson.

In the West, meanwhile, the key battle that raged was for control of the Mississippi. The Confederates, effectively blockaded from any maritime commerce, held a 250-mile stretch along the river in northern Louisiana and southern Mississippi that was their key lifeline to the Western Confederacy of Arkansas and Texas and, beyond that, to trade that could come overland through Mexico. The bulwark of its control of that vital stretch of river was Vicksburg, Mississippi, a natural fortress situated on a promontory commanding all traffic on the waterway. Through the summer of 1863, the Confederate forces along the river, with the benefit of friendly territory, were able to fortify Vicksburg and hold off the northern expeditionary force led by General Grant.[15]

So, to a sympathetic observer, one such as Johnnie who was not fully in touch with reality,[16] the war still appeared to be going well enough for the South. On June 5, 1863, the Union Army camped north of the Rappahannock discovered that Lee had moved his army north and west. Lincoln ordered Hooker to try to cut it in half. But in this they were unsuccessful. Soon reports came in that Confederate cavalry were raiding in southern Pennsylvania. Hooker got into conflict with the overall Commander-in-Chief appointed by Lincoln, the scholarly General Henry Halleck. As a result, Hooker was relieved of command. Lincoln replaced him with General George Meade. Meade forced a confrontation with the main Confederate invading force at Gettysburg, Pennsylvania, in a

CHAPTER 25: THE CRUSHING OF THE REBELLION

three-day battle starting July 1. This time, Lee's army got the worst of it. It was repulsed with appalling losses in trying to advance on an elevated position fortified with Union artillery. Gettysburg was another very bloody battle on both sides, one result of which was that the Confederates lost a huge number of the best soldiers in their Virginia army. But at the time the importance of that development still was not fully realized. The Confederates succeeded in retreating to Virginia, thus disappointing Lincoln, who had hoped for a total victory and capture of the entire invading Confederate army. But the very next day, on July 4, besieged Vicksburg surrendered to Grant, with the defending Confederate army captured. The military turning point of the war had occurred, although that fact would not be fully understood until later.[17]

The slow, arduous process of using the North's superior industrial, population, naval, and transportation resources to crush the rebellion was beginning to exert its effect. Yet Lincoln was by no means out of the woods politically. He faced significant opposition from within both major parties. The manpower needed for the war led the federal government to institute conscription for the first time. This news of a draft stirred major unrest. Resistance to it occurred throughout the North. Riots occurred in Boston, in Troy, New York, and in Newark, New Jersey. But the ugliest draft riots took place in mid-July 1863 in New York City, where well over 500 people were killed, over $1 million of property damage occurred, and African Americans were lynched on the streets by enraged protesters.[18]

The Emancipation Proclamation, the prolongation of the war with mounting casualties, the need for more military manpower with the attendant threat of a draft, and the general war-weariness of the people, all offered tempting and productive targets to the Democrats, many of whom abandoned their former support of the war effort.[19] Their sentiments were captured by Ohio Representative Clement Vallandigham, whom we have encountered previously in the capacity of one of John Brown's main interrogators at his Harpers Ferry post-capture "press conference." Vallandigham declared, in a speech made to a packed House of Representatives on January 14, 1863:[20]

> Debt, defeat, taxation, sepulchres are your trophies. In vain the people gave you treasure, and the soldier yielded up his life. War for the Union has been abandoned and war for the slave begun. With what success? Let the dead at Fredericksburg and Vicksburg answer. Ought this war to continue? I answer no – not a day, not an hour … Stop fighting. Make an armistice. Accept at once foreign mediation.

After another similar diatribe in Ohio on May 1, Burnside, who had been reassigned to command the Midwest, ordered Vallandigham's arrest. Vallandigham was quickly sentenced by a military tribunal to confinement for the duration of the war. Lincoln, again surprised at this independent initiative of one of his subordinates, was somewhat discomfited by this heavy-handed action. He "commuted" the sentence to an order of deportation behind Confederate lines. Rapidly, Vallandigham made his way to Canada, from where he conducted an unsuccessful absentee Democratic candidacy for Governor of his home state of Ohio.[21]

Even though Democrats were loudly protesting and holding rallies, they were slowly losing mass support. Unionist candidates got the better of the 1863 off-year election in all states except New Jersey. In October, Lincoln placed his victorious Western generals Ulysses S. Grant and William Sherman in command of the entire Western theater from Tennessee through northern Alabama to the Mississippi. They proved far more effective in winning battles than their predecessors. Lincoln soon gave Grant overall command of the

Abraham Lincoln, as President, in photo portrait by M. Brady & Co.

entire Union forces.

A single term for Presidents of the United States had become almost traditional. No President had run for re-election since Andrew Jackson in 1832. Thus, as of January 1864, most expected that Lincoln would not run for re-election. Lincoln, at that time, made no overt move to run. Political players, such as many Republican Senators and Secretary of the Treasury Salmon Chase, tried to cabal and plot against Lincoln, while the "popular sentiment" was perceived to be in favor of keeping him on for another term.[22] The Radical Republicans held their own alternative Republican convention in Cleveland. One of their "planks" was "a one-term Presidency." But the event was, overall, much more fizzle than sizzle. Lincoln easily received a unified party nomination for re-election. In the general election campaign he was opposed by, of all people, George McClellan. McClellan was in essence a compromise candidate selected by a Democratic party badly splintered between the point of view represented by Vallandigham and the point of view that favored prosecution of the war until the Union was restored.[23]

As the war continued to grind into its fourth year, 1864, Grant, who now commanded the campaign against the Confederate capital in Richmond, was far more aggressive than his predecessors. He refused to retreat after tactical repulses. Lee and Grant, with their armies, fought a series of bloody and devastating battles over the same terrain where Lee had previously repulsed Burnside and Hooker. Despite taking huge losses, Grant slowly began to apply a death grip. Many of the most daring and able Confederate commanders from the early days of the CSA rebellion, men like John's nemesis Jeb Stuart, were killed in action at this time.[24] In the meantime, Sherman was applying a similar grip moving southward from Chattanooga. Atlanta was finally occupied on September 2, 1864. Despite the slowness of the progress, and the horrific cost in killed and crippled, the Union was finally using its superior economic and industrial strength to strangle the South's organized resistance just as effectively as any python.

On February 1, 1864, Johnnie opened a two-week engagement in Nashville, Tennessee, as usual in the role of Richard III. He could hardly be oblivious to the signs of the Confederacy's imminent defeat. Newspapers in town ran accounts from Southerners, discussing how people in cities like Richmond were starving, "like skeletons," and predicting that the Confederacy was doomed and could not last. One of the quoted items remarked, of the rebellion: "[T]heir leaders were not good political economists, when they believed that a non-manufacturing could succeed in a contest with a manufacturing people."[25]

Nashville was then the residence of Tennessee's military governor Andrew Johnson, and the headquarters of the Union's theater of operations between the Appalachians and the Mississippi. Tennessee was racked by violence much different from the battlefield war unfolding in Virginia. It was the scene of a new and "unconventional" type of war:[26] "new in its intensity, ancient in its origin – war by guerrillas, subversives, insurgents, assassins – war by ambush instead of by combat, by infiltration instead of aggression – seeking victory by eroding and exhausting the enemy instead of engaging him."

East Tennessee, as the mountainous Appalachian portion of the state was called, was similar to Kansas in its demographics. Having very few plantations or slaves, it was majority pro-Union, and majority anti-slavery, in its orientation. In the early days of Tennessee's secession, paramilitary pro-Union guerrillas carried out clandestine attacks against the Confederate government and resources there. But by the time of Johnnie's arrival in Nashville in February 1864, the tables had totally turned. All major Tennessee cities were now in Union hands. The movements of Union armies within the state were now largely uncontested. When battlefield defeat for the Confederacy loomed as more and more inevitable, the focus of rebellion now shifted to so-called paramilitary "guerrillas." They committed atrocious and sometimes spectacular depredations on a largely unarmed civilian populace in the name of promoting the rebel "cause." Their means and methods were very similar to what we today call terrorism.

One such "guerrilla" leader was John Hunt Morgan. He was born into an upper class social context. His maternal grandfather, John Wesley Hunt, was extremely wealthy, a large-scale manufacturer, importer, and exporter of hemp products. His estate, Hopemont, was near Lexington, Kentucky. Hunt was a personal friend and political supporter of Henry Clay. On September 24, 1823, Hunt's daughter Henrietta was married at Hopemont to Calvin Morgan, son of Luther Morgan, himself a wealthy retail merchant in Huntsville, Alabama. After the wedding, the couple set up housekeeping in Huntsville. Their first son, born in 1825, they named John Hunt Morgan.

John Morgan was a poor student. He attended Transylvania University, a college in Lexington, for only a short time before being suspended for misbehavior toward the end of his second year. This terminated his schooling. He then enlisted in the military. He went to Mexico and saw action in the Mexican War. After returning, he married and moved, along with his mother, to Hopemont. He became one of the chief organizers of a volunteer militia in Lexington, called the Lexington Rifles. When the Civil War broke out, the Lexington Rifles at first dedicated themselves to protecting Kentucky's "neutrality." But the death of Morgan's first wife on July 21, 1861, freed him to participate more actively in the conflict. He successfully evaded the confiscation of the arms and equipment of the Lexington Rifles by federal troops. He took the Southern sympathizers among the "Rifles" and joined up with Confederate General Simon Bolivar at Bowling Green, Kentucky.[27]

Morgan's personality was described as "non-conformist" and "independent." He stood 6 feet, rather tall for the day. Numerous pro-Confederate soldiers of fortune were drawn to Morgan, and joined the "troop" he was forming. He named it the "Second Kentucky Cavalry." Before long, Morgan and the "Second Kentucky Cavalry" became notorious hit-and-run raiders, inflicting terror and attacking supply trains behind Union lines in Kentucky and Tennessee. Morgan was promoted by the CSA in 1862 to the rank of Brigadier General. The Confederates looked upon him as a hero. In December of 1862, when he remarried, the wedding was attended by CSA President Jefferson Davis as well as thirty Confederate generals.[28]

After this event, Morgan and his men continued to subsist off what they could steal during raids on pro-Union civilians and supply trains. Horses and weapons, in addition to food and money, were stolen. Morgan was highly successful at this plundering, and his "guerrilla raider" force swelled to approximately 4,000 men. In the summer of 1863, in direct disobedience to orders from the Confederate theater commander Braxton Bragg, Morgan decided on his own initiative to undertake a raid through Union-controlled territory in Kentucky and on into the states north of the Ohio. Morgan headed north with approximately 2,460 men. Initially, he benefitted from the element of surprise. At Lebanon, in central Kentucky, Morgan's force overwhelmed and forced the surrender of a smaller force of about 400 federal defenders on July 5, 1863. This, coincidentally, was immediately after the Battle of Gettysburg. His force proceeded northwest to Sheperdsville, south of Louisville, where it robbed and looted a train, stealing several thousand U.S. dollars. Ultimately, Morgan succeeded in moving around 2,000 armed men across the Ohio River into Indiana. There they started a burning and looting rampage. From Indiana they continued eastward into the state of Ohio, staying a few miles north of the Ohio River. Morgan and his men engaged in terrorist tactics, such as killing and maiming prisoners who were believed to have misbehaved or to be aligned with the enemy. Robbery was their everyday occupation. Another typical Morgan tactic was extortion. For example, he would threaten to destroy property, perhaps a mill, unless the owner paid him $1,000. The entire purpose and effect of Morgan's raid into Indiana and Ohio was to send a wave of terror through the civilian populace.[29]

Morgan evaded any confrontation with serious opposition forces. To do so, he avoided entering any large garrisoned cities such as Cincinnati. Rather, his men raided smaller towns in the outskirts. In addition, Morgan engaged in deceptive intelligence tactics. He had with him an expert on electronic communications, who was able to tap telegraph lines and decipher messages being sent about him. Additionally, he sent fake telegraph messages of his own that were deceptive and induced confusion as to his movements. Nevertheless, his force gradually diminished through attrition, as it came under constant fire from militiamen. A young school teacher named Joseph McDougal was captured while in the act of felling trees to block Morgan's advance, and met with the ire of Morgan as a result. He was placed in a small rowboat and summarily executed. His body, riddled with bullets, was used as target practice and left for an example. Morgan typically burned all bridges behind him to delay his pursuers. He had no intention of returning to the CSA. He acted like he was on a suicide mission.

Morgan and the remnants of his Ohio invaders were finally surrounded and captured in northeastern Ohio, near the Pennsylvania line, on July 26, 1863. He and his henchmen were legally prosecuted as criminals, not prisoners of war. They were convicted of felony horse stealing and placed in the Ohio Penitentiary. But in November, Morgan and six of his cadre escaped, in an event engineered by his chief lieutenant, Thomas Hines. The terrorists slowly and secretly chiseled out a tunnel leading downward from a cell into an air cavity, which they used to get out at night. Then they scaled a high wall using a makeshift rope with a grappling hook. Traveling mostly by train, Morgan made his way back into Confederate-controlled territory and on to the capital in Richmond. He was immediately feted as a hero. Despite his earlier insubordination, he was restored to command of the "Department of Southwestern Virginia." By now, Morgan and his followers had acquired a taste for the terrorist mode of inflicting violence against unsuspecting civilians. They plundered Union and Southern sympathizers alike. In the spring of 1864, he began another series of depredations against civilians in Tennessee and Kentucky, which led to his eventual death at the hands of pursuers on September 4, 1864.[30]

As 1864 got under way, people in the areas reclaimed for

John Hunt Morgan in his military garb

the Union were appalled not only at the ferocity, but also at the randomness and gratuitous nature, of the "guerrilla" violence. Massacres occurred, including chilling episodes of mass executions in cold blood of captured African Americans who had enlisted to support Union forces. Citizens could be plundered of everything of any value, could have their homes destroyed, and could be summarily hanged, if they were suspected of collaborating with the occupying force. But at times it was very difficult to tell why any particular victim, or group of victims, was selected. Some of the gangs appeared to be "mere marauders banded together, willing to rob and murder on either side."[31] The lawlessness spawned vicious reprisals. Whether or not there was any proof, suspected civilian Confederate or guerrilla sympathizers were frequently seized and stripped of their property, including food and clothes they needed to survive.

Life in Nashville went on as normal as possible at the time of Johnnie's engagement there in February 1864. But it was essentially a fortified garrison under military control in the midst of war-torn chaos and maelstrom associated with swirling partisan paramilitary violence.[32]

Johnnie received his usual glowing reviews from the pro-Union newspaper that was then publishing in Nashville. The following article was typical:[33]

> Mr. Booth came amongst us as a stranger, his reputation as a rising star having preceded him, creating a general desire amongst our play goers to get a "taste of his quality." His first night was a splendid ovation; the theatre being densely packed, every foot of standing room occupied, and numbers sent away unable to get in. Nobly did he fulfill expectations and establish himself as a favorite. Every succeeding performance has been but a repetition of his successes. In no part has he failed. His genius appears equal to

anything the tragic muse has produced; and the time is not distant when he will attain the highest niche of professional fame.

After two weeks, Johnnie returned north to Cincinnati. He had symptoms of a severe cold, which turned into bronchitis. The failing that his Boston reviewer had criticized three years earlier, improper development of his vocal capacities, started to hinder him. Several of his performances in Cincinnati were cancelled. Those that did go forward were lamented by reviewers due to Johnnie appearing "hoarse" and "weak."[34] But he went on with his nightly shows, concluding on February 26. His next engagement was in New Orleans. To get there he obtained a pass from General Grant, and he took a Mississippi riverboat south. While on board, he became friends with a Union officer, Colonel Richard M. Johnson, who had been on General Grant's staff. When he arrived in New Orleans, Johnnie was still feeling sick. His first week of scheduled performances had to be cancelled. Johnnie continued to feel poorly and had to cancel more nights in late March. Again, he was severely hoarse.[35]

Despite the continuing problems with his stage voice, which reviewers could not fail to notice, Johnnie led an active and prominent social life during his month in New Orleans. He spent much of his free time bowling and playing billiards with a swashbuckling companion who went by the name of Hiram Martin. Martin was reputed to be a blockade runner, one of a daring breed who made big money taking big risks smuggling goods from Confederate-held territory through the Union's increasingly tight naval grip on the few ports remaining in CSA hands.[36] Like Nashville, New Orleans was an occupied city. One night after playing billiards, Johnnie's companions challenged him, on a dare, to sing "Bonnie Blue Flag," a rebel tune then forbidden by the military authorities. Without a moment's hesitation, Johnnie broke out in the strains of the song. Reminiscent of his episode as a teenager in Baltimore, his playmates swiftly melted away, leaving Johnnie alone to deal with the Union soldiers who surrounded and confronted him in the street. With nonchalance and charm, Johnnie convinced them he had no idea what the song meant. He said he had merely heard it and liked the tune.[37]

Johnnie was described by people who got to know him in New Orleans as having an "ardent, sanguine temperament." He was highly charismatic. As an A-list celebrity, he tended to draw crowds during his visits to night spots, even when he was not acting in the theater. Though he was generally affable and courteous, to an observant boy who watched him he had one peccadillo, which became more pronounced when he was drinking. "His mind was haunted by strange ideas – particularly, the notion that he was the victim of conspiracies."[38]

Chapter 26: "To Strike at Wrong and Oppression"

No one can answer with certainty the question of exactly when Johnnie made the decision to abruptly throw off his lucrative stage career to become a terrorist. More than anything, that uncertainty is due to the fact that Johnnie himself was extremely cautious and close-lipped around the subject. As an experienced professional actor and aspiring undercover attacker, he proved capable of spending long amounts of time with family members, friends, colleagues, and social companions without betraying to them the slightest suspicion about his real intentions. But it is reasonable to conclude that Johnnie must have already had something of the sort in mind when he departed New Orleans on April 9, 1864.

Johnnie did not, as normal, schedule any more engagements to follow his upcoming month-long appearance in Boston. This Boston tour had been scheduled since before he went to Nashville at the beginning of February.[1] By his own account, Johnnie was then making $20,000 per year, the equivalent of about $400,000 today. Not touring meant turning his back on a large amount of money. So, there had to be a reason why. Johnnie's writings give clues which indicate he was deeply affected and influenced by his stay in the occupied

Chapter 26: "To Strike at Wrong and Oppression"

territories of Tennessee and Louisiana during the first months of 1864. In Nashville and New Orleans, people knew far more than what was written in the newspapers about the "dirty war" that was raging all around them. In his terrorist manifesto written a few months later, Johnnie explained his decision in these words:

> People of the north, to hate tyranny [and] to love liberty and justice, to strike at wrong and oppression, was the teaching of our fathers.... I know how foolish I will be deemed, for taking a step like this.... I have never been upon a battlefield, but, O my countrymen, could you all but see the reality or effects of this horrid war, as I have seen them (in *every* State, save Virginia). I know you would think like me.

Another important clue to the timing is Johnnie's peculiar flirtation with a 17-year-old Boston girl named Isabel Sumner. Johnnie's relations with Isabel need to be considered in the overall context of his relations with women generally. Johnnie, by the start of 1864, was a sensation, the nineteenth-century equivalent of a matinee idol. He was literally deluged on a daily basis with letters from female admirers. An actress who played supporting roles with Johnnie later remarked: "The stage door was always blocked with silly women waiting to catch a glimpse, as he passed, of his superb face and figure." While Johnnie was playing Boston in April and May of 1864, people waited in crowds after each performance in hopes of seeing him as he left the theater.[2] But from episodes such as his unfortunate experience with actress Henrietta Irving, Johnnie had learned his lesson about giving in to the warmth of admirers and crushes. He placed his need for sexual relations in the hands of professionals. Johnnie had a favorite brothel, and a favored comfort woman, in New York, Washington, and probably other cities as well.[3]

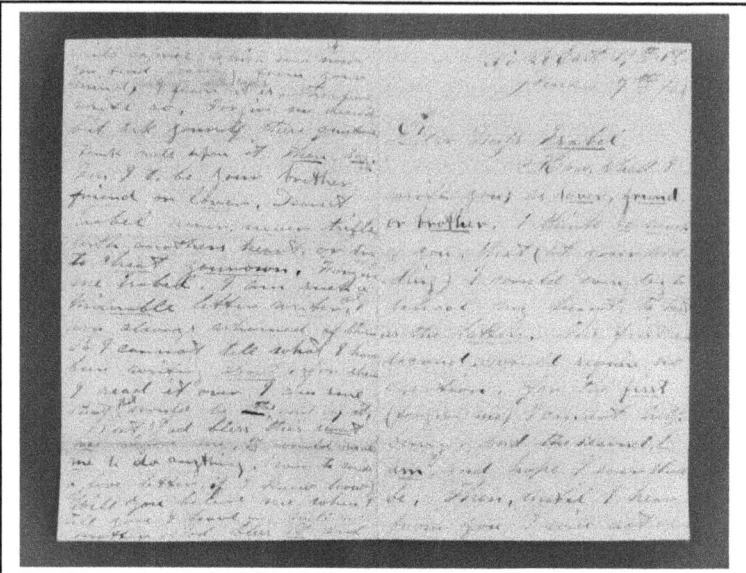

Portion of letter from John Wilkes Booth to Isabel Sumner, June 7, 1864. Image courtesy of Taper Collection owned by the Lincoln Presidential Foundation. Notice Johnnie refers to himself as "a *miserable letter writer.*"

    Johnnie wrote his first letter to Isabel on June 7, 1864, after he had finished his series of performances in Boston and was staying in New York City. The letter reveals that Johnnie had met the attractive girl, then a student who lived with her family near the Boston theater, and that the two had formed, in Johnnie's words, a "short acquaintance." Their "acquaintance" evidently was not particularly intimate, for Johnnie's letter begins with the question, "How shall I write you, as *lover, friend, or brother* [?]" The June 7 letter says virtually nothing of any substance. Its rhetoric has much of the feel of a Shakespearian sonnet. But Johnnie's prose does unwittingly betray the existence of suicidal ideation. "I know the *world*, and had begun to hate it. I saw you, Things seemed changed." The letter also dwells on "secrets." Johnnie was extremely emphatic that his letter to her must be kept secret. By mutual

CHAPTER 26: "TO STRIKE AT WRONG AND OPPRESSION"

arrangement he sent it to the Boston general delivery post office, so that she could retrieve it without her parents finding out.[4]

Ten days later, from the mountains of Pennsylvania, Johnnie wrote Isabel a second letter, which shows he had not yet received any answer to the first. In this letter he urged Isabel to "think of me sometimes" and to take up the proffered pen-pal exchange. This second letter dated June 17 sheds a little more light on the substance of their previous "short acquaintance" in Boston. Johnnie reminded Isabel: "You know you promised to teach me how to write."[5]

On July 14, 1864, Johnnie returned from Pennsylvania to New York City. Upon his arrival, he apparently found several letters from Isabel awaiting him. These letters do not survive but, from what Johnnie wrote Isabel that same day, we can glean something of their contents. Evidently Isabel, in response to Johnnie's question, had elected to call Johnnie a "friend" rather than any of his other suggestions. Nevertheless, he immediately composed a letter to her and sent it the next day. In it he insisted he planned to come to Boston to see her. The deliberately unemployed actor told her he would "be kept busy" with something undisclosed in New York for "a week or two yet" before this visit.

Johnnie did not receive any immediate response from Isabel to this missive. Ten days later, on July 25, he mailed her another letter. Its content, in the light of other information uncovered later, is very revealing. Johnnie told Isabel he was "uneasy" about her silence. He informed her he was going to "come at once" to Boston to see her. The ostensible purpose of the visit was the promised writing lesson. He remarked, "I am always – more or less – disgusted with my own bad writing etc." But Johnnie's real reason for going to Boston was very different. Investigators later discovered by accident that Johnnie did, in fact, travel to Boston to visit Isabel right away,

PRIMORDIAL AMERICAN TERRORISTS

just as he said he would. He arrived there July 26, the very next day after sending his letter. He checked into the Parker House, registering under his own name. Also arriving at the same hotel on the same day were four Confederate Secret Service agents, all of whom registered under false names, and all of whom gave false addresses in Canada.[6] The agenda of this secret gathering, of which Johnnie was an integral part, was to map out a terrorist plot. And Johnnie's insistence on coming to Boston to visit Isabel was, in reality, a cover for attending this meeting, which had been planned well in advance.

While in Boston, Johnnie presented Isabel with a gold ring, inscribed "J.W.B to I.S." It appears the young girl did, at that point, begin to pay attention to the star's unsolicited deluge of romantic overtures. Toward the end of August, she came to visit New York City, bringing Johnnie flowers. She also brought him a portrait photo of herself, in which she wore the ring. But Johnnie was at that time laid up with a severe case of erysipelas, a disfiguring skin infection, which required minor surgery. He could not see her. Their unlikely relationship did not progress any further.

Inscribed ring presented to Isabel Sumner by John Wilkes Booth, July 1864. Image courtesy of Taper Collection owned by the Lincoln Presidential Foundation.

As a matter of fact, Johnnie's whole dalliance with Isabel is most likely best explained as an opportunistic adjunct to his secret resolve to strike the dramatic irrational blow that is typical of terrorism. Isabel's father, a Boston native and business owner, was named Charles Sumner.[7] Johnnie may well have thought for a time that her father was the same Charles Sumner who, as we have seen, was an abolitionist U.S. Senator from Boston. The interest he pursued in the young student was probably intended to infiltrate and gain him a foothold he could use for the terror attack. At first glance, this seems like a rather far-fetched hypothesis. But Johnnie's later behavior with the daughter of a real abolitionist Senator lends it strong corroboration.

Johnnie's purpose in going to the Pennsylvania hills north of Pittsburgh in June of 1864 was to work on his investment in oil. At that time, the exploration of oil fields along the Allegheny River was fairly new. In view of emerging technology to use it, petroleum was becoming lucrative for those who succeeded in extracting substantial quantities. An oil craze of sorts led many prospectors to converge on the area. In December 1863, Johnnie first visited the Pennsylvania oil country. He persuaded John Ellsler, an actor friend and theater manager, to invest with him in an oil lease of 3.5 acres east of the Allegheny, across the river from the town of Franklin. They called their venture "the Dramatic Oil Company." Johnnie personally hired a local driller to install a well on the property.[8]

After finishing his final gig in Boston, then spending a week or two in New York, Johnnie headed back to the Pennsylvania oil country. He brought with him Joseph Simonds, an unmarried young man who was employed as a clerk in a Boston bank. Johnnie had recruited Simonds to leave his job in order to run the Dramatic Oil Company. For a few days Johnnie and Simonds shared a double room at the U.S. Hotel in Franklin with two other oil seekers. Johnnie and Simonds were only supposed to stay with them one or two nights, but wound up staying longer because of the crowded conditions in the oil boom town. Finally, they succeeded in finding a vacancy in a boarding house. But they continued to walk from there to the U.S. Hotel for meals. During this time, Johnnie developed a habit of playing every day with a little boy named Joe, who was stationed by his parents in the front window of their harness shop, as he walked by on his way to and from the U.S. Hotel. To attract the boy's attention, Johnnie whistled whenever he approached the shop. He often left a silver dollar or a closed pocket knife for little Joe to play with until Johnnie returned.[9] One day Johnnie came across a litter of stray kittens. He picked them up, bought them some milk, and took them back to his Franklin boarding house, asking his landlady to take care of them until a home could be found.[10]

With the townspeople he met, Johnnie soon established his typical reputation for being gentlemanly, convivial, and well-liked. He personally supervised work on the oil field, wearing a slouched hat, overalls, flannel shirt, and boots. When not working on the property, Johnnie went for long rambles about the pleasant springtime countryside. From boyhood, he was a lover of nature and pure air. With a companion who strolled along with him on some of these hikes, he engaged in long stream of consciousness conversations on poetry, the theatrical profession, literature, and other subjects. But he remained mostly silent about his feelings on politics and the war. The majority of the people he hung out with in Franklin accepted the pro-Union point of view. He never said a word to them about his passions on the subject.[11]

Johnnie spent about $5,000 in total on his investment in the Dramatic Oil Company. For another $1,000 he purchased an interest in a separate oil claim, slightly up the Allegheny near the confluence of Pithole Creek. The Dramatic Oil venture turned out to be a complete bust. Initially the well produced about twenty-five barrels a day, but that was deemed not enough. So the well was "shot" with explosives in an attempt to make it produce more. Instead, the explosion had the effect of ruining the well, drying it up completely.[12] The Pithole investment, on the other hand, turned out to be profitable. But

Chapter 26: "To Strike at Wrong and Oppression"

by that time Johnnie had already given away his entire interest in it.

Johnnie, as we have seen, returned to New York City on July 14. At that point, he told Isabel he would be "kept busy" with undisclosed business for a week to ten days. We can surmise this "business" involved what the Confederates called their "Secret Service." It had many hallmarks of a terrorist organization. Its operatives were men and women who were frequently expatriates in Canada, or, when in the United States, who lived underground and used aliases. It was financed with slush money. It conducted covert operations. It perfected and used sophisticated encrypted communications. Its agents were carefully organized into discrete "cells," so that the betrayal of any one cell would not infect the others. And the kinds of operations it carried out were typical of terrorism: propaganda; attacks on civilian property, including vessels; bank robbery; and attempts to free prisoners.[13]

New York City was a natural hub for the Confederate Secret Service. It was a major bastion of the Copperheads, as they were derisively called – holders of strong anti-abolitionist, anti-war sentiments. Much of the press, and many of the office holders, in New York were outspoken anti-war advocates. In the presidential election of 1860, and again in 1864, New York City voters rejected Lincoln by more than a two-to-one margin.[14] Some sympathizers with the rebel cause could be counted on to provide financial and logistical support. A clandestine underground organization affiliated with the Copperheads was called the Order of American Knights. Most likely, this shadowy group played a hand in fomenting the vicious anti-draft riots that occurred in New York City during the summer of 1863. CSA President Jefferson Davis and his top Cabinet ministers sent Confederate Secret Service agents to infiltrate the Northern states, including New York, from Canada to try to foment opposition to the war by the

Copperheads. They also charged these agents with a mission to try to build the Order of American Knights into an effective rallying point for uprising, as well as for sabotage. It is reasonable to surmise, from his subsequent actions, that Johnnie's "business" in New York City during June and July 1864 involved receiving briefing and training from agents of the Confederate Secret Service. Most likely, such agents participated with Johnnie in formulating a covert plan of action.

The granddaddy of terrorist plans, the notion of abducting President Lincoln, did not originate with Johnnie. It had actually been vetted in rebel circles ever since Lincoln's first inauguration. During those early years Confederate political leaders, including President Davis personally, had vetoed the concept. But by 1864 desperation had set in. Confederate government officials now became far more tolerant and even supportive of "dirty war" tactics, particularly guerrilla warfare and its close relative, terrorism. General Lee himself approved of systematic raids on civilians behind enemy lines in the northern Virginia theater. John Mosby, the leader of the Virginia Confederate dirty war, began reporting directly to Lee after Jeb Stuart, Mosby's former commander, was killed on May 12, 1864.[15]

In June 1864, the Confederate upper echelon gave their approval to a fairly elaborate plan to capture Lincoln and bring him to Richmond to be held as a hostage. This plan had been under development since the winter of 1863–1864. One who was involved in its conception was Bradley Johnson, a Confederate officer from Maryland. The plan reached the verge of execution after the cavalry battle of Trevilian Station in northern Virginia, on the outskirts of the District of Columbia area, on June 12–13, 1864. Years later, Johnson authorized publication of the following account of the plan by one of his subordinates at the time:

Confederate spies in Washington had kept General

CHAPTER 26: "TO STRIKE AT WRONG AND OPPRESSION"

> Lee thoroughly posted as to the disposition and force of every command of the enemy in and around the Capital. To carry out this daring enterprise, then, Colonel Johnson was to take the Maryland battalion, numbering two hundred and fifty sabres, and cross the Potomac above Georgetown, make a dash at a battalion of cavalry known to be stationed there, and push on to the Soldiers' Home, where it was well known President Lincoln lived, and after capturing him to send him across the river in charge of a body of picked men, whilst the main body was to cut the wires and roads between Washington and Baltimore, and then move back through Western Maryland to the Valley of Virginia; or, if that means of retreat was cut off, Johnson was to go up into Pennsylvania, and on west to West Virginia beyond Grafton. It seemed, indeed, a most desperate undertaking, but everything promised its successful accomplishment. Indeed, so sanguine was [Confederate commanding general Wade] Hampton that the plan of Johnson would succeed that he wanted to undertake it himself at the head of four thousand horse, and was only prevented by Sheridan's advance upon the Confederate Capital.

According to this account, Hampton gave orders for the logistical support of Johnson's venture but, before it could happen, Johnson and his men were recalled because they were urgently needed elsewhere.[16]

We do not have direct testimony that Johnnie, motivated by passion for an increasingly desperate cause, volunteered to join the pre-existing Confederate Secret Service plan to capture Lincoln. But the circumstantial evidence to that effect is overwhelming. In June 1864, the "Bradley Johnson" plan to capture Lincoln at the Soldiers' Home was organized and given logistical support, but it did not come off. A month later,

Johnnie met in Boston with four Confederate Secret Service agents to discuss an unknown agenda. Within the next two weeks, Johnnie began actively assembling his own terrorist cell. He expressly recruited its participants to carry out a secret plot to kidnap Lincoln while traveling unguarded to or from the Soldiers' Home.[17] The plot that Johnnie convinced his recruits to join was based on the same intelligence as Johnson's regarding Lincoln's habits regarding the Soldiers' Home – and, interestingly, that intelligence proved to be somewhat inaccurate, lending credence to the hypothesis that it came from the same source. Johnnie, whose travels are well documented, had not been in Washington since November 1863, so he had no opportunity to observe Lincoln's recent habits himself. Moreover, regarding the question of transport of Lincoln southward after the capture, a critical element of the scheme, Johnnie's plan depended upon the identical network of underground rebel operatives in southern Maryland and the Northern Neck of Virginia, which the Confederates called the Signal Corps, as did Johnson's. Without any doubt, the Confederate Secret Service furnished Johnnie with the identity and use of its prized clandestine smuggling network for this purpose.

And there is something more. George Kane, Johnnie's old friend from his days as the Police Marshal of Baltimore, was also involved in the Confederate Secret Service. Following his release from detention early in the war, Kane spent time as a Confederate expatriate in Canada, before returning to Richmond. He likely also participated during the winter of 1863–1864 in formulating the plot to kidnap Lincoln. General Lee, in a letter to Jefferson Davis of June 26, 1864, made a mysterious reference to a "project of Marshall Kane," commenting that it only could work "if the matter can be kept secret."[18] The inference that the "project" Lee was mentioning was the attempted Lincoln kidnapping fits very well with the rest of the chronology summarized above.

Chapter 26: "To Strike at Wrong and Oppression"

As his first recruits for the new terrorist cell, Johnnie turned to two people he knew from his boyhood in Baltimore. Johnnie had encountered Sam Arnold during his days as a student at St. Timothy's. Sam came from a wealthy family; his father owned a large Baltimore bakery. Johnnie remembered Sam as one of the more prominent leaders of the student uprising against Rev. Van Bokkelen. This dissident episode undoubtedly influenced Johnnie in his decision to tap Sam as a recruit. Johnnie thought Sam's willingness to buck authority would predispose Sam to join the plot against Lincoln. The Arnolds were a Southern family. When the war had broken out, Sam enlisted in Company C of the 1st Maryland Infantry, CSA. Discharged for medical reasons, he at first found desk jobs in the South. On hearing that his mother was ill, Arnold returned home to Baltimore in early 1864. So, in the summer of 1864, he was essentially unemployed. Johnnie learned that Sam was available. Through his brother Billy, who had also been a St. Timothy's schoolmate, Johnnie sent a message asking Sam to come to meet him at Barnum's Hotel in Baltimore. Sam had not seen Johnnie for twelve years. He found a confident, headstrong Johnnie who was much changed from the timid younger boy he remembered.[19]

Mike O'Laughlen, Johnnie's other recruit who was invited to join the same meeting, was a kid Johnnie knew from the streets of Baltimore. His older brother was one of Johnnie's closest friends during his teenage days. Like Sam Arnold, he was a former Confederate soldier. He had served in the same unit as Sam, but the two of them did not know each other. Like Sam, Mike had left the unit due to being sick. He then returned to Baltimore. Also like Sam, Mike was unmarried and unemployed, making him a perfect unattached candidate for a terrorist mission. Whereas Sam Arnold was three years older than Johnnie, Mike was two years younger. Genteel in appearance, Mike did not have the look of a doer of daring deeds. But he was smart, a keen observer, and talented with his hands.[20]

Over an offering of wine and cigars, Johnnie laid out his plan to Sam and Mike and soon convinced both to join. He spoke in earnest of the need for dramatic action to free the huge numbers of Confederate soldiers in Northern prison camps. Some 20–30,000 were now held in captivity, almost as many as were present in the entire Confederate army in the Virginia theater. Formulating proposals to free these prisoners of war had become a major obsession of the Confederate Secret Service. Such proposals now had gained the attention of the highest levels of the CSA government and military.[21] But Johnnie presented the idea to Sam and Mike as one he himself had devised. President Lincoln would be captured on his way to or from the presidential summer residence at Riggs Cottage, built in the 1840s by George Washington Riggs. This was located on the grounds of the Soldiers' Home in the northern part of the District of Columbia. The kidnap party would kill any guards, seize Lincoln, conceal him inside a horse-drawn carriage, and then make a rapid escape into southern Maryland. There, a network of agents would be waiting to help them cross over the Potomac River. They would escape, with the hostage, to Confederate-controlled territory in Virginia, and ultimately reach Richmond, where Lincoln's captivity could be used as leverage to secure the freedom of all of the prisoners of war and thus rescue the slipping Southern dream of independence.[22] The two recruits were won over by Johnnie's charisma and his air of total confidence. They agreed to join in his scheme.

Despite his general discretion around people who were not believers, after committing to make the ultimate sacrifice to the cause, Johnnie did betray his feelings on a few occasions. He had a severe quarrel with his brother Edwin over the cause of injustice to the South at the end of August, just after recovering in Edwin's home from his erysipelas. Edwin, as a result of the

CHAPTER 26: "TO STRIKE AT WRONG AND OPPRESSION"

unpleasantness of the fight, ordered Johnnie out of the house. Johnnie, for his part, announced to the family that he was going over to the South and from now on would do all his playing there.[23] After a brief sojourn in Baltimore, during which he again met with his recruits Sam Arnold and Mike O'Laughlen, he went to the Pennsylvania oil country to close out his affairs there. Johnnie spent the majority of September in Franklin, but to the locals it became clear that he had lost all interest in oil. He had Simonds prepare the necessary papers to dispose of his entire $6,000 investment. His ownership in the Dramatic Oil Company he gave away, one third to Simonds and two thirds to his oldest brother June. His interest in the Pithole property went to his spinster older sister Rosalie. Johnnie did not receive a dime.[24]

Shortly before his final departure on September 29, 1864, an incident occurred that revealed something of Johnnie's desperate temper. While in a barber shop, he became enraged over enthusiastic remarks made by Caleb Marshall, a black man, celebrating recent victories by the Union armies. Reacting in anger, Johnnie reached into his pocket, where he customarily kept a handgun. Tom Mears, one of Johnnie's oil business partners, saw what he was doing and reacted quickly. He grabbed Johnnie, pinned his arms at his sides and, with the help of another man, hustled him out of the barber shop before any more serious trouble could develop.[25]

By his dual actions of abandoning his stage career and giving away his oil investments, Johnnie demonstrated that he was not at all concerned with his financial fortunes. Typical of a terrorist, he had no need for money, except as necessary to fund his final desperate act. And for that funding, he relied now on an entirely different source: Confederate gold. The "Confederate Cabinet" in exile in Canada controlled a big chunk of the rapidly shrinking gold reserve of the slaveholding republics. And, among their other projects, these expats provided money to Johnnie to fund his terrorist activity.

When he left Pennsylvania on September 29, 1864, Johnnie told Simonds he was going to New York. To another local, he gave a much pithier and probably more insightful destination. He said, "I am going to Hell." Where Johnnie stayed in New York for the next two weeks, who he associated with, and what he did while there, are mysteries. Johnnie told family members he was preparing for an engagement in Canada. On Sunday, October 16, the actor was spotted in Newburgh, New York, an unlikely place for a celebrity. Newburgh is on the main train route along the Hudson, north to Albany from New York City. He was probably there to meet with Robert Coxe, an important Confederate Secret Service agent who was temporarily staying in nearby Poughkeepsie.[26] Johnnie was on his way to Canada. With him, he brought the accoutrements of his entire professional career, packed in two trunks and one long box. They contained his dressing case and wardrobe of velvet suits, crowns, caps, plumes, doublets, shoes, and accessories. Also included were fifty-six bound and pamphlet volumes of plays, many with handwritten stage notes, correspondence, photographs, and newspaper clippings, stage swords, and pistols.[27]

Johnnie arrived in Montreal two days later, on October 18. He checked into the St. Lawrence Hall, the unofficial local headquarters of the Confederate Cabinet. His first order of his business there was to seek out Patrick Charles Martin, better known as "P.C. Martin." Besides being a fellow Baltimorean, P.C. Martin was a Confederate Secret Service agent, and a close associate of George Kane. Johnnie apparently knew Martin from his pre-war days in Baltimore. P.C. Martin had spent the first year of the war as a blockade runner before escaping to Canada in the summer of 1862. By now, he was the head of clandestine Confederate maritime operations in Montreal. P.C. Martin entrusted Johnnie with a letter of introduction to critical operatives of the Confederate Secret

CHAPTER 26: "TO STRIKE AT WRONG AND OPPRESSION"

Service in southern Maryland. Johnnie, in turn, entrusted to P.C. Martin his packed theatrical wardrobe, to be shipped out of Canada and smuggled through the blockade into one of the few remaining Southern ports.[28] The very idea of sending his wardrobe so he could "play in the South" illustrates Johnnie's disconnection from reality. The theater venues in Richmond, Virginia, Columbus, Georgia, and Montgomery, Alabama, which Johnnie remembered as places where he was adored by Southern audiences, simply no longer existed. They would never, in that form, exist again.

On Saturday, October 24 Johnnie, to give credence to the cover story that he was in town to promote his career on stage, put on display a little of his own personal brand of fund raising. He performed a series of solo dramatic readings on the stage of Corby's Hall, Montreal. One of them was Mark Antony's famous Forum speech from Shakespeare's *Julius Caesar*.[29]

Chapter 27: Flocking With Birds of a Feather

Johnnie, in Montreal, by no means limited himself to a single night on stage and shipping out his baggage. He spent a great deal of time with George N. Sanders, who was staying at the nearby Ottawa Hotel in Montreal when Johnnie arrived. To observers, the two of them appeared to be fast friends. We have encountered this person earlier in our story. Yes, Johnnie's newest companion was the same George Sanders who was a great admirer of European revolutionaries, including the assassin who met his end on the guillotine, Felice Orsini.[1]

There are certain persons who turn out to be friends and supporters of terrorists, although they are not themselves terrorists.[2] George Sanders was one of those people. On a personal level, he was too connected to the political process to be a terrorist. Moreover, he lacked the asceticism and suicidal drive that terrorists generally manifest. However, George Sanders had many elements of the terrorist profile. He was:

1. born into a wealthy family;
2. a person with great native intelligence;[3]
3. strongly influenced in the direction of a parent (his father Lewis);

CHAPTER 27: FLOCKING WITH BIRDS OF A FEATHER

4. slightly divorced from reality, causing him to be a chronic "loser;"
5. confident in his own plans, no matter how unrealistic they seemed to others;
6. self-righteous;
7. exceptionally strong willed;[4]
8. possessed of personal charisma;
9. lacking in formal education;
10. a person who traveled extensively, including internationally;
11. a man of action, who always wanted to turn every idea into a plot or plan;
12. resistant to authority;[5] and
13. prone to adopting other people's causes.

And, in his life, George Sanders used "means and methods" that are typical of terrorists. He:

A. used aliases, and a false identity (in connection with blockade running);[6]
B. engaged often in clandestine activity; and
C. exaggerated the numbers and power of the terrorists he sponsored.[7]

George Sanders was born February 21, 1812 in Lexington, Kentucky. His father, Lewis Sanders, was a hemp tycoon. He was very active in Kentucky political affairs. Lewis, however, encountered financial difficulties after he was swindled by the former U.S. Vice-President, Aaron Burr. He sold his palatial estate in Lexington and moved out of town to a more rural location, where he established a manor called Grasslands. Young George grew up around thoroughbred horses. Lewis Sanders was not a large-scale slave owner. The labor force at Grasslands did include some slaves, but it also included hired workers. Lewis Sanders was a committed Democrat and, as such, his cornerstone political beliefs, which his son George absorbed, favored state's and individual's rights, limited government, strict construction of the Constitution, hard money, and free trade.[8]

Despite his intelligence and family wealth, George Sanders lacked any college or other formal education. He always retained something of the air of a country character. The story of how George met his wife is very curious. George, as well as his father Lewis, became avid readers of a miniature magazine called *The Passion Flower*. This magazine was published in New York City by Samuel Reid and his daughter, Anna. George wrote a letter to Anna praising the publication, and a correspondence between them ensued. George became enamored, and asked Anna to marry him without ever having met her, or even having seen a picture of her. She agreed. George found out on the day of the wedding that his bride was short and more than a little funny looking. But she was a good person who became popular with the Sanders family. The two were married on Tuesday evening, December 29, 1836, and they had four children.

On November 25, 1843, George organized a non-partisan meeting in Ghent, Kentucky, to promote the annexation of Texas. His father Lewis also took part in this event. The meeting helped bring the Texas annexation issue to large-scale prominence. In its wake, the relatively unknown James Knox Polk, who ran primarily on a Texas annexation platform, was elected U.S. President. This rather unexpected success brought George notoriety. In the aftermath of Polk's election, George in 1845 took his family from Grass Hills to New York City. There George continued in politics, even as he took a job on Wall Street. When a dispute emerged between the United States and Great Britain over the Oregon Territory, George plunged into it. He became an agent for the Hudson's Bay Company, which owned rights to the Oregon Territory. He

CHAPTER 27: FLOCKING WITH BIRDS OF A FEATHER

brokered a deal to sell these rights to the U.S. Government. He set himself up to make a huge personal profit on the transaction, since he obtained a commitment from the Company to sell for $410,000, while he was seeking to induce the U.S. Government to pay $1,000,000. But President Polk never fully trusted George. Partly, this was because he recognized that George was acting as a foreign entity's agent, but, even more so, it was because George's attempt to reap a large personal profit caused Polk to write in his diary that George was "unscrupulous and unprincipled." The Oregon deal brokered by George ultimately went nowhere.[9] But from his experiences, which took him to London, George acquired a certain cosmopolitan familiarity with international affairs.

From Oregon, George moved on to more fanatical and controversial schemes. He launched a political movement called "Young America." This was, in a sense, a counterpart to nationalistic groups emerging at the same time in Europe, including "Young Germany," "Young England," and "Young France." It billed itself as "progressive," and it was opposed above all else to "old fogies" of all stripes and denominations. Rather than backing a well-defined point of view, "Young America" was "primarily a slogan and a sentiment." As such, Young America caught on and rose to prominence during the period 1849–1853. To the extent that it had any political creed, it was a commitment to fulfilling the profound "destiny" of the United States. To many, this "manifest destiny" meant expansion on the American continent. But to George it emphasized overthrowing monarchies and replacing them with American-style republican governments. George found covert action and secret societies highly attractive ways to seek such change.

George "brought energy, (often unrealistic) optimism, influence, and a voice" to Young America. He was a short, stocky, cigar-smoking man whose "brains" were evident even to people who disagreed with him. His demeanor was described as:[10]

George Sanders

"one incessant action. He was constantly on his feet, moving in every direction ... He required little sleep, but strong meat and drink, although rarely guilty of excess. The vitality and volume of the man were gigantic, and seemingly inexhaustible ... He could find his man and make his statements, his argument, and his propositions in the shortest possible time, surpassing all men in his force, clearness, distinctness, and point ... At a dinner table, either private or public, he was a fine host, and was greatly devoted to champagne, for which he spent thousands while living in New York."

With Young America, age itself was elevated to become the central issue. Stephen Douglas was seized upon as a "young" Democratic presidential candidate whom the group would ardently support. In 1851, George purchased a publication called the *United States Magazine and Democratic Review*, changed its name to *Democratic Review*, and turned it into an organ to promote Young America and Douglas's nomination.

George had no veneration for authority figures. *Democratic Review* launched a crusade to personally and unapologetically attack all "old fogie" candidates, even if they were Democrats. Of course, this immediately alienated important people. George's crazed "support" for Douglas turned out to be something of an embarrassment. *Democratic*

Review was denounced repeatedly on the floor of the House of Representatives.[11] Arousing hostility almost seemed as if it were George's principal aim. On the pages of *Democratic Review*, he generally castigated "old fogies" as "drones," "vile toads," "elderly and incompetent good-for-nothings," "imbeciles," and "nincompoops."

Douglas hoped that at the June, 1852, national Democratic convention, he would be selected as the party's Presidential nominee on the rebound after an initial impasse between the other leading candidates, Lewis Cass and James Buchanan. Young America enthusiastically supported Douglas. However, it soon became clear that Douglas, like Cass and Buchanan, was unacceptable to the party as a whole. So a surprising compromise choice emerged – the political ingenue Franklin Pierce. Pierce was not a "Washington insider," and he was biologically somewhat "young," being in his 40s. So, with his nomination, George and Young America were able to declare themselves triumphant. The opposing Whigs nominated General Winfield Scott, who was indeed something of an "old fogie" and a weak candidate. Thus, Pierce had an immediate inside track to the White House.[12]

Young America vigorously supported Pierce in the general election. After his victory, he rewarded George with a recess appointment to become U.S. Consul-General to London. George left for England in August 1853. Upon arrival he promptly immersed himself in supporting "revolutionaries" – dissidents like Felice Orsini who, for one reason or another, were seeking to overthrow the governments of established European powers. George insisted Young America would not be content with anything less than a total embracing of the cause of republicans struggling against despotic rule. George became an ardent radical. Through his rabid outspoken "red republicanism," he quickly became fast friends with leading liberal and revolutionary figures of Europe. Lajos Kossuth, the apostle of Hungarian nationalism, and Giuseppe Garibaldi, the military genius behind Italy's eventual national unification, met for the first time at George's London home.[13]

At the dinner George and his wife hosted for their radical friends, including Felice Orsini, on February 21, 1854, George raised a toast "to do away with the Crowned Heads of Europe." In a later letter addressed to the people of France, George subtly urged the assassination of French Emperor Napoleon III. As we have seen, Felice ultimately attempted just that.

British leaders were not pleased with George's activities while on their soil, and neither was the U.S. Congress. On February 14, 1854 (and unbeknownst to George seven days later, at the time he gave his toast), the U.S. Senate rejected his confirmation as Consul-General by a vote of 29 to 10. George was bitter. He attributed his rejection to two of the "old fogies" he had attacked, Democrats Lewis Cass and Secretary of State William Marcy. A more accurate explanation is that George, as the holder of an appointive office, had long since lost touch with political reality.[14]

George Sanders was never an outspoken advocate of the slaveholding system. He viewed it as an unfortunate distraction from more important issues, such as America's geopolitical destiny. As a matter of fact, in 1858 George broke publicly with President James Buchanan, who had appointed him to another patronage position as Navy Agent in New York City, over Buchanan's support for the bogus slave-state Lecompton Constitution in Kansas. George's continuing brazen support for Stephen Douglas, who had feuded bitterly with Buchanan over the Lecompton Constitution, ended up costing him the Navy Agent job. It was another instance where George's lack of contact with political reality turned him into something of a loser. George once again strongly backed Douglas for the Democratic nomination at the Charleston convention in 1860. Although Douglas eventually got the nomination, the competing pro-slavery candidacy of Kentucky Democrat John

C. Breckinridge – one of the congressmen who had condemned *Democratic Review* on the floor of Congress nine years earlier – essentially doomed the Douglas campaign from its inception.[15]

Following Lincoln's election, George traveled to attend the formative convention of the CSA in Montgomery. There, he attempted to persuade the rebellious leaders to rejoin the United States in a parallel republic, with the two joined by a commercial compact and indissoluble except by mutual consent. His ideas were again unrealistic. They were ridiculed by the secessionist fire-eaters, who vehemently disavowed any notion of reconciliation.[16]

Unlike Douglas, George sided with the Confederacy in its attempt to secede from the Union. He volunteered his services to the CSA and, by the spring of 1862, the Confederate government found a use for George. It entrusted him to go to England to negotiate a large sale of cotton that would raise the funds necessary to purchase six iron-clad vessels. To get there, George had to somehow penetrate the Union blockade. He posed as an ignorant Welsh peasant under a fake name and, in disguise and using an alias, he successfully crossed into Canada at Niagara Falls. From there he made his way to England, arriving September 1, 1862. In an affair highly reminiscent of John Brown, George was a flop in his activities as an agent for selling cotton on the London market. George got into disagreements because the British only wanted to buy the Southern "cotton certificates" he was peddling at 8 cents per pound, rather than the 20 cents per pound that George was convinced the cotton was worth.

George then came up with another way to make a profit off the war. He organized his family to act as a courier service between Europe and the Confederacy. George negotiated compensation of $600 per month from the Confederate government for operating this service. He involved his sons in operating the courier service, which was, of course, carried on covertly in defiance of the Union blockade. This would prove fatal to one of them, who was captured repeatedly and later died in a prison in Boston Harbor.[17]

For most of the war, George stayed in England. But in the spring of 1864, like many others including Johnnie, he felt the growing sense of desperation of the Confederate cause. He decided to go to Canada to join the Confederacy's "Canadian Cabinet." George arrived in St. Catharine's, on Lake Ontario just across the border with the United States near Niagara Falls, at the beginning of June. Through his force of will, he was soon able to strongly influence two of the three official commissioners dispatched by the Richmond government to Canada, Clement Clay and James Holcombe. Clay regarded George as a good man to do the CSA's "dirty work." George associated with people with whom Clay himself could not. George immediately engineered a secret initiative, which resulted in a "peace" meeting between Clay and Holcombe, as well as George himself, with Union representatives in Niagara Falls on July 20, 1864. Horace Greeley was one of Lincoln's main emissaries to this meeting, along with Lincoln's personal secretary John Hay. They carried a handwritten "To Whom It May Concern" letter from Lincoln, which set forth his two most basic requirements of any settlement: "the integrity of the whole Union," and "the abandonment of slavery." These terms were wholly unacceptable to the Confederate commissioners, so the peace parley went nowhere.[18] The failing cause of the slaveholding republics grew even more desperate. George turned to "dirtier" work on its behalf.

Bennett Young had ridden as one of John Hunt Morgan's followers during his burn and pillage rampage through Ohio in the summer of 1863. He was captured along with Morgan on July 26, 1863, but, like Morgan, he escaped from Union custody. He made his way to Canada, where he met up with the pro-Confederates there. For a time Young attended theological school in Toronto, but he rapidly dropped out in order to resume his career in terrorism. With the approval of Clement Clay, who at this juncture did nothing of importance without consulting George, Young recruited a group of ex-Confederate soldiers that he called the "Retributors." Most of them had previously served with Morgan, with the even more rapacious William Quantrill (who during 1863 had led dirty war atrocities against civilians in the Kansas–Missouri theater), or with both. In late September, 1864, Young was given $2,000 by Clay to finance one of the most spectacular terrorist attacks of the American Civil War.[19] And George, despite his later protestations of ignorance, was one of the main supporters of this mission.[20]

Just before 3 o'clock on Wednesday, October 19, 1864, the bearded William Huntley, one of Young's men, strolled into the Franklin County Bank on Main Street in the bustling little town of St. Albans, Vermont.[21] St. Albans is located just east of Lake Champlain, about 18 miles south of the border between the state of Vermont, in the United States, and the province of Quebec, Canada. Huntley asked Marcus Beardsley, the bank cashier, the price of gold. Beardsley replied that the bank did not buy or sell gold. But he directed Huntley toward James Armington, a 27-year-old man who had just entered the bank to make a deposit. After making his deposit, Armington bought two $5 gold pieces from Huntley for $20 in U.S. paper currency. Armington then left the building, along with another customer named Saxe. While this little transaction was going on, four other men had entered the bank. As soon as Armington and Saxe left, one of these men stepped forward, drew a Colt revolver from his pocket, and silently pointed it at Beardsley. At that point Huntley announced, "We are Confederate soldiers, sir. There are one hundred of us in town. We have come to rob the banks and burn your town."

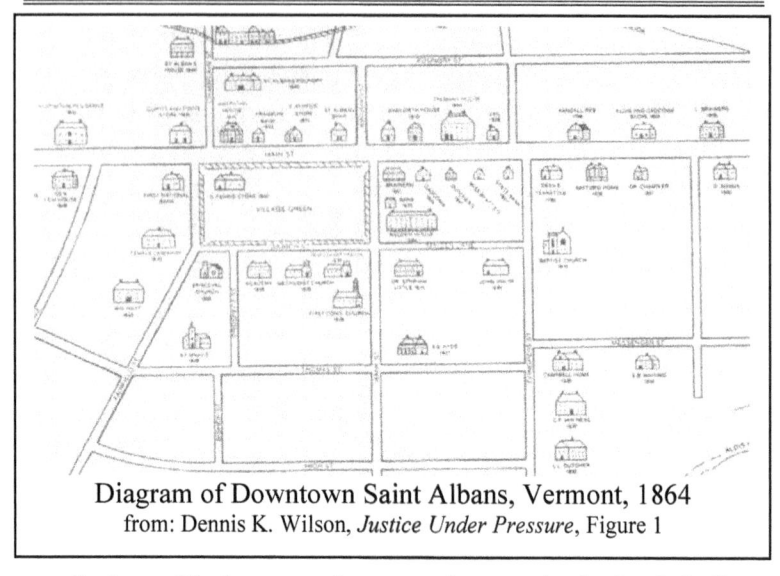

Diagram of Downtown Saint Albans, Vermont, 1864
from: Dennis K. Wilson, *Justice Under Pressure*, Figure 1

Jackson Clark, a wood cutter who was in the bank before Huntley came in, made a dash for the door. One of the raiders pulled him up short. He put a pistol to Clark's head and threatened, "I will blow your brains out if you stir another inch." Clark was forced into the bank's walk-in vault at the back of the room. Huntley instructed Beardsley to give his men all the bank's "greenbacks" and other paper money. Taking what Beardsley gave him, and having his men remove everything from the vault, the raiders gathered close to $70,000. They then forced Beardsley into the vault. Ignoring Beardsley's pleas that he and Clark would soon suffocate, Huntley locked both of them behind double iron doors. Fortunately, people who entered the bank shortly afterwards were able to hear the combination shouted by Beardsley from inside the vault, and used it to open the doors.

Just at the same time Huntley entered Franklin County Bank, two men peered through the front window of St. Albans Bank, also on Main Street several hundred feet to the north. They entered the bank and walked to the counter. Cyrus Bishop, the chief teller, moved toward them to be of service.

CHAPTER 27: FLOCKING WITH BIRDS OF A FEATHER

He thought they were reaching into their pockets for money. Instead, each removed a Colt revolver and pointed it directly at his chest. Bishop turned and fled into a private room. He tried to slam the door, but the pursuing raiders prevented him from doing so. They forced the door open, banging Bishop's head in the process. With pistols now pointed at his head, Bishop pleaded for his life. A man the robbers called "Captain," whose real name was Thomas Collins and who was a veteran of Morgan's terrorist raiders,[22] informed Bishop that if he stirred or made any resistance, his brain would be blown out. The invaders locked the front door of the bank. They forced Bishop and his assistant teller Martin Seymour to hand over three bags of silver coins. The bags were much too heavy and cumbersome to carry, so the men tore them open and stuffed as much of the silver as they could into their pockets. "Captain" Collins then got busy removing all the paper money from the bank's safe. A local businessman, surprised at finding the bank's door locked, knocked on it. The door was cracked open. He was greeted by a desperado with a pistol who grabbed him, forced him into the bank, and relieved him of $400 in cash he had planned to use to pay a debt. Soon another young man knocked at the door. He, too, was robbed of the funds he had come to deposit for his employer.

"Captain" Collins informed the victims that their treatment was retribution for the acts of Generals Sherman and Sheridan during their forays into the South. All four were forced to lie on a bed in the private room. Collins told them there were seventy-five armed men in the town, and that their intent was to burn all the public buildings, the Vermont Governor's home, and the train station. At that point, the invaders heard shots being fired outside. They withdrew from the bank, leaving the victims on the bed and warning them not to step outside. They took with them around $78,500.

At the same time the other robberies were in progress,

Caleb Wallace and another man who was never identified entered the First National Bank of Saint Albans, located across Main Street and a half block south of the other two banks. Only two people were inside, the cashier Albert Sowles and a 90-year-old retired Army general, who was quite deaf. The attackers rapidly put their pistols to Sowles's head. They informed him he was a prisoner and, if he resisted, he would be shot dead. Two other raiders now also entered. As directed by Wallace, one of them guarded the door while the other ransacked the premises for bank bills, treasury notes, bonds, and other securities, as well as paper money. A total of close to $58,000 was taken in satchels and pockets. Wallace informed Sowles that they were Confederate soldiers, a party of one hundred men from General Early's army, and that they were there "to avenge the actions of General Sherman in the Shenandoah Valley."[23] The deaf retired general, who looked up and saw the proceedings, remarked to Sowles, "What gentlemen are those? It seems to me they are rather rude in their behavior."

A local clothier named William Blaisdell entered the First National Bank just as the robbers were leaving. He asked Sowles what was going on. Sowles replied matter of factly that the strangers had just robbed the bank. Blaisdell turned around and went out into the street, accompanied by Sowles. Seeing Caleb Wallace point his gun, Blaisdell grabbed him and wrestled him down onto the unpaved Main Street, which was muddy from recent rains. As the two were rolling in the mud, two raiders who had been with Wallace inside the First National Bank came to his relief. They pointed their revolvers at Blaisdell and ordered him to stop fighting or else. Grudgingly, he surrendered and allowed himself to be marched, along with Sowles, across the street to the Town Green, a typical New England urban feature situated along Main Street and opposite the banks.

Just after this, Bennett Young came down Main Street

CHAPTER 27: FLOCKING WITH BIRDS OF A FEATHER

riding a horse he had hired from a livery stable just south of the Town Green. He was accompanied by three other raiders who were on foot. Young directed his men to go to a barn in the back, where they could each commandeer a horse. Young then rode in front of the American House hotel, which was next to the Franklin County Bank and diagonally across the intersection from the First National Bank. He held two pistols, one in each hand, which he brandished to the people on the veranda of the hotel. He then put one pistol back in its holster and brought out a proclamation which he intended to read. But the paper slipped out of his hand and dropped to the muddy street. So Young simply called out, to nine or ten civilians who were standing near him, "Gentlemen, I am an officer in the Confederate service. I have been sent here to take this town and I am going to do it! The first person that resists, I will shoot on the spot!" Alamanda Bruce, the raider who had guarded the door during the robbery of the First National Bank, ushered Young's audience across Main Street to the Town Green to join Blaisdell and Sowell, where they were all held under armed watch.

George Conger, a veteran of prior Civil War service in a Vermont cavalry unit, came into town driving a wagon with two horses. As he entered from the north along Main Street, a terrified rider passed him going the opposite way. The rider shouted to Conger, "What is going on? There are men with pistols taking horses from the stables!" Conger surmised that some kind of raid must be happening. He left his team and proceeded cautiously into the downtown area on foot, walking along a sort of boardwalk that provided less messy access to the shops, banks, and other buildings along Main Street. As he did, he encountered Young, mounted and in the street. Young ordered Conger to join the other captives being held on the Town Green. Conger declined to cross the muddy street. Instead, he kept going south toward a crosswalk in front of

American House. But when he arrived, instead of meekly crossing the street as ordered, he bolted in the opposite direction, entered the hotel, and burst out the back door opposite Main Street, yelling out that there was a crime in progress. He told a small crowd of bystanders that they needed to start gathering weapons and horses for a pursuit.

But the raid was not finished.

An elderly man named Collins Huntington was walking down the street in the same direction as Conger. When Young ordered him to cross the street, Huntington ignored him. Young threatened to shoot him. "No! Ye won't shoot me," Huntington replied. After Huntington continued for a few more steps, Young shot him in the back. Through good luck the bullet, even though it entered near his spine, did not hit any vital organs. It only caused a six-inch deep flesh wound. Huntington was finally cowed, though. He walked under his own power across the street to the Town Green, where the captives being held there worked to stanch his bleeding.

As Young and his followers continued to occupy Main Street, Conger and a few others came around the corner near St. Albans Bank into Main Street with weapons and began shooting at the raiders. The raiders returned their fire. The skirmish rapidly became chaotic, particularly because the horses that the raiders had commandeered were completely unused to gunfire. They rapidly became unmanageable, and several threw off their riders. Erasmus Fuller, the owner of the livery stable, quickly grasped that things were amiss. He told one of his employees to take a horse he knew to be sick back to the stable. His tone of command induced one of the raiders to take notice of Fuller. He was ordered to shut up, and to go into a store on the east side of Main Street to get a set of spurs for one of the terrorists. But Fuller, after entering, continued on through the store and out the back door in order to make his escape.

After fleeing the attackers in this way, Fuller soon came to

CHAPTER 27: FLOCKING WITH BIRDS OF A FEATHER

Weldon House, a new hotel that was being constructed about a block east of Main Street. The superintendent, Elinus Morrison, was standing on some scaffolding. When Fuller told him about the raid in progress, Morrison descended and went with Fuller in the direction of Main Street to investigate. When they turned the corner onto the block of stores north of the Town Green, they saw mounted raiders firing shots at civilians. Morrison remarked derisively that the terrorists were bad shots.

As Morrison and Fuller walked along the boardwalk in the direction of the Town Green, they encountered a raider attempting to commandeer a horse from a French-Canadian. Morrison shouted, "What do you want to take that man's horse for?" Taking advantage of the distraction, the would-be victim spurred the horse and quickly escaped. Fuller just then heard a voice cry out, "Look out, that fellow is aiming at you!" Fuller ducked behind an elm tree as Young, still on his horse, fired. Young's shot missed Fuller, but it struck Morrison in the left hand, then penetrated his body, punctured his intestines, and lodged near his spine. Morrison collapsed. His wound would soon prove fatal.

Young decided to get out of town. But, before doing so, he ordered the raiders to unleash a secret weapon. Terrorists commonly rely on bombs and other devices capable of inflicting widespread destruction. In the case of the St. Albans attackers, they had a liquid weapon. It was a form of "Greek Fire," the self-igniting forerunner of modern napalm. In the spring of 1864, the members of the "Confederate Cabinet" in Canada were visited for two weeks by R.C. Bocking, a "mad scientist" type based in Cincinnati. From Bocking, they obtained a formulation to produce a new version of the Greek Fire of ancient renown. The Confederates placed high hopes in this flaming weapon, probably in part because the educated among them had been strongly brought up to believe that the ancient civilizations of Greece and Rome (which, as everyone knew, included the institution of slavery) were morally and culturally superior societies. Huntley, in fact, had been deployed to join Young's group because of his supposed expertise with Greek Fire.[24] Before departing St. Albans, the raiders poured their liquid Greek Fire on several stores and buildings in an attempt to make good on their promise to burn the city. However, as the ancients themselves realized, Greek Fire is extremely tricky to deploy effectively as a weapon. On the damp Vermont surfaces to which it was applied by the terrorists, it quickly fizzled out, causing essentially no damage.[25]

After departing St. Albans, Young's party of approximately thirty made it back to Canada, extremely mud splattered, but loaded with cash. The raid caused a huge uproar in the press on both sides of the border, and the robbers were easy to identify. Over the next few days, some fourteen of them were taken into custody and placed in jail in St. Johns, near the U.S. border, by Canadian authorities.[26] Caleb Wallace, who had been the lead robber at the First National Bank, immediately telegraphed George Sanders in Montreal: "We are captured. Do what you can for us." On October 22, three days after the raid, George arrived in St. Johns and met with the prisoners. That same day, Clement Clay gave George $6,000 to use for the attackers' defense. George also made statements to the media which substantially exaggerated the attack. He said the terror was only beginning, that it was merely the starting point of a new system of warfare that would carry desolation all along the frontier. He predicted that other terrorists would soon attack and sack Buffalo, Detroit, and New York.[27]

Returning to Montreal on October 25, George checked into Room 169 at the St. Lawrence Hotel. John Wilkes Booth, his newest associate, was just down the hall in Room 150.[28]

Chapter 28: The Kidnapping Plot Thickens

Set honour in one eye and death in the other,
And I will look on both indifferently,
For let the gods so speed me as I love
The name of honour more than I fear death
    (Brutus, in Act I, Julius Caesar, by William Shakespeare, 1599)

Johnnie stayed in Canada for nine days, until October 27, 1864. That morning, he went to the Montreal branch of the Ontario Bank to arrange some financial matters. The Confederate Canada Cabinet regularly used this bank to handle its financial transactions. Johnnie opened an account there. Into it he deposited $455, which included $200 dollars in Canadian £20 bills and the rest in the form of a check from a Confederate-affiliated money broker who kept an office across the street from St. Lawrence Hall. Johnnie asked the chief teller about the merits of a bill of exchange. He disclosed that he planned to run the blockade into the South. If he were to be captured, he asked, could the captors cash a bill of exchange? The teller replied that the bill would be honored only if Johnnie personally endorsed it. With that, Johnnie used $300 of his money to purchase a bill of exchange carrying a face value of £61, 12 shillings, 10 pence of British currency. Johnnie figured he would keep it with him to use if he survived his mission to kidnap the President. And perhaps the Canadian bank account might prove useful if he were able to escape to Canada, like the St. Albans raiders.[1]

When he returned to the United States, Johnnie first went to New York. There, his brother Edwin was making preparations for a special charity benefit. The performance was to raise money to erect a statue of William Shakespeare in Central Park. Johnnie, as well as Junius, had agreed months earlier to take part in this benefit. The production on tap was Shakespeare's *Julius Caesar*. It was a highly attractive bill, being the first time the three famous Booth brothers would appear together professionally in a stage performance. The starring role of Brutus was to be played by Edwin, while Junius would play Cassius. Johnnie would play Marc Antony. One of the supporting characters, Trebonius, was to be played by Sam Chester, an actor Johnnie knew well from his days performing in the Richmond theater company, and also from his tour of the South during early 1861.[2] Johnnie's exact activities while in New York City following his return from Montreal remain a mystery. However, one person he definitely met with during this time was Sam Chester. Chester asked Johnnie why he was not acting. Johnnie answered that he did not intend to act in "this part of the country" again, that he had taken his wardrobe to Canada, and that he intended to run the blockade.[3]

By November 8, the day of Lincoln's victory in the presidential election, Johnnie was back in Baltimore. At around that time he exhibited a behavior that is remarkably consistent among terrorists who make their final psychological commitment to perform the ultimate act: He wrote out his manifesto. This document he ironically titled, "To Whom It May Concern." The heading was almost certainly intended as a mocking reference to the way Lincoln had titled his letter that

CHAPTER 28: THE KIDNAPPING PLOT THICKENS

had been presented at the peace talks organized by George Sanders in July.[4] Although Johnnie by his own admission was not much of a writer, his terrorist manifesto reflects that he devoted a great deal of time and attention to its diction and wording. He returned to it and made some substantive cross-outs and edits.

Throughout, Johnnie relied on two fundamental justifications for the atrocious act of kidnapping the President: God and Love.

Johnnie began his composition with a forthright, fatalistic appeal to religious authority. "Right or wrong, God judge me, not man ... All hope for peace is dead, my prayers have proved as idle as my hopes. God's will be done. I go to see, and share the bitter end." He invoked divine endorsement for his adopted cause of injustice, the crushing of the slaveholding republics:

> This country was formed for the *white* not for the black man. And looking upon *African slavery* from the same stand-point, as held by those noble framers of our Constitution, I for one, have ever considered *it*, one of the greatest blessings (both for themselves and us,) that God ever bestowed upon a favored nation. Witness heretofore our wealth and power. Witness their elevation in happiness and enlightenment above their race, elsewhere. I have lived among it most of my life and have seen *less* harsh treatment from Master to Man than I have beheld in the north from father to son. Yet Heaven knows *no one* would be willing to do, *more* for the negro race than I.

Johnnie rested his violent intentions upon passionate love for this cause of injustice. "People of the north, to hate tyranny to love liberty and justice, to strike at wrong and oppression, was the teaching of our fathers." He returned at length to the same theme:

> I love justice, more than I do a country, that disowns it. More than fame and wealth. More (Heaven pardon me if I am wrong) more than a happy home .... Alas, poor Country, Is she to meet her threatened doom. Four years ago, I would have given a thousand lives, to see her remain (as I had always known her) powerful and unbroken. And even now I would hold my life as naught, to see her what she was. O my friends, if the fearful scenes of the past four years had never been enacted, and if what has been had been but a frightful dream, from which we could now awake, with what overflowing hearts would we bless our God. And pray for his continued favor. How I have loved the *old flag* can never, now be known.... . I look upon my early admiration of her glories as a dream. My love (as things stand today) is for the South alone. Nor do I deem it a dishonor in attempting to make for her a prisoner of this man, to whom she owes so much of misery.

Suicidal ideation was sprinkled throughout. Besides the allusions set out above ("share the bitter end," "would have given a thousand lives," "hold my life as naught," etc.), Johnnie equated dying for the desperate Confederate cause with the classical Greek example of warriors suffering the most noble of hopeless battle deaths:

> Even should we allow, they were wrong at the beginning of this contest, *cruelty* and *injustice*, have made the wrong become the right. And they stand now, (before the wonder and admiration of the whole world) as a noble band of patriotic heroes. Hereafter, reading of *their* deeds, Thermopylae will be forgotten.

Later he returned to the same hyperbole: "The south can make no choice. It is either extermination or slavery for *themselves* (worse than death) to draw from. I would know my choice."

And Johnnie's concluding remarks again reflected a reverence for valiant suicide:

> They say she has found *that* "last ditch" which the north have so long derided, and been endeavoring to have her in, forgetting that they are our brothers, and that its impolitic to goad an enemy to madness. Should I reach her in safety and find it true, I will proudly beg permission to triumph or die in that same "ditch" by her side.

To his sister Asia, the lone person to whom he ultimately entrusted his manifesto, Johnnie frankly admitted his admiration for the example, and ensuing martyrdom, of John Brown. He remarked to her, "John Brown was a man inspired, the grandest character of this century."[5] Returning in his manifesto to the same ideas he had expressed four years earlier in "Alow Me a Few Words!", he wrote:

> When I aided in the capture and execution of John Brown, (Who was a murderer on our Western Border, and who was fairly *tried* and *convicted*, – before an impartial judge & jury – of treason), – And who by the way has since been made a God – I was proud of my little share in the transaction, for I deemed it my duty And that I was helping our common country to perform an act of justice. But what was a crime in poor John Brown is now considered (by themselves) as the greatest and only virtue, of the whole Republican party. Strange transmigration, *vice* to become a *virtue*. Simply because *more* indulge in it. I thought then, *as now*, that the abolitionists, were *the only traitors* in the land, And that the entire party, deserved the fate of poor old Brown.

Of course, Johnnie did not disclose the contents of his

manifesto to anyone. Terrorists almost never do. Later he placed it, together with a last letter to his mother, in a sealed envelope. With strict instructions not to open it unless something happened to him, he made Asia lock it in a safe in her home while he looked on.[6]

On November 9, 1864, Johnnie arrived in Washington and checked into the National Hotel, which would become the closest thing he had to a steady residence during his last six months. He was now in Washington for no reason other than full-time work on his kidnapping plot. Two days later he checked out of the National and headed down the peninsula bounded by the tidal portion of the Potomac River, on the south and west, and the Chesapeake Bay, on the east. Located directly across the bay from the birthplace of Frederick Douglass and Harriet Tubman, the peninsula was called then, as now, Southern Maryland. It was a region dominated by a slow-moving, archaic agricultural society, one very much in tune with the traditions of the slaveholding republics. In Southern Maryland the Confederate Secret Service had many of its most trusted operatives. Securing an introduction to this highly clandestine network had been one of the major objectives of Johnnie's visit to Montreal.

For the vital mission of smuggling information, money, and people through the battle lines to and from the Union-controlled North, the Confederate government relied heavily on physicians. Doctors could be expected to be mounted and traveling the roads at any hour of the day or night. They drew no particular suspicion when doing so. Two dependable operatives of the Confederate Secret Service in Southern Maryland were Dr. William Queen and Dr. Samuel Mudd. P.C. Martin, on behalf of the Confederate Cabinet in Montreal, wrote Johnnie a special letter of introduction to these doctors. So, when Johnnie set out to build a Southern Maryland mechanism for escape with an abducted President, the first agents he went about meeting were Dr. Queen and Dr. Mudd.[7]

CHAPTER 28: THE KIDNAPPING PLOT THICKENS

Johnnie was readily accepted by the elderly Dr. Queen, based on the P.C. Martin letter of introduction, and spent several nights with him at his home in Bryantown, in the heart of Southern Maryland. Johnnie quickly got to know Dr. Queen's son-in-law, John Thompson, who was much closer to Johnnie's age. On Sunday morning, the Queen family brought Johnnie with them to attend St. Mary's Catholic Church in Bryantown. Dr. Mudd, who was far younger than Dr. Queen, arrived at St. Mary's, which was not his usual parish, for the morning mass. Before the service, Thompson introduced Johnnie to Dr. Mudd. Dr. Mudd warmly welcomed Johnnie. He invited him to come and stay overnight at the Mudd home. Dr. Mudd's wife Sarah Frances Dyer, called "Frank," was a graduate of a Roman Catholic convent school in Frederick, Maryland. From her time there she was well acquainted with the Roman Catholic hierarchy. The Mudd home was located in an area called Beantown, the nickname for the region of upper Zekiah Creek. Johnnie probably spent more time in Beantown than is generally known. On the night of his most famous act, he would tell a bridge guard he was headed for Beantown. And on that night he in fact went straight to the Mudd residence in Beantown. Johnnie became good friends with Father Peter B. Lenaghan, the parish priest in Beantown. The Roman Catholic Church was oriented toward helping the Confederate cause, as we shall see.[8]

While Johnnie was visiting Beantown, he purchased a dark bay saddle horse from Dr. Mudd's neighbor, George Gardiner. The animal was blind in one eye, but in Johnnie's opinion he was a good mover and well configured. He envisioned the beast as suitable for pulling the buggy that would swiftly carry a bound and gagged Lincoln..[9] When he returned to Washington on this horse, Johnnie's terrorist designs were gaining momentum.

On November 16, 1864, Johnnie once again checked out

of the National, after depositing $1,500 into a new Washington bank account. Most likely, these were funds provided by Confederate-affiliated sponsors. What he did for the next week is unknown. Possibly Johnnie made another visit to Beantown, or visited his sister Asia in Philadelphia, or both. By the 24th, he arrived in New York City for the benefit production of *Julius Caesar*. In society, Johnnie's absence from the stage was an immediate and obvious topic of conversation. Friends joked with Johnnie about his oil speculations, the cover Johnnie generally invoked to explain his acting hiatus. He remarked privately to Sam Chester that he had a better speculation on hand, "one they wouldn't laugh at."

Johnnie started trying to recruit Sam Chester to join his kidnapping plot. This overture betrays the emergence of a new development in Johnnie's thinking. He was probably aware of Confederate intelligence that indicated Lincoln was now much better escorted on his trips to and from the Riggs Cottage, making the plan to capture him during such a trip unfeasible. Also, the intelligence revealed that Lincoln was now making few visits to the Soldiers' Home, which for him was more of a summer country getaway than a year-round second residence. Johnnie approached Chester because he wanted him to play a role in a new plan he had devised. This one would involve moving on Lincoln in a theater.[10]

William Shakespeare statue stands in Central Park, paid by the Booth brothers' 1864 fundraiser.
photo by author

Enormous public interest surrounded the joint appearance of the Booth brothers in *Julius Caesar*. "What a cast!" remarked a critic, "the three

CHAPTER 28: THE KIDNAPPING PLOT THICKENS

best tragedians in the land, and brothers at that, and sons by psychological as well as genealogical descent." Ticket prices were sky high and sold well, raising almost $4,000 for the Shakespeare statue. Scalpers obtained even more. The Winter Garden theater was packed beyond capacity, and police had to be on hand to preserve order among those attempting to get in. When the three brothers made their simultaneous stage entrance, the joyous crowd erupted. At the end of the first act, all three bowed to their mother Mary Ann, seated in a private box.[11]

During the second scene of the second act, at around 8.30 p.m., a most unexpected interruption occurred. Cries of "Fire, Fire!" were heard coming from the back of the audience. In a matter of moments, the entire crowd was in a state of pandemonium. Word quickly spread that the Lafarge House, next door to the Winter Garden, was indeed on fire.[12] This was just one of a whole series of blazes that had been set almost simultaneously, using "Greek Fire," in thirteen hotels and several other public places throughout the city. In its conception, the mass arson attack on New York was the most horrifying Confederate-sponsored act of terror yet.

It has not been established that the selection of the evening of November 25 for the mass arson, when Johnnie was on Broadway playing Marc Antony in *Julius Caesar*, was anything more than a coincidence. The attack was launched by a squad of eight terrorists, although two of them dropped out at the last minute. It was led by Robert Martin and John Headley, both veterans of John Hunt Morgan's terror expedition into Indiana and Ohio. They were assisted by a West Point dropout and escaped Confederate prisoner of war named Robert Kennedy. The financing and other sponsorship of the New York City arson attack are traceable primarily to Jacob Thompson, a Confederate government commissioner who stationed himself in Toronto. Confederate support for

Johnnie's operation against Lincoln appears connected more closely to George Sanders and his main patron in the Confederate government Clement Clay, who both had their headquarters in Montreal.[13] But our knowledge of the secret inner workings of this so-called "Canada Cabinet" remains sketchy. Clay, who was consulted by Thompson, also approved the New York attack. In an indiscreet moment, Robert Martin a year later confessed to a cellmate that he had known Johnnie, and that he had been aware of Johnnie's plot against Lincoln.[14]

Robert Martin and his terrorist squad filtered into New York at the end of October 1864. Their first initiative was to meet with the leaders of the "Order of American Knights" in an attempt to produce a coordinated uprising in connection with the outbreak of fires. But Henry Seward learned, through Union intelligence, about the existence of some kind of arson plot. He sent telegrams to the mayors of New York, Chicago, Buffalo, Detroit, and other cities, warning them that a plan was afoot to set fires to these cities on Election Day, November 8. Union soldiers were stationed in numbers in New York City. This demoralized the "American Knights" and caused them to abandon any ideas about a mass uprising. The garrisoning of troops forced Martin and his followers to lay low for the time being. But they were supplied by their sponsors with plenty of money, so they did not need to leave the city. Their funds were ample to enable them to live in hotel rooms all over the city for several weeks after the election.[15]

While awaiting developments, the attackers could not help but read the gleeful reports that appeared in New York newspapers about the total war of mass destruction that was being carried into the South by Union Generals William Sherman and Philip Sheridan. Articles trumpeted statistics: 1,000 barns burned; 300,000 bushels of corn, 500 barrels of flour, and 600,000 bushels of wheat, all destroyed. The news reinforced their terrorist resolve. Robert Martin refined his plan to burn the city, even without any plan for a simultaneous uprising. Emile Longuemare, a leader of the Order of American Knights, while declining to participate in the attack itself, assisted by procuring the "Greek Fire" chemical to be used to set the fires. Martin's followers picked it up from a chemist in 144 glass bottles containing four ounces each. They also bought chemicals such as turpentine and rosin to serve as accelerants.[16]

Martin and his group rented a cottage adjacent to Central Park to serve as their headquarters during the mission. There, they selected the places where they would set the fires. Typical of terrorists, they would avoid guarded facilities, such as federal and municipal buildings. Instead, they concentrated on civilian lodgings, softer targets that were easy to access and that could result in spectacular mass destruction and casualties. Already a world-class city, New York featured numerous large hotels with 500 or more rooms. Gigantic unprotected wood frame structures, these were ideal candidates for arson. Using a variety of fake names, all of the terrorists checked into rooms in multiple hotels.

At precisely 8 o'clock on Friday, November 25, just as Johnnie and his brothers were getting started with *Julius Caesar*, Robert Martin and his raiders began starting their fires. Typically, each arsonist stacked a hotel room's bedding in a heap, added movable wood furniture, doused the whole pile with "Greek Fire," and then left the premises quickly. However, their inexperience and lack of practice showed. In many instances, they failed to use all their "Greek Fire." In their haste, they also failed to use the accelerants. But worst of all, the terrorists failed to appreciate that, in order to spread and engulf entire buildings, a fire would need an ample supply of oxygen. They made the mistake of leaving the windows closed in the hotel rooms where they started the fires. As a result, even though their spectacular flames rapidly attracted attention, the fires turned out to be relatively easy to put out. Despite causing a major panic, they resulted in minimal damage.[17]

In the Winter Garden, word was quickly received that the fire at the neighboring Lafarge House was under control. Stepping out of his role as Brutus, Edwin Booth strode on stage and pleaded for order. The police, who initially were in the house to control the crowd, now took charge to prevent any panic. The audience milled about for half an hour, then returned to their seats. The performance resumed, with Johnnie giving the famous funeral oration of Marc Antony in the third act. At the play's end, the three brothers received lavish applause, with Johnnie perhaps drawing the greatest share.[18]

L to R, John Wilkes Booth, Edwin Booth, and Junius Booth, in posed photo, Nov. 27, 1864. By this time, Johnnie was already deep into his conspiracy to kidnap Lincoln

The next morning at breakfast, a heated argument erupted between Johnnie and Edwin. Johnnie tried to justify the terrorist attack, using the rationale that it was a justified form of retaliation for Union atrocities. Edwin was having none of it. He regarded Johnnie's passion for the Confederate cause as delusional, morally wrong, and highly foolish. However, the two of them patched things up well enough to pose together, with Junius, the next day for a portrait, posing in costume, just

CHAPTER 28: THE KIDNAPPING PLOT THICKENS

as they had appeared in Act 3 of *Julius Caesar*.[19]

As it happened, Johnnie's most trusted contact in the Canada Cabinet, the dashing blockade runner P.C. Martin, had less than two weeks to live. In early December his 73-foot schooner, the *Marie Victoria*, foundered in a winter storm on the St. Lawrence River near Bic, Quebec. P.C. Martin and everybody else on board perished. Johnnie's prized theatrical wardrobe, and with it any thought of returning to his theatrical career, was lost.[20]

On December 12, 1864, Johnnie returned to Washington. He plunged deeply into work on his own terrorist cell. Johnnie made another trip to Southern Maryland to network with Dr. Mudd and other Confederate operatives. Shortly afterward, on December 23, he was ready for a staged introduction by Dr. Samuel Mudd to an agent who would be very important to his organization.

Samuel Mudd came into Washington City and checked into the Pennsylvania Hotel, on C Street. He and Johnnie, who was residing as usual at the National, went for an evening walk. Acting as if it were purely by chance, they overtook a young man named John Surratt, walking along the sidewalk with a companion named Louis Weichmann who was dressed in a U.S. Army uniform. Mudd cried out, "Surratt, Surratt!" Mudd and Surratt shook hands warmly and greeted each other like they were long-lost friends. Surratt introduced Weichmann to Mudd, and Mudd introduced his companion to Surratt, referring to him as "Mr. Boone." "Mr. Boone" immediately invited Surratt and Weichmann to join him in his rooms at the National Hotel. He ordered everyone drinks. After taking them out into the hallway and out of Weichmann's earshot, Johnnie engaged in some conversation, first with Mudd, and then with Surratt. After returning to the room, Johnnie took out an envelope. On the back of it, he drew a diagram consisting of some lines while having an animated conversation with Mudd and Surratt in low tones that were unintelligible to Weichmann. Johnnie found something of a kindred spirit in Surratt. From that night forward, John Surratt became Johnnie's closest associate, replacing P.C. Martin as his primary link to the organized Confederacy.

In reality, Samuel Mudd and John Surratt were close associates in the Confederate Secret Service, which had been using John Surratt effectively as an agent for much of the war.[21] He was a clever and capable messenger, smuggling dispatches and information about Union troop movements back and forth across the Potomac and through the Southern Maryland border lands. Surratt and Johnnie had much in common. Like Johnnie, John Surratt had attended St. Charles College without graduating. Like Johnnie, his father drank liquor heavily, and, also like Junius Brutus Booth, Surratt's father died while John Surratt was a teenager. Similar to Johnnie, John Surratt quit school when his father died.[22] John Surratt came from a solidly upper middle class family. Like Johnnie, he grew up in a rural part of Maryland. The town of Surrattsville (where John Surratt's father had been the postmaster) was located in the heart of Southern Maryland, about two hours' horse carriage drive southeast of downtown Washington. This was John Surratt's home turf, which made him perfect for facilitating Johnnie's escape plans. And John Surratt immediately and wholeheartedly embraced Johnnie's plot. On January 13, 1865, Surratt quit his new job with the Adams Express Company to dedicate himself full time to the Lincoln kidnapping scheme.[23]

Johnnie soon met John Surratt's 43-year-old mother, the widowed Mary Surratt. Mary was an ardent Confederate supporter who was eager to provide covert aid and comfort to the rebels. From her late husband she had inherited both an urban boarding house, located at 541 H Street, NW[24] between Sixth and Seventh Streets in Washington City, and also the country tavern and lodging house in Surrattsville. Mary was aware of her son's role in the Confederate spy service. She did

CHAPTER 28: THE KIDNAPPING PLOT THICKENS

her best to fill for him in carrying on secret business while he was away on assignment. Surrattsville was located on the main illicit avenue of communication, and her tavern served as a way station and safe house for a steady stream of Confederate messengers. She volunteered its use for Johnnie's plans. She also made her city boarding house available, when necessary, to help Johnnie and his followers. Johnnie, after the beginning of 1865, became a regular caller at Mary Surratt's city house. On the many occasions when John Surratt was absent, Johnnie met privately with Mary Surratt, often for several hours.[25] She was well acquainted with his intentions, and was thrilled to be a party to them. On the day of the assassination, Mary would go out of her way to give Johnnie as much help as anyone.

Chapter 29: Enter the Muscle Hijacker

Terrorists typically engage in efforts to radicalize, and to co-opt into their plans for violent activities, persons who sympathize with their chosen cause. Johnnie was not an exception. His overtures to Mike O'Laughlen and Sam Arnold are good examples of radicalizing. Mike and Sam were perfectly happy to be done with the struggle to preserve the slaveholding republics at the time Johnnie approached them. But to Johnnie, his old friends Mike and Sam were basically Confederate soldiers on an informal leave. He felt they ought to be ready to be roused into supporting violent "last-ditch" efforts in support of the flagging cause.

In all probability, Johnnie also approached several others, unsuccessfully.[1] Sam Chester is the only one who later admitted to it. Johnnie repeatedly justified his absence from the stage by telling fellow actors he was engaging in oil speculation, and that he was already making money from it. To Chester, however, he confided that the real "speculation" was something much different. On a Manhattan night in late December, Johnnie took a walk with Chester on Fourth Street. He revealed that he was running a large conspiracy to capture the heads of the Government, including the President, and take them to Richmond. He asked Chester to aid in this effort by opening a back door of the theater, or by putting out the gas lights in the theater, at the critical moment.[2] Chester parried by saying he had to think of his wife and mother. To this, Johnnie replied that he would leave Chester's family "two or three thousand dollars." This provides some interesting insight into Johnnie's ideation. Implicitly it conceded that the attack Johnnie was asking Chester to join would almost certainly be a suicide mission for the cause.

Johnnie persisted in his overtures to Chester. In January, 1865, he sent him $50, together with a request that he travel to Washington to join his group. Chester did not go. On his next visit to New York the following month, Johnnie resumed his pressure. He told Chester he had previously approached another South-sympathizing actor, John Mathews, and that Mathews had declined to join because he was frightened. To Chester, Johnnie called Mathews a coward, "not fit to live," and made a veiled threat to kill Mathews. He also threatened to ruin Chester in his professional occupation if he did not join in the attack. Chester remained steadfast in declining for the sake of his "family." Chester returned the money, which Johnnie grudgingly accepted, conceding he was short of funds. Johnnie said to Chester that he, Johnnie, or an ally, would need to go to "Richmond" to secure more "means" to carry out the plot.[3]

Johnnie was more successful with followers who were sent to him by John Surratt and the Confederate Secret Service. Lewis Powell, who joined Johnnie's terrorist team in January 1865, was a prototype of the "muscle hijacker." His personality was described as sweet, lovable, and kind, but with a streak of stubbornness. He was born in Alabama but, shortly afterwards, his father received the calling as a Baptist preacher. The family moved to northern Florida where his father had a congregation. Lewis grew to be 6 foot 1 and 1/2 inches, broad and robust. Although he was only 17, when the war broke out he passed himself off as 19 in order to enlist, even before his two older brothers, in the Confederate army. After taking part in a series of important Virginia battles, Lewis suffered a gunshot wound in the right wrist at the battle of Gettysburg, Pennsylvania on July 2, 1863. The next day, when Lee's army was defeated in its most momentous assault of the entire war, Lewis was captured by the victorious Union forces. He was placed in a college hospital at Gettysburg. His wound quickly healed, and he took on duty as a male nurse. He was called "Doc Powell," a nickname given to him as a boy because of his fondness for taking care of injured and sick animals.[4]

While working at the Gettysburg hospital, Doc Powell became friends with Maggie Branson, a Confederate sympathizer who volunteered to help care for the war wounded. Like John Surratt, Maggie had a mother who owned and operated an urban boarding house, this one in Baltimore. Probably due to help from Maggie Branson, on September 1, 1863, Powell was transferred to duty at a hospital outside Baltimore. From there, the Branson family soon aided Powell in making his escape from Union custody.[5] Powell went to Warrenton, Virginia, 50 miles southwest of Washington, where he immediately became attached to John Mosby's rangers, the Confederacy's main guerrilla force operating in Virginia and occasionally Maryland.[6] He took up residence there with a family named Payne. The Paynes later remembered that Powell was "chivalrous, generous, gallant, and particularly fond of children." They also acknowledged that he was not particularly bright.[7]

Already an escaped prisoner, Powell was a perfect fit for Mosby's gang of raiders. Mosby basically only included in his force boys without any attachments, such as wives or children, who were willing to live on the edge.[8] They did not wear regular CSA uniforms. Their key defensive maneuver was the "skedaddle," a Viet Cong-like melting away in all directions after a violent raid. Mosby's "rangers" pretended to be ordinary

CHAPTER 29: ENTER THE MUSCLE HIJACKER

civilian non-combatants. They knew from experience that any who were caught would likely be swiftly hanged.

"Private Powell" is listed as a member of Mosby's Company B beginning October 1, 1863. Records show his continued presence in that group into the fourth quarter of 1864. There is no record that he was paid; however, Mosby's irregulars were generally supported by the proceeds of plunder. There is reason to believe Powell participated in Mosby's Greenback raid on October 14, 1864, in which a $170,000 payroll destined for Union soldiers was stolen from a derailed train. A month afterwards, Powell was involved when Mosby's forces at Kabletown, West Virginia, about 15 miles southwest of Harpers Ferry, ambushed and routed a Union cavalry squad, taking prisoner its commander Captain Richard Blazer.[9]

Powell is reported to have been part of an escort that accompanied the captive Blazer to Richmond.[10] Nothing really is known about what he did while he was there. In other circumstances, we know that Powell was a good soldier. He carried out orders faithfully. He did not desert, nor was he one to conjure up an elaborate plan of action all by himself. He must have been reassigned by someone in authority, probably in Richmond, from Mosby's guerrillas to another, even more irregular, rebel unit. This was the band of terrorists being assembled by Johnnie, with the active assistance of the Confederate Secret Service, to strike at President Lincoln.

On January 13, 1865, the same day John Surratt quit his delivery service job, Powell, adopting the false name by which he would be known to the time of his death, crossed the front as "Lewis Paine." He entered Union-controlled territory at Alexandria, Virginia. He immediately went to Baltimore and sought out Maggie Branson. Very likely the entire Branson family, including Maggie's father Joseph Branson (who was living in Richmond at the time), were active in the Confederate Secret Service. The Branson family probably also knew about the plan to kidnap Lincoln, which explains why Powell was sent to them. Powell promptly checked into a nearby residence hotel, where he stayed put until an opening developed ten days later at the Branson boarding house. The Branson sisters, Maggie and her younger sister Mary, practiced subterfuge by introducing Powell to the servants and the other boarders as "Mr. Payne, from Frederick County, Maryland." "Mr. Payne" lacked any visible means of support. Nor did he display any sense of urgency to look for employment. The Confederate Secret Service, after the assassination, succeeded in keeping its involvement with Powell in the shadows. But someone obviously provided him with both funds and instructions to travel to Baltimore and stand by for further duty.[11]

There is solid evidence that officials of the Roman Catholic Church were involved with the Confederate Secret Service, and that they took action to help Johnnie and John Surratt. Just after Powell's arrival in Baltimore, John McGill, the Bishop of Richmond, suddenly wrote two letters, one addressed to Louis Weichmann, and the other to Paul Dubreuil, father superior of St. Mary's Seminary in Baltimore. Weichmann, who was involved as we have seen in the December 23 introduction of John Surratt to Johnnie, considered himself to be an intimate friend of Surratt. He had been Surratt's roommate during his prior sojourn at St. Charles College. The two of them frequently shared a room in Mary Surratt's homes, both in the country and in the city. Louis had left St. Charles, shortly after Surratt, and moved to Washington, where he secured a job as a Union military clerk. He had moved into Mary Surratt's downtown Washington boarding house on November 1, 1864. Bishop McGill's letter greatly surprised Weichmann, because it responded out of nowhere to seemingly forgotten correspondence Weichmann had written over a year earlier, asking the Bishop's permission to resume his studies for the ministry.

Father Dubreuil responded to the Bishop's letter with

CHAPTER 29: ENTER THE MUSCLE HIJACKER

tremendous alacrity. He immediately invited Weichmann to take a Saturday off from his job and to come to Baltimore for a visit to discuss the matter. Weichmann eagerly reported this welcomed development to John Surratt. Surratt then informed Weichmann that he himself was, at that very moment, planning to go to Baltimore. Surratt suggested that the two of them should travel to Baltimore together.[12] This entire chain of events involving Weichmann's invitation to visit the Baltimore seminary was almost certainly a clever ruse, one engineered so that John Surratt would be accompanied by a U.S. government employee, Weichmann, on his covert mission. Thus, his travels to and from Baltimore would be less likely to arouse suspicion and attention from the authorities. Baltimore was basically a city under military occupation, where travelers were watched. Surratt was already a suspected spy.

On January 21, 1865, Weichmann and Surratt went to Baltimore and checked into a hotel room where they stayed together overnight. The next morning, a Sunday, Surratt left by himself in a carriage, after informing Weichmann that he, Surratt, had $300 in gold in his possession, and that he had business in town that Weichmann was not welcome to join. Weichmann went about his own meeting with Father Dubreuil. But he felt, in his word, "nettled" at being spoken to in a cold way by his intimate friend.[13] Surratt's actual business was to meet secretly with "Mr. Payne," which he did at the business premises of another Confederate agent, David Preston Parr.[14] Some of the money Surratt carried probably was conveyed to Powell. In fact, providing Confederate funds for Powell and Johnnie's other terrorist cell members was almost certainly Surratt's main reason for going to Baltimore.

Just before Surratt's Baltimore visit, he and Thomas Harbin, another Confederate agent who was part of Johnnie's kidnapping plot, went to Port Tobacco, on the Potomac in Southern Maryland. Their business was to purchase one or more small boats for use in ferrying a captive Lincoln, as well as his terrorist assailants, across the river into Virginia. They succeeded in buying a flat-bottomed boat, large enough to carry fifteen people, from a smuggler named Richard Smoot. Surratt told Smoot: "The need of the boat will be an event of unprecedented magnitude in the history of the country which will startle and astound the entire world." During this visit, Surratt and Harbin also recruited a local blockade runner, the German-born George Andrew Atzerodt, to take charge of the boat and to hide it while standing by to use it on a lucrative mission. Atzerodt was a tradesman, not a slave owner. He had no known convictions around the slavery issue beyond being racist, an attitude that was, in 1865, almost as ubiquitous among Northern whites as it was among Southerners. But he would soon become one of Johnnie's devoted followers.[15]

Another follower whom Surratt added to Johnnie's terrorist team was 22-year-old Davey Herold. Herold had met Johnnie briefly after one of his 1863 performances. He was taken with Johnnie's persona as a good fellow. But Herold knew John Surratt very well. Described by his family's neighbors as "light and trifling," Herold did not hold any strong political views. He had the spirit of a boy, constantly larking, playing with guns and dogs. He was employed for a period of time as a pharmacy clerk, but quit the job. As the only boy in the family, he was a little spoiled. After his father died in the fall of 1864, Herold apparently had no real need to work. This left him time to hang out with Johnnie and become involved in his plans. Herold was an asset to the kidnapping scheme because, like Surratt, he was intimately familiar with the roads and terrain along the planned escape route in Southern Maryland.[16]

After Powell's arrival in Baltimore and with the addition of Atzerodt and Herold, Johnnie's terrorist team was basically in position to strike when an opportunity arose. He had his Baltimore conscripts, Sam Arnold and Mike O'Laughlen,

CHAPTER 29: ENTER THE MUSCLE HIJACKER

make the six-hour journey to Washington City to transport into town his trunk filled with firearms and knives. Johnnie greatly surprised Arnold and O'Laughlen when he revealed to them his new idea of capturing Lincoln while he was in the theater. He brought both of them on a reconnaissance of Ford's Theater. Johnnie had Arnold and O'Laughlen check into a hotel near the National, where he himself continued to reside, to await developments.[17]

Johnnie, meanwhile, turned his attention to undercover work of an entirely different hue. In January 1865, former U.S. Senator John Hale, the long-time abolitionist stalwart who had recently lost a bid for re-election in his home state of New Hampshire, moved with his family to the National Hotel in Washington City. This hotel was also Johnnie's habitual Washington residence, as we have seen. Johnnie soon came into contact with Senator Hale's unmarried daughter, 24-year-old Lucy. Though charitably described as "rather stout," Lucy was both vivacious and flirtatious. She had previously encouraged romantic overtures from ambitious boys such as Bill Chandler, a future Senator and Cabinet officer, and Oliver Wendell Holmes, Jr., a future Supreme Court Justice. Now Johnnie made a big show, even to his family, of falling madly in love with Lucy. For instance, he stayed up all night with his brother June, painstakingly composing a Valentine's Day acrostic for Lucy. Lucy was thoroughly infatuated with Johnnie as well. The two of them became an item and were seen together in the National's ballroom. They began talking serious romance.[18]

The extreme oddity that the inveterate bachelor and passionate Southern-sympathizing Johnnie should suddenly be swept away by the daughter of a prominent abolitionist was not lost on his family. Johnnie's choice also seemed a little strange in that Lucy was by no means a beauty, and in that she was already 24 years old. Johnnie dedicated himself to the romantic chase by inviting Lucy's cousin John Wentworth, who was himself an aspiring politico, to room with him at the National. Reminiscent of his conduct with Isabel Sumner, Johnnie bought Lucy and himself engagement rings. He proposed marriage, which she accepted.

Johnnie was a master of misdirection and deception, even fooling several of his most studious biographers about Lucy.[19] It is wholly unrealistic and unreasonable to evaluate Johnnie's engagement to Lucy Hale as anything other than a highly skilled acting job. Johnnie never revealed to Lucy any hint of his true obsession, which was to become a righteous, unapologetic terrorist, abducting or assassinating the President. Johnnie was mad, by everyday standards, essentially planning to commit suicide. So, what did it matter if he made a promise of marriage that he did not plan to keep? To his inner self, Johnnie undoubtedly justified perfidy on the grounds that it was necessary for the cause, and probably, also, on the grounds that Lucy was the daughter of an abolitionist "traitor."

Even while he was courting Lucy, Johnnie continued to populate his sex life with prostitutes. His relationship with one of them, the young and pretty Ella Starr, flamed so hot that other men who knew the scene described her as "fierce as a tigress" in her devotion to him. Ella was a 20-year-old Baltimore native who had moved to Washington to take up the oldest profession in a brothel managed by her own mother. At the same time Johnnie was engaged to Lucy Hale, Ella was writing him notes such as: "[P]lease call this evening or as soon as you receive this note. I'll not detain you for five minutes – for God's sake come!" Another pleaded: "Please try and come down as soon after two as possible? You can *dine* privately with me. So do not mind your dinner. Be *very* good until I see you. Anything that pleases you will be acceptable."[20]

From mid-January 1865 Johnnie and his followers waited patiently for a chance to strike. Sam Arnold and Mike O'Laughlen, well funded, moved to a longer-term rental at a

CHAPTER 29: ENTER THE MUSCLE HIJACKER

Washington City boarding house.[21] But the President's schedule did not make Johnnie's mission easy. He stayed very busy directing the war effort. Lincoln did go to Ford's Theater on February 10, 1865 to see Asia's husband, John Sleeper Clarke, perform in *Everybody's Friend*. But Johnnie, perhaps not wanting his brother-in-law present at the scene of the terror attack, did not strike. He went to New York City to visit his mother, who was now living there with Edwin. He tried to enlist Chester, as we have seen, and he probably also met with Confederate agents to obtain more funds.[22]

Johnnie used his romantic liaison with Lucy Hale to obtain an official pass to the U.S. Capitol to witness Lincoln's inauguration for a second term on March 4, 1865. Exactly what he planned to do, and what he did, that day will always be a matter of some controversy. He later told Chester, in an animated manner: "What an excellent chance I had to kill the President, if I had wished, on inauguration day!"[23] But this could just be one of his many deceptions.

As part of the inaugural ceremonies, Lincoln and the Justices of the Supreme Court had to make their way from the Senate chamber, in the northerly wing of the Capitol, through the circular Rotunda modeled on the Pantheon of Rome, to the front portico, which is outside the eastern side of the Rotunda. The Rotunda that day was basically a mob scene, with many important dignitaries unable to plow through the crowd to enter the area near the portico where Lincoln was due to deliver his speech from a temporary platform. As Lincoln made his way across the Rotunda, a young man burst through the line of Capitol police who were holding open a path for the procession. He seemed frantic to approach Lincoln. Lieutenant John A. Westfall, who was one of the Capitol police, grabbed this man by the arm, and a physical and verbal struggle between them ensued. The man argued strenuously that he had every right to join the procession. He displayed to the officers his pass for the event. The man was handsome, spoke with the diction of someone cultured, and was so self-assured that the policemen began to wonder whether he was perhaps a new Congressman they did not yet know. So, while they did not let him join the procession, they did not arrest the man, either. They allowed him to go back into the crowd. After the assassination, multiple policemen who dealt with this intruder would have no doubt: The man who had tried so hard to approach Lincoln had been John Wilkes Booth.[24]

Oblivious to the turmoil in the Rotunda, Lincoln spoke moments afterwards on the east portico of the Capitol building. It was one of his most notable addresses, offering an olive branch to the defeated.

> With malice toward none, with charity for all; with firmness in the right, as God gives us to see the right, let us strive on to finish the work we are in, to bind up the nation's wounds; to care for him who shall have borne the battle, and for his widow, and his orphan – to do all which may achieve and cherish a just and lasting peace among ourselves, and with all nations.

Of course Johnnie, the terrorist, was not interested in harvesting olive branches.

If his after-the-fact identification by four policemen and the doorkeeper are true, then by March 4, 1865, Johnnie's thoughts had already definitively turned to killing, and not just kidnapping, Lincoln. This was just about the same time that the Confederate Secret Service changed its fifteen-character cipher key. The secret code had formerly been "Complete Victory," but now it became "Come Retribution." And Johnnie knew all about that cipher key.[25] By the beginning of March, the Confederate cause was becoming desperate, and so was Johnnie. Richmond, its capital, was crumbling under siege. Its beleaguered lines of defense were slowly weakening. In his final diary, Johnnie himself would explain his motivation in

CHAPTER 29: ENTER THE MUSCLE HIJACKER

this way: "For six months we had worked to capture. But our cause being almost lost, something decisive & great must be done."[26]

In forming his resolve to commit the ultimate act of terrorism, Johnnie was motivated by a strong desire to go down in posterity. He remarked to Chester that he could live in history if he assassinated Lincoln. He quoted from Act 3 of Colley Cibber's adaptation of *Richard III*, Johnnie's own signature play: "Fame not more survives from good than evil deeds. / The ambitious youth who fired the Ephesian Dome / Outlives in fame the pious fool who reared it." To a friend, Johnnie insisted that "the man who killed Abraham Lincoln would occupy a higher niche of fame than George Washington."[27]

Shortly after the inauguration, Johnnie faced difficulties within the ranks of his followers. On Monday, March 13, O'Laughlen failed to return promptly to Washington after a weekend in Baltimore. Meanwhile, Powell had been arrested by federal authorities in Baltimore based on a complaint against him by an African American woman employed by the Bransons. Powell and the Bransons later claimed the reason for this arrest was because Powell had given the woman a "whipping" because she was "insolent" and "failed to clean up his room."[28] This "whipping" story has the ring of a deception and a cover up. For one thing, it is out of character for Powell, based on everything else we know about him. For another, despite intense Government interest in "Paine" after the assassination, no alleged "whipping victim" was ever interviewed, or called as a witness. A white servant from the Branson boarding house, who accompanied Maggie Branson to the conspiracy trial to testify about the violence, actually gave testimony about the "whipping" in support of a proffered insanity defense for Powell. Much later, she admitted she "knew more" than she told at the trial.

Truth almost certainly is found in a small item that appeared in the *Baltimore Sun* on March 15, 1865. "Louis Paine," in fact, was arrested in Baltimore on Monday, March 13, but it was not for "whipping" someone. He was "charged with being a rebel spy." Most likely, a tip from the African American woman working in the Branson boarding home is what led to Powell's arrest. Federal authorities thus had one of Johnnie's most valuable muscle men in custody, and he was in their hands on a highly relevant charge. Had Powell been investigated thoroughly and questioned carefully, Johnnie's terrorist plot might well have been discovered and foiled. Just as an accurate report of John Brown's impending attack on Harpers Ferry went for naught, so the investigation of Powell was also bungled. Neither "Paine's" real identity nor his real reason for being in Baltimore were uncovered.

The federal detectives got "Paine" to admit he had some knowledge of Mosby's raiders. They also induced him to do some talking about them (but the names he gave the detectives were all fake). Although the lead investigator later said he "knew in his bones" he was dealing with some kind of spy, the detectives felt they lacked any tangible proof. The next day, "Paine" was required to take a new loyalty oath. He was released, but ordered to "stay north of Philadelphia." In effect, he was being banned from further association with the Bransons.[29] Powell, however, had no intention whatever of heading north. Following a last lunch with the Branson family, he took the next train to Washington City, where he would wait at the ready to serve John Wilkes Booth.[30]

Johnnie called together his entire band of followers the next night, March 15, 1865. This was the first time they were ever assembled and, for most of them, it was the first time they met the others. The evening started with Johnnie taking Powell, John Surratt, and two of Mary Surratt's young female boarders to see a play from the President's box at Ford's Theater.[31]

CHAPTER 29: ENTER THE MUSCLE HIJACKER

Disguised as a social outing, this theater visit was designed by Johnnie to acquaint his followers with the scene of the big event that he had planned for them. Johnnie had studied carefully the gleaming new architecture of Ford's Theater, which was only a year old. The President's box at Ford's Theater was well suited for his plans, in that it was physically isolated by a solid wall from the rest of the audience. It was very hard for anyone located elsewhere in the theater to see what was happening inside.[32] There was only one door to the box, which led into a passageway from the balcony level of the theater. During the existence of the plot, Johnnie got one of his friends who worked as a carpenter in the theater to customize this passageway entrance. After the assassination, it was discovered that a small niche had been carved in the plaster wall near this entry door. Johnnie used it, just before the assassination, to wedge a three-foot long wooden board in between the door and the niche. This effectively blocked the door from being opened by anyone outside.[33] In Johnnie's

John Wilkes Booth and his key followers: Counterclockwise, David Herold, George Atzerodt, Ned Spangler, Mike O'Laughlen, Lewis Payne (real name Lewis Powell), and Sam Arnold

kidnapping scheme, any other occupants of the box would be killed or otherwise incapacitated while Lincoln was being lowered to the stage. Jamming the door in this manner was intended to prevent possible rescuers from entering the box during this process.

After dropping off the girls at the Surratt boarding house just before midnight, Johnnie, Surratt, and Powell went to a private upstairs room, which Johnnie had reserved, in Gautier's Restaurant at 252 Pennsylvania Avenue. There they met up with Arnold, O'Laughlen and the two Southern Maryland connections, Herold and Atzerodt. The group played cards until the waiter, an African American, went home at 1.30 a.m. Then they got down to business, reviewing Johnnie's plan to kidnap the President at Ford's Theater.

Johnnie went over each participant's role. On his cue, O'Laughlen and Herold would put out the theater gaslights. In the ensuing darkness, Arnold, Johnnie and Atzerodt would rush into the President's box, jam the door shut, seize Lincoln, and kill or incapacitate any other occupants of the box. Johnnie and Atzerodt would handcuff the President and lower him to the stage, where Powell, code name "Mosby," would wait to "catch" him.[34] Others would gather around him there and, in the darkness, hustle him out the back of the building to a waiting carriage, which would be ready to make a quick dash out of the city before the pursuers could get organized.[35]

The meeting grew heated. Sam Arnold protested that the entire plan was unrealistic and, in his mind, had not a shadow of a chance of success. He raised the objection that the kidnap party would be required to cross a bridge that was guarded by troops. Johnnie responded that the raiders would overpower them. Sam protested that this skirmish would bring about a general alarm, which would lead to the entire party being caught. When Mike O'Laughlen started to agree with Sam, Johnnie responded with his own criticism of the doubters: "You find fault with everything" concerned with the plan. Sam

CHAPTER 29: ENTER THE MUSCLE HIJACKER

responded with words to the effect of, "No, I wanted to have a chance, and I intend to have it. I agreed that you could be the leader of my party, but not my executioner." Johnnie replied with a flash of authority, reminding Sam of the oath he had taken to support Johnnie's terrorist enterprise. "You know, you are liable to be shot." Sam persisted in his dissent. He had agreed to participate in an outdoor kidnapping, not one in a theater. Johnnie remained emphatic. The theater abduction was his day and night obsession. He had no thought of relenting. "Well, gentlemen, if the worst comes to the worst, I shall know what to do." It was a thinly veiled allusion to converting the kidnapping to a straight-up assassination.[36]

As a concession to Johnnie's leadership, Sam finally turned his protest into an ultimatum – either the attack would happen that week, or not at all.[37] The men finally left Gautier's at around 5 o'clock in the morning.[38]

Next day, Johnnie went to the room of John Mathews. Despite the story Johnnie had spun in his attempt to recruit Chester, Mathews remained one of his best actor friends. Mathews was staying in a home across the street from Ford's Theater. There Johnnie lounged on the bed while he chatted with Mathews and two others. This would be the same bed where President Lincoln would expire less than a month later.

From the chit-chat, Johnnie learned that the next day Mathews and others would give a charity performance of *Still Waters Run Deep* for the benefit of disabled veterans at Campbell Hospital, on the grounds of the Soldiers' Home. Johnnie seized on this as an opportunity for an elaborate deception aimed at his own followers. The next afternoon, at 2 o'clock, Johnnie sent urgent messages for all the conspirators to meet in front of the Mary Surratt boarding house. Within 45 minutes, they gathered. Johnnie told them President Lincoln was headed for the Campbell Hospital production, and that an outdoor abduction, as envisioned by the original plan, would now proceed. Johnnie and the others in his group rode out toward the Soldiers' Home, while Herold made his way across the Anacostia River, also known as the Eastern Branch of the Potomac, carrying rifles and supplies to be used by the escaping kidnapping party.[39] Separately, Surratt and Atzerodt crossed to Southern Maryland to stand ready for the flight. This Soldiers' Home expedition was bound to be fruitless, since Lincoln in fact had no intention of going to the Campbell Hospital performance. It was all merely a clever rehearsal, designed to test the sagging spirits of the two wavering conspirators, Arnold and O'Laughlen. Surratt made use of the occasion as an opportunity to stash the rifles and supplies that Herold had carried to Southern Maryland in an obscure crawl space within his family's Surrattsville tavern.[40] There, these items would await Johnnie's final flight from Washington.

Upon returning from the "failed" Campbell Hospital expedition, Johnnie told his followers they were dismissed. Arnold and O'Laughlen returned to Baltimore. Powell also left Washington, traveling to New York City.[41] Johnnie, after a single stage performance in a benefit the next night, joined him in New York. He watched his brother Edwin give the concluding performance in his widely acclaimed run of *One Hundred Nights of Hamlet*. However, there was never any ebb in Johnnie's passion for striking a terrorist blow, one virtually certain to result in the death of those involved. On March 25, Johnnie returned to Washington after paying a visit to his mother in New York City. A letter she wrote to him three days after his departure reveals she sensed his intent:[42]

> I did part with you sadly – & I still feel sad, very much so … I never yet doubted your love and devotion to me – in fact I always gave you praise for being the fondest of all my boys – but since you leave me to grief, I must doubt it – I am no Roman mother I love my dear ones, before Country or anything else. Heaven guard you is my constant prayer.

Chapter 30: As Brave a Man as General Lee

At 1.16 p.m. on Saturday, March 25, 1865, inside Fort Lafayette in New York Harbor, Robert Cobb Kennedy, one of the Confederate New York arsonists who had been caught, was executed using a device that yanked his body, by a rope connected to a noose around his neck, six feet upwards into the air with a swift jerk. His last bitter words were, "Gentlemen, this is murder. I warn you, Jefferson Davis will retaliate!"[1] That same morning, Johnnie left New York on a train, returning to Baltimore by way of Philadelphia. He summoned Sam Arnold to join him at Barnum's Hotel but, before Sam could arrive from his family home on the northwest outskirts of town, Johnnie had already left on another train to Washington City. Two days later, Sam wrote a letter, which Johnnie decided to keep rather than destroy as he generally did with all other correspondence related to his terror cell. Its wording gives a modicum of insight from Johnnie's closest counterpart to a Hugh Forbes:[2]

> Was business so important that you could not remain in Balto. till I saw you? ... How inconsiderate you have been! When I left you, you stated we would not

meet in a month or so. Therefore, I made application for employment, an answer to which I shall receive during the week. I told my parents I had ceased with you. Can I, then, come under existing circumstances, come as you request? You know full well the G—t suspicions something is going on there: therefore, the undertaking is becoming more complicated. Why not, for the present, desist, for various reasons, which if you look into, you can readily see, without my making any mention thereof. ….

None, no not one, were more in favour of this enterprise than myself, and today would be there, had you not done as you have – by this I mean, manner of proceeding. I am, as you well know, in need. I am, you may say, in rags, whereas to-day I ought to be well-clothed. ….

Do not act rashly or in haste. I would prefer your first query, go and see how it will be taken in R—d, and ere long I shall be better prepared to again be with you. I dislike writing, would sooner verbally make known my views, yet your non-writing causes me thus to proceed.

Do not in anger peruse this. Weigh all I have said, and as a rational man and a friend, you cannot censure or upbraid my conduct.

Johnnie, quite clearly, had presented Sam with a plan of action that no "rational man" could endorse. And Sam's suggestion that Johnnie "go and see how it will be taken in Richmond" strongly indicates that the new plan involved something other than the idea of a kidnapping, which Johnnie had long ago assured Sam met with the full support of the Confederate

Chapter 30: As Brave a Man as General Lee

Plan of downtown Washington City, 1865

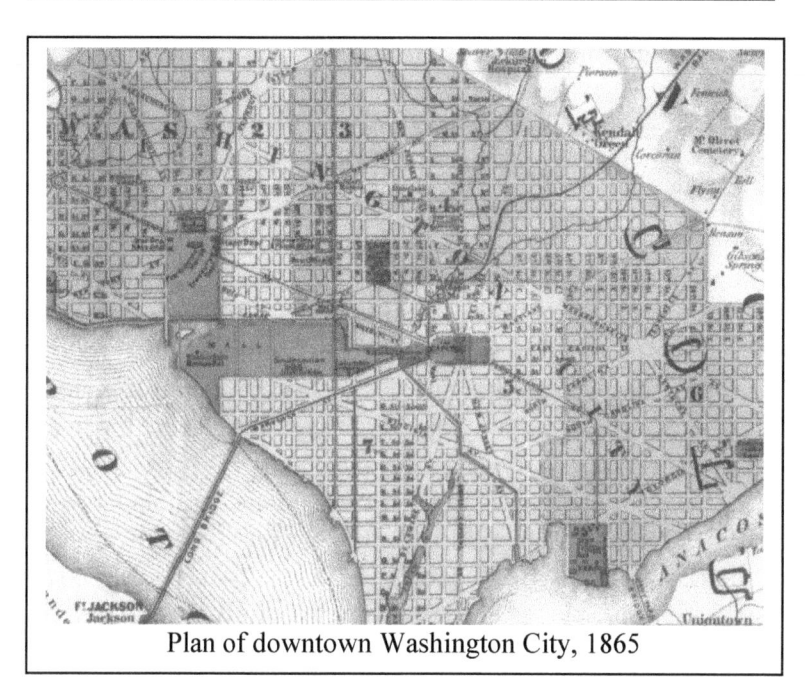

government.

On Monday, March 27, the *Washington Evening Star* published an announcement that President Lincoln would attend an opera two nights later at Ford's Theater. This news triggered Johnnie and John Surratt into action. Johnnie sent Mike O'Laughlen a telegram that said:[3] "Get word to Sam. Come on with or without him Wednesday morning. We sell that day sure. Don't fail." That same day, Powell arrived in Washington City, where he used yet another fictitious name to take a room at the Herndon Hotel that had been arranged for him by Surratt's friend, a Catholic school teacher named Annie Ward.[4] But the March 29 attempt was not to be. Contrary to what the newspaper had stated, Lincoln did not attend any opera at Ford's. He was not even in Washington, because he had left to travel to the front outside Richmond, where he would oversee the final assault on the beleaguered Confederate capital.

Johnnie had no intention of placing his terrorist project on hold, as Sam had suggested in his March 27 letter. He continued to orchestrate the people he had in Washington City. Powell, the former Mosby mounted raider, was now placed in charge of the group's horses.[5] Atzerodt, uprooted from Southern Maryland, was posted in a different Washington boarding house. Along with Herold, he was regularly treated to drinks and entertainment. While Powell, as a fugitive from his sentence of banishment, remained in seclusion in his room at the Herndon House, Johnnie, Herold, and Atzerodt frequently gathered. They generally did so at the stables where the horses were boarded.

Lodging Johnnie's followers in hotels, and his horses in stables, cost a substantial amount of money. To supplement his financing from Confederate sources, Johnnie turned to requiring his friends and followers to contribute money. This was typical terrorist behavior. Johnnie saw no need to repay his debts. He felt that, like Johnnie himself, the followers should sacrifice all their money, as well as their lives, to the cause. He borrowed $500, a hefty sum, from Mike O'Laughlen. He had John Surratt borrow money from Atzerodt.[6] From Simonds, who had finally achieved modest financial success with the Pithole oil well, he received another $500. The change in Johnnie's thinking was palpable. Since he would no longer need his buggy for transporting a kidnapped Lincoln, he had Ned Spangler, Johnnie's "groom" as some called him, but who was employed as a carpenter and scene shifter at Ford's Theater, put it up for sale. Eventually it brought $250. Johnnie's need for horses to carry off the kidnapping also came to an end. He got his men working to sell them off.[7] He failed to pay the balance due on the flat-bottomed boat that was reserved for crossing the Potomac with a large group of captors and the captive. This vessel, too, would no longer be needed.[8]

Richmond was evacuated and set afire by retreating

CHAPTER 30: AS BRAVE A MAN AS GENERAL LEE

Confederate forces on Sunday, April 2, 1865. When the news reached Washington City the following day, delirium ensued. Cannons boomed, rockets shrieked, bands blared, and crowds of revelers filled the streets. Johnnie, at that time, was on his way to a very brief visit to Montreal.[9] Probably, he was seeking more CSA Secret Service funds.

John Surratt finished his last covert trip to Richmond the day before the city fell. Among his other activities, he met with Jefferson Davis. The CSA Secretary of State, Judah Benjamin, gave him dispatches to take to Canada, together with $200 in gold pieces. Surratt also carried dispatches from Benjamin to the Confederate Canada Cabinet, which he cleverly concealed inside a copy of James Redpath's *The Life of John Brown*.[10] Surratt was well practiced in travels across federal lines. By the evening of Monday, April 3, he arrived at his mother's boarding house in Washington. After a quick dinner, he changed his clothes and left for the train station. Before departing for parts north, he briefly stopped to speak with his mother Mary. It would be their final goodbye.[11]

On April 5, Johnnie registered at a hotel in Newport, Rhode Island, as "J.W. Booth and Lady, Boston." The "lady" has never been identified. Some have speculated, without proof, that she was Lucy Hale. Just as likely, she was not a proper society "lady" such as Lucy, but one of his paid consorts. He was known to travel occasionally with Ella Starr.[12] From Newport, Johnnie went to Boston, where he presented an inscribed bloodstone ring to his close friend, theater manager Orlando Tompkins. Tompkins asked about the occasion for this unexpected gift. "I'll never see you again," was Johnnie's cryptic reply.[13] From Boston he went to New York, where he had his final conversation with actor Sam Chester.[14]

On Saturday, April 8, Booth returned to Washington, where he again checked into the National Hotel. That same day, General Lee surrendered the remnants of his haggard Confederate army to Grant at Appomattox. The news set off an even larger and wilder celebration than had the fall of Richmond, a week previously. In cities all across the United States candles and gas lamps were lit to pay tribute to the victory with a nighttime "illumination." At the same time there began a vindictive lashing out against those persons who had been perceived as Copperheads and Confederate sympathizers. Everyone was now expected to display the U.S. flag in a visible demonstration of patriotism. Those who did not fell under immediate suspicion. A mob threatened to seize a New York banker because he displayed a flag that was considered mockingly small.[15] All this ardor provided even more impetus to Johnnie's terrorist urge. He chafed at the suggestion that Lee's surrender effectively ended the Confederacy. One of his friends, a local restaurant owner, praised Lee as being the greatest general in the world. Johnnie rejoined, "He is a very good general but I don't like the way he surrendered." In Johnnie's eyes, Lee had received his sword in the Senate chamber in Richmond and swore he would never surrender, that he would die on the battlefield before he would surrender.[16]

Lincoln returned to Washington on April 9. Johnnie immediately intensified his attention to his terrorist plan. As celebrations unfolded the following day, Monday, April 10, Johnnie paid a lengthy visit to the Surratt boarding house. John Surratt was in Canada. In his absence, Johnnie spent most of his time with Mary Surratt. Exactly what he discussed with her is unknown. However, there can be little doubt that she knew exactly what was on his mind. The following day, Tuesday, Mary asked her boarder Louis Weichmann to take off work to drive her out to Surrattsville, where she was trying to settle some financial affairs. He easily obtained permission, because all of Washington City was still celebrating the great victory. Johnnie, whose own buggy was being sold by Spangler,

CHAPTER 30: AS BRAVE A MAN AS GENERAL LEE

provided $10 for Weichmann to rent a carriage for Mary. While Mary and Weichmann were on the road to Surrattsville, they encountered her tenant, the tavernkeeper John Lloyd, who was himself coming into the city. Mary advised Lloyd that the guns hidden in the tavern several weeks earlier by her son would be "needed soon."[17] This message must have been based on what Mary and Johnnie had discussed the day before. That same evening at 8 o'clock, Lincoln emerged at a White House window to make some public remarks. Johnnie, Herold, and Powell were all present in the large crowd of listeners outside. Johnnie's vehement remarks in response to Lincoln's appearance made it clear to Herold that Johnnie was determined for he and his followers to kill Lincoln. In fact, Powell later said that Johnnie tried to get him to shoot at Lincoln while the President was speaking.[18] With Lincoln now back in town, Johnnie was determined to take advantage of the first available opportunity to carry out the assassination.

The following day, Wednesday, April 12, Spangler finally sold Johnnie's carriage, netting $260. That evening, Johnnie came into Ford's Theater as a production was in progress. He proclaimed to his friend Harry Ford, the theater manager, "We are all slaves now." He proceeded to have a half-hour conversation with Ford and two other theater employees, in which he expressed bitterness about the fate of the Southern cause. He was ranting about African Americans. In particular, he was upset that they were guarding Confederate prisoners.[19]

On the evening of Thursday, April 13, Washington City had a grand illumination. The entire city was set aglow in celebration. Gas jets spelled the word "Union" over the Willard Hotel, the dome of the Capitol was lit, and the Patent Office displayed 5,000 candles. Crowds surged through the streets, and bands played. Bonfires blazed, rockets roared, and liquor flowed freely.[20] President Lincoln stayed home with a headache, but Mary Lincoln accompanied General Grant and his wife Julia on a carriage tour of the city.[21] The carriage passed by Ford's Theater. As it did, Mary Lincoln made a remark that revealed General Grant had already accepted an invitation from the Lincolns to join them in attending the next night's performance of the farce, *Our American Cousin*. Mary Lincoln had made herself thoroughly unpopular with Julia Grant during the Lincolns' recent visit to the front lines near Richmond. During that trip, Mary Lincoln had demonstrated, in front of Julia, her overbearing attitude toward her husband, her jealousy of people who spoke to him, and her habit of making unpleasant, snippy comments to his guests. From the moment Julia Grant heard about the theater invitation her husband had accepted, her mind churned over how to get out of it.[22]

Johnnie apparently worked off an educated guess that the Lincolns would attend the Friday night theater performance at one of Washington City's two theaters. Lincoln was a longtime devotee of stage comedies. He had reportedly once remarked, "Some find me wrong to attend the theater, but it serves me well to have a good laugh with a crowd of people."[23] Johnnie had a longtime close personal and professional relationship with John Ford, who owned Ford's Theater, and he was an even closer social companion of John Ford's brother Harry, who helped manage it. The Fords, like Johnnie, were Baltimoreans. Johnnie regularly hung out at Ford's the entire winter of 1864–1865, even though he performed only on one benefit night. The Fords cheerfully received his mail for him. Johnnie was also on good terms with Dwight Hess, the manager of Grover's Theater. Johnnie went to Grover's on the afternoon of Thursday, April 13, to urge Hess to invite the President to the theater.[24] He may have done the same thing with his friends the Fords, though they later denied it.[25] That same Thursday, Johnnie got word to his followers that the next day they would see action. He rapidly devised the final assignments. With his familiarity with, and command of, the

CHAPTER 30: AS BRAVE A MAN AS GENERAL LEE

theater, he would deal with Lincoln by himself. Atzerodt would kill Vice-President Johnson. And Powell, accompanied by Herold, would kill Henry Seward, the Secretary of State.

Johnnie's selection of Henry as a victim presents something of a puzzle. The notion that it was motivated by a political strategy lacks credibility. The Secretary of State, at the time, was not a successor in line for the presidency after the death of the President and Vice-President. Based on his remarks to people like Sam Chester, it seems Johnnie's main objective was simply to cause as much chaos and terror as possible. Additionally, Henry was hated by Johnnie because it was well known to Marylanders that, prior to the Civil War, he had sought the Presidency as a Republican abolitionist candidate.[26] George Kane, Johnnie's friend, held Henry responsible for his lengthy preventative detention early in the war. Johnnie was probably well aware of that sentiment. Henry, interestingly, was very taken with Johnnie's older brother Edwin. He had personally hosted Edwin for a dinner in his honor on March 11, 1864.[27]

Powell made his first scouting visit to Henry Seward's home, on Lafayette Square across Pennsylvania Avenue from the White House, on the morning of Thursday, April 13. He approached the window of the dining room and asked the male nurse inside about Henry's condition. The question made sense, because it was all over the newspapers that Henry, at that time, was laid up in bed. Henry had sustained serious injuries, including a broken jaw and a broken upper arm, in a carriage accident caused by a runaway horse just one week earlier.[28] In fact, Johnnie's decision to attack Henry may have been something of a crime of opportunity, born of an awareness of news coverage of his accident and resulting convalescence. Powell returned to the window the next morning and again asked about Henry.[29] The nurse would soon have plenty of reasons to remember being asked these questions by Powell.

On Thursday afternoon at 3.30 p.m. Mike O'Laughlen, accompanied by his friend Benjamin Early and two other Baltimore residents, boarded a train for Washington City. Their common purpose was to attend the grand illumination. The four of them arrived in Washington at around 5.00 o'clock, whereupon they started drinking in preparation for a night of partying. Soon afterwards, Mike and Early went to the National Hotel. Early waited while Mike went to look for Johnnie. Whether or not Mike actually met up with Johnnie and, if so, what they discussed, will never be known. Mike told his companions he would go back to the National to speak with his friend the next morning. Mike and Early soon rejoined the group from Baltimore. They continued with an evening full of drinking, eating, consorting with comfort women, and roaming about downtown Washington City. The real festivities started at around midnight, and continued until 2.00 a.m. At that point, the group of four checked into two rooms at the Metropolitan Hotel, about one block east of the National. In an arrangement that suggests O'Laughlen was responsible for funding much of the bacchanalia, he had one room to himself, while the other three shared the other room. The four of them arranged a wakeup call for 7 o'clock.[30]

Johnnie, too, wandered about the streets, looking over the grand illumination festivities. At just the same time that Mike and his companions finally turned in for the night, Johnnie put pen to paper for the last letter he would ever write to his mother:

April 14 2 A.M.

Dearest Mother:

I know you expect a letter, and am sure you will hardly forgive me. But indeed I have nothing to write about. Everything is dull; that is, has been till last night.

Everything was bright and splendid. More so in my

CHAPTER 30: AS BRAVE A MAN AS GENERAL LEE

eyes if it had been a display in a nobler cause.

But so goes the world. Might makes right. I only drop you these few lines to let you know I am well, and to say I have not heard from you [lately]. Had one from Rose. With best love to you all,

I am your affectionate son ever.

John

The next morning, Johnnie's core followers were activated early. Lewis Powell, for a second consecutive morning, scouted Seward's residence and spoke to the male nurse through the dining room window.[31] Before 8 a.m., George Atzerodt paid in advance and checked into a room at the Kirkwood Hotel, where Vice-President Andrew Johnson was staying. He left the hotel without even looking at the room.[32] Davey Herold reserved a roan horse named Charley, whose ride was so smooth he was generally reserved for ladies, to be picked up from John Fletcher's stable at 4.15 p.m. Johnnie, meanwhile, had breakfast at the National Hotel, even though he apparently spent the night somewhere else, possibly with Ella Starr. Johnnie was observed at the National chatting briefly with Lucy Hale. Mike O'Laughlen brought his Baltimore companions with him to the National and asked them to remain in the lobby while he looked for Johnnie. By the time they got tired of waiting around, both Johnnie and Mike were already gone.[33]

Johnnie walked over to nearby Ford's Theater, where he was very popular and had free run of the place. As soon as he arrived, one of the clerks employed in the theater ticket office went inside and brought out a long letter in a woman's handwriting that had arrived for Johnnie. Harry Ford, seeing him, immediately needled: "Here is a man who don't like General Lee." Johnnie muttered something to the effect that he was a "Southern man." He assured Harry that he was "just as brave a man as General Lee." Harry continued with his teasing. "Well, you have not yet got three stars to show for it." Johnnie did not take the bait any deeper. He went back to reading his letter. After taking his time, chuckling over some passages, he destroyed it, as was his usual practice. Johnnie acted extremely nonchalant when Harry Ford excitedly informed him that President Lincoln had accepted an invitation to attend the benefit performance of *Our American Cousin* at Ford's that evening. For Harry, it was excellent news. Harry was busy getting new posters printed up to announce Lincoln's plan to attend, which was bound to guarantee a large house and corresponding receipts.[34]

One of the most fateful days in the history of the United States, April 14, 1865, was Good Friday. Secretary of War Stanton circulated a note to all of his departments instructing that all employees "who are members of religious denominations that have religious services on this day" were to be allowed off work at noon. One devout Catholic employee was Louis Weichmann, Mary Surratt's boarder. Weichmann took off work, went to mass, and then returned to the Surratt boarding house. At around 2.30 p.m., Weichmann was summoned by Mary's knock on his bedroom door. She asked if he would drive her again that afternoon to "the country," meaning Surrattsville. Weichmann quickly assented. Mary gave Weichmann $10 to use to rent the carriage. As Louis was heading out the door, he came face to face with Johnnie, entering the house. Johnnie shook Weichmann's hand pleasantly.[35]

Weichmann went around the corner to rent the carriage. At the stable, he ran into Atzerodt, who was trying, unsuccessfully, to rent a horse from the same place. The talkative German volunteered to Weichmann that he intended to go into the country and that, once he found a horse to rent, he would send for "Payne." When Weichmann returned to the

CHAPTER 30: AS BRAVE A MAN AS GENERAL LEE

boarding house with the carriage, Johnnie was just finishing up his conversation with Mary. He left, and Mary stepped into the vehicle. Then she remembered that she needed to bring some "things" belonging to Johnnie on her journey. She went back in the house and returned with two paper packages, one of which was filled with documents, the other of which was 6–8 inches in diameter. She told Weichmann it contained glass.

On the way out of the city, the carriage passed a group of cavalrymen, lolling and enjoying themselves on the grass, which their horses were nibbling. Mary had Weichmann halt the buggy so she could ask a bystander what these soldiers were doing. "They are pickets," he replied. She asked if they would be out all night. He replied that no, they were generally called in at about 8 o'clock in the evening. "I am glad to know that," she responded. Personally scouting the route to Surrattsville was one of her real reasons for making the trip.

John Lloyd, keeper of Mary's Surrattsville tavern, returned there at 5 o'clock after having spent the day in court in Upper Marlboro, Maryland. When he arrived, he found Mary waiting to give him a message, one she made sure Weichmann did not overhear. The "shooting irons" previously left with him by her son John Surratt would be picked up that night, she told him, along with two bottles of whiskey. She asked him to have them ready. She handed Lloyd her package belonging to Johnnie, which turned out to be a pair of binoculars. Mary then had Weichmann drive her back to Washington City. During the

Mary Surratt

two-hour drive, Weichmann casually remarked on how Johnnie seemed to be without employment. "Booth is done acting," Mary replied. "He is going to New York very soon, never to return." When they were about a mile away, the carriage came over a small hill. Washington City, still swimming in "illumination," came into view. Raising her hands, Mary made a cryptic remark to Weichmann, "I am afraid all this rejoicing will be turned into mourning, and all this glory into sadness." When Weichmann asked her what she meant, she responded that after sunshine there is always a storm. The people are too proud and licentious, she said. "God will punish them." [36]

Mary Surratt was technically incorrect in her statement that Johnnie was done acting. Johnnie, in fact, had one final performance on his schedule.

By now, Johnnie had sold all his horses. Thus, like his small group of followers, Johnnie needed to rent one to use for the getaway. To do so, he went to the stable of James Pumphrey at around noon. Pumphrey informed Johnnie that the sorrel horse he was in the habit of riding was not available. He offered in its place a small bay mare, 14 or 14 1/2 hands high, with black legs, a black tail, and a white star on her forehead. Johnnie accepted the offer. After his visit to Mary Surratt at her boarding house just prior to her Surrattsville journey, where he encountered Weichmann, he returned to Pumphrey's stable to pick up the rented horse. When Johnnie asked for a tie-rein to hitch her while he stopped at a restaurant, Pumphrey strongly warned Johnnie against it. The feisty filly was in the habit of breaking a bridle. Johnnie, he said, would need to find a "boy" to hold her. Soon afterwards, while prancing about on 10th Street in front of Ford's Theater, Johnnie rode in front of the open door of Jim Ferguson's saloon next door, where he was a regular and often bought the whole house drinks. "Jim, see what a nice horse I have!" Johnnie called out. He expressed satisfaction at the way the small mare took off "like a cat" the

CHAPTER 30: AS BRAVE A MAN AS GENERAL LEE

moment she felt a spur.[37]

Riding up Pennsylvania Avenue, Johnnie encountered his friend and fellow actor, John Mathews. Mathews asked if Johnnie had seen the prisoners, former Confederate officers, being led in a group up the street. Johnnie acknowledged that he had. Placing a hand on his forehead, he exclaimed, "Great God, I have no longer a country!" Then he asked Mathews for a favor. "I may leave town tonight and I have a letter which I desire to publish in the *National Intelligencer*; please see to it for me unless I see you tomorrow before 10 o'clock." With that, he handed Mathews his latest manifesto, in a sealed envelope.[38]

Johnnie rode around the block to an alley leading from F Street into the area behind Ford's Theater. After practicing taking his rented horse in and out of the alley, he approached the back door of Ford's. He asked a boy standing nearby to go inside for James Maddox, the property man. Maddox was one of Johnnie's favorite companions in the theater crew. Three months earlier, Maddox and Ned Spangler had assisted James Gifford, the head carpenter at Ford's Theater and considered by his employer to be one of the most talented theater carpenters anywhere, in building a small stable for Johnnie, located on this very alley only steps from the theater's back door. They had customized Johnnie's rented stable to hold two items crucial for the kidnapping plot: a horse and a buggy. However, both the horse and buggy had recently been sold. So now the stable was empty. Johnnie planned to box his steed inside it until later that evening. For this he needed the key to the stable, which was normally kept on a nail in the theater.[39] Maddox and Spangler both accompanied Johnnie and the bay mare down the alley to the stable, and they opened it up for him. When they started to remove the horse's bridle, Johnnie objected. He informed them he intended to ride later, after dark, and he did not want to have to put the bit and bridle back on.

Acknowledging the animal was difficult to handle, he remarked to Spangler, "She is a bad little bitch." Maddox fastened the stable door in front of her and handed Johnnie the key. The three of them walked back through Ford's, crossed the stage, and went out the front door to 10th Street. They then had a drink together in Scipiano Grillo's restaurant, next door to Ford's on the opposite side from Ferguson's.[40]

Johnnie had known Gifford and Spangler ever since he was a boy. Both did significant construction work for his father on Tudor Hall. Gifford, Spangler and Maddox were popular with Johnnie because they quietly sympathized with his political views. And they did more than just build Johnnie a stable behind the theater. Someone, perhaps Johnnie himself but more likely one of the carpenters, at some point created a small niche in the plaster near the door to the President's box at Ford's. That niche had only one purpose: to hold the end of a two-by-two wooden brace, about 3 feet long, which when inserted into the niche and wedged against the door, would effectively bar the door and make it very difficult for anyone to enter the box. Someone also used a sharp knife to dig out an inconspicuous little peephole in the wooden door to the President's box.[41]

Grillo soon encountered Davey Herold, on the street in front of his restaurant. In response to Herold's query, Grillo informed him that Johnnie had just been in his restaurant for a drink. The two of them walked together for a while. At some point, Grillo noticed that Herold seemed to be limping. Davey then stopped and fooled around with his boot, at which point Grillo could see the reason for the limp. Herold was carrying a large dagger inside the boot. Grillo asked him why. Herold replied, "I am going into the country tonight on horseback, and it will be handy there."

Apparently, Herold caught up with Johnnie shortly thereafter. By 5.45 p.m., he arrived at the Kirkwood House to summon Atzerodt to a meeting with Johnnie and "Wood," the

CHAPTER 30: AS BRAVE A MAN AS GENERAL LEE

alias under which Atzerodt knew Powell. But first he asked Atzerodt to open his room. Inside, he took the knife out of his boot and tucked it underneath the sheets of the still-made up bed. He also left a large revolver. Then the two made their way together to the Herndon House, in the same block as Ford's Theater, where Johnnie assembled his action squad for the final time at around 6.30 or 7 o'clock.[42]

Exactly how Johnnie coordinated his group's terror attack in this meeting will never be known for sure. The accounts of the meeting that we have come from Atzerodt, who was using them unsuccessfully in an attempt to avoid execution, and his versions of the event changed over time.[43] We can surmise, from the results, that Johnnie decided to follow a strategy very similar to that used by the New York arson terrorists on the night of his Winter Garden performance in *Julius Caesar*. During the course of a theater performance, there would be a synchronized, simultaneous strike. All four of the raiders had arranged to have mounts to facilitate their travels. In the unlikely event that all went smoothly, they were to join up east of the Anacostia following their coordinated missions in an effort to head south together across the Potomac.

The Lincolns were late for the performance of *Our American Cousin*. The theater, which had been sparsely attended the previous evening, was now packed with spectators, most of whom were anticipating the arrival of the presidential party. The Lincolns arrived about 8.30, a half hour into the first act of the farce. Taking the places originally intended for the Grants were a young couple, a friend of Mary Lincoln named Clara Harris, and Clara's fiancée who was also her step-brother, an army major named Henry Rathbone. When the presence of the Lincoln party in the theater became known, even before they went into the President's box, the actors stopped playing and the orchestra struck up the familiar strains of "Hail to the Chief." The joyous audience rose in unison and received the President with vociferous cheering. The President and Mrs. Lincoln and their guests then entered the box.[44] Their seats, in reality, were two boxes, from which a partition had been removed to make a larger "Presidential" box.[45] There they sat down to watch the play continue.

 In darkness, after returning from his final briefing with Mary Surratt that had occurred at around 9 o'clock, Johnnie once again led his rented mare down the alleyways that led to the back door of Ford's Theater. He opened that door and called out for Ned Spangler, in a voice loud enough to spark the curiosity of some African American neighbors who lived nearby on the alley. Spangler did not respond right away, so Johnnie repeated his call three or four times. One of the neighbors chimed in by calling out, through a window, "Ned, Mr. Booth wants you." Finally, Spangler appeared briefly at the door. Johnnie needed someone to hold the fractious horse while he went inside the theater. Spangler was very busy helping to change the sets, a job he had to do punctually every few minutes for the duration of the performance. His absence would be swiftly missed, so he could not hold the animal. Ultimately, either Spangler or Maddox corralled a young stage hand named John Burrough, who was generally called "Peanuts" because he used to sell peanuts to the theater goers. Spangler rapidly ordered Peanuts to hold Johnnie's horse. Peanuts protested that he had a stage door to watch. Spangler said watch the horse anyway, that he would take the blame if anything untoward happened at the door in the absence of Peanuts. Peanuts obeyed. He sat down on a bench in the dark alley, holding the reins to the mare. The neighbors soon noticed she was loudly stamping and fidgeting with impatience. Peanuts had to walk her back and forth to try to calm her.[46]

Chapter 31: A Tragedy in Three Acts

Johnnie's command performance was carefully scripted to occur during the third act, second scene of *Our American Cousin*. Thus, he had to allow some minutes to pass before his entrance. After making his way into the audience portion of the theater by a passageway underneath the stage, Johnnie left the building and entered the bar next door. He wanted some whiskey and water to help steel his nerve.[1] John Buckingham, the front doorkeeper at Ford's, saw Johnnie leave, then return a few minutes thereafter. Johnnie asked Buckingham what time it was. Buckingham suggested he check for himself at a clock in the theater lobby. Johnnie then ascended to the theater's dress circle, or balcony. He made his way past spectators who were sitting along the wall of the dress circle outside the President's box. One of them had to scoot forward, so that Johnnie could pass behind. A lone aide, who was not a trained bodyguard, sat outside the passageway leading to the President's box. Johnnie smoothly and confidently presented his card, with a look that quickly satisfied the aide Johnnie was expected.[2] He let Johnnie pass without further question.

Once inside the box, Johnnie tightly secured the passageway door with his wooden wedge. He quickly and quietly advanced toward Lincoln, who was facing the front of the box in a cushioned rocking chair to the left of his wife Mary. Lincoln's chair was located in the front left corner of the box, at the point farthest from the stage below, and thus giving the best view.[3] Before anyone had any inkling he was present, Johnnie cocked and fired a single shot from a small pocket handgun, a Philadelphia Deringer, into the President's head from point blank range.[4] The ball entered the back of Lincoln's head, not far from the base of the skull, about an inch and a half left of center. It crossed over the centerline of the brain, at a level too high to sever the brain stem and cause instant death. The bullet lodged just behind and above Lincoln's right eye.[5] Due to the application of artificial respiration and his prodigal physical strength,[6] the President would go on breathing until morning, but he would never regain consciousness.

Major Rathbone was sitting to the right of the President, about 7 feet away and closer to the stage, when he was startled by the report of Johnnie's Deringer. Peering through a cloud of smoke, he saw a man standing behind Lincoln. He rose to his feet and tried to grab the intruder. Discarding the pistol, Johnnie pulled free, then lunged back toward him, brandishing his dagger inscribed with the words, "America, Land of the Free."[7] Johnnie tried to stab Rathbone in the chest. Instinctively, Rathbone threw up his arm to block the knife. Suffering a deep flesh wound in his left arm, between the elbow and the shoulder, he reeled backward. Johnnie did not continue with

The President's Box at Ford's Theater, Washington, D.C.
photo by author

CHAPTER 31: A TRAGEDY IN THREE ACTS

the combat. Fast as lightning, he mounted the railing on the forward half of the box, and then leaped down onto the stage 12 feet below the balustrade. His spur caught on one of the flags hanging in front of the President's box. After landing awkwardly and falling on one knee, he staggered to his feet and exited, with extreme haste, stage right, dragging a piece of the flag along with him.[8]

As he ran across the stage, Johnnie cried out the words, "*Sic semper tyrannis.*" Many in the audience heard him, but only a few actually understood the line he would immortalize. Translated as "Thus always to tyrants," the Latin phrase was attributed to Marcus Junius Brutus, just after he had plunged his knife into Julius Caesar. However, the line does not appear in the script of Shakespeare's *Julius Caesar*. Another of Johnnie's stage improvisations, its origin appears to rest with George Mason of Alexandria, Virginia, who has been dubbed America's "thoughtful revolutionary." Mason proposed that the phrase "*sic semper tyrannis*" be adopted as the state motto of Virginia at the time of its constitutional convention in 1776. Despite its repeated association with notorious acts of terrorism, the phrase today remains legislatively enshrined on the field of Virginia's state seal.[9] As an occasional Virginia militiaman, Johnnie knew about the phrase, and its association with the assassination of Caesar. Thus, he adapted it into the script for his own tragic performance.

Few people in the audience immediately realized what had happened. But one of them, a large man named Joseph Stewart who was sitting in the front row, climbed on stage in a matter of seconds to go after Johnnie. His pursuit was delayed for just a moment as he fumbled to figure out how to open the back door of the theater through which Johnnie had just disappeared. This gave Johnnie all the lead time he needed. Once in the alley, after brushing aside "Peanuts" with the butt end of his dagger, Johnnie deftly climbed astride his waiting mare, spun her around and was off at a gallop, disappearing out of the alley just as Stewart emerged.[10]

One mile away, the second act of Johnnie's play was set to begin.

The home of Henry Seward was located at 17 Madison Place in an area, then called Lafayette Park, that was diagonally across Pennsylvania Avenue from the official presidential residence. At about 10.15 p.m., just as Johnnie was starting his performance at Ford's Theater, Lewis Powell made his presence known by ringing the doorbell. William H. Bell, a 19-year-old African American employed as a waiter in the Seward household, opened the door in response. Powell, looking well dressed with a pink and gray overcoat and a white collar, entered and showed Bell a small package that he was carrying in his hand. This package, Powell said, contained important medicine sent by Dr. Verdi for Mr. Seward. Almost certainly aided in devising this ruse by the former pharmacy clerk David Herold, Johnnie and his followers knew Dr. Verdi was Henry's attending physician. Dr. Verdi had given very specific instructions, Powell continued. Powell was to personally direct Mr. Seward on how to take the medicine.

Bell resisted Powell. He told him he could not go up to see Secretary Seward, that it was against his orders to let anyone go upstairs. Powell, in response, kept repeating the same thing over and over. Dr. Verdi had given very specific orders. Powell must personally tell Mr. Seward how to take the medicine. While Powell spoke with Bell, he inched his way slowly toward the staircase that led to the second floor, where Henry's bedroom was located. Bell kept telling him over and over, "No." Powell kept inching toward the stairs. Finally, Powell started up the stairs. Bell nimbly jumped around Powell, and started backing up in front of him as Powell ascended. However, the thought crossed Bell's mind that Powell might indeed be right. Maybe he really was sent by Dr. Verdi.

CHAPTER 31: A TRAGEDY IN THREE ACTS

When Powell reached the top of the staircase, he and Bell were met by Frederick Seward, Henry's son. Frederick was currently acting temporarily as Secretary of State in his father's absence, as Henry was laid up in bed following his carriage accident the previous week. Only that afternoon, Frederick had attended a Cabinet meeting with President Lincoln and General Grant, a session in which Lincoln insisted all present should get on their knees and pray with humility and thanksgiving for the war victory. Powell repeated to Frederick Seward his orders to see Henry personally. At that moment, Frederick's sister, Fanny Seward, emerged from the patient's bedroom and unhelpfully informed everyone, "Fred, father is awake now." Frederick went into his father's bedroom briefly. He emerged and told Powell, "You cannot see him." Powell then began pleading with Frederick Seward. Frederick was steadfast. "I am the proprietor here, and his son. If you cannot leave your message with me, you cannot leave it at all."[11]

Powell pretended to accept this decision. He mumbled something and turned as if to descend the stairs. He went down about three steps, treading so hard he prompted Bell to scold him so he would not wake the Secretary: "Don't walk so heavy." Then, suddenly, Powell turned around and sprang back up the steps. He drew a revolver from his pocket which he pointed at Frederick Seward's temple and tried to fire. But the

Lewis Powell, aka Lewis Payne
Library of Congress

pistol just clicked. Had Powell cocked the gun properly, he could have killed five people. Instead, he used the butt of the gun to smash Frederick over the head.[12] The weapon fell apart from the force of the blow. Frederick was struck so hard that his skull was fractured in two places. He would afterwards lie in a coma for five days.[13] Frederick collapsed, bleeding profusely, into the doorway to his sister Fanny's bedroom. Meanwhile, the terrified Bell bolted down the stairs and ran out of the house shouting, "Murder!"

Powell immediately rushed into Henry's bedroom. The room was dimly lit by a gas light turned down low so the patient could try to sleep. A male nurse, George Robinson, was in the room keeping Henry company, along with Fanny Seward. Just as soon as he opened the door, Powell sprang right at Robinson wielding a knife. Robinson instinctively parried the blow, which struck him hard in the forehead and knocked him to the floor. Powell then brushed Fanny Seward aside and rushed toward Henry, his arms outstretched. Henry was sitting up in his bed. Powell quickly went to slit his throat with his bowie knife. But because of his broken arm and jaw, Henry's body was being supported by a metal frame that acted as a backrest. In the dimness, Powell's knife hit this metal, which deflected the main force of his thrust. In the moment before Robinson succeeded in climbing to his feet and jumping on his back, Powell was able to slash his knife into Henry two times, the first inflicting a deep slice in Henry's right cheek, sweeping down to his neck, the second cutting along the left side of his neck. But Henry had enough agility and presence of mind to roll off the bed into the crack between the bed and the wall, which kept Powell from finishing him off. His wounds, although bloody, were superficial. Henry's face was permanently disfigured, but he would survive the attack.[14]

Augustus Seward, another son of the Secretary, was awakened by screams. When he entered his father's bedroom, he saw two men, one trying to hold the other. His first

CHAPTER 31: A TRAGEDY IN THREE ACTS

impression was that his father was delirious and that the nurse, Robinson, was trying to restrain him. But then he realized that the man being held was much bigger than his father, and then he thought it must be Robinson who had gone delirious. Augustus grabbed Powell, the actual person who Robinson was holding, and tried to pull him back out of the bedroom. As he did so, Powell struck him over and over on his forehead, and also on the hand, with his knife. The wounds cut Augustus to the bone. During this horrifying struggle, Powell kept repeating, in a voice Augustus would describe as "intense, but not strong," the words "I'm mad, I'm mad." Finally, Powell powerfully shrugged himself loose from Augustus, exited the room, and hastily bounded down the stairs.[15] As he descended, he encountered a State Department messenger who was coming up. Powell knocked the messenger aside, at the same time inflicting a deep stab wound on his back with his knife, and kept going.[16] Bursting out the door, Powell quickly untied a horse he had left in an alley nearby, mounted, and rode off.

Bell, who was outside, saw Powell exit and mount the horse. He chased after him, running almost as fast as the mounted Powell. Powell's horse, the "one-eyed" specimen Johnnie had purchased in Beantown several months earlier, was selected for his ability to pull a wagon. He was not accustomed to a rapid gait. Eventually, as Powell was able to stimulate the horse to move with a little more speed, he pulled away from Bell. He headed east on I Street, then turned north on Vermont Avenue. As he did, he disappeared from the view of Bell and other soldiers who had responded to the Seward residence.[17] Like Booth's performance at Ford's Theater, Powell's assault on Henry was so surprising he was able to use the advantage of a waiting horse to make a clean getaway.

The third act of Johnnie's scripted play did not come off. We will never know exactly why not. Johnnie intended that a third major U.S. public official, Vice-President Andrew

Johnson, should be assassinated at the same time as Lincoln and Henry Seward. Johnnie and Johnson likely knew each other from the time Johnnie spent performing on the stage in Nashville in February 1864.[18] At that time, Johnson had been the Union's military governor of Tennessee and, as such, he had a reputation for being hard on Confederate sympathizers. Perhaps that was one reason why he was targeted; but, more likely, the main reason was that Johnnie wanted the perception of his attack to be as broad a threat as possible, and to generate as much terror as possible. Johnson was staying by himself in a hotel, where he was not guarded. Johnnie decided to use Atzerodt to handle the attack on Johnson. As early as Wednesday, April 12, Johnnie had Atzerodt scout Johnson to determine what he looked like and where he was staying in the Kirkwood Hotel.[19]

After reporting back to Johnnie, the next day Atzerodt was given money and sent by Johnnie to take a room at the Kirkwood Hotel, although it appears he did not actually sleep there. He checked into Room 126 early in the morning on Friday, April 14. He spent much of the day working on renting a horse. At some point, a handwritten card was left in the box in the hotel office for Johnson's private secretary, William Browning. It read: "Don't wish to disturb you; are you at home? J. Wilkes Booth." Browning was handed the card between 4 and 5 o'clock in the afternoon, when he returned to the Kirkwood, where he was also staying, from Johnson's chambers in the Capitol. Browning, who without any doubt knew Johnnie from Nashville, interpreted the card as being for him. However, after the assassination he then theorized that the card actually may have been intended for Vice-President Johnson, who was away at the Capitol during most of the day. Browning and Johnson had boxes next to one another in the hotel office, and frequently there was confusion on the part of hotel staff about what items were intended for whom.[20]

Davey Herold left his revolver and knife in Atzerodt's

CHAPTER 31: A TRAGEDY IN THREE ACTS

room, as we have seen. He also left an overcoat and some personal items such as gloves and handkerchiefs, which indicates he was probably planning to return for them later in the evening.[21] According to Atzerodt, in the Friday evening meeting at Powell's room, Johnnie instructed Atzerodt to kill Johnson.[22] Atzerodt claimed he declined the assignment, and that Johnnie then ordered Herold to kill Johnson. Maybe this was true. In any event, Atzerodt shortly after this meeting told a stable hand, John Fletcher, that he planned on using his rented horse at 10 o'clock. Atzerodt indeed picked up the horse and, after having a glass of ale with Fletcher, was seen by him tying the horse and entering Kirkwood House a few minutes after 10 p.m. This was just about the time he was supposed to commence the third act of Johnnie's play, according to the script. Atzerodt remained inside the Kirkwood a few minutes. The hotel desk clerk's wife, at a little after 10 p.m., heard someone running down the hall where Room 126 is located, apparently trying without success to open the doors of three separate rooms. She then heard the person run down the stairs. Fletcher saw Atzerodt exit the Kirkwood at about 10.20 p.m. At that moment, he also saw Davey Herold approach, riding on Fletcher's overdue horse Charley. Herold was coming down Pennsylvania Avenue from the direction of Henry Seward's residence, where he had hung around long enough to hear the screams and other commotion that told him Powell was successful in his terror attack there.

Fletcher was very interested in reclaiming his horse. But Herold spotted Fletcher, spurred Charley, and turned off onto 14th Avenue to avoid him.[23]

Apparently, Atzerodt lost his nerve, changed his mind, or never intended to go along with the plan to attack Johnson in the first place. Whatever the reason, he soon returned his horse to the stable from which it was rented. By around 11 o'clock he was riding aimlessly toward the eastern end of the city in a street car.[24]

Silas D. Cobb, a sergeant in the Third Massachusetts Heavy Artillery, was acting as the sergeant of the guard at the Navy Yard bridge over the Anacostia River. At about 10.25 p.m., a horseman came to the bridge riding rapidly. He was halted. Upon being asked who he was, he gave his name as Booth. Cobb had not yet heard about the assassination. He informed Johnnie that there was in effect a 9 p.m. curfew, after which the bridge was closed. Nonchalant, Johnnie countered that he was new in the city from Southern Maryland, and that he did not know about the curfew. He deftly parried Cobb's questions. "I am going home, down in Charles," he told Cobb. Asked what town, he replied, "I don't live in any town, I live close to Beantown." Cobb said he did not know that place. "Good God, then you never been down there!" Johnnie exclaimed. He then told Cobb he had figured it would be better to return home after the moon rose (and, in fact, the 89% sunlit gibbous moon had just risen at 10.10 p.m.). Cobb noticed that Johnnie's small bay mare looked winded from a short burst. The horse was very restive and uneasy, "much more so than the rider." Despite the curfew, Cobb decided to let Johnnie and his little bay mare pass. He made Johnnie walk the horse over the quarter-mile long bridge.[25]

Within 10–15 minutes, a second horseback rider approached Cobb's guard post. He did not seem to be riding quite as rapidly as the first. This man informed Cobb that his name was Smith, that he was from White Plains, and that he was going home. "Smith" was also informed of the 9 p.m. curfew. He replied he had been to see a woman in the city and could not get away any earlier. After looking the man over thoroughly, Cobb let him pass over the bridge.[26] This second rider, of course, was not really named Smith. He was Johnnie's helper and Southern Maryland guide, Davey Herold.

John Fletcher, the Washington City stableman, was not at all pleased when Herold evaded him on Pennsylvania Avenue.

He was worried it meant Herold planned to abscond with a horse that was very popular with ladies. He went back to his stable, quickly put a saddle and bridle on another mount, and rode east, toward the Capitol. Some bystanders told him yes, they had recently seen two riders passing by very fast. Fletcher continued on to the Navy Yard bridge, where he asked Cobb if a man had just passed riding his roan horse, giving a description. Cobb replied that a man giving the name "Smith" had just passed on this horse. He also informed Fletcher that he would let him pass if he wished, but that he would not allow him to return to the city afterwards. Fletcher decided the pursuit of Herold was not worth having to stay out all night, so he turned back.[27] Once again, good fortune aided Johnnie in making a clean getaway.

After 11 p.m., a teamster named Polk Gardiner encountered a mounted rider on the road at Good Hope Hill, about a mile east of the Navy Yard bridge. Gardiner was riding toward Washington City, while the rider was approaching rapidly in the opposite direction. It was Johnnie, traveling on the rented bay mare. Gardiner, who drove horses for a living, noticed that Johnnie's mount was "quite spirited, requiring no urging with the whip." Johnnie asked if Gardiner had seen another rider pass. No, he had not. Johnnie also asked about the way to Upper Marlboro. Gardiner did not observe any sign of distress. Leaving Gardiner, he rode on very rapidly. About 5 minutes later, Gardiner encountered "Smith," aka David Herold, riding quickly in the same direction on Charley, the grayish roan horse. Without stopping, just slowing slightly, Herold called out to ask some wagon teamsters stopped along the road whether or not another horseman had passed them. Gardiner remarked to his companion that the two men they had encountered were "wearing their horses out chasing each other."[28]

But around the time the clock struck midnight, somewhere

along the dimly moonlit road leading to his next intended stop at the tavern in Surrattsville, Johnnie's remarkable run of good luck ended. As with so many aspects of Johnnie's terrorist career, we will never know the details. His spirited but tired bay mare, in all likelihood, took a fall. In this postulated accident, the horse rolled over on his leg and the crushing caused a broken left tibia, one of the two long bones in his lower leg, approximately 2 inches above the ankle. Johnnie, as we have seen, was prone to misdirection, even with his friends and followers. He was not above falsifying to create the preferred legend about himself. His subsequent claim of, "in jumping broke my leg," which implies the injury was suffered when he hit the stage in his descent from the President's box at Ford's, was not supported by the statements of the numerous eyewitnesses who saw his brief stage performance, and who saw him during the first part of his getaway. In the days immediately following the event, not one of the theater full of people who discussed Booth's swift exit from the stage at Ford's reported any sign of injury, or cry of pain, when he landed on stage. The overwhelming majority of the naïve eyewitness accounts reported a brief moment of unsteadiness followed by recovery, much like a gymnast after a stumbling dismount. Nor did any of the many witnesses – in the accounts given before the legend grew that his injury was suffered in the fall – detect the slightest hint of a limp or discomfort, when Johnnie ran off the stage. Johnnie shoved aside the people who happened to be in his way, departed the building, mounted his waiting horse with a leap from the ground, and dashed away, all with exceptional alacrity. When he encountered Silas Cobb at the Navy Yard bridge, Johnnie's demeanor was extremely smooth. No hint of pain or distress was noted by Cobb, who conversed with Johnnie at some length. Johnnie had no problem walking his unruly horse across the long Navy Yard bridge. And Polk Gardiner, in conversing with Johnnie, did not notice anything amiss.

CHAPTER 31: A TRAGEDY IN THREE ACTS

In stark contrast, everybody who observed or encountered Johnnie subsequent to Polk Gardiner immediately recognized that Johnnie was seriously injured. He was unable to walk, or to mount a horse, unaided. And an additional detail was that Johnnie now only rode Charley, the roan horse with the smooth gait. Johnnie and Herold had switched horses, so that Herold was now atop the wild little bay mare.[29] This mare, one witness said, was also noticeably lame, with a bad cut on her left front leg.[30] Johnnie's leg fracture could have been the result of the kind of a twisting injury that might be sustained in an awkward fall, but it was also consistent with a relatively common type of horse accident in which the weight of the animal fell on the leg.[31]

At approximately 12.15 a.m., John Lloyd was awakened by the arrival of two mounted men outside his Surrattsville tavern, 10 miles southeast of the Navy Yard Bridge. Going outside to investigate, he found that one of them was Herold. The other rider, whom he had never met before, was Johnnie. Lloyd observed that Herold was riding a medium-sized bay horse, while the other man was seated on a larger horse that was gray or roan. Herold told Lloyd to "hurry up and get those things." Both of them perfectly well understood this request to refer to the rifles, binoculars, and whiskey that Mary Surratt had, the previous afternoon, instructed Lloyd to have ready and waiting. Lloyd went upstairs and brought down one carbine and the box of cartridges for it. Herold went into the bar and got a bottle of whiskey for Johnnie, who remained seated on Charley the entire time. When Lloyd asked if Herold wanted the other carbine, Johnnie spoke up and told him he could not carry the gun, because his leg was broken. He said he wanted to find a surgeon to have it set. Johnnie then asked Lloyd if he wanted to hear some news. Lloyd responded that he did not particularly care one way or the other. Lloyd already was apprehensive, from the drama of Mary's visit, that something overly bold for his taste was afoot. Johnnie volunteered, "We have killed President Lincoln and Secretary Seward." Lloyd decided to keep his mouth shut. He did not ask any questions.[32] Herold and Johnnie took off, continuing along the road south.

Johnnie's midnight visit to Lloyd's tavern, even though it lasted no more than perhaps 5 minutes, was a watershed moment. Like all terrorists, Johnnie was inwardly convinced of his utter righteousness. Lloyd's cold reaction to the "news" about the assassination was Johnnie's first exposure to the fact that people he expected to welcome him as a hero in fact would regard him as something more akin to a monster. And the rude awakening would continue.

Intentionally or unintentionally, Johnnie added extra spice to the piece by performing it on Good Friday. The striking parallel between the undeserved death of Lincoln and the death of Christ was instantly perceived.[33] Intent on immortalizing himself, Johnnie more than anything else succeeded in withdrawing Lincoln from the rough and tumble world of political warfare and, instead, canonizing him in the pantheon of saints.

All over the North, the flags of celebration of victory were taken down and immediately replaced with black flags of mourning. April's weather was typically rainy. Walt Whitman wrote: "Black clouds driving overhead. Lincoln's death – black, black, black – as you look toward the sky, long broad black like great serpents." From Washington City, to Des Moines, Iowa, to San Francisco, California, the news spread. As it did, the shock and grief set in. People wrote of feeling as if an "eclipse of the sun" had occurred.[34]

Johnnie's act produced the two most typical responses to terrorism – utter revulsion of the public and a tremendous overreaction. In the days immediately following the attacks, hundreds died, thousands were beaten or jailed, and many more were forced to flee for their lives. In Indiana and Illinois, those who celebrated the news from Washington were shot down on

CHAPTER 31: A TRAGEDY IN THREE ACTS

the spot. One man was cut to ribbons by fifteen bullets. Both real and mock lynchings of perceived "Copperheads" and other Southern sympathizers occurred in the North and West. Some victims were tarred and feathered or otherwise humiliated. Numerous deaths were reported as alleged, but questionable, "suicides." Homes and businesses of suspected Copperheads were looted and destroyed. John's terrorist acts had succeeded in inflicting a degree of anarchy.[35] When a man on the Brooklyn ferry was heard muttering "disloyal" sentiments, he was seized and flung over the side. He was swept under the boat and crushed to death by the paddles.

In Cincinnati, Ohio, one of the most drunken celebrations in the city's history had just ended hours earlier when the tragic news from Washington arrived. Two men, perhaps rashly overreacting to what they perceived as an excess of jubilation by the revelers, stepped into the street and announced they were "glad." A man nearby drew a pistol and shot one on the spot. The other was set upon by a mob and literally cut to pieces. June Booth, Johnnie's oldest brother, was performing a theater engagement in Cincinnati when the assassination happened. Hearing the news at a Saturday morning rehearsal, he collapsed with shock. Several hundred rioters soon surrounded the hotel where he was saying. He was saved from lynching only because a quick-witted hotel clerk informed them that June had already left.[36]

Chapter 32: An Underground Railroad in Reverse

The southward flight of Johnnie and Herold in the days following the assassination bore a perverse resemblance to the northward journeys of Harriet Tubman and her charges escaping the yoke of slavery in the days of the "Underground Railroad." At bottom their strategy was the same as Harriet's: Hole up during the day, when they would run a far bigger risk of discovery, and then travel by night. Also, Johnnie made use of a similar type of underground railroad. Confederate Secret Service agents more or less acted as his "stationmasters." For instance, after Johnnie left the first planned stop at Lloyd's Surrattsville tavern, there was never any doubt about his next destination. It was the country home of the Confederate agent, Samuel Mudd. Though it lay a little out of the way in terms of the direct route to cross the Potomac, what Johnnie now needed most urgently was a doctor. Mudd was a physician, even if he was not a surgeon. Johnnie knew Sam and his wife Frank well, having previously stayed in their home, and they had already helped him procure a horse to use in his kidnapping plan. The Mudds could be counted on to help. The way to their country home could be

CHAPTER 32: AN UNDERGROUND RAILROAD IN REVERSE

confusing, but Johnnie was familiar with it from several prior visits. So, with Herold helping as a guide, the two of them managed to wend their way through the moonlight to the Mudd residence a few miles east of Beantown.

They arrived at around 4 a.m. Surely Johnnie bragged to Sam and Frank Mudd right away about his successful terrorist exploit, just as he did with Lloyd, and as he did with others later. But, like Lloyd, the Mudds were rational beings bent on survival. As sympathizers, they would indeed help, but they would also keep their mouths shut. Permanently. With their lives on the line, the Mudds had every motive to conceal the truth. We must be highly skeptical of their claims about what happened at their home on April 15, 1865, except for what is corroborated by other evidence. For example, both Sam and Frank Mudd later made the ludicrous contention that they did not recognize Johnnie, and that, in fact, they had no idea who he was when he was in their home on April 15. Sam Mudd claimed both men were "strangers." Knowing as much as we do now about the Mudds' prior connections with Johnnie, it is obvious that they lied. Using a tested tactic, they took refuge behind the fact that Sam Mudd was a physician. By doing so, they were successful in saving Sam Mudd from the gallows. Their nonsense has even fooled numerous authors.[1]

Samuel Mudd residence, near Beantown
photo by author

According to Sam and Frank Mudd, Herold and Johnnie told them one of the horses had fallen, causing Johnnie to break his leg. Johnnie also reported that he had seriously injured his back in the fall. He complained of severe pain. He had to be helped by both men to get off his horse and into the house. Sam Mudd decided to carry Johnnie upstairs, where he could lie in bed in a small room, out of the sight of servants who would be up at the break of day. Johnnie's pants were spattered with mud in many places. Mudd had to cut a vertical slit in Johnnie's left boot to remove it. It took around three quarters of an hour for him to examine Johnnie's leg and to set the fracture, which he did not regard as a particularly painful or dangerous wound. He fashioned a makeshift splint out of a wooden hat box. Later in the day he asked his English gardener, John Best, to make a pair of crutches for Johnnie.[2]

After finishing his work with Johnnie's leg, Dr. Mudd awakened his African American servant, Frank Washington, and asked if he would tend to the horses that had arrived during the night. Herold, too, asked Frank to rub the horses.[3] For a time, the exhausted Johnnie and Herold slept. The Mudds managed to feed them without Johnnie being observed by any servants. Johnnie asked for a razor and soap, so that he could shave. Johnnie broached the idea of borrowing a carriage in which to continue his southward journey. To Sam Mudd, he expressed doubt about whether he could ride a horse with the broken leg. As a result, after lunch, Mudd and Herold struck out together in search of a carriage that might be serviceable. They went together to the nearby home of Mudd's father Henry, with Herold riding Pumphrey's small bay mare. But after some conversation with family members, the notion of borrowing a carriage was abandoned. There was no suitable carriage available and, in any event, the family was not anxious to sacrifice a vehicle. Moreover, it was not clear to them why Johnnie's ride south would be any easier in a bumpy carriage than it would be on a horse.[4]

Sam Mudd continued into Bryantown, while Herold hid out in a swamp. Mudd rapidly ascertained that the town was completely abuzz with the sensational news of the previous

CHAPTER 32: AN UNDERGROUND RAILROAD IN REVERSE

night's terror attacks in Washington City. After some indecision about waiting for Mudd, Herold rode back alone to the Mudd residence. When he arrived, he told Frank Mudd that he and her husband had been unable to secure a carriage. Johnnie then announced that the pair would leave that evening on their horses. Johnnie hobbled down the stairs to test his ability to mount a horse. Meanwhile Sam Mudd, returning home, stopped about halfway for 10 or 15 minutes to exchange pleasantries with two local residents. Mudd told them what everybody was talking about, the Lincoln assassination and that John Wilkes Booth was suspected of it. He did not mention anything at all about the two men who were staying at his home.[5]

Johnnie and Herold left the Mudd residence at dusk, without speaking to anyone other than Frank and Sam Mudd. Sam Mudd, six days later, claimed to investigators that they had told him they were going to the residence of Parson Lemuel Wilmer 4 miles away. He told them "the men" said they knew Parson Wilmer. This report was almost certainly an obfuscation. Wilmer had a reputation as a staunch Unionist.[6] Johnnie and Herold left the Mudd manor not on the main driveway but via a back trail, through a swampy area. They made sure to turn off the trail and ride their horses through a heavily disturbed field, in order to conceal their tracks. They had no intention of visiting Parson Wilmer. Where they in fact headed, probably coached to do so by the Mudds, was to the home of Ausy Swan, a mixed-race local who was willing to act as a paid guide. Swan's home was 2 miles east of Bryantown, not at all in the direction of their intended route to cross the Potomac. Apparently they got mixed up, because when it was almost dark, near Henry Mudd's residence, Herold dismounted and approached an African American named Eluctus Thomas. After Thomas showed Herold the way for getting back to "the swamp," Herold headed in the direction indicated. Reoriented, he and Johnnie arrived at Swan's home at 9 o'clock.[7]

Johnnie asked if Swan could show them the way to the home of William Burtles, which the Confederate Secret Service had used often as a safehouse.[8] Swan agreed to lead them there, for $2. He also gave them some bread and whiskey. But before getting to the Burtles place, Johnnie came out and asked Swan whether he could instead guide them to their preferred destination, a farm called Rich Hill, which was the home of their next intended stationmaster, Samuel Cox. We can surmise Johnnie had reviewed both Burtles and Cox with the Mudds before leaving their home. Rich Hill was much farther from Bryantown, and thus preferrable from the standpoint of eluding pursuers. Getting there at night, however, was a difficult trek through the dark, dank Zekiah Swamp. Swan, though, agreed to take them for $5 more. The three of them arrived at Rich Hill at approximately 4 a.m. In the end, Johnnie gave Swan a total of $12. Ausy evidently was loyal to his customers, because even though federal detectives were soon swarming all over the Bryantown area offering big rewards, and even though Swan had to be aware that his charges fit the profile of the assassination suspects, he said nothing to anyone about his midnight escapade for a full week. The delay was critical in avoiding an immediate descent of the detectives on Rich Hill.[9]

Whatever his personal feelings about the assassination, as a Confederate stationmaster Cox handled the challenge of Johnnie's arrival with a great deal of aplomb. After emerging with a candle to greet Johnnie and Herold, he managed to bring them into the house, feed them, and figure out what to do with them, all within a short period of time and all without exposing them to curious servants who might be interested in mentioning their presence to federal detectives. He had Johnnie and Herold leave the house and return to dismiss the waiting Ausy Swan, while muttering imprecations about Cox such as, "he was supposed to be a man of Southern feeling." Johnnie pointedly

CHAPTER 32: AN UNDERGROUND RAILROAD IN REVERSE

made Swan and Herold help him get up on his horse so that they could leave. This was pure acting, subterfuge, and misdirection.

In reality, Johnnie and Herold were only pretending to depart from Rich Hill. They never actually left its grounds that night. Cox, meanwhile, was busy finding help for the fugitive terrorists. Confederate operatives in Southern Maryland were used to stashing smuggled guests in the dense woods in order to evade detection. Cox had his overseer, Franklin Robey, conduct Johnnie and Herold to a particular spot a mile west of Rich Hill, a place off the road where the Maryland pines grew so thick no one could see through them for more than a few feet. In the early morning hours of Easter Sunday, April 16, Robey positioned them in the woods to await their next stationmaster.[10]

Thomas Jones was the 44-year-old foster brother of Samuel Cox. He was originally from Port Tobacco, home of George Atzerodt. In 1861 he acquired a 500-acre farm in Charles County bordering the Potomac on the west and Pope's Creek on the north. The home was situated on a bluff 80 feet high, with a grand waterfront view. This made it perfect for sending and receiving line of sight messages across the river. Jones was suspected by federal authorities of being a sympathizer of the CSA. In September 1861 he was arrested and, like George Kane, he was held without charges in Old Capitol Prison. He was released in March 1862. Jones used his time in confinement to meet other militants, several of whom were already Confederate Secret Service agents. Soon after his return home, Jones's wife died. Jones was embittered. He held it against the Union that he had been imprisoned and not able to take care of her.

After his release, Jones remained active in smuggling Confederates across the Potomac. Jones was approached about making his home one of the way stations in the Confederate

Signal Corps, a vital communications network that enabled the secessionist republic to stay connected with its allies and partisans in the North. He accepted, but only after the organizers granted him total control over the entire operation. Jones was the brother-in-law of Thomas Harbin who, as we have seen, introduced Johnnie to Atzerodt during the winter of 1864–1865. Undoubtedly, Jones also knew Sam Mudd. Jones in his communications work used doctors on a regular basis because they were able to travel freely due to their profession. He had them conceal large quantities of correspondence in various pockets of their clothing. Jones was a high-quality spy. He was intelligent, inventive, and highly cautious. He trusted no one who it was not absolutely necessary to trust.[11]

Through his spy work, Jones was aware of Johnnie's conspiracy to kidnap Lincoln. On the evening after the assassination, although he had since moved to another farm called Huckleberry, Jones was taking care of some business at his old residence, the former Signal Corps station. Two federal soldiers rode up and asked about a boat they saw in Pope's Creek. Jones told them it was his. "Well, you had better keep an eye on it," one of them replied. "There are two suspicious characters somewhere in the neighborhood who will be looking to cross the river." The soldiers told him about President Lincoln's assassination the night before. They suggested that the desperadoes who did it might try to steal the boat. In this way Jones was alerted that he might somehow be called upon to assist in connection with Johnnie's flight. So, when Samuel Cox, Jr. visited Jones at Huckleberry on the morning of Easter Sunday and told him his father wanted him to come to Rich Hill to speak about getting some seed corn, Jones knew very well that the real business at hand had nothing to do with spring planting. Jones immediately suspected it was about the assassination. Jones immediately saddled his horse and, without exchanging a word other than casual pleasantries about the weather, rode with the young man to his father's

CHAPTER 32: AN UNDERGROUND RAILROAD IN REVERSE

house.[12]

After several minutes of small talk, Cox got to the point. He told him how Johnnie, after verifying Cox's identity, had shown him the initials JWB tattooed on his own arm. Out of earshot of Swan, he had then told Cox about his terrorist feat. He called upon Cox, as a Confederate agent, for assistance. Cox immediately agreed to help. And now Cox was calling upon his foster brother to get Johnnie ferried south across the Potomac.[13]

Jones, for his part, was a little disturbed about this task. True, he had risked his life many times for the cause of the rebellious slaveholding republic. But that cause was now lost. He felt a sense of horror and dread about the assassination itself. He knew anything done to help Johnnie would put his life in imminent jeopardy. Southern Maryland was literally swarming with detectives and soldiers, all seeking justice for the outrageous act of terrorism against their nation's leader. But Jones's sense of loyalty to the cause was also strong. After a moment of reluctance, he agreed to meet with the fugitives. Soon he rode out to the area where Cox told him they were hiding. The first thing he saw was a bay horse, wearing a saddle and bridle, grazing in a clearing that had been made for planting tobacco. Jones used a predetermined signal, a whistle, to make contact. Herold soon emerged and led Jones into the dense woods where Johnnie lay hiding. He found him, even in the midst of his desperate situation, to be still handsome, gentlemanly, and courteous.[14]

From that moment forward, Jones became Johnnie's most valuable protector. He did everything for him personally, never delegating to even his most trusted servants and associates. The very first thing Jones told Johnnie and Herold was that they must get rid of the horses. They would certainly betray their presence in the area, and it would be impossible to feed them. Heeding this advice, Johnnie had Herold march both horses deep into the swamp, to an area filled with quicksand, and shoot them with his revolver. After they were destroyed, they sank into the muck and were never seen again, not even by Cox, who had heard the shots, when he later came to make a close inspection.[15] It would turn out to be the only deadly use of the substantial arsenal of firearms Johnnie and Herold carried with them.

Day after day, as they remained hidden in the woods, Jones every morning prepared food and coffee, which he brought to the fugitives. He also brought something else Johnnie craved even more: Newspapers. Johnnie was obsessed with scrutinizing his press coverage.[16] On Monday, April 17, as Jones was visiting with the fugitives, a squadron of cavalry passed along the road, within 200 yards of where Johnnie and Herold were hiding. They all held their breath as the clanking of sabers and tramping of horses passed. After that scare, Johnnie became less impatient to be on his way, and more willing to trust in Jones's judgment. The following day, Tuesday, April 18, Jones went to the town of Port Tobacco. There he encountered a federal officer who loudly proclaimed, right in front of Jones: "I will give a hundred thousand dollars to anyone who will give me the information that will lead to Booth's capture." Jones remarked, "That is a large sum of money, and ought to get him if money can do it."[17]

While Johnnie had the benefit of Confederate stationmasters who helped him remain concealed, along with Herold, in Southern Maryland, federal detectives made progress in identifying and arresting his other followers. In the frantic melee that ensued the night Lincoln was shot, it was quickly brought to the detectives' attention that John Surratt was a known associate of Johnnie. Well after midnight on the night of the assassination, Washington City detectives arrived at Mary Surratt's boarding house. They roused all the residents and searched the place thoroughly for any trace of John Surratt or Johnnie himself. Neither of these suspects were present, but

CHAPTER 32: AN UNDERGROUND RAILROAD IN REVERSE

the visit was still an investigative success. From residents of the Surratt boarding house, the detectives learned about Mary Surratt's many visits with Johnnie, including several on the day of the assassination. Louis Weichmann told them about her Good Friday trip to Surrattsville. Over Easter weekend, the Surratt boarding house was kept under watch, probably in hopes that Johnnie or John Surratt would show. The night of Monday, April 17, federal authorities finally decided to move in. They arrested Mary Surratt and everyone else living at her boarding house. At approximately 11.30 p.m., while they were preparing to transport all the residents to jail, Lewis Powell unexpectedly showed up at the front door. It was a critical stroke of luck for the investigation.[18]

After getting away clean following his attack at the Seward residence, Powell had been unsuccessful in leaving Washington City. The bridge over the Eastern Branch that he intended to take in order to head north to Baltimore was closed with a gate. So he was forced to take another route northward, one that did not connect to a highway. His blood-spattered overcoat was later found discarded, 3 miles northeast of the city limits. Powell also abandoned the one-eyed horse. He hid out in some woods. Fearing discovery by dogs, for a time he climbed up a tree. He became aware of swarms of cavalry searching nearby. He also saw reward placards that were posted everywhere. They bore a remarkably detailed and accurate description of him:

> Height 6 feet 1 inch, hair black, thick, full and straight; no beard or appearance of beard; cheeks red on the jaws; face moderately full; 22 or 23 years of age; eyes, color not known – large eyes, not prominent; brows not heavy, but dark; face not large, but rather round; complexion healthy; nose straight and well formed, medium size; mouth small; lips thin; upper lip protruded when he talked; chin rounded and

prominent; head medium size; neck short and of medium length; hands soft and small; fingers tapering; shows no signs of hard labor; broad shoulders; taper waist; straight figure; strong looking man; manner not gentlemanly, but vulgar; overcoat double-breasted, color mixed of pink and grey spots, pockets in side and one on the breast, with lapells or flaps; pants black, common stuff; new heavy boots; voice small and thin, inclined to tenor.

After spending three nights and three days hiding on the outskirts of the city, on Monday Powell, after dark, walked all the way back into town to seek help at the Surratt boarding house. He had lost his hat at Henry's house, so he tore off a sleeve of his undershirt and used it to fashion a crude head covering. He found an abandoned coat, which he donned. He took a pickaxe from a gravedigger's shed and carried it with him, thinking he could pose as a workman.[19]

Officers in charge of the party that had seized Mary Surratt's boarding house answered Powell's knock at the door. Powell's legs were covered with mud up to his knees. He claimed he was a laborer who had come to dig a gutter for Mary Surratt. The officers rapidly saw through this story. They asked Mary Surratt if she knew the visitor. She answered, "Before God, sir, I do not know this man, and have never seen him." However, others living in her house quickly helped the detectives establish that the same man, then traveling under the name Wood, had previously stayed at the boarding house. It became obvious to the Government that Mary Surratt was deeply involved in the terrorist conspiracy, and that she was lying about not knowing "Wood." Powell fit the description of the Seward attacker perfectly. William Bell and Augustus Seward would identify him without hesitation.[20]

Federal authorities also bagged George Atzerodt. Atzerodt's identity as one of Johnnie's followers had been uncovered very quickly after the assassination. Shortly after the

CHAPTER 32: AN UNDERGROUND RAILROAD IN REVERSE

assassinations, a detective named John Lee went to the Kirkwood House and checked the entire hotel for any sign of a threat to Vice-President Johnson. The bartender, knowing what Lee was doing, approached him and mentioned a suspicious-looking man – a grubby-looking German fellow – who had checked into the hotel that morning. The bartender thought Atzerodt looked out of place in an elegant hotel. Checking the hotel register, management quickly identified this man as having checked into Room 126 under his real name, Atzerodt. The locked door to the room was forced open and the room was searched. Herold's bowie knife and loaded pistol were found. There was also a coat hanging on the wall. In its pockets were found a handkerchief embroidered with "Mary A.H. Booth," and Johnnie's bankbook from the Bank of Ontario. This was very tangible evidence tying Atzerodt to Johnnie.[21] Thus, Atzerodt like Johnnie became the object of an intense manhunt.

After hearing the rapidly spreading news of the assassination, Atzerodt at first wandered aimlessly about Washington City. He asked to stay the night with an acquaintance he encountered on the streetcar, who turned him down. Then, at 2 a.m., he tried to get back his old room at the Pennsylvania House. This was also unsuccessful, but he did manage to get a bed in a room with five other men. He woke at 5 a.m. and left without paying his bill.[22]

After his early morning departure from the Pennsylvania House, Atzerodt got out of the city, heading northwest to Germantown, in Montgomery County, where he had relatives. By Sunday afternoon, he reached the home of Hezekiah Metz, a family friend, where he introduced himself to other dinner guests as Andrew Atwood. The table talk at the Metz residence, as everywhere else, was all about the assassination. "Atwood" could not resist making a rash statement. "If the fellow that had promised to follow Grant had done his duty, we would have got General Grant, too." This extremely odd statement was remembered and reported to others. In three days' time it came to the attention of U.S. Army officers. At around 4 a.m. on Thursday, April 20, a detachment of soldiers sent to find "Atwood" traced him to the Germantown home of his uncle, Frederick Richter. Atzerodt, who was sleeping with two other men, was awakened and arrested in his underwear.[23]

Meanwhile, Johnnie and Herold continued to lead a patient, almost boring existence hiding out in the woods near Zekiah Swamp. Jones's wisdom in handling by himself all the arrangements for Johnnie bore fruit when cavalrymen and detectives repeatedly visited and scoured his Huckleberry home. They interviewed Henry Woodland, an African American former slave who, after emancipation, continued to work as Jones's trusted servant. Woodland did not "know" anything, no matter what he might suspect. He told the detectives nothing.[24]

Finally, on Friday, April 21, which was one full week after the assassination, the monotony ended. Jones made his daily afternoon visit to Allen's Fresh, a small village about 3 miles east of his house. While Jones was sitting in the town's only hotel bar, a detachment of cavalry rode in. The leader, who was from St. Mary's County to the southeast, came in and announced, "Boys, I have news, they have all been seen in St. Mary's." At that, all of the men instantly remounted and scurried over a bridge leading in the southeasterly direction of St. Mary's County. Jones, watching their departure, realized that his opportunity to move Johnnie and Herold had finally arrived. After prudently awaiting the passing of a few minutes, Jones rode slowly out of Allen's Fresh at about dusk. Then he went rapidly to the place where Johnnie was concealed. It was the first time he had ever tried approaching his charges after dark. Telling them "the coast seems to be clear" for a nighttime river crossing, he rapidly got them organized to depart.[25]

Very slowly, dreading an encounter with curious neighbors or their barking dogs at every step, Jones led

Chapter 32: An Underground Railroad in Reverse

Johnnie, on his horse, and Herold, on foot, for the 3.5-mile journey to the small inlet where Jones had asked Woodland to stash the rowboat he planned to give Johnnie for the crossing. Between 9 and 10 o'clock, the party arrived in front of Jones's house. Jones told them he was going to go in to get them some supper. Johnnie, terribly weary of living outdoors, appealed to Jones to let him come in for one cup of hot coffee. With a feeling of pity, Jones firmly told him no. There were people inside, and it would not be safe. Later, Jones would write that to refuse Johnnie's plea was the hardest thing he ever had to do.[26]

Herold and Jones had to leave the horse behind and carry Johnnie the last 300 yards to the river. They reached the boat, a flat-bottomed vessel 12 feet long. Jones had bought it the previous year for $18. Now he accepted that sum, and nothing more, from Johnnie in exchange for the boat Johnnie so badly needed to continue his "underground railroad" journey on the other side of the Potomac. Johnnie was placed in the back, where he could steer, while Herold took the front to provide the power.[27]

Johnnie's navigation was not very successful. Due to the inky darkness, fog, and an incoming tide, he and Herold got turned around. Instead of rowing across to Virginia as planned, they veered off course. On a pitch-black night and without the benefit of any navigation lights, this is very easy to do. By the time day broke, Herold recognized where they had come to shore as being Nanjemoy Creek, still on the Maryland side of the river. For much of the war, it had been a favored launching point for surreptitious Potomac crossings. Originally, it was an area brimming with Confederate sympathizers. But now, with their terrorist act reviled far and wide, Johnnie and Herold were not about to receive a warm reception. They approached the home of a local resident, one Herold knew from a prior hunting expedition, to ask for bread. The resident told them brusquely that he did not have any, nor was he about to bake. Rebuffed also in an effort to buy whiskey, all they succeeded in purchasing was a small amount of milk from a boy. They had to spend a long day in hiding before another opportunity to make the crossing under cover of darkness.[28]

In January of 1864, when Johnnie was performing in St. Louis, he had acquired a leather-bound pocket diary. The diary was set up in the format of a daily calendar for the year 1864. But Johnnie never used it as a diary. He used its nifty pockets to store miniature photos of five women, including Lucy Hale. He used its pencil holder to carry a pencil. When Johnnie left the National Hotel to go to the assassination, he took along the calendar.[29] It was in his pocket when he shot Lincoln. It was in his pocket when he jumped onto the stage at Ford's Theater. Later, while he was in hiding, he pulled out the pencil and used several of the diary's pages to write. On Saturday, April 22, lying in wait for dusk, Johnnie gave us an emotional window on his inner thoughts.

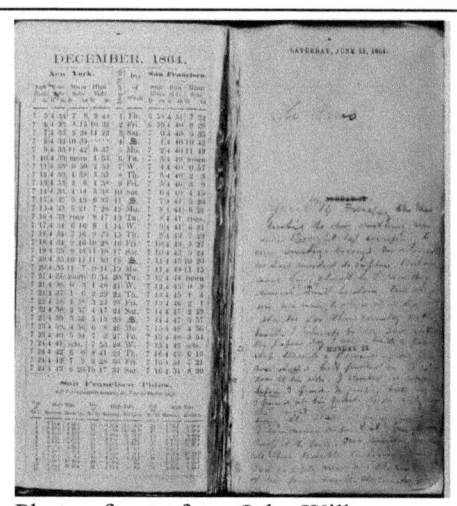

Photo of page from John Wilkes Booth's leather pocket diary, on which he began his final manifesto

"Ti amo," he began in very large letters. That small phrase, in Italian, means "I love you." Johnnie continued to regard his terrorist act as, above all, one of utmost devotion and sacrifice. In his final paragraph, he would write, "I bless the entire world. Have never hated or wronged anyone. This last was not a

CHAPTER 32: AN UNDERGROUND RAILROAD IN REVERSE

wrong, unless God deems it to be." He wrote his own version of the assassination, disputing some of the press coverage he had studied so avidly.

Not only does his last writing reflect how profoundly influenced Johnnie was by literature, but it also actually contained his own comparative analysis, setting himself up beside mythic assassins:

> After being hunted like a dog through swamps, woods, and last night being chased by gun boats till I was forced to return wet, cold and starving, with every man's hand against me, I am here in despair. And, why? For doing what Brutus was honored for, what made Tell a Hero. And yet I for striking down a greater tyrant than they ever knew am looked upon as a common cutthroat. My action was purer than either of theirs. One hoped to be great himself. The other had not only his countrys but his own wrongs to avenge.

Johnnie emphasized one striking element of our developing profile of the terrorist: the total absence of any personal motive for giving up his career and his life for the cause: "I hoped for no gain. I knew no private wrong. I struck for my country and for that alone." But he expressed profound disappointment and "despair" – his word – over the reaction to his deed:

> A country groaned beneath this tyranny and prayed for this end. Yet now behold the cold hand they extend to me. God cannot pardon me if I have done wrong. Yet I cannot see any wrong in serving a degenerate people ….

> I think I have done well, though I am abandoned, with the curse of Cain upon me, when if the world knew my heart, that one blow would have made me great, though I desired no greatness.

Primordial American Terrorists

Unbeknownst to Johnnie, John Mathews had never turned over his intended manifesto to the *National Intelligencer*. In the furor that erupted following the assassination, Mathews instead prudently destroyed it. Johnnie, however, assumed the federal government had suppressed its publication. He returned to the theme of his ultimate personal sacrifice:

> The little, very little I left behind to clear my name, the Govmt will not allow to be printed. So ends all. For my country I have given up all that makes life sweet and Holy, brought misery upon my family, and I am sure there is no pardon in Heaven for me since man condemns me so.

He expressed a delusion peculiar to terrorists, the sense that if only given the opportunity, he could persuade the world to adopt his own passionately held view:

> To night I will once more try the river with the intent to cross; though I have almost a greater desire and almost a mind to return to Washington and in a measure clear my name, which I feel I can do. I do not repent the blow I struck. I may before my God but not to man.

Finally, Johnnie recognized that the ending of his story was imminent. It was an inevitable death. He prayed it would happen without the humiliation of surrender and execution. "I have too great a soul to die like a criminal. O may he, may he spare me that and let me die bravely ... I do not wish to shed a drop of blood, but 'I must fight the course.' Tis all that's left me." Johnnie's last quotation, "I must fight the course," was taken directly from the script of *Macbeth*. In the most radical development of his personality, Shakespeare's tragic figure utters these words when he is on his way to fight, even though he knows his fate is to die.

Chapter 33: "O Let Me Die Bravely"

Johnnie and Herold ventured back onto the Potomac with far less difficulty on the night of Saturday, April 22. They did not take the shortest route across. Instead, they rowed downriver until they found the original Virginia destination pointed out to them by Jones. They were seeking out their next planned station mistress, Elizabeth Quesenberry. For much of the war, Quesenberry's home called Cottage Farm near the mouth of Machodoc Creek had been operated as a safehouse for Confederate agents.[1] A schoolhouse on Quesenberry's property was being staffed at the time by Thomas Harbin, the same Confederate agent who had earlier introduced Johnnie to George Atzerodt in Port Tobacco, along with Joseph Baden, a soldier in the Confederate army. Sunday morning, upon learning of the arrival on shore of Johnnie and Herold, Harbin and Baden went down to meet them. They found both in a pitiful, filthy condition. Johnnie and Herold were wanted men, the objects of an intense ongoing manhunt that was scouring every corner of Southern Maryland and the Northern Neck of Virginia (the peninsula north of the Rappahannock). Harbin and Quesenberry knew better than to allow Johnnie and Herold anywhere near Cottage Farm, where they would inevitably be seen by servants. Quesenberry instead arranged to bring them food. Then, she and Harbin arranged for them to be conducted after sunset on horseback to their next station by a poor white farmer named William Bryant.[2]

Harbin accompanied the group part of the way. En route, he had an opportunity to chat with Johnnie. He was riding with his right leg in one stirrup, the left, broken leg dangling. To Harbin he projected an attitude of optimism. He did not appear nervous or apprehensive. Now that he was in Virginia, he hoped he would soon find friends. Johnnie continued to express a glow of satisfaction with his terrorist exploit. He accepted with equanimity the knowledge that he was almost certainly doomed. Pointing to the revolver he carried, Johnnie assured Harbin that he would never be taken alive.[3]

The next stationmaster was another physician, Richard Stewart. Stewart had been identified to Johnnie by Samuel Mudd as a loyal Confederate agent who could check on his broken leg and adjust the splint as needed. Stewart knew and worked with Samuel Cox and, very likely, also worked with Harbin and Jones. During the war, Stewart had smuggled drugs, languished on a prison ship, and harbored agents. He owned a magnificent mansion on the banks of the Potomac as well as a separate inland summer home that he called Cleydael. Stewart was also a relative of the Confederate General-in-Chief, Robert E. Lee. But, like Lee, he felt the war was over and lost. The desperation of martyrdom had no appeal for him. He was not at all happy to have Johnnie and Herold deposited on his doorstep. Stewart did his minimum duty, giving them some dinner, but he did not invite them to stay the night at Cleydael, nor did he give Johnnie any medical attention. He begged off on the ground that he, like Mudd, was not a surgeon. As soon as Johnnie and Herold ate, Stewart had Bryant take them to the very modest nearby home of William Lucas, a free-born African American. Lucas was in need of money. Stewart predicted that, for a fare, he would be willing to provide

Chapter 33: "O Let Me Die Bravely"

transportation to the banks of the Rappahannock, the crossing of which was Johnnie's next objective.[4]

They arrived at the Lucas home about midnight. Lucas was very apprehensive at their arrival. All his dogs were barking. Only the fact that he knew Bryant induced him to open the door. When told that Johnnie and Herold wished to stay with him, Lucas protested. "I am a colored man and have no right to take care of white people." Hobbling on his crutches, Johnnie elbowed his way past Lucas and into the one room house. He said he and Herold were brothers, two of Mosby's men returning home from three years of service. After displaying his revolver and knife, Johnnie succeeded in negotiating for permission to sleep inside the house and then to get a ride to Port Conway, on the Rappahannock, 10 miles to the south, in exchange for $10 in gold. Lucas and his wife spent the night outside, on the porch.[5]

In the morning, Lucas had his adult son transport the visitors in a carriage to Port Conway, taking an indirect route to avoid the main road. Before they left, Johnnie tore two pages from his pocket diary. On one he wrote a draft, on the other a final version, of a note to be taken back to Richard Stewart. Johnnie's words, including a line from the script of *Macbeth*, betray the frustration and bitterness he felt at the lack of support from a man he had been assured would be a loyal ally of the cause:[6]

> Forgive me, but I have some little pride. I hate to blame you for want of hospitality; you know your own affairs. I was sick and tired, with a broken leg, in need of medical advice. I would not have turned a dog from my door in such a condition. However, you were kind enough to give me something to eat, for which I not only thank you but on account of the reluctant manner in which it was bestowed, I feel bound to pay for it. It is not the substance but the manner in which a

kindness is extended that makes one happy in the acceptance thereof. 'The sauce in meat is ceremony; meeting were bare without it.' Be kind enough to accept the enclosed two dollars and a half (though hard to spare) for what we have received.

Yours respectfully,
Stranger
April 24, 1865

Johnnie and Herold arrived in Port Conway at about noon. The driver pulled up at the gate to the house of a local fisherman named William Rollins. Herold got down and asked Rollins, who was outside, for a drink of water. He introduced himself to Rollins as David Boyd. He said his brother with a broken leg in the wagon was James Boyd. He asked if he could take a drink of water to "James" in a large tin ladle, to which Rollins agreed. Herold asked Rollins if, for $10, he would take them to Orange Court House. This was an interesting objective, in that it lay west, not south, of Port Conway, and in that it was over 60 miles away, actually farther from Port Conway than Richmond. Evidently, Johnnie had heard that there was still a Confederate garrison at Gordonsville, which is not far from Orange Court House.[7] Rollins refused to consider going as far as Orange Court House, but he agreed to take them to Bowling Green, which was only 13 miles away, to the southwest, in exchange for ten greenback dollars.

Their trip had to wait, because the tide was so low that the ferry was stuck on the south side of the river and could not come across. In the meantime, Rollins went down to the water to tend to his fishing nets. While he was gone, three rebel soldiers who were also intent on crossing the Rappahannock rode over the hill and down to the wharf. These were not just any Confederates. They were all Mosby guerrillas heading south. One of them, Mortimer Ruggles, was the son of a general and an officer in the Confederate Signal Corps, who

CHAPTER 33: "O LET ME DIE BRAVELY"

between July and September 1864 had served directly under Thomas Conrad, a major participant in the plot to kidnap Lincoln.[8] Johnnie and Herold immediately seized on the opportunity to travel along with them. Herold politely informed Rollins that his services would no longer be needed. One of the soldiers, 18-year-old Willie Jett, borrowed ink from Rollins. In a precaution oddly reminiscent of that of Harriet, the two of them created fake parole slips, including the forged signature of the U.S. Provost Marshal, that they could show in the event they should be questioned while on the road.[9]

The three Confederates were well aware of who they were escorting. They felt some admiration for Johnnie's feat of terrorism, as well as his cool courage, despite his obvious pain, in the face of a huge and highly publicized reward placed upon his head. While carrying his crutches, Ruggles let Johnnie ride on his horse aboard the ferry. As soon as they crossed over to Port Royal, the escorts took Johnnie to the home of Sarah Jane Peyton, whom Jett knew. Jett asked if she would "take care" of an injured solder named "Boyd" for two days. At first she said yes. Johnnie got off the horse, hobbled into her house, and sat down. But after getting a good look at the bedraggled ex-actor, Sarah changed her mind. She told Jett privately that her brother, a lawyer, was not at home, and that she was not at liberty to accept a house guest in his absence. Instead, she suggested that Jett and the others should take "Boyd" to the farm of Richard Garrett, 5 miles to the southwest just off the road to the next large town of Bowling Green. Jett accepted this idea.[10]

Late in the afternoon of Monday, April 24, Jett and Ruggles brought Johnnie to the door of Garrett's farmhouse, about a quarter mile off the main road. They knocked, and introduced their companion as "James William Boyd," a wounded Confederate soldier. They asked Garrett if "Boyd" could stay with him a day or two. "Certainly," Garrett replied.

Garrett had two sons at home who were themselves Confederate soldiers, just returned from the war. Jett and Ruggles rejoined Herold and Absalom Bainbridge, the third rebel soldier, who were waiting at the gate, and the three of them continued toward Bowling Green. They dropped Herold off to spend the night at the home of another CSA sympathizer, Virginia Clark.[11]

Johnnie, meanwhile, immediately warmed to Garrett's hospitality. After taking a nap, he had dinner with the large family. Then he smoked a pipe on the front porch while engaging in some pleasant conversation. At about 10 o'clock, he went to sleep in the bed of one of Garrett's soldier sons. Johnnie slept very soundly. The following morning, Tuesday, he got up late. It was the warmest day in months. Without an apparent care in the world, Johnnie lounged about on the lawn. The Garretts had four children under the age of 10. As usual, Johnnie related very well to them. They romped about and played with him, tugging at his shirt sleeves. At lunch, the topic of the Lincoln assassination came up. One of Garrett's soldier sons mentioned that a $140,000 reward had been posted for the capture of the killer. Johnnie took umbrage at the figure. It should be at least $500,000, he remarked. Later he noticed a large map of the United States hanging over the living room fireplace. He asked if he could take it down and study it. He told the Garretts he was planning to go from Richmond to Mexico. With a pencil, he marked out on the map the route he intended to follow.[12]

The news of Johnnie and Herold crossing the Rappahannock in the company of three Confederate soldiers did not take long to reach the ears of federal detectives. Lafayette C. Baker, an Army Colonel, was the head of the Federal Detective Police. He foresaw that Johnnie, if he made it to Virginia, was likely to head to Bowling Green, a railroad stop, and from there, to try to take a train to Orange Court House. His son, Luther Byron Baker, was a detective working

Chapter 33: "O Let Me Die Bravely"

under his father's supervision. Colonel Baker sent into Virginia, by way of the Potomac, a detachment of twenty-five cavalrymen, essentially a posse, under the command of Edward Doherty, to go to Bowling Green with another of his detectives, Everton Conger, and Baker's son Luther. They reached the Port Conway wharf at about 1 o'clock in the afternoon on Tuesday, April 25. The detectives quickly ascertained, from Rollins, that two men exactly matching the descriptions of Johnnie and Herold had crossed the river in the company of three rebel soldiers the day before. Rollins's wife Bettie volunteered that she knew one of the Confederate soldiers, Jett, and that he could be expected to be found with his girlfriend Izora Gouldman in a hotel in Bowling Green.[13]

The posse, taking turns using the ferry, crossed the Rappahannock and headed to Bowling Green. Their approach along the road was noted. Ruggles and Bainbridge, after dropping Herold at the Garrett farm, went in to warn Johnnie he was being pursued. The news swiftly ended Johnnie's period of relaxation. He asked one of Garrett's sons to fetch his guns, which he had stored in their bedroom. Johnnie sent Ruggles and Bainbridge on their way, assuring them he would never be taken alive. Then he hobbled into the woods, in case Garrett's home should be searched. Soon the sound of trampling hoofs was heard coming from the road. It was Conger's posse. The detectives did not, however, stop at Garrett's. They were bent on reaching Bowling Green to look for Jett. Johnnie and Herold remained concealed in the trees until after dark. By the time the senior Richard Garrett sent word to "Boyd" to come in for supper, the family was thoroughly nervous about the developments. Johnnie and the Garretts agreed it would be best for Johnnie and Herold to sleep outside, in a tobacco barn that was currently being used to store hay. Because Garrett's soldier sons suspected Johnnie and Herold might be thinking about making off with horses, they locked them into the structure for the night. The sons slept outside as well, in an adjacent grain storage shed.[14]

Conger, at the head of his posse, made it to the Star Hotel where Jett was staying well after 11 p.m. The matron of the house, Julia Gouldman, was the mother of Jett's girlfriend. She showed the way to where Jett was sleeping in a bed with one of her sons. At gunpoint, the detectives brusquely ordered him to get up and get dressed. Jett, although he had done loyal service to the Confederate cause, was a rational person. He was not particularly in sympathy with terrorists. He asked to speak privately with Conger. Conger asked his fellow detective Baker, as well as Doherty, to step out of the room. Jett told Conger, "I know what you want, and I will tell you where they can be found." He truthfully told him that Johnnie and Herold were at Garrett's. He even volunteered to show Conger and his men the way to get there on this dark, moonless night. The interminable manhunt finally was nearing its end.[15]

The posse arrived at the Garrett farm at 2 a.m. Luther Baker dismounted and forced the outer gate. The troops then entered. They circled the house before Baker went up to the kitchen entrance. Baker rapped and yelled lustily. The patriarch, Richard Garrett, unbolted the door and came out. He was seized by the throat and threatened with a pistol. The old man at first did not talk. He then claimed that the visitors had gone into the woods. The soldiers prepared to search the house. Richard protested that there were undressed women in there. Baker did not care. He burst into the other room. Everybody denied knowing the strangers' whereabouts. The detectives began making arrangements to hang Richard Garrett on the spot.

One of Garrett's soldier sons appeared. A rational being, he said, "Don't hurt the old man; he is scared. I will tell you where the men are. In the barn." At that, one soldier was left to guard Richard Garrett and the rest went out to surround the barn. Baker and Conger approached the door to the barn. They

Chapter 33: "O Let Me Die Bravely"

heard rustling as if from someone walking around on the hay. They held a cocked pistol to the head of Garrett's son Jack. Baker opened the padlock that locked the door.

Then the petrified Jack Garrett was forced into the barn. Immediately Baker locked the door on the outside. The youth appealed for the outlaws to surrender. Johnnie growled: "Damn you. Get out of here. You have betrayed me." At the same time, he placed his hand in his pocket as if for a pistol. Jack Garrett slipped quickly through the reopened door, reporting that his errand had failed. Baker yelled out: "Either surrender your arms and then give yourselves up, or we'll set fire to the place. We mean to take you both, or to have a bonfire and a shooting match." No answer came.

All this time a candle was lighting the area beside the two detectives. So, it would have been fairly easy for someone inside the barn, especially a crack shot like Johnnie, to shoot them. The light was cautiously removed. Baker called out: "There is no chance for escape. Give yourselves up!" A "bold, clarion reply" came from within: "Who are you, and what do you want with us?" Baker responded: "We want you to deliver up your arms and become our prisoners." "But who are you?" asked the same strong voice. Baker responded, "That makes no difference. We know who you are, and we want you. We have here fifty men, armed with carbines and pistols. You cannot escape." After a long pause, Johnnie called out, "Captain, this is a hard case, I swear. Perhaps I am being taken by my own friends." The detectives did not reply. Johnnie continued to palaver. He said, "Well, give us a little time to consider." Baker said "Very well. Take time." He said his party would allow 5 minutes, and then the barn would be set on fire.

Another long pause, more than 5 minutes and much more like a half hour, went by.[16]

Baker finally broke the silence. "Well, we have waited long enough; surrender your arms and come out or we'll fire the barn." Conger ordered one of Garrett's sons to pile up highly flammable pine boughs next to a corner of the barn. Johnnie replied: "I am but a cripple, a one-legged man. Withdraw your forces one hundred yards from the door, and I will come. Give me a chance for my life, captain. I will never be taken alive." Baker responded. "We did not come here to fight, but to capture you. I say again, appear, or the barn shall be fired." Those listening outside could hear a long, audible breath. Johnnie then called out, "Well, then, my brave boys, prepare a stretcher for me." The long back-and-forth continued. Johnnie said at another time: "Well, Captain, make quick work of it; shoot me through the heart," or words to that effect. Another pause followed, broken by low discussions from within. Herold seemed to be trying to persuade Johnnie to give up.[17]

It was next Johnnie who called out, "Captain, there's a man inside who wants to surrender mighty bad." Baker responded, "Let him come, if he will bring his arms." Johnnie called out: "I declare before my Maker that this man here is innocent of any crime whatever." Herold, at the door, said "Let me out; open the door; I want to surrender." Baker responded: "Hand out your arms, then." "I haven't got any," said Herold. Johnnie volunteered: "He hasn't got any arms; they are mine, and I have kept them." Baker: "Well, he carried the carbine, and must bring it out." Johnnie: "On the word and honor of a gentleman, he has no arms with him. They are mine, and I have got them." Herold by now was by the door, within whispering distance of Doherty.[18]

Doherty told him to put out his hands to be handcuffed, at the same time opening the door slightly. Herold thrust out his hands, and was handcuffed, then jerked out. He began to blubber about being innocent. Conger threatened to gag him unless he shut up. Johnnie then made a last appeal in a strong, clear voice. "Captain, give me a chance. Draw off your men and I will fight them singly. I could have killed you six times

Chapter 33: "O Let Me Die Bravely"

tonight, but I believe you to be a brave man, and would not murder you. Give a lame man a show."

Before he stopped speaking, Conger, who had slipped around to the rear of the barn, threw some loose straws through a crack, and lit a match on them. They were dry and blazed up in an instant. A fire soon started inside the barn. Now, with the fire blazing up, Johnnie could be seen from outside by the troops looking in. He was standing upright on a crutch. Johnnie approached the fire and looked around for a way to stamp out the flames. He saw that it was impossible, because the flames were rising too rapidly. He turned, and started moving toward the door, carrying his carbine. As he did, Sergeant Boston Corbett, who was watching through a crack, fired a single shot. Johnnie fell headlong to the floor, landing in a heap. Baker rushed in. He at first thought Johnnie had shot himself. Conger grabbed Johnnie's arms and felt that they were limp. Conger lifted Johnnie up and saw that he had a bullet hole in the right side of his neck.[19]

Conger and two sergeants quickly entered the barn, picking up Johnnie's body and moving it hastily away from the advancing flame. They laid him outside on the grass, which was moist with dew. Conger called for a bucket of water, which he dashed on Johnnie's face. This revived Johnnie slightly. He was paralyzed, but able to move his lips. Conger put his ear very close to Johnnie's mouth. Johnnie made several efforts to speak. Conger was barely able to make out the words that Johnnie was trying to say. "Tell Mother I die for my country." Conger pronounced these words himself, and then asked, "Booth, do I repeat it correctly?" Johnnie was able to indicate "yes."[20]

By now, the tobacco barn was completely engulfed in flames. Johnnie was carried away from it and was placed on a mattress on the porch of the Garrett residence. The single rifle bullet had bored through two vertebrae of John's neck, severing his spinal cord. Thus, although he did not bleed to death, the wound instantly paralyzed him from the neck down. He was unable to cough to clear the blood that gradually entered into his lungs from the neck wound. In a mechanism similar to crucifixion, Johnnie slowly suffocated. In his agony, he was able to mouth to Conger, two or three times, the words, "Kill me, kill me." This was to no avail. The detectives declined to shoot him, as Johnnie requested.

Instead, the women of the Garrett household applied water and brandy to his lips. Johnnie remained alert while his body gradually weakened. He was able to indicate to those present, by facial gesture, that he wanted to be turned over into different positions. The onlookers obliged. Johnnie had them alternately place him on his back, belly, and side, but none of these positions succeeded in relieving his discomfort and his increasing difficulty breathing. Shortly after sunrise, Johnnie asked that his hands, which he could not feel, be held up so that he could see them. "Useless, useless," he muttered. Those were to be his last words.[21] Before the sun reached the height of a man on Wednesday, April 26, 1865, Johnnie suffered his last twitch of death.[22]

And, along with him, the legally-sanctioned institution of slavery in the United States of America coughed its last, and died.

Epilogue

The Constitutional Amendment

Passed by Congress on January 31, 1865, and swiftly ratified on December 6, 1865, the Thirteenth Amendment to the United States Constitution abolished the institution of slavery in the United States. It provides, very simply: "Neither slavery nor involuntary servitude, except as a punishment for crime whereof the party shall have been duly convicted, shall exist within the United States, or any place subject to their jurisdiction."[1]

The Hangings

Little time was wasted putting Johnnie's followers on trial. Like other Confederate spies captured during the war, they would be tried by a military tribunal rather than a regular criminal jury. None of the defendants was allowed to speak. At the trial's conclusion, David Herold, George Atzerodt, Lewis Powell, and Mary Surratt were all sentenced to hang. Scant attention was paid by the judges to arguments by defense attorneys that Atzerodt, for sure, had withdrawn from the assassinations, and that Herold really had done nothing relating to them other than helping Johnnie and Powell get away. Samuel Mudd, Ned Spangler, Michael O'Laughlen, and Samuel Arnold were also found guilty of participating in the

Preparing the condemned to die on the gallows, July 7, 1865.
L to R: Mary Surratt, Lewis Powell, David Herold, George Atzerodt.
Library of Congress

assassination conspiracy, and were sentenced to life imprisonment at hard labor.

The condemned learned of their sentences on the night of July 6. The executions were set to occur at 1 p.m. the following day. Mary Surratt's daughter Anna, encouraged by the existence of a dissent in the tribunal to her mother's death sentence, made a hysterical visit to Andrew Johnson, pleading with him to spare her mother. It was to no avail. Roman Catholic Church officials protested that at least three days were needed in order to administer the prescribed rites prior to her death. Johnson was unmoved. He was used to approving wartime hangings as the former military governor of Tennessee.

Friday, July 7, 1865 was one of those miserably hot, humid summer days for which the Maryland and Virginia region is justly infamous. The muggy air was filled with hum and excitement. A reporter for the *New York Tribune* that day wrote: "So great a crime required an equally signal punishment, not only as a just retribution upon the guilty, but as a warning to any who might hereafter be tempted to imitate their atrocious example."

Johnnie's followers were executed behind prison walls at Fort McNair, located at the southern tip of the District of Columbia where the Potomac meets the Anacostia. Some 200 highly coveted passes were distributed to newspaper reporters and other favored witnesses. Three thousand soldiers stood guard outside the prison. The entire scaffold was constructed from the ground up in the early morning hours, in the prison yard just outside the cells of the condemned, who were easily able to hear the noises of the hammering and sawing. Four holes to hold the bodies were also dug that morning, right below the gallows. The condemned were led in front of their graves on their way to mount the stairs to the platform. Mary Surratt, the first of the prisoners brought out, collapsed. She had become sick during the trial, requiring her to be moved to a special cell,[2] and the thought of being hanged did nothing to improve her condition. Trembling and fainting, she had to be carried up to her seat facing the noose. Powell, on the other hand, received the general approbation of the audience for the calm, soldierly demeanor with which he met his destiny. Umbrellas were held over the heads of the condemned, to fend off the stifling solar heat, as they received their final rites. Then, they were made to stand, their arms and legs were wrapped with bindings, the nooses were placed and tightened around their necks. White hoods went over their heads to hide the horror of their strangled faces. The last words heard from any of the condemned just before the dual traps were sprung were shouted by Atzerodt in his heavy German accent. "Gentlemen, beware. Goodbye, gentlemen. May we meet in another world!"

Only Mary Surratt died with the drop. The bodies of the

three males visibly contorted and convulsed as they slowly died of asphyxiation.[3] But, after hanging 30 minutes, their still bodies were ready to be examined and pronounced dead.

The Backers

The Government's investigations into the terrorist raids of John Brown and John Wilkes Booth bore unmistakable similarities. In each instance, the foot soldiers were hanged on a scaffold, but the deeper involvement of the financial backers was entirely swept underneath a rug. Largely this occurred for political reasons. The financial backers had helpful friends, and even helpful enemies, in high places. Thus, even though plenty of documentary "tracks" were left behind,[4] the backers were able to deflect and deny their way out of trouble. In this they were aided and abetted by those in power who wished to deny credence to the cause of the terrorists. With respect to Senator Mason's committee, which handled the John Brown investigation, Jeffrey Rossbach summed up the dynamic brilliantly:[5]

> Mason's analysis was not an "unskillful" one. Indeed, anyone who reads the report can recognize it as a piece of master craftsmanship. The Virginia senator implied a full understanding of how and why the conspiracy took place. Yet he succeeded in doing to the general public what the conspirators tried to do to him. In the report he successfully obscured the relationships of Brown and his supporters so as to prevent the public from learning of their tacit agreement on the principles of justified political violence. Mason accepted statements about Brown's 'remarkable reticence' and his 'secretiveness,' not so much because he believed that this was the case, but because he wanted to turn those claims to his advantage. Brown's friends might escape prosecution by pleading that they were not informed of his

intentions, but Mason then used the same argument to prove they did not condone Brown's acts at Harpers Ferry.

The Confederate leaders who financed Johnnie similarly escaped the noose. The prosecutors completely ignored ample evidence of a direct connection between Lewis Powell and the regular CSA army, including his commander John Mosby, who was the darling of Jefferson Davis. In fact, the prosecutors' efforts to look into his identity and history were so lax, Powell was tried, sentenced, and hanged under his pseudonym of "Lewis Payne."[6] Republican politicians who held supreme power after Lincoln's death were no longer concerned with the defeated Confederates. They were far more concerned with getting rid of Andrew Johnson, the accidental President from the opposing Democratic party.[7] For purposes of his impeachment trial, they would concoct a conspiracy theory that Johnson secretly was friends with John Wilkes Booth; that Johnnie and Johnson had together kept two sisters as mistresses in 1864 when Johnnie was in Nashville and Johnson was the military governor of Tennessee.[8]

Jefferson Davis fled south into Georgia, where he was taken into custody at a town called Irwinville on May 10, 1865. He was put in prison at Fortress Monroe, where he remained for two years. Although the House of Representatives voted to have him prosecuted for treason, the trial never occurred. Eventually he was released on bail (with Gerrit Smith signing on as one of his bondsmen), and left for Canada. On Christmas Day, 1868, Davis, along with all other past CSA leaders, was granted a pardon by the outgoing President Johnson. He returned to prosperity, and he lived on through the 1880s, ultimately collaborating on a series of articles with John Brown's friend and biographer, James Redpath. Upon his death on December 5, 1889, Jefferson Davis was buried as a great national hero.[9]

Judah Benjamin, Davis's Secretary of State, who coordinated the financing of Confederate terrorism and who on September 17, 1864 provided Thomas Conrad with $400 in gold to be used for the kidnapping plot against Lincoln, avoided capture and escaped from Florida with the help of a blockade runner. Eventually he made his way to England, where he pursued a highly successful career as a barrister into the 1880s.[10]

George Sanders was instrumental in bringing about the discrediting of the case for conspiracy against Confederate leaders. He played a mysterious double agent role, helping plant a man named Charles Dunham, whom Sanders had previously produced to give false testimony in the St. Albans proceedings, to give false testimony under the false name of Sanford Conover in the Lincoln assassination trial. When "Conover" was thoroughly impeached as a perjurer, other witnesses, who probably were testifying truthfully when they told of a close connection between Sanders and Johnnie, were discredited along with him. The net effect was that the case for a Confederate Cabinet conspiracy involving Johnnie collapsed.[11] Little effort was made to revive it. Sanders fled Canada to Europe, where he rejoined the same expat community he had once assisted in his role as U.S. Consul. He was involved in supporting revolutionaries in Italy and in the short-lived Paris Commune of 1870, before finally returning to the United States in 1872. He died shortly afterwards.[12]

The Survivors

Hugh Forbes returned to Italy after John Brown's capture and hanging. There he rejoined Garibaldi's forces and participated in the famous conquest of all of southern Italy by the revolutionary *Mille* (Garibaldi's force of only 1,000) in 1860. Following the reunification of Italy, accomplished as a result of Garibaldi's heroics in which Forbes took a part, he moved with his family to the city of Pisa, where he led a modest life.

He died on July 22, 1892.[13]

Owen Brown, John Brown's lone son who survived his father's terrorist ventures both in Kansas and at Harpers Ferry, moved back to the original family home in Ohio. After the Civil War, he was for some time a grape grower, in association with two other brothers. Then, with a number of Brown family members, he relocated to California. He took up residence on a hilltop near Pasadena, where he lived on until 1891.[14]

Osborne Perry Anderson was the lone African American survivor among John Brown's Harpers Ferry followers. He wrote an eyewitness narrative, called *A Voice from Harpers Ferry*, which remains the only available account of the planning and execution of the raid by one of John Brown's men. Having found his way out of Harpers Ferry before the final attack by the force commanded by Robert E. Lee, Anderson escaped to Canada. Then, during the Civil War, he enlisted and fought on the side of the Union. He died in Washington City on December 13, 1872.[15]

Although Henry Seward bled profusely from Powell's knife attack, he never lost consciousness. He was able to direct his servants to "call for the police and a surgeon, and close the house." Dr. Verdi, whose messenger Powell had pretended to be, arrived a few minutes later. Henry's son Frederick was much more seriously injured from his head bashing with Powell's pistol. He fell into a coma for days, and his imminent death was feared. However, Frederick eventually recovered. Henry's face was permanently disfigured from Powell's slashing knife. Henry's wife died at the age of 59 two months after the attack. The death of his daughter Fanny at the age of 21 followed a year later.[16]

In a strange irony typical of terrorism, Johnnie's two most prominent victims, Abraham Lincoln and Henry Seward, were also, by the end of the war, two of the most moderate Union leaders. Thus they were, in reality, the most important politicians favoring forgiveness of the defeated Southern aristocracy. In Lincoln's absence, Henry became a steadfast advocate of reconciliation. He became a close ally and supporter of the new President, Andrew Johnson. In that capacity he came into sharp conflict with so-called Radical Republicans, personified by Charles Sumner. Charles and other radicals disliked the Johnson Administration's tendency to continue the old-guard Southern leadership. They favored the federal government's active intervention to assure civil rights for African Americans. Johnson severely antagonized the radicals and their supporters by vetoing civil rights legislation.[17] But, despite facing popular wrath for his backing of Johnson, during March and April 1867 Henry as Secretary of State accomplished the achievement for which he is now best known, the acquisition for the United States from Russia of "Seward's Folly" – then called Russian America and now the state of Alaska – for a total purchase price of $7.2 million. Henry died on October 10, 1872.[18]

John Surratt, at the time of the assassinations, was in Elmira, New York, scouting a project to free Confederate soldiers imprisoned in a prisoner of war camp there. By April 18, he returned to Montreal, where he registered under the alias of "John Harrison." Finding that he was the subject of a manhunt and a $25,000 offer of reward, Surratt soon left the hotel and was hidden for a time in the home of a Confederate agent. On April 22 he was taken out of Montreal and conveyed to the residence of a Catholic priest named Father Charles Boucher. Here he used the fictitious name, "Charles Armstrong." "Armstrong" resided secretly with Father Boucher for almost three months. Some people became suspicious about why Father Boucher was keeping a young man in his house. To stop whispers, Surratt had to leave. He was taken back to Montreal and placed with another Catholic priest, a Reverend LaPierre, in a lodging virtually in the shadow of the Bishop's residence.

Eventually it was decided by the Church to send Surratt to Rome. Preparations were made to enlist him in the army of the Papal State. Surratt sailed from Quebec on September 16, 1865. This time he used the alias of "McCarty." He carried letters of introduction to Catholic clergymen in England. After a brief stay there, he was forwarded on to Rome, which he reached in November or December 1865. In Rome he was again assisted by Catholic clergy. Now he went by a new fake name, "John Watson." In January 1866, "Watson" enlisted in the Papal Zouaves. But, as fate would have it, he was recognized by one of his old St. Charles College classmates. His tip led Henry Seward, as Secretary of State, to authorize an official inquiry with the Vatican about Surratt.

Surratt was arrested at Veroli, about 10 miles northwest of Frosinone, Italy, on November 7, 1866. However, the next morning he surprised everyone with an acrobatic vault over a balustrade, which far surpassed Johnnie's leap from the President's box at Ford's Theater. Surratt tumbled down into the valley below, got up, and made a clean getaway. Several days later, he came across a camp of Garibaldi's followers who were fighting against the Papal State in their efforts to unify Italy. They gladly befriended the renegade American. With their help, Surratt was able to board a steamer bound for Alexandria, Egypt, this time traveling under the alias of "Walters," on November 17, 1866. However, Surratt's luck finally ran out. Word of his departure on the ship was telegraphed ahead and, when Surratt disembarked at Alexandria on November 23, 1866, he was arrested. He was shipped back to the United States and arrived in the middle of February, 1867. He was promptly indicted for conspiracy to murder President Lincoln, and was placed on trial in June.[19]

By that time, the ardor for more war-related hangings had totally cooled. Under President Johnson, there was a growing willingness to allow former rebels back into the political arena.

There was also now some popular sympathy for John's deceased mother, Mary Surratt. Southern sympathizers referred to her hanging as a "murder." Catholic prelates very publicly supported the defense of Surratt, sitting right beside him in court. They brought twenty students from St. Charles College into the courtroom to shake hands with the celebrity defendant, while pointedly shunning Louis Weichmann, the would-be Catholic priest and the prosecution's star witness. On Friday, August 9, 1867, after three days of deliberation, the jury was discharged after it announced that it was hopelessly deadlocked.[20]

Surratt was never retried. On December 6, 1870, at the courthouse in Rockville, Maryland, he gave a public lecture in which he set forth his full version of his participation in the Lincoln kidnapping conspiracy. Surratt lived on into the twentieth century. He had seven children and a career as a steamship line accountant. He died in 1916.[21]

The Deranged

Henry Rathbone, who bled profusely from his arm after being stabbed by Johnnie in the box at Ford's Theater, healed from the physical wound. However, he seemed to have lingering psychological after-effects. In 1867, he married Clara Harris, his portly stepsister who had accompanied him, with the Lincolns, to the theater on that fateful evening. They had three children. However, Rathbone began suffering from serious hypochondria and mental instability. He became convinced that Clara was unfaithful. He relocated, with the family, to Europe, where he sought treatment in a variety of doctors' offices and spas. On December 23, 1883 in Hanover, Germany, he attacked his wife with a revolver. Rathbone then stabbed himself six times as an attempt at suicide. Clara died; Rathbone recovered. Charged with murder, he was declared insane and spent the rest of his life, until 1911, in an asylum. One of the children, Henry Riggs Rathbone, later became a U.S.

Congressman.[22]

Boston Corbett, the man who shot John Wilkes Booth, was born Thomas Corbett. A hat maker by trade, he might well be termed a mad hatter. He was noted for his erratic behavior and incoherent speeches, which usually had overtones of religious fanaticism. He became paranoid that people were out to get him because he had deprived them of the pleasure of prosecuting and executing Johnnie. Ultimately, he moved to Kansas, where he spent some time as a preacher. He got into serious trouble by brandishing a revolver in the Kansas House of Representatives. As a result, he was committed to the Topeka Asylum for the insane. He escaped. Then he moved to Minnesota and lived as a hermit. He is believed to have died in a wildfire on September 1, 1894.[23]

The Resurrected

Samuel Mudd, along with Johnnie's other followers who were tried and not hanged, was sent to imprisonment and labor at Fort Jefferson in the Dry Tortugas, a stifling desert island in the Florida Caribbean 70 miles west of Key West. In September of 1867, a yellow fever outbreak occurred that infected all non-African Americans on the island. At first, the officers and their families were hit harder by the epidemic than the prisoners. The post's doctor died, after which Mudd was pressed into service as the hospital physician. Sam Arnold caught yellow fever, and recovered. Mike O'Laughlen, too, caught it, and died after a struggle. Mudd's body acted as if he had a prior immunity. Ultimately, he contracted the fever, but the case was relatively mild. He remained in charge of medical duties. The officers of the post wrote out a petition of appreciation for his services, urging the immediate release of Mudd from custody.[24] On February 13, 1869, after the election of Grant as his successor but prior to the end of his term, President Johnson issued Mudd a pardon, resulting in his release about a month later. Ned Spangler, who had become a close friend of Mudd during the four years the two of them were imprisoned together at Fort Jefferson, came to live with the Mudds at their Southern Maryland property near Zekiah Swamp, until Spangler died of natural causes eighteen months later. Mudd himself passed away at age 50, on January 10, 1883.[25]

George Kane, the Baltimore Police Marshal whose lengthy confinement without charges provided a cause for Johnnie to become angry and who, very likely, helped encourage Johnnie's participation in the plot to kidnap Lincoln, returned after the war's end to his native city. He again became involved in politics. In 1877, he was elected Mayor of Baltimore. Less than a year later, he died in office.[26]

Thomas H. Hines was John Hunt Morgan's chief lieutenant when he burned his terrorist swath through Kentucky, Indiana, and Ohio during the summer of 1863. Captured and imprisoned along with Morgan, he was instrumental in devising Morgan's escape. Afterwards he made his way into Canada, where he was welcomed into the CSA's "Canada Cabinet." Hines rapidly was entrusted by the Confederate leadership with coordinating terrorist attacks. In addition to various plots to instigate uprisings by Copperheads, Hines was involved in planning both the St. Albans raid and the conspiracy to burn New York City. Undoubtedly, he was also in on Johnnie's plot to kidnap Lincoln. However, the highly intelligent Hines was a very cautious, capable spy, which means he excelled at keeping secrets. As a result, although some of his terrorist exploits were revealed, the full scope of his involvement in CSA-financed terrorist activities will never be known.

When his arrest was sought after the terror attacks on Lincoln and Seward, Hines managed to escape back into Canada. In Toronto, he began studying law with John C. Breckinridge, the former Vice-President whom Lincoln had defeated in the Presidential election of 1860, and who had served as a Confederate general during the war. Taking advantage of a general decree of amnesty issued by President Johnson to former Confederates, Hines returned to Tennessee, where he passed the bar examination on June 12, 1866. He then relocated to Kentucky, where he took up law practice. He was elected first a county judge, and then, in 1878, to the Kentucky Court of Appeals, at that time Kentucky's highest court. He became Chief Justice, a capacity in which he served from 1884 until 1886. At that time, in consultation with Jefferson Davis, he published a series of articles dedicated to "the Lost Cause of the Confederacy."[27]

Charles Hamilton, evading capture after his terrorist massacre near Trading Post, Kansas on May 19, 1858, made his way into the Deep South. He returned to the relative safety of Georgia. Hamilton was never brought to justice for his crimes. Only one member of his band was ever caught and hanged for the offense, and that did not occur until five years later, when the Civil War was in progress. After moving to Texas, where he farmed and bred horses, Hamilton later returned to Georgia and became a state legislator in 1878. He lived on until 1880.[28]

The Heroes

Prudence Crandall, on August 12, 1834, suddenly married a widower named Calvin Philleo, who was a highly eccentric and borderline mentally ill Baptist minister. Philleo had placed an advertisement, seeking a new wife, after his first wife died. The marriage was a development that befuddled Prudence's abolitionist friends, such as Lloyd Garrison. Philleo fell into a burning fireplace, in a horrifying accident that left him grossly disfigured and blind in one eye.[29]

Once, when asked why she had married Philleo, Prudence replied, "Someone had to take care of him." Saddled with a troubled husband, Prudence perpetually struggled financially.

Eventually she moved west, first to Illinois, where she spent the Civil War years, and then to Kansas. She resumed teaching.[30] Prudence was in Kansas in 1879 when it became the objective of the "Exodusters." This was a mass exodus of African Americans, mostly former slaves, who left the South by the thousands in an effort to free themselves from the taint of racial bigotry and segregation that remained long after racially-based servitude was outlawed. They hoped to find in Kansas and Nebraska a land free from inherited prejudices. Of course, this was a pipe dream. They found plenty of racism waiting for them among the former "free white state" advocates who had largely populated Kansas and Nebraska during the 1850s.

In her later years, Prudence became a passionate supporter of women's rights, networking with leaders in the national women's suffrage movement. In the media, she was fondly remembered and canonized as a heroine and a martyr. Finally, in 1886, Prudence was granted a pension by the state of Connecticut in partial recognition of the state-sponsored abuses committed against her. Prudence lived until January 28, 1890.[31]

On October 22, 1859, in the immediate aftermath of John Brown's terrorist raid at Harpers Ferry, Frederick Douglass fled to Canada to escape arrest. Papers left behind by John implicated Frederick in John's planning activities. On November 12, 1859, Frederick boarded a vessel from Quebec, Canada to Liverpool, England. There he was hosted by old friends, including Julia Griffiths (now married). He remained in "exile" in England for six months, supporting himself by giving lectures. He finally returned to the United States in April 1860.[32]

During the Civil War, Frederick was asked by George Stearns, the former member of John's "Secret Six," to assist in raising African American regiments to take the field on behalf of the Union. He succeeded in raising two regiments, which acquitted themselves very well in North Carolina and South Carolina. But Frederick was disappointed that the African American troops were not treated on an equal footing with white soldiers, particularly with respect to their treatment after being captured as prisoners of war. Frederick himself was not granted an officer's commission, apparently because African American officers were not wanted, but three of his sons enlisted in the Union forces.[33]

When the war was over and slavery formally abolished for good, Frederick felt a strange tinge of sadness. It was as if the cause he had fought for all his life was ended. But Frederick continued to fight, on a personal level, against the ingrained habits of racial prejudice. He recognized that though African Americans "were not slaves, they were not quite free." He therefore found that, in his own words, "the Negro had a cause."[34] Frederick became a leading advocate of the Fifteenth Amendment to the U.S. Constitution, passed by Congress in February 1869 and ratified a year later, which guaranteed to African Americans, and expressly to ex-slaves, the right to vote. Frederick was appointed by President Grant to be on the governing council of the District of Columbia, although he soon resigned the position and elected to have the balance of his term filled by his son Lewis. Later he was appointed by President Hayes to be U.S. Marshal for the District of Columbia.[35]

Frederick strongly opposed the "Exodus," as he called it, of the late 1870s. He viewed it as a "premature, disheartening surrender." "The business of this nation," he bitterly pointed out, "is to protect its citizens where they are, not to transplant them where they will not need protection."[36]

Frederick died, shortly after giving a speech, on February 20, 1895.

During the Civil War, Harriet Tubman served with the U.S. Army as a scout and spy in the Carolinas. Afterwards, she continued to live, with her extended family, in the property she had acquired from Henry Seward in Auburn, New York. In that home she had "a great deal of young and old, black and white, all poorer than she." Finally, in 1903, when she was infirm and financially incapable of continuing to maintain it, she gave the residence to the African Methodist Episcopal Zion Church.

Harriet disagreed with Frederick in his support of the Fifteenth Amendment. She strongly believed that this amendment should also encompass a guarantee of the right to vote for women. She became a prominent advocate of women's suffrage. She continued to appear at meetings to raise support and funds for the cause of a woman's right to vote into the early twentieth century.

Harriet was recognized as a virtual living legend, the "Black Joan of Arc." Queen Victoria invited Harriet to attend her Diamond Jubilee in 1897, although Harriet declined. She died on March 10, 1913, at the age of 91.[37]

As of 2022, there is a proposal to replace the official portrait of President Andrew Jackson with a portrait of Harriet Tubman on the $20 bill used as everyday currency in the United States. This initiative was delayed during the four-year Trump administration, but it has been revived under President Joe Biden. The Biden Administration has announced plans to speed up the transition to eliminating the image of one of America's most pro-slavery Presidents and substituting that of the woman called "Moses."[38]

Endnotes

Endnotes to Chapter 1: The Coming of the Prophet

[1] This chapter's narrative is taken directly from Nat's own personal account, as reported to Thomas R. Gray the day after his arrest, November 1, 1831. Gray assures the reader that Nat personally verified the accuracy of what Gray wrote out before the court that pronounced him guilty. Numerous aspects of the account are so startling that they could not plausibly be viewed as fabrications or embellishments. Gray served as defense counsel in at least five of the capital trials related to the terrorist attacks that proceeded before Nat was captured. Gray soon published Nat's account as the major element of *The Confessions of Nat Turner, the Leader of the Late Insurrection in Southampton, Virginia*, (T. W. White, printer, Richmond, Va., 1832). As to the sequence of events and other factual matters, Nat's account as reported by Gray is substantially consistent with the testimony that was recorded in the Minutes of the Court for the trials. Some names and other details in this chapter's narrative were supplied from this testimony. In a few instances, names and details were also supplied by an account written at the end of the nineteenth century by William Sidney Drewry. W.S. Drewry, *The Southampton Insurrection* (Neale, Washington, D.C., 1900). Drewry

claimed he interviewed old timers in Southampton County who recalled either Nat's raid itself or local lore about the raid. Drewry's version is written from a largely pro-Southern point of view, and likely contains some significant inaccuracies and embellishments. A few other details were supplied by the careful research reflected in Patrick H. Breen, *The Land Will Be Deluged With Blood, A New History of the Nat Turner Revolt* (Oxford Univ. Press, Oxford, 2015).

[2] Drewry, p. 67.

[3] See Drewry, p. 73.

[4] From these statistics, it is evident that there was a large disparity between the number of African Americans who joined Nat's motley army, which is reported as having been as many as fifty to sixty both by Nat himself and by eyewitnesses to the attacks, and the much smaller number who were hanged after trial. Two of the seventeen hanged, it should added, were not even accused of being participants in Nat's army itself; they were merely persons of color who were heard to voice sympathy for the terrorists. How to explain this numerical discrepancy is necessarily a matter of conjecture. Some of the rebels were killed in battle. The trials mostly involved defendants who were in some sense borderline cases. It is likely that many of those persons readily identified as participants were summarily executed – lynched, if you like the term -- within a day or two after the raid was quelled and did not survive to be tried. The bulk of the participants, once the cause was lost, quietly returned to their plantations. If confronted with witnesses or other evidence to substantiate their presence during the eighteen hours of rampage, they then claimed that they had been coerced by the terrorists into joining (there was much trial testimony to this effect). Their owners had a financial incentive to believe these kinds of claims.

[5] Drewry, pp. 90-92.

[6] Gray, p. 22.

Endnotes to Chapter 2: Fighting the Serpent

[1] Laqueur, pp. 8–9; see also Bernard Lewis, *The Assassins: A Radical Sect in Islam* (Perseus Books Group, New York, 2003).

[2] Laqueur, p. 9; see also Mike Dash, *Thug, the True Story of India's Murderous Cult* (Granta Publications, London, 2011); Kim A. Wagner, *Thuggee: Banditry and the British in Early Nineteenth Century India* (Palgrave MacMillan, Basingstoke, UK, 2007).

[3] Laqueur, "introductory note," April 1977.

[4] See generally, Robert Riggs, *Sofia Perovskaya, Terrorist Princess* (Global Harmony Press, Berkeley 2017).

[5] Gray, p. 10.

[6] See, e.g., Charles Edward Banks, *History of York, Maine* (Regional Publishing Co., Baltimore, 1967), pp. 279–299; S. C. Gwynne, *Empire of the Summer Moon* (Scribner, New York, 2010), pp. 17–22; see generally, Archibald Loudon, *A Selection of Some of the Most Interesting Narratives of Outrages Committed by the Indians in their Wars with the White People*, vol. 1 and vol. 2 (Garland Publishing, New York, 2007).

[7] Hinton Rowan Helper, *The Impending Crisis of the South* (A. B. Burdick, New York, 1860), pp. 31–32.

[8] Helper, p. 14.

[9] Helper, pp. 14–17.

[10] Helper, pp. 17–23.

[11] Eugene D. Genovese's survey in *Roll, Jordan, Roll* (Pantheon Books, New York, 1972), pp. 587–597, revealed that, besides the massacre led by Nat, alias Nat Turner, there were only two significant slave revolts in the approximately seventy years between the formation of the United States and the American Civil War. Both of these, unlike Nat's, were abortive. Of the three American revolts, including Nat's, Genovese makes the seminal observation that, "Each had literate leaders drawn from the ranks of privileged slaves."

Endnotes to Chapter 3: A Precocious Frontier Puritan

[1] Autobiography of Owen Brown, reprinted in F.B. Sanborn (ed.), *John Brown, Life and Letters* (The Torch Press, Cedar Rapids, Iowa, 1910), p. 8.

[2] John Brown autobiographical letter, Letter to Henry L. Stearns, Red Rock, Iowa, July 15, 1857, reprinted in its entirety in Sanborn, p. 14.

[3] John Brown autobiographical letter, in Sanborn, pp. 13, 15.

[4] John Brown autobiographical letter, in Sanborn, pp. 14–15.

[5] Letter of James Foreman to James Redpath, Dec. 26, 1859, original handwritten and typed versions at Kansas Historical Society, Lawrence, Kansas, p. 2.

[6] Sanborn, p. 31; Richard J. Hinton, *John Brown and His Men* (Funk & Wagnall's, London, 1894), p. 13.

[7] John did complain of trouble with his eyes in a letter to his son some thirty years later, in January of 1846. Sanborn, p. 62.

[8] See, e.g., Sanborn, pp. 30–31; Villard, p. 17; Stephen B. Oates, *To Purge This Land With Blood: A Biography of John Brown* (Harper & Row, New York, 1970), p. 13. Although he too engages in a certain amount of hero-worship, Richard Boyer does give the "bitter defeat" of John Brown's failure in the Plainfield and Morris Academies some of the attention it deserves. Richard O. Boyer, *The Legend of John Brown: A Biography and a History* (Alfred A. Knopf, New York, 1973), pp. 202–206.

[9] Remarks of Anna Perkins, daughter of John Brown's business partner Simon Perkins in Akron, Ohio, quoted in Boyer, p. 349.

[10] See Hinton, p. 24; Villard, p. 26.

[11] Sanborn, pp. 449–450; William E. Connelley, *John Brown* (Crane & Co., Topeka, 1900), p. 92.

[12] John Brown autobiographical letter, in Sanborn, p. 16; see also Villard, p. 24, quoting recollection of John's young Randolph neighbor, George Delamater.

[13] Letter of Milton Lusk, written in 1882, quoted in Sanborn, p. 33.

At p. 36, n.1, Sanborn prints a detailed history and genealogy of the Lusk family, provided to him from a family Bible by John Brown, Jr. (who was Milton's nephew). Sanborn states that the Lusks were distantly related to President John Adams, which no doubt helps explain their "federalist" political orientation. Sanborn here reports that before marrying Amos Lusk, Mary Lusk was previously married to a man named Hull. General William Hull (b. 1853) was the commander of the American army that surrendered Detroit without a battle in August 1812, for which he was later court-martialed. John Brown's autobiographical letter implies that, as a result of his involvement in supplying cattle to Hull's force, he had as a boy acquired some inside knowledge of the leaders in the American force including "some who have figured before the country since that time" Lewis Cass, who was one of Hull's key generals, later became a nationally prominent pro-slavery figure and was the Democratic presidential candidate in 1848. At the time John Brown wrote his autobiographical letter, Cass was serving as Secretary of State under President James Buchanan.

[14] Milton Lusk Letter.

[15] See Richard Baxter, *The Saints' Everlasting Rest* (American Tract Society, New York (c. 1830); originally published 1650), pp. 16–17, 211–212.

[16] Foreman letter, *passim*. In quoting from the Foreman letter in this text, we will honor James's express request to anyone publishing it by correcting his spelling and punctuation errors and by modernizing the language where appropriate.

[17] Sanborn, p. 31, n.1.

[18] Account of John Brown, Jr., reprinted in Sanborn, pp. 91–93.

[19] Account of Ruth Thompson, reprinted in Sanborn, pp. 93–94.

[20] Account of Ruth Thompson, reprinted in Sanborn, p. 95.

[21] Foreman letter, p. 2.

[22] Foreman letter, p. 5.

[23] Foreman letter, p. 3; see Boyer, p. 249, citing letter of John Brown to Seth Thompson, Aug. 13, 1832.
[24] Villard, pp. 24–25; Boyer, p. 251, citing letter of John Brown to Seth Thompson, Aug. 13, 1832, and unpublished 1908 manuscript interview notes by Villard's assistant K. Mayo; Account of Ruth Thompson, quoted in Sanborn, pp. 91, 93; Boyer, p. 252, citing unpublished 1908 manuscript interview notes by Villard's assistant K. Mayo.

Endnotes to Chapter 4: The Rising Cause of Injustice

[1] See Ronald Walters, *The Antislavery Appeal* (Johns Hopkins Univ. Press, Baltimore, 1976), pp. 19–24.

[2] Thomas Earl (ed.), *The Life, Travels and Opinions of Benjamin Lundy* (William Parrish, Philadelphia, 1847) ("Lundy Autobiography"), p. 12.

[3] Alice Dana Adams, *The Neglected Period of Anti-Slavery in America, 1808–1831* (monograph) (Ginn & Co., Boston, 1908), pp. 11–12.

[4] See generally Sven Beckert, *Empire of Cotton, a Global History* (Vintage Books, New York, 2014), pp. 98–135.

[5] The majority of the material on Benjamin Lundy in this chapter is taken from Lundy Autobiography, pp. 13–29. Some gaps in the autobiography are filled in by the works on William Lloyd Garrison, cited *infra*.

[6] See Adams, pp. 26–28, 39–40.

[7] Lundy Autobiography, p. 29. Lundy inaccurately gives the date of the assault as the winter of 1828–1829. On the Woolfolk slave trading enterprises, see also Kate Clifford Larson, *Bound for the Promised Land, Harriet Tubman, Portrait of an American Hero* (Ballantine Books, New York, 2004), pp. 29–30.

[8] On William Lloyd Garrison's history as a typesetter, printer, and editor up until the time he met Benjamin Lundy, see, generally,

Henry Mayer, *All on Fire, William Lloyd Garrison and the Abolition of Slavery* (St. Martin's Press, New York, 1998), pp. 17–51.

[9] Mayer, pp. 90–94.

[10] During the first half of the nineteenth century and extending throughout the period addressed in this book, the developed portion of the District of Columbia was referred to by the term "Washington City." We will use that term throughout this text.

[11] Fehrenbacher, p. 68.

[12] John Jay Chapman, *William Lloyd Garrison, 2nd Ed.* (Atlantic Monthly Press, Boston 1921), p. 46.

[13] Chapman, p. 37.

[14] Chapman, p. 64; Mayer, pp. 134–138.

[15] Mayer, pp. 120–123.

[16] Chapman, pp. 48-88.

[17] Letter, John Brown to Frederick Brown, Nov. 21, 1834, reprinted in Sanborn, pp. 40–41.

[18] Much of this account of the Prudence Crandall persecution is taken from the account of a Unitarian minister who was a close associate and supporter of William Lloyd Garrison, and who became involved in representing Prudence. Samuel J. May, *Some Recollections of Our Antislavery Conflict* (Fields, Osgood & Co., Boston, 1869), pp. 39–72. Notwithstanding his personal involvement, May's account is inaccurate on some points and it glosses over some others.

[19] May, *Some Recollections*; Susan Strane, *Whole Souled Woman, Prudence Crandall and the Education of Black Women* (W. W. Norton & Co., New York, 1990), pp. 4, 9–26.

[20] Strane, pp. 28–45.

[21] Strane, p. 79. Strane points out that May and others in the abolitionist press exaggerated the number of students in the school.

[22] Oates, pp. 29–30; see also Boyer, pp. 228–229, 254–255, 283.

Endnotes to Chapter 5: Sacrificing Life for Liberty

[1] *The Liberator*, vol. 5, no. 2, Jan. 10, 1835, pp. 5–6.

[2] The account given here of Amos Dresser's pilgrimage into Tennessee is taken from "The Narrative of Amos Dresser" that was written by Dresser for the *Cincinnati Gazette*, dated August 25, 1835, and was promptly reprinted in *The Liberator* on September 26, 1835.

[3] Joseph C. and Owen Lovejoy, *Memoir of the Rev. Elijah P. Lovejoy*, (John S. Taylor, New York, 1838) (hereafter, "Lovejoy Brothers"), p. 23.

[4] Henry Tanner, *History of the Rise and Progress of the Alton Riots, Culminating in the Death of Rev. Elijah P. Lovejoy on November 7, 1837* (James D. Warren, Buffalo, NY, 1878), p. 3; Lovejoy Brothers, pp. 32–38.

[5] Lovejoy Brothers, pp. 81–88, 103–109.

[6] Lovejoy Brothers, pp. 136, 138–139, 149–150, 156.

[7] Slightly different accounts of this event are given in different sources. What is given here is an amalgam from Paul Simon, *Freedom's Champion: Elijah Lovejoy* (Carbondale, Illinois: Southern Illinois University Press, 1994), pp. 45–50; Tanner, p. 4; and an article by Elijah Lovejoy published in the *St. Louis Observer* dated May 5, 1836, reprinted in Lovejoy Brothers, pp. 168–171 (inaccurately dated May 5, 1835).

[8] May 5, 1836 *Observer* article by Elijah Lovejoy, reprinted in Lovejoy Brothers, pp. 173–174.

[9] July 21, 1836 *Observer* article by Elijah Lovejoy, reprinted in Lovejoy Brothers, p. 175; see also, Robert M. Pallitto (ed.), *Torture and State Violence in the United States: A Documentary History* (Johns Hopkins Univ. Press, Baltimore, 2011), p. 687. In view of various disruptions in printing of the *Observer*, discussed in text *infra*, it is unclear if the date of this article given by Lovejoy Brothers is correct.

[10] Letter reprinted in Lovejoy Brothers, p. 186.

[11] Elijah Lovejoy Letter of Nov. 10, 1835, reprinted in Lovejoy

Brothers, p. 158.

[12] *Observer* editorial of July 6, 1836, reprinted in Lovejoy Brothers, p. 215.

[13] The *Observer*, July 20, 1837, reprinted in Lovejoy Brothers, pp. 234–244.

[14] Letter from Elijah Lovejoy to B.K. Hart, L.J. Clawson, N. Buckmaster, A. Olney, and John A. Halderman, dated July 26, 1837, reprinted in Lovejoy Brothers, p. 228.

[15] Lovejoy Brothers, pp. 232–234; see also account in *The Liberator*, Sept. 15, 1837, p. 3.

[16] See *The Liberator*, August 18, 1837, p. 3; Sept. 8, 1837, p. 2; Sept. 15, 1837, p. 3.

[17] Lovejoy Brothers, p. 246; see https://mississippi encyclopedia.org/entries/james-smylie/ (accessed May 23, 2020).

[18] Tanner, p. 4; Lovejoy Brothers, p. 251.

[19] Letter by Elijah Lovejoy dated Oct. 3, 1837, reprinted in Lovejoy Brothers, pp. 252–253.

[20] Oct. 3, 1837 letter, reprinted in Lovejoy Brothers, pp. 254–255.

[21] Oct. 3, 1837 letter, reprinted in Lovejoy Brothers, pp. 257–258; Lovejoy Brothers, p. 262; see also Edward Beecher, *Narrative of Riots at Alton in Connection with the Death of Rev. Elijah P. Lovejoy* (George Holton, Alton, 1838), pp. 44–45.

[22] Lovejoy Brothers, pp. 263–267; Tanner, p. 6; see also Beecher, pp. 28–34.

[23] Speech by Elijah Lovejoy, Nov. 3, 1837, reprinted in Lovejoy Brothers, pp. 279–281.

[24] Tanner, p. 8.

[25] Tanner, p. 9; Lovejoy Brothers, pp. 282–283.

[26] Tanner, pp. 9–12; see also, Lovejoy Brothers, pp. 281–291; Beecher, pp. 103–107. The exact circumstances and details of Elijah Lovejoy's death differ in the various accounts. Of these, Henry Tanner's version of these events is deemed the most reliable. Tanner

says Elijah was killed as he and the others stepped outside with rifles poised to fire at the person on the ladder setting fire to the building, while the other two contend that, when Elijah was gunned down, he was merely standing in the doorway. Tanner is the only one of the three authors who was actually present at the time Elijah's death occurred.

[27] Tanner, p. 12.

[28] See, generally, *Alton Trials of Winthrop S. Gilman, et al., for the Crime of Riot* (John F. Trow, New York, 1838).

[29] *Alton Trials*, pp. 75–77.

[30] *Alton Trials*, pp. 7–81.

[31] *Alton Trials*, pp. 127–143, 158.

[32] *Liberator*, Nov. 24, 1837, p. 3; see also *All on Fire: William Lloyd Garrison and the Abolition of Slavery* (St. Martin's Press, New York, 1998), pp. 237–239.

[33] Justus Newton Brown, "Lovejoy's Influence on John Brown," *The Magazine of History*, Nos. 3–4 (September–October 1916), pp. 100–101. The story was told by Edward Brown, a cousin of John Brown, who was a 23-year-old divinity student at Western Reserve College at the time. Interestingly, John Brown's noted biographer Oswald Garrison Villard wrote a response to the 1916 publication of Edward's reminiscence, calling it a trap for the unwary historian. Lora Case, another Hudson citizen and a lifelong correspondent of John Brown, who was also present at the meeting called by Professor Hickok, gave a slightly different version in a separate recollection. She says: "John arose and in his calm, emphatic way says: 'I pledge myself with God's help that I will devote my life to increasing hostility toward slavery'." Lora's recollection of the event was found in a scrapbook in the possession of George A. Miller of Hudson.

Endnotes to Chapter 6: A Star Bursts on the Scene

[1] Mayer, pp. 193-94.

[2] Mayer, pp. 200-07.

[3] Mayer, pp. 230-33.
[4] Mayer, pp. 254-55, 259-60.
[5] *Liberator*, July 23, 1841, p.2; Mayer, pp. 304-05.
[6] Mayer, pp. 304-05; Frederick Douglass, *My Bondage and My Freedom* (Miller, Orton & Co., New York and Auburn, N.Y., 1857), pp. 357-58; see also *Liberator*, Aug. 20, 1841, pp. 2-3.
[7] William Lloyd Garrison, in the Preface to the First American Edition of Frederick Douglass, *Narrative of the Life of Frederick Douglass, an American Slave, Written by Himself* (Webb and Chapman, Dublin, 1846), p. viii.
[8] Douglass, *My Bondage and My Freedom*, pp. 358-59; Mayer, pp. 305-06.
[9] Douglass, *My Bondage and My Freedom*, pp. 33-38, 51-52, 342; David W. Blight, *Frederick Douglass, Prophet of Freedom* (Simon & Schuster, New York, 2018), pp. 9-14.
[10] Douglass, *My Bondage and My Freedom*, pp. 40-41.
[11] Douglass, *My Bondage and My Freedom*, pp. 85-88.
[12] Douglass, *My Bondage and My Freedom*, p. 77; see Blight, pp. 21-22.
[13] Douglass, *My Bondage and My Freedom,* pp. 129-32; see Blight, pp. 23, 30-31.
[14] Douglass, *Narrative*, pp. 32-33; Douglass, *My Bondage and My Freedom*, pp. 64, 141-45.
[15] Douglass, *Narrative,* p. 47; Douglass, *My Bondage and My Freedom*, pp. 173-79. Blight, pp. 48-49, without explanation gives a different chronology in which Lucretia died before her father. However, both of Douglass's autobiographies remember this otherwise.
[16] Douglass, *Narrative*, p. 33; Douglass, *My Bondage and My Freedom*, pp. 145-47.
[17] Douglass, *My Bondage and My Freedom*, pp. 158-60.
[18] *The Columbian Orator: Containing a Variety of Original and*

Selected Pieces, Together With Rules, by Caleb Bingham (Boston, 1817).
[19] Douglass, *My Bondage and My Freedom*, pp. 155-58.
[20] Douglass, *Narrative*, p. 51; Douglass, *My Bondage and My Freedom*, pp. 166-72, 182-83.
[21] Douglass, *Narrative*, pp. 51-54; Douglass, *My Bondage and My Freedom*, pp. 181-84, 186-87.
[22] Douglass, *Narrative*, p. 55; Douglass, *My Bondage and My Freedom*, pp. 199-200.
[23] Douglass, *My Bondage and My Freedom*, pp. 206-07.
[24] Douglass, *My Bondage and My Freedom*, pp. 215-16.
[25] Douglass, *My Bondage and My Freedom*, p. 219.
[26] Douglass, *My Bondage and My Freedom*, pp. 228-46.
[27] Douglass, *My Bondage and My Freedom*, pp. 246-49.
[28] Douglass, *My Bondage and My Freedom*, p. 263.
[29] Blight, pp. 69-75.
[30] Frederick Douglass, *Life and Times of Frederick Douglass, written by himself (1881 Autobiography)* (Pathway Press, New York, 1941), pp. 199-207.
[31] Douglass, *Life and Times*, pp. 211-13; Blight, pp. 79-80.
[32] Douglass, *Life and Times*, pp. 219-23; Blight, pp. 81-83.
[33] Douglass, *My Bondage and My Freedom*, pp. 340-43.
[34] Douglass, *My Bondage and My Freedom*, pp. 349-58; Douglass, *Life and Times*, p. 237.

Endnotes to Chapter 7: He Was an Honest Thief

[1] Oates, p. 44.
[2] Villard, p. 28; Boyer, p. 264, 273–274.
[3] Boyer, p. 265; Oates, p. 34.
[4] Boyer, pp. 267, 270, 275–276.
[5] Boyer, pp. 271, 272, 278.
[6] Boyer, p. 276 & n. 26, citing letter from John Brown to Seth Thompson. Even Richard Boyer, the sympathetic biographer,

grudgingly admits that John Brown had poor contact with reality when it came to business matters. "In the end, his hope and need were sufficiently desperate to overcome any sense of reality." Boyer, p. 325. Boyer deserves credit for being sufficiently honest, intellectually, to probe carefully John Brown's financial failures and their exact causes. Brown's other worshipful biographers ignored this side of their hero.

[7] Boyer, pp. 277, 314–318.

[8] Boyer, p. 319.

[9] Boyer, p. 326, quoting John Brown letter to Mary Brown, June 12, 1839.

[10] Receipt dated June 15, 1839, in collection of Vernon Historical Society, Vernon, Connecticut.

[11] John Brown letter to George Kellogg, in collection of Vernon Historical Society, August 22, 1839.

[12] Boyer, pp. 329–330, quoting John Brown letter to George Kellogg, Sept. 20, 1839.

[13] Boyer, p. 341; see 5 Stat. 440 (27th Congress, 1st Sess, Ch. IX, enacted Aug. 19, 1841).

[14] Boyer, p. 337.

[15] Boyer, pp. 338–339.

[16] Boyer, pp. 280, 336–337; Sanborn, pp. 134–136.

[17] Letter of John Brown to John Brown, Jr. of Jan. 11, 1844, reprinted in Sanborn, pp. 59–60.

[18] Letter of Samuel Lawrence to Simon Perkins, Jr., dated July 22, 1844, later published in *Ohio Cultivator*, Sept. 1, 1845. On the manner in which John Brown used labor by his children in his sheep-herding business, see Boyer, p. 350, quoting interview with Salmon Brown that appeared Oct. 10, 1906 in Portland (Ore.) *Telegram*. John was able to travel extensively to New England to promote his fleeces and to start his wool cooperative because he could, with confidence, leave his wife and unpaid older boys in charge of the flock during his

absences. Boyer, p. 363; see, e.g., letters reprinted in Sanborn, pp. 60–65.

[19] See, e.g., article entitled *Perkins & Brown's Fine Sheep*, under dateline Mt. Vernon, Ohio, July 29, 1845, and published in *Ohio Cultivator*, Aug. 15, 1845, as well as the comment of editor M.B. Bateham which follows: "We had at several times seen commendatory notices of Mssrs. Perkins' and Brown's sheep, in the newspapers, but we paid but little attention to them, supposing they were too highly flattered. The samples of wool received with the foregoing, however, and more especially the opportunity for personally inspecting the sheep, which we have enjoyed since, has removed that impression entirely, and we can assure our readers, that too much cannot well be said in praise of the care and skill displayed by Mr. Brown."

[20] Article under byline John Brown dated March 1846, titled *Remedy for Bots or Grubs in the Heads of Sheep; Remarks on the Fine Sheep of Ohio and Other States*, in *Ohio Cultivator*, April 15, 1846.

[21] Boyer, p. 348.

[22] Quoted in Boyer, pp. 273–274.

[23] Account of E.C. Leonard, reproduced in Sanborn, pp. 63–64.

[24] Oates, p. 56; regarding the scalding death of John's daughter Amelia, see Reynolds, p. 81; Boyer, p. 383; Oates, p. 55; regarding the death from dysentery of John's four children in September 1843, see Reynolds, p. 78; Boyer, p. 343.

[25] *Life and Times* does not give an exact date of this visit, except to say it was around the time he started *North Star*, which happened in November 1847. In a contemporary published reference quoted below, Frederick discussed his meeting with John Brown in a travel report about a just-completed trip to Springfield published Feb. 11, 1848.

[26] Blight, p. 169; Douglass, *Life and Times*, p. 288–294, 301.

[27] Douglass, *Life and Times*, pp. 301–302.

[28] Reprinted in its entirety in Sanborn, pp. 128–131.

[29] See Boyer, p. 388, where he comments: "if the pen is more powerful than the sword ... it was evidently not so at this juncture of his life."
[30] See Boyer, p. 363, and letters to *Ohio Cultivator* there cited.
[31] Boyer, p. 379.
[32] Ibid.
[33] Boyer, p. 380.
[34] Ibid.
[35] Boyer, pp. 380–381.
[36] Boyer, p. 394.
[37] Boyer, pp. 395–396.
[38] Boyer, p. 397.
[39] Boyer, p. 398.
[40] Boyer, p. 405.
[41] Boyer, p. 409.
[42] Boyer, p. 411.
[43] Boyer, p. 412.
[44] Boyer, pp. 412–413.
[45] Boyer, p. 414.
[46] Boyer, p. 417.

Endnotes to Chapter 8: Henry Seward, a Boy Wonder

[1] Walter Stahr, *Seward, Lincoln's Indispensable Man* (Simon & Schuster, New York, 2012), pp. 9–10.
[2] Stahr, pp. 11–14.
[3] Stahr, p. 86.
[4] Stahr, pp. 16–25, 33.
[5] Stahr, pp. 41–44.
[6] Stahr, p. 69.
[7] Stahr, pp. 45–70.
[8] Stahr, pp. 78–80.

[9] Stahr, p. 85.
[10] Stahr, p. 90–95.
[11] Stahr, pp. 98–99.
[12] Stahr, pp. 112-17.
[13] Stahr, pp. 121–123.
[14] Daniel Webster's March 7, 1850 speech is reprinted in Appendix to the Congressional Globe, 31st Congress, 1st Session, pp. 269–276.
[15] William Henry Seward's March 11, 1850 speech is reprinted in Appendix to the Congressional Globe, 31st Congress, 1st Session, pp. 260–269.
[16] E.g., Mayer, p. 413.
[17] Stahr, p. 125.
[18] Stahr, pp. 128–129.
[19] Credit is due to John Brown's biographer Richard Boyer, p. 430, for stating this valuable and fundamental insight.
[20] Boyer, p. 435.
[21] John Brown's "Words of Advice" to the "Branch of the United States League of Gileadites" dated Jan. 15, 1851 is reprinted in Sanborn, pp. 124–128. Sanborn, p. 124, tells us that he "somewhat condensed" the presentation he reprinted from John's original manuscript, which has been lost.
[22] Boyer, p. 434.
[23] Boyer, p. 438; see also Oates, p. 75. William Wells Brown, an African American orator, in 1870 wrote a reminiscent account in which he suggests that, as of a visit he made in June, 1854, there was an African American resistance militia in Springfield, featuring women prepared to dump scalding water on slave catchers, which was the descendant of John Brown's putative Gileadite organization. This may or may not be true, but there is no evidence that the capture of fugitive slaves ever became an issue in Springfield.

Endnotes to Chapter 9: A Nightmarish Family Outing

[1] William Uhler Hensel, *The Christiana Riot and the Treason Trials of 1851* (New Era Printing Co., Lancaster, Pa., 1911), pp. 20–21; Thomas P. Slaughter, *Bloody Dawn: The Christiana Riot and Racial Violence in the Antebellum North* (Oxford Univ. Press, New York, 1991), pp. 3–6.

[2] Slaughter, p. 3; Hensel, p. 22.

[3] Slaughter, pp. 10–11; Hensel, pp. 22–24.

[4] Hensel, p. 22; Slaughter, pp. 14–15.

[5] Letter reprinted in: David R. Forbes, *A True Story of the Christiana Riot* (Quarryville, PA, 1898), pp. 11–12.

[6] Slaughter, p. 14 & n. 26, crediting this observation about motivations to Larry Gara, "The Liberty Line: The Legend of the Underground Railroad," *The Journal of Negro History*, vol. 46 (4), 1961), p. 141.

[7] James J. Robbins (ed.), *Report of the Trial of Castner Hanway for Treason* (Philadelphia, 1852) (hereafter, Hanway Trial Transcript"), pp. 54, 56, 73; "Find-a-Grave.com," https://www.findagrave.com/memorial/6138708/Edward-gorsuch; Hensel, p. 25.

[8] Forbes, pp. 7–8; see Hanway Trial Transcript, p. 100 (testimony of Dr. Augustus Cain).

[9] Memoirs of William Parker, reprinted in Forbes, pp. 138–150; see also Slaughter, pp. 47–52.

[10] Hanway Trial Transcript, pp. 56–57 (testimony of Kline).

[11] Hanway Trial Transcript, p. 57 (testimony of Kline); Hensel, p. 25.

[12] Hanway Trial Transcript, pp. 99–100 (testimony of William Proudfoot); Forbes, p. 23 (quoting testimony by Henry Cloud), p. 33 (testimony of Josephus Washington); pp. 33-34 (testimony of Charles Smith); 150 (quoting memoir by Parker). Regarding the uncertainty about Abraham Johnson, see Hensel, p. 29. Parker was

employed, at the time, by Joseph Scarlett operating a thresher machine. Forbes, p. 148.

[13] Hanway Trial Transcript, pp. 56–57, 69 (testimony of Kline).

[14] Hanway Trial Transcript, p. 58 (testimony of Kline); p. 74 (testimony of Pearce); p. 80 (testimony of J. Gorsuch); p. 83 (testimony of D. Gorsuch); p. 85 (testimony of Hutchings).

[15] Hanway Trial Testimony, pp. 58, 63 (testimony of Kline); p. 74 (testimony of Pearce); pp. 83, 85 (testimony of D. Gorsuch); Hensel, pp. 20–21; Forbes, p. 12.

[16] Hanway Trial Testimony, p. 58; Parker memoir, quoted in Hensel, p. 104.

[17] Hanway Trial Testimony, pp. 58, 61 (testimony of Kline); pp. 74–75 (testimony of Pearce); p. 81 (testimony of J. Gorsuch); Parker memoir, quoted in Hensel, p. 107.

[18] Hanway Trial Testimony, p. 58 (testimony of Kline); p. 74 (testimony of Pearce); pp. 82–83 (testimony of J. Gorsuch); p. 83 (testimony of D. Gorsuch); p. 85 (testimony of Hutchings); p. 86 (testimony of Nelson); Parker memoir, quoted in Hensel, pp. 106–110.

[19] Hanway Trial Testimony, pp. 59–60, 73 (testimony of Kline); pp. 86, 91 (testimony of M. Nott); p. 101 (testimony of Roberts); p. 120 (testimony of Lewis); Slaughter, pp. 64–66; Hensel, p. 25.

[20] Hanway Trial Testimony, pp. 59, 62, 63 (testimony of Kline); p. 77 (testimony of Pearce); p. 86 (testimony of Nelson); pp. 120–121 (testimony of Lewis).

[21] Hanway Trial Testimony, p. 59 (testimony of Kline); p. 74 (testimony of Pearce); p. 81 (testimony of J. Gorsuch); p. 83 (testimony of D. Gorsuch).

[22] Hanway Trial Testimony, p. 83 (testimony of D. Gorsuch); see also *id.* at p. 74 (testimony of Pearce); p. 85 (testimony of Hutchings); p. 86 (testimony of Nelson).

[23] Hanway Trial Testimony, pp. 59, 61 (testimony of Kline); pp. 75, 77 (testimony of Pearce); p. 81 (testimony of J. Gorsuch); p. 84

(testimony of D. Gorsuch); p. 91 (testimony of M. Nott); Parker memoir, reprinted in Hensel, p. 112.)

[24] Hanway Trial Testimony, p. 59 (testimony of Kline); pp. 75–76 (testimony of Pearce); p. 81 (testimony of J. Gorsuch); p. 84 (testimony of D. Gorsuch); pp. 85–86 (testimony of Hutchings); p. 89 (testimony of J. Nott); Parker memoir, reprinted in Hensel, p. 113.

[25] Hanway Trial Testimony, p. 60 (testimony of Kline); p. 84 (testimony of D. Gorsuch); p. 100 (testimony of Cain).

[26] Douglass, *Life and Times*, pp. 312–313; Parker memoir, reprinted in Hensel, pp. 117–120.

[27] Hensel, pp. 38–39.

[28] Terry Alford, *Fortune's Fool, the Life of John Wilkes Booth* (Oxford Univ. Press, Oxford, 2015), pp. 25–27; Asia Booth Clarke, *The Unlocked Book, a Memoir of John Wilkes Booth* (G.P. Putnam's Sons, New York, 1938), pp. 50–51.

Endnotes to Chapter 10: For Brutus Was an Honorable Man

[1] See Francis Wilson, *John Wilkes Booth: Fact and Fiction of Lincoln's Assassination* (The Riverside Press, Cambridge, 1929), p. 3.

[2] See Kimmel, p. 38.

[3] Kimmel, pp. 15–16.

[4] Stephen M. Archer, *Junius Brutus Booth, Theatrical Prometheus* (Southern Ill. Univ. Press, Carbondale, Ill., 1992), pp. 7–14; Kimmel, p. 17.

[5] Archer, pp. 1–2, 18–27.

[6] Archer, pp. 41–67.

[7] Kimmel, pp. 25–26, 35.

[8] Wilson, pp. 7–8; Kimmel, pp. 37, 59; Michael W. Kauffman, *American Brutus: John Wilkes Booth and the Lincoln Conspirators* (Random House, New York 2004), p. 82 & notes 3–4. Junius, Jr., the

oldest, was born in Charleston, South Carolina; Joseph, the youngest, was born after the family moved to a city home in Baltimore. Technically, the Farm was leased by Junius on a 1,000-year lease, rather than purchased, because Junius was an alien.

[9] Alford, pp. 17–19, 25, quoting various sources; see generally, letters reproduced in John Rhodehamel and Louise Taper (eds.), *Right or Wrong, God Judge Me: The Writings of John Wilkes Booth* (Univ. of Illinois Press, Urbana, 1997).

[10] Clarke, pp. 58, 75; Rhodehamel and Taper, pp. 37–38, reprinting letter by John Wilkes Booth to Bill O'Laughlen dated April 30, 1854 that he signed Billy Bowlegs;" on Junius and his bow legs, see Archer, p. 10; on John Wilkes's bow legs, see Stanley Kimmel, *The Mad Booths of Maryland* (Bobbs-Merrill, New York, 1940), p. 70; on Junius's similarities to John Wilkes Booth, see Kimmel, pp. 153–154; George A. Townsend, *The Life, Crime, and Capture of John Wilkes Booth* (Dick & Fitzgerald, New York 1865), p. 26.

[11] Archer, pp. 94, 111–114, 116, 120–121, 135, 137, 148.

[12] Archer, pp. 139–140 (quoting article April 16, 1836 article reprinted in *Spirit of the Times*); pp. 148–155; see also Kimmel, pp. 23, 57–58.

[13] Reproduced in Archer, p. 136.

[14] Clarke, p. 34; Kimmel, pp. 39, 45.

[15] Archer, p. 98.

[16] Archer, pp. 146–148.

[17] Arthur Richard Shileto (ed.), *Plutarch's Morals* (Covent Garden, London, 1888), p. 1.

[18] Archer, pp. 167–168, 176, 196, 197; Alford, p. 23.

[19] Kimmel, pp. 60–62.

[20] Archer, p. 168.

[21] Kimmel, pp. 72–77.

[22] Kimmel, pp. 85–89; Archer, pp. 215–218.

[23] Clarke, p. 58; see also http://www.mdhs.org/finding-aid/muller-van-bokkelen-allison-papers-1878-1889-ms-2752.

[24] Clarke, p. 60.
[25] Clarke, p. 72.
[26] Clarke, pp. 74, 84–90.
[27] Clarke, pp. 99–101.
[28] Alford, pp. 34–35; see Rhodehamel & Taper, p. 38 (reprinting letter from John Wilkes Booth to T. William O'Laughlen, Aug. 8, 1854).
[29] Clarke, pp. 47–49.
[30] Clarke, p. 107.
[31] Clarke, p. 73.
[32] Clarke, pp. 102–104.
[33] Clarke, p. 71.
[34] Ernest C. Miller, *John Wilkes Booth - Oilman* (The Exposition Press, New York, 1947), pp. 33-34.
[35] Clarke, p. 67.
[36] Clarke, pp. 74, 80–81; Alford, p. 15.
[37] Stahr, pp. 147–152.
[38] Clarke, pp. 105–106; Alford, pp. 35–36.

Endnotes to Chapter 11: A Battleground Called Kansas

[1] Appendix to the Congressional Globe, 31st Congress, 1st Session, p. 264.
[2] See Stahr, pp. 123–128.
[3] Stahr, p. 141; Mayer, p. 436.
[4] Stahr, p. 143.
[5] Michael A. Morrison, *Slavery and the American West: The Eclipse of Manifest Destiny and the Coming of the Civil War* (Univ. of North Carolina Press, Chapel Hill, 1997), p. 154; Stahr, p. 143.
[6] See Boyer, pp. 468–484. Seward's statement is quoted in Oates, p. 80.
[7] Boyer, pp. 471–481.

[8] Sanborn, p. 164; Boyer, pp. 487–491.

[9] Letter quoted in Sanborn, p. 191; see also, John Brown letter of Nov. 2, 1854, reprinted in Sanborn, pp. 110–111.

[10] See generally, O.B. Frothingham, *Gerrit Smith* (Negro Universities Press, New York, 1877), pp. 7–9, 99–113; see also Sanborn, pp. 96–97. A more cynical view of Smith's land giveaway is that Smith, by his own admission, unloaded lands that were tax-defaulted and scheduled to be sold to pay the tax debt within a year or two. See Letter of Gerrit Smith to Dr. J. McCune Smith et al. dated Aug. 1, 1846, reprinted in Frothingham, p. 105.

[11] Sanborn, pp. 97–104; Oates, pp. 67–68; Boyer, pp. 398–401, 422; Frothingham, p. 253.

[12] Oates, p. 68; see also Sanborn, pp. 102–103.

[13] See, e.g., Boyer, pp. 349, 423, 431, 435, 439, 442–443, 446; Sanborn, pp. 68, 75–79, 80, 81, 82–83, 84, 85–86, 107, 108–111, 124–126. Boyer concurs with the conclusion expressed here that John Brown's statement to John Jr. that he felt "committed" is referring to an unfulfilled commitment to Gerrit Smith. Boyer, pp. 457–459.

[14] Letters by John Brown, reprinted in Sanborn, pp. 91, 110–111, 191–192, 192–193; Boyer, pp. 460, 461.

[15] Letter of John Brown dated June 28, 1855, reprinted in Sanborn, pp. 193–194; Blight, pp. 293–294; Boyer, pp. 521–527.

[16] Letters of John Brown dated Oct. 13, 1855, Oct. 14, 1855, Nov. 2, 1855, and Nov. 23, 1855, reprinted in Sanborn, pp. 200–205; as to traveling on foot, see Boyer, p. 562.

[17] See Sanborn, p. 181.

[18] Boyer, pp. 494–503; Frank W. Blackmar, *The Life of Charles Robinson, First State Governor of Kansas* (Crane & Co., Topeka, 1902), pp. 172–173.

[19] Blackmar, pp. 168–170; Boyer, p. 502.

[20] Sanborn, pp. 214–216.

[21] Article in Kansas *Herald of Freedom*, June 30, 1855, p. 1.

[22] Oates, p. 48; see Boyer, pp. 449–453; Connelley, pp. 85–86. John Brown, Jr. attended Grand River Institute, a boarding school in Austinburg, Ohio for four years between 1843 and 1847. See http://www.morganohiolibrary.com/GrandRiver.html.

[23] Sanborn, p. 183; Oates, p. 101; Boyer, pp. 566–568; Blackmar, pp. 137, 166–167, 174–177, 180.

[24] Major James Abbott's typed account of the Branson rescue, complete with his handwritten interlineations, is in the Kansas State Historical Society collection. The account in text is taken largely from his version of events. See also Blackmar, pp. 140–143; Sanborn, pp. 206–210; Oates, p. 106.

[25] Blackmar, p. 147; Sanborn, p. 214.

[26] James C. Malin, *John Brown and the Legend of Fifty-Six* (Haskell House, New York, 1971), pp. 16–17. Regarding the bayonets being mounted on makeshift spears, see Sanborn, p. 264, fn. 1.

[27] Oates, p. 108.

[28] *Herald of Freedom* article by G.W. Brown, Oct. 29, 1859, quoted in Malin, pp. 20–21.

[29] Boyer, p. 566.

[30] Blackmar, pp. 153–154; Letter of John Brown dated Dec. 16, 1855, reprinted in Sanborn, pp. 217–220.

[31] See Letter from Salmon Brown to William Connelley, May 28, 1913 (available through West Virginia State Archives) (hereafter, "Salmon Brown statement"), p. 2. The "Treaty of Peace" of December 8, 1855 is reprinted in Blackmar, pp. 148–149.

[32] John Brown letter of Dec. 16, 1855, quoted in Sanborn, p. 219.

[33] Villard, pp. 125–126; Oates, p. 109; Salmon Brown statement, p. 4. G.W. Brown, in an article published in *Herald of Freedom* on Oct. 29, 1859, recalled that John *"retired in disgust"* (his italics) from Lawrence after peace was established. Malin, pp. 20–21.

Endnotes to Chapter 12: A Primordial Terrorist Erupts

[1] Sanborn, pp. 224–227; Blackmar, pp. 190–191, 194; Malin, p. 35; Oates, p. 114.

[2] Sanborn, pp. 204–205.

[3] Blackmar, pp. 194–195; Sanborn, pp. 227–228.

[4] Oates, p. 118.

[5] Malin, pp. 532–533, gives by far the most complete information on the background of Martin White prior to April 16, 1856. White has been misrepresented, and his account of events at the April 16 meeting has been incorrectly rejected, by worshipful biographers of John Brown. See Malin, p. 532 & fn. 61 & p. 533 fn. 65. See also, http://the-history-nut-of-missouri.blogspot.com/2010/08/MartinWhite.html (accessed online Oct. 21, 2018).

[6] A letter from John Brown, Jr. dated April 29, 1856 to the *Herald of Freedom*, published in its May 10, 1856 edition, p. 3, set forth John Jr.'s version of the sequence of events leading up to the April 16 settler meeting, and published the Brown resolutions in their entirety. See also Malin, pp. 532–534; Oates, p. 118.

[7] Malin, pp. 717–718.

[8] John Brown, Jr. letter of April 29, 1856; Malin, p. 24; Oates, p. 119.

[9] John Brown, Jr. letter of April 29, 1856; Malin, pp. 539–559.

[10] The sequence of events given here is taken from an article that appeared on p. 1 of the Lawrence, Kansas, *Herald of Freedom*, April 24, 1856 edition.

[11] *Herald of Freedom*, April 24, 1856 edition, p. 1.

[12] Article in the *Border Times*, Westport, Missouri, reprinted in *Herald of Freedom*, May 3, 1856 edition, p. 2; see also *Herald of Freedom*, April 24, 1856 edition, p. 1; Sara T.D. Robinson, *Kansas, Its Interior and Exterior Life* (Lawrence, 1899), p. 231.

[13] *Herald of Freedom*, April 24, 1856 edition, p. 1; S. Robinson, pp. 232–234.

[14] *Herald of Freedom*, May 10, 1856 edition, p. 3, "Original

Correspondence;" see undated Grand Jury Indictment on file with Kansas State Historical Society, reprinted in Sanborn, p. 235; Malin, pp. 49–50. The Johnson County resolutions mentioned in the grand jury indictment apparently were published in other newspaper, the *Free State*. However, the *Herald of Freedom* published other materials that could have been found "treasonable" on a similar rationale: "Message" of the "Governor" (referring to "Governor" Robinson) of March 4, 1856, published in March 8, 1856 edition, pp. 1, 4, and including the "Big Springs" Resolutions of Sept. 4–5, 1855; draft "Resolutions" of the Massachusetts Legislature, published in April 5, 1856 edition, p. 1; "Resolutions" from an Emigrant Aid Society in Wisconsin, published in April 12, 1856 edition, p. 4.

[15] Article by James C. Malin, titled "Judge Lecompte and the Sack of Lawrence," *Kansas Historical Quarterly,* Vol. 20, No. 7 (August 1953), pp. 465–494; Malin, pp. 50–51; Sanborn, pp. 231–232. On May 20, indictments were also handed down charging Andrew Reeder, Charles Robinson, G.W. Brown, Samuel Wood and James Lane with treason. Malin, p. 51.

[16] Malin, pp. 560–561.

[17] Oates, p. 125.

[18] Oates, pp. 126–127.

[19] Oates, p. 127; see statement of Townsley dated Dec. 6, 1879, reproduced in S. Robinson, pp. 407–408.

[20] David S. Reynolds, in his 2005 biography of John Brown, makes the claim that John Brown was aware of the Sumner beating recounted at length in Chapter 14, *infra*, and that this event was his substantial motivating factor in undertaking Pottawatomie massacre. This claim does not withstand scrutiny. At the time of the attack on Sumner, John Brown was camped in a remote area of frontier Kansas where there were no newspapers or other media. Reynolds in his biography is not very careful, because he discusses Jason Brown as recalling this happening. This is not correct. What Reynolds in his

footnotes cites is a mention of the alleged incident in Villard, p. 154. Villard made the claim based on a reminiscent account of Salmon (not Jason) Brown about a messenger named "Gardner" who supposedly came to the camp with a message about the Sumner assault "hidden in his boot." Apparently, this particular reminiscent account was unpublished. However, another version of it was set forth in a letter from Salmon Brown to John Brown biographer William Connelley dated May 28, 1913, cited above. This detail of the reminiscence is not credible, for a few reasons.

1. It is implausible that news of the attack on Sumner reached John Brown by the following morning, May 23, at which time he left the common camp to take his party on its deadly mission to the Pottawatomie. John would have had to have received the news by the morning of May 23, because that day he was already heading with his raiders south toward the Pottawatomie on his self-declared "secret mission," according to a highly contemporaneous grand jury statement of eyewitness Amos Hall who met the party on the road, quoted in Malin, pp. 572–573. The sacking of Lawrence several days earlier destroyed all free state presses in that town. No newspapers elsewhere mentioning the event could have been delivered in time to reach Lawrence. The information we have from reasonably contemporaneous sources, including John Brown himself (see Sanborn, p. 236), is that the news reached the camp that Lawrence had been sacked, that order had been restored, and that there was no need for a rescue party to go to Lawrence. Nothing was said by these sources about receiving news of the attack on Sumner.

2. Assuming news of the attack on Sumner did somehow reached John Brown the next day, it does

not explain a reaction of killing settlers on the Pottawatomie who had absolutely nothing to do with the Preston Brooks attack. John had an entirely separate agenda for the terror attacks.

3. The details of Salmon's 1913 letter to Connolley differ somewhat from the version described by Villard. In the letter version, the news about Sumner was told verbally to a gathering of free state supporters who were observing the Free State Hotel burn while on the south bank of the Wakarusa. The letter is confused and incorrect about many known details. John Brown, Sr., at this time, was not anywhere near Lawrence. By his own account he was camped many miles to the south. Also it is demonstrable that one cannot "gaze" at the Free State Hotel burning from the south bank of the Wakarusa, which is a specific claim Salmon makes on p. 7 of the letter. The motivation for the murders of the Doyles and Wilkinson is discussed later on in the letter. The attack on Sumner is not mentioned. Thus, Salmon's 1913 letter does not repeat the claim quoted by Villard that news of the Sumner assault made John Brown's men go "crazy."

4. In his accounts far closer to the events (written in 1859 and 1860) Salmon Brown denied that his father had anything at all to do with the Pottawatomie massacres. See Malin, p. 268, quoting letter, Salmon Brown to Redpath, Jan. 10, 1860. Nothing was said about John Brown Sr. hearing the news on the Sumner attack, or that news making John or his men "go crazy."

5. James Townsley, a member of the John Brown's party, who gave a far more complete and contemporaneous account of the massacre events

than did Salmon, does mention news about the sack of Lawrence, but he says nothing about any news on Sumner. See Sanborn, pp. 262–264.

6. Although full of hero worship for his martyred friend John Brown, and although he was obviously on the lookout for any possible extenuation for the Pottawatomie horror, Sanborn says nothing about the atrocity against Sumner being a factor.

7. John Brown himself, in the letter he wrote after the massacre (reprinted in Sanborn, pp. 238–239), says nothing about the attack on Sumner. He does talk explicitly about the sack of Lawrence.

[21] Salmon Brown statement, pp. 8–10; Hinton, p. 63.

[22] Malin, pp. 556–559; see also Malin, p. 546, describing the indictment of David Baldwin, a free state settler who lived south of Pottawatomie Creek, for an assault by firing a rifle ball with intent to kill George Wilson. Wilson brought a civil suit against James Townsley, which was eventually dismissed for lack of prosecution. The gravamen of that suit is not disclosed by surviving court records. Thus, it is a conjecture that the indictment of Townsley may have also had something to do with Wilson.

[23] Sanborn, pp. 262–263 (quoting statement of Townsley); Connelley, pp. 210–215 (quoting various witnesses); Malin, pp. 562–563.

[24] Salmon Brown statement, p. 9; Townsley statement, reproduced in Sanborn, pp. 262–263; Connelley, pp. 193, 210–215. Malin, e.g., pp. 387–393, 539–559, provides a dispassionate analysis of the grounds for doubt about the veracity of various statements and silences of the Pottawatomie massacre perpetrators, all of whom were motivated to justify John Brown's acts and to avoid implicating themselves in the crimes.

[25] Salmon Brown statement, p. 9; statement of Townsley in S. Robinson, p. 408.

[26] Affidavits of Mahala Doyle, June 7, 1856, and John Doyle, June

7, 1856, published in *Report of the Special Committee appointed to Investigate the Troubles in Kansas; with the Views of the Minority of Said Committee.* House Report No. 200, 34th Cong., 1st Sess. Washington: Cornelius Wendell, printer, 1856, pp. 1193–1199; see Salmon Brown statement, pp. 9–10; James Townley statement, in S. Robinson, pp. 408–409; Oates, p. 119.

[27] Affidavit of Louisa Jane Wilkinson, June 13, 1856, published in *Report of the Special Committee appointed to Investigate the Troubles in Kansas; with the Views of the Minority of Said Committee.* House Report No. 200, 34th Cong., 1st Sess. Washington: Cornelius Wendell, printer, 1856, pp. 1193–1199; see Salmon Brown statement, p. 10; James Townley statement, in S. Robinson, pp. 408–409; Malin, p. 540 (regarding court records of proceedings of April 21, 1856 (available through Kansas State Historical Society)).

[28] Malin, p. 544.

[29] Affidavit of James Harris, June 6, 1856, published in *Report of the Special Committee appointed to Investigate the Troubles in Kansas; with the Views of the Minority of Said Committee.* House Report No. 200, 34th Cong., 1st Sess. Washington: Cornelius Wendell, printer, 1856, pp. 1193–1199; see Salmon Brown statement, pp. 10–11; James Townley statement, in S. Robinson, p. 409.

[30] James Townsley statement, in S. Robinson, p. 409; Salmon Brown statement, pp. 10–-11.

[31] Salmon Brown statement, p. 14; Villard, p. 165.

[32] Oates, p. 140; Villard, pp. 166–167; Sanborn, pp. 273, 276, n. 2 (quoting an eyewitness, John Brown's half-sister's husband, Samuel Adair); Salmon Brown statement, p. 12 (John's brother Owen went to see him in the woods but "he could do nothing with him as his head was wild"); Malin, p. 367 (citing G.W. Brown). S. Robinson, p. 353, discusses her observations while incarcerated with John Jr. Annie Brown Adams to John Brown biographer R.J. Hinton, June 7,

1894.

[33] In a letter of June, 1856 to his family, John wrote: "God, who has not given us over to the will of our enemies, but has moreover delivered them into our hand, will, we humbly trust, still keep and deliver us. We feel assured that He who sees not as men see, does not lay the guilt of innocent blood to our charge." Reprinted in Sanborn, p. 240.

Endnotes to Chapter 13: A Brutal Beating in the Senate

[1] Walter G. Shotwell, *The Life of Charles Sumner* (New York: Crowell & Company 1910), pp. 3-25. Charles Sumner, as a student, also became the librarian at Harvard's law school library.

[2] Shotwell, pp. 27-33.

[3] Shotwell, pp. 96-97, 110-12, 117; Jeffery Rossbach, *Ambivalent Conspirators* (Univ. of Pennsylvania Press, Philadelphia, 1982), pp. 26-28.

[4] Shotwell, pp. 140-59, 179.

[5] Shotwell, pp. 189-99.

[6] Shotwell, pp. 223-32.

[7] Fehrenbacher, pp. 75-77.

[8] Shotwell, pp. 251-56.

[9] Charles Sumner's August 26, 1852 oration is reprinted in Appendix to the Congressional Globe, 32nd Congress, 1st Session, pp. 1102-13; see Shotwell, pp. 256-67.

[10] James O. Farmer, Jr., *An Edgefield Planter & His World, the 1840's Journals of Whitfield Brooks* (Mercer Univ. Press, Macon, Georgia 2019), Introduction p. xli.

[11] Paul Christopher Anderson, *Andrew Pickens Butler* (South Carolina Encyclopedia, University of South Carolina, Institute for Southern Studies, May 17, 2016), retrieved Oct. 24, 2020 at https://www.scencyclopedia.org/sce/entries/butler-andrew-pickens/; on Judge Butler's residence with his mother, see Farmer, p. 245; see

also Biographical Directory of the United States Congress, "Butler, Andrew Pickens," retrieved Oct. 24, 2020 at https://bioguideretro.congress.gov/Home/MemberDetails?memIndex=b001173..

[12] Regarding the failed attempt to rescue Anthony Burns, see generally, Rossbach, pp. 12-34.

[13] Congressional Globe, 33rd Congress, 1st Session, p. 1515.

[14] *Id.*, p. 1516.

[15] *Ibid.*

[16] *Id.*, at p. 1517.

[17] 2 Kings 8:13 (King James version).

[18] Congressional Globe, 33rd Congress, 1st Session, p. 1517.

[19] Appendix to the Congressional Globe, 33rd Congress, 1st Session, pp. 1011-1015.

[20] Congressional Globe, 34th Congress, 1st Session, pp. 848-51 (proceedings of April 10, 1856), 862-63.

[21] Charles Sumner's five hour speech of May 19 and 20, 1856 is printed in the Appendix to the Congressional Globe, 34th Congress, 1st Session, pp. 530-544.

[22] Quoted in Edward L. Pierce, *Memoir and Letters of Charles L. Sumner, Vol III* (Roberts Brothers, Boston 1893), pp. 376-77, 394; Shotwell, p. 329.

[23] Pierce, p. 461-62.

[24] Congressional Globe, 34th Congress, 1st Session, pp. 1353-54 (testimony of C. Sumner); *id.*, pp. 1363 (testimony of D. McNair); *id.*, p. 1365 (testimony of J. Davis); *id.*, p. 1365 (testimony of A. Glossbrenner); see also Pierce, *op. cit.,* pp. 470-71 & diagram at p. 468.

[25] Congressional Globe, 34th Congress, 1st Session, p. 1354 (testimony of W. Gorman); *id.,* pp. 1354-55 (testimony of J. Pearce); *id.,* pp. 1355-56 (testimony of R. Toombs); *id.,* p. 1356 (testimony of L. Foster); *id.,* pp. 1356-57 (testimony of A. Murray); *id.,* p. 1357 (testimony of E. Morgan; *id.,* p. 1359 (testimony of J. Crittenden);

id., p. 1361 (testimony of W. Winslow); *id.*, p. 1361 (testimony of J. Simonton); *id.*, p. 1363 (testimony of R. Sution); *id.*, p. 1363 (testimony of D. McNair); *id.*, pp. 1364-65 (testimony of A. Iverson); *id.* at p. 1367-68 (testimony of Nicholson); see also Pierce, *op. cit.*, pp. 470-71 & diagram at p. 468.

[26] Congressional Globe, 34th Congress, 1st Session, p. 1361 (testimony of J. Simonton); see also *id.* at p. 1354 (testimony of W. Gorman); *id.* at p. 1354-55 (testimony of J. Pearce); *id.* at p. 1355-56 (testimony of R. Toombs); *id.* at p. 1356 (testimony of L. Foster); *id.* at p. 1356-57 (testimony of A. Murray); *id.* at p. 1357 (testimony of E. Morgan); *id.* at p. 1357-58 (testimony of I. Holland); *id.* at p. 1359 (testimony of J. Crittenden); *id.* at p. 1359 (testimony of C. Jones); *id.* at p. 1363 (testimony of R. Sution); *id.* at p. 1367-68 (testimony of Nicholson).

[27] Congressional Globe, 34th Congress, 1st Session, p. 1356-57 (testimony of A. Murray); *id.* at p. 1357 (testimony of E. Morgan); see also *id.* at p. 1355-56 (testimony of R. Toombs); *id.* at p. 1359 (testimony of C. Jones); *id.*, at p. 1361 (testimony of J. Simonton).

[28] Congressional Globe, 34th Congress, 1st Session, p. 1356 (testimony of L. Foster); *id.* at pp. 1356-57 (testimony of A. Murray); *id.* at pp. 1357 (testimony of E. Morgan); *id.*, at p. 1360 (testimony of C. Boyle); *id.*, at p. 1360 (testimony of N. Darling); *id.*, at p. 1364 (testimony of M. Perry); see also Pierce, pp. 473-75.

[29] Shotwell, pp. 342-48, 384.

[30] See generally, Farmer, Introduction, p. xxv; and the Whitfield Brooks diary, 1840-49, published in Farmer, passim.

[31] In a strange twist, neither Preston Brooks nor Andrew Butler would survive more than a year following Preston's attack on Charles. Preston died in January 1857, at age 37, of apparent complications following a cold. Judge Butler died May 25, 1857. Shotwell, pp. 340-41.

[32] Farmer, pp. 2-10; see also Farmer, Introduction, pp. liv – lix.

[33] Farmer, pp. 287-88.

[34] Farmer, Introduction, pp. lvii – lviii.

[35] Appendix to the Congressional Globe, 34th Congress, 1st Session, p. 886.

[36] Keitt served as the de facto advocate and counsel for Brooks when he avoided expulsion from the House for his assault on Charles Sumner. See Congressional Globe, 34th Congress, 1st Session, passim. Edmundson admitted that he knew of Brooks's intentions beforehand, did nothing to dissuade him, and in fact accompanied Brooks in his efforts to find Sumner so that he could attack him. Congressional Globe, 34th Congress, 1st Session, pp. 1361-63. Other witnesses testified that they had heard statements, after the speech, that violence or "punishment" should be inflicted against Sumner. E.g., *id.* at p. 1363 (testimony of James Marriott); *id.* at 1365 (testimony of Edwin Coleman); *id.* at 1366 (testimony of James Ricaud); *id.* at 1367 (reporting statement of Brooks, accompanied by Keitt, to ex-Governor Brown of Virginia, shortly after the attack).

[37] Pierce, p. 478.

[38] Pierce, pp. 490-92; Congressional Globe, 34th Congress, 1st Session, p. 1639.

[39] Appendix to the Congressional Globe, 34th Congress, 1st Session, p. 886. Hall here spoke in direct response to remarks by Brooks and Keitt.

Endnotes to Chapter 14: Fleeing to Escape the Peace

[1] Oates, p. 144; Boyer, pp. 113–114; Malin, vol. I, pp. 87–88.

[2] See account of John Brown, Jr., reprinted in Sanborn, pp. 237–238 & n. 3; Reynolds, p. 181.

[3] Affidavit of Henry Sherman, July 7, 1856, on file with Kansas State Historical Society. The author has discovered a discrepancy that escaped James Malin as well as KSHS. Malin, p. 733, erroneously reported that Sherman said the theft happened "May 13," which

makes little sense as it was before the massacre. However, the Sherman affidavit, which is available for inspection online in the KSHS collection, actually says the cattle theft happened on the "thirtieth" day of May. This is consistent with being a further attack on Sherman's property in the aftermath of the Pottawatomie massacre. See also, Reynolds, p. 190.

[4] Oates, p. 147.

[5] Oates, pp. 150–151.

[6] The account of the Battle of Black Jack in this text is based principally on a combination of two relatively contemporaneous sources: (1) John Brown's account in a letter he wrote in June 1856, published in Sanborn, pp. 237–240, and (2) Captain Pate's account, published in the St. Louis *Republican* on June 9, 1856.

[7] Brown's and Pate's accounts agree remarkably well on the general time frame and sequence of events of the battle. Brown's account, however, omits any mention of his treacherous taking advantage of the white flag to secure the surrender of Pate and his force.

[8] The original signed "Articles of Agreement for the exchange of prisoners following the battle of Black Jack" is on file at the Kansas State Historical Society in Lawrence, Kansas and may be viewed on line at the KSHS website.

[9] *New York Tribune,* June 17, 1856, p. 6; Villard, p. 210.

[10] Shotwell, pp. 1–2.

[11] Pierce, p. 419.

[12] Letter of John Brown, reprinted in Sanborn, pp. 238–239; Letter of John Sedgwick, June 11, 1856, reprinted in C. Stoeckel, *Correspondence of John Sedgwick, Major General, Vol. II* (De Vinne Press, New York, 1903); Oates, pp. 151–156; see also Villard, pp. 208–210. Malin points out that some aspects of later Brown family reminiscences on this incident are incorrect. Malin, pp. 85–88.

[13] See William Stanley Houle (ed.), *A Southerner's Viewpoint of the Kansas Situation, 1856–1857: The Letters of Lieut. Col. A. J. Hoole,*

C.S.A. (Kansas Historical Society, 1934), pp. 43–56.

[14] See Sanborn, pp. 331–332.

[15] See Malin, p. 576 (discussing change in account by George Grant); Villard, pp. 168 (discussing statement of George Thompson), 174–175 (discussing statement of Grant).

[16] See Villard, p. 216; Malin, pp. 604–607; Charles Robinson, *The Kansas Conflict* (Harper & Bros., New York, 1892), pp. 298, 318. Villard, p. 264, sums up well the summer of 1856: "The carnival of crime and the civil war inaugurated by the sacking of Lawrence and the midnight assassinations in the hitherto peaceful region of Osawatomie, had brought eastern Kansas to the lowest state of her fortunes."

[17] Letter of John Brown, reprinted in Sanborn, pp. 238–239; Robinson, p. 299; Malin, pp. 589–590, 603–604; Villard, pp. 210–211 & p. 230 (quoting R.G. Elliot, of Lawrence).

[18] Villard, p. 229.

[19] Villard, p. 234; Malin, pp. 607–611.

[20] Narrative of Thomas Bedoe, Dec. 2, 1856, on file with Kansas State Historical Society, p. 2; see Malin, p. 616.

[21] Bedoe narrative, p. 3; Narrative of James H. Holmes, Dec. 7, 1856, on file with Kansas State Historical Society, p. 7; see Malin, p. 617.

[22] Bedoe narrative, pp. 3–4; Malin, pp. 617–618; Villard, p. 238.

[23] Bedoe narrative, p. 4; Villard, p. 238; see also Sanborn at pp. 326–327 (quoting Richard Mendenhall).

[24] Villard, p. 250.

[25] That Frederick was feeding the horses" rather than acting as a lookout is according to a "tradition" reported in Villard, p. 241. On Frederick Brown previously acting as a sentry at Camp Brown, as well as his wild appearance, see Redpath account quoted in Oates, pp. 149–150. On problems within the John Brown family caused by Frederick acting "wild," see letter of John Brown to John Jr., Dec. 1, 1851, reprinted in Sanborn, p. 82. On Frederick being mentally

disturbed, see Oates, pp. 324, 330.

[26] Account of Luke F. Parsons, reprinted in Sanborn, p. 285–287; Villard, pp. 241–242 (reprinting portion of account by Martin White); Sanborn, pp. 317-18 (reprinting letter of Sept. 7, 1856 by John Brown); *id.*, pp. 318–319 (reprinting newspaper account of Sept. 8, 1856 by John Brown).

[27] Quoted in Villard, p. 246.

[28] Holmes account, pp. 9–10; Parsons account; John Brown letter of Sept. 7, 1856; Bedoe account; see Villard, pp. 243–246.

[29] Quoted in Villard, p. 248.

[30] Sanborn, p. 328; Villard, p. 253.

[31] See, in particular, Letter from Charles Robinson to Sara Robinson, dated Sept. 20, 1856, reprinted in Malin, pp. 633–634, which betrays the free staters' initial lack of trust in Geary. Robinson's later writings, and even his subsequent edits after he first wrote the letter, backtracked on this point of view.

[32] Reprinted in Sanborn, p. 329.

[33] Reprinted in Sanborn, pp. 330–331.

[34] John Brown's account of these events is reprinted in Sanborn, pp. 332–333; see also Villard p. 257; Sanborn pp. 333–334 (reporting statement by H.A. Dunlop), 335; Malin, pp. 633–634.

[35] Malin, pp. 142–143, 637.

[36] Quoted in Malin, p. 640.

[37] Quoted in Malin, pp. 638, 640.

[38] Robinson, pp. 341–354.

[39] Sanborn, p. 473, quoting John Brown as reported by Hinton.

[40] Villard, pp. 270, 275; Sanborn, pp. 342–343.

[41] See Rossbach, pp. 15–39, for an insightful discussion of Howe, Parker, and their rôles and attitudes with respect to the failed Burns rescue.

[42] Villard, p. 272, citing F. J. Garrison, *William Lloyd Garrison, By His Children* (Houghton Mifflin, Boston and New York, 1894), vol. 3, pp. 487–488.

[43] Rossbach, pp. 83–84.
[44] Sanborn, pp. 359–360; Rossbach, p. 90; Villard, p. 275.
[45] Villard, pp. 275–276.
[46] The notes for John's speech are in the collection of the Kansas State Historical Society. See also, Rossbach, p. 101; Villard, pp. 277–278, 281.
[47] Villard, p. 277.
[48] The original of John Brown's March 30, 1857 contract with Charles Blair, as well as his other correspondence with Blair, are in the collection of the Kansas State Historical Society. See also, Villard, pp. 283-85; Oates, pp. 199-200, 211, 272.
[49] Letter from John Brown to F. B. Sanborn, Oct. 1, 1857, reprinted in Sanborn, pp. 398–401.
[50] Sanborn, p. 114.

Endnotes to Chapter 15: A Terrorist Replaces an Un-Terrorist

[1] See Sanborn, p. 431.
[2] George Macaulay Trevelyan, *Garibaldi e la Difesa della Repubblica Romana*, translated by Emma Rice Dobelli (Nicola Zanichelli, Bologna, 1909), p. 281 & Appendice N.
[3] Trevelyan, pp. 281–281; Alfonso Scirocco, *Garibaldi* (Il Sole 24 Ore, Milan, 2010), p. 169.
[4] Trevelyan, pp. 286–315.
[5] Trevelyan, pp. 331–338 & Appendice N. For Hugh Forbes's personal account of his barricade work in support of Garibaldi at Cesanatico, see Hugh Forbes, *Compendio del Volontario Patriotico* (Stamperia Nazionale, Napoli, 1860) p. 121 & n.
[6] See Forbes letter to Sanborn of Jan. 9, 1858, reprinted in *New York Herald*, Oct. 27, 1858, p. 3.
[7] Forbes letters reprinted in *New York Herald*, Oct. 27, 1859, p. 3; Reynolds, pp. 191, 234; Villard, p. 285; Oates, p. 200; Rossbach, p.

132.

[8] Testimony of William H.D. Callender of January 23, 1860, transcribed in Senate Select Committee Report on the Harper's Ferry Invasion, 36th Congress, 1st Session, Senate Rep. Com. No. 278 ("Mason Report").

[9] John Brown admitted that he did, indeed, have an agreement to pay Forbes $100 per month in a letter he ghost-wrote in February 1857 for his son John Brown, Jr. to send to Forbes. Sanborn, pp. 432–433.

[10] Rossbach, p. 118; Sanborn, p. 390.

[11] Rossbach, pp. 115–117, 121, 124, 127; Sanborn, pp. 111–112 & fn.1; Frothingham, p. 237 (Gerrit Smith diary entry about visit July 24, 1857 with Hugh Forbes "on his way to Kansas" and noting that Smith gave him some money); Villard, p. 279. On John Brown's continuing efforts to raise funds for his family, see also Letter of John Brown to George Stearns, Aug. 8, 1857, reprinted in Sanborn, p. 412; Letter of S.G. Howe dated Nov. 7, 1857 excerpted in Appendix to testimony of Samuel Howe in Mason Report.

[12] Sanborn, p. 431.

[13] Letter from Hugh Forbes to Samuel Howe, May 14, 1858, reprinted in *New York Herald*, Oct. 27, 1859, p. 4; see also Villard, p. 313–315; Rossbach, p. 133.

[14] *Ibid.*

[15] Letter from John Brown *sub nom.* Nelson Hawkins to Wife and Children, Aug. 17, 1857, reprinted in Sanborn, p. 414.

[16] Hugh Forbes, *Manual of the Patriotic Volunteer* (W. H. Tinson, New York, 1855) Vol. II, pp. 59–95; on the comparison with *Catechism of a Revolutionary,* see Philip Pomper, *Sergei Nechaev* (Rutgers Univ. Press, New Brunswick, New Jersey, 1979), pp. 90–95; Robert Riggs, *Sofia Perovskaya, Terrorist Princess* (Global Harmony Press, Berkeley 2017), pp. 95–98.

[17] Sanborn, p. 431; Rossbach, pp. 129, 133; Malin, p. 706; Villard, pp. 299, 308; Connelley, p. 316; Reynolds, p. 243.

[18] "Connecticut Births and Christenings, 1649-1906", Family Search

database (7 January 2020), Aaron Dwight Stevens, 1831; see also "United States Census, 1850," Family Search database with images (9 April 2016), Connecticut > New London > Norwich > image 184 of 245; citing NARA microfilm publication M432 (Washington, D.C.: National Archives and Records Administration, n.d.).

[19] See generally, Will Gorenfeld & John Gorenfeld, *Kearney's Dragoons Out West* (University of Oklahoma Press, Norman, OK, 2016).

[20] See Edwin L. Sabin, *Kit Carson Days, 1809 – 1868* (A.C. McClurg & Co., Chicago, 1914), pp. 345-50, 365.

[21] These treaties are now, of course, regarded as notoriously unfavorable to the aborigines. See Sabin, supra, pp. 359-62.

[22] See, Letter from Aaron Stevens to his sister Lydia dated Nov. 9, 1854, reprinted in Vic Butsch & Tommy Coletti, *A Journey to the Gallows, Aaron Dwight Stevens, the Story of a Forgotten American Hero* (Next Century Publishing, Las Vegas, NV, 2016), p. 299.

[23] Letter from E. T. Conley, Brigadier General, to Hon John Taber, House of Representatives, July 23, 1935, summarizing Aaron D. Stevens military file (in National Archive Record Group Record Group 153: Records of the Judge Advocate General's Office (Army), Entry 15: Court-Martial Case Files, (1809-94).) On the action seen by Company F, 1st Dragoons, see Edwin L. Sabin, *Kit Carson Days, 1809 – 1868* (A.C. McClurg & Co., Chicago, 1914), pp. 380-90; on the casualties suffered by members of Company "F," see Muster Rolls of the Battle of Cieneguilla, April 30, 1854 ("Muster Roll") reprinted at https://web.archive.org/web/20110807172303/-http://musketoon.com/2005/01/17/muster-rolls-battle-of-cieneguilla-30-march-1854/.

[24] Stevens letter of Nov. 9, 1854, reprinted in *Journey to the Gallows*, supra. On the campaigns conducted by forces which included Company F against the Apaches in the wake of Cieneguilla, see Sabin, supra, pp. 380-84.

[25] Compare Muster Roll, supra (identifying Stevens as a "private" in Company F), with Taos May 1855 Court Martial, supra (identifying Stevens as a "bugler" in Company F). In addition to the choir director job of his father, confirmed in numerous sources, the 1850 census also identifies Stevens' older brother as being a "music teacher" by occupation. Supporting the inference that Stevens was appointed Company F bugler after the desertion of a former bugler, see Muster Roll, supra (Bugler James Cook deserted on April 9, 1854).

[26] On Blake's penchant for fault-finding with both officers and men, and being excessively restrictive and overly hard on the men of Company F, see Record Group 153: Records of the Judge Advocate General's Office (Army), Entry 15: Court-Martial Case Files (1809-1894), Court of Inquiry HH-496 pertaining to Major Philip R. Thompson, 1st Dragoons that occurred May 23, 1855 – May 28, 1855 at Taos, NM containing circa 90 pp. (hereafter, "Thompson Court of Inquiry"), testimony of Stevens (May 26, 1855), testimony of Cameron (May 26, 1855), testimony of Fitzsimmons (May 26, 1855, testimony of Asst. Surgeon Barry (May 26, 1855), testimony of Lt. Johnston (May 28, 1855). On Blake's point of view that the soldiers tended to be rowdy when they were in town, see Record Group 153: Records of the Judge Advocate General's Office (Army), Entry 15: Court-Martial Case Files (1809-1894), Court-Martial Case File HH-660 pertaining to Major George A. H. Blake, 1st Dragoons that took place January 29, 1856 – June 10, 1856 at Santa Fe, NM containing circa 170 pp. (hereafter, "Blake Court Martial"), testimony of Joseph (Jan. 29, 1856); testimony of Depew (Feb. 4, 1856). On Philip Thompson's severe alcoholism, see Thompson Court of Inquiry, testimony of Barry (May 26, 1855); Blake Court Martial, testimony of Barry (Feb. 1, 1856), testimony of Johnston (Jan. 30, 1856). On Blake's frequent absences from Cantonment Burgwin on private business, see Thompson Court of Inquiry, testimony of Johnston (May 28, 1856); Blake Court Martial, testimony of Fitzsimmons (Jan. 31, 1856); testimony of Barry (Feb.

1, 1856).

[27] On the stop at St. Vrain's mill to get liquor, see Thompson Court of Inquiry, testimony of Barry (May 26, 1855), testimony of Fitzsimmons (May 24, 1855). On Blake passing the Company on his way to Taos, see Thompson Court of Inquiry, testimony of Stevens (May 26, 1855), testimony of Maj. Blake (May 24, 1855).

[28] The time Company F entered Taos Square is the subject of conflicting testimony. Compare Thompson Court of Inquiry, testimony of Blake (May 25, 1855) ("2 p.m."), with Blake Court Martial, testimony of Barry (Feb. 1, 1856) ("11 a.m."). The author deems the estimate that is most reliable and consistent with the overall time sequence to be that of Kit Carson. He recalled that the Company came into town after 12 p.m., shortly after he finished his lunch. Blake Court Martial, testimony of Carson (Feb. 2, 1856). On Thompson's order for the "ones and threes" to dismount and shop while the "twos and fours" held their horses, see Thompson Court of Inquiry, testimony of Fitzsimmons (May 24, 1855); Blake Court Martial, testimony of Johnston (Jan. 30, 1856). That the bugle call to recall the first group was in fact sounded, see *ibid.* That citizens began complaining to Blake and urging him to order the Company to leave town, see Thompson Court of Inquiry, testimony of Judge Brocchus (May 25, 1855); testimony of Blake (May 24, 1855).

[29] That Thompson had Stevens "blow" a second assembly, see Record Group 153: Records of the Judge Advocate General's Office (Army), Entry 15: Court-Martial Case Files (1809-1894), Court-Martial Case File HH-497 pertaining to Bugler Aaron D. Stevens, Private John Cooper, Private Joseph Fox, and Private John Steel that took place May 21, 1855 – May 25, 1855 at Taos, NM containing circa 52 pp. ("Stevens-Cooper-Fox-Steel Court Martial"), testimony of Thompson (May 21, 1856 and May 24, 1856); Thompson Court of Inquiry, testimony of Fitzsimmons (May 24, 1855), testimony of Barry (May 26, 1855); Blake Court Martial, testimony of

Fitzsimmons (Jan. 31, 1856). On Blake's order to arrest Fitzsimmons, see Thompson Court of Inquiry, testimony of Blake (May 24, 1855), testimony of Barry (May 26, 1855), testimony of Fitzsimmons (May 24, 1856).

[30] Thompson Court of Inquiry, testimony of Fitzsimmons (May 24, 1855), testimony of Blake (May 24, 1855), testimony of Johnston (May 28, 1855); Blake Court Martial, testimony of Johnston (Jan. 30, 1856).

[31] According to E. N. Depew, a deputy federal marshal who was present when the charge occurred, the mood of the riotous troops in Taos Plaza at the time was such that anyone who tried to interfere with them was risking his life. Blake Court Martial, testimony of Depew (Feb. 2, 1856). Regarding Blake's emergence from Joseph's store to order the Company out of town, and Fox's reaction to that order, see Thompson Court of Inquiry, testimony of Blake (May 24, 1855), testimony of Fitzsimmons (May 24, 1855 and May 26, 1855), testimony of Fox (May 26, 1855); Blake Court Martial, testimony of Fitzsimmons (Jan. 31, 1856).

[32] Cooper Court Martial, testimony of Fitzsimmons (May 22, 1855), testimony of Blake (May 22, 1855), testimony of Gould (May 22, 1855); Thompson Court of Inquiry, testimony of Fitzsimmons (May 24, 1855), testimony of Blake (May 24, 1855).

[33] Thompson Court of Inquiry, testimony of Barry (May 26, 1855), testimony of Blake (May 24, 1855), testimony of Baca (May 25, 1855), testimony of Carson (May 25, 1855); Cooper Court Martial, testimony of Blake (May 22, 1855), testimony of Baca (May 22, 1855), testimony of Gould (May 22, 1855).

[34] Thompson Court of Inquiry, testimony of Fitzsimmons (May 24, 1855 and May 26, 1855), testimony of Steel (May 26, 1855); Steel Court Martial, testimony of Blake (May 25, 1855), testimony of Fitzsimmons (May 25, 1855)

[35] On Johnston's role as Thompson's second-in-command, see Blake Court Martial, testimony of Barry (Feb. 1, 1856). On Johnston's

request to Stevens to hold his horse, see Blake Court Martial, testimony of Johnston (Jan. 30, 1856). On the difficulty of getting through the crowd to help Blake, see Thompson Court of Inquiry, testimony of Carson (May 25, 1855); Fox Court Martial, testimony of Johnston (May 25, 1855). On how the fight ended, see Steel Court Martial, testimony of Blake (May 25, 1855), testimony of Thompson (May 25, 1855); Fox Court Martial, testimony of Fitzsimmons (May 25, 1855) Thompson Court of Inquiry, testimony of Blake (May 24, 1855), testimony of Fitzsimmons (May 26, 1855), closing statement of Thompson (May 28, 1855).

[36] On Blake's injuries, appearance and demeanor after the fight, see Blake Court Martial, testimony of Carson (Feb. 2, 1856), testimony of Barry (Feb. 1, 1856). On Blake's challenge to the Company, and Stevens's response to it, see Stevens Court Martial, testimony of Fitzsimmons (May 21, 1855), testimony of Johnston (May 21, 1855), testimony of Blake (May 21, 1855), testimony of Stevens (May 21, 1855), testimony of Johnston (May 21, 1855) Thompson Court of Inquiry, testimony of Fitzsimmons (May 24, 1855); Blake Court Martial, testimony of Johnston (Jan. 30, 1856 and Jan. 31, 1856), testimony of Fitzsimmons (Jan. 31, 1856), testimony of Smith (Feb. 5, 1856). Johnston is the only witness who claimed Stevens brandished a pistol as he responded to Blake's challenge, so his testimony is deemed inaccurate on this point. On Johnston's order to Stevens to take the three horses he was holding to the far side of Joseph's store, see Thompson Court of Inquiry, testimony of Johnston (May 28, 1855); Blake Court Martial, testimony of Johnston (Jan. 31, 1856). On Blake's direction to Brocchus to have Cooper, Fox, Steel and Stevens arrested, see Thompson Court of Inquiry, testimony of Blake (May 24, 1855), testimony of Fitzsimmons (May 24, 1855); Blake Court Martial, testimony of Johnston (Jan. 30, 1856 and Jan. 31, 1856), and testimony of Depew (Feb. 4, 1856).

[37] Stevens Court Martial, testimony of Brocchus (May 21, 1855), testimony of Johnston (May 21, 1855), testimony of Carson (May 21, 1855), testimony of Stevens (May 21, 1855); Thompson Court of Inquiry, testimony of Brocchus (May 25, 1855); Blake Court Martial, testimony of Joseph (Jan. 29, 1856).

[38] Stevens Court Martial, testimony of Brocchus (May 21, 1855), testimony of Carson (May 21, 1855), testimony of Johnston (May 21, 1855), testimony of Thompson (May 21, 1855), testimony of Blake (May 21, 1855), testimony of Stevens (May 21, 1855). On Stevens's hot temper, see Villard, Appendix, p. 680 (quoting George Gill as recalling Stevens as "rash" and "hasty"); Hinton, pp. 498-99, reprinting final letter of John Brown to Aaron Stevens, dated Dec. 2, 1859, admonishing Stevens in a biblical phrase to be "slow to anger." Hinton, though demonstrably wrong about the reasons for Stevens's court-martial, described him as "hard to discipline" and "hasty," having a "disposition to resist the daily tyrannies" of military life. Hinton, p. 493.

[39] Letter of Jefferson Davis, Aug. 9, 1855, reprinted in Stevens Court Martial record. Davis further ordered that Major Blake and Major Thompson be court-martialed, and that Company F be broken up with its men disbursed throughout other companies.

[40] Hinton speculated that the alias "Whipple" was selected by Stevens because it was a family name. See Hinton, pp. 493-94. Just as likely, he adopted the name because of Amiel Weeks Whipple, an American military officer from Massachusetts who led survey teams in the same American Southwest theater where Stevens served in Company F of the First Dragoons.

[41] Villard, p. 254; Malin, p. 233.

[42] See Malin, p. 233; Hinton, pp. 462, 493–496.

[43] Hinton, pp. 455–463.

[44] Much of the history of John Brown's recruitment tour in Kansas during the fall of 1857 is taken from the first person so-called "Confession of John Cook" written in November 1859, reprinted in

an appendix to Hinton, pp. 700–717; see also, Hinton, pp. 466–468; Villard, p. 308; account of Henry Clay Pate in Norfolk *Argus*, and reprinted in the online site of West Virginia Archives and History, in which Pate recalled that he met Cook in "Camp Brown" after he was taken prisoner at the Battle of Black Jack. Pate recalled that he had already met Cook during the "siege of Lawrence" two weeks earlier.

[45] Sanborn, pp. 238–239 (recalling that planned timing of attack was mid-May); Villard, pp. 311–315; see also Sanborn, p. 425 (quoting account of C.W. Moffat).

[46] See letter ghost-written in early February 1858 by John Brown for John Brown, Jr. to send to Hugh Forbes, reprinted in Sanborn, pp. 432–433.

[47] Sanborn, pp. 431–432. The existence of this letter from John Brown shows, contrary to what Sanborn later wrote, that John anticipated that Hugh would engage in professional abolitionist-type canvassing. John revealed many details to Hugh which indicate that he supported at least some of Hugh's canvassing. The tenor of Hugh's correspondence lends credence to the inference that John, in discussions with Hugh, blamed his inability to continue to pay Hugh on the failure of the NKC and other groups to fulfill the financial pledges they had made to John Brown in the spring of 1857.

[48] Sanborn, pp. 431–432.

[49] Letter from H. Forbes to F. Sanborn, Jan. 9, 1858, reprinted in *New York Herald*, Oct. 27, 1859, p. 3.

[50] Sanborn, p. 427; Letter from F. Sanborn to H. Forbes, reprinted in Sanborn, pp. 429–430.

[51] Sanborn claimed that $500 of the $5,000 pledged by the NKC had been paid; but in his January 23, 1858 response, Hugh Forbes said this statement was in error and that only $150 had been paid. Hugh also said that the person who delivered the $150 took $40 for expenses, leaving John Brown with only $110. Letter from H. Forbes to F. Sanborn, Jan. 23, 1858, reprinted in *New York Herald*, Oct. 27,

1859, pp. 3–4. The NKC figure of $110 used by Forbes in his letter to Sanborn is the exact same figure John Brown himself reported to Sanborn on Aug. 13, 1857. Letter from John Brown to F. Sanborn, Aug. 13, 1857, reprinted in Sanborn, p. 412.

[52] See Letter from John Brown to George Stearns, Aug. 8, 1857, reprinted in Sanborn, p. 411.

[53] Letter from H. Forbes to F. Sanborn, Jan. 9, 1858.

[54] Letter from F. Sanborn to H. Forbes, reprinted in Sanborn, pp. 429–430; Rossbach, p. 130.

[55] Letter from H. Forbes to F. Sanborn, Jan. 23, 1858, reprinted in *New York Herald*, Oct. 27, 1859, pp. 3–4.

[56] Rossbach, p. 134; Sanborn, pp. 432–433.

[57] Reprinted in Hinton, pp. 619–620.

[58] A reference to the deprecating language of the U.S. Supreme Court in its majority opinion in *Dred Scott v. Sandford*, 60 U.S. (19 How.) 393 (1857).

[59] See Hinton, pp. 619–634.

[60] F. Douglass, *Life and Times*, pp. 346–349.

[61] Rossbach, pp. 142–143, quoting letter from Sanborn to Higginson, Feb. 23, 1858; Frothingham, p. 239–240; Sanborn, pp. 439, 440–441.

[62] Letter from John Brown to F.B. Sanborn dated Feb. 24, 1858, reprinted in Sanborn, pp. 444–445.

[63] Letter from John Brown to F.B. Sanborn dated Feb. 26, 1856, reprinted in Sanborn, pp. 443–444.

[64] See Malin, pp. 698–699.

[65] Rossbach, pp. 144–146, 150–157; Villard, p. 325.

Endnotes to Chapter 16: A Society Feeling Insecure

[1] *Scott v. Sandford*, 60 U.S. 393 (1857).

[2] Matthew Karp, *This Vast Southern Empire* (Harvard Univ. Press, Cambridge, 2016), pp. 137, 140.

[3] Genovese, *The Political Economy of Slavery*, p. 3.

[4] Karp, pp. 8, 12, 15-16.

[5] Karp, pp. 86-89, 105.
[6] Karp, p. 57.
[7] See Karp, p. 61; see also Randall W. McGavock, *A Tennessean Abroad* (New York, 1854), pp. 213-14.
[8] Karp, pp. 141-42, 153.
[9] Karp, pp. 154-59.
[10] Karp, pp. 138-39.
[11] Karp, p. 137.
[12] Karp, p. 17.
[13] Karp, p. 6.
[14] Karp, pp. 49-51.
[15] The facts as stated in the Supreme Court's opinion were treated as stipulated. These stipulated facts actually deviated from the real facts in various respects.
[16] For instance, the Court could have based its decision on a determination of whether or not Dr. Emerson, due to his military service, changed his domicile from Missouri to Illinois or Wisconsin Territory. See 60 U.S., at p. 494 (Campbell, J., concurring); *id.* at p. 597 (Curtis, J., dissenting). Or, the Court could have sent the case back for a determination of whether or not Dred Scott was ever recognized, de facto, as a "free" man. See 60 U.S. at p. 517 (Campbell, J., concurring).
[17] 60 U.S., at p. 407.
[18] 60 U.S., at pp. 414–415; see also, *id.* at pp. 415–417.
[19] 60 U.S., at pp. 477–479 (Daniel, J., concurring).
[20] 60 U.S., at p. 450; see also, *id.* at p. 517 (Campbell, J., concurring); *id.* at p. 527 (Catron, J., concurring).

Endnotes to Chapter 17: She Saw John's Head on a Serpent

[1] Harriet Tubman, *Affidavit in Pension Claim Case*, Jan. 1, 1898, reprinted in Jean M. Humez, *Harriet Tubman, the Life and the Life*

Stories (Univ. of Wisconsin Press, Madison, 2003), p. 287.

[2] Kate Clifford Larson, *Bound for the Promised Land, Harriet Tubman, Portrait of an American Hero* (Ballantine Books, New York, 2004), introduction p. xvi and pp. 94–96. Larson points out that, in the wake of Frederick's 1845 publication of *My Bondage and My Freedom,* Frederick engaged in a public exchange of letters relative to his account of life on the Eastern Shore with A.C.C. Thompson. A.C.C. Thompson was the nephew of Anthony C. Thompson, with whom Ben Ross, as well as Harriet Tubman herself, had a lengthy, complex and intimate master and servant relationship. See Larson, p. 333, fn. 39. In fact, Harriet probably made her 1849 escape from a Caroline County property that was under development by Anthony C. Thompson. Larson, p. 80; Humez, pp. 215–216.

[3] See reports quoted in Humez, pp. 257–263; Sarah H. Bradford, *Harriet, the Moses of Her People* (Lockwood & Son, New York, 1886), p. 23.

[4] Humez, p. 209; Larson, p. 35.

[5] Humez, p. 178; Larson, p. 54.

[6] Humez, pp. 204–205; Larson, p. 5.

[7] Larson, pp. 18–21.

[8] Larson, pp. 37–38

[9] Humez, p. 212.

[10] Humez, p. 211; Larson, pp. 42–44.

[11] Larson, p. 62.

[12] Larson, p. 65–67.

[13] Initially, upon the death of Harriet's insolvent owner Edward Brodess, his "negroes" were excepted from the probate court's order that all of his personal property must be sold off to pay his debts. See Larson, p. 76. However, his widow Eliza soon decided that "liquidating" the family's human possessions was the only way to attempt to get out of debt.

[14] Larson, p. 64.

[15] Larson, pp. 73–74.

[16] Larson, pp. 74–76.
[17] Larson, p. 79 (reprinting reward notice).
[18] See Larson, p. 80; see also, *id.* p. 329, fn. 128.
[19] Larson, p. 84.
[20] Larson, pp. 99–100.
[21] See Humez, p. 218
[22] Larson, pp. 89–90.
[23] Larson, pp. 90–91, Humez, pp. 218–219.
[24] Larson, pp. 92–93; Douglass, *Life and Times*, p. 296.
[25] Larson pp. 100–101; Humez, p. 233.
[26] Larson p. 101; Humez, pp. 233–236.
[27] Larson pp. 111–116; see details at Humez, pp. 219–222.
[28] Larson pp. 119–120.
[29] Larson, pp. 128–129; also discussed at Humez, pp. 233–234.
[30] Larson, p. 133.
[31] Larson, pp. 131–132; see Humez, pp. 223–224 for a reprinted report of Harriet's account about the rescue of Tilly.
[32] Larson, pp. 133–137.
[33] Larson, pp. 143–144.
[34] Larson, pp. 144–149.
[35] Larson, pp. 156–157.
[36] Larson, p. 159 & n.18.
[37] Letter from John Brown to John Brown, Jr., reprinted in Sanborn, p. 452.
[38] Larson, pp. 159–160.
[39] Quoted in Humez, pp. 243–244.
[40] Humez, pp. 215–216.
[41] George Orwell, "Reflections on Gandhi" (first published, *Partisan Review* (January 1949)).
[42] Sarah H. Bradford, *Scenes in the Life of Harriet Tubman*, (W. J. Moses, Auburn, NY, 1869), pp. 112–113, quoted in: James A. McGowan, *Station Master on the Underground Railroad, the Life*

and Letters of Thomas Garrett (McFarland & Co., Jefferson, NC, 2005), p. 101.

[43] Rossbach, p. 166; Larson, p. 161.

[44] Letter from H. Forbes to S. Howe, April 19, 1858, reprinted in *New York Herald*, Oct. 27, 1859, p. 4.

[45] Rossbach, pp. 160–161.

[46] Letter from H. Forbes to S. Howe, May 6, 1858, reprinted in *New York Herald*, Oct. 27, 1859, p. 4.

[47] Letter from S. Howe to H. Forbes dated May 10, 1858, reprinted in Appendix to testimony of Samuel Howe in Mason Report.

[48] Quoted in Rossbach, p. 164.

Endnotes to Chapter 18: A Massacre and a Midnight Murder

[1] See generally, Walter L. Fleming, "The Buford Expedition to Kansas," *American Historical Review*, Vol. 6, No. 1, pp. 38–48 (1900); see also sources quoted in Villard, p. 622, fn. 93. In the words of Villard, p. 265:

> Climate and soil fought in Kansas on the side of the Free State men. The Southerners themselves complained that their settlers who did reach Kansas were inoculated with the virus of liberty, became Free Soilers and often freed their slaves. The familiar slave crops could have never been raised in Kansas with its bleak winters. Moreover, the South was never a colonizing section; the history of the settlement of our Western communities proves this, if the fate of Buford's band and its inability to settle down anywhere did not. The final failure of the slave power to hold the great advantage it had in Kansas in 1855 was due not to fear of weapons, but to inability to place farmers and pioneers on the battle-ground.

[2] See *New York Tribune*, May 31, 1858, p. 5.

[3] C. Robinson, *The Kansas Conflict* (Harper & Bros., New York, 1892), p. 391.
[4] William P. Tomlinson, *Kansas in Eighteen Fifty Eight* (H. Dayton, New York, 1859), pp. 164–166.
[5] Tomlinson, pp. 168–174.
[6] As recorded by Tomlinson, pp. 134–136.
[7] Harvey Hougen, *The Marais des Cygnes Massacre and the Execution of William Griffith* (Kansas State Historical Society, Lawrence, Kansas, 1985), pp 77–78.
[8] See Robinson, p. 392.
[9] Tomlinson, pp. 63–65; Statement of William Hairgrove, quoted in *The Daily Exchange*, Baltimore, MD, June 9, 1858; Hougen, pp. 78–79. Charles A. Hamilton's own version of events actually appears in print. The *New York Tribune* of May 31, 1858 ran an item attributed to the *St. Louis Republican*, May 21, 1858, giving an account by "Captain A. C. Hamilton" about the raid. Charles Hamilton, due to his Mexican War service, was commonly called the honorific "Captain Hamilton," whereas his brother George, who was a physician, was called "Dr. Hamilton." This "Captain A.C. Hamilton" account confirms that Hamilton, prior to May 8, was required to leave Kansas Territory; that he took his wife and children "to safety," and that he returned "to save life and property." According to this account, the "abolitionists" subsequently let some of the expelled settlers return, but not Charles.
[10] Tomlinson, pp. 65–66.
[11] See *National Era*, June 3, 1858; *New York Daily Tribune*, May 10, 1858; *Herald of Freedom*, March 5, 1858; see also Indictment in *United States v. Walter B. Brocket*, dated April 27, 1858, on file with Kansas State Historical Society.
[12] Account of Sarah Read in *National Intelligencer*, June 17, 1858; Account of B.L. Read in *The Daily Exchange* of June 7, 1858; Hougen, p. 80.

[13] Hougen, p. 80. There are sharply conflicting accounts about the prelude to the Marais des Cygnes massacre, as well as the massacre itself. In addition to what is to all indications Charles Hamilton's own account, noted above, there are multiple eyewitness accounts from two survivors of the massacre, South Carolina-born William Hairgrove and a Baptist minister named B.L. Read, that were published in *The Daily Exchange* of June 7, 1858. Another account by B.L. Read was published in the *National Era* of Washington City on June 17, 1858, together with the eyewitness account of Read's wife, Sarah Read. Other accounts deemed sufficiently credible to factor into the history given here are those of William P. Tomlinson, in the work cited above, pp. 68–75 (Tomlinson arrived in the area on the day of the massacre, and collected information from eyewitnesses and survivors), and Hinton, pp. 194–195. Hinton was in Kansas acting as a newspaper correspondent at the time of the massacre; see Sanborn p. 471.

[14] B.L. Read Account in *National Era*; Sarah Read Account in *National Era*.

[15] Account of William Hairgrove, published in *Herald of Freedom*, July 31, 1858.

[16] William Hairgrove Account in *The Daily Exchange*; B.L. Read Account in *The Daily Exchange*; Tomlinson, pp. 69–70; Account of "A.C. Hamilton" from *St. Louis Republican*, May 21, 1858, reprinted in *New York Tribune* edition of May 31, 1858. For John Brown's description of Snyder's shop as it existed on May 19, 1858, see Hinton, pp. 213–214.

[17] Brocket's act in turning his horse away rather than participating in the massacre, enraging Hamilton, is described by victim B.L. Read in his account in *The Daily Exchange*.

[18] B.L. Read Account in *National Era*; account of William Hairgrove, discussed in Tomlinson, pp. 241–242; Sarah Read Account in *National Era*; Hougen, pp. 83–84; see also "A.C. Hamilton" Account in *St. Louis Republican*, May 21, 1858.

[19] B.L. Read Account in *The Daily Exchange*; Tomlinson, pp. 74–83.
[20] "A.C. Hamilton" Account in *St. Louis Republican*, May 21, 1858.
[21] *Arkansas True Democrat*, Little Rock, Arkansas, June 29, 1858, p. 1.
[22] Sanborn, p. 463; Rossbach, p. 170.
[23] Account of George B. Gill, reprinted in Hinton, p. 734; see Villard, p. 344.
[24] Sanborn, pp. 471–474; Villard, pp. 354–357.
[25] Malin, p. 711; Villard, p. 358.
[26] Villard, pp. 358–360; Oates, p. 258.
[27] Hinton, pp. 216–217; Villard, pp. 364–366; on McDaniel and Mitchell as the leaders of the posse sent out after Marais des Cygnes, see Tomlinson, pp. 77 & ff.; on the identity of McDaniel see Daniel W. Wilder, *Annals of Kansas, Vol. I* (Topeka, 1875), p. 154.
[28] Gill Account, reprinted in Hinton, pp. 217–219; Malin pp. 711–712; Villard, p. 366; Robinson, p. 405.
[29] Eyewitness Account of Harvey G. Hicklin, reprinted in W.A. Mullies, *John Brown's Raid in Vernon County* (Hume, Missouri, 2008).
[30] Statement of David Cruise's son Rufus, from Mullies. The surname of the victim shot to death by Stevens, aka "Whipple," is reported in various published sources as David "Cruse," "Cruise," or "Crews." See *Herald of Freedom*, Lawrence, KN, Jan. 8, 1859, p. 1 ("Crews"); *The Spirit of Democracy*, Columbus, OH, Jan. 5, 1859, p. 2 ("Crews"); *Cleveland Morning Leader*, Cleveland, OH, Dec. 28, 1858, p. 3 ("Cruse"); *Staunton Vindicator*, Staunton, VA, Jan. 22, 1859, p. 1 ("Cruse"); *1887 History of Vernon County* (Brown & Co., St. Louis, Mo.), pp. 228-32, reprinted as US Gen Web project, found online as https://sites.rootsweb.com/movernon/bios/cruise_david.htm ("Cruise"). The marriage certificate of David and Lucinda dated July 28, 1841 gives David's name as "Cruse." Rufus later served as

a Confederate Missouri cavalry soldier in the Civil War. His surname is listed in records both as "Cruse" and, more often, as "Cruise." There is no detailed contemporary published account of the killing of David Cruise, although his murder was nationally reported. John Brown and Aaron Stevens later gave self-serving versions which, while claiming that David Cruise was shot while engaging in armed resistance, admit that Cruise was killed by Stevens while trying to defend his home from a midnight ransack and robbery. Other accounts say Cruise when shot either was unarmed, or was armed with a revolver that did not fire and that he threw down before being shot.

[31] Gill Account in Hinton, pp. 221–222; Malin, p. 712; Villard, pp. 367–368, 377.

[32] Quoted in Robinson, pp. 406–407.

[33] Reprinted in Sanborn, pp. 481–482 and Villard, pp. 375–376.

Endnotes to Chapter 19: Gathering for the Storm

[1] The primary narrative regarding events of January 27–31, 1859 are taken from an eyewitness account of William F. Creitz to James Redpath dated Dec. 17, 1859, on file with the Kansas State Historical Society ("Creitz Account"). Corroborating but less detailed accounts are found in Sanborn, pp. 484–488, and Villard, pp. 381–383.

[2] Creitz account, pp. 3–4.

[3] Creitz account, pp. 4–8; see also Letter of Cyrus Kurtz dated Feb. 6, 1859, in collection of Kansas State Historical Society; Villard, p. 381; Sara Robinson, p. 351 (on Wood); Hinton, pp. 106–107 (on Wood).

[4] Sanborn, p. 488.

[5] As reprinted in http://www.wvculture.org/history/jbexhibit/shepherdstownregraid.html, the document found after John's capture read as follows:

> VINDICATION OF THE INVASION, &C.
> The Denver truce was broken &

  1st It was in accordance with my settled policy
  2nd It was intended as a discriminating blow at Slavery
  3 It was calculated to lessen the value of Slaves
  4th It was (over & above all other motives) Right.
  Duty of all persons in regard to this matter
  Criminality of neglect in this matter
  Suppose a case
  Ask further support.

Oates, pp. 283–284, is incorrect in ascribing this manifesto to the Harpers Ferry period. The opening reference by John to the "Denver truce," referring to Kansas acting Governor James Denver's agreement with James Montgomery in June of 1858 following the Marais des Cygnes massacre, is a clear attempt at an excuse for why John himself broke the peace with his Missouri raid. The concluding line, "Ask further support," suggests that this "Vindication" note was actually the outline for one of John's fund raising speeches.

[6] See Villard, pp. 387–395.

[7] W.E.B. DuBois, *John Brown* (Oxford, Oxford Univ. Press, 2007), p. 125; James Redpath, *The Public Life of Capt. John Brown* (Boston, Thayer & Eldridge 1860), p. 239; Villard, p. 393.

[8] Reprinted in Sanborn, p. 467; see also Frothingham, p. 237; Rossbach, p. 195; Villard, p. 395.

[9] Rossbach, pp. 204–206.

[10] Quoted in Villard, pp. 398–399.

[11] Rossbach, p. 204–205.

[12] See generally, E. Nason & T. Russell, *The Life and Public Services of Henry Wilson* (Philadelphia, 1876) pp. 31–272.

[13] Rossbach, p. 205; on Hugh Forbes and Henry Wilson, see Rossbach, p. 162.

[14] Rossbach, pp. 107, 206–207.

[15] Hinton, p. 239.

[16] See Reynolds, p. 300.

[17] Larson, pp. 169–173.

[18] See Larson, pp. 171–174.

[19] Testimony of John C. Unseld, reported in *Report of the Select Committee of the U.S. Senate on the Harpers Ferry Invasion*, Chaired by J.M. Mason "Mason Committee Report," testimony appendix, pp. 1–3 ("Unseld Senate Testimony").

[20] Unseld Senate Testimony, p. 2.

[21] Hinton, p. 249; Anderson, p. 19.

[22] Hinton, p. 248.

[23] Anderson, p. 24.

[24] Villard, p. 419.

[25] E.g., Letter of John Brown, Jr., Sept. 8, 1859, quoted in Villard, p. 414; letter of Jeremiah Anderson, late September, 1859, quoted in Sanborn, p. 545.

[26] Hinton, pp. 249–250; see also, Unseld Senate Testimony, p. 11.

[27] Reprinted in Hinton, pp. 537–538.

[28] Excerpt from Letter of "C. Whipple" to Jenny Dunbar, Oct. 1, 1859 (on file at Kansas State Historical Society).

[29] Villard, pp. 409, 413.

[30] John's anxiety over the small number of African Americans among his followers is reflected in a letter by his son Watson, quoted in Sanborn, p. 549, remarking that there were "only" two black men in the company.

[31] Eugene L. Meyer, *Five for Freedom* (Lawrence Hill Books, Chicago, 2018), pp. 19–24.

[32] F. Douglass, *Life and Times*, pp. 351–353.

[33] Villard, pp. 410–411.

[34] Meyer, p. 72. Green went by the name "Shield Emperor" in his Rochester advertisement for cleaning services, one that was probably written for him by Frederick Douglass or one of his assistants.

[35] Meyer, pp. 40–41.

[36] Meyer, pp. 29–34, 40.

[37] Meyer, pp. 34–35, 42–43.
[38] Meyer, pp. 42–45, 80.
[39] See Hinton, pp. 273–274, 505, 508; Villard, pp. 684, 686; Boyer, p. 31 note; Reynolds, p. 289. Hinton contradicts himself, by saying in one place that Leary and Copeland arrived in Harpers Ferry on October 2, and in another that they arrived in Chambersburg on October 12. Compare Hinton, p. 266 with Hinton, pp. 273–274. An excerpt from the diary of John Henry Kagi, quoted in Sanborn, p. 549, records that Leary and Copeland arrived at the Kennedy Farm on Wednesday, October 12.
[40] DuBois, p. 124.
[41] Villard, pp. 420–421, 686; DuBois, p. 123; Hinton, pp. 275–276.

Endnotes to Chapter 20: The Other Washington

[1] Washington gave a detailed description of the night of his kidnapping in testimony before the U.S. Senate on January 6, 1860, less than three months after the event. Washington's testimony is transcribed in the Report [of] the Select committee of the Senate appointed to inquire into the late invasion and seizure of the public property at Harpers Ferry, section titled "Testimony," pp. 29–41 (hereafter, "Washington Senate Testimony"). The majority of the details in the present narrative are taken from Washington's account in his Senate testimony.

However, there is reason to think that Washington, whether intentionally or not, omitted some important details in his Senate testimony account. Washington's account is at variance in some respects with the report of the other extant primary source, Osborne P. Anderson. Anderson, a man of mixed race African American descent, was one of Brown's raiders. In 1861 he published a monograph, titled *A Voice from Harper's Ferry, a Narrative of Events at Harper's Ferry, with incidents prior and subsequent to its capture by Captain Brown and his men* (Boston: 1861, Harvard

College Library) (hereafter, "O. Anderson Narrative").

The most important single discrepancy between the two accounts is that Washington did not recall either Osborne Anderson, nor any "colored" man meeting Anderson's description, as being among of the band of six raiders who kidnapped him (Washington Senate Testimony, p. 31). Anderson, on the other hand, vividly recalled that Aaron Stevens, the leader of the squadron assigned to kidnap Washington, ceremoniously forced Washington to hand over the "Frederick the Great sword" to Anderson personally, and that this act had a symbolic importance to the raiders, in that Anderson was a black man (albeit, a freed man and one who had mixed race ancestry). (O. Anderson Narrative, pp. 30–31 (John Brown's "orders" explicitly required the sword to be handed to Anderson) & p. 35).

Other evidence suggests Anderson was truthful in reporting that he was among the six men who took part in the Washington kidnapping. Anderson's narrative agrees with Washington on the general sequence of events that occurred during the post-midnight raid, including several otherwise trivial and "unimportant" details. For example, Washington and Anderson both agree on Stevens's role as the leader of the kidnap squadron. They also both agree on the general sequence of events and conversation that transpired between Washington and Stevens. Unless Anderson, prior to producing his narrative, obtained and studied a transcript or other version of Washington's testimony, he would be unable to produce an account that would agree with Washington's account on these matters if he had not been personally present on the night of the kidnapping.

The appendix to then Colonel Robert E. Lee's official report on the raid, submitted the day after the collapse of Brown's insurrection, lists "O. P. Anderson" as a "negro" insurrectionist from Pennsylvania, who was "unaccounted for" (Letter of Colonel Lee to the Adjutant General, dated Oct. 19, 1859 ("Lee Oct. 19 Letter", Appendix "B," reprinted in Senate Select Committee Report, p. 44).

Lee must have assumed that Anderson was an otherwise unidentified African American killed in the Harpers Ferry fighting, as his report states that John Cook is the only raider known to have escaped (Lee Oct. 19 Letter, p. 42).

Since the Stevens party's principal and crucial goal, apart from taking hostages, was to recruit slaves and other local residents of color to immediately rise up and join the insurrection, the decision of John Brown and Stevens to include three men of African American descent (Shields Green, Lewis Leary, and Osborne Anderson) in the nighttime raiding party seems logical and plausible.

The one man Washington positively identifies as one of his six kidnappers, but who was not present with the Stevens-led nighttime raiders according to Anderson's account, is Stewart Taylor. Taylor, a "white," was a 23-year-old Canadian-born follower of Brown. He was killed in the fighting at Harpers Ferry the next day after the kidnapping (Du Bois 141). According to Anderson's narrative (p. 30), Brown's orders assigned Taylor on the night of October 16–17 to assist Brown's son, Watson Brown, in "holding" the "Maryland Bridge" leading into Harpers Ferry over the Potomac until morning. Anderson and other extant accounts suggest that this is indeed what Taylor did on the night of the Washington kidnapping.

Is it plausible that Washington failed to notice that the raider to whom he was forced to hand over his beloved Frederick sword was of African American descent? Given the conditions of darkness that prevailed in Washington's home during the kidnapping, this is the most probable explanation for Washington's omission of any mention of such a raider. Washington likely paid far more attention to the revolver and to the loaded, cocked rifles that were pointed directly at him at all times during the home invasion than he did to the faces of the invaders. He may have been misled as well by Anderson's speech. Literate and educated, Anderson was neither a Southerner nor an ex-slave. He did not speak with the deferential patois of the local African Americans with whom Virginia slave owners such as Washington were familiar (see, for example, the transcription of the slave's speech in the report of a conversation between Alexander Botelier and a Harpers Ferry area slave in Botelier, "Recollections of the John Brown Raid by a Virginian Who Witnessed the Fight," *Century Magazine*, 26 (July 1883), pp. 399–411).

We must assume Washington's mistaken "identification" of Taylor as one of his kidnappers was based on error in an attempt by Washington and others, after his rescue, to reconstruct which men from Brown's party had been the home invaders. At that time, Anderson's role as one of the raiders, and his escape from the Harpers Ferry area, appear to have been overlooked as noted above. The captured raiders including John Brown, Aaron Stevens, and John Cook were not offered clemency for assisting the investigation and had no reason to bring Anderson's involvement to the authorities' attention.

The accounts of both Washington and Anderson were given in the heat of passions that prevailed in the wake of the John Brown raid, as the storm clouds of civil war gathered. What is said by both needs to be evaluated in this light.

Lewis Washington's accounts were colored by a desire, which was shared by many Virginians in the aftermath of the Brown raid, to promote and propagandize the conception of an alleged benevolent, harmonious relationship between master and slave. The Southern landed gentry, of which Washington was a member, clung desperately to this world view. Additionally, it must be remembered that in Virginia in the 1850s, the automatic punishment for any slave who joined an anti-slavery insurrection was a swift and humiliating death. Such a fate also, ironically, inflicted a financial loss upon the slave's owner. Thus, it is likely that in Washington's statements and testimony after the John Brown raid, he consistently and purposefully disregarded and understated the willingness with which his slaves, and the slaves of others, joined the insurrection. Washington also, in the author's view, omits many details about the terrifying sequence of events, which Washington probably regarded as dishonorable, embarrassing, or both, but which are evident from the Anderson narrative.

The narrative by Anderson is suspect because it was written with a more or less explicit propaganda objective, and also because it is demonstrably false in some important particulars. Anderson's narrative claims he remained in the Arsenal with fellow raider Albert Hazlett, across the street from the Armory's engine house, to witness the final assault of the U.S. Marines on Brown's position in the engine house on the Armory grounds (Anderson Narrative, p. 45). However, from the testimony of numerous witnesses, it is not reasonably controvertible that by the time of the final assault on the morning of Tuesday, October 18, the Arsenal was already secured and under the control of the authorities (Villard, pp. 445–446). Anderson and Hazlett, in all likelihood, left the Arsenal and escaped to higher ground away from the central part of Harpers Ferry in the general confusion sometime around dusk on the prior evening (Monday, Oct. 17), then stole a rowboat and used it to cross the Potomac. From the Maryland side, Anderson made his escape northward (Oates, p. 298 & n.12).

Anderson's agenda in writing his narrative was to emphasize two issues: (1) the slaves in the Harpers Ferry area were, contrary to slave-owner propaganda, generally receptive to the uprising promoted by John Brown, and generally joined it voluntarily; and (2) the Southern slave owners, such as Washington, conducted themselves in a cowardly fashion during the raid and thus were not worthy of a great deal of personal respect or deference. The possibility must be considered that Anderson, to promote this agenda, in his narrative of events fabricated his entire role in the Washington kidnapping, basing the details on published accounts by

Washington and others. The author concludes that this theory, though it cannot conclusively be ruled out, is highly unlikely due to the narrative's mention of numerous "unimportant" details of the raid that are confirmed by Washington's testimony. It has generally been accepted by historians that Anderson's account is mostly reliable, with some "exaggerations."

[2] Washington and Anderson each state that four of the armed raiders entered the house and encountered Washington at the door to his bedroom (Washington Senate Testimony, at p. 31; O. Anderson Narrative, p. 34 (after four members of the raiding party entered the house, "Colonel Washington opened his room door, and begged us not to kill him")).

[3] Washington Senate Testimony, pp. 31–32.

[4] O. Anderson Narrative, p. 34.

[5] Washington Senate Testimony, p. 30.

[6] Washington Senate Testimony, pp. 30–31; W.E.B. Du Bois, *John Brown* (Oxford: Oxford University Press, 2007) ("Du Bois"), p. 124; Stephen B. Oates, *To Purge This Land With Blood, a biography of John Brown* (Harper & Row, New York, 1970) ("Oates"), p. 275.

[7] Washington Senate Testimony, p. 30.

[8] O. Anderson Narrative, p. 34.

[9] O. Anderson Narrative, p. 34; Washington Senate Testimony, p. 30.

[10] Washington Senate Testimony, p. 32.

[11] Washington Senate Testimony, p. 32. One discrepancy between Washington's testimony and Anderson's account of the home invasion and kidnapping concerns the presence of "females" in Washington's house. Washington, in his Senate testimony, answered a leading question by agreeing he was the only "white man" in the house at the time of the invasion. He also said that his daughter, who had previously been staying with him, left for Baltimore with some friends the morning prior (Washington Senate Testimony, p. 31). Anderson's narrative describes "females" looking out from the upper story windows of the Washington home as the raiding party knocked,

without response, prior to entering (O. Anderson Narrative, p. 34). Anderson also dramatically describes the "females of the family" as howling in protest with "great outcries" when the raiders refused their entreaties to leave Lewis Washington at home (O. Anderson Narrative, p. 35).

This difference between the two accounts can be reconciled upon the hypothesis that the "females of the family" described by Anderson were, in fact, Washington's house servants who slept in the main house. That Washington had "house servants" with him on the night of the invasion is clear from his testimony (see Washington Senate Testimony, p. 30 (he at first thought the raiders were friends admitted by the servants)). Washington testified that he went into the dining room after his capture, in part hoping to find a lighted fire there. It is logical to suppose that the house servants, well aware of the raiders' intrusion, were at work in this regard.

[12] O. Anderson Narrative, p. 34.

[13] *The Life, Trial, and Execution of Captain John Brown Known as "Old Brown of Ossawatomie"*, Robert M. De Witt, 1859 (hereafter, "Brown Trial Transcription") (testimony of Armistead Ball).

[14] "John Brown at Harper's Ferry," Account of Capt. John E.P. Daingerfield, published in *Century Magazine*, June 1885, pp. 265–267 (hereafter, "Daingerfield Century Magazine Account").

[15] Washington Senate Testimony, pp. 34–35.

[16] Washington Senate Testimony, p. 36.

[17] Testimony of Terence Byrne, transcribed in Report [of] the Select committee of the Senate appointed to inquire into the late invasion and seizure of the public property at Harpers Ferry, section titled "Testimony," p. 15 (hereafter, "Byrne Senate Testimony").

[18] Oates, p. 293; Anderson, p. 42.

[19] E.g., Anderson, p. 36; Redpath, p. 251.

[20] DuBois, p. 116; see also Map, reprinted in Oates, p. 277.

[21] DuBois, p. 119; see also Oates, pp. 278–280.

[22] DuBois, pp. 135–137.

[23] Account of Israel Green, in *The North American Review*, December 1885 ("Green Account").

[24] Byrne Senate Testimony, p. 18; see also Green Account (as to the location of the prisoners).

[25] Daingerfield Century Magazine Account.

[26] Brown Trial Transcription (testimony of Joseph Brewer).

[27] Byrne Senate Testimony, p. 19.

[28] Brown Trial Transcription (testimony of Armistead Ball).

[29] Brown Trial Transcription (testimony of Captain Simms).

[30] Allstadt Senate Testimony, p. 43.

[31] Brown Trial Transcription (testimony of Joseph Brewer, John Daingerfield, Captain Simms).

[32] Daingerfield Century Magazine Account, p. 266.

[33] Israel Green, "The Capture of John Brown," *North American Review* (December 1885), reproduced at http://www2-.iath.virginia.edu/jbrown/igreen.html ("Green Account").

[34] Daingerfield Century Magazine Account, p. 267.

[35] Green Account.

[36] Lee Dispatch.

[37] There is an interesting discrepancy in eyewitness reports concerning the subject of whether or not Brown's raiders fired on the Marines as they attempted to break down the doors of the engine house. Colonel Robert E. Lee's Report Concerning the Attack at Harper's Ferry, Oct. 19, 1859, reprinted at http://law2.-umkc.edu/faculty/projects/ftrials/johnbrown/leereport.html ("Lee Account"), Green's account, and the contemporary official dispatch by Colonel Lee (Colonel Robert E. Lee's Report Concerning the Attack at Harper's Ferry, Oct. 19, 1859, reprinted at http://law2.umkc. edu/faculty/projects/ftrials/johnbrown/leereport.-html ("Lee Account")), both state that firing by Brown's force occurred while the door was under assault, although no one was hit. On the other hand, Congressman Alexander R. Boteler wrote an

account twenty-four years later in which he stated that the raiders held their fire at this juncture ("Recollections of the John Brown Raid by a Virginian Who Witnessed the Fight, by Alexander Boteler," *Century Magazine*, 26 (July 1883), pp. 399–411, reprinted at http://www2.iath.virginia.edu/jbrown /boteler.html ("Boteler Account"). John Brown, in his "post-game interview" on the same day of the attack, claimed that he and the raiders had already effectively surrendered, did not fire at the entering Marines, and that even his wounds had been inflicted gratuitously by Green at a time after he and the other raiders had already surrendered. This claim, however, was not supported by the 1885 *Century Magazine* account of engine house hostage John Daingerfield, which was otherwise fairly sympathetic to Brown. Daingerfield stated that the raiders "fired incessantly" while the door was under assault.

[38] Green Account.

[39] John's raiders are generally profiled, and their roles in the attack as well as their fates summarized, in Hinton, pp. 275–276, 476, 488–489, 505–507, 513–514, 534–545; see also Villard, p. 686; DuBois, pp. 122, 134–135; O. Anderson Narrative; Meyer, *passim*.

Endnotes to Chapter 21: The Ecstasy of the Martyr

[1] Lee Account.

[2] Oates, p. 321.

[3] Reprinted in James Redpath, *The Public Life of John Brown* (Boston, Thayer & Eldridge, 1860), p. 370.

[4] Reprinted in Redpath, pp. 350–351

[5] Rossbach, p. 113.

[6] Brown Letter of Nov. 21, 1859, quoted in Oates, p. 342.

[7] Reprinted in Redpath, pp. 354–355.

[8] Reprinted in Redpath, pp. 349–350. With respect to the tenor of letters from abolitionists which declined to approve of John's methods, see, e.g., letters reprinted in, Redpath, pp. 345, 348, 352,

[9] Oates, pp. 318–319.
[10] Oates, pp. 318–319.
[11] Rossbach, pp. 219–222, 229.
[12] Rossbach, pp. 226–228.
[13] Blight, pp. 305–309; Douglass, *Life and Times,* p. 354.
[14] Letter from George Henry Hoyt to J. W. LeBarnes, Oct. 30, 1859, reprinted in Hinton, pp. 367–368; see also Sanborn, pp. 622, n.2 & 623; Hinton, p. 365 & n.1.
[15] Hinton, p. 373.
[16] Alford, pp. 65, 68–71.
[17] George Alfred Townsend, *The Life, Crime and Capture of John Wilkes Booth* (Dick & Fitzgerald, New York, 1865), p. 21; Kimmel, pp. 149–150.
[18] Clarke, p. 249.
[19] Wilson, p. 10.
[20] Alford, pp. 52–53.
[21] John Mathews statement, in William C. Edwards & Edward Steers editors, *The Lincoln Assassination: The Evidence* (Univ. of Illinois Press, Illinois, 2009) (hereafter, "Edwards & Steers"), p. 848.
[22] George W. Libby, *John Brown and John Wilkes Booth,* published in *Confederate Veteran* (S.A. Cunningham, founder, Nashville, TN, 1930), p. 138.
[23] Alford, p. 71.
[24] Alford, pp. 70–75.
[25] Clarke, p. 75.
[26] E. Lawrence Abel, *John Wilkes Booth and the Women Who Loved Him* (Regnery History, Washington, D.C., 2018), p. 63.
[27] Alford, p. 77; John Wilkes Booth draft speech, titled "Alow Me a Few Words," reprinted in Rhodehamel & Taper, p. 60; see also Redpath, p. 384; Townsend, p. 22.
[28] Report of Cleon Moore, reprinted in Boyd B. Stutler Database, accessed online at http://www.wvculture.org /history/wv-memory/images/jb/RP06-0119G.jpg ("Stutler On Line Compil-

ation").
[29] Letter of H. H. Riker to C. S. Gee, April 10, 1952, , reprinted in Stutler On Line Compilation.
[30] Declaration of John Avis, April 25, 1882, reproduced in Villard, pp. 670–671.
[31] Villard, note reproduced at p. 555.
[32] Letter of Thomas J. Jackson dated Dec. 2, 1859, reprinted in Stutler On Line Compilation.
[33] Oates, p. 352.

Endnotes to Chapter 22: A Primordial Political Genius

[1] Benjamin P. Thomas, *Abraham Lincoln, a Biography* (Southern Ill. Univ. Press, Carbondale, Illinois, 1952), p. 202.
[2] *New York Herald*, Feb. 28, 1860, p. 2.
[3] *New York Herald*, Feb. 28, 1860, pp. 2–3.
[4] See Ellis P. Oberholtzer, *Philadelphia: A History of the City and Its People, Vol. II* (S. J. Clarke, Philadelphia, 1912), p. 354.
[5] F. Venosta, *Felice Orsini, Notizie Storiche* (Milano, 1862), p. 7.
[6] Venosta , p. 8.
[7] Venosta, pp. 21–23.
[8] Venosta, pp. 27–29.
[9] Melinda Squires, "The Controversial Career of George Nicholas Sanders" (Western Kentucky Univ. Masters Theses & Specialist Projects, Paper 704, 2000), pp. 5–6, 83–84; see Venosta, p. 63.
[10] Venosta, p. 65.
[11] Venosta, pp. 66–70.
[12] Venosta, pp. 92–96.
[13] Venosta, p. 99.
[14] Venosta, pp. 100–101 & n.1.
[15] Venosta, pp. 103–106.
[16] Venosta, pp. 107–111.

[17] William H. Herndon and Jesse W. Weik, with notes by Paul Angle, *Herndon's Life of Lincoln* (Albert & Charles Boni, New York, 1930), pp. 2–12.
[18] Herndon & Weik, pp. 21–33.
[19] Herndon & Weik, pp. 50–53.
[20] Thomas, p. 45; Herndon & Weik, pp. 131, 329–330.
[21] Thomas, pp. 58, 60–61; Herndon & Weik, p. 141.
[22] Herndon & Weik, pp. 153–154; Thomas, pp. 74–75.
[23] Herndon & Weik, pp. 163–164, 167.
[24] Herndon & Weik, pp. 167–181.
[25] Thomas, p. 78; Herndon & Weik, pp. 218–220, 238; Michael S. Green, "Lincoln, the Organizer," in *The Election of 1860 Reconsidered*, edited by A. James Fuller (Kent State Univ. Press, Ohio, 2013), p. 12.
[26] Herndon & Weik, pp. 238, 291–294; Thomas, p. 138.
[27] Thomas, p. 72. Lincoln recognized, in a statement published in the wake of the Elijah Lovejoy controversy in Alton, the injustice and bad policy involved with slavery. But he also emphasized that the sanctity of Southern rights should be protected. Thomas., pp. 56–64.
[28] Eric Foner, *The Fiery Trial, Abraham Lincoln and American Slavery* (W.W. Norton & Co., New York, 2010), p. 61.
[29] Lincoln actually derived this saying from the words attributed to Jesus in three of the synoptic gospels, Matthew, 12:25, Mark, 3:25, and Luke, 11:17. In this context, Jesus used this logic to rebut the accusation of the Pharisees that he was using the power of the devil to perform miracles such as exorcism. He was saying, if he uses the power of the devil to cast out the devil, then the house of the devil is divided against itself. Thus, "if Satan is divided against himself, how will his kingdom stand?" Herndon & Weik, p. 325.
[30] Thomas, pp. 176–178; Green, in Fuller, p. 14; see Herndon & Weik, p. 319.
[31] Herndon & Weik, pp. 328–329.
[32] See Foner, pp. 105–106.

[33] Foner, p. 64.
[34] Quoted in Herndon & Weik, p. 332.
[35] Green, in Fuller, p. 15.
[36] Thomas, pp. 188–193; Mayer, p. 511.
[37] Green, in Fuller, p. 15.
[38] Herndon & Weik, p. 337; Thomas, pp. 194–195; Stahr, pp. 182–183, 186, 191.
[39] Green, in Fuller, pp. 18–22.
[40] Stahr, p. 189–190.
[41] James M McPherson, *Battle Cry of Freedom* (Oxford Univ. Press, New York, 1988), p. 214.
[42] James L. Huston, "The Southern Sojourns of Stephen A. Douglas and the Irrepressible Separation," published in Fuller, pp. 30–33; A. James Fuller, "A Forlorn Hope," in Fuller, pp. 75–77.
[43] A. James Fuller, "The Last True Whig," in Fuller, pp. 114–119; see also Fuller, "A Forlorn Hope," in Fuller, p. 89; Douglas G. Gardner, *"An Inscrutable Election,"* in Fuller, pp. 249–250.
[44] McPherson, pp. 223–224.
[45] Huston, in McPherson, pp. 29-44. On Douglas's speech, see David R. Barbee and Milledge L. bonham, Jr. (eds.), "The Montgomery Address of Stephan A. Douglas," *Journal of Southern History*, vol. 5, no. 4 (Nov. 1939), pp. 527–552.
[46] Eric Foner, *The Fiery Trial, Abraham Lincoln and American Slavery* (W.W. Norton & Co., New York, 2010), pp. 142–144.

Endnotes to Chapter 23: "Alow Me a Few Words"

[1] Gordon Samples, *Lust for Fame, The Stage Career of John Wilkes Booth* (McFarland & Co., North Carolina, 1982), p. 46.
[2] Quoted in Arthur F. Loux, *John Wilkes Booth, Day by Day* (McFarland & Co., North Carolina 2014), p. 133.
[3] See Alford, pp. 161–162.
[4] Samples, p. 49; see also Samples, pp. 55, 59.

[5] Samples, pp. 50 (illustration)–51.
[6] Samples, pp. 47–49; Alford, pp. 89–92; E. Lawrence Abel, *John Wilkes Booth and the Women Who Loved Him* (Regnery History, Washington, D.C. 2018), pp. 71–72.
[7] Louise C. Wooster, *The Autobiography of a Magdalen* (Birmingham, 1911), pp. 50–52.
[8] See Alford, pp. 97–98.
[9] Wooster, pp. 51–52. The circumstances of Johnnie's hasty flight were corroborated in accounts he himself subsequently gave. See Rhodehamel & Taper, p. 50; Alford, p. 98.
[10] McPherson, p. 231.
[11] The analysis given here of President Buchanan's December 3, 1860 State of the Union message is based on the full text of that message as printed in the *Bedford [Pennsylvania] Inquirer*, on Dec. 14, 1860, pp. 1–2.
[12] Oberholtzer, p. 357; see *Baltimore Daily Exchange*, Dec. 14, 1860, p. 1; *Shepardstown, Jefferson County, VA, Register*, Dec. 17, 1860, p. 1.
[13] Michael W. Kaufman, *American Brutus* (Random House, New York, 2004), pp. 111–112.
[14] The analysis and quotations from John Wilkes Booth's "*Alow Me a Few Words*" are taken from the unedited text of the draft speech as reprinted (with editorial notes) in John Rhodehamel and Louise Taper (eds.), *Right or Wrong, God Judge Me: The Writings of John Wilkes Booth* (Univ. of Illinois Press, Urbana, 1997), pp. 55–69.
[15] See *Report of the Warren Commission: The Assassination of President Kennedy* (McGraw Hill, 1964), Exhibit 24, vol. 16, pp. 94–105.
[16] See Rhodehamel & Taper, p. 50.
[17] See Niccolò Machiavelli, edited by L. Arthur Burd, *Il Principe* (Oxford Univ. Press, Oxford, 1891), ch. XVIII, pp. 303–319; see also Revital Refael-Vivante, *Of Lions and Foxes: Power and Rule in Hebrew Medieval Fables* (Universidad de Grenada, Grenada, Spain,

2009), pp. 25–26.

[18] Stahr, pp. 223–224.

[19] Alford, p. 103, citing *Union and Advertiser,* and *Rochester Evening Express*, Jan. 26, 1861; Samples, pp. 57–58.

[20] Quoted in Samples, p. 58.

[21] Alford, p. 103, 105; Samples p. 59–60 & Chronology appendix.

[22] Abel, p. 86.

[23] McPherson, pp. 258–274; Stahr, p. 280.

[24] Stahr, p. 281; McPherson, p. 285; Alford, pp. 106 & n.76, 109; Abel, p. 90.

[25] Abel, p. 86.

[26] Abel, pp. 93–94; Samples, p. 61; Kaufman, p. 117; Alford, pp. 106–107; Townsend, p. 24.

[27] See Alford, p. 248; *New York Times*, April 18, 1858; *Morning Cleveland Herald*, April 28, 1865.

[28] McPherson, pp. 276, 297; see Helper, pp. 144, 284–286.

[29] McPherson, pp. 290–291.

[30] Stahr, pp. 283–287; Alford, pp. 112–113.

[31] Alford, pp. 108–109; Kimmel, p. 168; Rhodehamel & Taper, pp. 72, 75; Samples, p. 62 & Chronology Appendix.

Endnotes to Chapter 24: An Extraordinarily Lifelike Villain

[1] John J. Jennings, *Theatrical and Circus Life* (Sun Publishing, St. Louis 1883), pp. 484–487.

[2] Quoted in Samples, p. 82.

[3] Samples, p. 44; Alford, p. 153.

[4] Alford, p. 144.

[5] Alford, p. 109; Abel, p. 97.

[6] Alford, p. 150.

[7] Alford, pp. 155–156; *Washington Post*, July 17, 1904.

[8] Quoted in Wilson, p. 11

[9] Quoted in Alford, p. 52.
[10] Alford, pp. 156–157.
[11] Alford, p. 167.
[12] Alford, p. 150.
[13] Townsend, p. 26.
[14] Alford, p. 146.
[15] Quoted in Wilson, pp. 15–16.
[16] From *New York Herald*, April 7, 1962, quoted in Samples, p. 85; see also Samples, p. 88.
[17] Samples, pp. 54-55.
[18] *The Spirit of the Times*, April 5, 1862, quoted in Samples, pp. 83–85.
[19] Quoted in Wilson, pp. 15–16.
[20] Kimmel, p. 168; Samples, pp. 88–89.
[21] Samples, Chronology Appendix; see Alford, p. 135; *New York Herald*, April 7, 1962, quoted in Samples, p. 85. As to the $20,000 per year estimate, see Alford, p. 163, and sources quoted there.
[22] Stahr, pp. 299–300; Thomas, pp. 270–271, 274; McPherson, p. 289.
[23] Foner, p. 179; Thomas, pp. 275, 278–279.
[24] Thomas, pp. 289–291; Foner, p. 193.
[25] Thomas, pp. 279–283.
[26] Foner, p. 190.
[27] Foner, p. 102, comparing the pre-war views of Seward with those of Lincoln.
[28] Thomas, pp. 259–260.
[29] See Foner, pp. 118, 222.
[30] Foner, pp. 110, 112–115, 123.
[31] Foner, pp. 211–212.
[32] Thomas, pp. 291–293, 305, 308.
[33] Thomas, pp. 316–320.
[34] Thomas, pp. 81–84, 321–325.
[35] Thomas, pp. 325–330.

[36] Thomas, pp. 333–338.
[37] Alford, p. 134.
[38] McPherson, pp. 296–297, 519–520, 522, 858; Thomas, pp. 340–341, 347–348.
[39] Thomas, pp. 340–341; Samples, Chronology Appendix, p. 217.

Chapter 25: The Crushing of the Rebellion

[1] See Thomas, pp. 347–348, 422–423.
[2] Foner, p. 210.
[3] Foner, pp. 164–168, 174.
[4] Foner, pp. 175, 208–209.
[5] Foner, pp. 169–171, 206–207.
[6] Foner, pp. 182, 186, 187.
[7] Foner, p. 197.
[8] Foner, pp. 189–190, 200, 203–204.
[9] Foner, pp. 209–210, 215–216, 217.
[10] Foner, pp. 219–220.
[11] Foner, pp. 213, 217, 223–225.
[12] Foner, p. 230–234.
[13] Thomas, pp. 347–355; Foner, pp. 235, 238.
[14] Foner, pp. 242–244; Thomas, pp. 361–364.
[15] Thomas, pp. 365–374.
[16] Johnnie had a habit of rationalizing away bad war news. Per his brother Junius, "whenever I would mention any success of federal arms, he would say he had not heard it ... or that it was a false report and would be corrected." He contended, "for each fact in a newspaper, there are a hundred lies." Alford, p. 151.
[17] Thomas, pp. 381–390.
[18] Thomas, pp. 391–392.
[19] Thomas, p. 378.
[20] Quoted in Thomas, p. 379.
[21] Thomas, pp. 379–380, 396, 398–399.

[22] Thomas, pp. 394–395, 405, 409–412.

[23] Thomas, p. 425; Foner, p. 308.

[24] McPherson, p. 728; see generally Burke Davis, *Jeb Stuart, the Last Cavalier* (New York, Rinehart, 1957).

[25] *Nashville Daily Union*, Feb. 4, 1864, p. 2.

[26] Paul A. Whelan, in the Preface to "Unconventional Warfare in East Tennessee, 1861–65," a Graduate Thesis, March 1963, quoting a speech by President John F. Kennedy to the graduating class at West Point, June 6, 1962.

[27] R. Max Gard, *Morgan's Raid Into Ohio* (Published by Author, Lisbon, OH, 1963), pp. 2–5.

[28] Gard, pp. 6–9.

[29] Gard, preface, pp. XV, 9–14, 21; Cooling, p. 121.

[30] Benjamin Franklin Cooling, *To the Battles of Franklin, Nashville, and Beyond* (University of Tennessee Press, Knoxville, 2013), pp. 179–181, 257–260; Gard, pp. 53–59.

[31] Daniel E. Sutherland, *American Civil War Guerrillas* (Praeger, Santa Barbara, 2013), pp. 73–77, 81.

[32] Cooling, pp. 113–120.

[33] *Nashville Daily Union*, Feb. 12, 1864, p. 3.

[34] Rhodehamel & Taper, p. 101; Alford, p. 168.

[35] Rhodehamel & Taper, p. 102 & nn. 2 & 3; Samples, pp. 144–145 & Chron Appendix, p. 222.

[36] See Hamilton Cochran, *Blockade Runners of the Confederacy* (University of Alabama Press, Tuscaloosa, 1958), pp. 43–65.

[37] John S. Kendall, *Golden Age of the New Orleans Theater* (Louisiana State University Press, Baton Rouge, 1952), p. 498 (quoting reminiscent account of Ed Curtis, in whose home John Wilkes Booth boarded while in New Orleans).

[38] Curtis account, quoted in Kendall, p. 499.

Endnotes to Chapter 26: "To Strike at Wrong and Oppression"

[1] Johnnie kept this engagement even though Edwin Keach, the manager of the Boston Museum who had booked him, had passed away. Rhodehamel & Taper, pp. 98–99; Samples, Chronology Appendix, p. 222. He confirmed the Boston engagement to the theater's new manager, Richard Montgomery Field, while he was in Cincinnati on February 21, 1864. Rhodehamel & Taper, p. 101.

[2] Rhodehamel & Taper, pp. 106–107.

[3] See Abel, pp. 187–192, 223–226, 297–300; Alford, pp. 147–148.

[4] Johnnie's June 7, 1864 letter to Isabel Sumner is reprinted in Rhodehamel & Taper, pp. 110–111; see also Abel, p. 155; Alford, pp. 148–149.

[5] The June 17, 1864 letter is reprinted in Rhodehamel & Taper, pp. 113–114.

[6] William A. Tidwell, with James Hall and David Gaddy, *Come Retribution, the Confederate Secret Service and the Assassination of Abraham Lincoln* (University Press of Mississippi, Jackson, 1988), pp. 19, 262–263.

[7] Rhodehamel & Taper, p. 108.

[8] Rhodehamel & Taper, p. 66 n.12, pp. 96–97 & n.2; Miller, pp. 27–28.

[9] Miller, pp. 29–30.

[10] Alford, p. 172.

[11] Rhodehamel & Taper, pp. 113–114 & n.1; Miller, pp. 33, 48, 63; Alford, p. 172.

[12] Miller, pp. 35, 48–50.

[13] See generally Tidwell, *Come Retribution*, pp. 155–224.

[14] Nat Brandt, *The Man Who Tried to Burn New York* (Syracuse Univ. Press, Syracuse, 1986), pp. 5–7, 91.

[15] Tidwell, *Come Retribution,* p. 110.

[16] W.W. Goldsborough, *The Maryland Line in the Confederate Army, 1861–65* (Guggenheimer, Weil & Co., Baltimore, 1900), p. 203.

[17] Confession of Samuel Arnold, reprinted in Louis J. Weichmann, *A True History of the Assassination of Abraham Lincoln and the Conspiracy of 1865* (Alfred A. Knopf, New York, 1975), pp. 380–381.

[18] Quoted in Tidwell, *Come Retribution*, pp. 153–154; see also Tidwell, *Come Retribution*, pp. 250–251, 275.

[19] First Confession of Samuel B. Arnold, April 18, 1865, reprinted in Weichmann, pp. 380–381; Kauffman, p. 133 & fn. 9; Alford, p. 30.

[20] Alford, pp. 177–178; Kauffman, p. 86.

[21] E.g., Letters of Robert E. Lee, quoted in Tidwell, *Come Retribution*, pp. 145–147. On the Confederate Secret Service emphasis on the tactic of freeing large numbers of prisoners of war, see Tidwell, *Come Retribution*, pp. 146–147 (plans against Point Lookout in Maryland); 172, 178–180 (plans on freeing Confederate officers held on Johnson's Island, off Lake Erie); p. 198 (plans to instigate simultaneous risings of the Confederate prisoners of war in Johnson's Island, Camp Chase in Ohio, Camp Morton in Indianapolis, and Camp Douglas in Chicago).

[22] First Arnold Confession, in Weichmann, p. 381; Kauffman, pp. 133–134.

[23] Alford, p. 183.

[24] Miller, pp. 48–50.

[25] Miller, pp. 35–36.

[26] Tidwell, *Come Retribution*, pp. 193–195.

[27] Alford, p. 185.

[28] Edward Steers, Jr., *The Essential Civil War Curriculum: The Lincoln Assassination* (Virginia Center for Civil War Studies at Virginia Tech, July 2011), pp. 4–5.

[29] Samples, Chronology Appendix, p. 233.

Endnotes to Chapter 27: Flocking With Birds of a Feather

[1] Tidwell, *Come Retribution,* p. 333; Squires, introduction at vii; pp. 5–6.

[2] One good example we have profiled elsewhere is the Russian radical, Mikhail Bakhunin. See generally, Robert Riggs, *Sofia Perovskaya, Terrorist Princess* (Global Harmony Press, Location, Berkeley, CA 2017), pp. 38–53.

[3] See Squires, p. 110.

[4] See Squires, p. 118

[5] See Squires, p. 49.

[6] See Squires, p. 109.

[7] See Dennis K. Wilson, *Justice Under Pressure: the St. Albans Raid and Its Aftermath* (University Press of America, Lanham, Maryland, 1992), p. 43: "Sanders made a number of public pronouncements to the effect that the Raid was only the first part of a wide-ranging Confederate effort; that there were two thousand armed troops of the South in Canada; and that other raids along the frontier could be expected momentarily. These statements were widely reported in the press with predictable results. Panic swept the United States side of the frontier."

[8] Squires, pp. 12–15.

[9] Squires, pp. 20–35.

[10] Squires, p. 44, quoting Cincinnati lawyer and editor William M. Corry; see also Squires, p. 110, quoting a Northern newspaper editor who, in warning about Sanders during the Civil War, commented that Sanders "has a large head well-stocked with brains."

[11] Squires, pp. 66–67. The House remarks of John C. Breckinridge on March 3, 1852 regarding *Democratic Review* and "old fogyism" are reprinted the Appendix to Congressional Globe, 32nd Congress, 1st Session, p. 302. The remarks of Representative William A.

Richardson seven days later, which specifically condemned Sanders by name, are reprinted in the Congressional Globe (main volume), 32nd Congress, 1st Session, pp. 710–715.

[12] Squires, p. 68.

[13] Squires, pp. 77–80.

[14] Squires, pp. 83–87.

[15] Squires, pp. 93–98.

[16] Squires, pp. 104–107.

[17] Squires, pp. 108–111, 123.

[18] Foner, pp. 303–304; see Tidwell, *Come Retribution,* pp. 197–198. On Sanders as dominating the two official Confederate commissioners in St. Catharine's, see Squires, pp. 117–118. On Clay's reported statements about Sanders doing "dirty work" and associating with men with whom Clay could not, see Testimony of Richard Montgomery, summarized in Benn Pitman, *The Assassination of President Abraham Lincoln and the Trial of the Conspirators,* (P. Van Doren Stern edition, Funk & Wagnalls, New York, 1954) pp. 25–26.

[19] Wilson, pp. 6–10.

[20] See Squires, pp. 124–125.

[21] The narrative which follows is taken from Wilson, pp. 17–26.

[22] See Wilson, p. 9.

[23] General William T. Sherman did not command any forces in the Shenandoah Valley. Moreover, none of the St. Albans raiders had any known involvement with General Jubal Early's command that had operated in the northern Virginia theater during the summer of 1864.

[24] Tidwell, *Come Retribution,* p. 196; Wilson, pp. 8–9,

[25] Wilson, p. 24.

[26] Only Young was captured by pursuing vigilantes from St. Albans, led by George Conger and Erasmus Fuller. However, he quickly managed to escape and place himself in the hands of Canadian authorities.

[27] Tidwell, *Come Retribution,* pp. 201–202, 333; Wilson, pp. 32, 42–43; Squires, pp. 125–126; testimony of Henry Edson, June 10, 1865, summarized in Benn Pitman, *The Assassination of President Abraham Lincoln and the Trial of the Conspirators* (P. Van Doren Stern edition, Funk & Wagnalls, New York, 1954) p. 53. The excellent Canadian lawyers George hired were ultimately able to keep any of the raiding party from being convicted of criminal offenses, largely on jurisdictional grounds, and arguing that the attack was a military mission. They even got most of the stolen money that was confiscated upon their arrests returned to the defendants.

[28] Tidwell, *Come Retribution,* p. 333.

Endnotes to Chapter 28: The Kidnapping Plot Thickens

[1] Testimony of Robert Anson Campbell, summarized in Benn Pitman, *The Assassination of President Abraham Lincoln and the Trial of the Conspirators* (P. Van Doren Stern edition, Funk & Wagnalls, New York, 1954) pp. 46–47; see also at 63 (testimony of Daniel Eastwood, June 16, 1865); Alford, p. 188.

[2] See Samples, pp. 226–227, 234; Alford, pp. 47, 98. Kauffman, pp. 149–150, points out that this fund-raiser was Edwin's project. The event raised $3,500 for the erection of the statue by J.Q.A. Ward.

[3] Testimony of Sam Chester, summarized in Pitman, p. 44.

[4] Rhodehamel & Taper, p. 127 n.1. John Wilkes Booth's "terrorist manifesto," as quoted in the text here, is reprinted in full in Rhodehamel & Hamel, pp. 124–127.

[5] Clarke, p. 124.

[6] Clarke, p. 126

[7] On Mudd's involvement as a Confederate station agent, see William Tidwell, *April '65* (Kent State Univ. Press, Kent, Ohio & London, England, 1995), p. 74.

[8] Alford, pp. 189–190, 215; Kauffman, p. 145. On the use of physicians for Confederate secret service work, see Thomas N. Conrad, *A Confederate Spy* (Ogilvie Publishing Co., New York, 1892), p. 39. On the Catholic convent background of "Frank" Mudd, see Nettie Mudd (ed.), *The Life of Dr. Samuel A. Mudd* (Neale Publishing Co., New York & Washington, 1906), pp. 26–27. Regarding the details of Johnnie's first visit to Bryantown, see Testimony of John Thompson, summarized in Pitman, p. 178; see also Testimony of G.W. Bunker, summarized in Pitman, p. 46. All of the later accounts of Johnnie's activities in Southern Maryland need to be regarded with great caution. After the assassination, everyone involved had a motivation to minimize and falsify their involvement with his plot. They also shaded their testimony where possible to try to exculpate Samuel Mudd.

[9] Account of Frank Mudd in Nettie Mudd's *Life of Samuel Mudd*, pp. 29–30; Testimony of Thomas L. Gardiner, summarized in Pitman, p. 71; Testimony of John Thompson, summarized in Pitman, p. 178. There are discrepancies in the accounts of various people with personal knowledge as to how many visits John Wilkes Booth made to Southern Maryland in late 1864, exactly when they occurred, and on what visit, exactly, he purchased the one-eyed saddle horse. As noted above, all of these accounts are potentially unreliable. It is likely that Booth made more visits than the one mentioned here, which is taken from Frank Mudd's reminiscent account as well as Thomas Gardiner's and John Thompson's trial testimony. Thompson remembered two such visits, as did another Southern Maryland doctor, William Bowman. Testimony of William Bowman, summarized in Pitman, p. 178. See also Alford, pp. 193, 200, 231.

[10] Testimony of Samuel Chester, summarized in Pitman, p. 44.

[11] Samples, pp. 162–165; Alford, pp. 193–197; Rhodehamel & Taper, p. 119.

[12] Nat Brandt, *The Man Who Tried to Burn New York* (Syracuse

Univ. Press, Syracuse, New York, 1986), p. 14; Alford, pp. 195–197.

[13] See Brandt, pp. 66–67, 71–72.

[14] Tidwell, *Come Retribution,* pp. 335–336.

[15] Brandt, pp. 83–91.

[16] Brandt, pp. 100–101.

[17] Brandt, pp. 109–120.

[18] Alford, pp. 196–197.

[19] Alford, pp. 197–198.

[20] Tidwell, *Come Retribution,* p. 331; Weichmann, p. 46.

[21] See, in particular, the testimony of Mary Simms, Elizee Eglent, Melvina Washington, Milo Simms, Rachel Spencer, William Marshall, and Daniel J. Thomas, in Pitman, pp. 170–174.

[22] Kate Clifford Larson, *The Assassin's Accomplice, Mary Surratt and the Plot to Kill Abraham Lincoln* (Basic Books, New York, 2008), p. 25.

[23] Tidwell, *Come Retribution,* p. 339.

[24] Testimony of Weichmann, summarized in Pitman, p. 113; William C. Edwards, *The Lincoln Assassination Trial: The Court Transcripts* (accessed on line via Google Books) ("Lincoln Assassination Court Transcripts"), p. 76 (testimony of Weichmann). The property has since been renumbered as 604 H Street, NW.

[25] Weichmann, p. 78.

Endnotes to Chapter 29: Enter the Muscle Hijacker

[1] See Alford, pp. 206–207, 214.

[2] Chester claimed he was merely asked to hold open the back door of the theater. Interview with Samuel Knapp Chester, April 18, 1865, reprinted in Edwards & Steers, p. 346. However, Johnnie told his followers he "had tried to procure a man in New York to turn off the gas," but that this was unsuccessful. M. Kauffman (ed.), "Samuel B. Arnold," in *Memoirs of a Lincoln Conspirator* (Heritage Books, Bowie MD, 1995) ("Arnold Memoir"), p. 34; see also Confession of

George A. Atzerodt of July 6, 1865, reprinted in Weichmann, p. 387. Arnold explicitly asserted that Johnnie tried to induce Chester to turn off the gas lights to create darkness and confusion. Arnold Memoir, p. 46.

[3] Testimony of Samuel Knapp Chester, summarized in Pitman, pp. 44–45. Despite what Johnnie said to Chester, he in fact remained friendly with Mathews up until the time of the assassination. See Statement of John Mathews, in Edwards & Steers, pp. 845–847.

[4] Betty J. Ownsbey, *Alias Paine: Lewis Thornton Powell, the Mystery Man of the Lincoln Conspiracy* (MacFarland & Co., Jefferson, North Carolina, 1993), pp. 7, 11, 15, 21.

[5] Ownsbey, p. 16.

[6] The official Confederate military did not acknowledge any awareness that Powell had escaped. The military records continued to show that Powell was a prisoner of war when Powell was captured in April 1865.

[7] Ownsbey, pp. 25, 174.

[8] See generally, Wikipedia article, "43rd Battalion Virginia Cavalry," http://en.wikipedia.org/wiki/Mosby%27s_Raiders_(American_Civil_War).

[9] Ownsbey, pp. 26–28.

[10] Kauffman, p. 165.

[11] Ownsbey, pp. 28–30, 33, 35–36. Kauffman, to the contrary, argued Powell "followed his heart" by crossing the front to go to Baltimore to seek out the Branson sisters. Kauffman, pp. 165–166. This hypothesis cannot be endorsed. Powell never previously deserted military duties for personal reasons. Additionally, Powell already had a local romantic interest in Warrenton, an 18-year-old girl from a well-to-do family named Betty Meredith. Ownsbey, pp. 26, 141. Kauffman's hypothesis that Powell left Warrenton to go to Baltimore due to a sudden romantic impulse lacks logical appeal. As Kauffman himself summed up, Powell "was a good soldier – the kind of man who does what he is told." Kauffman, p. 161. Tidwell, *Come*

Retribution, pp. 339–340, rightly concludes that "[w]ord went out that the capture of Lincoln needed a fearless recruit," and that Powell was the man chosen.

[12] Weichmann, p. 74.

[13] Weichmann, p. 75.

[14] Ownsbey, pp. 39–40.

[15] Kauffman, p. 161; Alford, p. 211.

[16] Alford, pp. 221–222; Kauffman, p. 160. Regarding Herold's personality as "light and trifling" and a "person easily led," see Pitman, pp. 96–97 (summarizing testimony of Francis Walsh, Dr. Charles Davis, James Nokes, and William Keilitz). Regarding Herold's familiarity with John Surratt prior to the John Wilkes Booth terrorist plot, see Weichmann, p. 22.

[17] Alford, pp. 213–214; Weichmann, p. 371 (quoting account of Arnold).

[18] Abel, pp. 180–182; Rhodehamel & Taper, pp. 135–136. Regarding the Valentine's Day acrostic, Clarke, p. 121; Rhodehamel & Taper, p. 135 n.4, quoting Junius Booth diary.

[19] See, e.g., Alford, pp. 217–218; Kauffman, p. 169.

[20] W. Edwards and E. Steers (eds.), *The Lincoln Assassination: The Evidence* (University of Illinois Press, Urbana and Chicago, 2009), p. 1192; Abel, pp. 187–191.

[21] Kauffman, p. 169.

[22] Johnnie was able to get money by going to New York City, according to Arnold. Arnold Memoir, p. 46; see Rhodehamel & Taper, p. 120.

[23] Testimony of S. Chester, summarized in Pitman, p. 45.

[24] The most contemporaneous report concerning the incident at Lincoln's inauguration came from the U.S. Commissioner of Public Buildings, Benjamin French, who was in charge of physical arrangements for the ceremony. See Edward Achorn, "On the Anniversary of the Murder of Abraham Lincoln by John Wilkes

Booth," lithub.com, April 14, 2020, https://lithub.com/on-the-anniversary-of-the-murder-of-abraham-lincoln-by-john-wilkes-booth/. Eleven years afterwards, affidavits were collected from four Capitol policemen, and a Capitol doorkeeper, which were all to a similar effect. These officers when shown a photo of Johnnie had no doubt that he was the intruder who had attempted to break into the Presidential procession.

[25] Tidwell, *Come Retribution,* p. 346. A Confederate Secret Service secret cipher decoding device, as well as a message coded using the secret cipher, was found in Johnnie's trunk in his hotel room after the assassination. Pitman, pp. 41–42 (summarizing testimony of W. Terry, W. Eaton, T. Eckert, C. Dana).

[26] Quoted in Rhodehamel & Taper, p. 154.

[27] Alford, pp. 227, 244, 250; see also Alford, p. 215, quoting Weichmann, regarding Surratt saying if he succeeded in his speculation, "his country would love him forever and that his name would go down green to posterity."

[28] See Pitman, p. 161 (testimony of M. Kaighns).

[29] Ownsbey, pp. 45–49; see also, Edwards and Steers, pp. 1356–1357 (letters by W. Weigel); H. Smith, *Between the Lines: Secret Service Stories 50 Years After* (Booz Brothers, New York, 1911), p. 255. The March 1865 dates as given by Smith much later do not jive with the Weigel letter of April 18, 1865 and other contemporaneous records, and thus are suspect.

[30] Ownsbey, p. 49.

[31] Kauffman, p. 179; Weichmann, pp. 99–100.

[32] See generally Norman Gasparro, "The Architecture of Ford's Theater and Laura Keene," gratzpa.org, Jan. 23, 2012, http://civilwar.gratzpa.org/2012/01/the-architecture-of-fords-theatre-laura-keene/.

[33] Pitman, pp. 77 (testimony of J. Gifford), 78 (testimony of H. Rathbone), 82 (testimony of I. Jacquette).

[34] Though never proven, it is likely that the hands of stage carpenter

Ned Spangler (discussed below) were involved in installing the mechanism for barring the door to the President's box at Ford's Theater. Also, it is probably no coincidence that, after his arrest, Ned's carpet bag was found to conceal an 81-foot length of rope. Pitman, p. 98 (testimony of C. Rosch). When Ned Spangler was arrested after the assassination, legitimate theatrical explanations were found for this rope. But, when viewed in the context of Booth's earlier plan to kidnap Lincoln from the President's box, it is a logical inference that Spangler's possession of this long rope had something to do with Booth's intent to "lower" Lincoln onto the Ford's stage as part of his kidnapping. Perhaps there was also a plan to fasten some kind of pulley onto the box railing, a mechanism that would have made this seemingly ludicrous aspect of the kidnapping plan more physically feasible.

[35] Kauffman, p. 180.

[36] Arnold Memoir, p. 45; Speech of John H. Surratt, Rockville, Maryland, Dec. 6, 1870, reprinted in Weichmann, pp. 429–440 (hereafter, "Surratt Speech"), at p. 431; Alford, p. 238; Kauffman, pp. 180–182.

[37] Pitman, p. 235 (testimony of E. Horner, describing Arnold confession).

[38] Kauffman, pp. 180–181; Surratt Speech, at p. 432.

[39] Kauffman, p. 184; see also, Surratt Speech, at p. 432.

[40] Lincoln Assassination Transcripts, pp. 108–111 (testimony of Lloyd); Kauffman, pp. 187–188; Weichmann, p. 118.

[41] When Powell was captured after the assassination, he was found to have some Canadian coins in his pockets. It is possible that his itinerary away from Washington included a brief visit to Canada, as well as New York.

[42] Kauffman, p. 199.

Endnotes to Chapter 30: As Brave a Man as General Lee

[1] Brandt, pp. 228–231.
[2] Arnold's letter is reprinted in *Arnold Memoir*, pp. 9–10. Its wording and spelling are slightly better preserved in a reprint in Clara E. Laughlin, *The Death of Lincoln, The Story of Booth's Plot, His Deed & the Penalty* (Doubleday, New York, 1909), pp. 52–53. Arnold did, in fact, see Johnnie again after writing this letter. He and Mike O'Laughlen traveled to Washington City to visit Johnnie at the National Hotel on Friday, March 31. According to Arnold's later account, one of their purposes was to try to collect the $500 that Johnnie had borrowed from Mike. Johnnie told both of them that the project was abandoned and that they should keep the weapons they had acquired to use in it. *Arnold Memoir*, p. 29.
[3] Reprinted in Weichmann, p. 126.
[4] Weichmann, pp. 120–122, 124–125; Alford, p. 243.
[5] Weichmann, p. 127.
[6] George A. Atzerodt statement of April 25, 1865, in Edwards & Steers, p. 62.
[7] Pitman, p. 145 (testimony of J. Fletcher); see also Pitman, p. 45 (testimony of S. Chester).
[8] Alford, p. 231; Kauffman, pp. 209–210.
[9] Thomas Goodrich, *The Darkest Dawn, Lincoln, Booth and the Great American Tragedy* (Indiana Univ. Press, Bloomington & Indianapolis, Indiana, 2005), p. 10. Johnnie checked out of the National Hotel on April 1, 1865. Pitman, p. 46; Weichmann, p. 127. His whereabouts are not known with any degree of certainty until April 5, when he signed the register of a hotel in Newport, Rhode Island. It is likely that he made a secret brief trip to Canada during this four-day interlude. Alford, p. 252 & n. 45; see also Atzerodt statement of April 25, 1865, reprinted in Edwards & Steers, p. 64: "when Booth went to New York last, he said he was going to Canada." On the evening of April 3, Surratt, who had Confederate

gold and dispatches with him, told Weichmann he was headed to Montreal the next morning. Weichmann, p. 128.

[10] Surratt Speech, reprinted in Weichmann, p. 433.

[11] Kauffman, p. 201.

[12] Abel, p. 190.

[13] Quoted in Kauffman, p. 204.

[14] Testimony of Sam Chester, summarized in Pitman, p. 45.

[15] Goodrich, pp. 17–21.

[16] Testimony of Harry Ford, in Edwards & Steers, p. 518.

[17] Weichmann, pp. 133–134; Pitman, p. 85 (testimony of J. Lloyd).

[18] Alford, p. 256–257; Atzerodt statement of April 25, 1865, in Edwards & Steers, p. 52.

[19] J. Burroughs, in Pitman, p. 75; Kauffman, p. 210; Harry Ford, statement of April 20, 1865, in Edwards & Steers, p. 516. Spangler, in a statement reprinted in Nettie Mudd (ed.), *The Life of Samuel A. Mudd* (Neale Publishing Co., New York and Washington, 1906) (*"Life of Mudd"*), p. 323, said he got $260 for the buggy.

[20] Kauffman, p. 214; Goodrich, p. 28.

[21] Kauffman, p. 214.

[22] Goodrich, pp. 25–28.

[23] Timothy Good (ed.), *We Saw Lincoln Shot* (Univ. Press of Mississippi, Jackson, Mississippi, 1995), p. 3, citing a sermon by the Rev. Justin Fulton.

[24] Statement of C.D. Hess, in Edwards & Steers, p. 687.

[25] Harry Ford told investigators that Johnnie never pressed the Fords to invite Lincoln to the theater. Statement of Harry Ford, in Edwards & Steers, p. 522. At the conspiracy trial Harry Ford, who was then acting as one of the managers of Ford's Theater, testified that the President's visit could not have been known to anyone at the theater until 12 noon on Friday, April 14, the day of the assassination. Pitman, p. 100. However, the Fords had a strong motive to minimize, in their testimony, any involvement of someone associated with their

theater in providing advance word to Johnnie of the President's impending visit. John Ford and Harry Ford were suspected of complicity with Booth and consequently were arrested immediately after Lincoln's assassination. John Ford was confined in prison for most of the forty-five days that elapsed before their testimony was given May 30 and 31, 1865. Edwards & Steers, "Evidence," pp. 530–531 (letters of John T. Ford). The third brother, James Ford, testified that the President "had been previously invited to the theater that night," but claimed he did not know for sure they were coming until a messenger from the White House arrived at the theater at 10.30 a.m. Pitman, pp. 100–101.

[26] Kauffman, pp. 93–94.

[27] Kauffman, p. 127.

[28] Kauffman, p. 203.

[29] Edwards & Steers, "Evidence," p. 1111 (letter of Private George Robinson).

[30] Statements of Edmund Murphy, in Edwards & Steers, pp. 955–958; Benjamin Early, in Edwards & Steers, p. 458; John Henderson, in Edwards & Steers, p. 661. O'Laughlen never gave any credible explanation about his business in Washington City with Johnnie. When arrested, he told Baltimore Police Marshal Thomas Carmichael that he had lent Johnnie $500 and had been to Washington several times to see him about it, including Friday, April 14. Fragmentary Statement of Thomas H. Carmichael, quoted in Edwards & Steers, p. 332. The burden of the evidence indicates Johnnie made a last-minute decision to move forward with the concerted assassination plan using only the followers furnished to him directly or indirectly by the Confederate Secret Service, and without Mike's knowledge or participation.

[31] Statement of George F. Robinson, in Edwards & Steers, p. 1111.

[32] Statements of R.R. Jones and James Kipp, desk clerks at the Kirkwood Hotel, in Edwards & Steers, pp. 60–61.

[33] Statement of John Fletcher, in Edwards & Steers, p. 513;

Weichmann, pp. 135, 142; Abel, p. 187; Murphy, in Edwards & Steers, p. 957; Early, in Edwards & Steers, p. 459. The sequence of events as narrated in statements by both Murphy and Early is both very confusing and somewhat implausible, which raises an inference that both men were probably trying to serve as alibis for O'Laughlen. O'Laughlen right after his arrest admitted to Baltimore's Police Marshal that he did see Johnnie on April 14. If so, what they discussed remains a mystery. O'Laughlin does not appear to have had any further direct involvement in the day's events with respect to Johnnie's terrorist plot. Multiple witnesses besides Early and Murphy agree that O'Laughlen was in a restaurant the entire evening until the assassination occurred. E.g., Statement of George Grillet, in Edwards & Steers, pp. 617, 618; Statement of Dan Loughran, in Edwards & Steers, p. 820.

[34] Statement of Harry Ford, in Edwards & Steers, p. 518; see also Statement of John Ford, in Edwards & Steers, p. 529.

[35] Weichmann, pp. 164–165.

[36] Weichmann, pp. 166–171.

[37] Testimony of James W. Pumphrey, summarized in Pitman, p. 72; Pumphrey statement of April 15, 1865, in Edwards & Steers, p. 1065; Statement of James P. Ferguson, in Edwards & Steers, p. 485; Testimony of James P. Ferguson, summarized in Pitman, p. 76.

[38] Statement of John Mathews, July 17, 1867, quoted in Weichmann, pp. 139–140.

[39] Statement of Spangler, reprinted in *Life of Mudd*, p. 323.

[40] Statement of Spangler, April 15, 1865, in Edwards & Steers, p. 1174; Statement of Maddox, April 17, 1865, in Edwards & Steers, p. 831; Statement of John Miles, described as "colored," in Edwards & Steers, p. 898; Statement of John Morris, described as "colored," in Edwards & Steers, p. 921. Morris puts the time at 3 p.m. See also, Statement of Margaret Rozier, described as "colored," in Edwards & Steers, p. 1121. On Grillo's restaurant being opposite Ferguson's, see

Statement of Harry Ford, in Edwards & Steers, p. 517.

[41] Testimony of Joseph Plant, reported in Pitman, pp. 111–112; Testimony of Isaac Jacquette, reported in Pitman, p. 82; testimony of Judge A.B. Olin, reported in Pitman, p. 82. Harry Ford, who spent two hours preparing the President's box between 4 and 6 p.m., told investigators that he did not think he would have noticed either the hole in the door or the niche in the plaster. Statement of Harry Ford, in Edwards & Steers, p. 521. Johnnie's many and varied activities on April 14 as reported by witnesses do not include any visits to the Presidential box. Also, investigators found no trace of any dust or shavings on the floor of the box near these holes. This leads to the conclusion that the scheme to bar the door, and the associated hole in the plaster, was already created, probably by someone more of a construction professional than Johnnie, as part of the kidnapping plan. On Spangler being acquainted with Johnnie since he was a boy, see Statement of Edward Spangler, reprinted in *Life of Mudd*, pp. 322–323.

[42] Pitman, p. 70 (testimony of R. Jones); Grillo statements reported in Weichmann, p. 142 and Kauffman, p. 221; Atzerodt statement of April 25, 1865, in Edwards & Steers, p. 63. It is likely that Atzerodt's very first statement, given on April 25, was also his most accurate.

[43] See Atzerodt statement of April 25, 1865, reprinted in Edwards & Steers, pp. 62–63, 64; Confession of Atzerodt dated July 8, 1865, reprinted in Weichmann p. 385. A helpful compendium of all of Atzerodt's confessions is online at https://lincolnconspirators.com/2020/08/30/the-confessions-of-george-atzerodt/ . Atzerodt claimed he told Johnnie that he refused to have anything to do with killing Vice-President Johnson; that Herold was then assigned to do so, and that Atzerodt only agreed to assist Johnnie in the mounted getaway on the other side of the Anacostia.

[44] Good (ed.), pp. 9–10; Pitman, p. 78 (testimony of H. Rathbone); Kauffman, p. 212.

[45] Pitman, p. 100 (testimony of H. Ford).

[46] Pitman, pp. 74 (testimony of J. Burroughs); 75 (testimony of M. Turner, M. Anderson), 77–78 (testimony of J. Gifford); Edwards & Steers, "Evidence," pp. 1174–1175 (statement of E. Spangler, 15 April, 1865).

Endnotes to Chapter 31: A Tragedy in Three Acts

[1] Pitman, p. 72 (testimony of P. Taltavul).
[2] Pitman, pp. 73 (testimony of J. Buckingham), 76 (testimony of J. Ferguson); 78 (testimony of T. McGowan).
[3] Townsend, p. 7.
[4] Kauffman, pp. 46, 226–227.
[5] Kauffman, pp. 67–68, 242.
[6] Kauffman, pp. 28, 33; Goodrich, p. 118.
[7] Statement of Henry A. Rathbone, April 17, 1865, in Edwards & Steers, pp. 1080–1081; Kauffman, p. 212.
[8] The reliable eyewitness accounts provide strong evidence that Johnnie's leg was not broken in the course of his jump from the box to the stage. Good, pp. 17, 19–20.
[9] "What is the State Motto of Virginia," http://www.wisegeek.com/what-is-the-state-motto-of-virginia.htm; see also Jack D. Warren, "George Mason, the Thoughtful Revolutionary," Gunston Gazette (Gunston Hall Plantation's Membership Newsletter), vol. 6, no. 1 (2001): 6–8, http://www.gunstonhall.org/georgemason-/essays/warren_-essay.html.
[10] Pitman, pp. 74 (testimony of J. Burroughs), 75 (testimony of M. Anderson), 79–80 (testimony of J. Stewart).
[11] Pitman, p. 154 (testimony of W. Bell); Ownsbey, pp. 78–79.
[12] Kauffman, p. 23; Ownsbey, p. 79.
[13] Pitman, p. 157 (testimony of J. Barnes); see Kauffman, p. 247.
[14] Pitman, p. 155 (testimony of G. Robinson); Ownsbey, p. 82; Kauffman, pp. 23, 26.
[15] Pitman, p. 156 (testimony of A. Seward).

[16] Pitman, p. 157 (testimony of T. Verdi).

[17] Pitman, pp. 154–155 (testimony of W. Bell); Kauffman, pp. 24, 27.

[18] Rhodehamel & Taper, p. 100 n.5, citing Tidwell, *Come Retribution*, p. 261. While in Nashville, Johnnie definitely met "several times" with Johnson's private secretary, William Browning and, in Browning's mind, as a result, he knew Johnnie personally. Testimony of W. Browning, reported in Pitman, pp. 70–71. This supports an inference that Johnnie had also met Johnson.

[19] Testimony of William R. Nevins, in Pitman, pp. 144–145; Edwards & Steers, p. 312 fn. 2 (citing Nevins testimony).

[20] Testimony of W. Browning, in Pitman, pp. 70–71.

[21] See Statement of John Lee, in Edwards & Steers, p. 799. Interestingly, among the items found in the overcoat left in Kirkwood Room 126 was the passbook evidencing Johnnie's account with $455 in the Ontario Bank. See also Confession of George Atzerodt, May 1, 1865, in which Atzerodt states that Herold is the person who left his coat in Room 126, along with the pistol and knife.

[22] However, Atzerodt's accounts are not reliable, as noted in text. It is interesting that one of the very few people who had the opportunity to speak with Johnnie about his terrorist exploits after the assassination, and perhaps the only one who was never caught and placed on trial and thus had no solid motive to prevaricate, believed that Atzerodt's actual mission was to kill Secretary of War Edwin Stanton. Thomas A. Jones, *J. Wilkes Booth* (Laird & Little, Chicago, 1898), p. 46.

[23] Statement of John Fletcher, in Edwards & Steers, pp. 512–513. On Herold staying outside Seward's house long enough to know Powell was successful, see Alford, p. 274. This is virtually a required inference from Johnnie's subsequent awareness that Seward had been assassinated.

[24] Kauffman, p. 229.

[25] Pitman, p. 84 (testimony of S. Cobb); Statement of S. Cobb in

Edwards & Steers, pp. 363–364; Kauffman, p. 228. The time of moon rise is calculated courtesy of a widget maintained by the U.S. Naval Observatory, http://aa.usno.navy. mil/data/ docs/RS_One-Day.php. See also, Edwards & Steers, p. 365 n.1.

[26] Pitman, pp. 84–85 (testimony of S. Cobb).
[27] Pitman, pp. 83–84 (testimony of J. Fletcher).
[28] Pitman, p. 85 (testimony of P. Gardiner); see also statement of P. Gardiner in Edwards & Steers, pp. 585–586.
[29] Statement of John Lloyd, in Edwards & Steers, p. 808; see also Pitman, p. 86 (testimony of John Lloyd).
[30] Statement of Thomas Davis of April 29, 1865 in Edwards & Steers, pp. 419–421. However, in a statement on April 28, 1865, Frank Washington, an African American servant of Samuel Mudd who actually curried both horses, stated that they were not splattered with mud, and that he did not see on them any evidence of a fall. Statement of F. Washington in Edwards & Steers, p. 1314. As often happens, the evidence on this point is contradictory and there is nothing to definitively reconcile it. However, it is difficult to fathom why Herold and Mudd would have elected to take a lame horse on a 6-mile round trip to Bryantown on the afternoon of April 15.
[31] Johnnie's leg fracture was not carefully examined or described. There is a contradiction between the report of the "treating physician" Dr. Mudd, who described it as a tibia fracture 2 inches above the ankle, and the autopsy report, which described it as a fibula fracture 3 inches above the ankle. Two authors who have examined the evidence in depth arrived at the conclusion that Johnnie did not break his leg jumping to the stage. Michael Kauffman, in *American Brutus*, focused on this issue at pp. 272–274 & nn. 9–11; Timothy Good evaluated the issue in *We Saw Lincoln Shot* at pp. 18–20. Both deemed decisive the fact that none of the eyewitnesses who discussed Johnnie's fall to the stage and exit immediately after the assassination mentioned any cry of pain, limp, or other sign of distress. It is

noteworthy that David Herold, in a statement otherwise filled with fibs he gave following his arrest on April 27, 1865, did say Johnnie told him his horse "had fallen or he was thrown off," causing the leg injury. Statement of Herold, in Edwards & Steers, p. 671. Detectives investigating in Southern Maryland in the chaotic aftermath of the assassination immediately realized the importance of the fact that Johnnie and Herold had changed horses. They theorized that Pumphrey's frisky bay mare had fallen or thrown Johnnie off, breaking his leg. Statement of William P. Wood, in Edwards & Steers, p. 1372. The author has consulted with a horse-riding expert, Lanora Voegtly, who advised that keeping the rider's leg in its boot after an injury suffered in a fall would be the normal and advisable method of keeping the broken limb as stable as possible until better medical attention could be provided.

[32] See Kauffman, p. 233. Like most witnesses who were suspected of complicity in Johnnie's terrorist plot, Lloyd, after finally being forced to talk, ultimately gave several exculpatory versions of the night's events. The facts cited here are taken from his early version of April 22, 1865, which appears in Edwards & Steers, pp. 807–808; see also p. 814 where Lloyd admitted in a subsequent interview that he covered up the existence of Johnnie's visit when first questioned by guards who came by looking for the murderers. Lloyd's trial testimony of May 13, 1865 about the nighttime visit is summarized in Pitman, p. 86.

[33] Goodrich, pp. 152–153.

[34] Goodrich, pp. 132–133.

[35] Goodrich, p. 138; see also Kauffman, p. 236 & n.14.

[36] Goodrich, pp. 137, 144.

Endnotes to Chapter 32: An Underground Railroad in Reverse

[1] See, e.g., Kauffman in *American Brutus*, pp. 231, 243–244; Alford in *Fortune's Fool*, pp. 277–278; Laughlen in *The Death of Lincoln*,

pp. 123–126. Even though Samuel Mudd was removed from imprisonment and other legal disabilities arising from his role in helping Johnnie by virtue of a presidential pardon in 1869, he and Frank were not about to publish any "tell all." They continued with efforts to try to "clear his name" for the remainder of their lives, largely denying Mudd's role in Johnnie's conspiracy. Their daughter in 1906 published a biography, *Life of Mudd*, for the same purpose.

[2] The initial statements of Samuel Mudd about his visit from Johnnie and Herold on April 15, 1865 were given to investigating detectives six days later, on April 21, 1865. They are reported in Pitman, p. 168, and in Edwards & Steers. Interestingly, Mudd's very first statement implicitly conceded that Johnnie did not regard him as a "regular physician" (in Johnnie's own words) for purposes of treating the broken leg. Mudd actually gave two statements that day, first a so-called "voluntary statement" that he wrote out himself, which appears in Edwards & Steers, pp. 942–946, and then a second statement that resulted from an interrogation, which is reprinted several times in Edwards & Steers, including at pp. 939–942. Other witnesses corroborated parts of these statements. Thomas Davis, a white servant employed by the Mudds, in Edwards & Steers, p. 419 et seq., put the time of arrival of Johnnie and Herold as "between 4 and 5 o'clock." Frank Washington, an African American servant, in a statement at Edwards & Steers p. 1313 et seq., stated they arrived at "just about daylight" (sunrise was at 5.35 a.m.). In a statement published in the 1906 work *Life of Mudd*, at p. 30, Frank Mudd, like her husband Samuel, said they arrived at 4 a.m. John Best, the English gardener, made Johnnie a wooden crutch, per a footnote in Edwards & Steers, p. 240, and specifically alluded to in a contemporaneous letter on that page.

[3] Statement of Frank Washington, in Edwards & Steers, p. 1314; Statement of Thomas Davis, in Edwards & Steers, pp. 419, 420–421.

[4] Statement of Thomas Davis, in Edwards & Steers, p. 419;

Statement of Frank Washington, in Edwards & Steers, p. 1314; Kauffman, p. 243; see also Report of H.H. Wells, in Edwards & Steers, p. 1338.

[5] Testimony of Becky Briscoe in Pitman, p. 177; "Voluntary" statement of Dr. Mudd, reported in Edwards & Steers, p. 945; Testimony of Frank Bloyce in Pitman, p. 176; Statement of Electus Thomas, in Edwards & Steers, p. 1268; Statement of Frank Mudd in *Life of Mudd*, p. 31; John Hardy testimony in Pitman, p. 218; Francis Farrell testimony, in Pitman, p. 218; Statement of Dr. Mudd, April 21, 1865, reported in Edwards & Steers, p. 941.

[6] Jones, p. 56.

[7] Statement of Eluctus Thomas, in Edwards & Steers, p. 1268; Statement of Ausy Swan, in Edwards & Steers, p. 1251; see also Jones, p. 62; Tidwell, *Come Retribution*, p. 446.

[8] See Tidwell, *Come Retribution*, p. 446.

[9] Statement of Ausy Swan, in Edwards & Steers, pp. 1251–1252; Statement of May Swann, in Edwards & Steers, p. 1252; see also Tidwell, *Come Retribution*, pp. 447–449. Jones, at p. 68, quotes Cox himself as saying Johnnie and Herold arrived at about 4 a.m.

[10] Statement of Ausy Swan, in Edwards & Steers, p. 1251; Jones, pp. 68–72; see also Tidwell, *Come Retribution*, pp. 446–448.

[11] Jones, pp. 8, 11, 20, 22–24, 28, 29, 31. Dr. Stoughton Dent, whom Jones mentions in his account, may have networked with Dr. Samuel Mudd. Jones says "Dr. Dent" regularly took Confederate mail from Port Tobacco to Bryantown, which is essentially Dr. Samuel Mudd's town of residence. See also, Tidwell, *Come Retribution*, p. 98.

[12] Account of Thomas Jones in Thomas A. Jones, *J. Wilkes Booth* (Laird & Little, Chicago, 1898) ("Jones account"), pp. 66–68.

[13] Jones account, pp. 71–72.

[14] Jones account, pp. 73–79.

[15] Jones account, pp. 80–82.

[16] Jones account, pp. 80, 81, 96–97.

[17] Jones account, pp. 88–93.

[18] Kauffman, pp. 265–266.
[19] Ownsbey, pp. 86–90; Kauffman, pp. 268–269.
[20] Pitman, pp. 121–123 (testimony of H. Smith, R. Morgan), p. 157 (testimony of A. Seward); Kauffman, p. 267.
[21] Kauffman, pp. 31–32.
[22] Pitman, p. 146 (testimony of J. Greenawalt); p. 147 (testimony of J. Walker).
[23] Kauffman, p. 283–284.
[24] Jones account, pp. 95–96; see Statement of Henry Woodland, April 30, 1865, in Edwards & Steers, pp. 1377–1378.
[25] Jones account, pp. 98–101. Reports were circulating that on Thursday, April 20, Johnnie had attempted unsuccessfully to cross the Potomac from Point Lookout, at the southeasternmost tip of St. Mary's County. See *New York Herald,* p. 1, April 28, 1865.
[26] Jones account, pp. 101–106.
[27] Jones account, pp. 106–110.
[28] Jones, p. 111; Alford, pp. 287–288.
[29] William Hanchett, *Booth's Diary,* Journal of the Illinois State Historical Society, 1979, p. 48.

Endnotes to Chapter 33: "O Let Me Die Bravely"

[1] Alford, p. 288; Statement of Elizabeth Quesenberry in Edwards & Steers, pp. 1074–1075; see also p. 1074 fn. 1, added by Edwards & Steers. As in the case of Samuel Mudd, Confederate agents such as Quesenberry had every reason to conceal their knowledge of Johnnie as well as the help they gave him. Their statements to investigators are highly suspect and cannot be trusted as to any aspect that cannot be independently corroborated. Other knowledgeable sources include Jones, p. 111.
[2] Alford, pp. 289–290.
[3] Reminiscent account of Thomas Harbin, quoted in Alford, p. 290.
[4] Statement of Richard H. Stuart, also called Stewart, of May 6, 1865,

reprinted in Edwards & Steers, pp. 1201–1202; see also, Statement of David Herold, reprinted in Edwards & Steers, pp. 674–675; Alford, pp. 290–293; Tidwell, *April '65*, pp. 189–190; Kauffman, pp. 298, 299–300.

[5] Statement of William Lucas, May 6, 1865, in Edwards & Steers, pp. 824–825; *New York Herald*, May 4, 1865, p. 1; see also Statement of D. Herold, in Edwards & Steers, p. 675.

[6] Quoted in Alford, p. 293; see also Edwards & Steers, p. 1202 fn. 2. Johnnie actually wrote out two versions of this note; a first draft, which he kept with him, and a slight revision, which he actually sent to Stuart. See Alford, p. 293 fn. 76; Rhodehamel & Taper, pp. 157–158 & fn. 1. The quotation is a line of Lady Macbeth from the banquet scene of Shakespeare's tragedy *Macbeth*, Act III, Scene 4.

[7] See Tidwell, *April '65*, pp. 184–185, 186, 190.

[8] Tidwell, *April '65*, p. 190; see Tidwell, *Come Retribution*, p. 19.

[9] Dual Statements of William Rollins, May 6, 1865, in Edwards & Steers, pp. 1112–1114 & fn. 1; Statement of Willie Jett, May 6, 1865, in Edwards & Steers, pp. 745–749.

[10] Statement of Willie Jett, in Edwards & Steers, pp. 747–748; Testimony of Willie Jett, May 17, 1865, summarized in Pitman, pp. 90–91; Alford, pp. 296–298; see also *New York Herald*, May 4, 1865, p. 1.

[11] Statement of Willie Jett, in Edwards & Steers, p. 748; Alford, pp. 295, 299; *New York Herald*, May 4, 1865, p. 1; see also Kauffman, p. 310; Edwards & Steers, p. 1113 fn. 3.

[12] Letter to Hon. W. McKee Dunn from R.B. Garrett, Jan. 13, 1880, in Edwards & Steers, pp. 587–588 & fn. 2; Alford, pp. 299–301; *New York Herald*, May 4, 1865, p. 1.

[13] *New York Herald*, April 28, 1865, p. 1; Edwards & Steers, p. 587 & fn. 2; Statement of William Rollins, in Edwards & Steers, p. 1112 & fn. 2.

[14] *New York Herald*, May 4, 1865; Alford, pp. 304–306.

[15] Testimony of Everton J. Conger, May 17, 1865, summarized in

Pitman, p. 91; Statement of Willie Jett, p. 749; Kauffman, pp. 313–314; Alford, p. 306.

[16] Townsend, pp. 30–37; Testimony of Conger, in Pitman, pp. 91–93; Testimony of Boston Corbett, May 17, 1865, summarized in Pitman, pp. 94–95.

[17] Testimony of Corbett, in Pitman, pp. 94–95.

[18] Townsend, p. 35; Testimony of Corbett, in Pitman, p. 94; Testimony of Edward Doherty, May 22, 1865, in Pitman, p. 95.

[19] Testimony of Conger, p. 93; Testimony of Corbett, in Conger, p. 94.

[20] Townsend, pp. 30–37; "John Wilkes Booth's Last Days," an account by R.B. Garrett, published in the *Milwaukee Sentinel*, July 30, 1896; Wilson, p. 214; Testimony of Conger, in Pitman, p. 93; Corbett account in *New York Herald*, April 28, 1865, p. 1.

[21] Townsend, p. 37; Wilson, p. 216; R.B. Garrett account.

[22] Townsend, p. 37.

Endnotes to Epilogue

[1] See https:// www.archives.gov/ historical-docs/ 13th-amendment#:~ :text = Passed%20by%20 Congress%20on%20January, within %20the%20United%20States%2C%20or (accessed June 4, 2022).

[2] See Kauffman, p. 354.

[3] Account of the execution published in the *New York Tribune*, July 8, 1865, available on line at http://law2.umkc.edu/faculty/projects/ftrials/lincolnconspiracy/herald78.html.

[4] See, e.g., Rossbach, pp. 218–235, 238–260.

[5] Rossbach, p. 260. On the political motivations of the failure to pursue John Brown's financial supporters, see also, Blight, p. 315.

[6] Sentence of Lewis Payne, in Pitman, p. 248.

[7] See Weichmann, p. 376.

[8] Hamilton Gay Howard, *Civil-War Echoes, Character Sketches and State Secrets* (Howard Publishing Company, Washington, D.C.,

1907), pp. 78–85; see also Kauffman, pp. 214–215; Tidwell, *Come Retribution*, p. 261 & n. 29; Rhodehamel & Taper, p. 100 n.5.
[9] See Armistead C. Gordon, *Jefferson Davis* (Scribner & Sons, New York, 1918), pp. 238–291; Donald E. Collins, *The Death and Resurrection of Jefferson Davis* (Rowman & Littlefield, Lanham, Maryland, 2005), p. 49.
[10] Pierce Butler, *Judah P. Benjamin* (George W. Jacobs, Philadelphia, 1907), pp. 347–348, 363–415.
[11] Squires, pp. 134–137; Tidwell, *April '65*, pp. 151–154.
[12] Squires, pp. 143–144.
[13] Trevelyan, p. 393.
[14] Villard, p. 685.
[15] Villard, p. 685.
[16] Stahr, pp. 436–438, 450.
[17] Stahr, pp. 452, 461, 475.
[18] Stahr, pp. 482–491, 517, 543.
[19] Weichmann, pp. 330–349.
[20] Weichmann, pp. 376–379.
[21] *Life of Mudd*, p. 221; *The New York Times*, April 22, 1916, p. 11.
[22] Gene Smith, *"The Haunted Major," American Heritage Magazine*, vol. 45, issue 1, February / March 1994; see also James L. Swanson, *Manhunt* (Harper Collins, New York, 2009), p. 372; Frederick Hatch, *Protecting President Lincoln: The Security Effort, Thwarted Plots, and the Disaster at Ford's Theater* (McFarland & Co., North Carolina, 2011), p. 161.
[23] "Abraham Lincoln's Assassination: Boston Corbett," https://rogerjnorton.com/Lincoln32.html (accessed May 3, 2022).
[24] *Life of Mudd*, pp. 257–295.
[25] *Life of Mudd*, pp. 318–320, 321–322, 326.
[26] Wilbur F. Coyle, *The Mayors of Baltimore* (reprinted from *The Baltimore Municipal Journal*, 1919), pp. 139–1151, Archives of Maryland, Biographical Series, https:// msa.maryland.gov/ megafile/ msa/ speccol/ sc3500/ sc3520/012400/ 012478/ html/12478bio.html.

[27] Tidwell, *April '65*, p. 126; see generally, James D. Horan, *Confederate Agent: A Discovery in History* (Crown Publishers, New York, 1954); Gary G. Matthews, *Basil Wilson Duke, CSA: the Right Man in the Right Place* (University Press of Kentucky, Lexington, 2005).

[28] Kansas State Historical Society, "Hamilton Charles," https://www.kshs.org/kansapedia/charles-hamilton/19728 (accessed Dec. 27, 2020).

[29] Strane, pp. 134–149.

[30] Strane, pp. 175–178.

[31] Strane, pp. 203-05, 213–221.

[32] Blight, pp. 305–309.

[33] Douglass, *Life and Times*, pp. 376–377, 385.

[34] Douglass, *Life and Times*, pp. 403–415.

[35] Douglass, *Life and Times*, pp. 437–438, 455, 462.

[36] Strane, p. 205; see also Douglass, *Life and Times*, p. 477.

[37] Larson, pp. 272–288.

[38] *New York Times*, Jan. 25, 2021, https://www.nytimes.com/2021/01/25/us/politics/tubman-20-dollar-bill.html.

Index

Abbott, James 192, 195-196, 204
Adair, Samuel 250
Adams, Annie Brown ... 218
Adams, Charles Francis 223
Adams, John 228
Adams, John Quincy 223
Aesop's Fables (book) .. 398
Alton, IL   63, 67-70, 72-80, 83, 86, 402-05
American Colonization Society 52, 59
Anderson, Jeremiah 331
Anderson, Jerry 335
Anderson, Osborne 353, 605
Anthony, Aaron 94, 98
Arnold, Sam. 483, 520, 526, 528, 534, 536-37, 609
Assassins 20, 233-34
Assing, Ottilie 278, 383
Atchison, David .. 185, 191, 210, 254
Atzerodt, George.. 526, 534, 536, 540, 545, 547-48, 552-53, 562-63, 575-76, 580-82, 587, 599, 601
Auld, Hugh 98, 100, 106-07
Auld, Lucretia 97-98
Auld, Rowena 100
Auld, Sophie 97-98, 100
Auld, Thomas 100, 103, 105-06, 121
Auld, Tommy 97, 106
Avis, John 380, 387

Baca, Ramon 272
Baden, Joseph 587
Bailey, Betsy 92
Bailey, Isaac 92
Bainbridge, Absolom.. 592, 593
Baker, Lafayette 592
Baker, Luther ... 592, 594-95
Barber, Thomas 199, 311
Barron, John 385
Battle of Black Jack 245, 257, 277, 314, 332, 368
Beecher, Edward. 73, 76-77, 381
Beecher, Henry Ward ... 381
Beecher, Lyman 76
Bell, John 408-09
Bell, William 558, 561, 580
Benjamin, Judah ... 541, 603
Best, John 572
Bible (book)   1, 35-36, 38, 61, 73, 101, 371, 398
Biden, Joe 614
Bishop, Lyman 82
Black Law (state of Connecticut) 56-57
Blair, Charles 259
Blake, George .. 269, 270-74
Blakeslee, Levi 37
Blazer, Richard 523
Bocking, R.C. 503
Bolivar, Simon 466
Bonaparte, Louis 393
Bonaparte, Napoleon . 393,

INDEX

428
Book of Martyrs (book) 147, 180, 379, 387
Booth, Adelaide 166, 172-74
Booth, Asia.. 176, 179, 509, 529
Booth, Edwin ..174-75, 432, 441, 506, 515, 529, 536
Booth, John Wilkes
   1864 visit to Canada.. 505
   1865 visit to Canada.. 541
   Admiration for Felice Orsini 428
   Admiration for John Brown 419, 509
   As a Know-Nothing supporter................ 180
   Asceticism.................. 176
   Assembly of terrorist cell 482-83, 517, 532
   Assisted by Confederate agents during flight after assassination. 577, 582, 587
   Attempts to negotiate with federal posse.....595-96
   Attends Great Union rally in Philadelphia........... 416
   Attitude of resistance to authority 176, 470
   Born into wealthy family 165
   Capacity for self-discipline 385
   Changes plan from kidnapping to assassination 540, 542-43
   Charisma .. 435, 437, 438, 471, 473
   Condemns advocacy of abolition as treason 417, 419, 423, 528
   Criticized for unstudied performances. 439, 440
   Date of birth 168
   Death 598
   Decision to become a terrorist .. 472, 475-76, 484-85, 528
   Disconnect with reality.... 460, 471, 487, 586
   Doubts about story that broken leg occurred at Ford's Theater 566
   Early embarrassments on stage...................... 384
   Empathy for animals and children 179, 436-37, 478
   Erysipelas........... 476, 484
   Estimated income....... 441
   Exceptionally creative and emotive interpretations 411, 425, 439
   Exit from Ford's Theater 557
   Expresses strong feelings of patriotism....... 180, 542
   Final manifesto 584
   Flirtation with Isabel Sumner 473-75

Good qualities .. 385-86, 434, 478
High IQ 168
Horsemanship 169
Influenced by literary works 585-86
Investment in Pennsylvania oil properties 477-78, 485
Invocation of divine approval 507, 585
Lacks faith in his powers of persuasion 418, 423
Last words 597-598
Leap to stage after shooting Lincoln 557
Leaves acting job to volunteer for militia after JB Harpers Ferry raid .. 384
Obsessed with press coverage 578
Opposition to prevailing political sentiments 413, 427, 542
Passionate love for idea of the Union 413, 420, 423
Performs with brothers to raise funds for Central Park Shakespeare statue 512, 515
Plans to abduct President Lincoln. 482, 484, 517, 534, 610
Poor student 164, 168, 176
Portrayal of Shakespeare's Richard III 433, 450, 464
Possible attempt to assassinate Lincoln at second term inauguration 530
Preparatory visits to Southern Maryland 511
Presence in occupied Confederate territory ... 469-70, 473
Purported romance and engagement with Lucy Hale 527-28
Quarrels with brother Edwin over Confederate sympathy 484, 516
Rave reviews for portrayal of villains 411, 424-25, 434, 439
Receives funding from Confederate government 486, 512, 521, 541
Receives logistical support from Confederate government 486, 510, 521
Recitations of Shakespeare 387, 487
Relationships with comfort women... 412, 473, 528
Rents horse to use the night of assassination 550-52, 565
Shakespearian roles 410-11, 439, 506, 512
Suicidal ideation 420, 474,

INDEX

508, 521, 541, 586
Talks of plan to escape to Mexico 592
Talks way past guard at Navy Yard Bridge 564, 566
Terrorist manifesto . 506, 509, 551
Thoughtful and sensitive . 178-79, 436
Use of code words and false names... 512, 534, 539, 564, 580-81, 590-91
Voice problems .. 440, 470
Writes card to Vice-President Johnson . 562

Booth, John Wilkes -- Victims
Johnson, Andrew .. 562-63
Lincoln, Abraham 556
Lincoln, Mary Todd... 556
Rathbone, Henry 556, 608
Robinson, George 560
Seward, Augustus 560, 580
Seward, Fanny 559-60, 605
Seward, Frederick 559, 605
Seward, William Henry 558, 560

Booth, Junius Brutus 165-67, 169, 170-71, 174-75
Booth, Junius Brutus Jr. 168, 174-75, 485, 506, 569
Booth, Mary Ann .. 167-68, 170, 172-73, 428, 536, 541
Booth, Richard (JWB's grandfather) 165-66, 168, 180
Booth, Richard (JWB's half-brother) 172
Booth, Rosalie 485
Bossieux, Louis 386
Boucher, Charles 606
Bragg, Braxton 450
Branson, Jacob 196-97
Branson, Joseph 523
Branson, Maggie 522-23, 531
Branson, Mary 524
Breckinridge, John 408, 409, 495, 610
Brocchus, Perry 274
Brocket, Walter 245, 314, 317
Brodess, Edward 295
Brodess, Eliza 296-97
Brooks, Preston 238, 239-40, 257
Brooks, Whitfield 238-39
Brooks, Whitfield Jr. 239
Brown, Anne 336
Brown, Dianthe 37-38, 44
Brown, Frederick . 197, 211, 250, 259
Brown, G.W. 198, 209
Brown, Jason .. 41, 188, 210, 212, 217, 243, 251, 339
Brown, John 393
Activities in Kansas 197-98, 201, 206, 210, 267, 319-20
Ascetic lifestyle 125
Attempts to recruit Harriet Tubman into plot 302-04, 306, 333, 334

719

Attitude of resistance to authority 35
Becomes a terrorist . 211, 256, 313
Capacity for moral turpitude 116
Confessions of guilt to patrons 115, 130
Convinced of his righteousness 324, 330-31
Creation of fictitious organization .. 146, 319
Date of birth 30
Dedication of life to destruction of slavery 87, 113
Disdain for organizational work 188, 204
Emergence of terrorist thinking 145
Emotional shock of losing mother 32
Empathy with animals . 32, 42, 118
Execution 387-89
Expertise on the Bible 36, 44, 125, 146, 257
Final manifesto 388
Fund raising from wealthy sympathizers 280, 284-85, 319-20, 331, 333
Hatred toward slave owners 305
High IQ 32, 35, 131
Interview session after capture 370
Invocation of divine approval 217, 219, 246, 251, 283, 369, 370
Leather tanning 34
Living underground 243-44, 247
North Elba, NY settlement project 186-89, 259
Obsession with crime and punishment 41, 116
Partnership with Simon Perkins 118-19, 121, 128
Partnership with Wadsworth & Wells 114-15
Partnership with Zenas Kent 110-11
Perceived by Lincoln as terrorist .. 397, 453, 457
Pioneer skills 190, 310
Plans attack on Harpers Ferry 265, 277, 280, 282
Poor sense of reality . 113, 120, 127, 303
Poor student . 34, 168, 194
Pottawatomie Creek massacre .. 212-15, 218, 243, 246-47
Raid into Missouri 321, 323
Rejection of political solution 332
Strange inaction after success of terrorist attack 360

INDEX

Suicidal ideation 332, 334, 379
Telling lies 32
Trial and conviction ... 378
Urge to adopt cause of another 120
Urge to die as a martyr 251, 284, 368, 370, 379, 380-81, 384
Use of code words 337, 346
Use of false names 319, 333, 335
Use of pikes for use as weapons 336
Westlands farm .. 112-13, 115, 117
Willingness to sacrifice family for the cause 305

Brown, John -- Victims
Allstadt, John 355, 362
Ball, Armistead 361
Brewer, Joseph 364
Brown, John E. 249
Byrne, Terence ... 359, 362
Cruise, David 323, 327
Cruise, Lucinda 323
Daingerfield, John ... 357, 362-63
Doyle, Drury 214
Doyle, James 213
Doyle, John 213-14
Doyle, Mahala 213, 381
Doyle, William 213
Harris, James 216

Hicklin, Harvey 321-22
Kitzmiller, Archibald. 363
Larue, John 322
Sherman, Henry 216
Sherman, William 216
Washington, Lewis 349-52, 354-55, 357, 361, 363, 367-68, 387
Wilkinson, Allen ... 214-15
Wilkinson, Louisa 214

Brown, John Jr. 41, 118, 188, 192, 194, 197, 202, 204, 207, 210, 212, 217, 243, 252, 258, 278, 281, 334, 339
Brown, Martha 336
Brown, Mary ... 44, 188, 190
Brown, Oliver .211, 335-36, 367, 369
Brown, Owen 30, 44-45, 59, 86, 114, 188
Brown, Owen (JB's son)197, 211, 265, 369, 605
Brown, R.P. 203
Brown, Ruth Mills 32
Brown, Salmon 198, 211, 339
Brown, Watson 335, 367, 369
Brown's Station . 190, 193, 197, 198, 201, 203-05, 212-13, 243
Browning, William 562
Bryant, Joseph 278
Bryant, William 588
Buchanan, James .. 383, 391, 394, 407-408, 413-15, 421, 424, 493-94

Buckhorn.................... 12
Buckingham, John 555
Buell, Don Carlos . 443, 450
Buford, Jefferson 309
Buley, Noah .. 150, 152, 161
Burns, Anthony..... 228, 257
Burnside, Ambrose .. 458, 460, 462
Burr, Aaron................... 489
Burrough, John "Peanuts" 554, 557
Burtles, William............ 574
Bush, Sally.................... 398
Butler, Andrew 227, 229-31, 232, 238-39
Butler, Behethland 227, 238
Butler, Benjamin........... 454
Butler, Pierce Mason 239
Butler, William 227
Calhoun, John 227
Camp Brown 244, 246, 250, 277
Campbell, James 388
Canning, Matthew... 410-11, 424, 427
Canterbury, CT 54, 55, 56, 57, 58
Carson, Kit............ 272, 275
Cass, Lewis...... 223, 493-94
Catechism of a Revolutionary (book)...................... 267
Cato, Sterling........... 206-07
Chamberlain, Amos 117
Chandler, Bill................ 527
Channing, William........ 222
Charley (horse) .. 547, 563, 565, 567, 577
Chase, Salmon 225, 256, 446, 459, 463

Chester, Sam... 506, 520-21, 529, 541, 545
Christiana, PA. 152-56, 159, 162-64, 226
Clark, Virginia.............. 592
Clarke, George.............. 311
Clarke, John Sleeper..... 529
Clarkson, Isaiah 159, 162
Clay, Clement....... 496, 513
Clay, Henry.. 135-36, 138, 465
Cline, James.................. 250
Cobb, Jeremiah 17
Cobb, Silas............... 564-65
Coffin, William............. 109
Coleman, Frank 195
Collins, Thomas............ 499
Columbian Orator (book) 99
Compromise of 1850 225
Confederate Secret Service 476, 479-82, 484, 486-87, 510, 517, 521, 523-25, 530, 541, 574, 575
Conger, Everton....... 593-96
Conrad, Thomas.... 591, 604
Cook, John . 276, 319, 346, 350, 357
Cooper Union address.. 390, 406, 408
Cooper, John.... 271-72, 275
Copeland, John 345, 388
Copperheads 479, 542, 569, 610
Coppoc, Barclay 346
Corbett, Boston............. 609
Covey, Edward 101-05
Cox, Samuel.. 574, 577-78, 588
Cox, Samuel Jr.............. 576

INDEX

Coxe, Robert 486
Crandall, Prudence ... 54-59, 291, 611-12
Crawford, George 323
Creitz, William 328
Crittenden, John 236
Cross Keys 14
Crutchfeld, George 434
Cuyler, Theodore 417
Daniels, Jim 321-22
Daniels, Narcissa 322
Davis, Henry Winter 180
Davis, Jefferson ... 203, 246, 275, 407, 426-27, 466, 479, 482, 541, 603, 611
Democratic Review (newspaper) . 492-93, 495
Doherty, Edward 593
Donaldson, Israel 210
Douglas, Stephen . 183, 227, 232, 399-410, 413, 492, 494-95
Douglass, Anna 107
Douglass, Frederick.. 91-93, 98-99, 101, 104-09, 121, 124, 149, 153, 163, 189, 257, 278, 281, 283, 293, 299, 302, 339, 383, 403, 612-13
Douglass, Lewis 613
Dow, Charles 195
Draft riots of 1863 . 461, 479
Dramatic Oil Company 477-78, 485
Dresser, Amos 37, 61-65, 324
Drew, Louisa 440
Dubreuil, Paul 524, 525
Dutch Henry .. *See* Sherman, Henry
Dutch Henry's Crossing 206, 213, 215
Dyer, Sarah Frances ...... *See* Mudd, Sarah
Early, Benjamin 546
Edgefield, SC ... 227, 238-39
Edmundson, Henry 240
Edwards, Ninian 401
Ellsler, John 477
Emancipation of slaves in the United States 455-56
Emancipation of slaves in United States 455
Emancipation Proclamation 457-59, 461
Evans, Kathryn 435
Everett, Edward 408
Ferguson, James 434
Ferguson, Jim 550
Fillmore, Millard ... 136, 145
Fish, Hamilton 137
Fitzsimmons, Thomas .. 271, 273
Fletcher, John ... 547, 563-64
Floyd, John 15, 342-43
Flynn, Tom 170
Forbes, Hugh 260-67, 276-77, 279-80, 306-08, 394, 604
Forbes, Hugh Jr. 262
Forbes, John 332
Ford, Harry 543, 547
Ford, John 544
Ford, Nelson. 150, 152, 155, 157
Ford's Theater 434, 527, 529, 532-35, 539-40, 543-44, 547, 550-54, 558, 561, 584,

607-08
Foreman, James 34, 38-41, 43-44
Forrest, Edwin............... 440
Fort Sumter 424, 426-27, 429, 453
Fox, Joseph........... 272, 275
Franklin, OH... 110-14, 133, 204, 485, 497
Franklin, PA.............. 477-78
Frederick the Great....... 353
Free Soil Party.. 223-25, 227, 333
Free State Hotel....... 209-11
Freeland, William......... 105
Frémont, John 442, 447, 455
Fugitive Slave Law 145, 151-52, 164, 192, 224-26, 228-32, 414
Gandhi, Mohandas........ 305
Gardiner, George.......... 511
Gardiner, Polk............... 565
Garibaldi, Anita....... 262-63
Garibaldi, Giuseppe 262-63, 394, 604, 607
Garnet, Henry Highland 121-22
Garrett, Jack.................. 595
Garrett, Richard 591, 593-94
Garrett, Thomas............ 299
Garrison, William Lloyd 50-53, 59, 88-91, 109, 122, 141, 153, 171, 222, 257, 403
Geary, John... 252-53, 255, 276, 310
Gettysburg (battle).. 461, 467, 522
Giddings, Joshua........... 402

Gifford, James.............. 551
Gill, George.......... 321, 338
Gilman, Winthrop...... 81-85
Godwin, William......... 167
Gomez, Antonio............ 396
Gorsuch, Dickinson 152, 159-62, 164
Gorsuch, Edward.. 149-53, 156, 158-63
Gorsuch, Joshua... 152, 158, 160, 162
Gorsuch, Thomas.......... 164
Gouldman, Izora........... 593
Gouldman, Julia............ 594
Grant, Julia.................... 544
Grant, Ulysses S. . 453, 460-464, 470, 542-44, 559, 581-82, 609, 613
Gray, Thomas 25, 620
Greek Fire........ 503, 513-15
Greeley, Horace.... 404, 496
Green, Israel............ 368-69
Green, Rit ... 293-94, 296, 300, 302
Green, Shields... 339, 344, 354, 388
Griffiths, Julia....... 163, 612
Grillo, Scipiano............ 552
Grimké, Angelina........... 89
Grimké, Sarah................. 89
Grover's Theater........... 544
Gue, Benjamin.............. 343
Gue, David.................... 343
Hale, John .. 225, 232, 234, 308, 527
Hale, Lucy....... 527-29, 547
Hall, Joe........................ 180
Hall, Robert.................. 241
Halleck, Henry.............. 460

INDEX

Hamilton, Al..........313, 315
Hamilton, Charles ...313-14, 316, 318, 611
Hamilton, Charles -- Victims
   Campbell, James........317
   Campbell, John..........314
   Colpetzer, William. 315, 317
   Hairgrove, Asa..........315
   Hairgrove, William.. 315, 317, 319
   Hall, Amos.................315
   Hall, Austin.. 315, 317-18
   Nichols, Sam..............314
   Read, B.L............314, 317
   Robertson, Michael....315
   Ross, Patrick.......314, 317
   Snider, Charles...........315
   Stillwell, William........314
Hamilton, George..........313
Hamilton, Thomas.........313
Hammond, George 150, 152
Hammond, Joshua 150, 152, 155, 157
Hampton, Wade...........481
Hancock, John..............228
Hanks, Lucy..................397
Hanway, Castner... 159-60, 162, 164
Harbin, Thomas... 525-26, 576, 587-88
Harpers Ferry, VA 267, 277, 281, 283, 303-04, 308, 319, 335-36, 339-40, 345-47, 350, 353-54, 357, 360-61, 365, 367, 369, 378, 382-86, 392, 413, 419, 428, 429, 443, 523, 532, 605, 612
Harris, Clara.........553, 608
Harris, Sarah....................54
Harrison, William Henry 135, 289, 400
Harvard...........220-22, 246
Hay, John......................496
Hayden, Lewis..............334
Hayes, Rutherford.........613
Headley, John................513
Henderson, Richard.......354
Henry, Alexander..........416
Herald of Freedom (newspaper).198, 209-11
Herndon Hotel...............539
Herndon House.............553
Herold, Davey.526, 534-36, 540, 543, 545, 547, 552, 558, 562-65, 567-68, 570-75, 577-78, 581-83, 587-94, 596, 599
Herzen, Alexander........394
Hess, Dwight.................544
Hickok, Laurens..............86
Higginson, Thomas... 285, 308, 319, 334
Hines, Thomas.........610-11
Hodges, Willis...............125
Holcombe, James..........496
Holmes, James..............248
Holmes, Mary Ann...... *See* Booth, Mary Ann
Holmes, Oliver Wendell Jr. 527
Hoogland, Edward........244
Hooker, Joseph..............460
Howe, Julia Ward..........257

Howe, Samuel. 222-23, 228, 257, 279, 285, 306-08, 382
Hudson, OH 31, 34, 36-39, 43, 53, 59-60, 86, 110-14, 117-18, 121
Hunt, John Wesley 465
Hunter, David 455
Hunter, Robert 226
Huntley, William . 497-98, 504
Hutchings, Nicholas 152
Illinois Anti-Slavery Society 69, 75-76
Ingraham, Edward 152, 154, 160
Institutes of Justinian 292
Irving, Henrietta 427
Irving, Maria 428
Jackson, Andrew.. 113, 223, 463, 614
Jackson, Francis 347
Jackson, Thomas ("Stonewall") 447-48, 460
Jeanne d'Arc ... 17, 300, 614
Jett, Willie 591-92, 594
Johnson, Abe.. 150-51, 155, 163
Johnson, Andrew . 445, 459, 464, 600, 603, 606-09
Johnson, Bradley 480-81
Johnson, Richard 470
Johnston, Joseph 447
Johnston, Robert 273
Johnston, William 151
Jones, Samuel 196-97, 207-09
Jones, Thomas 575-77, 582-83
Joseph, Peter 270
Kagi, John Henry . 276, 339, 344, 359, 369
Kane, George   .. 430, 482, 486, 545, 575, 610
Kansas-Nebraska Act... 227, 310, 402
Kean, Edmund 166, 168
Keating, Edward 81-82
Keitt, Laurence 236, 240
Kellogg, George 115-16
Kennedy, Mary 350
Kennedy, Robert ... 513, 537
Kent, Marvin 110, 120
Kent, Zenas 59, 110-11
Kickapoo Rangers 202
King, William 185
Kirkwood Hotel .. 547, 552, 562, 563, 581
Kline, Henry 152-54, 156-62
Kossuth, Lajos 394, 493
Krum, John 74, 80, 82, 84-85
Lane Rebels 60-61
Lane, James .. 199, 232, 251
Laqueur, Walter 21
Lawless, Luke ... 67, 85, 191
Lawrence, Amos . 184, 192, 257
Leary, Lewis 345
Lecompte, Samuel 210
Lee, John 581
Lee, Robert E .. 367-68, 377, 444, 448-49, 459-63, 480, 482, 542, 588, 605
Leeman, Will 277, 337
Lenaghan, Peter 511
Letters on American Slavery (book) 62
Lewis, Elijah 159
Lexington Rifles 466
Liberator, The (newspaper)

INDEX

52-55, 59-60, 73, 88-89, 222
Lincoln, Abraham 291, 390-93, 397-409, 413, 415, 424-27, 429-30, 441-49, 453-63, 479, 480, 481, 482, 483, 484, 495, 496, 506, 511-14, 518, 523-24, 526-27, 529-36, 539-45, 548, 553-54, 556, 559, 562, 568, 573, 576, 578, 584, 591, 603-08, 610
Lincoln, Mary Todd 400-01, 543, 554
Lincoln, Thomas 397-98
Linder, Usher 76-77, 84, 400
Little, J.H. 321
Lloyd, Daniel 97
Lloyd, Edward 94
Lloyd, John. 543, 549, 567, 570
Loguen, Jeremy 121
Longfellow, Henry Wadsworth 221
Longuemare, Emile 514
Lovejoy, Celia 74
Lovejoy, Elijah 63-77, 79-83, 85-86, 110, 147, 195, 203, 400, 402-403
Lovejoy, Joseph 75
Lovejoy, Owen 75, 403
Lucas, William 588-89
Lundy, Benjamin 46-51, 171
Lusk, Milton 36-37
Lyon, Nathaniel 429, 442
Mace, Harriet 175
Maddox, James 551
Madison, James 139, 415

Manual of the Patriotic Volunteer (book) .. 264, 266, 337
Marais des Cygnes massacre 318-20
Marcy, William 133, 494
Marshall, Caleb 485
Martin, Hiram 470
Martin, P.C... 486-87, 510, 516
Martin, Robert 513-15
Mason, James 232, 371, 375, 443
Mass arson attack on New York 513
Mathews, John .. 386, 521, 535, 551, 586
Mazzini, Giuseppe .. 261-62, 394-95
McClellan, George .. 441-42, 446-49, 453, 457-58, 463
McDaniel, C.W. 320
McDougal, Joseph 467
McGill, John 524
McIntosh, Francis 65
McLeod, Alexander 135
Meadville, OH 40
Mears, Tom 485
Merriam, Francis 347
Metz, Hezekiah 581
Mills, Ruth 42
Milton School ... 164-65, 169
Missouri Compromise .. 137, 183, 290, 292
Mitchell, Robert 320
Montgomery, James 310-13, 319-21, 323
Moore, Hark 3-5, 12-16

Morgan, Calvin............ 465
Morgan, Edwin............ 236
Morgan, John.. 465-68, 496, 513
Morgan, Luther............ 465
Morris Academy .. 34-35, 40
Morris, Clara......... 436, 438
Morton, Edwin............ 331
Mosby, John.. 480, 522, 603
Mudd, Henry................. 573
Mudd, Samuel. 510-11, 517, 570-73, 609
Mudd, Sarah..... 511, 570-73
Murray, Ambrose.......... 236
Nancy Hanks................. 398
National Hotel 510, 512, 517, 527, 541, 546-47, 584
Nelson, Nathan............. 152
New Bedford, MA .. 90-91, 108-09, 334
Newby, Dangerfield...... 339
North Star (newspaper) 121, 126, 163
O'Laughlen, Michael... 483, 485, 520, 526-28, 531, 534, 536, 539-40, 546-47, 599, 609
Oberlin College... 117-18, 187, 344-46
Observer (newspaper) 64-77
O'Laughlen, Michael..... 483
Orsini, Andrea............... 393
Orsini, Felice... 393-97, 488, 493-94
Osawatomie, KS .. 204, 206, 210, 248-55, 310, 314, 320, 351-52, 356
Oswald, Lee Harvey 417
Otis, James.................... 228

Our American Cousin (play) 544, 548, 553, 555
Oviatt, Heman.. 113-14, 116
Padgett, William 151-52, 156
Parker, Eliza.................. 159
Parker, James................. 11
Parker, Theodore . 257, 285, 307
Parker, William... 153, 155, 158-59, 163
Parnell, Levi................. 158
Parr, David.................... 525
Pate, Henry Clay... 245, 332
Pattison, Atthow ... 294, 296
Pattison, Gourney 296
Pattison, Mary............... 294
Pearce, James................ 236
Pearce, Thomas... 150, 152, 156, 158, 160-62
Perkins, Simon...... 119, 130
Peyton, Sarah Jane........ 591
Philleo, Calvin.............. 611
Phipps, Benjamin............ 17
Pickens, Francis............ 426
Pierce, Franklin... 184-85, 191-92, 197, 203, 275, 493
Pieri, Andrea................. 396
Plumb, Ralph................ 346
Plutarch's Lives (book).. 36, 180, 284
Plutarch's Morals (book) 173, 180
Polk, James...... 136, 490-91
Pope Gregory XVI........ 393
Pope Pius IX................. 393
Pope, John.................... 448
Pottawatomie Rifles... 204, 207, 210, 212, 217
Powell, Lewis 521-26, 531-

INDEX

34, 536, 539-40, 543, 545, 547-48, 553, 558-61, 563, 579-80, 599, 601, 603, 605
Pownell, Levi 155, 163
Price, C.H. 217
Price, John 344
Proposals to colonize freed slaves 455, 458
Provost, Mary 432
Pumphrey, James 550
Quantrill, William 497
Queen, William 510, 511
Quesenberry, Elizabeth 587, 588
Ram's Horn (newspaper) 124
Randolph, PA .43-44, 53, 59
Rathbone, Henry ... 553, 608
Read, Sarah 317
Redpath, James 244
Reed, Roland 437
Reeder, Andrew 191, 203
Reid, John... 250-51, 254-55
Reid, Samuel 490
Rice, Ben 321
Richmond Grays .384, 386, 444
Richter, Frederick 582
Ridley, Thomas 12
Roberts, Ned 94-95
Robinson, Charles 199, 201, 202, 209, 218, 252, 253
Robinson, Sara 218
Rockwell, Julius 228
Rollins, Bettie 593
Rollins, William 590
Roman Catholic Church 511, 524, 600, 606, 608

Ross, Ben .293-94, 300, 302
Rossbach, Jeffrey 602
Rudio, Carlo 396
Ruggles, David 90, 108
Ruggles, Mortimer ... 590-93
Saints Everlasting Rest (book) 37
Sanborn, Franklin 257, 278-84, 307-08, 320, 331, 382
Sanders, Anna 490
Sanders, George 394, 488-97, 504, 507, 513, 604
Sanders, Lewis 489-90
Sandford, John 289
Scarlett, Joseph 159
Scott v. Sandford (court decision) .. 289, 391, 403, 406, 416, 456, 459
Scott, Dred 289, 291-92
Scott, Winfield 441, 493
Secret Six .. 285, 306, 308, 319, 332, 334, 382-83, 612
Seward, William Henry 131-37, 142-43, 145, 180, 182, 184, 232, 234, 288, 308, 334, 406, 424, 426, 429, 430, 441-44, 455, 457-59, 514, 545, 605, 607
Shakespeare's Julius Caesar (play) 180, 487, 506, 513, 515-16, 557
Shannon, Wilson .. 197, 199-200, 248
Shelley, Percy 165, 167
Sheridan, Philip 514
Sherman, Henry 206, 216
Sherman, William . 462, 514
Shields, James 447

Shore, Samuel 244
Simonds, Joseph 477, 485-86, 540
Simonton, James 237
Slidell, John 443
Smith, Gerrit 118, 134, 186, 188-89, 192, 278-80, 283, 285, 303, 331, 373, 382, 603
Smith, J. McCune 189
Smoot, Richard 526
Snyder, Elias 315-19
South Carolina College 227, 239
Southall, Joseph 434
Southern Literary Messenger (newspaper) 288
Southern Maryland . 510-11, 517, 518, 525-26, 534, 536, 540, 564, 575-78, 587, 610
Spangler, Edward "Ned" 540, 542-43, 551-52, 554, 599, 609-10
Speed, Joshua 400-01
St. Albans (terror attack) -- Victims
  Beardsley, Marcus 497-98
  Bishop, Cyrus 498
  Blaisdell, William. 500-01
  Clark, Jackson 498
  Conger, George 501
  Fuller, Erasmus 502-03
  Huntington, Collins ... 502
  Morrison, Elinus 503
  Seymour, Martin 499
  Sowles, Albert 500
St. Charles College .. 518, 524, 607-08

St. Timothy's Hall 175, 483
Stanton, Edwin 446, 548
Starr, Ella 528, 541
Stearns, George.. 257, 264, 285, 307, 332, 382, 612
Steel, John 273, 275
Stephens, Alexander 426
Stevens, Aaron 267-70, 273-77, 320, 323, 327-29, 338, 352-55, 359, 363-64, 369, 388
Stewart, Joseph 557
Stewart, Richard 588
Story, Joseph 220-21
Stowe, Harriet Beecher. 381
Stuart, Jeb .. 246, 368, 371, 382, 464, 480
Sullivan, Jeremiah 270
Sumner, Charles ... 220-32, 234-35, 237-40, 246, 257, 279, 288, 295, 306, 308, 442, 453, 456, 606
Sumner, Charles Pinckney 220
Sumner, Edwin .. 197, 208, 245-46, 277, 328
Sumner, Isabel 473, 476, 479
Surratt, Anna 600
Surratt, John ... 517-18, 521, 523-26, 532, 534, 536, 539-41, 578, 606, 608
Surratt, Mary ... 518-19, 524, 542-43, 548-50, 554, 567, 579-601, 608
Swan, Ausy 573-74
Taney, Roger 290-91
Tappan, Arthur 51, 57
Taylor, Zachary .. 136-38, 144, 223

INDEX

Terrorism
- And threatened cultures... 26, 28
- As anti-democratic.. 28-29
- As desperation tactic used by Confederate rebels 466-68, 480, 530
- As giving rise to extreme counter reaction .. 408, 455, 568
- As having effect of creating uproar 209
- As having very little precedent in Anglo-American culture 25
- As mode of supporting hopeless cause.......... 25
- As new and unconventional form of warfare 464
- As perverted form of political action.......... 19
- As related to suppression of free speech............... 28
- As resembling attacks from bands of aboriginal peoples..................... 25
- Revulsion felt by ordinary citizens regardless of ideology 217, 330, 369, 568
- Use of attempts to free prisoners................ 479
- Use of propaganda 479
- Use of robbery and attacks on civilian property 479

Terrorists
- As being convinced of their righteousness. 330, 568
- As being in search of a cause of injustice to champion unto death 422
- As being in search of a cause to champion unto death 585
- As disdaining political engagement 69
- As motivated by desire to achieve fame in posterity 531, 578
- As rejecting political solutions 418, 530
- As requiring followers to give money.... 346, 540
- As slightly divorced from reality....... 24, 260, 420
- As suicidal................... 25
- Desire to publicize cause. 370
- Radicalization of sympathizers and friends 520
- Selection of soft targets 515, 555
- Tendency to exaggerate... 504, 508, 562
- Use of fake names 276, 319, 335, 515, 517, 524, 603, 604, 606-07

Use of unmarried and unattached followers ... 483, 522
Use of weapons of widespread destruction 503
Writing of terrorist manifestoes ... 337, 506

Thayer, Eli 323
The Genius of Universal Emancipation (newspaper) 48-51
The Philanthropist (newspaper) 48
Thomas, Eluctus 573
Thompson, George ... 88, 89
Thompson, Henry 188, 211, 337, 339
Thompson, Jacob 513
Thompson, John 511
Thompson, Philip 269-71
Thompson, Ruth 188
Thompson, Seth 111-12
Thompson, William 369
Thugs 21, 233-34
Tidd, Charles 277, 354
Tompkins, Orlando 541
Toombs, Robert 236
Townsend, George 435
Townsley, James 212-13
Tubman, Harriet.. 293-305, 333-34, 570, 591, 613-14
Tubman, John 295
Tuckahoe 92, 107
Turner, Nat 1-16, 17, 19, 24-25, 30, 53, 58, 65, 84, 101, 212, 259, 369, 392, 414, 457, 620

Turner, Nat -- Victims
  Barrow, Mary 8
  Barrow, Tom 8
  Bryant, Henry 7
  Francis, Salathiel 5
  Harris, Newit 13
  Jones, Clarinda 10
  Moore, Putnam 5
  Newsome, Sarah 6
  Prebles, Hartwell 6
  Reese, Piety 6
  Reese, William 6
  Travis, Joseph 4
  Travis, Sallie 4, 5
  Turner, Elizabeth 6
  Waller, Levi 8-10, 16
  Westbrook, Joel 5
  Whitehead, Caty 7-8
  Whitehead, Peggy 8
  Whitehead, Richard 7
  Williams, William 10
Tyler, John 135, 289
Underground Railroad . 108, 299-300, 302, 360, 570
Unseld, John 335-36
Upstart republics of 1848-49 261-62
Vaill, H.L. 380
Vallandigham, Clement 371, 373, 377, 462
Van Bokkelen, Libertus 175, 483
Van Buren, Martin 113, 223
Vicksburg (battle) 460-62
Wallace, Caleb 500, 504
Walsh, Hugh 320
Ward, Annie 539

INDEX

Washington, Frank 572
Washington, George ... 227, 352, 353, 391
Watters, Thomas 327
Webster, Daniel... 135-36, 138, 141
Weed, Thurlow 133-34
Weichmann, Louis 517, 524-25, 543, 548, 579, 608
Weiner, Theodore 212
Welles, Gideon 457
Wentworth, John 528
West, Henry 81-82
Western Reserve Bank 112-13
Western Reserve College 86
Westfall, John 529
White, Martin 135, 145, 205, 206, 248, 250
Whitfield, J.W. 203
Whitman, Walt 568
Wigfall, Louis 239
Wilkes, John 165
Williams, H.H. 217
Williams, Samuel 154
Wilmer, Lemuel 573
Wilson, Henry 333
Winthrop, Robert 223
Wise, Henry ..372, 383-84, 386, 428
Wood, J.P. 328-29
Wood, Samuel 207
Woodland, Henry 582
Woodson, Daniel 250
Woolfolk, Austin 49
Wooster, Louise 412-13
Wright, Martin 436
Wye Plantation 94, 97-98
Wyndham, Charles 438
Yale 277
Young America 491-93
Young, Bennett ....
.... 496-97, 500-01, 503
Zealots 20

Milton Keynes UK
Ingram Content Group UK Ltd.
UKHW020032271124
451585UK00014B/1593

9 780999 155